Contemporary Authors®
Autobiography Series

ISSN 0748-0636

Contemporary

Authors

Autobiography Series

Joyce Nakamura
Editor

Shelly Andrews
Associate Editor

volume **22**

An ITP Information/Reference Group

I(T)P
Changing the Way the World Learns

NEW YORK • LONDON • BONN • BOSTON • DETROIT
MADRID • MELBOURNE • MEXICO CITY • PARIS
SINGAPORE • TOKYO • TORONTO • WASHINGTON
ALBANY NY • BELMONT CA • CINCINNATI OH

EDITORIAL STAFF

Joyce Nakamura, *Editor*

Linda R. Andres, Shelly Andrews, and Motoko Fujishiro Huthwaite, *Associate Editors*
Marilyn O'Connell Allen and Paul Zyskowski, *Assistant Editors*
Carolyn C. March, Heidi J. Hagen, Alan Hedblad, Laurie Collier Hillstrom, and
Lori J. Sawicki, *Contributing Copyeditors*

Victoria B. Cariappa, *Research Manager*

Hal May, *Publisher*

Mary Beth Trimper, *Production Director*
Shanna Philpott Heilveil, *Production Assistant*

Cynthia Baldwin, *Art Director*
C. J. Jonik, *Keyliner*
Randy A. Bassett, *Image Database Supervisor*
Robert Duncan, *Scanner Operator*

Theresa Rocklin, *Manager, Technical Support Services*

10 9 8 7 6 5 4 3 2 1

Contents

Preface   vii
A Brief Sampler   ix
Acknowledgments   xi

Preface

A Unique Collection of Essays

Each volume in the *Contemporary Authors Autobiography Series (CAAS)* presents an original collection of autobiographical essays written especially for the series by noted writers.

CA Autobiography Series is designed to be a meeting place for writers and readers—a place where writers can present themselves, on their own terms, to their audience; and a place where general readers, students of contemporary literature, teachers and librarians, even aspiring writers can become better acquainted with familiar authors and meet others for the first time.

This is an opportunity for writers who may never write a full-length autobiography to let their readers know how they see themselves and their work, what brought them to this time and place.

Even for those authors who have already published full-length autobiographies, there is the opportunity in *CAAS* to bring their readers "up to date" or perhaps to take a different approach in the essay format. In some instances, previously published material may be reprinted or expanded upon; this fact is always noted at the end of such an essay. Individually, the essays in this series can enhance the reader's understanding of a writer's work; collectively, they are lessons in the creative process and in the discovery of its roots.

CAAS makes no attempt to give a comprehensive overview of authors and their works. That outlook is already well represented in biographies, reviews, and critiques published in a wide variety of sources. Instead, *CAAS* complements that perspective and presents what no other ongoing reference source does: the view of contemporary writers that is shaped by their own choice of materials and their own manner of storytelling.

Who Is Covered?

Like its parent series, *Contemporary Authors,* the *CA Autobiography Series* sets out to meet the needs and interests of a wide range of readers. Each volume includes essays by writers in all genres whose work is being read today. We consider it extraordinary that so many busy authors from throughout the world are able to interrupt their existing writing, teaching, speaking, traveling, and other schedules to converge on a given deadline for any one volume. So it is not always possible that all genres can be equally and uniformly represented from volume to volume, although we strive to include writers working in a variety of categories, including fiction, nonfiction, and poetry. As only a few writers specialize in a single area, the breadth of writings by authors in this volume also encompasses drama, translation, and criticism as well as work for movies, television, radio, newspapers, and journals.

What Each Essay Includes

Authors who contribute to *CAAS* are invited to write a "mini-autobiography" of approximately 10,000 words. In order to give the writer's imagination free rein, we suggest no guidelines or pattern for the essay.

We only ask that each writer tell his or her story in the manner and to the extent that feels most natural and appropriate. In addition, writers are asked to supply a selection of personal photographs showing themselves at various ages, as well as important people and special moments in their lives. Our contributors have responded generously, sharing with us some of their most treasured mementoes. The result is a special blend of text and photographs that will attract even the casual browser. Other features include:

Bibliography at the end of each essay, listing book-length works in chronological order of publication. Each bibliography in this volume was compiled by members of the *CAAS* editorial staff and submitted to the author for review.

Cumulative index in each volume, which cites all the essayists in the series as well as the subjects presented in the essays: personal names, titles of works, geographical names, schools of writing, etc. To ensure ease of use for these cumulating references, the name of the essayist is given before the volume and page number(s) for every reference that appears in more than one essay. In the following example, the entry in the index allows the user to identify the essay writers by name:

> Auden, W.H.
>   Allen **6:**18, 24
>   Ashby **6:**36, 39
>   Bowles **1:**86
>   etc.

For references that appear in only one essay, the volume and page number(s) are given but the name of the essayist is omitted. For example:

> Stieglitz, Alfred **1:**104, 109, 110

CAAS is something more than the sum of its individual essays. At many points the essays touch common ground, and from these intersections emerge new patterns of information and impressions. The index is an important guide to these interconnections.

For Additional Information

For detailed information on awards won, adaptations of works, critical reviews of works, and more, readers are encouraged to consult Gale's *Contemporary Authors* cumulative index for authors' listings in other Gale sources. These include, among others, *Contemporary Authors*, *Contemporary Authors New Revision Series*, *Dictionary of Literary Biography*, and *Contemporary Literary Criticism*.

Special Thanks

We wish to acknowledge our special gratitude to each of the authors in this volume. They all have been most kind and cooperative in contributing not only their talents but their enthusiasm and encouragement to this project.

A Brief Sampler

Each essay in the series has a special character and point of view that sets it apart from its companions. A small sampler of anecdotes and musings from the essays in this volume hint at the unique perspective of these life stories.

Tom Clark, living the challenge of New York City: "My first month or so in the city was spent in an apartment on the nether reaches of East First Street, borrowed from the poet Dick Gallup. . . . The building was a testament to some unknown slumlord's legend. The graffiti-scrawled, piss-pooled, creaking, swaying ancient elevator was an adventure one wouldn't want to risk twice. Climbing the Raskolnikovian stairs, on the other hand, was not only depressing and exhausting but about as safe as a solo patrol in what weird-eyed street guys just back from Nam called Indian Country. Dick's place was on the third-floor rear, with an exposed fire escape that offered perfect entry and exit routes for emergency 'movers.' During my stay, prospective burglars showed up every few days, peering over my shoulder past the chain lock to case the place, just on the chance a new TV set might have been brought in (no such luck). One particularly brazen prospector, a beat-up-looking guy in a big baggy overcoat, ogled the scene for at least a slow half-minute before remembering to pretend to explain to me what he'd come for. Producing from deep within his coat a balled-up out-of-date copy of *Muhammad Speaks*, he asked, 'Want to buy a newspaper?'"

John Robert Colombo, recalling the legendary Northrop Frye: "I enrolled in his Blake course and the following year audited his popular course in literary symbolism. . . . Frye made little attempt to 'relate' to his students other than to relate to them everything that they needed to know about the imagery at hand. But he did not disdain or demean his students as did so many of the popular professors of the day. When Frye asked a question, he would wait for an answer. And wait. And wait. Even when he asked what we felt was a rhetorical question, he would wait for an answer. The pause would grow in length. It was not the pause that refreshes, but the pause-as-Black-Hole into the maw of which everything local disappears. The silence elicited thoughtless answers to thoughtful questions. I timed one pause, occasioned by a question about Blake's 'Beulah,' that lasted two minutes. It would have lasted longer, but the class was nearing its end, so Frye himself, grimly, supplied the answer."

Carolyn See, experiencing the lure of writing as a child: "Every weekend, Daddy would come over to take me out. Often we went to afternoon literary parties—this would be in the late forties in L.A. The sun would be shining and the windows open, and witty Los Angeles journalists (Matt Weinstock, Gene Coughlin, Virginia Wright) would be knocking back scotch-and-sodas and laughing hard. They'd be talking about how, when they were writing their short stories, they'd weep from the pathos of it all. They'd tell stories from their City Side days. They worried about whether a magazine called *Fortnight* would continue. (It didn't, of course.) These afternoons were like paradise to me. Then, as darkness fell, he'd take me home to Mother. She'd have been crying all day long. It didn't take a genius to see that fun was where the writing was; writing was where the fun hung out."

Lewis Putnam Turco, reliving youthful memories: "When I was in the eighth grade my father sent me off to Suffield Academy in Suffield, Connecticut. He told me that he was doing it to give me the best education he could, but he evidently told Gene that he sent me away to save my brother's life. I don't recollect that I was all that homicidal toward my sibling. The worst thing I remember doing was tying him to the porch of the parsonage on Windsor Avenue when I was supposed to be baby-sitting him. I wanted to play with my neighborhood buddies instead, and I knew he was safe because I could hear him screaming."

Gerald Vizenor, reviewing the police reports of his father's murder, years later: "I was, that summer, the same age as my father when he was murdered. There was some resistance by the police, of course, some concern that my intentions were not personal but political. The police must be defensive about homicides that were never solved. A thin folder was recovered from the archives. Inside, the chief of detectives was surprised to discover that his name was on the report. . . . The coincidence seemed to please him for a moment, as he explained that he was a new police officer then. His mood turned when he defended his trivial report. 'We never spent much time on winos and derelicts in those days. . . . Who knows, one Indian vagrant kills another. . . . Look kid, that was a long time ago,' he said and then looked at his watch. 'Take it on the chin, you know what I mean?' I certainly did know what he meant. Homicide investigations are political, and notice of my father, a descendant of the crane and native newcomer from the reservation, was minimal in the city. That detective could have been the same man who told my mother to move out of town, and, as she told me later, 'forget forever what happened.'"

C. D. Wright, sharing a mysteriously enchanting moment in her childhood: "The swing had been hung by the previous owners, rumored to have been accomplished with arrows—so that I could pump perilously high and ever so slowly descend; slowly slowly come to a full stop. Then I could begin to busy myself as architect of stick towns for the fat, black ants. . . . I quit pumping and started to drift down toward my ant kingdom. Leaves of oak passed downward, then surprisingly upward, opening and closing in their passage, becoming winged. They lighted on the rusted chains of my swing. By the thousands, tens of thousands, the monarchs materialized in certain migration. The entire eastern population fluttering through our backyard on Cherry Street en route to Mexico. The yard noiselessly exploded with their black-veined pinions. I filled the lap of my dress and stroked the settled ones while countless others extravasated in the splotches of sun about me. I sat still. Silent. 'I did not move my arms so much. It was an exotic moment without rush, without engines . . . ,' wrote Neruda. Maybe such an occurrence cannot be called numinous. Or can it?"

These brief examples only suggest what lies ahead in this volume. The essays will speak differently to different readers; but they are certain to speak best, and most eloquently, for themselves.

Acknowledgments

Grateful acknowledgment is made to those publishers, photographers, and artists whose works appear with these authors' essays.

Photographs/Art

John Robert Colombo: All photographs courtesy of Hawkshead Services.

Garrett Hongo: p. 87, Alice Anderson.

Mark Jarman: p. 100, Larry's Photography.

M. T. Kelly: p. 107, © Judy Nisenholt.

Maurice Kenny: p. 121, Jodi Buren; p. 123, Murray Studio; p. 163, Coordinating Council of Literary Magazines (CCLM) Newsletter, spring 1981.

James Laughlin: p. 173, © Virginia Schendler, 1993; p. 177, Alice B. Toklas; p. 188, Dick Durrance; p. 190, Miggs Durrance; p. 194, Eberhart Kneisl; p. 200, Gregory Harvey; p. 202, C. Zumwalt; p. 206, Dick Ziegfeld.

Carolyn See: p. 211, © Marilyn Sanders; p. 216, Joan Weber.

Gerald Vizenor: p. 255, Thomas King.

Tobias Wolff: p. 279, © Jerry Bauer; p. 297, © Catherine Wolff.

Text

Garrett Hongo: Essay "America Singing: An Address to the Newly Arrived Peoples" originally appeared in *Parnassus: Poetry in Review,* vol. 17, no. 1, 1992. Reprinted with permission of Garrett Hongo. Poem "Ministry: Homage to Kilauea," Blue Heron Publishing, Inc. Reprinted with permission of Garrett Hongo.

James Laughlin: Essay includes parts of "Byways" from *The Country Road* by James Laughlin. Cambridge, Massachusetts: Zoland Books, 1995. Copyright © 1995 by James Laughlin. Reprinted with permission of Zoland Books, Inc./ Parts of "Byways" have also appeared in *Ambit* (London) and other periodicals, including *Agni, Conjunctions, Grand Street,* and *Iowa Review.*

Lewis Putnam Turco: Poem "Cancer" from *The Shifting Web: New and Selected Poems* by Lewis Turco. University of Arkansas Press, 1989. Copyright © 1989 by Lewis Turco. Reprinted with permission of University of Arkansas Press./ Poem "The Shadowman"

Contemporary Authors®

Autobiography Series

Tom Clark

1941-

CONFESSIONS

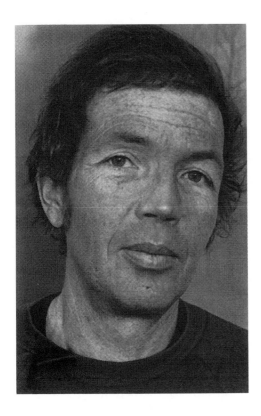

Tom Clark, 1984

Dowsing

He was a thoroughly delightful man, when sober," my cousin Jim says of his uncle Bud, Arthur Clark, my father. Jim has researched family history in recent years, and much of what I know about the earlier generations of my father's family comes from him. But though my dad was the youngest of four children and an early darling, seemingly favored by fate and certainly much loved then and later

by the two older sisters who survived him, something in him went terribly wrong, and that wrong-going, in retrospect, looks increasingly less like an accident or aberration than the sad expression of some ingrained canker in the blood. What makes some people not fit into the world that surrounds them? Is it just that they don't like feeling so surrounded?

An older brother of my father's, John Clark, a quiet, serious man who was said to spend a lot of time reading, appears in one poor reproduction of a family photo I've seen. In a dark suit, gravely handsome, enigmatic, unsmiling, he stands in the center of the back row, the tallest figure in the photo (my father, looking about thirteen at the time, always the most "outgoing," smiles winningly at the camera from down in front). Next to my uncle John in the back row stands the head of the family, Willard Clark, itinerant sign painter, veteran of the Great War, jaunty in a boater, with a cocked grin, worldly, dapper-looking. Seated in a chair before Willard is his plump, dark-haired wife, Irene *née* Cann—daughter of Mary Burke, an immigrant girl who'd been born in steerage, arriving orphaned in the New World (both a twin sister and her mother had died at sea), and of the equally unfortunate John Cann, who'd entered America from Nova Scotia just in time to serve with the Illinois Volunteers in the Civil War and lose his right arm at Peach Tree Creek, Georgia ("They gave him a shot of whiskey and sawed it off"). A year or two after this backyard Chicago family-gathering photo was taken, Willard, my second namesake—I would be called Thomas Willard—was dead. By then his two daughters had married, leaving the two sons alone with their mother.

My dad left high school and went to work, while his brother John stayed at home. One day Bud walked into the house and found their mother stricken on the kitchen floor with a sudden, catastrophic stroke. He ran for help, but before it came Irene was dead. That was August 1936. The following April there came a further blow, when the quiet, serious, book-reading older brother took his own life by walking east into Lake Michigan until his hat floated. (Not to make too much of it, but to my knowledge my father never swam. Our few family vacations to the Wisconsin lake country, to me a land of F. Scott Fitzgeraldian mythic glamor, were short and unhappy. I remember him taking me fishing once or twice in leaky rented rowboats; that was clearly an ordeal for him. Of course back then I couldn't have guessed why. I didn't learn about my uncle's suicide until many, many years later—just recently, in fact; all through my life at home that suicide remained a shameful, painful secret, unknown not only to me but to my younger brother John, who was named after that unfortunate man.) My father seems to have spent the rest of his days doggedly dowsing bottle after bottle in search of his own black lake of forgetfulness to wade off into. Had life in this world

of surprising, gratuitous cruelty and pain taken off its mask for him at too early an age?

Through one of his sisters who'd married a stockbroker, Bud got a job as a bond trader on the Chicago Exchange, and did well for a time, until the relentless seriousness of his drinking problem reared its vicious head. A good-looking, wavy-haired fellow much favored by the ladies—"quite the collar ad," one of them later recalled him—he dated a pretty, vivacious, young Irish-American woman named Rita Kearin, who at the time was working as a shopgirl and living at home after graduating from a west suburban Catholic college. They saw a little of one another, but he seemed to lose interest, and disappeared for some months. Then he was hauled in by the law for drunken driving. To forestall formal charges he showed up, sober and contrite, at the front door of Rita's father, a local police captain. The captain helped him out, and shortly afterwards, in 1939, the quick-witted, fast-talking Buddy married my mother.

Exempted from service in World War II because of high blood pressure, he was put to work at a Douglas Aviation plant located west of the city in raw Illinois countryside later to become O'Hare airport; the DC-3 was then in development, and his draughtsman's skills were employed in helping design it. Those skills had been inherited from his father, the sign painter, though whether his father or anyone else had ever formally instructed him in drawing I don't know. At any rate, he drew with a strong, bold, flowing line. (He taught or anyway inspired me to draw, too—an avocation absorbing enough to earn me many a brisk rap across guilty knuckles from ruler-brandishing nuns irritated by my inattention in religion and arithmetic classes.) Later on he continued to make use of this gift, as and when he could. That was, however, only marginally. He made silk screens and decals for a while, and as a hobby did decorative art, sometimes of remarkable quality; I recall his movie-star-caricature wall murals done for the basement barroom of the South Oak Park house of his stockbroker brother-in-law, where we later lived (by then, like other forgotten reminders of his once-promising future, they'd long since been painted over). In his last days as an invalid, when drinking had destroyed his health, he took up his old oils to turn out knock-off Renoirs and Van Goghs on wooden trivets, to be sold in his sister's inte-

Mother, Rita Kearin, in her engagement photo, 1938

*As an altar boy at St. Catherine's Church,
Oak Park, Illinois, 1948*

rior-decorating showrooms. Considering his diminished circumstances, even these rather kitschy late productions were surprisingly competent. Then again, they represent the sad testament of a wasted talent.

In his middle years, the years of his heaviest drinking, before a series of strokes confined him to the house, he went through a series of increasingly depressing traveling salesman's jobs, peddling first decals, then later cans and cardboard boxes for a number of different firms. I remember riding along with him at age nine or ten on one midsummer box-selling junket across the Mississippi into Iowa. We stopped at John Deere and International Harvester farm equipment plants in hot, dusty nowhere burgs like Moline and Davenport, whose mundane Midwestern ordinariness did not dim their electrifying away-from-home aura for me, and spent a night at the Blackhawk Hotel in Des Moines, where the Indian murals in the dining room convinced me I'd finally entered the fabled territory of the West—I remember

being quite excited about that. However, I also remember my father's tenseness and jumpiness throughout the trip. The dingy, unromantic traveling salesman's life, worse than Arthur Miller ever conceived it, was my father's professional reality. While being good at thinking on his feet when sober helped him land salesman's job after salesman's job, selling inevitably made him hate not only those he had to sell to but himself, and in the long run contributed no little to his ultimate humiliation. He seldom held *any* job very long; as the years went by and his range narrowed, he drank more and more, and finally seemed to leave his paycheck in West Madison Street bars far more often than he showed up at home with it.

As my father's sharp wit grew dull with progressive alcohol poisoning, and a general sense of bitterness and disappointment overcame his natural charm, the bloom of life was taken away from my mother in predictable proportion, till all pretense to domestic harmony buckled under the strains of their unfortunate union. From the turmoil and damage of life at home, my own sole secure refuge came to be that provided in my maternal grandfather's relatively much happier household. Accordingly, I spent longer and longer periods of time there, relieved to be safely away from the violent battle-ground of home and increasingly reluctant to return to it.

My parents aside, perhaps the most important person in my early life was Thomas Patrick Kearin, my mother's father, on whose birthday (March 1) I came into the world, and whose first name I was accordingly given. A hale, robust young man from a large family whose origins lay in the romantic Gaelic-speaking wilds of County Kerry on Ireland's southwest coast (he retained a strong west-country brogue throughout his life), he'd come down around the turn of the century to Chicago from South Dakota, striking out on his own in the rough-neck city of that era, first as a street lamplighter, then as a streetcar driver, before settling into his life's work as a policeman. A physically imposing man, he possessed also great energy, and a cheerful Celtic good-heartedness and generosity exceptional even in a race noted for those traits. In 1912 he married a tiny, pert young Irish girl named Kathleen Gaynor, a pub-keeper's daughter and telegraph operator from the crossroads town of Mullingar in County

*Officer Thomas Patrick Kearin, the author's grandfather, front and center in the parade,
Oak Park, Illinois, about 1948*

Westmeath, who'd emigrated at age eighteen in order to avoid an arranged marriage. My grandfather devoted himself thenceforth to an extended family that soon included not only his and Kathleen's two daughters but seven of his own eight siblings, who'd also landed in America, as well as his mother and father. When his parents' health failed in the 1920s, he personally fetched them home from California in dutiful Old Country fashion to take their final rest in his own house. I have a photo of his father, Humphrey Kearin, laid out amid flowers in the front room of that Harlem Avenue house in Oak Park, and my mother recalls quite vividly as one of the most affecting events of her own girlhood the traditional Irish wake afforded there to her grandmother, Johanna Horan Kearin. It was an event of nightlong drinking, dancing, and storytelling—a kind of mourning, as she is still moved to remember it, that seemed not so much woeful grieving as joyful lamentation, the communal celebration of a life valued in its passing. Indeed that

same house at Harlem and Augusta remains the site of many of my own happiest early memories: a tree-shaded homestead, adjacent to daisy-filled fields and woods (all paved concrete and suburban development now); also to the western arterial thoroughfare of Harlem Avenue, and, a little farther off, the Chicago and North Western railroad tracks, sources of those nocturnal sounds of long-distance truck tires and train whistles that to my dreamily listening ears, as I lay awake late at night in the upstairs bedroom, summoned vistas of wide-open prairies beyond.

By the time I got to know him, my grandfather was already a man of broad experience that ranged from seeing action in the line of duty at the scene of the St. Valentine's Day Massacre to busting up beer and whiskey barrels in the streets during Prohibition. While enforcing the Volstead Act was professionally required of him, he remained himself no disrespecter of the good uses of an occasional glass of spirits, and whether or not it's just my imagination, the news photo I have of him in plainclothes supervising the destruction of a bootlegger's haul seems to indicate, only partially concealed beneath his straw boater, a look of mild dismay over the unfortunate waste involved.

Prominent among my childhood memories of him are those involving the protracted festivities of Christmases in his household, a time when a veritable magic bounty of tribute invariably arrived from his grateful constituency, the doorbell steadily ringing with messenger deliveries "for the Chief," fat turkeys by the dozen, potted poinsettias, hand-packed boxes of fancy fruit and nuts from the Pacific Northwest (a place I imagined as a remote forested factory of spectacular benisons), an annual year's supply of Mars bars and Eskimo Pies (the sheer plenitude of which, along with the turkeys, required two large basement freezers to contain them), and, most notable of all to my childish eyes, a cornucopia of cases of fine bourbon, generously offered to seasonal visitors for convivial social consumption. The climax of this mysterious torrent of gifts was of course Christmas morning, when my grandfather always left out a shot of bourbon for Santa Claus, and I myself without fail rose hours before all others to hungrily attack my own small treasure-trove of gifts. One year, I'm informed—I must have been about three or four—my great joy over some wooden racing cars I'd been given spilled over into a misguided attempt to share it by opening up everyone else's packages too, and painting the contents with red nail polish, a task I was able to accomplish just in time for the rest of the family to walk in and find their presents coated with a wild crimson lacquer.

My grandfather, who'd never had a son of his own, lavished vast transferred paternal indulgence on me; on this occasion, as on all too many others subsequently, he warded off any possible criticism of my excessive deed with the injunction, "Just give the lad another month." He was always ready to forgive me anything. One winter when I was in seventh or eighth grade I was caught—and, for good measure, cuffed around by the civic-minded juice-truck driver who'd caught me—tossing snowballs into a mail van; beat cops who were summoned had no choice but to haul me into the station house, where my grandfather's discomfort was so evident I for once actually regretted my transgression. He attempted to demonstrate my in-

nocence to his bemused police cronies by having me exhibit my gloves, which he claimed were dry as a bone even though they were obviously caked with ice from furious snowball making.

Just how far his protection may have extended beyond the bounds of his beloved family to other interests always remained a matter of some question to me. At the borders of that shadow of a doubt, just across Harlem Avenue in the neighboring village of River Forest, a number of alleged crime bosses were known to make their homes—some, like the notorious Tony Accardo, in plush mansions with rolling lawns, tennis courts, ballrooms, and bowling alleys, some in abodes that were at least to the casual eye much more modest. One of the more discreet reputed-mobster domiciles was in fact visible from my grandfather's front-window easy chair, into which, putting up his big pearl-handled pistol out of child's reach and whistling a few bars of some old Killarney ballad, he settled for his daily noontime "forty winks." How much he knew or didn't know about the secrets that lay behind those shuttered windows across the avenue *I* of course can't know, but considering that as early as 1946 he'd risen to the position of chief of the Oak Park police force, I'd guess he knew quite a bit. Of those particular neighbors, anyway, he spoke with the wry distance of someone who appeared relieved to have them outside his jurisdiction. When I was in high school with the family's scion, a pleasant enough fellow whose well-oiled ducktail and pegged slacks declared his membership in a "hoody" set that definitely was not mine, a nightclub in an adjacent town unaccountably burned down one evening just before a school prom had been scheduled to occur there. That nightclub had moreover been selected as prom site over the objections of the son of my grandfather's Italian-American neighbor, who'd held out for another establishment to which his family was speculated to have a more than passing connection.

Indeed there sometimes seemed to be invisible sympathies and affiliations, unspoken connections and dependencies, locked into place almost everywhere in this primordial landscape, at once silently sustaining and implicitly inhibiting. Social as well as religious understandings in our little corner of the world were based not so much on the cold relations of logic as on more emotional or imaginative ones of faith and trust, often requiring irrational leaps as a matter of course. These were in many respects a hardheaded as well as hard-working people, yet a certain semimystical suspension of disbelief generally prevailed. On my mother's side of the family, superstitions were commonplace, including but not limited to an orthodox Catholic credence in miracles. Irish folk wisdom did little to separate the available mythologies in this regard. My grandmother had brought over with her from the Old Country a stereopticon in whose binocular viewer one could glimpse hand-tinted misty twilit Celtic copses where strange "little people" wandered the gloaming, doing the supernatural things little people were presumed to do. The legendary kingdom of these diminutive fairy beings both intrigued and scared me. For all I could tell, in my youthful unknowingness, the same stretched time-space envelope roamed by the little people also contained, to cite just two among a thousand instances, such places as that spooky grotto at Lourdes where Saint Bernadette, played by the somewhat inappropriately sexy Jean Peters in a Hollywood movie we were shown every year by the nuns, had witnessed the Virgin striking water from the rocks; or those unearthly North Polar zones where, according to the theories of an oddball Irish Catholic soft-water magnate whose pamphlet on the subject received great currency in our parish during the cold war's fearful early stages, a continuous series of aurora borealis displays had begun to signal the incipient fulfillment of the promised eschatology of the biblical Abomination of Desolation. The Apocalypse was soon to erupt in the form of global thermonuclear conflict, it was commonly thought. At school, we curled up in practice fetal poses beneath our desks, and at home, blankets were tacked up over the basement windows in dry-run exercises aimed at preparing us for avoiding blinding from the flash of the blast.

In my earlier, even more impressionable years, when a hot war I knew of only through the fraught tones of adults' conversation still raged on in Europe and the Pacific, I was plagued by secret anxieties about something or someone hiding in my bedroom closet after the lamp went out; lights shifted and flickered outside our South Austin Boulevard tenement apartment window, shadows crawled across the walls, and words inexplicably lost their meanings. What was in that closet? A ghost? A "dirty Nazi"? How could I know, I'd never seen one. All too often in those first years of my life I was bedridden with assorted illnesses, and it seems fever too acted as a kind of solvent of meaning, sending me swirling into a vertigo of lost sense. The first movie I recall, *The Spiral Staircase*, was one I probably should not have been taken to: all my concealed fears and phobias were confirmed and afterwards ran amok in uncontrolled visions of dangers hidden in dark places; like the deaf-mute heroine in the film, I could neither be sure of the grounding of my private terrors in any tangible reality, nor find words to utter them. I suppose all of this is perfectly normal personality development in certain respects, the predictable problems of adjustment any child experiences in coming to terms with a world that is at least in part a place of unintelligible and inexpressible menace.

Across Austin Boulevard from the large brown brick apartment house that was my first home lay a Chicago city park with scrubby woods and public golf links—Columbus Park, *terra incognita* of my earliest psychic geographizing. In the beginning it was forbidden territory. The tree-shaded landfill hillock with cinder path that ran parallel to the boulevard, defining the park's western boundary, was the supposed lair of unpleasant characters who lurked in wait to snare any insouciant children happening past. Though "God only knew" exactly what these bogeymen did to their victims, one suspected the adults had a clue but weren't telling. Once permitted out on my own, of course, I spent as much time there as possible, foraging with pals through the patchy foliage beside the dandelion-pocked fairways, surreptitiously scavenging lost golf balls and then peddling them back to the golfers for a dime apiece, nicked or waterlogged ones going for a nickel. This was, I believe, the first mercantile enterprise in which I ever took part.

My father had been an excellent golfer in his youth. I have a photo of him, at age thirty-one, holding his driver, lined up in a row with three other local amateur champs, all of them much older than he, taken on the occasion of the Evanston Rodeo Tournament at Evanston Country Club on the North Shore in the summer of 1942. That was before he'd lost the job as a bond trader—perhaps the peak moment of his hopes in life. Though drinking has already begun to bloat his face in this photo, there is still intelligence in the wide-set, curi-

*The author's father, Arthur Clark (far right), at age thirty-one, Evanston Rodeo
Tournament at Evanston Country Club, Illinois, 1942*

ously penetrating eyes. But it is the intelligence of someone who's seen the darker side of himself, the face of a man to whom damage is on its way to happen. When I was about ten he gave me his old clubs and taught me to play. I have scorecards of some of our ancient rounds on the Columbus Park links—even when I was thirteen and getting stronger, and he was forty-three and in bad shape, the best I could ever do was come within two strokes of him on the nine-hole course. It was the only sport he ever practiced seriously, though he was fairly astute about how baseball was meant to be played, and played it himself with an adeptness that made our occasional games of catch a useful teaching experience for me.

He took me to my first big-league games at Comiskey Park on the city's South Side. These were intense adventures indeed. The car ride through the most infernal neighborhoods I'd so far ever seen was an education in itself; in the broken-glass-littered streets where we parked, aggressive urchins boldly demanded tribute

("Watch your car, fifty cents," they promised, fleeing if you paid—or, if you didn't, hanging around to slash your tires). Then once inside the big old brick ballpark we marched up long dark grandstand ramps for what seemed an endless time until finally and suddenly emerging through a tunnel into the radiantly illuminated, enchanted emerald green space. The first game I attended, sometime in 1948 or 1949, was a night contest, won by the Yankees, 11 to 8, on the strength of a bases-clearing double in the top of the eighth by a hobbled and aging but still elegant Joe DiMaggio. The night left me exhausted but exultant, unable to sleep. My father took me to other games now and then, of course not as often as I would have liked. His own grown-up's problems prevented his sharing my religious involvement in the game.

Perhaps religious is the wrong term, though. Part hobby, part escape hatch from endarkened household, for me baseball opened up a secret door in the wall to numinous worlds religion promised but never delivered. Before long

I was collecting baseball cards with a passion that defied reason. Hanging out at penny candy shops on Harrison Street, waiting for the season's new shipment of cards to come in, I risked the wrath of the nuns, several times getting caught ditching classes—and, on one infamous occasion, Sunday mass—for the sake of a wafer of cardboard containing the painted figure of Tommy Holmes or Felix Mantilla, Sam Jethroe or Johnny Groth, Eddie Yost or Irv Noren. Along with each packet of cards came several thick powder-coated slabs of sugary pink bubble gum which I dutifully chewed all through my bike-riding and pickup ballgame days, thus contributing directly to the early stages of the erosion of my now long-gone dental apparatus. Some twenty-five or thirty years later, after I'd left home for good, these vast early collections, having done nothing for decades but gather dust in my mother's attic while concurrently also unbeknownst to her gathering increasing monetary value, were taken out by her into the back alley one day and burned with the rest of the trash. These three facts, the third being the crowning consideration, allow my collecting to remain in my mind one of the few instances of pure sacrifice in my life.

From the age of eight or nine onwards, I listened to White Sox games broadcast by "Commander Bob" Elson on WCFL radio with an intensity of imaginative involvement rarely equalled in my participation, say, as an altar boy at mass; indeed the two forms of attention were so linked that I felt no qualms about enlisting the latter in the service of the former, often praying through an entire Sunday morning ceremony for a double-header sweep by the Sox, and deliberately fixing my mind, in the moment of receiving the eucharist upon my tongue, on certain hoped-for achievements of the day by my current favorite player, be it Billy Pierce, Minnie Minoso, or Nelson Fox.

As an adolescent it was one of my great joys to actually get up close to big-league players through the happy chance of picking up work as a ballpark usher. Over three summers I probably worked some three hundred games at Chicago's two major league parks, met many players, had more than a few interesting conversations with them (Dick Stuart, the home-run-hitting "Dr. Strangeglove" first baseman of the Pittsburgh Pirates, once explained to me his philosophy of dealing with the opposite sex, a subject on which I could use all the coach-

ing I could get), and was even several times (thrill!) mistaken for them by autograph seekers, when in my pre- or post-game white-shirt-and-slacks mufti.

Blue Boy in a Green Shade

In that little urban neighborhood of working-class or lower-middle-class pseudorespectable lace-curtain Irish where I grew up, three categories of human being were recognized as more or less warily coexisting: churchgoing Catholics, who dwelt within the familiar limits of that invisible social frontier, the parish; non-Catholics, who dwelt on the exotic other side; and the "fallen away," or embarrassed-circumstance ex-Catholics, who, for all the unknowing child could tell, inhabited some shadowy nether zone of their own, bound in by disillusion, disappointment, and private shame.

It was difficult to be sure exactly why anyone might be tempted (or for that matter—who knew?—driven) into falling away. If the first stirrings of puberty brought hints sex must have something to do with it, still these inklings had to await, and rather impatiently at that, any kind of tangible confirmation. College would inevitably provide it. In the meantime, however, the few hundred dollars that had somehow to be found to pay my tuition at a private Dominican high school were likely well spent, though you'd perhaps have had a hard time putting that fact across to my father. A reluctant Catholic at best, he'd taken up the faith only under duress, in order to enter a matrimonial state that had anyway turned out somewhat less than entirely blissful, and was besides no great admirer of the confident dogmatic wisdom of the priests. (In the Catholic cop world of his wife's family, he was always a stranger in a strange land, and as the darkness in his nature more and more revealed itself, was increasingly *non grata* there.) My mother, though, insisted. In consideration of the by then already evident unruly aspects of my character, her view in this matter was probably the more sensible. Noted citywide for its several disciplines—religious, athletic, scholastic—the school did an excellent job not only of keeping potential hard cases like me off the streets and out of reformatories, but also of moving its graduates (all save a very few of them, and not just the small minority of rich kids) on to college. Thus provided a classical education good enough to qualify me for a small scholarship to a Jesuit liberal arts college in Ohio, I found myself faced with the highly desirable prospect of living away from home for the first time.

Hopeful images of Joe College days, footballs falling through the leaves, lasted but a few weeks. My year with the Jesuits turned out to be for the most part strange and lonely. By midwinter I had moved in with an old high school friend from back home, with whom I probably spent more hours in a certain beer joint on Euclid Avenue in Cleveland than I ever put in studying. Sad and blue, down to my bottom dollar, I learned from an obliging senior—a lieutenant from my ROTC unit, if memory serves—how to twist a wire coat hanger so that it would, upon insertion, retrieve coins from pay phones, thus making possible nightly hours of long-distance sweet talking with my teenage main squeeze, an Illinois state champion high school butterfly stroker and (naturally) the daughter of a Chicago cop.

In *The Psychopathology of Everyday Life* Freud suggested there are no accidents, and perhaps it is true that someone who gets into so-called accidents throughout life must in some unconscious sense be self-propelled into them. Recklessness, in any case, has more than once been my undoing. Rushing down dormitory stairs one day, I tripped and plunged headlong through a double-pane, wire-reinforced "safety" window, nearly severing my left arm just above the wrist. Long nights in a Cleveland hospital ensued; a generous Italian-American specialist treated me for months without charge, performing a series of skin-graft surgeries. The folks back home never heard a word about any of this. Further difficulties followed. The complications of a romantic liaison with a local high school girl, daughter of a trucking company boss, caused the embarrassment of a series of increasingly late and disorganized arrivals at a daily 8:00 A.M. history class. Then the phone company started making belated inquiries, and school officials began to diplomatically suggest everyone concerned might be better off if this particularly trouble-prone student were to seek a transfer.

At that age there is still a certain feeling of living a charmed life—a delusion further impressed upon me by what happened next, my seemingly serendipitous admission to the University of Michigan. My first collegiate venture had been an utter washout, and probably should have doomed me for life to the drab working-class existence I so dreaded. Instead I found myself actually welcomed by a much larger and more prestigious institution, which would prove not only much better equipped scholastically, but considerably broader in its tolerance of my often noisome presence. At any rate, things worked out somewhat better there. After a final flourish during a brief fling at fraternity life, my determined wild-oat-sowing mercifully gave over to a first demonstration of serious intent to acquire knowledge. Perhaps forcible body painting on a frosty midnight and the subsequent dousing-with-firehose during pledge week helped diminish my loyalty to Sigma Chi; certainly I do recall rueful thoughts afterwards upon finding my photo in the house album, naked, wet, and shivering, humorously captioned "Blue Boy."

Ann Arbor became for me a place of dark weeping trees under which long solitary night rambles took me down to the New York Central tracks that ran through the sleepy valley of the Huron River. There, one night, I witnessed a violent quarrel between two strangers that spilled from a car onto the shaded railroad embankment and ended—I was certain, from the *in extremis* sounds that issued out of the invisible trees by that unforgetting river—in bloody murder. Sleepless in my deracinated asceticism, I experienced a derangement of the senses made more acute by month after month of living on apples and coffee to stretch my few final dollars, burning the midnight oil, staring at the light bulb in the ceiling fixture while silent snow piled up in the blackness outside. With the belated arrival of spring, an intensity of lilacs burst upon the surprised air. I had been reading Rilke and Wallace Stevens, but when my spooky-normal landlord, a German-American fellow who wore an Elmer Fudd-style hunting cap every day of the year, informed me that he'd known the family of the poet Theodore Roethke, and that Roethke himself had lived in this neighborhood while at the university, I also began to intuit a darker presence underlying the profuse erotic greenness of the late Midwestern spring. The lofty imperatives of Rilke's angels and the sober contemplative clarities of Stevens's snowy evenings gave way briefly to Roethke's muddier psychic landscape, with its ominous inevitabilities, nurturings of womb and birthplace, mushy, loamy oozings of life-throes circling back to the dark closure of grave-humus. Then I found Boris Pasternak's *Safe Conduct.* Pasternak's testament to another kind of virid lyric springtime—a prism through which the life of poetry appeared such a delicate yet powerful thing, trembling with its singular impossible demand for grace—seemed the most resonant of all.

The poets of the university circuit who came through Ann Arbor, however, were hardly my idea of role models. A recent Pulitzer Prize winner and college-circuit darling of the moment from the Iowa Writer's Workshop read his famous "confessional" lyrics, then at the compulsory professors' party afterward keened disconsolately on a freezing sidewalk during a blizzard. I'll never forget seeing him there on his hands and knees weeping melodramatically into the driving snow—feet clad only in lightweight loafers meant for gently treading fallen leaves, index finger hooked into a Chianti bottle—and remarking inwardly on the tendency of poets to act out the *personae* of their work in public.

The poet of the Library of Congress, a hulking crew-cut Southerner, former air force bomber pilot, and successful advertising man, came through to do a reading just a few weeks after the appearance in the *New York Times* of an essay he'd penned about the heavy spiritual toll and sincere Platonic satisfactions of being a touring campus poet. From his reaction at the post-reading party to my enthusiastic comments about the new Grove Press anthology of "alternative" poets, I sensed he regarded me as a rather dubious character—and not just because a knee in the groin had been his disappointing reward for following my girlfriend, a diminutive but feisty New Yorker, upstairs to a bedroom and falling upon her atop a pile of coats.

Indeed such opportunities for up-close viewing of the "major" American poets of the day left me with a strong and lasting negative impression. I now look back on this as unfortunate, not so much because I presumed judgment as because, once offered the chance some four or five years later to become a university poet

Standing with friends as a young collegian, Cleveland, Ohio, 1959

myself (at Iowa, among other proffered places), I turned it down, thus irrevocably exiting, with a headstrong lack of foresight surely to be regretted, the moving staircase of academic poetry-careering. Once you step off that escalator-to-a-secure-mediocrity, you can never step back on.

Meanwhile, of course, Ann Arbor proposed not just poetry's but quite a few other possible voices and ways of life. On the Diag, the open space in front of Rackham Library that served not only as heavily traveled pedestrian thoroughfare but informal center of campus political activity, *soi-disant* radicals, mostly from New York and Chicago, gathered to hear speakers who stood on large stone benches to debate the urgent issues of the hour. I heard a smart, intense, pimply faced young student politician named Tom Hayden debate Fulton Lewis, Jr., about civil rights on those benches once, and, another time, a rousing speech by Martin Luther King. Ramblin' Jack Elliott came through town, camped under a tree adjacent to the Diag to pick and sing for his next meal, and included in his repertoire the first Woody Guthrie and Bob Dylan songs I'd ever heard.

Folk singing I understood—hadn't I gone to hear the Kingston Trio in high school?—but Realpolitik meant nothing to me as yet (if it ever would). I'll never forget the image of a rather unworldly, eccentric professor of English—a noted scholar of Spenserian Neoplatonism and brilliant lecturer on Renaissance literature who'd taught me Shakespeare—emerge from the library into the bleak twilight of the scariest day of the Cuban missile crisis, listen silently to a few minutes of the back-and-forth Diag debate about the momently anticipated cataclysm, and walk off sadly shaking his head. There was obviously no place for nuclear war in his world of Ideal Forms. Nor in mine. While elsewhere on campus co-eds were picked up from dorms by their dads to be driven home to Kalamazoo or Grand Rapids for Doomsday, I spent the final few hours of nervous indecision in sweaty argument with my downstairs neighbor, an eighteen-year-old Jewish prodigy from Horace Mann School, before word came through that the Russian ships had turned back. I can't remember the exact details of our disagreement now, except that it hinged on some obscure question of one's choice of logics for opposing war; as I recall, his reasoning was based on pacifist principles supported by citations from Gandhi, whereas mine was based on a desire not to be burned up, supported by citations from Beckett's *Watt*.

The denizens of the campus beatnik fringe, on the other hand, seemed way too cool ever to work up much of a sweat about political issues, or for that matter anything else—save possibly drugs, which they approached with a bizarre, exotic seriousness I found fascinating in a glass-bottom-boat sort of way. Wild tales circulated about beatnik naked parties, at which guests of both sexes were said to arrive wearing nothing but raincoats that were immediately removed, but I was never invited to one. A red-bearded renegade philosopher, rumored scion of old Prussian aristocracy and going by the name of Count Leopold von Bretzel, was bruited to be an organizer of naked parties at other people's houses. Once he intercepted me on the steps of a classroom building and attempted to sell me his tennis shoes for a dollar. Ratty, smelly, and full of holes, these were shoes one would have paid good money to have removed from one's presence. Before this encounter, the last time I'd seen the Count—who often appeared somewhat less studiedly cool than many of the local hipster set, yet also quite a bit crazier—he'd been plunging through crowds of mystified sorority and fraternity types on South University Avenue, waving a fist in the air and chanting, "Human heads shrunk to the size of baseballs!" I was more than a little intimidated by him. I offered to purchase enough hamburger to make a meal for both of us, provided he would cease to wave his awful sneakers in my face. He accepted, threw them in a trash can, and accompanied me barefoot to my room, where I cooked the ground beef on my plug-in frying pan, and we ate it together in total silence. In his eyes I detected the sullen, remote contempt of the true beatnik, seeing right through me even as he gnawed on my meat.

Exile

After three years of increasingly intense and compulsive scholastic effort ultimately at the expense of all pretension to social existence, a degree with highest honors was awarded. Thus armed, one embarked on real life.

The first thought was to somehow cash in on all that work by turning it into freedom. The next thought was to leave the country. In

Returning to the University of Michigan for a reading, Ann Arbor, 1968

1963 I went abroad to "study," i.e., learn to live. The generous proposal of a gentlemanly progress to a Harvard doctorate, by way of a Henry Fellowship, was passed over for a Fulbright to Cambridge because England spelled at once liberty and the past—that unlikely tandem of values which would in the long run provide the excuse for a cranky way of life, a turning both inward and backward, eventually to become the author's perverse distinction.

But just as I was so earnestly struggling to shed my national identity in order to become a citizen of the world, that identity sneakily reasserted itself. Passing by an out-of-focus television screen in the junior common room of a Cambridge college notable for its scientists and explorers, my new home in this first year abroad, my eye was caught by the image of an American naval ship at sea, as a news announcer reported its taking enemy fire in the Tonkin Gulf. In months and years that followed, when fulsome, fatuous, Ugly American politician voices droned on promulgating the pressing of a war,

I found myself hard put to listen. But the embarrassment of one's own real if involuntary sharing in that voice was inevitably to become a necessary self-chastisement. Not choosing sides in the conflict involved an almost impossible luxury of evasion in those years. I'm reminded of doing a magazine feature interview, some twenty years after his involvement in the war, with that disenchanted think-tank strategist, ex-military-advising circuit rider of the New Frontier, Daniel Ellsberg. My assumptions as to the naiveté of those who'd believed in the war in those early days were shaken somewhat when Ellsberg related to me the surprising depth of his initial commitment to the American cause, the practical application, as he explained it, of a high-minded ideal of scholar-warriorhood inherited from twentieth-century western imperialism's most notable cockeyed-intellectual-ascetic-soldier-of-fortune-spook role model, T. E. Lawrence. Ellsberg showed me a photo of himself in Vietnam—a Harvard Ph.D. crouched in the elephant grass of the Delta, M-16 poking belligerently between tall reeds—then with his next breath wept over the enormous toll of human suffering in which the acting out of his high Lawrentian ideals had implicated him.

Well, at least he'd believed in *something.* Having once waited hours through the northern night frost for a chance to shake Jack Kennedy's hand in a college-town motorcade, perhaps I myself ought to have proven more loyal to that clever Irishman's war. Instead, avoiding both the commitment and the suffering, the cleansing with filth and the shame of the slaughter, at whatever sacrifice of career advantage, became a personal goal. Staying on in Europe represented in this respect an act of omission, more telling in terms of what I was *not* doing than of what I *was.*

Two years of fairly desultory scholarship at Cambridge were followed by two more years of same—accompanied by a little teaching work—at the then newly opened University of Essex, where I halfheartedly attempted to get a thesis on Ezra Pound off the ground.

What Lawrence of Arabia was to Dan Ellsberg, I suppose Ezra Pound was to me. While still at Cambridge, I'd used my first long vacation to set off in search of the sacred places of *The Cantos,* hitchhiking in Pound's long-cooled footsteps through the troubadour country of the south of France, at first dutifully, out of the simple loyalty of the pilgrim, but then with increasingly particular delight. After close encounters with Provencal landscape and Romanesque church architecture, I passed on into Italy to get next to the radiant stones of Venice and examine firsthand that Pound-proclaimed triumph of fifteenth-century paternalistic economics, Sigismondo Malatesta's glorious neo-pagan *duomo* at Rimini (where a joyless little curate inconveniently appropriated my passport, penalty for my trespass into a closed-off chapel to inspect Piero della Francesca's portrait of Malatesta). Finally I ascended the Dolomites into the alpine village of Merano in search of the Master himself.

Pound, I'd been told, was residing on a mountaintop above the town, at the familial castle of an Austrian baron who'd wed his daughter Mary. Armed with an ostensible "official" reason to visit, as the delegate of English art-collecting interests—I'd been appointed, in my innocence, to solicit the donation of the poet's collection of Gaudier-Brzeska sculptures to the Tate Gallery—I made the grueling hike up that sacred mountain, toiling sweatily past hefty vacationing Viennese in lederhosen and Tyrolean hats. My mission, though, proved fruitless. Leaning out a tower window, her striking high cheekbones remarkably evoking the leonine "Hieratic Head of E. P." carved from marble by Gaudier in London some half-century before and now planted on a slope in the castle garden whence its blind eyes stared up a spectacular valley between snowy peaks toward Innsbruck, the Baroness Mary de Rachewiltz informed me her father, no longer able to endure the chill of the brisk alpine nights, had gone off to Venice. As a reward for my persistence, however, I was asked in for tea. Suddenly embarrassed by my petty toe-in-the-door pretext of an errand, I downplayed the Tate solicitation as best I could; my hostess made it emphatically clear, once I'd got up the nerve to spill out my appointed purpose, that the English had never particularly endeared themselves to her father. What, she pointedly inquired, were the English prepared to pay in order to have what they were asking? Nothing at all, I was forced humbly to confess. My intended homage simply amounted to a fresh insult from a nation that had never really meant her father any good, any more for that matter than it had my own forefathers. This chastening conclusion to my trip contained a lesson I was as yet too young to understand, but appreciate in retrospect.

In and out of school, poetry provided a life—of sorts. At a poetry festival in Bristol, Allen Ginsberg turned up unexpectedly, read a dolorous lament for Neal Cassady, then, when I stood up next to him in our little circle of poets to read, even more unexpectedly goosed me. He and I rode through the Somerset night in a motorcycle sidecar, me coming on about poetry, him just coming on. We hitchhiked together to Bath, then on to Glastonbury, where we visited the ruins of King Arthur's Avalon and Allen gleefully scandalized some old ladies in a tea shoppe. In open country miles west of Reading, rideless for hours as night and rain began to fall, I grew desperate, but an unfazed Allen calmly tried out his Buddhist hand signals, an alternative to thumbing that brought the next lorry driver screeching to a halt. This obliging Lancelot conducted us back to London. A few days later, with Ginsberg, Gregory Corso, Andrei Voznesensky, Diter Rot, Patrick Kavanagh, Robert Graves, Anselm Hollo, Christopher Logue, Harry Fainlight, Simon Vinkenoog, Adrian Mitchell, and other poets of all nations, I participated in a "Wholly Communion" mega-reading at the Albert Hall. Dolled up like some wastrel son of Omar the tent maker in a several-sizes-too-large mod leather jacket I'd purchased for three pounds earlier that day at a cut-price tailor's in the King's Road, I recited my poem "Superballs" and was heckled for my nasal Chicago accent by some wag in the third balcony.

The evening, like many spent in London's poetry *demimonde* of those years, segued into further confusions, reversals, adventures. I'd been camping across the river at the amazing Dickensian-dockside East End council-house digs of a young woman I'd met at a poetry festival in Nottingham, but at the Albert Hall found myself spontaneously befriended by a charming if rather fallen-looking duchess in a white vinyl minidress and shut-eye shades. She generously invited me back to her flat off the Fulham Road, and the next morning we staggered off on a bleary-eyed day trip to Winchester, a cathedral town of old buildings as beautiful as Oxford's or Cambridge's, but set among hills, trees, streams. Revived by the stroll past the west front of the cathedral, down College Street and through water meadows Keats had walked on another summer's day, I marveled at my poet's good fortune—then an hour later sank into deep gloom when it developed we'd missed the last bus to London, and had to thumb.

By and large life back at Cambridge left me feeling lonesome for my own kind, though there were happy discoveries of common ground with a couple of student poets who fancied the same kind of new verse I did. One was John Temple, a gentle, shambling, undergraduate scholarship boy from the working classes up north. My first year at Gonville and Caius College, John dwelt in ground-floor rooms beneath my own in St. Michael's Court, adjacent to Trinity Church and the town market square. John became my best friend in college. He invested wistful yearnings for the American West in his poetry enthusiasm, and found in the lyricism of Edward Dorn, a maverick bard of those lonely western spaces he himself had never seen, the same purity of longing that he discovered in the poems of his fellow underclass countryman John Keats. Donald Davie, the lecturer in English who tutored us both in poetry, had alerted John and me to the articulate energy of syntax in verse; together quaffing congenial brews deep into the quiet college evenings, we earnestly compared the sinuous lines of Keats's *Hyperion* with those of Dorn's poems about that equally remote and mythy locale *Nyew* Mexico, as John pronounced it—to him an almost unimaginable paradise; to me, in my memory of my one youthful enthralled passage west at age thirteen with my grandfather, almost as fantastic. About all I could actually recall of New Mexico by then was my long-yearned-for first sighting of an actual mountain, the large, loaf-shaped mesa with a big white *T* on it at which I'd stared transfixed from the Cactus Motor Lodge in Tucumcari. Still, these pub talks of ours, continuing after closing time back in our rooms, often took on, as they advanced into the night, a curious tone of bittersweet sadness, almost as if we'd really experienced that wild locale whereof we spoke. In my new exile, I already found myself able to work up a powerful nostalgia for a homeland of big skies and painted canyons that never really had been mine, except through the same agency it had been my English friend's, i.e., that of a fanciful poetic imagination. Perhaps part of the appeal of such conversations lay in the peculiar exotic quality of lostness that places you've always desired take on for you when you begin to recognize they are getting farther and farther out of reach. Standing on Municipal Pier in Santa Monica, drinking in my first awed sighting of the green Pacific in 1954, I'd developed my own individual fantasy of the West—about as unique as the banal longings of every other Irishman who'd ever left home to be burnt by an alien sun on that far shore.

A second Cambridge friend, Andrew Crozier, a diffident, earnest young Londoner, graduate of Dulwich School and at this time an undergraduate at Milton's college, Christ's, was a devotee of another American "outsider," the notoriously difficult Black Mountain master Charles Olson. Later, after both he and John Temple had put in time among Olson's little corps of disciples at Buffalo, Andrew joined me back in England as a grad student at Essex, where we reverently followed Olson's directive in plastering the recently discovered Vinland map on the cover of the inaugural issue of a magazine we coedited, *The Wivenhoe Park Review*. (A chance to meet Olson himself on his November 1966 trip to England proved a surprising pleasure, the imposing behemoth of *The Maximus Poems* turning out to be a friendly giant who wanted to keep me up all night yakking about connective tissue and fish people from outer space.) Hearing of a budding poetry scene in the far north of England, Andrew and I hitchhiked together from Cambridge to Newcastle, a bleak, gray city then economically devastated by the decline of its traditional shipbuilding industry. There we found a little enclave of youthful working-class poets led by a dashing blond-mopped teenager named Tom Pickard, who on his minuscule weekly dole stipend was not only raising a family but running a poetry-reading series in the Morden Tower on the city's old medieval wall. (This enterprising youth had single-handedly spurred back into verse writing the long-silent Basil Bunting, former Objectivist colleague of Pound and Louis Zukofsky and, though totally disregarded at that time, still one of England's finest living poets.) The lack of electric lights at our reading in the medieval tower was not for quaintness' sake but because impoverished young entrepreneur Pickard hadn't been able to foot the bill that month. We went ahead anyway with candles, and it felt like poetry was meant to be read that way. To college boys Andrew and me this trip was an altogether marvelous adventure. We were invited to read our poems on local television—certainly a first for both of us. We drank dark brown ale with young Geordi poets in Tyneside pubs rocking with a life and atmosphere that defied the gloom of the streets outside, and went dancing in a subterranean club filled by long-haired guitar boys with the throbbing din of Marshall amps and flashing with the pulse of black-light strobes. This, too—so far from our world of Oxbridge and London—was England, perhaps much closer to the "real" England circa 1964.

Eric Burdon's then-popular song "We Gotta Get Out of This Place" made a particular kind of poetic sense in that context. Obvious differences in scale notwithstanding, the tiny underground poetry movement and the exploding electric rock minstrelsy of the period were essentially linked, the former as it were standing on the latter's shoulders; both constituted expressions of a generalized resistance against England's dead-end prospects. The Beatles and the Rolling Stones could still be heard in town dance-hall venues, as could up-and-coming mod bands like the Yardbirds, the Kinks, the Who, and the Small Faces. Allegedly fueled by "diet pills" obtained from national health doctors by their dolly-girl consorts, young British musicians appeared to tap inexhaustible energy resources, memorizing their favorite R & B licks, distorting them into new dimensions, and then playing them all night long.

Around this time a band of fairly typical going-nowhere Cambridge town kids, learning to play their instruments as they went along, started what in later years would have been called a "concept" band—if one can speak of calculated irrationalism as a concept—and began putting on England's first psychedelic light shows in a gloomy church hall near Notting Hill Gate in London. Pharmaceutical LSD was just then hitting England, and this band's shows at All Saints Hall amounted to unsolicited testimonials for it: prolonged baths in an acid ambiance still too inchoate to be a cliché, and not yet quite controllable enough to be successfully exploited (that phase wouldn't last long). Meanwhile their leader and guiding genius, Syd Barrett, zoomed through half-hour shoe-gazing guitar explorations on "Interstellar Overdrive," his signature composition, while bassist Roger Waters, a tall, expressionless zombie type, lay prone on stage, staring up into the flashing cellular blob projections as though mesmerized by a giant amoeba. Milling rather than dancing, we in the audience mimed the determined spaciness of the group, contributing our own semicomatose, vaguely participatory looniness to the occasion. One of my Essex students, also a

On the evening of their wedding, Clark's wife, Angelica Heinegg, stands with poet Ted Berrigan, who gave the bride away, New York City, March 22, 1968

Cambridge townie, showed me strange color drawings of cartoonoid hulk figures Syd Barrett had done on LSD. Later Barrett reportedly went off to India and "blew his mind" even beyond professional barriers. At Essex we still brought in the remnants of the band—Pink Floyd, they called themselves—to play for student dances. They'd learned to play their instruments, but without their certified loony leader would never again be quite the same. It seemed true madness was after all not easy either to simulate or to survive.

Another, tamer distraction from my nominal academic chores was my growing involvement with magazines both little and not-so-little. An opportunity to edit the poetry section of *The Paris Review*—arising out of an introduction supplied by my Ann Arbor teacher Donald Hall to that journal's editor, George Plimpton, who would prove a generously noninterfering if sometimes uncomprehending boss over the decade of my tenure—provided a pretext for contact with as well as occasion to promote the work of most of those contemporary poets I had latterly come to admire: both older ones (Olson, Dorn, Creeley, Ashbery, O'Hara, Schuyler,

Duncan, Zukofsky, Whalen, et al.) and younger ones of my own generation (Berrigan, Padgett, Sanders, Saroyan, Coolidge, et al.).

Though at best only thirty to forty pages of poetry could be squeezed into any given issue of *The Paris Review*, before long I was swamped with at least five times that much interesting incoming material. The runoff, it soon became apparent, would require its own place. To the creation of such a place I devoted my nights at Essex, parlaying my own manic industry with the mechanical and postal resources of the university to crank out a dozen issues of a freewheeling, spur-of-the-moment giveaway mimeograph magazine, the "Once" series (*Once, Twice, Thrice*, etc.). It went out to a mailing list of seventy-five to a hundred poet-friends on both sides of the Atlantic. Of the works to appear therein, perhaps the most notable in literary terms would be the seed-poem of the masterly mock-epic *Gunslinger*, whose author, the brilliant, craggy Ed Dorn, I had the good luck to befriend when he arrived at Essex as a visiting poet in September 1965. But immortal works were perhaps less to the point of the "Once" series than extremely transitory ones. The more-or-less instantaneous nature of the mimeo-mag project allowed it to keep up with an epoch whose essence seemed a Heraclitean flow: looking back now, much of what I published seems at once ephemeral and curiously indicant, a kind of unintended readout on times that were a-changin' faster than any culture that pretended to contain them. For example, in a brief poetic manifesto titled after his own folk-rock group "The Fugs," New York peace-and-love activist Ed Sanders made a free-verse bow to the Rolling Stones, declaring their music as important as the Magna Carta. The Stones LP Sanders singled out as news of the final tender human solution was the appropriately titled *Out of Our Heads*. Thought evidently had given up the ghost, now it all came down to bodies. Again, Ted Berrigan, another New York poet, to whom I'd mailed some mimeo stencils so that he could inscribe poems directly into my pages, sent back one stencil with just four words etched into it in huge block capitals beneath the heading "Poem for Ed Sanders": I AIN'T GONNA DIE. An Immortality Ode for the new consciousness?

My strange nighttime office labors, though, once reported back by university porters, precipitated a moment-of-truth interview with my department boss, Donald Davie. My erstwhile Cambridge research sponsor, whose good graces were furthermore responsible for my position in this new program he'd come to head, Davie had by this time grown somewhat impatient with my failure to proceed in acceptable academic manner. Indeed, looking back, I think he had good reason to look askance: my penchant for guerilla publication was only the latest in a series of manifestations that also included my long hair, irregular period attire, and evident preference for the company of my rock-and-rolling, hash-smoking students (as versus that of my Oxbridge-bred, pipe-smoking colleagues). Summoning me to his inner sanctum, he inquired sternly whether I intended to be *a scholar or a bohemian?*

Caught no more than a moment on the horns of that impossible dilemma, I abandoned my Ph.D. candidacy and teaching assistantship at the progressive university in Constable country. Cleaning out my bachelor digs in a quaint but bleak little North Sea fishing village, where the bemused gnomic eye of the Wittgenstein duck-rabbit figure I'd painted on the wallpaper to keep me company in my nocturnal poetry solitudes stared down upon two years of dirty laundry, I now had no job and virtually no assets save a somewhat battered trunkful of books and a steamship ticket for passage from Southampton to New York.

"White man, tomorrow you die"

White man, tomorrow you die!" Ted Berrigan's *noir humoresque* line had a prophetic half-life he couldn't have calculated when he applied it to his own little sphere of influence on Lower East Side streets. Passionate winds of the times blowing crossfire from several directions at once rang out their siren changes beneath the phrases of rock songs. History had caught a bunch of rootless, impoverished, foot-loose white kids confused and adrift at point-blank range in its expiring backdraft. If it looked more certain every day that history in its received version might actually soon be *over*, there was equally little certainty as to what might be coming to replace it. In social terms especially this funny posthistorical vacancy was felt; in fact it sometimes seemed there was no class structure left at all. In terrain where the overlay of pot smoke and incense could neither eradicate

With daughter, Juliet, Bolinas, California, 1978

nor mask for long those other odors in the grit-charged air—dread, adrenaline, amphet-aminoid anxiety, rotten garbage, too-closely-packed, overheated human bodies—utopian collectivist philosophy just couldn't seem to take root, communal households inevitably devolving by stages into crash pads, then shooting galleries, then drifter graveyards. In the summer of '67, flowers and love settled over San Francisco in a soft psychedelic storm, but on the streets of the East Village there lingered more than enough fear and resentment to go around. Here the period hippie tribalism of the West Coast would never really get off the ground.

My first month or so in the city was spent in an apartment on the nether reaches of East First Street, borrowed from the poet Dick Gallup. Dick and his family, out of money and plagued by a discouraging siege of robberies, had retreated home to Tulsa, Oklahoma, for a few square meals and a respite from the trials of the city. The building was a testament to some unknown slumlord's legend. The graffiti-scrawled, piss-pooled, creaking, swaying ancient elevator was an adventure one wouldn't want to risk

twice. Climbing the Raskolnikovian stairs, on the other hand, was not only depressing and exhausting but about as safe as a solo patrol in what weird-eyed street guys just back from Nam called Indian Country. Dick's place was on the third-floor rear, with an exposed fire escape that offered perfect entry and exit routes for emergency "movers." During my stay, prospective burglars showed up every few days, peering over my shoulder past the chain lock to case the place, just on the chance a new TV set might have been brought in (no such luck). One particularly brazen prospector, a beat-up-looking guy in a big baggy overcoat, ogled the scene for at least a slow half-minute before remembering to pretend to explain to me what he'd come for. Producing from deep within his coat a balled-up out-of-date copy of *Muhammad Speaks*, he asked, "Want to buy a newspaper?" In fact I felt fairly invulnerable; the only vaguely stealable object I'd brought into the apartment was a vintage British-made Magnavox phonograph, but this machine—a big boxy white imitation-leather-covered console model, pawnshop value about five dollars—appeared hardly worth the trouble of any self-respecting burglar. I, however, valued it unduly highly. It was the shrine of that spaced-out muse whose ghostly electrical visage, staring out from the museum of infinity, had kept me up past dawn spinning my half-dozen or so essential rock LPs for several years on sundry continents, and I didn't want to lose it (or them) now.

I went off to Chicago for a week, and left the apartment key with Ted Berrigan. On my return, I learned he'd left it in turn with a third party. When finally I retrieved the key and went to the apartment, I was startled to find both front door and fire-escape window gaping open, ancient Magnavox gone and my stash of precious albums vanished. My heart sank. I went over to Ted's to share my woes. It was late afternoon. A ray of sunlight slanted warmly from somewhere over by the East River into the tiny book-strewn front room. Ted was in a great mood, feet up on his desk, savoring the sugar rush of his second breakfast Pepsi, wagging his head from side to side in time with the rhythms of my Jefferson Airplane LP playing on the Magnavox. He'd come over to Dick's and picked it up to take care of it for me while I was away, he explained. Ted's social philosophy hinged on the adage, "*Mi casa, tu casa.*" What was his was yours, and what was yours was his. Living out his hero Kerouac's brave proposition—everything belongs to me because I'm poor—Ted was New York City's poet-realist answer to tribalism.

Eventually I found an apartment of my own, one tiny, tacky room on East Fourteenth Street near Avenue B. The sixty-dollar rent represented for me a princely sum, scraped together every month with no little difficulty out of my microscopic earnings from *The Paris Review* and from pickup labors like moving chairs around for poetry readings at St. Mark's Church—a fact which no doubt helped the place look better to me at the time than it does now in the mind's unsentimental eye. There was a hideaway bed that wouldn't hide properly (it had a "bent frame," handyman Ted astutely speculated), a dingy, unlit kitchen containing a cockroach watering hole of a sink and a minimal portable shower rigged precariously atop a cinder block that required a Right-Stuff-level sense of balance, a nonfunctioning turn-of-the-century brick fireplace containing a huge bass drum bearing the inscription of a Polish neighbor-

hood social club, and some cast-iron-and-wire bookshelves found on the street. I lined the latter with books which immediately accumulated a thick layer of dust and grime that sifted in through the barred but screenless windows from the Con Ed plant on the opposite bank of the turbulent traffic stream that was Fourteenth Street. (A decade later when Mount Saint Helens blew up and the volcanic dust drift spread as far as Colorado one morning, surprisingly depositing a sudden gray residue on everything, the first image that flashed into mind was a recollection of that apartment.)

Across a deep dismal courtyard, there was a view down into a household of Hare Krishna freaks, who in the sweltering dog days of summer liked to hang out the windows in their gaudy, gauzy veils, no doubt half-asphyxiated by the steam of boiling rice stews, burning patchouli, and sheer crush of physical overcrowding. Downstairs from me, a heavy covey of Puerto Rican junkies ruled the roost, up all night doing a serious trade in heroin and stolen goods, relentlessly playing the same Wes Montgomery track over and over at revving-jetliner volume on what had probably once been someone's very expensive stereo speakers. Paul Simon may have heard the sounds of silence echoing in tenement walls, but what I heard as I traveled up and down the vomit-coated staircases and landings of my building was a thunderous "A Day in the Life." This particular tenement was pressed smack up against a Chemical Bank whose power system hummed super-vibrantly all night long. I learned to live with my building's ambient noise, swallowed up in that general ungodly hum. Oddly, the daytime traffic racket on Fourteenth Street had a way of muting everything, like white noise.

Days were when I did my sleeping, anyway. One day I woke abruptly to the sensation of fluid dripping on my face from somewhere overhead. As there were several floors above me, rain would not explain this. Upstairs, a young unmarried mother who didn't speak English had broken a water pipe. I went up there, but could not explain the problem to her. The slumlord, a wizened old Russian, also pretended not to understand, until I threatened to withhold my rent payment.

The gentrification process that would turn these mean streets into a neighborhood where "nice" people lived wasn't yet so much as a gleam in a slumlord's eye. Beneath the thin surface veneer of hippie entrepreneurism—the sandwich stands, trendy boutiques, and record shops—an indigenous domain still ominously remained, its lower depths cruised by potentially dangerous unfriendlies who dictated nervous rules of engagement, retreating into invisibility by day but scary ghost presences emerging to rule the night.

After dark, not merely *where* you walked but *with whom* could quickly get to be a serious matter. After my first few months in town I ceased rambling the neighborhood at night with my otherwise good friend, the poet Michael Brownstein, who lived a block or two away. I couldn't help noting that Michael's particular sympathetic magic seemed to draw down upon us an inordinate share of street "bummers": having firecrackers thrown at us from tenement windows, being chased for blocks by crazed demanders of cigarettes, etc. My speculation was that Michael somehow brought these episodes upon us by neurotically anticipating them. For all I know, he may well have blamed them on *me*, and probably with equally good cause. Indeed it often seemed as though bad things happened to you in the streets in reverse proportion to your ability to handle them.

Foolish and intrepid in my long hair and Carnaby Street remnants, I must have shown up on those hostile street sensors as a perfect target. And with reason. Decked out in my purple madras potato-dyed surgical attendant's jacket, I dropped in one day my first week in town to play my English Jimi Hendrix 45s for a Nigerian fellow I'd met at Cambridge, who was now living with Sun Ra's Solar Arkestra in a collective flat down around Third Street. Four bars of "Purple Haze" were enough to get me chased out, followed by ominous scowls, the double bolt slammed shut behind me. If *I* didn't know who I was, that didn't mean it wasn't visible to others. And in fact my nocturnal rambles of the neighborhood did not take long to pitch me into the clutches of troubles of all kinds. Mugged, bugged, ragged on, and ripped off, I didn't require a microscope to get the joke. Territorial consciousness, developing almost overnight, suggested that finding a suitable hangout partner was not just a good idea but an absolute imperative.

This need had a lot to do with the growth of my relationship with Ted Berrigan, which was in basic practical terms largely a matter of defensive strategy. Thinking back on it now,

I'd moreover have to concede the strategy was probably one I'd learned long before, dealing with the minatory aspect of growing up on the West Side of Chicago, an environment in many ways unlike yet not always all that much kinder than this present one. My chosen best friend in grade school was the affable, burly captain of the football team, and in high school it was the six-foot-eleven-inch-tall basketball center. Having a large ally, I'd learned early, never hurt. Ted, for his part, was a fairly big guy who projected himself even larger; in the NBA they call this "playing big." Streetwise in summertime army fatigues or fur-lined Jim Bridger mountain-man cold-weather windbreaker, striding slightly bowlegged with arms swinging out at his sides in a sort of rolling sea captain's gait, the bluff, swaggering Providence Irish tough I found buried not too far under the skin in Ted brought out a goofy reckless Chicago Irish punk sidekick in me; wandering Alphabet City together, security actually seemed the least of our problems, well behind where to find, say, speed pills, danceable music, congenial friends, interesting books, or free cookies.

One night after a party at the Avenue D apartment of poet George Kimball, Ted had gone off in the opposite direction, toward Houston Street and home. Negotiating the bad stretch of Ninth Street between B and C at 2:30 in the morning, I paired up with Lewis Warsh, an angular, bespectacled, hypersensitive young poet from the Bronx. We hadn't ventured far when the "vibes," those all-sensing tutelary deities of the period, started to feel wrong; like shrinking walls in a nightmarish expressionist movie, the dark streets seemed to narrow in on us, looming up larger and larger as we ambled fake-casually along. Soon we had company: a quiver of slim shadows silently dividing off from the massed darkness of the other side of the street and gliding toward us with the unmistakable menacing purposiveness of serious misfortune incoming. We were trapped between our assailants and the parked cars that blocked off our route of flight. Honed-down blades of linoleum cutters pressed unsteadily against our throats, we surrendered our wallets. Watching my last forty dollars dissolve into the night, I choked back any useless—and possibly risky—protest. A tense eternity of five seconds or so went by, and then Lewis quite unexpectedly let out a strange, half-strangulated wail, clearly involuntary, somewhat resembling an animal's panic-stricken moan. It was a sound that could only have welled up from somewhere deep inside his trembling poet's soul. The tension broken, for his show of weakness Lewis was rewarded by having his glasses knocked to the pavement and stamped on. Tumbling in a pathetic cascade from curb to street, the broken pieces of plastic and glass added to the grit that was general all over our common world. For a moment the resonant echo of my friend's otherworldly howl of fear still hung in the concrete-encanyoned night. Standing in that echo I was as far from home as I'd ever be in my life, though still too young and foolish to understand it.

Uncloudy Day

In January 1968, I met my future wife, Angelica Heinegg, at an uptown party I attended with Lewis Warsh and Anne Waldman, who were acquaintances of the host. It was a party full of young short-haired stockbrokers. One of them asked sarcastically if I were "a member of the Byrds." My reply was to dance all evening with the prettiest girl in the room. Some weeks later this lovely young woman came along on a trip to Ann Arbor, where Ted Berrigan, Ron Padgett, and I were all to read our poems as part of a week-long arts festival. We stayed in guest rooms in the Student Union. Angelica and I locked ourselves up in our room and acted like fiancées are supposed to. I remember Ted pounding on the door minutes before a scheduled poetry reading, loudly announcing, "You two are jeopardizing the future of American Poetry! Come out!"

Ted spent the days in Ann Arbor paying respectful homage to the ghost of Frank O'Hara, who'd written many of his early poems while in graduate school there. O'Hara had won a Hopwood Prize, as had I—Michigan in both his time and mine having been one of the few schools where a young writer could actually make a few hundred dollars out of poetry. A memorial reading of Frank's poems took place—eerily for me—in what once had been the pool where I'd swum lonely college-boy laps,

Clark's own paintings can be seen in the background of this photo,
Boulder, Colorado, 1979

now filled in with concrete and serving as a student union lecture hall. Ron, Ted, and I all took part; Ted's O'Hara reading was wistful and tremulous, and not without tears. One very cold day we all walked off campus to the rooming house on South University Street where Frank had lived. It looked like any other tree-lined street in Ann Arbor. We stood there shivering on the sidewalk, trying to share Ted's glow of holy-proximity-with-the-great. It was difficult. Ted was our Wordsworth and our Shelley rolled into one. No one else had that romantic sense of poetry's immortality.

Back in New York, store-window TV images on icy Second Avenue flickered a cold strobe vision of the present. At the end of the third week in January, *now* became a place in the middle of nowhere called Khe Sanh. TV showed us dark-green, brooding, mist-shrouded jungle-highland hills, red dirt, explosions, white smoke, blood, wrecked planes, wounded men, marines scrambling under mortar fire, close-in jet strikes, followed by the stock "Are you scared?" interviews—the shaking, exhausted boy-men in the bunkers, scared shitless, rocked out of their minds by an impossible history. A kid who'd played guard on my high school football team was there, trapped inside that ring of death. And where was I? I hardly knew, some nights, to be honest. Ten days later, on January 30, the Tet offensive hit network television. CBS showed the marine air base at Da Nang lit up by the impact of salvo upon salvo of rockets and heavy mortars, climaxed by a Fourth-of-July starburst of illumination when a storage depot took a direct hit, and ignited chemicals and electrical supplies went up in towering flames. Angelica's twenty-fourth birthday fell a week after that, and we celebrated in my dingy hide-a-bed to the reverberating strains of the Staple Singers's *Uncloudy Day.*

In late March, we got married in St. Mark's Church. Two days before the wedding, while my fiancée and I were out securing a New York City marriage license, my apartment had been robbed and ransacked by the junkies downstairs. *A Day in the Life.* When I confronted them about this, they feigned remorse, but for the next two nights they kept climbing back up the fire escape to see if there was anything left to steal. It was time to go. After the wedding, I never went back to the apartment. I left what was there for the landlord to dispose of, and forfeited my deposit.

At the wedding, Ron was the best man, Ted gave away the bride. All three of us wore heavy wool double-breasted psychedelic gangster suits that looked like something left over from *Bonnie and Clyde.* These came from a poetry groupie named Shelley Lustig, whose husband ran a used-clothing store. Not only were they similar to the outfits once worn by guys like Larry Fay and Frankie Marlow (from the Damon Runyon era), these may have been *the same suits!* Ted's was a gray three-piece pinstripe, worn over a dark blue shirt and white-and-green floral necktie. With his bushy reddish whiskers, this neighborhood Irish-American patriarch looked very colorful strolling up the aisle, the visionary bride in white lace on his arm. Poets David Shapiro, Dick Gallup, Larry Fagin, and the painter Mike Goldberg (who'd provided my Italian wedding shirt) played and sang the wedding music during the ceremony: "I Love You Truly." Afterwards, there was a party at Anne and Lewis's. In those few moments when he wasn't busy kissing the bride, Ted proffered upon me solemn paternal advice on my new condition as a married man.

Jack of All Trades
(Little Grub Street Testament)

In Liffey Street had furniture bugs and
    fleas I sold it,
And at the Bank a big placard I often
    stood to hold it.
In New Street I sold hay and straw and
    in Spitalfields made bacon,
In Fishamble Street was at the grand old
    trade of basketmaking.
In Summerhill a coachmaker, in Denzille
    Street a gilder,
In Corn Street was a tanner, in Brunswick
    Street a builder,
In High Street I sold hosiery, in Patrick
    Street sold all blades,
So if you wish to know my name they call
    me Jack of all trades.

            —Old Dublin Street Ballad

Once out of school there is the temptation never to look back: also the concurrent temptation never to look ahead. Almost-idyllic country-comfort family-founding years of a poet's life on a shoestring in a windy, eucalyptus-lit rural Pacific coastal hamlet called Bolinas—where, to paraphrase a poem by Robert Creeley, one of the many poet-friends who over the next decade would flock there, each day for all its flaws was as much as each wave washing up on that shore, perfect—dissolve in the late 1970s, as hard economic reality sets in, to relatively aimless wanderings wherever temporary employment beckons, from California to Colorado and back again, from west to east, east to west, south to north, and north to south, subsisting day by day through a long contagion of free-lancing.

The man of letters who gives Grub Street as his address may wear his unprincipled professionalism as a badge of shame, but will not swear his allegiance till he cashes the check, his independence thus becoming a form of principle ironically doubled back upon itself. Implication follows hard upon implication: cumbrous months and years of a writing life all too rashly thrown into projects no more substantial than the wind, and all too frequently about as profitable. Executing literary labors assigned with variable degrees of attention by people one had for the most part never met, one found oneself doing many things one had never supposed the trade of literature might entail. The elements of surprise, challenge, and adventure in these labors moreover before very long gave way to tedious sieges of oppression, tension, and drudgery, interrupted now and then by outright catastrophe.

In these years I now speak of, I went everywhere I was told to go, read everything I was told to read, but didn't say everything I was told to say, and when questioned about it had only my own stubborn self-belief to fall back on as defense; and then that too fell away. I was edited to death, over the years, but each time like a phoenix staggered up from the ashes of my once-burnt-out, twice-shy sentences to be edited all over again. I learned eventually to expect that despite what was promised by those who'd put me to my toils, once the product was in their hands, the mail could be counted on almost never to contain the check. I'd once pretended to something more, but after a while I no longer recalled what.

Much though I professed to abhor it, however, this dubious business of free-lancing probably became me more than I was inclined to admit to myself. My character was always to betray my fate. I combined my father's self-destructiveness, artistic talents, and dogged wrongheadedness with my grandfather's energy,

though that also ran out after a while, and his good judgment I had always lacked. My affiliations were fierce, but unsoundly intense. I adopted groundless causes as though they were my long-lost offspring.

In this regard, the Grub Street pamphleteer-poet Tom Brown at times appeared to me in the light of a sort of perverse patron saint. Dean Swift once called Brown "the greatest genius of his age," by which he meant not the most delightful writer but the one most able to cause discomfort. Such gifts don't come cheap to the bearer. To chalk up to Tom Brown's influence the polemical pamphleteering of *The Great Naropa Poetry Wars* or *Stalin as Linguist*—to name the best-known of my Grub Street-style assaults on the pretensions of *soi-disant* literary avant-gardes of my own age—would of course be stretching a point. Still, there *are* some telling parallels. Reckless habits of living paired with a certain defiance, which prevented his simply giving up, kept Tom Brown going, but his was a poor progress, ever deeper into debt. Recently an unsuspecting student inquired about the retirement plan at the fly-by-night institution where I have, for the past decade or so, supplemented meager free-lancing income by serving as a part-time teacher of literature. Images of a golden rope ladder gently descending from the sky, ready to pick one up, soon faded into a view of Tom Brown translated forcibly from his garret to the public sponging house. Grub Street has never had a retirement plan.

Epilogue: Poetry and Biography
(Notes of a Lighthouse Keeper)

Is all true autobiographical writing in some sense elegiac? The subject is forever vanishing, lost like water seeping into sand as the wave retreats. Beneath the sand lie forgotten secret cities. . . . The work of a lifetime could be sunk into a self-excavation project such as this without ever getting to the bottom of it. To see oneself as others see one, let alone as one *is*—who's capable of that unimaginable feat? Perhaps it was when poised precariously at the brink of not only physical extinction but the further ignominy of eradication from human memory—forgetfulness, as each of us must instinctively suspect, is the *real* river of no return—that some saint or martyr once speculated that the power of self-knowledge would allow one to raise the dead. The ultimate eleventh-hour reprieve. . . . But, upon further reflection, who'd really want to be the instrument of such fatal clarity?

I recall the shock of seeing home videotape for the first time, walking with my friend, the poet Aram Saroyan, into an apartment in Cambridge, Massachusetts, in the spring of 1967. It was the same week *Sergeant Pepper* came out; an amiable draft dodger who was hiding out *chez* Aram kept playing "Lucy in the Sky with Diamonds," a supposed LSD anthem, over and over, but even that latest ratcheting of cogs in the cultural-consciousness loop had not prepared us. Entering that apartment in real time, we watched the previous moments played out by the inhabitants in a serial tableau incredibly unfolding before us. Presumably when *we* left, *our* presences, thus frozen into an instant past, would be equally so exposed. But watching oneself on videotape, what is it that one really sees—oneself, or the self one *was* a moment ago yet now no longer *is*, having shed it in passing like a snake's skin? Sex, lies, and dreams . . . I think this amazing experience delighted Aram, whose avidity to participate in the brave new electronic world very much exceeded my own; I myself found it bewildering and disorienting. I've always been anxious to *get on with* time, and reluctant to go back to it.

Thus the present project's challenge for me: I confess the exercise of "telling" my life has proved difficult in the extreme. Everything connected with the concept of myself as a "public figure"—to start with—makes me terribly uneasy; of all one's several selves, that dwarf-grand "public" one must surely be the silliest, most insubstantial and deceiving. On the other hand, given you will never see yourself as you are, why deny the possible truth of that *other* you, which "others" think they see: your "identity" insofar as you have a name. Further, though, a name can go only just so far toward describing anyone. As the seventeenth-century poet Robert Herrick wrote in "Dreames,"

> Here we are all, by day: By night w'are hurl'd
> By dreames, each one, into a sev'rall world.

Not knowing oneself, when all's said and done, is a little like breathing, a habit one can give up only for a minute or two before serious consequences start to set in. Given *that*

fact, imagine how uncomfortable things might quickly get if one were able to actually see one's various unidentical selves strutting their ridiculous pretensions to coherence through the eyes of others. Some levels of complication were probably meant to be borne only by language, in whose surprising reflections and sudden transparencies things take on for moments at a time a clarity that's spellbinding—or perhaps more accurately spell breaking, shattering the data-hypnotized, stressed-out, hurry-up stupor of a life in a technologically administered society.

Within that society, to *be* oneself is almost too great a burden to bear, even, and maybe especially, in the chilling revelation of the lyric moment, the moment of negative capability when one's party to the projection of a kind of self-knowledge that's not individual but species-specific. As deep into the substratum of a collective life the undercurrent of our language seeps, the lyric never loses its power to follow, tapping the convergences of all those tributary streams, drawing off primary metaphors as trace elements from word roots. That underground current is the medium in which a submerged poetics can always be detected, rising back up to the surface like air bubbles behind a swimmer in water. Out of *mourning's* unending pining history of sorrow and care—its riverine night of trembling and lamentation, reflective, mindful, unable ever to leave off remembering—the first faintly glowing buoyant light-geyser of *morning* again rises, abiding promise of mercy and forgetfulness, of a morrow beyond all compromise with death: the ultimate Irish wake.

Then again, there's nothing like the writing or reading of biographies to bring home to one the vanity and futility of individual human enterprise, and in particular of all attempt to discover in it some larger meaning or fulfillment, a role in some destiny greater than one's own minute, pathetically personalized private fate. The aphorist E. M. Cioran had it right when he suggested that every life is the story of a collapse. Heroes, villains, geniuses, achievers, cowards—all subjects of biography—ultimately seem equally ridiculous in their obdurate failure to recognize the oblivion of their furious undertakings, that rushing toward a dead-heat last-place finish which sometimes seems the only thing that really involves one with one's fellows in the race.

Each clinging as best he or she can to a losing ticket, all winners have their distinct unlucky stars to thank for their particular negative triumphs. The prototypical story of a life in the capitalist petit-bourgeoisie, the East German writer Heiner Müller once suggested to me apropos a life of Céline I was trying to write, is that of a dog chasing its tail; the only story of the twentieth century to attain tragic dimension, that of the failure of communism. (Our conversation occurred seven or eight years back, when the collapse of communism still appeared to have some meaning beyond its invitation to intellectual despondency.) I think it was Heiner Müller's identification of the B-movie-villain quality in Klaus Kinski—who at the time wanted to play Céline—that prompted these observations. But Kinski had learned the secret of overacting from his theater experience in the early years of his career. On stage, the futility of a life must be amplified to reach the back rows—what we now call the demographic bottom line. (Aim low, aim true, Céline once advised.)

The lyric poet, who is the playwright of the deepest and purest voices of the human collective's several selves, is briefly released from those selves' several internal conflicts by setting their baffling "characters" at each other's throats: his refusal of harmony while continually courting reconciliation is mimetic of the human struggle. What else are the figures of poetry but the extrapolations of all the continually collapsing lives that quarrel within us? These figures make it clear to us that a life's absence of meaning is finally the only reason to live. Such clarities, however, are once again not easy to bear. Burdensome as the writing of others' lives has increasingly become for me—after suffering through a half-dozen or so of them, I've finally learned to give the whole business up—autobiography seems an even more acute kind of torment. Not knowing oneself is the universal law, Cioran also suggested, and no one transgresses it with impunity.

I've sometimes thought the most honest approach to autobiography might be the scatter-shot-schizoid "method" adopted by Rousseau in his *Dialogues*, a crazy conundrum of a work; though once conventionally regarded as at least semidemented, like some other historical works whose apparent evocations of madness have come later to possess for us a certain diachronic resonance, it now seems to have that quality we call "being ahead of its time." Rousseau's work is staged as a conversation of three voices, two

Tom Clark, Berkeley, California, 1992

of them variously identified with the author himself, the third that of an "impartial" outside observer. The mystery their extended conversation seeks to unravel is no less than the understanding of the author's life—and in particular of the disproportion between the "objective" literary value of his books and the bad reputation of their author. What makes this compelling text more than just the fascinating document of a hallucinated paranoia (it's also that, of course; Edmund Burke, who disliked everything about Rousseau, called it "the mad confession of his mad faults") is its curious verisimilitude, an almost uncanny truthfulness-to-life suggestive at once of mania and everyday reality. By splitting himself into three selves, each allowed only a partial knowledge, Rousseau re-creates those discrepancies of awareness which in real life separate not only the parts of one's selves but each person from any other. Much as persons fated to remain forever unreconciled—Rousseau's method implies—the quarreling simulacra of one's several selves may occasionally strike sparks that for a moment illuminate everything.

The late poet Jim Brodey was a particular friend of those "revolutionary" years when one's own sundry and various selves seemed conspiratorially shuffled every day like a deck of cards in the hands of some invisible dealer who had nothing to do with anything as coherent as Providence and everything to do with an intriguingly aleatory force of Chance. Back in 1967, he titled a book of his poems *Identikit*, implicitly likening the reconstructive technique of the police composite image to the reconstruction of the authorial self in lyric poetry. The usual suspects, however, once released into the dispersive field of the lyric, seem to flee too quickly even for that kind of quasi-random identification. Autobiography would by that same trope be a way of rounding them up and bringing them in.

The evidence of an old baby-book notation in which my mother comments that I seemed happiest when playing alone, the critical check marks against the column "works well with others" inscribed by concerned nuns in my elementary school report cards, and the fate of being a writer—what do these things have in common? To confess that one's often felt most comfortable with one's own company is certainly not a proud admission. Among trades with which this character defect is compatible, writing must rank right up there with lighthouse keeping. Solitaries apply. Rubbing up against one's own kind, anyway, has always seemed a pleasure more attractive in the being longed for than in the being gratified. Of course one's status as social animal justifiably suffers in ratio with the evidence of such a failure in natural sympathy. The ruined church of the old gods stands vacant on the wind-swept promontory watched over by the lonely lighthouse keeper, in his crabby, sullen art.

Let's for the sake of the story place this lighthouse out in Dingle Bay, on the wild Kerry coast. Closing out a sixth decade on a loved, soon-to-be-lost planet, one inevitably tumbles into genealogy as into a grave one mistakes for home. "As we grow old we become more and more the stuff our forebears put into us," Willa Cather wrote in her tale "My Mortal Enemy." "We think we are so individual and so misunderstood when we are young; but the nature our strain of blood carries is inside there, waiting, like our skeleton." As if it were an X-ray of bones un-

dergoing a shanty-Irish cell mutation, herewith our strain of blood offers you these notes.

BIBLIOGRAPHY

Poetry:

Airplanes, Once, 1966.

The Sand Burg: Poems, Ferry, 1966.

(With Ron Padgett) *Bun*, Angel Hair, 1968.

(With Lewis Warsh) *Chicago*, Angel Hair, 1969.

Stones, Harper, 1969.

Air, Harper, 1970.

Green, Black Sparrow, 1971.

Neil Young, Coach House, 1971.

The No Book, Ant's Forefoot, 1971.

(With Ron Padgett and Ted Berrigan) *Back in Boston Again*, Telegraph, 1972.

John's Heart, Grossman, 1972.

Smack, Black Sparrow, 1972.

Chicago, Black Sparrow, 1974.

Suite, Black Sparrow, 1974.

At Malibu, Kulchur, 1975.

Blue, Black Sparrow, 1975.

Baseball, Figures, 1976.

Fan Poems, North Atlantic, 1976.

How I Broke In and Six Modern Masters, Tombouctou, 1977.

35, Poltroon, 1978.

When Things Get Tough on Easy Street: Selected Poems, 1963–1978, Black Sparrow, 1978.

The Mutabilitie of the English Lyrick (parodies), Poltroon, 1979.

The End of the Line, Little Caesar, 1980.

Heartbreak Hotel, Toothpaste, 1981.

Journey to the Ulterior, Am Here/Immediate, 1981.

Nine Songs, Turkey, 1981.

The Rodent Who Came to Dinner, Am Here/Immediate, 1981.

A Short Guide to the High Plains, Cadmus, 1981.

Under the Fortune Palms, Turkey, 1982.

Dark as Day, Smithereens, 1983.

Paradise Resisted: Selected Poems, 1978–1984, Black Sparrow, 1984.

Property, Illuminati, 1984.

The Border, Coffee House, 1985.

Disordered Ideas, Black Sparrow, 1987.

Easter Sunday, Coffee House, 1987.

Fractured Karma, Black Sparrow, 1990.

Sleepwalker's Fate: New and Selected Poems, 1965–1991, Black Sparrow, 1992.

Junkets on a Sad Planet: Scenes from the Life of John Keats, Black Sparrow, 1994.

Like Real People, Black Sparrow, 1995.

Biographies:

(With Mark Fidrych) *No Big Deal*, Lippincott, 1977.

The World of Damon Runyon, Harper, 1978.

One Last Round for the Shuffler: A Blacklisted Ballplayer's Story, Truck, 1979.

Jack Kerouac: A Biography, Harcourt, 1984.

Late Returns: A Personal Memoir of Ted Berrigan, Tombouctou, 1985.

Charles Olson: The Allegory of a Poet's Life, Norton, 1991.

Robert Creeley and the Genius of the American Common Place: Together with the Poet's Own Autobiography, New Directions, 1993.

Nonfiction:

Champagne and Baloney: The Rise and Fall of Finley's A's, Harper, 1976.

The Great Naropa Poetry Wars, Cadmus Editions, 1980.

Kerouac's Last Word: Jack Kerouac in Escapade, Water Row, 1987.

Stalin as Linguist, Crank Case, 1987.

The Poetry Beat: Reviewing the Eighties, University of Michigan Press, 1990.

Fiction:

A Conversation with Hitler (stories), Black Sparrow, 1978.

Who Is Sylvia? (novel), Blue Wind, 1979.

The Last Gas Station and Other Stories, Black Sparrow, 1980.

The Master (novel), Pentagram, 1984.

The Exile of Céline (novelized biography), Random House, 1986.

Also author of *The Emperor of the Animals* (three-act play), first produced in London, 1966. Contributor of book reviews to the *Los Angeles Herald-Examiner*, *Los Angeles Times* and the *San Francisco Chronicle*.

John Robert Colombo

1936-

"The newspaper photographer for the Toronto Star *and I spent a lot of time arranging this 'personality' shot. I am reclining on a wall of books, resting on* Colombo's Canadian Quotations *and displaying* Colombo's Canadian References.*"*

The historian Merrill Denison began his memoirs with these words: "I have always felt confused about my birth and, for that matter, I still am. The trouble is, I seem to remember so many things that happened before I was born."

I have no such confusions, being untroubled by the circumstances surrounding my birth. I recall no events prior to that event. What I do recall are scenes that must have followed my birth by four or five years. For instance, I remember the sight of a living-room wall. I distinctly see a window to the left, a doorway in the centre, and to the left, on the wall, a picture. It is a framed picture, a photograph in sepia or the reproduction of a painting of a subdued scene in Europe, perhaps a bridge over a canal in Holland, a fashionable interior decoration at the time.

I also remember an incident that occurred to me in the bright sunlight of summer. I was standing on the sidewalk across the street from the house in which I was born. I was part of a group of young boys older than I. One of them had a BB gun, and I was both impressed with it and frightened by it.

"It shoots babies," they teased me.

"No," I protested. "It shoots BB's, not babies!"

My final memory of my earliest years seems to relate to the sense of smell. I was standing alone on the sidewalk a little farther down the street and staring at the small factory at the corner. It was a chocolate factory, and I was entranced by the aroma of cocoa beans that came from the factory. So strong was the sensation that my mouth was watering. I could literally taste the dark sweet chocolate. I have had a sweet tooth ever since.

Childhood memories are the most personal and precious of memories, recalled with interest, recounted with a sense of unease. Who else could possibly care about them? By their nature they are meaningless to others, although no doubt they could be seen to be significant by artists and therapists.

I was born, a healthy, chubby child, at St. Mary's Hospital in Kitchener, Ontario, Canada. The delivery took place on Tuesday, March 24, 1936, at 10:15 p.m. Kitchener was then and is today a middle-sized industrial city located in what was picturesquely called "the heart" of south-central Ontario. Despite its English-sounding name, the community was founded by German immigrants, many of them hard-working farmer folk known as the Pennsylvania Dutch who in the early nineteenth century arrived by Conestoga wagon from Lancaster County, Pennsylvania. Kitchener and nearby St. Jacobs are known today for their farmers' markets. Workers were soon attracted to the area by two rubber factories, B. F. Goodrich and A. R. Kaufman, and Kitchener and to some extent Waterloo acquired a number of small plants and industries.

The original name of the community was Berlin. The Great War brought about deep divisions in German-speaking families, so that a plebiscite was held to change the town's name. The citizens opted to rename Berlin after the British General, Lord Kitchener. In my childhood Kitchener and Waterloo were known, far and wide I assumed, as "the twin cities." They shared this honour with Port Arthur and Fort William, until they merged as Thunder Bay, and Minneapolis and St. Paul in the United States. But there never seemed to be any talk of the consolidation of Kitchener and Waterloo, although there was a Kit-Wat Dairy. "Clean as a Kitchen" seemed to be the unofficial motto of the city. Kitchener had a larger population than Waterloo, so Kitchenerites furtively felt that anyone foolish enough to make his home in Waterloo was somewhat lesser in stature. It was not until the establishment of the University of Waterloo in 1959 and the rapid growth of its forward-looking engineering and computer science specialization that Waterloo completely eclipsed Kitchener in reputation.

Colombo, an Italian name that means "dove" or "pigeon," was considered a foreign name in southern Ontario when I was growing up. Despite the prominence of Italian immigrants and native-born Canadians of Italian background in Ontario in the years following the Second World War, the name did not become North Americanized until the 1970s, when Peter Falk created the role of the bumbling detective for the NBC-TV series *Columbo*. My sole complaint with the program is that the surname should be spelled with an *o*, not with a *u*.

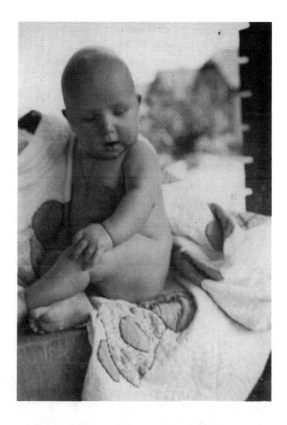

"I was a chubby baby and a bald-headed one at that, judging by this sepia snapshot taken in summer 1936 on the porch of our house on Chestnut Street in Kitchener, Ontario"

"George Nicholson, my maternal grandfather, is playing games with me outside his restaurant, U-Eat-A Lunch, next door to my future father-in-law's store, Prince Fashion Mens' Wear, on King Street, then and now Kitchener's main street"

Why do I have an Italian surname? Whatever was an Italian family doing in Kitchener? The truth is that the Colombo family is not really Italian. Family tradition has it that our branch of the family began about 1870 with the arrival on Canadian soil of one John Fermo Colombo. A stone mason from Genoa, Italy, it is said that he worked on some of the larger private homes that stand in some splendour in the Baden area, between Kitchener and Stratford, home of the well-known Shakespeare Festival. John Fermo married Barbara Bachman, a local girl of German background, and among their children was John Louis Colombo, my grandfather. I remember him well: a stocky, farmerish figure of a man, well over six feet in height. A gruff manner hid a gentle disposition. He married Rosemary Lorentz, a petite and delicate figure of a woman, the daughter of a couple who had emigrated to the Baden area from Alsace-Lorraine. As she stood less than five feet in height, they made an unusual couple. He farmed, sold tombstones, and operated a gas station. He was a hard worker, as he had to be to support their fourteen children. (One of

them died in infancy.) The fifth child was my father, John Anthony Colombo, who was raised in a large, red-brick house on Queen Street South, now torn down, but once the setting for many generations of family events. Visitors to Kitchener can visit historic Schneider Haus. Across the street from it stood the Colombo family home.

So much for the paternal side of the family. I vividly recall my maternal grandparents. George Nicholson was a wiry and energetic little man. Born George Nikotopolis in Athena, he taught grade school in Greece before apprenticing as a chef. He decided to seek his fortune in Canada, and when his boat landed he changed his name to Nicholson. He worked in the kitchens of the larger hotels in Montreal and Toronto. In the former city he met and married Ernestine Morisette, lively daughter of a family long established at Valleyfield, Quebec. The young couple moved to Toronto. Their desire to own and operate their own restaurant brought them to Kitchener, where they opened a popular eatery. They gave it the quaint name U-Eat-A Lunch, and offered the diner a four-course dinner for thirty-five cents. It was located on King Street, next door to Prince Fashion Men's Wear, the clothing store operated by my future in-laws. The Nicholsons had five children. Their fifth and last child, the loveliest of the lot, was Irene Mary Nicholson, my mother. The Nicholsons, like the Colombos, were good Catholics, although my maternal grandfather felt more at home with Greek Orthodoxy than he did with Roman Catholicism.

My father left school early to help to support the family. As he had a knack for mechanical and electrical work, he learned to repair refrigerators and then joined Ellis and Howard, a firm of electrical suppliers. My mother completed elementary school, learned shorthand and business practice at the Euler Business College, and after marrying my father assisted him in the operation of his fledgling business. A newspaper clipping that dates from the late 1920s shows my father as a young man standing in front of a model of a moving-picture stage that he built, complete with flashing electric lights, moving curtains, and still-picture projections. In the clipping he is described as an electrical "wizard," and I often think of him resembling the inventive Edison, the ingenious Marconi, and the testy Tesla. Over the years he acquired photographic and developing equip-

"Here is my favourite photograph of my father and mother, John A. and Irene M. Colombo. I took it in July 1951."

ment and taught himself how to be a first-rate still photographer. That led him to 16mm motion-picture photography and the business of shooting short industrial movies for local and Toronto-based sponsors. This in turn caused him to construct black-and-white and then colour-film processors, immense motor-driven units with tanks full of hypo and fix, which brought him the franchise for processing all Ansco 8 and 16mm film in Canada. Along the way he branched out into sound recording, acquiring equipment to make 78 rpm transcription disks for radio replay. He never wanted to work with anyone else. John A. Colombo Ltd. was always a one-man operation.

My parents were married in 1932, when the Depression was at its height. I was raised in two houses in Kitchener. My early years were spent in the rented brown brick house on Chestnut Street in a middle-class residential district. The sturdy corner house is still standing at the foot of a hill; the summit of the hill was crowned by the Breithaupt mansion, occupied by L. O. Breithaupt, a local businessman and political power broker who subsequently served as Lieutenant Governor of Ontario. The sole auspicious event during my early life involved "L.O." in his pre-vice-regal days. It also involved a minor car accident. I was being taken for a ride by my father and he had an accident not far from home. Mr. Breithaupt, driv-

ing by, observed that something was amiss and stopped to offer assistance. My father asked him if he would take me home. He agreed and drove me back, carrying me up the stairs to the porch. Handing me to my mother he had to assure her that while there had been a minor accident, nobody was hurt. Being cradled in the arms of the future Lieutenant Governor, while meaning little, may signify something!

Immediately after the war, we moved about a mile away into our own house at 114 Pandora Avenue. The dark brick house with wooden pillars on the porch is also standing. It looks smaller today than it appeared to me when I was in my pre-teens. It was here that I first became aware of my father's varied work. In the kitchen the telephone sat on a small shelf along with a pencil and a pad of paper for taking important business messages. On the baby grand piano that dominated the living room, I practised the piano for eight years. It was not a luxury having such a fine piano, for it was used for making sound recordings. Also in the living room was a microphone on a boom and a bulky machine capable of making "master" disks. In the basement was the darkroom, where I made photographic prints and enlargements. A small machine shop was attached to the back of the house and soon expanded to include a motion-picture recording studio. Aladdin's cave had nothing over the shop and studio with its desk, workbench, control panel, lathe, drill press, jars full of nuts and bolts, spools of wire, canisters of film, public address equipment, sound-on-film cameras and projection equipment, as well as an insulated projection room which doubled as a recording studio. By the time I was in university, the rest of the available space was taken up by the immense processors for 8 and 16mm black-and-white and colour movie film. Much of the equipment was homemade and was eventually purchased by CHCH-TV for use in the preparation of its local news broadcasts during the three decades between the inauguration of television and the arrival of portable videocams. In later years, when my parents moved into their "dream house" in the Stanley Park subdivision, much of the equipment was moved to a studio on John Street.

My primary school education is a series of images, more a succession than a progression. The teachers I remember from Grade I to Grade VIII at St. Mary's School were the black-dressed Sisters of Notre Dame. They were dedicated teachers but their principal interests lay with catechism and religious instruction. Each morning began with these subjects. Only when they were finished were we told to open our spellers and other texts. The highlight of the week was the Friday afternoon visit of the black-robed priest from St. Mary's Church next door who also had religion on the mind. One of the priests, Father Murphy, had a sense of humour to leaven the didacticism and moralism. He was unbeatable and unforgettable on the subject of the sin of stealing. I relish one of his formulations. He assured us, the youngsters that we were, that the theft of something worth $5.00 or more was a "mortal sin," whereas stealing something worth $4.99 or less was merely a "venial sin." (This was in Ontario in 1949, so the ravages of inflation must be kept in mind.) Even in those days, as innocent as we were, a number of us were unimpressed with this logic. The pupil who sat next to me asked the question that was on everyone's mind: "Suppose someone steals something worth less than $5.00 but believes it to be worth more?" Unfortunately I have forgotten the formula that dealt with this objection (no doubt there is one in Aquinas or Augustine). But I never have forgotten the instruction that we sit on our seats in front of our desks to the right, so our "guardian angels" could sit comfortably at our side.

St. Mary's School lacked a library, but located not two blocks away was the Kitchener Public Library, and it had lots of good books. Like the other libraries built by Andrew Carnegie in North America, it was housed in a graceful and gracious building. It was well maintained. During morning recess, pupils with library cards were permitted to race to the library, borrow books (bound volumes of *Popular Mechanics* were more popular with the boys than with the girls), and race back again, barely making the recess bell. Throughout my primary and secondary school years, I would make good use of the borrowing privileges at this library. Kitchener has been described as the only community in Ontario lacking an Anglo-Saxon elite. Whatever the truth of this, the community did possess a superb library system. It was under the direction of Mabel Dunham, Ontario's first fully trained librarian, an author in her own right. I would see her from time to time, sorting books, checking shelves, even stamping books out for patrons. To the extent that I am educated, libraries educated me.

At the end of Grade VIII, it was a simple matter of crossing the street to go from St. Mary's School to St. Jerome's College for Grade IX. Despite its name, St. Jerome's was a collegiate institute, not a college, and it was run by the black-robed Augustinian fathers. I took Grades IX and X in the building with its sepulchral air. Today one finds the same atmosphere in the older seminaries in Quebec. The feeling of being adrift was especially pronounced in the residential wing; many of the boarders were problem students sent by their parents in the United States and Latin America.

There was no library worthy of the name. The collection of old textbooks and German-language theology that masqueraded as a collection was presided over by a retired priest who kept the doors of the cramped quarters locked more often than unlocked. Readers of the novels of Graham Greene and Brian Moore will recognize the priests and laymen who tried to teach us languages—French, Latin, and English—and the sciences, social studies, and religious knowledge. They were men who had problems with the bottle or the body. Some were as dry as dust; others were unsteady and unable to tame their tempers. These were not the characteristics of Father Jerome, the rector, who worked long hours, making the best of the situation. There is reason to believe that the situation at St. Jerome's College has improved since the early 1950s, but I have not ventured back to see for myself.

Transferring from St. Jerome's College to the Kitchener and Waterloo Collegiate and Vocational Institute was the equivalent of climbing from the dungeon to the penthouse. Suddenly there were qualified teachers, counselling services, cafeteria, even a library. In fact, there was a literary tradition at KCI. In the rotunda for all to see were plaques that honoured two native sons, essayist Archibald MacMechan and poet William Wilfred Campbell. The presence there of Margaret Millar and Ross Macdonald was still being discussed by staff and teachers. They had been students and then young teachers at KCI. After the war, in Santa Barbara, California, they wrote their widely read mystery novels. John Smallbridge, a teacher of English, did his best to interest us in literature and composition, to use the terms that described the subject of English in those days. Fresh from the Ontario College of Education, he organized a small circle of avid readers and would-be writers and called it Symposium. We met evenings to read and discuss poems and essays written by the masters of English literature and by ourselves.

As well as writers, there were girls at KCI. One girl in particular was a student named Ruth F. Brown, whose family ran the clothing store on King Street. It turned out that Ruth and I were practically neighbours. She lived on Borden Avenue, I on Pandora. We were both interested in English and attended the circle for would-be writers.

If I had to describe myself during my high school years, I would do so with some degree of diffidence, but the word I would use is *reader*. I had no interest in sports or athletics, but I was interested in everything else. I was an omnivorous appreciator of ink on cellulose, from the advertising that appears on bilingual cereal boxes to pamphlets handed out on the street. I had a special interest in historical mysteries. I haunted (if that is the right word) the occult section of books at the public library—Dewey Decimal 001.94 and 133. I was immediately attracted to the books of P. D. Ouspensky, the Russian philosopher, and, as if in counterbalance, the mystery novels of Sax Rohmer, creator of Dr. Fu Manchu. Both interests have remained strong over the years.

I was not much of a student. Although I wrote nine Grade XIII subjects and passed the much-dreaded departmental examinations, my marks were not the highest. I was too busy elsewhere with an active social life. I met irregularly to listen to classical music with friends Charles Westfall and Charles Ruby. I discussed drama and theatre with Robert Hallman; yearning to be an actor, like James Dean, he left to study at the celebrated Pasadena Playhouse. I had philosophical discussions about the nature of society and the universe with a class chum, Hugh Washburn, who soon left for Los Angeles and now lives in Spokane, Washington. I associated with a blind piano-teacher named Peter Lipnicki whose appreciation of classical music on 33's and 45's far transcended that of any sighted person I knew. I worked my way through the shelves on the two floors of Kuhl's secondhand bookstore on King Street, only to discover that a trap door led to a basement full of unsorted hardcover books. With Harold Kurschenska, who later moved to Toronto, I learned to set type from a California job case

in the William English Printing Company and printed leaflets of early poems. I visited Alex Potter, who wrote a column on local history for the local newspaper; his homosexuality was of no interest to me, but he was willing to share with me fascinating tales of his student days in Paris and Zurich. It seems he had an automobile in those days and he would be asked to drive James Joyce to visit his daughter in the asylum. It was Potter's view that Joyce was as unhinged as his hospitalized daughter. Joyce took great delight in the fact that his name was pronounced differently in each of the languages he heard spoken around him in Zurich. I shook Potter's hand, so if you shake my hand, you are shaking the hand of a man who shook the hand of the man who shook the hand of Joyce.

One day, perusing the personal columns of the *Kitchener Record,* I saw an announcement of a forthcoming meeting of the Kitchener Chapter of the Theosophical Society. This surprised me. I knew there was a lodge in Toronto, about one hundred miles away, but I had not known that there was one in Kitchener. So I attended the Thursday evening meeting and there I met Alexander Watt, a man who played a major role in my life. More than thirty years later I completed the manuscript of *Mysterious Canada,* which surveys the country's major and minor "mysteries." It was inevitable that I would dedicate the book to his memory. Mr. Watt was then in his late fifties and an imposing figure, part trickster, part instructor. He had once held a seat on the Toronto Stock Exchange, and he was still buying and selling speculative stocks. He was also a dealer in used coins, and he took great pride in owning and then selling a rare "dot-dime." Through his connections with book dealers in London and New York, he had amassed an impressive private collection of books devoted to all aspects of the occult. These volumes lined the hallway and master bedroom of the Queen Street apartment that he shared with his wife Mary, a mild-mannered, perceptive, if long-suffering woman. Included among the books were rare works on the Cabbalah and Freemasonry, and many privately printed books and much mimeographed material that derived from Aleister Crowley, England's "black magician" and so-called Great Beast. There were also curious volumes like *The Book of Oahpse* that remain in print but are seldom seen in bookstores. What a treasure trove! Where else in the country was there a collection of occult literature in private hands to match this one? Mr. Watt was delighted with my curiosity about this cache of material. He extended borrowing privileges, so on a weekly basis I signed titles in and out. In 1959, the Watts died tragically in a car accident. In the late 1980s, the collection of books and papers, kept intact by Hugh and Betty Watt, son and daughter-in-law, was donated to the Douglas Library of Queen's University. Finding much of value in the printed books, but little of worth in the personal papers, the Douglas librarians rejected the files, correspondence with fellow occultists, including missives to and from Aleister Crowley in England (not to mention one of his original oil paintings, a work of great though unsettling power). The cache of papers was eventually presented to me for safekeeping.

Mr. Watt could play various roles, that of the magistrate, that of the iconoclast, in an attempt to balance his messiah-like desire to teach and lead with his Mencken-like detestation of bunkum. His passion was occultism, by which he meant all and everything from Anthroposophy to Zen. He lectured on the Tarot cards and on "Shakespeare's Greatest Secret" (the secret being that Shakespeare was really Sir Francis Bacon). His usual audiences were members of the lodges of the Theosophist Society in Kitchener and the nearby cities of Hamilton and London. He went as far afield as Toronto, talking on a number of occasions in the TS's old lodge on Isabella Street, the one designed and painted by members of the Group of Seven. He may or may not have been a Rosicrucian. He considered himself a member of the organization founded by Crowley (known as the OTO). I could continue, but the relevant point is that even in the circle of his followers, there was no one who knew him very well. He could be delightful or devilish by turns, ever tricksterish. One member of his circle in the mid-1950s was Alice M. Neal, a social worker. Now retired, she lives in Toronto, not far from the Metropolitan Toronto Reference Library, where since the 1980s she has assisted me with my research into Canadiana and the country's "mysteries."

I still had no clear conception of what I wanted to do in life, except that I knew it would have to do with my literary and other interests. The easiest thing to do was enroll at Waterloo College, a small liberal arts college

"This studio portrait was taken of Alexander Watt in the early 1950s. Note the ring with the inset hieroglyphics. The researcher Alice Neal presented me with this sepia photograph in 1995."

maintained by the Lutheran Church but affiliated with the University of Western Ontario whose degree it granted. On campus there was a small but adequate library. The faculty consisted of a clutch of professors who maintained intellectual interests, notably J. A. S. Evans, a classicist, and Flora Roy, the head of the English department. I enrolled in a course called "English and Philosophy" and found the lectures exciting, especially the psychology course I took from Professor Bexton, who some years earlier had worked on the McGill "perceptual isolation" experiments. There was also calculus (I loved the theory but hated deriving the formulae) and Ancient Greek (Mondays and Fridays at 8:30 a.m., a real pain). There was, as well, an active, after-hours social life on campus that often took us off campus. On one occasion a group of us (including a complex fellow named Wally Ryerson who turned up as the central character in Graeme Gibson's first novel, *Five Legs*) drove to the University of Western Ontario in London to hear E. J. Pratt drone through a reading of his poetic narrative *The Roosevelt and the Antinoe.* On another occasion, driving to Stratford, we saw the McGill musical production *My Fur Lady,* which proved that satire and Canadiana could be side-splittingly funny.

After two years at Waterloo College, I was yearning for wider horizons. The obvious place to head was Toronto, the city that everyone in Kitchener seemed to despise. Toronto may have been less than a hundred miles away, but through "the magic of radio" its influence was felt throughout Ontario and the rest of Canada. One did not have to live in that city to tune into CFRB to enjoy the news reports and views broadcasts of veteran newsman and broadcaster Gordon Sinclair. The Canadian Broadcasting Corporation operated two national, English-language radio services, the Dominion Network and the National Network. On one or other of the networks, I was a regular listener to the thrilling "Stage" series of dramas directed for radio by Andrew Allan, and the occasional plays written or adapted by Lister Sinclair. Max Ferguson's daily "Rawhide" program offered no end of offbeat records and chatter, particularly his character Marvin Mellobell, the sweet-voiced CBC announcer from Halifax. Every Saturday radio-waves brought us the Metropolitan Opera broadcasts, live from the stage of the Metropolitan Opera in New York City, sponsored by Texaco Canada. (The CBC is still broadcasting live performances from "the Met"—thank you, Texaco, "The Star of the American Road"!) Radio was our ear to the world. Television's appeal is primarily to the eye, hardly to the ear. TV may be a more powerful medium than radio, but it is a far less intimate one. One does not love television the way one used to love radio.

In the early 1960s, Toronto, including its radio broadcasts, changed its character, doffing its staid, provincial gown, donning a lively, cosmopolitan garb. It did this within a handful of years. I arrived in Toronto in 1957; within ten years, the transformation of the "new city" was complete. It eclipsed Montreal in population and emerged as the country's bellwether city.

I enrolled at University College, the nondenominational college within the University of Toronto, and was awarded a room on the third floor of St. Daniel Wilson Residence. When not attending classes, I worked as a proofreader at the University of Toronto Press. Many a night I covered events for the student newspaper, the *Varsity,* when they had their offices in the basement of the Old Observatory. The first event I covered was an on-campus appearance of the comedy team of Wayne and Shuster. Like other radio listeners, I was unable to tell them apart, at least until they opened their mouths. I also "covered" a séance held at Casa Loma and attended lectures at the old Toronto Theosophical Society as well as concerts at old Massey Hall (one directed by H. Villa-Lobos which received a critical lambasting in the provincial press of the day; I wrote him a fan letter and received a pleasant reply); and poetry readings at the old Greenwich Gallery on Bay Street and then at the Isaacs Gallery on Yonge Street, organized by Raymond Souster; not to mention meetings of the Guild of Hand Printers (memorably in the workshop in the Richmond Hill studio of Carl Dair) and the Society for Typographical Designers (where I met Allan Fleming, designer of Canadian National's CN logo, the first of the country's major corporate reimagings). One memorable afternoon I shook hands with three of my favourite people: Nathan Cohen and Gordon Sinclair, as they were dining together at Winston's Theatre Grill, and Lister Sinclair, as he was holding forth on all subjects under the sun at a gathering in a flat in Rosedale.

I was an undergraduate student at University College from 1957 to 1959 and even then it was apparent that there were two intellectual currents crisscrossing the campus, the city, and hence the country. Would it be disrespectful to characterize these currents in cosmological terms: Steady State and Big Bang? The Steady State was the emanation from Victoria College, where Northrop Frye was formulating his views on the nature of myth and the social function of criticism and the arts. The Big Bang was the blast from St. Michael's College, where Marshall McLuhan was holding seminars and collecting his insights on the media, which he brought together in a marathon whirl of xeroxing in the preparation of the manuscript of *The Gutenberg Galaxy.* It was McLuhan's first major book, and it was designed by Harold Kurschenska, my Kitchener friend, a student of Carl Dair, who joined the University of Toronto Press as its typographer.

"A festival book launch was held by Les Editions du Jour of Montreal in the fall of 1963 for the publication of the anthology Poetry 64/Poésie 64. *I am standing beside my co-editor, poet, novelist, and filmmaker Jacques Godbout."*

In the 1950s, the colleges at the University of Toronto offered four-year honours courses, as distinguished from the general three-year undergraduate courses. These were in addition to thirteen years of Ontario high school. The honours system, modelled on that of Oxford and Cambridge, had great merit, so it was a sad year when it was replaced by the more general, nonspecialist system. Is it by accident that the successor system saw classes being taught by teaching assistants rather than being conducted by assistant or associate or full professors? Class size was small by any standard. From ten to twenty-five students might enroll in any one course; a seminar would consist of half a dozen students. Five years later, when I began a term of teaching English and humanities at Atkinson College, York University, I found to my surprise that a seminar consisted of from twenty-five to fifty students, and the number of students attending any given lecture might be as high as two hundred.

What I found exceptionally exciting was the fact that the faculty of the University College comprised so many scholars and authors. In the philosophy department were the varied talents of the rambunctious Marcus Long, saturnine Emil Fackenheim, aloof Fulton Anderson, gentle David Savan, thoughtful Thomas Goudge, and youthful Lionel Rubinoff. A. S. P. Wodehouse, the eccentric and cantankerous head of the English department, was a leading authority on John Milton. The course in eighteenth-century thought was conducted by Douglas Grant, author of the standard book on the Cock Lane Ghost as well as a volume of memoirs of serving as a pilot with the Royal Air Force. Dr. Grant was a lean, intense man whose life seemed devoted to literature and scholarship and the excitement of ideas. Some years later we met by accident on the stage of the Royal Court Theatre in London. I was deeply moved to discover that while he had long since left the country, he was aware of my own writing and of my editorial labours on behalf of the *Tamarack Review*.

Students who enrolled in humanities courses were always aware of the academic and scientific achievements of Banting and Best who discovered insulin; of the legacy of the scholar Harold Adams Innis; of the ongoing contributions of political scientist C. B. Macpherson and his activist wife Kay Macpherson; of the poetry and painting of Robert Finch; of the poetry and prose and painting of German scholar Barker Fairley. The tradition of enlightenment and learning seemed to be embodied in the person of English scholar Claude T. Bissell, later appointed president of the university.

Across Queen's Park was St. Michael's College, with its formidable if not forbidding Pontifical Institute of Mediaeval Studies. Every St. Mike's student I met was studying Thomism, and it seemed St. Thomas Aquinas had a multitude of answers to questions unasked. Marshall McLuhan's star was to rise in the 1960s, but years earlier students and the city's journalists were well aware of some of his key concepts: "Gutenberg era," "acoustical space," "electronic village." These expressions studded his public appearances and interviews and abounded in the well-designed pages of *Explorations,* the annual journal that he edited and published with Edmund Carpenter. The indelible contributions made by Carpenter to the development of McLuhanism have yet to be properly appreciated. An American anthropologist of delightful dash and considerable daring, Carpenter had firsthand knowledge of Eskimo life and, unlike McLuhan, was a through-going iconoclast. McLuhan was like St. Thomas Aquinas in that he had answers for unasked questions. If Carpenter had a patron saint it was St. Socrates (I borrow the phrase from the poet George Faludy), who had a question for every question. I took Carpenter's introductory anthropology course, and what I most remember is the energy with which he flailed the bureaucrats at Queen's Park for failing to enact legislation to protect the Peterborough Serpent Mounds; the way he dismissed the claims of authenticity made on behalf of the Beardmore Relics (then on open display at Royal Ontario Museum; later to be relegated to the vaults); and the lively discussions of social mores over coffee in the basement of the ROM where the anthropology classes were then held.

Victoria College also lay across Queen's Park. It was the domain of Northrop Frye, even then a man approaching legendary status. In subsequent years he would be appointed head of the English department, president of Victoria, and then chancellor of the college. Frye brings to mind the remark that Charles de Gaulle made to André Malraux: Remoteness inspires respect. Remoteness may not be the ideal word to use to describe Northrop Frye. Yet he did seem to bask in "splendid isolation" (to use Sir George Foster's words). No one I knew as a student knew him personally. All I knew about him was the fact that his friends called him "Norrie." I was incredulous when I subsequently learned from someone who knew him in Moncton that as a child his bright-coloured head of hair had earned him the epithetical description "Little Buttercup." The stories that were told about Frye turned out to be either trite or untrue. I enrolled in his Blake course and the following year audited his popular course in literary symbolism. It is one of Frye's axioms that the authority in the classroom is not the teacher but the subject. Frye embodied his subject to such a degree that fellow students grumbled all the time that "Frye thinks he's Blake" or "Frye thinks he invented the Literary Archetype." I felt otherwise. I reasoned that in the lecture room we were privileged to witness an impersonation of an ideal. Frye's performance was like that of the lawyer who so identifies his interest with his client's that he presents it more effectively, selectively, and abstractly than could the client himself. Yet the analogy breaks down because Frye would present a completely balanced view of the subject at hand, rather in the manner of the judge or magistrate who weighs merit on one side and then on the other before striking a balance and delivering a verdict. Frye made little attempt to "relate" to his students other than to relate to them everything that they needed to know about the imagery at hand. But he did not disdain or demean his students as did so many of the popular professors of the day. When Frye asked a question, he would wait for an answer. And wait. And wait. Even when he asked what we felt was a rhetorical question, he would wait for an answer. The pause would grow in length. It was not the pause that refreshes, but the pause-as-Black-Hole into the maw of which everything local disappears. The silence elicited thoughtless answers to thoughtful questions. I timed one pause, occasioned by a question about Blake's "Beulah," that lasted two minutes. It would have lasted longer, but the class was nearing its end, so Frye himself, grimly, supplied the answer.

At the last meeting of the influential Blake course, with about fifteen minutes to spare, Frye asked us if there were any further points to discuss. There were about thirty of us there, it was the end of the term, and nobody wanted to imply that some point or other had not been completely covered over the course of the year. After all, it might reflect poorly on the professor; besides, we were all certain that Frye had made certain that everything relevant had been discussed. I raised my hand and said, as courteously as possible, "Many of us are not planning to take graduate courses in English. It would be a special favour if you could present on the blackboard the diagram that shows the Declining Power of the Hero to Act in Western Literature."

Frye squinted at me through his thick, Coke-bottle glasses. A description of this scheme appears in *Anatomy of Criticism*, but nowhere was it reproduced as a diagram. He said, "Yes," and proceeded to give a formal demonstration of how representative characters from classical times to contemporary times illustrated a progressive decline in physical action, social status, psychology, and self-awareness. Then he looked at me and asked, "Is that what you wanted?"

"Thank you, sir," I said. "As I understand it, the demonstration is based on actual instances of heroes in literature. It clearly moves from the mythic mode to the ironic. If someone pointed out important heroes who have greater or lesser powers, would you abandon the scheme?"

"Yes," he said. He did not have to repeat my word "if."

But I was not yet finished. "Is the scheme original with you?"

"Yes."

"It seems to me to be an extraordinary insight. It strikes me as curious that by the late twentieth century, today, the hero's power to act has diminished to such a degree that he lacks even the power to react. You must have an answer to the following question: 'What happens next in literature?'"

He had given the matter much thought because he had a ready reply. "I find in the ironic literature of the present day many of the elements of the mythic."

The insight struck me with great force. It seemed to me to be central to an understanding of much of the most imaginative of contemporary poetry, drama, and fiction. Some years later, when I found myself attracted to the pantheon of superheroes of the popular imagination, I reasoned that the appeal of characters like Superman and Clark Kent is precisely the admixture of the mythic and the ironic—superhuman abilities encased in an oh-so-human body. This seed produced the found poems in my collection *Mostly Monsters*.

Throughout the fifties, Frye chronicled the year-by-year development of Canadian poetry in the "Letters in Canada" feature in the *University of Toronto Quarterly*. In those years not all that many books of verse were being published, so perhaps that is why he turned his attention to campus activity, and in one review article referred to me as being "conspicuous" on campus. He was right, for at the time I was, conspicuously, printing broadsheets and pamphlets, contributing to the campus newspaper the *Varsity*, co-editing University College's the *Undergrad*, and editing the first all-campus literary magazine, *Jargon*.

I attended the monthly Contact poetry readings that were being organized by the poet Raymond Souster at the old Greenwich Gallery on Bay Street before it became the Isaacs Gallery on Yonge Street. Ray, who became a friend, felt strongly that there should be a meeting of "town and gown" in contemporary North American poetry. (This was prior to the "beat" versus "the establishment" dichotomy that so marked and marred the literary scene of the 1960s.) He corresponded with the Black Mountain poets, published their poems in his little magazine *Combustion*, and all the while wrote poems that could be respected by readers of both persuasions. In the Contact reading series, Ray was assisted by two other poets, Kenneth McRobbie and Peter Miller (who wrote a moving poem called "The Prevention of Stacy Miller" that I have never understood yet quite loved). I assisted Ray in running a later series of readings, which acted as a focal point for the city's writers as well as a venue for visiting readers (among them Charles Olson and Robert Creeley). Margaret Avison and Jay Macpherson might be readers or audience members. Alden Nowlan took the train all the way from Hartland, New

Brunswick, to give his first public poetry reading. The train was late, so when he arrived at the Greenwich Gallery, he found that a local poet was pinch-hitting for him. Alden took a seat in the audience, rather than disturb the substitute reader, before being recognized and urged to continue the reading, to the delight of the attentive audience. Perhaps when he was seated in the audience he found himself sitting beside Gwendolyn MacEwen, then in her late teens, even then lovely and lonely looking, the most Celtic-looking member of the audience. Her great round eyes seemed to absorb all shapes and sounds and colours.

For me the highlight of the Contact Reading Series at the Greenwich and Isaacs galleries was the evening devoted to translations of Hungarian poems. The translations had been commissioned by Ilona Polanyi, the tough-as-steel wife of the warm-hearted historian Karl Polanyi. Margaret Avison had contributed a sensitive translation of Gyula Illyes's amazingly sustained denunciation of tyrannical thinking called "One Sentence on Tyranny." Such were the powers of Mrs. Polanyi, that she prevailed upon Marshall McLuhan to appear and recite the text. He did so with incredible authority, progressively lowering his voice until the audience had to strain and almost wince in pain to not hear but overhear the poem's final syllables. That performance was met with silence, then applause, and an intermission. I watched McLuhan make his way to the door, step out onto Bay Street, and gradually disappear into the night.

In the 1950s, all the coffeehouses in Toronto seemed to be located in the area known as Little Italy. But by the mid-1960s, there were coffeehouses in operation throughout the city. One of the first coffeehouses was the First Floor Club, which occupied a decrepit warehouse building that once stood on the present-day site of the Metropolitan Toronto Reference Library. The First Floor Club was an "after-hours club." The operating principle was that the management could bypass the need for a public hall licence (costly and unlikely to be issued by the city authorities) by organizing as a private club, with a nominal annual membership fee and service restricted to coffee, soft drinks, and light refreshments, rather than as a public hall, open to all. It did not take long for the authorities to catch on to this ruse,

but in the meantime the club-operators were opening their doors to patrons and offering them folksongs and jazz. Howard Matthews, later associated with the performer Salome Bey, operated the First Floor Club. He turned to Michael John Nimchuk, like me at the time an undergraduate and a poet, to supply some literary fare. Michael John asked me to be part of it, and I agreed. Soon we were joined by Jack Winter, a graduate student who wrote poems but who eventually joined forces with the producer and director George Luscombe and became the dramaturge at Toronto Workshop Productions. We called the series of literary evenings "Vocal Magazine," and on my tiny Adana handpress I printed a program or "table of contents" for each of the programs. We staged a number of evenings of literary cabaret that showcased local writers and performers. The theatre personality Mavor Moore, then drama critic for the old *Toronto Telegram,* attended one evening and devoted a column to it. He called the overall production "an evening of courage." Of my own poetry, he said that the poet "succeeds in making the difficult clear, not the clear difficult." He was right on both accounts.

The First Floor Club proved that there was a small but regular audience for literary cabaret and prose and poetry recitals. It was succeeded by the fabled Bohemian Embassy, which was opened in a second-story loft above a garage at 7 St. Nicholas Street, an alleyway near Gerrard and Yonge. From the alleyway a narrow flight of stairs led to a narrow loft with a high ceiling. Despite the narrowness of the room, there was enough room for a dais, perhaps two dozen tables and four dozen chairs. There was a coffee bar that dispensed a delicious drink: hot mulled cider. It warmed the innards, vital in winter because the heating system was known to break down and the temperature would drop, leaving patrons at small tables huddling in their bulky parkas. As they recited their poems, the poets left vapour trails in the air. Like the First Floor Club, the Bohemian Embassy operated only in the evenings, and it operated without a licence. Patrons were required to go through the fiction of purchasing for fifty cents a year's membership.

Don Cullen, actor and performer, was the prime mover of the Bohemian Embassy. Don is a sprite-like figure with a gleam in his eye and a quaver in his voice. He most represents the idea behind "La BoEm," as it was soon

The author and his wife, Ruth. "In those days, I wore my hair long—longer than my wife's!"

dubbed. Don saw me at the First Floor Club and decided I would be an ideal "literary manager." He wanted the club to be open six nights a week. Friday nights were reserved for folksingers ("hootenannies," Don called them). Saturday nights were the domain of Brian Westwood and his jazz group. Thursday nights would be perfect for poetry readings, Don decided. Naturally I agreed, and the fee for services was five dollars a night, collectible if and when gross receipts topped expenses, which happened now and then. The not-inconsiderable expenses ranged from postage for mailers, rental fees of documentary films made by the National Film Board to show between eight and nine o'clock, to talent fees.

The resident poet of the Bohemian Embassy was a lanky fellow named George Miller. A friend of Don's, George was as suave and as cool as his Ferlinghetti-like poems, performed to the accompaniment of a jazz guitar. The visiting poet was Milton Acorn, fresh from Montreal, where, in a gesture of faith in himself and fealty to the muse of poetry, he sold his carpenter's tools and dedicated himself to the life of the Bohemian poet. One of the reasons I accepted Don's offer to host the Thursday evenings was to keep Milton at bay. With no job and no interests outside his own writing and public reading, he had time on his hands. He wanted to spend his days talking about poetry and his evenings drinking and reading his poems. It was more convenient to

meet him at 7 St. Nicholas Street than it was at our flat. To generate some spending money for Milton, I printed a broadsheet of his poems called *Against a League of Liars,* and he hawked the broadsheet at his readings. Members of the audience kept buying them to help Miltie along. On a number of occasions, patrons, young lawyers as I recall, would slip me a five- or a ten-dollar bill to pass on to him to buy a fresh shirt or tie. Acorn lived for the exposure he got on the dais of the Bohemian Embassy.

The poets had to be paid, and so did the singer. Our regular singer, another of Don's friends, was a strong woman with a strong voice, Sylvia Fricker. I paid her the sum of $5.00 to perform two sets of songs. She was very talented and very professional and knew what to sing and when to stop. Her performances were quite professional, unlike the performances of the poets who were inclined either to mumble or to declaim. Sylvia usually appeared alone with her guitar. One evening she arrived with a young dude named Ian Tyson. At the time Ian was known as a designer, not as a singer or composer. He brought with him an autoharp and an able-looking person who turned out to be a talent manager from New York City. Ian and Sylvia proceeded to perform for about forty minutes, to great effect and to rapturous applause. Then they promptly up and left with the manager. The rest of the evening, being limited to the spoken word, was a quiet occasion.

As Canada's premier coffeehouse, the Bohemian Embassy attracted widespread press attention. If San Francisco could have coffeehouses, so could Toronto. While there was some coverage of the readings, the press was fixated on the fate of the Embassy in its ongoing struggle against the dark forces at City Hall. Curiously, today what is recalled is the minor contribution made by the Bohemian Embassy to the city's literary, musical, and cultural life. The club was eventually closed by the city. I arranged for the *Montrealer* to print an edited version of the proceedings of the court case that did in "La BoEm."

Many talented poets made literary debuts at the Bohemian Embassy. Names that immediately come to mind include Gwendolyn MacEwen, Margaret Atwood, and David Donnell. Names of a dozen or so other writers, unknown to the general reading public, also come to mind, because the Embassy existed for them, too. It also was a force that led to the formation of a listening public. A high school student who lived in the Toronto suburb of Mimico, too young to visit the Embassy on his own, read about its activities in the daily newspaper and resolved to be an impresario, too. His name is Greg Gatenby, and after attending York University he joined the Harbourfront Corporation where he was finally able to attend an evening at the Bohemian Embassy. This was a revival of the Embassy, staged by Don Cullen, who had again asked me to perform as the literary manager. Over two years we held literary evenings at Harbourfront which drew audiences that ranged in size from twenty to over three hundred. To me it was apparent at the time that there was a new and educated audience that would buy tickets to see and hear writers of poetry or prose who were being commercially published. Gatenby was able to benefit from the sophistication of the audience and launch Harbourfront's justly famous Reading Series and then its International Festival of Authors, now the world's largest literary "hootenanny" (to use Don Cullen's word).

Words should be heard; they should also be seen. The evenings I was not acting as master of ceremonies at some reading or other, I was busy printing on my small handpress. Under the influence of Harold Kurschenska, I used an Adana press that weighed about fifty pounds and could print an area the size of a postcard—large enough for a short poem. Harold and I imported type from Holland and I handset programs for the First Floor Club and the Bohemian Embassy, as well as booklets of my own and other peoples' poems; other items were sold to libraries with special collections devoted to incunabula. I acquired a respect for the principles of typography, as distinct from the practices of art directors. Nothing commands more respect for the text than standing in front of a California job case, typestick in hand, setting line after line of justified or unjustified text. I attended informal meetings of the Guild of Hand Printers at the home of Carl Dair in Richmond Hill, and also formal meetings of the Society of Typographical Designers of Canada at the Architect's Club. McLuhan sometimes attended the latter sessions; printers felt that "the oracle of the electronic age" knew something about typography because he talked knowingly about the "Gutenberg era."

The Guild of Hand Printers sponsored an annual gathering of the contributions of its members, and I printed pamphlets for a number of these. Most of what I issued appeared over the imprint of the Hawkshead Press, a reference to the Hawkshead Mountains in the Lake District where William Wordsworth dedicated his life to the ideals of art. Thus the Hawkshead imprint appears on dozens of pieces of ephemeral or incunabula—booklets and broadsheets. Two poetic broadsheets were designed and illustrated by then little known artists William Kurelek and Mike Snow. One highly collectible item is a booklet of poems titled *Double Persephone*. It was Margaret Atwood's first separate publication. With David Donnell, she handset the poems and designed and cut the linoblock used in the printing of its green cover. The press run was extremely limited.

While a student at the University of Toronto, I would spend as much time as I could spare in the stacks of the Sigmund Samuel Library, then the university's main library, where I would make use of any carrel that was vacant. I loved nothing more than to wander up and down the aisles, tall shelves of books on either side, and pluck at random those titles that interested me. I would take them to the carrel where I would devote to them the time they required. Every week or so I would browse through a secondhand bookstore and occasionally make a purchase. Prices were cheap in those days. In a used-magazine shop on Queen Street East, I snapped up first editions of a number of Edgar Rice Burroughs's Tarzan novels, paying the marked price of twenty-five cents apiece. I probably never read more than one of them, but later I resold them at an impressive profit when I was short of cash.

Prices were higher and the stock was strictly Canadiana at Dora Hood's Book Room, then located on Spadina Avenue. The mail-order service was presided over by Dora Hood, the author of a biography of Davidson Black, the discoverer of Peking Man, and the retired librarian W. Stewart Wallace. I bought a small book from Dr. Wallace. He was immediately suspicious of me when I mentioned that I was a student. "I'm enrolled at University College," I explained. "I live in the Sir Daniel Wilson Residence." He looked uncertain. "My house is Wallace House." Not until I uttered that piece of information did I realize that the man who was standing in front of me, wearing a dark suit and bow tie on a hot day, was the house's namesake. If he felt surprise, he never showed it.

In a secondhand bookstore on Yonge Street I purchased a copy of Oswald Spengler's *Technics and Man*. Neither the author of the book nor its subject commanded my interest, but its bookplate did: "This Book Belongs to Norman Bethune and His Friends." That evening I paged through it, hoping to find some of Dr. Bethune's marginalia, but there was none. Acting on a hunch, I held the flyleaf with the bookplate on it up to the light, and there, under the bookplate, appeared Bethune's copperplate signature. I have had many adventures with books, but I have never been a collector of editions. I regard a book more as a way of conquering time and space, of capturing experiences and ideas, than as an object in itself, no matter how beautiful. Yet I find I can recall the appearance of each and every book I have read. I find it harder to warm up to a paperback book than I do a hardbound book.

When I arrived in Toronto in the summer of 1956, I immediately looked for work. I was extremely lucky. At the suggestion of Harold Kurschenska, I walked into the editorial offices of the University of Toronto Press, which occupied the new, yellow-brick building on the university quadrangle, and asked if there were any openings in the editorial department. A Miss Harmon greeted me. She was familiar with some of my small-press activity. I did not realize it at the time, but the UTP was then poised to become one of the leading university presses of North America. Under the able direction of Marsh Jeanneret, with financial control in the hands of future director Harald Bohne, the press began to make its mark in the field of trade publishing to match that in the field of scholarly publishing. The editorial reins were in the hands of two women: Eleanor Harmon, a wraith-thin woman in the manner of a headmistress of a private school, and Frances Halpenny, a large woman with a passionate interest in books and theatre. Miss Harmon led

"All five of us look happy (and rather goofy) seated on the church pew in the living room of our house on Dell Park Avenue, Toronto, Ontario. That's Jonathan sitting between Ruth and me, Theo on Jonathan's lap, and Cathie on my lap."

me to the Editorial Reading Department where she introduced me to Katie Sheldon who was in charge of five "readers," two full-time and three part-time. One of the readers was on sick leave. I would replace the part-time reader for the interim. Mrs. Sheldon had been educated in Germany and was exceedingly meticulous, as well as kind and considerate. She took an interest in my literary work and printing endeavours and managed to employ me a few hours a week throughout the academic years from 1957 to 1960 and full-time for two summers.

What Mrs. Sheldon ran was the proofreading department. She sat at a desk at the head of the room and we sat at four tables. In twos and in tandem we read copy and corrected galleys and then page proofs, marking corrections in pencil in the time-honoured manner. One of my first tasks was to check the proofs of the *University of Toronto Quarterly* for the copy editor who worked in the office down the hall. Later on we took great pains with the proofing of a book called *Late Archaic Chinese* which consisted of the Roman text that had been monotyped on campus (the printing department was located in a building immediately south of Simcoe Hall) with intricate Chinese characters (typeset at Harvard or Princeton and dispatched by post to Toronto where they arrived out of sequence and out of order). The work resembled a mammoth jigsaw puzzle. We were reduced to describing Chinese characters in words: "I need three horizontal lines and one short comma." Before long I was assigned a task connected with a new project, the *Dictionary of Canadian Biography*. We were visited by the historian George Brown; he shared his enthusiasm for this exciting project with the editors and the assistants. He asked us to cut and mount entries from other biographical encyclopedias on five-by-eight cards and alphabetize them. A courtly man, he inquired about my interests in Canadiana. I mentioned that I was reading *Walt Whitman* by Richard Maurice Bucke. He suggested that he might add my name to the card reserved for Dr. Bucke. I demurred, suggesting that it might be better to wait until I had undertaken some scholarly research on the man and his work. It seemed every week a publisher from abroad was given a tour of the press. On one occasion the portrait photographer Yousuf Karsh made the rounds. The Editorial Reading Department was one of the few

rooms that looked "editorial." In function it did not really differ greatly from the mediaeval scriptorium familiar to Erasmus.

I learned a great deal about the editing process and production techniques at the University of Toronto Press during summer breaks and at odd times throughout the academic year. It paid less but was more intellectually stimulating than my previous summer jobs, working in the shipping departments of Kitchener's two meat-packing plants, Burns' Meats and J. M. Schneider Ltd. On the shop floor I learned to appreciate manual labour and manual labourers. But because of my copy-reading training and my familiarity with editorial procedure, I was able to think in terms of a career in publishing.

I canvassed a number of trade publishing houses for openings and was eventually hired by the Ryerson Press. The company had its own offices and printing presses, and these were located in the neo-Gothic Wesley Building. The building is now the swinging operations centre of CITY-TV and MuchMusic. In its nonswinging days, the Ryerson Press and its predecessor, the Methodist Publishing House, had trained three or more generations of book editors and book salesmen who left for greener pastures or founded their own book publishing or distribution operations. By 1960, Ryerson was a survivor from another era, a brontosaurus lumbering among the mastodons. Originally founded by the Methodist Church, it was being operated at a loss by the United Church of Canada. It printed and published its own books and operated as a general printing company. Its flatbed and rotary presses were antiquated even then, and the highspeed press that it imported from Germany during my time at Ryerson was out of date before it was installed. Yet the Ryerson imprint had probably appeared on the title pages of one thousand books, many of them worthwhile, many of them well designed by Thoreau MacDonald and other artists. Certainly the presence of the Ryerson imprint enriched and ennobled the history of Canadian literature.

The Rev. Dr. Lorne Pierce served as the editor-in-chief of the "Mother Publishing House of Canada" from 1920 to 1960. The description was recalled dismissively by John Gray of Macmillan and Jack McClelland of McClelland and Stewart, heads of the leading publishing companies, and it was an embarrassment to the

Rev. Dr. John Webster Grant, Dr. Pierce's successor as editor-in-chief. I spent many an evening with Dr. Pierce, recalling the writers he had known and had published, but he was chronically hard of hearing so it was difficult to learn much about anything. Dr. Grant, the new editor-in-chief, redirected his intelligence and attention away from the problems of "clergy reserves" to the possibilities of "balanced lists." I was the new assistant editor of trade publications. I shared an office with Miss Enid Thornton, an educational editor and permissions editor who had been with the firm for many years.

I had surprising success adding books to the Ryerson list, although this would not be apparent from the first two incidents that happened on my first day on the job. There was a knock on the editorial door, which was always left half open, and the department's receptionist appeared, looking apologetic and hopeful. She had a question. "Will you join the department's bowling league?" she asked. I am afraid my answer disappointed her.

My first phone call was equally irrelevant. As the junior editor I had to field outside telephone calls, so anyone who phoned the company with a general inquiry probably reached me. The first call went like this:

"How do I publish a book?" a woman wanted to know.

"If you send us the manuscript, with return postage," I said, "we will consider it for publication."

"How much do you pay?"

"We don't pay, but we offer the author a royalty, a percentage of earnings."

The caller sounded suspicious. "What percentage?"

"Ten percent for the first five thousand copies?"

Now she was really suspicious. "And who gets the other ninety percent?"

To offset such callers, as well as callers who wanted to know the cost of rebinding the tattered family Bible, there were businessmen's lunches with literary figures. I wanted to suggest to the Toronto press that there was a "new spirit" at Ryerson. Dr. Grant and I met over lunch with Nathan Cohen, Robert Fulford, Robert Weaver, and many movers and shakers of Toronto's literary establishment.

Dr. Grant eyed the annual Governor General's Literary Awards with envy. "I wish we could win one of those for one of our books," he

said. It had been ten years or so since a Ryerson book had qualified for the coveted award. I take some pride in the fact that during the three years I spent at Ryerson, I personally added three Governor General's Award winners to the list. These were James Reaney's *Twelve Letters to a Small Town,* Hugh Garner's *Best Stories,* and Alice Munro's *The Dance of the Happy Shades.* (The latter book, Munro's first, appeared five years after the ending of my apprenticeship at Ryerson. At the time Munro was wary of publishing a collection of short stories, the wisdom in the book trade being that a volume of stories should follow the appearance of a major novel. With the years she felt more sure of herself and the hard attitude towards short fiction softened.) Hugh Hood, another natural-born short-story writer, felt much the same way about producing a novel before a collection of fiction. Nevertheless he was delighted when we accepted the stories in *Flying a Red Kite.* Among the stories he wanted to include was a vivid evocation of Toronto titled "The End of It." We both felt the story would be the best possible culmination of the collection, but the story was under consideration by the *New Yorker.* If accepted, it would have to be withdrawn from the MS of the book because of time constraints. But if declined, it would be available for the book. One evening Hugh telephoned me from Montreal to say that the story had been returned to his agent. To Hugh's surprise, I expressed considerable pleasure. Hugh dedicated *Around the Mountain,* his next collection of stories, to Ruth and me, perhaps in gratitude. I was the in-house editor of many books, notably George F. G. Stanley's *Louis Riel* and John Coulter's popular play *Riel.* I was able to arrange for Carl Dair to be commissioned to give that play its unusual, native-influenced typographic design.

The Ryerson period introduced me to the world of contracts, company policies, and sales conferences. Throughout the 1960s the company was losing money, some estimates being as high as a million dollars a year. The educational market had changed, but Ryerson under the leadership of its book steward, the Rev. C. H. Dickinson, had not. One instance of lack of judgement was the purchase of an immense, German-built rotary printing press for the purpose of printing the the *United Church Observer,* but it could not be operated effectively or efficiently. Offset presses were what were required.

"The late Nikola Roussanoff and I examine a book in front of an entire wall of books in our basement. This photograph appeared on the dust-jacket of The Balkan Range. *In Sofia, they claimed they could not tell which author was the Bulgar!"*

Nor was Ryerson successful with textbooks. Long gone were the days when a phone call from the superintendent of a provincial department of education would authorize the production and automatic purchase of 30,000 copies of a textbook. In the 1960s, the textbook department went through the motions, reimbursing teachers for reports on manuscripts when it was known that those very teachers recommended books for inclusion on Circular XIV (the Ontario Department of Education's list of books for which provincial subsidies were available). The trade department, with its five editors, broke even. But the significant books, the books that were being reviewed and bought in quantity, were appearing on the lists of more enterprising publishing houses. Even the printing and binding departments were uncompetitive. Ryerson was losing money and by the end of the decade the United Church resolved to sell it to the American publishing giant McGraw-Hill—to the consternation of cultural nationalists.

In the meantime, on the Ryerson salary, I could no longer support myself and my family—payday was every two weeks and by day twelve I would be borrowing a few dollars from Miss Thornton to tide me over—so I supplemented my salary with writing assignments that came my way. I contributed occasional articles to the *Montrealer* and reviews of Toronto art

shows to *Canadian Art*, which Paul Arthur so ably edited from Ottawa. The *Canadian Forum* had a long history of encouraging new talent, so under the editorship of Milton Wilson, I contributed cultural commentary. As its sometime movie reviewer, I had a pass to the Famous Players theatre chain. I also wrote reviews of current books for Frank Moritsugu of the *Toronto Star* and William French of the *Globe and Mail*. All this was in addition to volunteer work on the board of the *Tamarack Review*.

The country's most exciting publishing house was McClelland & Stewart. Its swinging image was one thing; its reality was a rabbit warren of offices fronting the warehouse located off Bermondsey Road in the depths of Scarborough, Ontario. J. G. (Jack) McClelland, newly in control, decided to expand its list and "go for gold." The country was approaching the Centennial of Confederation in 1967, and various levels of government were generously making grants available for cultural projects, including books. It was the place to be—but on contract, not on staff.

The first time I saw Jack McClelland I thought I was seeing Adonis in person. It was at a book launch, and I realized right away that he must be one of the handsomest men in the world. He was not *the* handsomest man—according to Sir Kenneth Clark that distinction belonged to another Canadian, the youthful Alan Jarvis, who subsequently became director of the National Gallery in Ottawa and succumbed to alcoholism—but Jack was certainly the most dashing and electric personality in the world when it came to the promotion of Canadian authors and their books. Jack's secret was that he believed in people more than in books. He claimed he never read most of the books he published, yet I soon found he could be an astute critic of text and design, copy and illustration, a good judge of people. Above all, he could distinguish between books and "koobs," his term for books that make sense in book-trade terms but otherwise were unloved. It is at odds with his image, but I recall that he once thought that what he would be most remembered for was the Carleton Library, a multi-volume series of history texts.

I introduced myself to Jack and he arranged for me to meet his educational and trade editors Jim Totten and Clare Pratt, the daughter of E. J. Pratt, who began to make use of my round-the-clock willingness to work on assignment. The first manuscript I was assigned to copy edit was "a book about the church." I thought I had left all that behind at Ryerson, but the manuscript turned out to be by Pierre Berton and its title was *The Comfortable Pew*. Because of controversy and promotion, it became an outstanding trade bestseller. On another occasion I was asked if I would check the quotations and the style and spelling of "a book about social philosophy." Miss Pratt added, "The feeling here is that it will need a new and better title. It's currently called 'Lament for a Nation,' but nobody here likes the title." I took the ninety-nine-page manuscript home and read it one weekend with rapt fascination. I dutifully drew up a list of alternate titles, knowing in my heart that no one could ever better Professor Grant's formal "lament." His arguments and analysis convinced me that while it was a moral good to struggle for an independent Canada, the outcome was all but certain; we were battling for points. My immediate task was to convince Professor Grant that his prose would be more understandable if it were more idiomatic. At one point he had ideas "issuing into" rather than "issuing out of," and the development of his arguments paid little heed to chapter breaks. Our first meeting took place in the M&S canteen in the warehouse. Coffee was served but for some reason no spoons were in evidence. Professor Grant took off his glasses—I noticed that they were held on by one arm, the other being unaccountably missing—and with its arm he simply stirred his coffee. He lit a cigarette, and before long there were cigarette ashes and coffee stains over everything. Oblivious of the mess, he held forth with considerable gusto and authority on major matters of moral philosophy and minor matters of social improprieties. Everyone within earshot was dumbfounded with astonishment.

To this day I take pride in the minor yet significant contribution I made to the appearance of *Lament for a Nation*. (The sole change I would make to the text is to turn the "further" to a "farther" where it appears on the final page.) Professor Grant asked permission to acknowledge my assistance in the appropriate section of the book, but at the time it was not yet accepted practice for authors to thank anybody and everybody—agent, secretary, typist, publisher, editor, etc. Some years later I caught a glimpse of him on a television show. Professor Grant and Dalton Camp were the guests of Peter Gzowski. The subject of the authorship of Camp's book came up. Professor Grant quipped, "Was it written by John Robert Colombo, too?"

In all, as an editor at large, I edited close to one hundred trade titles for McClelland and Stewart and other publishers, including the memoirs by Judy LaMarsh, the political biography of Walter Gordon, whom I greatly respected and to whom I dedicated my first "quote book," and books of poetry by Earle Birney and Irving Layton. One of the last books I edited for the company was a collection of speeches delivered over the years by Brian Mulroney, then on the verge of being elected leader of the Conservative Party. The collection was called *Here I Stand*. All authors are anxious to please their publishers and editors. I found this author to be anxious lest he displease even one single member of the public.

Throughout the 1970s and 1980s, I undertook various assignments for trade publishers and others but, all the while, I was researching my own books. I started collecting "quotable quotes" during the Centennial year. If there is one book of mine that the public knows, it is *Colombo's Canadian Quotations*. For readers who have never seen it, I am talking about a fat tome of over seven hundred, double-column pages. It was published with great success by Hurtig Publishers in Edmonton in the fall of 1974. Mel was an amazing publisher. He made more headlines than all of his authors combined as the country's most vocal economic nationalist. As a publisher of well-designed and well-promoted books, he seemed to add Prairie enthusiasm to Eastern enterprise. He would "chat up" his books with influential people he encountered on his busy speaking schedule.

Here is how I compiled the quote book and in the process came to be known as John "Bartlett" Colombo and "the Master Gatherer." It struck me with some force that I should collect notable and quotable quotations by Canadians on any subject or by foreigners about Canada. I should do so on three-by-five slips and organize them into a book-length collection. (This was at a time when electric typewriters and sore wrists were common, not yet computers and carpal-tunnel syndrome.) At the time I was researching and writing programs on Canadian history and society for CBC Radio, often on assignment from the ever-helpful Robert Weaver. On one occasion, I spent the better part of a morning trying to pin down where and when Sir Wilfrid Laurier had actually uttered the celebrated remark "The Twentieth Century belongs to Canada." The only place to turn was the book of Canadian quotations and phrases that had already been published, but it was badly out of date and hardly encyclopaedic. I was the right person to trace familiar and important quotations, as I was and remain a determined browser, one who takes as much pleasure in reading lesser-known works as very well-known works. I was fairly knowledgeable about current Canadiana. After all, the writers we were championing at *Tamarack* and at the Bohemian Embassy coffeehouse were making their reputations. Unlike most cultural commentators, who seemed caught in the current of events, I was as much interested in the drama of the past as I was in the theatre of the present. I had a fair knowledge of major and minor writers of the past and the present. Why not capitalize on that knowledge and collect those quotations? Some (like Sir Wilfrid's) were widely known; others (like Stephen Leacock's "Many a man falls in love with a dimple and marries the girl") deserved to be better known. I estimated that there might be as many as two hundred important remarks, too few to issue in book form, but enough for the core of a substantial book. In the end I prepared a collection of six thousand quotations by Canadians of the past and the present and from all walks of life, about all subjects, or by foreigners who had found occasion to write or speak knowledgeably or devastatingly about Canada. Copying the quotations correctly was one thing; supplying the sources and the contexts as required was quite another. Dealing with so many quotations called for a sense of organization, but it also called for "determined browsing," to use fellow compiler the late George Seldes's term. I spent mornings and afternoons in the old Metropolitan Toronto Reference Library at the corner of College and St. George Street, requesting books from the stacks, checking issues of *Hansard,* and consulting standard reference volumes. At the library, I copied in longhand those passages I did not photocopy; at my desk at home, I typed them all on my manual typewriter onto three-by-five slips. (Decades later personal computers and laptops would be available to lighten the compiler's load, but

much is gained by the concentration needed to write out passages by hand.)

The organization of a vast body of quoted matter calls for careful planning. From the first I reasoned that organizing the book by contributor would make it more interesting and impressive than organizing it by topic. Opinion is divided on the matter. Most people want direct access to a quotation, and so prefer a collection organized alphabetically by topic than they do one organized alphabetically by contributor, as long as there is an index of contributors. Yet I noted that the two most important and influential quote books, *Bartlett's Familiar Quotations* and the *Oxford Dictionary of Quotations,* had a contributor arrangement. (Few users of these books seem to realize that *Bartlett* has an arrangement by author and the arrangement of authors is chronological, while *Oxford* presents its authors alphabetically.) I had no second thoughts about the alphabetical author arrangement of my book, at least until it came time to tackle the problem of indexing the six thousand quotations. The book would obviously benefit from an extensive index of keywords and subjects. It took me a couple of weeks to

"In 1987, Ruth took this snapshot of the author resting his arm on the stone marker that identifies the site of the Birthplace of Modern Spiritualism. It all took place in 1848 in the Fox family cottage outside Hydesville, upstate New York."

prepare the twenty-thousand index slips, and to sort them into rough alphabetical order. One Sunday afternoon Ruth and I invited about a dozen friends to a "sorting bee." Upon arrival the guest was handed the cards that began with one letter of the alphabet and was asked to undertake the fine sort. I handed writers George Jonas and Barbara Amiel the S's, and Barbara later admitted to me that sorting through the Saints, St.'s, Ste.'s, and St.-'s, was the hardest task that she had performed since sitting for the Ontario Grade XIII departmental examinations. We supplied pizza and beer. At the end of the day about half the index was more or less sorted. The next day I prevailed upon Philip Singer to come to my aid. Philip was able to take a few days of holiday leave from the Bathurst Heights Area Branch of the North York Public Library where he worked as a librarian and go through the index with the proverbial fine-tooth comb. It took me close to a week to type the index and proof it. I am quite proud of that index, as it covers eighty-four, three-columned pages. Although the book generated a lot of positive newspaper, magazine, radio and television coverage, hardly any reviewers noticed the bulky but useful 20,000-entry index.

Early on, I made a presentation of the undertaking to Robert I. Fitzhenry, a canny Scot if there ever was one, head of Fitzhenry and Whiteside, then a new and growing publisher and distributor. I requested an advance large enough to permit me to devote three or four months to the completion of the work, and we signed a contract that specified that he would publish a work called *Colombo's Canadian Quotations*. While I was labouring over the index, he expressed approval of the finished manuscript and assigned the experienced editor Diane Mew to make spot checks and to see it through the press. But the day earmarked for the first of the typesetting, he called a meeting at which he said, "The name 'Colombo' is a good name, but not the name for this book."

I was not entirely committed to having my name appear in the book's title. In the 1970s the name Colombo sounded more foreign than North American. (Peter Falk was shortly to make his appearance in a rumpled raincoat.) So I asked Fitzhenry, "Do you have a better title in mind?"

"Yes, I do," he said. "We should call it *Quotations Canada*."

I could hardly believe my ears. Was my book going to sound like a department of the fed-eral government, like Health and Welfare Canada? To explain what he meant, he continued, "We will call the first edition of the book *Quotations Canada*. Then, if you insist, you can call the second edition of the book whatever you want." The logic of that escaped me.

At that point negotiations broke down. I repaid in full the advance of $5,000. When he tried to dun me for a $265 photocopying bill to copy the MS, I severed all connection with the firm. A few months later his company placed an advertisement in a librarian's journal requesting the services of a knowledgeable person to edit a quote book. About two years later F&W issued its own book, *The Fitzhenry and Whiteside Book of Quotations,* a collection of English-language "quotable quotes" based on little research and a lack of sources. I noticed that it was not called *Quotations Canada.*

By chance, Mel Hurtig phoned me the next day about another matter. I told him what had happened. "Why not send me the manuscript? That sounds like a book for Hurtig Publishers." I did, and Mel and his editor Jan Walter read through the entire manuscript, made many annotations, and offered me a contract with an advance of $10,000. The sum of money may not sound very large in the mid-1990s, but it was a substantial advance in those days, especially from a smaller publishing house to a freelance writer. There was no discussion of the title; it was to be *Colombo's Canadian Quotations*. When broadcaster Larry Zolf learned that I was collecting Canadian quotations for a book, he surmised, "It'll be a short and dull book." But when he saw the beautiful, bulky book that Mel published, Larry generously recanted, adding that he found it "remarkable." Robin Skelton, the poet and editor, reviewing a later book, dubbed me "the Master Gatherer." An editorial writer said, "It's a book to launch a thousand editorials." In that edition it sold about 35,000 copies at the then unheard of price of $25.00 a copy.

In its wake, I compiled a concise paperback edition with a topical arrangement, then two, large-scale collections of brand-new quotations, plus *Colombo's All-Time Great Canadian Quotations,* a sort of "selected quotations." As a result of all this activity, I am frequently asked to identify my favourite Canadian quotations. Without hesitation I say, "It's by J. Castell Hopkins, a Toronto editor at the turn of the century. He wrote, 'Canada only needs to be known in order to be great.'" One does not have to be a chauvinist to take delight in that remark. Knowledge is a necessary good, and there is no knowledge without self-knowledge. To some degree there is no self-knowledge without national knowledge. No one exists outside a context. Self-knowledge leads to an awareness of the needs of others as individuals and as groups. I like to add that as long as Canadians say interesting things, I will be there to collect them.

In the 1970s, William Toye was the very busy general editor of the Canadian Division of Oxford University Press. Bill, a designer as well as an editor, is a man of great taste and discernment. He established the high editorial and design standards of the *Tamarack Review.* On behalf of Oxford, Bill commissioned me to research and write *Colombo's Canadian References,* which I visualized as the companion of the big "quote book." There are six thousand entries in *References;* as it happens, the same number of quoted passages make up *Quotations.* The idea was to prepare a ready reference book for the general reading public, the men and women Robertson Davies describes as "the clerisy." *Benêt's Reader's Companion* was my model for the new book, for it identified and briefly described major and minor references throughout world literature. *Colombo's Canadian References* would do the same for people, places, things, and ideas. Bill supplied superb editorial and writing support. I wrote about eighty-five percent of the book; specialists like historian Jack Grantstein produced capsule biographies of the prime ministers, etc. I see the 6,000 entries in the book as an alphabetical arrangement of 6,000 ways in which Canadians are distinct from the people of other lands. My favourite entry is the one devoted to "Cartier," Canada's first commercial typeface, designed by Carl Dair. Bill arranged for it to be set, unlike the rest of the book, in "Cartier." No reviewer noted the fact or commented on it.

Colombo's Canadian References went through two editions and then went out of print. Librarians and editors, writers and scholars, regularly ask me, "When are you going to prepare a new edition?" My ready answer is, "When I find a publisher or a sponsor for it." But given the parlous state of the Canadian economy in the 1990s, and the even worse state of Canadian publishing, that time is not now and probably will not return. Yet my responsible answer

to that question is, "Hurtig's four-volume *Canadian Encyclopaedia* does the job." I am still intrigued with the notion of compacting a country between the covers of a book, but modern media, including CD-ROMS and online data bases, make the prospect of packaging it between covers less appealing than it once was.

By the mid-1990s, I have written, edited, or translated over one hundred books. Some are short, others are long. Many are compilations, so I take no great pride in numbers and will never rival the imaginative productivity and scientific knowledge of an author like Isaac Asimov. Occasionally an interviewer will ask me to name my own favourite among my books. I have no quick answer. But I do have an answer when the question is "Which book gave you the most pleasure?" The book that I most enjoyed researching and editing is *Other Canadas.* I like to call it "the world's first anthology of Canadian fantastic literature."

Anthologies have played an important role in the development of science fiction and fantasy. Indeed, anthologies have had a great influence on the world—the King James version of the Bible is an anthology, and the lyric poem owes much of its popularity to another anthology, *Palgrave's Golden Treasury.* Awaiting to be assessed is the role played by anthologies in establishing national traditions in fantastic literature. In the meantime, here is how *Other Canadas* came into being.

On a flight between Edmonton and Toronto, I was skimming through an issue of my favourite publication, the *Times Literary Supplement,* when three words leapt out at me. In one review I saw the word "national," and in another review on another page, I saw the words "science fiction." These words are not commonly associated. In the mid-1970s, the words "national science fiction" sounded like a contradiction in terms. Although SF is considered to be supra-national, in practice the genre has always been heavily affected by American writers and publishing practice. I asked myself, "Why has nobody ever compiled an anthology of Canadian science fiction?" Nobody had bothered because, despite the fact that anthologies are important in the SF world, few people were familiar with the available material. There were no checklists, no bibliographies. A longtime reader of fantastic literature as well as Canadian literature, I could easily take excerpts from novels, reprint short stories, and commission an original work or two. A truly Canadian anthology of science fiction would be like no other country's. It would feature stories by mainstream authors as well as genre writers. It might be an anthology of "fantastic literature," including not only science fiction but also fantasy fiction and weird fiction. It could showcase poems and dramas, forms seldom found in American or British anthologies. In much of my thinking I was responding to my conception of the "mosaic" of Canadian writing as well as to the expansive thinking of Judith Merril, the veteran SF anthologist who (like Jane Jacobs) had immigrated to Canada and settled in Toronto to protest in a personal way the American involvement in Vietnam.

If *Other Canadas* had a catalyst, it was Judy Merril, the knowledgeable, opinionated, experimental, and irreplaceable author and editor. One of my prized possessions is the Bantam paperback edition of *Shot in the Dark*, Judy's first SF anthology and the first SF book I ever bought and read. I pondered the stories in the books and the editor's headnotes to them, and I cannot imagine a better introduction to "the sense of awe" (the foundation and firmament of fantastic literature) than her anthology. I could hardly believe my luck when I learned, by accident, that Judy had moved to Toronto. I sought her out shortly after she had made a donation to the Toronto Public Library of her collection of 5,000 paperbacks, including *Shot in the Dark,* to form the backbone of the Spaced Out Library, the world's largest public collection of highly imaginative literature. The library is now known as the Merril Collection of Science Fiction, Speculation and Fantasy and nicknamed MC=SF². With Judy's goading and the collection at hand, I quickly acquainted myself with the world highways and Canadian byways of the literature I most loved to read and ponder.

The sole problem was that no one had ever compiled a bibliography of Canadian fantastic literature. I began to work on one with a librarian friend, Michael Richardson, and for the French-language titles we enlisted the aid of Professor Alexandre L. Amprimoz. Then we were joined by archivist John Bell, who had independently sifted through mainstream Canadiana for uncharacteristically imaginative literary works by E. J. Pratt and Sir Charles G. D. Roberts and others. The result of our labours was *CDN SF&F,* which identified and annotated some six

"On a trip to Los Angeles in 1990, Ruth and I made a point of seeking out A. E. van Vogt, one of science fiction's "greats," and his lovely wife Lydia, in their hillside home on Belden Drive, Hollywood. Ruth poses alongside them. I took the snapshot."

hundred titles. In the process it became obvious that this hitherto unknown and hence unexplored body of writing had a number of characteristics: the prevalence of fantasy over science fiction, the accent on the polar world, and the notion of the "alienated outsider."

Other Canadas was one of those books that found a publisher right away and made its mark quickly. Published by McGraw-Hill Ryerson in cloth and paper editions, it traced the tradition of fantastic literature in the country from 1657, with Cyrano de Bergerac's imaginative account of the crash-landing of an ancient astronaut in New France, to Colombo in 1979. In all, the book includes thirty-six contributions: stories, poems, an article on fantasy (by Margaret Atwood), another on SF (by David Ketterer), and even the script of the National Film Board of Canada's superb and influential documentary film *Universe.* At first, reviews of the anthology were mixed. Mainstream reviewers objected to the inclusion of genre writers among the mainstream writers. SF specialists objected to the mainstream writers being treated as genre writers. One reviewer quipped that my definition of "Canadian" was so broad that it would embrace anyone "who had ever flown over Canada in a rocket ship." Indeed, I have always felt that national boundaries are blurred by concentrating on the issue of nationality or citizenship. I have since argued that the "greatest" Canadian science-fiction novel is *Roadside Picnic,* a work set in a small community in northern Ontario rather like Sudbury, written by the Strugatsky brothers, Russian authors who never set foot on Canadian soil, flew over it in a space ship, or crossed the Atlantic. But it was not long before a new generation of writers (among them Robert J. Sawyer) began to make contributions to the field that could be widely appreciated at home and abroad.

The compilation of *Other Canadas* gave me the opportunity to collect more material than could be printed between the covers of a single book, so I followed it with an anthology of weird fiction, co-edited with Michael Richardson, and a study of fandom in the guise of a commentary and a collection of the writings and opinions of Leslie A. Croutch of Parry Sound, Ontario. In the process, I greatly enjoyed the task of evolving a narrative history of "Four Hundred Years of Fantastic Literature in Canada," a talk, illustrated with forty coloured slides, that I delivered almost two dozen times in varied venues in various parts of the country. Audiences were appreciative, yet I found that hardcore fans who profess an interest in the future display a disinterest in the past. In my adolescent years, science fiction was a secret and hence a guilty pleasure. In my more mature years, it has challenged me to discover and uncover writers and works of quaintness or quality. Today, although much fine fantastic literature is being written, I find I have little time for it, much preferring to re-experience the "fine, careless rapture" of the early fiction of A. E. van Vogt or the works of H. G. Wells, Arthur C. Clarke, etc. In cartons in the basement of our house reside the manuscripts of four anthologies of Canadian fantastic literature—two of them of stories that predate the Golden Age—which I trust will someday see the light of day. After all, the axiom of the science-fiction writer is that the future is what we make it.

Outer space has fascinated me, and so has inner space, by which I mean the mysteries of the supernatural and the paranormal. Although the words are often taken to be synonymous, there is a simple distinction between them. A supernatural event or experience is one for which there is no reasonable explanation, no cause-and-effect relationship that is a sufficient cause. The occurrence is, in effect, a miracle. A paranormal event or experience is one for which

there exists a reasonable explanation, the sole problem being that scientific and rational inquiry have yet to establish that cause. The cause is the occurrence that has yet to be understood. My curiosity about such mysteries is, like outer space, boundless.

At the same time as I began to collect quotations, I started to collect references to mysteries connected with Canada. I soon realized that far from being an "unmysterious" country, Canada was the domain of a multitude of mysteries, many of them of historical interest to readers around the world. Here are three instances: First, the famous mystery ship the *Mary Celeste,* which was found abandoned on the high seas, was built and launched in Parrsboro, Nova Scotia, and considered a "hoodoo" ship from the day of its maiden voyage. Second, Spiritualism, as a modern movement, dates from the activities of the Fox Sisters in upstate New York in 1848. I learned that Maggie and Katie Fox were two farm girls born in Consecon, a farming community in Upper Canada, now Ontario. Third, Borley Rectory. As a youngster I was fascinated with the description of Borley Rectory as "the most haunted house in England." To my surprise, it turned out that all the mysterious comings and goings at Borley in the modern period were a replay of events that had taken place three quarters of a century earlier as part of the Great Amherst Mystery, again in Nova Scotia. Before long, I had references to over five hundred major and minor mysteries that covered all provinces and territories and pretty well every manifestation of the supernatural and the paranormal from appearances of ghosts and poltergeists to experiments in psychokinesis and simultaneity. These were described and sometimes dramatized in *Mysterious Canada,* a tome that includes 114 illustrations.

What I realized, working as a researcher in the study rather than as an investigator in the field, was that there was much evidence of the operation of the mysterious, but little in the way of proof. What did present itself as proof was, by and large, firsthand, narrative accounts that had been prepared by observers or participants for purposes of their own. I found myself by turns arguing and agreeing with two earlier scholars, R. S. Lambert and A. R. G. Owen, authors of fine books devoted respectively to the supernatural and the paranormal in Canada. Pondering their work and the books of such of such folklorists as Helen Creighton and Edith Fowke—I benefited from many conversations with Edith—I came to a couple of conclusions. The first is that the first-person accounts make fabulous reading and the accounts should be preserved and collected for their own sake and for the sake of readers with a taste for true-life mysteries. The second is that, except for such reports, there is no proof of the existence of abilities, beings, or worlds other than our own. (The jury is still out on the results of the laboratory testing by scientists who place psychics in sensory-deprivation chambers or pit them against random-number generators.) I found these narratives in old newspapers and books, and through media appearances, and by writing to the editors of daily and weekly newspapers and asking them to run my letter requesting their readers to contact me. There is no shortage of "experiencers." So far I have published six collections of "personal accounts." I call the accounts in these books *memorates,* taking the term from folklore studies, and in the prefaces to these collections I consider the various characteristics of these memorates which constitute the best evidence for the objective reality of ancient, historical, modern, and contemporary mysteries in space and time.

How do I see myself? I see myself as an editor-at-large (to use Ruth's term) and as someone who has not had full-time employment since 1963. I was nervous about economic conditions and prospects when I left the Ryerson Press. Robert Weaver of the CBC promised me some freelance radio work, and he lived up to his promise in every way. A fine omen marked the first full week of self-employment. I was phoned, out of the blue, by Edward Weeks, editor of the *Atlantic Monthly,* which was then the leading literary magazine in North America. Weeks had been given my name by Jack McClelland, and he wanted to know if I would be willing to subedit a gathering of Canadian poetry for a special feature devoted to Canada that was scheduled to appear in a forthcoming issue. I found the offer hard to credit. Only two years earlier I had heard Weeks speak at University College in the course of a memorial to Mazo de la Roche. He spoke warmly about the distant woman, coolly about her romantic writing. Now here he was offering me a wonderful opportunity with a small fee attached to it. Accordingly I "rounded up the usual suspects," and poems by all the poets whose works I forwarded to him were accepted for publication, including my own piece of satiric verse

"I delivered a keynote address at a conference on Russian-Canadian relations in Moscow in summer 1993. Ruth and I are photographed alongside Yeltsin and Gorbachev, or life-size facsimiles thereof, on the prospect of Lenin Hills. Political economist Abraham Rotstein, who also spoke at the conference, snapped the picture."

"Recipe for a Canadian Novel." Thereafter, when asked where I had been published, I would boast that I was "published" in the *Atlantic Monthly!*

Perhaps the reason that my name popped into Jack McClelland's mind when Weeks had contacted him, was that I was then the youngest member of the editorial board of the *Tamarack Review.* The quarterly literary journal had been founded in 1956 by a group of Toronto writers and editors that included William Toye, Robert Weaver, Anne Wilkinson, and Ivon and Patricia Owen. Bob Weaver was invited to talk about Canadian writing and literary broadcasting on campus, and I attended. It turned out that he was familiar with some of my publications. When he learned I was serious about pursuing a career in publishing or letters, as distinct from teaching or scholarship, he convinced the other *Tamarack* editors that the publication needed "new blood" and that I might be "a future Bob Weaver." I was surprised and flattered by the invitation and accepted with alacrity. But being the youngest editor on the board for many years turned out to be a mixed blessing.

Tamarack differed from almost all the other "little magazines" and literary journals published in Canada in that it defined itself as a professional publication, produced by professional editors for the general reading public, not by writers or academics for the benefit of a clique of writers or a school of academics. That is how it saw itself. Other writers often saw it as representing the "Toronto literary establishment." It was difficult for younger writers to be critical of Bob Weaver who, as the chief literary officer of the Canadian Broadcasting Corporation, was in a position to purchase already written poems and stories for broadcast or commission original works for broadcast. At the same time it was easy for younger writers to be critical of the magazine's youngest editor and dub him "the lieutenant of the Canadian literary establishment" (Robin Matthews' phrase). The truth is that Bob has a sixth sense when it comes to assessing quality in contemporary writing and a sense of forbearance when it comes to showing loyalty to people of talent through thick and thin. He encouraged such writers as Margaret Laurence, Norman Levine, Timothy Findley, Mordecai Richler, Alice Munro, Hugh Hood, and Margaret Atwood from the first, not to mention innumerable writers who continue to

feel close to him and to his taste and preferences. He was never one for cliques or schools of writing. Whether for the printed page or the airwaves, he favoured prose and poetry that could be read and heard and reread and reheard with pleasure decades later. *Tamarack* appeared quarterly between 1956 and 1982, years that saw changes not only in the country's writers but also in the country itself. During those twenty-six years, the word "national" lost much of its appeal to the word "regional." Those years also saw the rise (and fall) of the dichotomy between "beat" and "establishment" writing, and the appearance of schools of literary criticism and cliques of writers. Yet, as George Woodcock noted about the magazine, "It set the standard by which later Canadian literary magazines have been judged."

I find in these memories that I have yet to write much about my "other" life. The other life refers to family life. I married Ruth Brown, a childhood sweetheart, not the country singer by that name, shortly after we both graduated from the University of Toronto. Ruth immediately enrolled in the Ontario College of Education and I entered the Graduate School. We moved into a furnished, two-room, third-floor flat in Rosedale, at 48a Dale Avenue, just down the street from Morley Callaghan's residence. We were happy there and entertained literary guests—on one memorable afternoon we hosted A. J. M. Smith and F. R. Scott. Thereafter we moved into an unfurnished, ground-floor apartment at 120 Millwood Road. There we entertained large gatherings that on one evening drew both Irving Layton who loved to "explain" current movies and Leonard Cohen who had eyes only for Sylvia Jonas, the fiery, red-headed, Hungarian-born wife of poet and radio producer George Jonas. Thereafter we moved into a graceful, six-room flat at 85 Burnside Drive, where we entertained no end of writers including such unlikely ones as Phyllis Webb and George Bowering. In my tiny study in the early 1960s, George Jonas and I translated over a hundred poems from the Hungarian. A frequent visitor was Robert Zend, another Hungarian intellectual. Our son Jonathan was born here. Our daughter Catherine was born in the house which we rented on 60 Ellis Park Road overlooking Grenadier Pond. Raymond Souster, who also lived in the city's west end, was an occasional visitor. I like to think that it was in our living room, with Ray, Earle Birney, and others present, that the League of Canadian Poets was effectively formed.

William Ready, the amazing librarian of Mills Memorial Library at McMaster University, who secured the literary papers of the late Bertrand Russell for one of his special collections, purchased my own papers. With the down payment in 1968, we were able to buy the house in which we now live at 42 Dell Park Avenue. The house is located in an area of North York that is part Italian and part Jewish, known locally as "the Kosher Nostra." Our third child, Theo, was born here. In the early years we hosted a great many literary events and gatherings. Margaret Laurence, Andrei Voznesensky, and Marcel Marceau (brought by Robert Zend) were some visitors. Wherever we lived, Ruth was immensely supportive of my work and interests. Without her regular salary as a teacher, first on the high school level, then at a community college, little if any of these activities would have been possible. It is important to make that point, but a larger point must also be made. Ruth and I share not only a background, but also emotional concerns and intellectual interests. Like me, Ruth has so great a curiosity about people, ideas, and current events, that others see it as inquisitiveness. We have evolved a form of "shorthand" in speech and gesture which other people find difficult to follow. Sometimes I think we must be twins. A recent visitor suggested that after thirty-five years of marriage, we are still enjoying a honeymoon. She was right.

Only someone who is a father or a mother can appreciate the pride and joy that parents can take in their children. Jonathan, Catherine, and Theo are now adults. Jonathan is a lawyer whose specialty is the growing field of intellectual property. Catherine works with a famous physician as a medical administrator. Theo is a student of history who loves the world of ideas. All three have "significant others."

Missing from these memoirs are many friends whose values have influenced our own. Among them is Cyril Greenland, longtime family mentor. Together Cyril and I compiled *Walt Whitman's Canada,* the first-ever examination of the influence of Whitman and of Whitmanism on three generations of Canadians. There is also the unforgettable Nikola Roussanoff, a native of Bulgaria, a mature student at the University of Toronto during the time I was on campus. Nick forced me to pay attention to the literature of

his native country by claiming, "Dora Gabe is a better poet than Dorothy Livesay." To prove it, he translated a line of Gabe's about the secrets of a people that could be found only "under the eaves of a forgotten village." I put the poem into fluent English. Thus began a collaboration that resulted in the publication of five books of translations of Bulgarian prose and poetry, not to mention numerous trips to that country under the shadow of the Balkan Range. From its capital, Sofia, Bulgaria is seen as the crossroads of civilization. It is certainly the domain of poets, including Dora Gabe, Elisabetta Bagrayana, Andrei Germanov, Lyubomir Levchev, to name a handful of the remarkable and talented men and women whom we met and translated with the help of the Slav Committee and the Writers' Union. I must not forget Tony Hawke, publisher of Hounslow Press, whose heart beats faster and quicker than those of most publishers. Then there are friends found in the last few years: Jane Dachs and David A. Gotlib. Dr. Dave, as we call him, is a physician and therapist with a special concern for clients who report anomalous experiences. Our discussions of these matters has led to a deeper understanding of the nature of ordinary as well as extraordinary experiences.

In my professional work as an author, editor, and anthologist, I am inclined to downplay my interest in writing poetry in favour of promoting projects of more widespread interest. The public is not much interested in poems, or at least my poems, and I find increasingly that what I expect from the Muse is not what the media or the public wants. Being the professional poet does not appeal to me. Until about fifteen years ago, I enjoyed giving poetry readings and conducting creative writing courses. Now I can barely stand the idea of participating in them. I have always seen myself as someone who experiments or innovates, yet unlike most experimenters and innovators, what I produce is not complicated. Characteristic of my writing has been a concern with "found art." My feeling is that only the aesthetic response separates art from non-art, and the response is built into the reader and not added to the work itself. Some works of art are deeper than others, to be sure, and they may even be dramatic constructions, but unadorned nature offers the possibility of aesthetic experiences that match those of well-wrought villanelles. There is no gainsaying the power

"January 1995 saw us in Japan, where I delivered a keynote address at a conference on the subject of cryptozoology held in Ibusuki City, Kyushu. In the background is Lake Ikeda, said to be the haunt of the monster Isshei; in the foreground is the fabulous Isshei itself."

of a few words from a poem—witness W. H. Auden's line about "the long littleness of life"— but the response may come from prose as well as from poetry, from the world of nature and from human nature as well as from the world of art. *The Mackenzie Poems,* my first full-length book, was a collection of found poems—the "redeemed prose" of a rebel journalist, W. L. Mackenzie. A subsequent book, *John Toronto,* took the uncollected writings of the reactionary bishop, John Strachan, and presented them as found poetry. Hugh Hood once referred to me as the *abordist* of Canadian poetry, someone who explores the borderlines, the extremities, who makes end-runs, and reworks the borders. He is right.

After exploring the possibilities inherent in "found poetry" in half a dozen such books, I investigated the possibilities of neo-surrealism. Textbooks tend to regard surrealism as a movement in time and not as a tendency of thought and personality. There are natural-born surrealists. Not too many years after I completed the surreal contents of *Neo Poems,* I met and worked with two surrealist spirits: Robert Zend, Hungarian-born, Toronto-based broadcaster and writer; Ludwig Zeller, Chilean-born poet and artist of collage. Ludwig and his wife, the painter Susana Wald, who is of Hungarian birth and Argentine and Chilean background, are latter-day surrealists. I assisted the Zellers in the co-

translation and publication of some of their books. We became great friends who would see in each others' work the sight of configurations denied to others.

Following the surrealist stage, there was what I like to call my Euro-modernist period, when I took more than a passing interest in modern European poetry. The period began with my work with George Jonas on modern Hungarian poets and continued with a collaboration with George Faludy, the contemporary Hungarian master, that resulted in the appearance of two books. With Nikola Roussanoff, I co-translated those five volumes of Bulgarian prose and poetry. The Polish poet Waclaw Iwaniuk and I undertook to translate the first book in English of Ewa Lipska. This period in my life reached its apotheosis when Waclaw and I prepared our version of the most incisive of modern poems, Zbigniew Herbert's "Fortinbras's Elegy." What it says is that now that the Hamlets (the superheroes of the past associated with the Second World War) are dead and gone, it is time to put things in order; it is the postwar day of the common-born Fortinbrases.

The Euro-modernist period was succeeded by the Nativist period, during which I prepared basic texts of Inuit and Indian lyric poems, producing a series of books—*Songs of the Indians* (in two volumes) and *Poems of the Inuit* and *Songs of the Great Land*—not to mention the prose collections, *The Mystery of the Shaking Tent* and *Voices of Rama.* These periods gave me a taste for translations and for the "translated" tone, something that comes through in the writings of European poets like Miroslav Holub or Hans Magnus Enzensberger or an innovative American poet like Richard Kostelanetz. Every native lyric I have ever read sounds "translated." Much of the post-Modern literature sounds like it has been translated.

If there is a word to describe the current state of my poetry, it is probably "spacy," not in the sense of drugs but in the sense of outer space. A recent collection, *Off Earth,* bears the subtitle "Poems and Effects." When the poet Fraser Sutherland reviewed the book, he noted that "there are more 'effects' than 'poems,'" I did not regard it as criticism, for my intention was to create aesthetic, literary, and cultural effects in the sense of 'special effects' for films and 'sound effects' for radio programs. Poems may be dramatic entities like stories; they may also be aphoristic-like insights.

I have hardly ever suffered from a "writer's block," but I have from time to time suffered from what I like to call a "publisher's block." There are not enough publishers for the book-length manuscripts that I wish to write, compile, and translate. This may sound like a strange admission—or complaint—from someone whose name appears on the title pages of more books than any other Canadian author. (Cultural commentator Robert Fulford described me as the most persistent collector of words in the history of Canadian letters.) To find an outlet for future books, especially those of a semi-commercial nature, I finally created a publication platform for my own work. In the late 1950s, I used the Hawkshead Press imprint for private printing. Throughout the 1970s and 1980s, I was able to add a number of titles to the list of Hounslow Press, then owned and operated by Tony Hawke. So I was no stranger to private printing and one-man publishing. It seemed inevitable that at one time or another I would create the imprint of Colombo & Company, which since 1994 has been the publisher of record of ten books. The imprint first appeared on *Voices of Rama,* a collection and commentary on Ojibwa traditional tales collected at the Rama Reserve near Orillia, Ontario. The typescript had been lying around for fifteen years, so all I had to do was to scan it, pre-

pare book-size pages, print the text with a LaserJet printer, and arrange to have the pages photocopied, trimmed, covered, and cerlox-bound by an instant printer. A small edition was then offered for sale. I call the finished product— more a photocopied report than a printed book, to be sure—a QuasiBook. McLuhan mused about the day that the electronic media would make "every writer his own publisher." That day dawned for me in December 1994 with *Voices of Rama.* In the future I see increasing numbers of creative-minded writers, some of whose works may lack an economically defined market, turning to "sanity" (not "vanity") publication. Why stop at the printed page? Why not move toward the Internet with an electronic "home page"? As of this writing I have yet to establish a home page, but I do have an Internet address (*jrc@inforamp.net*). Initiatives like these may seem to be departures from "the norms" of the past, but they seem to me to be ways to ensure that creation and communication are not confused with market conditions and dynamics, so that no matter what conditions may prevail at any one time, ideas and ideals will find innovative expression.

I began these professional memoirs by quoting some lines written by Merrill Denison about the confusion that he felt that so many things had happened to him before he was born. Nearing my sixtieth year, I find I am surprised to realize that so much has happened to me *since* I was born. It has happened to me, often because I have made it happen, little knowing the consequences or the lack of them. There are so many more stories to tell. For instance, I would delight in sharing my thoughts on being chosen by Carl Sagan of the Planetary Society and the space artist Jon Lomberg to prepare the bibliography of Mars-related science fiction for inclusion on the CD-ROM disk that is being affixed to the Mars Observer spacecraft which will soon be launched from the planet Earth and landed on the planet Mars. As a youngster I yearned to be a space-farer, an astronaut. I may never set foot on another world, but for me there is some small consolation in the realization that one of my undertakings, with my name attached, will appear on that disk, in digital form, affixed to that spacecraft that will cast its shadow across the sands of the Red Planet.

BIBLIOGRAPHY

Poetry:

Lines for the Last Day, Hawkshead, 1960.

Miraculous Montages, illustrated by Don Jean-Louis, Heinrich Heine, 1966.

Abracadabra, McClelland & Stewart, 1967.

Neo Poems, Sono Nis Press, 1970.

The Great Collage, Oasis, 1974.

The Sad Truths, PMA Books, 1974.

Variable Cloudiness, Hounslow, 1977.

Private Parts: New Poems by John Robert Colombo, Hounslow, 1978.

The Great Cities of Antiquity, Hounslow, 1979.

Recent Poems, League of Canadian Poets, 1980.

Selected Poems of John Robert Colombo, Black Moss, 1982.

Off Earth, Hounslow, 1987.

Luna Park: One Thousand Poems, Hounslow, 1994.

Space Poems, Colombo & Company, 1995.

"Found" poetry:

The Great Wall of China: An Entertainment, Delta Canada, 1966.

The Mackenzie Poems, Swan, 1966.

William Lyon Mackenzie Rides Again!, The Guild of Hand Printers, 1967.

John Toronto: New Poems by Dr. Strachan, Oberon, 1969.

The Great San Francisco Earthquake and Fire, Fiddlehead Poetry Books, 1971.

Leonardo's Lists, Weed Flower, 1972.

Praise Poems, Weed Flower, 1972.

Translations from the English: Found Poems, PMA Books, 1974.

Proverbial Play, The Missing Link, 1975.

Mostly Monsters, Hounslow, 1977, Colombo & Company, 1995.

Humor & lore:

Colombo's Little Book of Canadian Proverbs, Graffiti, Limericks and Other Vital Matters, illustrated by P. Whalley and D. Shaw, Hurtig, 1975.

Colombo's Hollywood: Wit and Wisdom of the Moviemakers, Collins, 1979; as *Wit and Wisdom of the Moviemakers,* Hamlyn (England), 1980; as *Popcorn in Paradise,* Holt, 1980.

The Canada Colouring Book, illustrated by Emma Hesse, Hounslow, 1980.

222 Canadian Jokes, illustrated by Peter Whalley, Highway, 1981.

Colombo's Last Words, illustrated by Peter Whalley, Highway, 1982.

Colombo's Laws, illustrated by Peter Whalley, Highway, 1982.

Colombo's Canadiana Quiz Book, Western Producer, 1983.

Colombo's 101 Canadian Places, illustrated by Peter Whalley, Hounslow, 1983.

René Lévesque Buys Canada Savings Bonds, and Other Great Canadian Graffiti, illustrated by David Shaw, Hurtig, 1983.

Canada First Quiz: A Quiz Game about Canada, Petro-Canada, 1984.

Great Moments in Canadian History, illustrated by Peter Whalley, Hounslow, 1984.

The Toronto Puzzle Book, McClelland & Stewart, 1984.

Toronto's Fantastic Street Names, Bakka Books, 1984.

Quotations from Chairman Lamport, Pulp Press (Vancouver), 1990.

Ogdenisms, Hounslow, 1994.

Compiler:

The Varsity Chapbook, Ryerson, 1959.

(With Jacques Godbout) *Poetry 64/Poésis 64*, Ryerson, 1963.

(With Raymond Souster) *Shapes and Sounds: Poems of W. W. E. Ross*, Longmans, Green (Canada), 1968.

How Do I Love Thee?, Hurtig, 1970.

New Direction in Canadian Poetry, Holt, 1971.

Rhymes and Reasons, Holt, 1971.

Trio: 21 Poems . . . in English Translation, International Festival of Poetry, 1975.

Colombo's Book of Canada, Hurtig, 1978.

The Poets of Canada, Hurtig, 1978.

(With Michael Richardson) *We Stand on Guard: Poems and Songs of Canadians in Battle*, Doubleday (Canada), 1985.

Walt Whitman's Canada, Hounslow, 1992.

(With Cyril Greenland) *Worlds in Small: An Anthology of Miniature Literary Compositions*, Ronsdale, 1992.

Translator:

Robert Zend, *From Zero to One*, Sono Nis Press, 1973.

(With Irene Currie) Paul Eluard and Benjamin Péret, *152 Proverbs Adapted to the Taste of the Day*, Oasis, 1975.

(And editor with Nikola Roussanoff) *Under the Eaves of a Forgotten Village: Sixty Poems from Contemporary Bulgaria*, illustrated by Maryon Kantaroff, Hounslow, 1975.

(And editor with Nikola Roussanoff) *The Balkan Range: A Bulgarian Reader*, Hounslow, 1976.

(With Susana Wald) Ludwig Zeller, *When the Animal Rises from the Deep the Head Explodes*, Mosaic, 1976.

(With Nikola Roussanoff) Lyubomir Levchev, *The Left-Handed One: The Poems of Lyubomir Levchev*, Hounslow, 1977.

(With Susana Wald) Ludwig Zeller, *Mirages*, Oasis, 1977.

(With Nikola Roussanoff) Dora Gabe, *Depths*, Hounslow, 1978.

(And editor) George Faludy, *East and West: Selected Poems*, Hounslow, 1978.

(With Nikola Roussanoff) Andrei Germanov, *Remember Me Well*, Hounslow, 1978.

Dark Times: Selected Poems of Waclaw Iwaniuk, Hounslow, 1979.

(And editor) Waclaw Iwaniuk, *Evenings on Lake Ontario: From My Canadian Diary*, Hounslow, 1981.

Far from You: Selected Poems of George Skvor/Pavel Javor, Hounslow, 1981.

(And editor with Waclaw Iwaniuk) Ewa Lipska, *Such Times: Selected Poems*, Hounslow, 1981.

Robert Zend, *Beyond Labels*, Hounslow, 1982.

Selected Translations, Black Moss, 1982.

(With Petronela Negosanu) Marin Sorescu, *Symmetries: Selected Poems*, Hounslow, 1982.

(And editor) George Faludy, *Learn This Poem of Mine by Heart*, Hounslow, 1983.

Some Hungarian Poets, Colombo & Company, 1995.

Quotation collections:

Colombo's Canadian Quotations, Hurtig, 1974.

Colombo's Concise Canadian Quotations, Hurtig, 1976.

New Canadian Quotations, Hurtig, 1987.

The Dictionary of Canadian Quotations, Stoddart, 1991.

Colombo's All-Time Great Canadian Quotations, Stoddart, 1994.

Reference works:

Probings (essays), Canadian Mental Health Association, 1968.

Colombo's Names and Nicknames, NC, 1974.

Colombo's Canadian References, Oxford University Press (Toronto), 1976; Oxford University Press (London and New York), 1977.

(With others) *CDN SF&F: A Bibliography of Canadian Science Fiction and Fantasy,* Hounslow, 1979.

Blackwood's Books: A Bibliography Devoted to Algernon Blackwood, Hounslow, 1981.

Canadian Literary Landmarks, Hounslow, 1984.

1001 Questions about Canada, Doubleday (Canada), 1986.

999 Questions about Canada, Doubleday, 1989.

Writer's Map of Toronto, Colombo & Company, 1991.

Writer's Map of Ontario, Colombo & Company, 1992.

Canadian Global Almanac 1993, Macmillan (Canada), 1992.

Canadian Global Almanac 1994, Macmillan, 1993.

Canadian Global Almanac 1995, Macmillan, 1994.

Omnium Gatherum, Colombo & Company, 1994.

Fantastic literature:

Other Canadas: An Anthology of Science Fiction and Fantasy, McGraw-Hill Ryerson, 1979.

Friendly Aliens, Hounslow, 1981.

(With Michael Richardson) *Not to Be Taken at Night: Classic Canadian Tales of Mystery and the Supernatural,* Lester & Orpen Dennys, 1981.

Native studies:

Poems of the Inuit, Oberon, 1981.

Windigo: An Anthology of Fact and Fantasy Fiction, Western Producer Prairie Books, 1982; University of Nebraska Press, 1983.

Years of Light: A Celebration of Leslie A. Croutch, Hounslow, 1982.

Songs of the Indians [Volume I: Beothukan, Algonkian, Iroquoian, Athapascan, Kootenayan], Oberon, 1983.

Songs of the Indians [Volume II: Salishan, Wakashan, Tsimshian, Haidan, Koluschan, Chinookan], Oberon, 1983.

Songs of the Great Land, Oberon, 1989.

The Mystery of the Shaking Tent, Hounslow, 1993.

Voices of Rama, Colombo & Company, 1994.

Mysteries:

Colombo's Book of Marvels, NC, 1979.

Mysterious Canada: Strange Sights, Extraordinary Events, and Peculiar Places, Doubleday, 1988.

Extraordinary Experiences: Personal Accounts of the Paranormal in Canada, Hounslow, 1989.

Mysterious Encounters, Hounslow, 1990.

Mackenzie King's Ghost, Hounslow, 1991.

Dark Visions: Personal Accounts of the Mysterious in Canada, Hounslow, 1992.

Little Blue Book of UFO's, Arsenal Pulp, 1992.

UFO's Over Canada: Personal Accounts of Sightings & Close Encounters, Hounslow, 1992.

Close Encounters of the Canadian Kind: Personal Accounts of Flying Saucers and UFOs in Canada, Colombo & Company, 1994.

Ghosts Galore!: Personal Accounts of Hauntings in Canada, Colombo & Company, 1994.

Strange Stories: Weird and Wonderful Events and Experiences from Canada's Past, Colombo & Company, 1994.

Ghost Stories of Ontario, Hounslow, 1995.

Also author of plays and documentaries for Canadian Broadcasting Corporation. Contributor to periodicals, including *Canadian Art, Canadian Forum, Globe and Mail, Montrealer,* and *Toronto Star.* Member of editorial board, *Tamarack Review,* 1960–82.

Jonathan Holden

1941-

Jonathan Holden, 1993

Probably the two greatest influences on my life have been my father, Alan Nordby Holden, and the fact of having been born an identical twin. Stephen and I were born on July 18, 1941, in what was then rural New Jersey. Our mother, Jaynet Conselyea, and our father were intellectually inclined. Alan had graduated summa cum laude from Harvard in 1925. He had majored in chemistry. He had always been regarded as "different" and, like J. Robert Oppenheimer, he had been teased in high school for his intellectuality. A genius, he would have gone to graduate school, except that his parents were not well off, and so, after graduation, he worked in New York City as an accountant to support his mother, who was dying of tuberculosis. He was a very thorough man, half German, and when he had dispatched that obligation he managed by dint of his brilliance to get work at the Bell Telephone Laboratory in Murray Hill, New Jersey, as a physical chemist—a crystallographer—but for the rest of his life he felt that he was playing catch-up ball. In World War II, he developed a crystal used in sonar antisubmarine detection.

In 1939, Jaynet and Alan bought an old farmhouse on seven acres of land on Pleasantville Road, five miles from the nearest town. There they lived until their deaths, five weeks apart, in the fall of 1985. It was in that quiet, creaky farmhouse where Stephen and I grew up. It was lonely. We were their only children, and there were few other children around. Pleasantville was a narrow, gravel road. Occasionally a cow would wander across it. Though we were only thirty miles west of the Holland Tunnel, Pleasantville Road seemed like the uttermost end of the earth.

What do I remember about my childhood? Atmosphere, mainly, not detail. Pleasantville Road is on the northern edge of what is now the Great Swamp National Wildlife Refuge, and the landscape was primeval—slow fetid rivers, cattails, mosquitoes, briars. There were dangers everywhere: strange dogs, bees, hornets' nests, rumors of "quicksand." Jaynet read bedtime stories to us—all of the Oz books, all of Hugh Lofting's Dr. Dolittle books, and all the books by Arthur Ransome of *Swallows and Amazons*. There was no television back then, but there were comics, and by the time I was ten I had graduated from Donald Duck and Scrooge to E.C. comics—*Two-Fisted, Weird Science Fantasy*. The stories were better than Disney stories. They had irony. But what I liked best about them was the art. William M. Gaines hired serious artists, and I quickly learned to distinguish the style of each artist: Joe Orlando, Wally Wood, and (the best) Al Williamson. *Weird Science Fantasy* devoted an entire issue to Ray Bradbury's *Mar-*

tian Chronicles, illustrated by Williamson. I pored over it many times like a poem, and, in truth, it was a kind of poem. *Two-Fisted,* when it had exhausted Korean War material, began to retell famous battles such as the Battle of Lexington and Concord and various Civil War battles. It was realist art, and Gaines insisted that all the weaponry and uniforms be rendered with historical accuracy. The mortars discharged with a PONG! Rifles discharged with a KA-POW! I became a connoisseur of comic-book gunshot noises.

Around the age of nine, I became interested in baseball, and in the summers, when there wasn't enough to do, I would lie on my bed, the electric fan going (there was no air-conditioning), listening through the static to Mel Allen broadcasting New York Yankees games. I read Claire Bee's sports stories starring a boy named Chip Hilton. I began to construct an imaginary baseball team, its star pitcher a gaunt, seedy veteran like Sal Maglie except that he was, like me, left-handed. Gray had a slow curve that (as I put to myself verbally) "curled" away from the batter. With no other kids to play with, I began playing imaginary innings alone, hitting a threadbare tennis ball into the air and judging the result: a low liner for a single, a higher liner that ricocheted off the pear tree for a double, a homer if it carried over Thompsons' hedge. I would announce the games to the woods: "There's a long drive! Woodling going back, back . . ."

In the sixth grade, I received my first *C* in class. Stephen and I were bored to the point of desperation. My parents had heard about a progressive school in Short Hills, New Jersey, called Far Brook, a school like the Putney School, but for locals. Its director was a graduate of Bennington College, Winifred Moore. Mrs. Moore was a sort of contemporary version of Margaret Fuller, and Far Brook School was not unlike the famous transcendentalist commune Brook Farm described in Hawthorne's *Blithedale Romance.*

When our parents announced to us the school change, we bawled, but the school radically changed our lives for the better. A major part of the curriculum involved art and music. Each spring, classes stopped and the seventh, eighth, and ninth graders produced and performed a Shakespeare play. In the ninth grade there were just six students, three girls and three boys—Stephen, I, and a boy named Bob

Gabriner. Far Brook was like a three-year honeymoon before we had to return to public high school. We were given tennis lessons, and I was allowed to be a baseball pitcher. At home, my boyhood companion, Pat Burke, had been taken out of public school and sent to a parochial school, Delbarton. Pat and I had lost touch with the local kids, and so, in summer, we spent time together teaching each other tennis. In his senior year, Pat was second singles on the Delbarton team. In my senior year, I was first singles and captain on the Morristown High team.

At Morristown High, the education I received was unusually good. In 1957, when the Russians embarrassed the United States by being the first country to put a man in orbit, there was a frantic rush to upgrade curricula in science and mathematics. The curricula of Morristown High had tracks, and in the college prep track the teaching was intense. We could take Latin. Stephen was in the National Honor Society. He did some acting. Stephen attracted and hung out with the intellectual kids, the geeks. He had a slightly effeminate manner, and he couldn't throw a baseball correctly. He threw like a girl. I affected a macho manner, though I was so scrawny I looked like somebody from a concentration camp. Some of the tougher guys in the high school would tease Stephen. I was terrified of them, of being mistaken for Stephen. Though I was timid and hypersensitive, I pretended to be "one of the guys." At the end of high school, Stephen was accepted into Yale; I was accepted into Oberlin.

Oberlin was a shock. For the first time in my life, I found myself in a student body that was at least as smart as I was. Those who weren't smarter were more worldly and had greater intellectual sophistication. My freshman roommate, Paul Levy, had graduated from the Bronx High School of Science. He majored in music and physics. From 1960 on, I had the feeling, like Alan, of playing catch-up ball. All through high school, whenever I'd been asked what I wanted to be when I grew up, I would guess "an engineer"; but at Oberlin I saw that the only thing I knew how to do was read. I became an English major.

The two most fashionable sets of ideas at Oberlin in the early sixties were Wittgenstein and Sartrean existentialism. I bought a tattered, army surplus jacket and began to play the part

With identical twin brother, Stephen (left)

of an existentialist, smoking unfiltered Camels and imagining myself like Camus. After my sophomore year, I dropped off the tennis team. I had been "first alternate." My homemade game couldn't stand up to the trained, tutored games of kids like Phil Page, from St. Louis, or our first singles player Jon Erickson, who had been a Michigan junior champion at Kalamazoo. Besides, tennis was too bourgeois an activity for my new persona, and my cigarette addiction (two packs a day) left me out of shape.

In my junior year, I became interested in the game of bridge. It was a popular game at Oberlin, and it was a good way to meet girls. My best friend at Oberlin was a brilliant, eccentric student named Ted Ulrich. Ted and I decided to memorize a new bidding system called the Kaplan/Sheinwold system, whose wrinkle was that the stronger your hand the lower your bid: that way you would have more opportunity to exchange information to find a good "fit." Much of my junior year at Oberlin I spent playing bridge. That summer, the summer of

1962, I went to Chautauqua, New York, where my uncle David was a music critic for the *Chautauqua Daily.* Through the local employment agency, I got a job as a yardboy for a minister from Chicago who summered there, Dr. Carl S. Winters. Ted arrived, and we began playing in local bridge tournaments. Our bidding system was so new that it confused many of our opponents, and we came in second in a tournament in Jamestown, New York. We each earned half a master point. The world of serious bridge was eye-opening to me. After that summer, I didn't play much bridge, but the bridge-world that I glimpsed is described in my first novel, *Brilliant Kids,* where the town of Powawathia is another name for Chautauqua. The character Clifford Bell is a conflation of Carl Winters and Norman Vincent Peale. I had intended to call the Winters character Peale, but because in the book Peale's daughter, Linda, undergoes an illegal abortion, the University of Utah Press, fearing a lawsuit, insisted that I change Peale's name, so Norman Vincent Peale became Norbert Victor Bell. The character Barbara is based upon Georgia Clark, my first serious girlfriend at Oberlin.

I hated Oberlin and swore to all my friends that I would never set foot in a blankety-blank college again, but it educated me in spite of myself. In 1969, when I was taking a class called the "Origins of Continental Fiction," at San Francisco State College, the professor, Donald Doub, was remarking how, in the second book of Don Quixote, Quixote keeps running into characters who have heard about the exploits of a knight named Don Quixote. I raised my hand and said, "So the entire second half of the story takes place at an entirely different ontic level than the first." Doub was flabbergasted. The class was puzzled. One of the girls said, "Antic?" "Ontic," I explained.

In my senior year at Oberlin, I began carrying a pint of gin around, like a baby bottle to pull on. Oberlin had hired a poet/scholar, David Young, and a professor of German, Stuart Friebert. One of the most powerful aesthetic experiences I can remember is hearing Friebert

read Paul Celan's "Todesfuge" in German. There was a burst of literary activity at Oberlin. X. J. Kennedy, Lewis Turco, Miller Williams, and Judson Jerome visited in a group. Williams left the strongest impression on me. He read a poem in which Christ was a cowboy. In the last line, which was dialogue, a girl declared: "He could have me." The audience was deliciously shocked. This was a long way from stuffy poetry in the tradition of T. S. Eliot.

That year, I met and began to court Gretchen Weltzheimer, the girl I would later marry. Gretchen lived with her mother, Margaret, and her younger sister, Kristin, in a house designed by Frank Lloyd Wright. Gretchen had the most beautiful auburn-red hair I have ever seen. Margaret was intellectual, with a master's degree in literature. She was an alcoholic, and since the age of thirteen Gretchen had managed the household, bought the groceries, kept a brave front to the world. Whereas I was paralyzed with timidity and shyness, unable to break the ice with strangers, Gretchen had chutzpah and charm, and the gift of gab. Being with her was easy, because as she gabbled happily along her presence was a sort of panoply running ahead of me. This was especially true when I brought her to my parents' house. She could front for me to my parents. Jaynet, seeing that I was in love with Gretchen and sensing how desperately in need of parental love Gretchen was, admitted her into the charmed circle of my family. When I graduated from Oberlin, I would need a practical, extroverted partner like Gretchen to run interference for me.

When Gretchen graduated at midyear, in January 1963, she moved to New York, got a job as an investigator for the New York City Department of Child Welfare, and found an apartment on the Lower East Side of Manhattan. That June, after graduation, I moved in with her. I saw an ad for "writer" in the *New York Times.* I went to the employment agency to inquire. The job was to turn out formula fiction for a series of schlock romances. I was unqualified, but as the lady began politely to dismiss me, she remarked, "Oh, I see you're from Oberlin. Do you know my niece Susan Howell?" Susan was the fiancée of Ted Ulrich. The lady said, "Sit down again. Maybe I can find you something." She placed me in my first job, working as an editorial assistant at a textbook company called Cambridge Book Company

In sixth grade at Harding Township School, New Jersey

in Bronxville, New York. I worked there for two years. Cambridge produced review books. Its main competition was a company called AMSCO, which had cornered the review market on texts designed to help high school students prepare for the New York State regents exams.

One of the trends in public education was New Mathematics, started by the School Mathematics Study Group at Yale. SMSG was part of the continuing fallout from *Sputnik,* part of the attempt by the American education establishment to upgrade teaching in science and mathematics. The Doubleday Science Series, in which my father and Phylis Singer published the book *Crystals and Crystal Growing,* was another part of this effort. New Mathematics added a few high mathematical frills and jargon such as set theory and logic to ordinary high school algebra. The solution to an equation became the "solution set." The best of the SMSG texts was an *Introduction to Matrix Algebra,* which included some number theory. It made fascinating reading, but it was mainly to please mathematicians with gestures toward mathematical elegance which only the most brilliant high school students could appreciate. As I began editing the text Cambridge was pushing, I realized that I liked mathematics more than I had realized in high school, and as I began to talk about mathematics with Alan, we both realized that we had something in common and that he could be of substantive help to me. Our relationship changed. With me grown-up and in my first adult job, Alan could see that I was not going to be dependent upon him economically. We approached each other as adults, and Alan was able to introduce me to a world in which he was an authority and to a mind that was truly unusual; for he was, as his colleagues would freely admit, a polymath—one with style.

On November 16, 1963, Gretchen and I married, and we began a marriage that would last twenty-seven years. At the time, our immediate needs were exigent: married men were exempt from the draft. Gretchen needed a family; I needed a caretaker. The marriage, like that in Henry James's *The Golden Bowl,* was deeply flawed from the beginning. Gretchen was too much a mother; I was too much a child.

We moved from the Lower East Side to a clean apartment near Ninety-fourth Street on Lexington Avenue. It was close to the Ninety-second Street YMCA, where I heard Muriel Rukeyser and John Montague read. But white-collar life in New York seemed a dead end. The Peace Corps was new. In January 1965, Gretchen and I boarded a TWA 707 and flew to Albuquerque, New Mexico, where we would train for a project in urban community development in Chile. I had never been further west than Oberlin, Ohio, and the dry air and the sense of possibility in the Southwest was like a revelation. We received daily political indoctrination, an attempt to *liberalize* the trainees. While we were there, the U.S. Marines invaded Santo Domingo, and there were heated arguments among trainees about imperialism.

Each of us was interviewed by a psychologist, and, a week later, there was a "feedback" session. My psychologist browsed through his notes and concluded of me: "Solid citizen type. Mature." I was appalled. I had fooled them. When, in the initial interview, he had dropped his voice and said gravely, "Tell me, Jon, do you love your father?" I'd said, "Well gosh, yes, I . . . I really do!" And when taking the Minnesota multiphasic, I reached the question, "Have you ever had a black tarry bowel-movement?" I'd checked "no," reasoning that no straight, well-adjusted American man would say "yes." "Have you ever had feelings of unreality?" "No." By far the most liberal person in our batch was Gretchen, and by the time our training was over, she had succeeded in antagonizing many of the trainees. But Gretchen had been by far the most successful in her fieldwork, and at the end of the training, she was swarmed by grateful locals. In a process called peer nominations, however, a bunch of the trainees conspired to get back at Gretchen for her shrill political opinions.

On the final evening, all of us gathered in a lecture room. You'd approach the podium, be handed an envelope, take it out to the foyer and open it. It would either say "Congratulations, go on to next phase" or "Please see Dr. Napoli immediately." That night, Gretchen and I waited forlornly outside Napoli's office. Somebody came out. We rose to go in. "Just you," Napoli said—to Gretchen. I waited outside for an hour. Finally the door opened, and Napoli said gravely, "Jon, you'd better come in." Inside I found Gretchen dissolved in tears. Both the other psychologists were there, vulturelike. I had the feeling that she'd been beaten up. Napoli said that she was "a flaming vehicle." I told them sincerely that she had been the most effective in her field placement and would probably have been more effective than any of the trainees. "I'm glad you feel that way, Jon," Napoli said. "You know, we have couples here on the verge of divorce." I told him that we were treated like statistics in terms of risk. Napoli replied, "What other kind of risk is there?"

Another trainee who had been deselected drove us to El Paso. I had Alan and Jaynet wire us money. We bought a Volkswagen Bug and decided to drive west, then up the California coast to Seattle, where my parents would be for the summer at a conference on the teaching of college physics. That summer the Gulf of Tonkin incident happened, the Kennedy amnesty was rescinded, and it became immediately obvious that if I didn't get some kind of deferment I would be drafted. We drove back to New Jersey, and I called up every private school in a twenty-mile radius of New Vernon. One school, Carteret School for Boys, in West Orange, New Jersey, offered me a job: to teach Spanish and remedial math for $3,500 per year.

There is a set of private schools that are reformatories cloaked by a respectable ivied veneer. Carteret was one of these. I had never taught before. I was petrified, not only of teaching but of the students, who were tough, the very kinds of kids I'd tried to avoid in high school. For the first week, before heading the forty-five minutes east toward Newark, I would sit in the car in my parents' driveway trying not to throw up. As a teacher, I was a fraud. The school was fraudulent. Both the students and the teachers knew it. The motto of the school was "Success equals I.Q. + I Can + I Will." The students referred to me as "Pin-head." Many of the younger teachers were, like me, evading the draft. Two months after I started, I received my notice to appear for a physical. The headmaster, George Douglas Hofe, wrote the draft board a letter. I was reclassified 2A. While I was teaching, Gretchen commuted to Rutgers University to get a master of social work degree.

For the next three years, until I turned twenty-seven, Vietnam dominated the very weather of my life. Gretchen wanted to have a baby. I refused to, until I had gotten a terminal degree. From a friend I'd met in New York, Francis Silenzi, I was invited to read some poems with other young poets over WBAI. The two other poets I read with were, like me, virtually unknown: Grace Shulman and Charles Simic. I

began sending poems to journals. My first acceptance was the poem "El Paso" by the *Antioch Review.*

After two years, I found a better job, teaching four classes of Algebra II, the advanced placement course in calculus at Rutgers Preparatory School, and coaching the tennis team. We moved into a small farmhouse near Bernardsville, New Jersey, a forty-minute drive to New Brunswick and a five-minute drive to my parents'. My parents' Bell Labs friends took an interest in us. Alan had been put out to pasture at the Bell Labs and was tinkering with educational projects and giving lectures at schools around the country. The students at Rutgers Prep, well-groomed children of doctors and lawyers, were preparing for places like Brown and Cornell, and I had the uncomfortable sense of them walking over my back into an upper-middle-class life, leaving me stuck as a teacher.

In the summer of 1967, I resigned from Rutgers Prep. Gretchen had her M.S.W. I had been accepted by San Francisco State College in its M.A. creative writing program. Gretchen and I spent the early summer in Europe on a student tour. We had ordered a Volkswagen Squareback to be picked up in Wolfsburg, West Germany. We'd drive it around Europe, then have it shipped to the United States. It was forlorn and drizzling in northern Germany. We drove the new car south until, near Munich, the sun came out. We continued south, down the Dalmatian coast, winding up in Dubrovnik.

Back in America, we drove to San Francisco and found an apartment on Corona Heights. Gretchen was hired by Marin County Legal Services as a social worker. I attended San Francisco State. The Vietnam War was going on more intensely than ever, but the only sign of it was the occasional grey aircraft carrier that would roost for awhile across the bay. There was a peace march, but instead of the marches I'd joined in Washington, D.C., and in New York City—grey, somber affairs in which thousands of grim citizens walked silently past FBI photographers, past the members of the American Nazi party holding up cans of gasoline and matches inviting us to use them—it was like Mardi Gras. Marchers passed joints around, jugs of wine. The entire city was happily stoned. Nothing was serious in San Francisco. It seemed awash in acid, devoted to pleasure and dissipation. The city was too pretty, littered like white bric-a-brac beside a bay too blue to be real.

Meanwhile, the college was under siege from student demonstrations: the campus buildings were guarded by the San Francisco Tactical Squad. President Summerskill had been replaced by S. I. Hayakawa. Many of our classes were held in the homes of the professors. I studied poetry with William Dickey at his house on Chenery Street. The star creative writing student in poetry then was Gene Berson, and we hung out together. Berson was one of the best storytellers I've ever heard. Most of his stories were about high school experiences. Berson's storytelling gave me permission to be personal. Toward the end of my stay in San Francisco, I wrote the first poem based directly on my personal experience: "How to Have Fourth of July." The poem simply described the great Fourth of July parties which my parents threw for their friends and colleagues. It utilized an instructional format which I'd picked up from reading some of Gary Snyder's "Things to the Do" poems in *Poetry*. Snyder was the inventor of that form. My master's thesis, though, was a novel based on my Carteret experience. My advisor was Herb Wilner. I called up Donald Allen at Grove Press, and he invited me to his offices. He was an elegant, shrewd man, and we had a civil conversation. I sent him a copy of the novel *The First Lesson of Richard Grubb*. When I wrote them a year later, from Colorado, they had lost it.

Most of our social life centered around Gretchen's friends in Legal Aid, especially her boss, Jim Kovacs. To me, Kovac's pursuit of pleasure seems in retrospect to epitomize the entire San Francisco Bay culture around the time of the famous flower summer of 1967 when the term "hippie" was invented. Kovacs was a pothead. He would argue cases before the judge stoned. We began having laughing-gas parties. Everybody would be issued a balloon. You'd inflate it off the tank and breathe in and out. On weekends we would have great rambling "office" parties in Mendocino County along the banks of the Navarro River.

As I neared the end of my master's, I decided to go for a Ph.D., and the criteria which Gretchen and I followed for programs was the physical beauty of the place. I would have gone to Eugene, Oregon, but the University of Or-

egon would not support a student for the first year. I ended up going to the University of Colorado. Because of my publishing experience, I had qualified for a fellowship as an editorial assistant for the journal *English Language Notes*.

My four years at the University of Colorado were the most important years of my life. Gretchen and I had made an exploratory trip to Boulder two weeks earlier. We had driven around the foothills asking people if they knew of any houses to rent, and by sheer luck we were steered to Dick and Kathy Ralston. Dick was a computer engineer at IBM. They had a cabin on Magnolia Road, a winding dirt road which levelled off at around eight thousand feet. The country was rolling pastures and groves of ponderosa pine. It was all owned by a family named Skates, but it was about to be sold and subdivided. In 1970, Boulder was a quaint, almost rustic town that was about to be ruined by wealthy out-of-towners and turned into a version of San Francisco, a city of fern bars, elegant restaurants, and brokerages. But Boulder was also the Midwest: CU's football team under coach Eddie Crowder was ranked third in the nation. It was a town about to boom. The university English department, however, was highly traditional. There were only two creative writing classes, both taught by an instructor named R. D. Lakin. The man who turned out to be the best poet on the staff, Reg Saner, was a Shakespeare scholar, a closet poet.

The National Endowment for the Arts had started its Poets-in-the-Schools program, and Colorado was one of the states participating. Gene Berson, who had been invited to direct California's Poets-in-the-Schools program, recommended me to Judith Wray, the new director of Colorado's program, and early in the fall of 1971 all the poets in Colorado were invited to Denver to meet the arts council and to read poems. It was a curious occasion, because, unlike the scene at San Francisco State, the poets were amateurish. The great boom in university creative writing—what Louis Simpson was later to dub Po-Biz—had not yet started.

Between 1970 and 1974, I supported Gretchen. Poets-in-the-Schools money (one hundred dollars per day), plus the *ELN* Fellowship, plus the extra money from teaching freshman composition went far enough. Gretchen had taken a pottery course in San Francisco. We ordered

*Jonathan, age thirty-two, beside self-built
geodesic dome near Boulder, Colorado*

a kick wheel, and she took more courses in Boulder. She bought a female palomino named Misty and took up horseback riding in the mountains. Gretchen believed that we should buy some of the land around us. My parents made an interest-free loan to us to buy three lots—nine acres for about eleven hundred dollars per acre. We had a well drilled and electric power installed. We decided to build a geodesic dome on the land. A group of idealistic young men had formed a construction company called the Alternative Housing Construction Company. They sold a dome kit and would help you put it together if you wanted. In July 1971, we had a circular concrete slab poured, and we erected the dome—three-eighths of a sphere—and had it sprayed with polyurethane. I bought a Skil saw and began constructing the interior. It was the first time I had ever done any building. It filled me with a kind of confidence I had never known before, forever changing me. At night, I would write poems about it.

There were no poets in the CU English department, but people told me that Professor Saner wrote poems, so I visited with him and asked to see some. As I went through them, I could see that he had exceptional talent, and I told him so, pointing to particular phrasings and also to his prosody. He could see that I knew what I was talking about. We became literary confidants—two poets using each other as resources, admiring each other. Reg had always wanted to be a poet and had studied contemporary poetry and poetry-gossip intensively. One of his closest friends was Wayne Dodd, the editor of the *Ohio Review.*

One day, in the halls of Hellems where I worked at *ELN* and where the English department resided, I noticed a poster for something called the Devins Award: five hundred dollars plus publication by the University of Missouri Press. On a whim, I threw together what poems I had, beginning the book with a poem about the dome, "Design for a House," ending it with a poem called "After Building" and placing in the middle a poem called "Cross Bracing." I called the book *Design for a House.* Several months later, the phone rang and a suspicious woman named Mary Ellen Cruff asked me about the circumstances of the book. She then told me that I had won the Devins Award. There had been some 360 entries. The three judges had been Bruce Cutler, Donald Finkel, and Carolyn Kizer. Could I be present to accept the award in person?

I asked the department chairman, Harold Kelling, if the department would pay my airfare to Kansas City, and he immediately agreed. When I told Reg of the award, he blanched, and I realized that he was jealous, that he was wondering why Holden instead of Saner, though Reg hadn't applied for the Devins. My award started him competing for awards (and he was extremely successful: he won the first Walt Whitman Award, in 1975, for his collection *Climbing into the Roots,* and not long afterwards *So This Is the Map* was selected by Derek Walcott for the National Poetry Series).

On a mild April morning, I flew to Kansas City, attended the awards banquet to accept the award, and met Howard Nemerov, the featured reader of the evening. Tan, brawny, in his early fifties, he reminded me of a powerful executive. He had not yet won any of the major prizes he was later to win. His attitude toward my enthusiasm was one of patriarchal indulgence. I was familiar with his work but had never been taken with it. It was too hedged with irony. I wanted poems which transcended the academic, poems like the "spots of time" in Wordsworth's *Prelude,* which gave you the taste of raw experience. I would return again to Kansas City that fall for my own reading.

The University of Colorado was almost insultingly easy. There was a particularly severe young professor of Anglo-Saxon from Brown University named John Kirk, and I began toying with making medieval literature my major field, but one day, driving from Boulder into Denver for a Poets-in-the-Schools gig, I saw with a sort of visionary clarity what I should do. I should abandon the medieval nonsense of trying to please some scholarly father figure. I should major in twentieth-century American. I would do a thesis on William Stafford. Because it would be the first book on Stafford, it would probably be published. Best of all, Gretchen and I could drive out that summer to Lake Oswego, Oregon, and I would interview him in person.

Meanwhile, Gretchen and I, unable to spawn a child, decided to adopt. We had friends who had adopted a Korean child through the Holt Agency in Oregon, so we submitted an application and went through the screening process. We were sent a photograph of a child whom we named Elizabeth. The time for her arrival came, and there was no word. Several weeks after the arrival date, we received a letter saying that Elizabeth had died in the orphanage. With the letter came a picture of a second child. We decided to name her Alanna.

That July we drove out to Oregon, and I interviewed Bill Stafford. Ever since I'd encountered his poem "Traveling through the Dark" in the *Penguin Anthology of Contemporary Poets* in 1960, Stafford had been my role model. In the early sixties, that poem seemed to many of us almost revolutionary. Its sincerity, its autobiographical directness, seemed audacious. And its stern, almost didactic tone ran squarely against the dominant style of that time. That style—a style which has come to be known as "late modernist"—was dictated by academics and relied heavily on irony as a replacement for raw emotion. But "Traveling through the Dark" was different. The voice speaking the poem sounded like somebody you'd trust—a man bound to a rigid code of moral responsibility. The ethos

of this man was so unflinching, so obviously authentic, that it compelled admiration.

The first time I met him was in July 1972, at his home. He was fifty-eight. It was thrilling to meet him, but it was daunting, too, because he was so much like my own father. Wiry, elfin, with the face of a fox, Stafford was curious about everything around him, absolutely alert. From being in the presence of Bell Labs geniuses for my entire childhood, I'd learned to recognize them, like a bird-watcher. (I'd had to. It was a kind of survival technique to avoid making a fool of oneself in the presence of some of the most high-powered intellectuals in the world. Some of them had worked on the Manhattan Project.)

In his book *Alone with America,* Richard Howard refers to the "arrogant otherness" of the persona in Bill's first poetry collection, *West of Your City,* but it was not the "otherness" of some kind of regional pride. It was the "otherness" of every major mind I've had the privilege to observe, though Bill camouflaged under a folksy demeanor his true nature.

In the fall, I started studying for the Ph.D. comprehensives—in eighteenth-century British, in the English Romantics, in Victorian, and in twentieth-century American. My major professor was one of the most popular teachers in the department, a younger man named James Folsom. Folsom had studied at Yale and felt superior to most of the older men around him. He was an alcoholic but highly charming. He lived in the old mining town of Gold Hill, and he kept horses. He would often compare working with his stable of graduate students to the breaking of horses. He was the only professor who would support my Stafford thesis, partly because Stafford was a "western" writer, and Folsom's special field was Western American literature.

In April, Gretchen and I received a call that our baby daughter, Alanna, was to arrive in San Francisco. Gretchen went to fetch her. I was doing another Poets-in-the-Schools gig. I met Gretchen and the baby at Stapleton International the next day. As Gretchen handed me the baby, I remembered what a friend of mine had once said—that the places where you weren't touched enough as a child are the places where you need extra attention as an adult. Later, in a poem entitled "Making Things Grow," I would write about that theme, the need for physical love. I passed my comprehensives and, in the fall, began writing the thesis. I had noticed, from reading Stafford, that certain words such as *dark, deep, far, near, cold* recurred with an almost symbolic meaning. In a slender thesis, *The Mark to Turn: A Reading of William Stafford's Poetry*, I "deciphered" Stafford's symbolic vocabulary. It followed the classic "new critical" approach to texts that I had been taught at Oberlin and which, except for Freudian analysis, was the only approach I knew.

Gretchen was pregnant. We had heard of other couples who, unable to get pregnant, had adopted a baby only to become pregnant immediately. One older lady we knew, after adopting a baby, had begun to menstruate again. On March 4, 1974, my son, Zachary, was born in Boulder, Colorado. We named him Zack after Zachary Fisk, a childhood chum who had been best man at our wedding. Baby Zack's hair was an apricot-colored haze. The dome was cold, heated mainly with a wood fire, and after we brought Zack to the dome, he came down with a cold which turned into a hacking cough. We called Zack's pediatrician at Boulder Memorial who insisted that we were being alarmists. We borrowed a humidifier, made a tent of blankets, fortified Zack there, and kept the fire going, but there was no improvement. Finally we prevailed upon the doctor to test him for pneumonia. Zack tested positive. He was hospitalized in an oxygen tent. Gretchen sat with him round the clock.

That spring I graduated, and in August we loaded up our Squareback, I rented a Ryder truck, and we headed east to Columbia, Missouri, where I had been offered a job at Stephens College. Descending from the pristine mountain air into the heat and haze of the plains was depressing, even vaguely humiliating. We had to stop regularly so that Gretchen could nurse Zachary. The heat and the humidity increased steadily the further east we went. At around 3:00 P.M. the radio began to mention tornado warnings. We were near the town of Paxico, about twenty miles west of Topeka. The west had become preternaturally dark, like the famous painting *Line Squall* by John Steuart Curry. The lightning strikes were so constant and frequent that it was as if a marching band were coming toward us briskly with fife and drum. I pulled the truck off the highway, on a rise so that Gretchen and the kids would find me, for we had been separated. When the storm struck,

the force of the line squall nearly blew the truck over. Coming through the melee of rain was Gretchen, screaming that there were tornadoes everywhere. She and the kids were sheltered in the underpass. But the storm was short-lived. We followed it the rest of the way to Columbia, arriving after midnight at a dilapidated house which we had rented sight unseen. The kitchen was filthy; the refrigerator had spoiled food in it. The house had been rented by some actors. Later that morning, I would be attending Stephens' fall faculty conference.

Thus began the worst four years of my life. In 1962, Stephens and Sweet Briar had been the best two-year women's "finishing schools" in the country. Then Stephens had decided to be a four-year college, and it had lost its uniqueness. Its enrollment had peaked at about two thousand, but now enrollment was declining, and the college was entering a period of retrenchment. The first thing the acting president did was show us the latest enrollment figures and begin what during my four years there would be a litany: "retention is the key to enrollment" and (to us) "advising is the key to retention."

Stephens had hired as its star poet Heather McHugh. Heather had graduated magna cum laude from Radcliffe and gotten an M.A. in creative writing from the University of Denver. She was accompanied by her partner, Gregory Biss, a composer. Heather was brilliant, brash, ambitious. She had many connections with famous writers, and she invited Richard Howard to read at Stephens. Howard came pro bono: all he demanded was expenses. His reading was memorable to me. He read from *Two-Part Inventions* the poem "Wildflowers," an argument between Walt Whitman and Oscar Wilde.

The University of Missouri had just hired Larry Levis. There was a vital poetry scene there, and Larry's readings were jammed. He was and still is one of the best readers that I have ever heard. He would read softly, with the sultry demeanor of a hood—a sort of tropical James Dean—but his poems gave me a kind of vertigo. It was what Robert Bly called "leaping poetry," though Larry was and is the only poet in America able to write it. Other poets there from Iowa were Leslie Ullman (who would, in 1977, win the Yale Younger Poets Prize), and Larry's girlfriend, Marcia Southwick. Larry might be a genius; the others I found mannered, like spoiled upper-middle-class children who regarded creativity as a birthright. A poet named David Steingass had satirized them perfectly in a poem called "The Workshop Poem" which "insists on real cream with oatmeal / but call me plain toadstool."

From the moment I arrived at Stephens, I resolved somehow to get out. It was possible to do, but the competition was enormous. I submitted my thesis to the University Press of Kansas, and, in 1976, they published it. I began working on various critical essays about poetry. One was called "Affected Naturalness and the Poetry of Sensibility." It was aimed at exposing the manners of Iowa workshop poetry.

Stephens was intent on maintaining an image of wealth. When I arrived and when I left it was still possible for a student to board her horse in Stephens's stables and to major in equestrian science. My second year there, Stephens hired a new president, an elegant scion of the upper classes: Arland Crist-Janer. I had been hired at a salary of eleven thousand dollars. When I left, four years later, I was making twelve thousand dollars. Stephens's enrollment had steadily decreased. It had cut several departments, including the music department.

After a year and a half, Heather left for a better job at SUNY Binghamton, and their aging fiction writer, Andrew Jolly, retired. We hired a young fiction writer named Fred Pfeil. Fred had graduated summa cum laude from Amherst College and gotten his master's degree at Stanford where he had been a Stegner fellow. A doctrinaire Marxist, Fred was a brilliant teacher and, for me, a necessary friend and ally, almost the only person on the staff or administration who was not either lesbian or bisexual. I felt terribly out of place there. The workload and the advising load were crushing, and publication was not, as in most universities, rewarded. But Stephens offered a bachelor of fine arts in creative writing, and the better students I had are still among the most brilliant and serious students that I have ever taught. By far the best, though, was Leslie Miller, a young woman from Zanesville, Ohio, where her father was a judge. Leslie was high-spirited, full of chutzpah, and she was a virtual fountain of creativity: to this day I have never seen anybody write so much so well so steadily. After Stephens, she attended the Iowa Writer's Workshop and then got a Ph.D. in creative writing

at the University of Houston. She has since published two collections with Carnegie-Mellon University Press. Meanwhile, we had a succession of fine writers on campus: Diane Johnson, Tillie Olsen, Denise Levertov, Jonathan Penner, William Stafford, Stanley Plumly.

Plumly had taught at Iowa. He was bringing news from the front line. He had just published, in the *American Poetry Review,* a two-part essay entitled "Chapter and Verse," in which he talked about poetry as "rhetoric." There were two kinds of rhetoric in poetry, a rhetoric of image and a rhetoric of voice. Both parts of his essay talked about the issue of "credentials." In a milieu in which free verse was the norm, the issue of credentials, Plumly pointed out, was particularly crucial. How could one distinguish quality? Most of the essay consisted of examples of contemporary poetry and explications of these poems. From Plumly, more than anybody else, I acquired the notion of poetry as an art of "rhetoric."

Stephens also had a nationally known little magazine called *Open Places,* edited by Eleanor Bender. Immediately upon my arrival, Eleanor

Daughter, Alanna

asked for some poems from me and she published them. One of them was published in the *Borestone Mountain Best Poems of 1975.* The poem was called "Making Things Grow," and it described my feeling when Gretchen had placed Alanna in my arms, at six months old. There was a beautiful poem by Gene Berson which had ended with the line: "God is moist. I forget the rest." I ended "Making Things Grow" in a similar way, by pointing toward experience which couldn't be described in words: "what all unkissed places everywhere / expect, the tongue expects, what this / lonely place on the neck expects and / what, on tiptoe, this place on the / throat expects and what this / neglected place expects. And this place / here. And here."

One of the results of my feeling left out of the poetry scene, left to play catch-up ball, was that I studied the manners of more successful poets with suspicion, as if they had discovered a kind of trick by which they could induce awe and even hero worship in an audience. Perhaps, as Plumly argued, successful presentation of poetry *was* a rhetorical art. At Oberlin, I had read Aristotle's *Rhetoric,* and as I continued to write essays, they focused around poetry as "rhetoric," as an art of persuasion. Plumly's essay was a significant confirmation of all that I had suspected.

A friend of mine at Stephens, Tom Dillingham, brought back for me from the 1976 MLA convention in New York a copy of a paper by a young critic named Paul Breslin, "Nihilistic Decorum in Contemporary American Poetry." The paper described the diction of much of what was soon to be called "deep image" poetry as "codified" and "generic." It was the latest "period style." Fashion, then, was a kind of rhetoric.

In the fall of 1976, I applied for a creative writing position at Kansas State University, to replace Helen Williams, who had died of cancer. Every winter I had interviewed for creative writing jobs at MLA. The first winter, I had been interviewed for Dartmouth College by Noel Perrin and been confused when the door opened. Was this pale-haired, svelte man a graduate student? Or was he an old man? Perrin inquired delicately about the nature of teaching at a women's college. I told him that I had ceased to be conscious of the students as girls at all. He raised his eyes and remarked, "I should have thought one would be teaching in a con-

stant state of semiarousal." Years later, when I was talking with Ripley Hugo in Missoula, she related a story of when she was married to a young English professor who taught eighteenth-century literature at Dartmouth and both were asked to a cocktail party in honor of Richard Eberhart. Early in the party, Perrin edged over to them and whispered in confidential tones, "We asked you here as 'buffers.'" The moral of the story seemed to speak for itself.

In August 1977 we moved from Columbia, Missouri, to Manhattan, Kansas. We had found an older home on Fairview Avenue, a short walk to campus. The street was filled with children, and across the alley from our backyard was the playground of Eugene Field School, the very school where Zachary and Alanna would be going—an authentic, old-fashioned "neighborhood" school.

The English department of Kansas State was, at that time, highly traditional and dominated by older professors. In *Lovejoy's College Handbook,* the university had been called "Silo Tech," and the last words in the entry were "No place for a poet." Which meant it would be the ideal place for a poet, a place where poetry was a precious resource like water in the desert, a place where the office of "poet" might be more than decorative, and where "research and publication" were not only honored but financially rewarded. For the first time that I could remember, everything seemed to fall into place and make sense. I could live as my father had at the Bell Labs. What he had shown me, more by example than by precept, was the desirability of (to quote Robert Frost in "Two Tramps in Mud Time") uniting "My avocation and my vocation / As my two eyes make one in sight," of finding one's identity through work and of working for an institution that would leave you some leeway to play, to experiment. "Keep your needs modest," he had said, "and make enough to satisfy them." Time was money, and there was a trade-off: physicians and attorneys sold away their leisure. Teachers were paid less but could enjoy whole summers to do what they wished.

In 1979, the book I had been assembling, *The Rhetoric of the Contemporary Lyric,* was accepted by the Indiana University Press, and a poem of mine, "God," which I had submitted to *Kansas Quarterly,* won first prize in its annual best poetry awards. The judge was Maxine

Kumin. In 1980, *The Rhetoric of the Contemporary Lyric* was published, and I was told that it was being read avidly at the Iowa Writer's Workshop. I was promoted to associate professor, with tenure. I began a series of visiting writer's grants with funds from the National Endowment for the Arts, hosting Gerald Costanzo, Susan Fromberg Schaeffer, George Garrett, Winston Weathers, Marvin Bell, and Richard Hugo. I had always temperamentally been inclined to Hugo's poetry, and the reading which he gave was one of the best readings I would ever hear. Heavy, troll-like, nearly bald, he stumped back and forth before the first row of seats in the audience, yakking in a loud, guffawing, yet oddly confidential way about his childhood. Then suddenly his speech had crossed a threshold, become more organized, and he was reciting from memory, as though still talking, "What Thou Lovest Well, Remains American."

It was a trick, but it opened my eyes to the subtle difference between poetry and speech. It suggested that a poem had to exceed in passion and eloquence the best conversation in order to have a raison d'être. The thermostat in the shabby lecture room had broken, and the temperature was at least eighty degrees. Sweat rolled off Hugo's head, but the audience was transfixed. The next year, when, visiting him in Missoula, I mentioned to his wife Ripley how odd it was that various poets like Reg Saner and David Wagoner were accomplished magicians. Ripley said that Dick was too, only his magic was storytelling. After the reading, Gretchen and I held the reception at our house. Dick had brought with him a type of superdrug for his ulcer. He chugged it down, then, chain-smoking and guzzling Cutty Sark, he settled in a corner of the living room and held court.

In the 1979–1980 academic year, I procured another NEA visiting writer's grant and this time brought Jerry Bumpus, H. E. Francis, Stephen Dunn, Jorie Graham, and Dave Smith. I had always felt a special simpatico with Stephen Dunn's poetry and had written about it in *The Rhetoric,* in the chapter "Stephen Dunn and the Realist Lyric." It was Dunn who once confided to me that in order to be a writer it was necessary to live in "a landscape of desire" and that New Jersey, where he resided and where I had grown up, was just such a landscape. As Dunn's reputation had grown and he was offered various jobs—jobs I would have given my eyeteeth for, such as at the University of Colorado—he had spurned them. He seemed to have intrinsic common sense and emotional honesty. He knew that he was a poet who had charisma, star power, but he distrusted that charisma as much as he liked it. He was on guard against vanity. He told me that the best feeling in the world he had ever experienced was when he had hit the winning jump shot at the buzzer of a college basketball game and been mobbed by the fans.

When Jorie Graham visited campus, her beauty stunned people, and she gave one of the best readings I have ever heard. One of my students was so bewildered by the power of it that at the end of the reading she ducked out to the lady's room and cried. She couldn't figure out what had happened to her. I felt the same way, and I tried to describe my reaction in a poem called "The Third Party." Although the "she" in the poem was actually one of my students who was a genius but schizophrenic, the poem's praise of "mind" was inspired by Jorie. How much rhetorical power Jorie's physical beauty added to a reading was impossible to say. If contemporary American poetry has a diva, it is Jorie.

In the 1980–1981 academic year, we had hired a brilliant young fiction writer, Steve Heller, whose presence on the staff decisively changed my life for the better; for Steve was a real writer and an excellent reader of poetry. For the first time since coming to Kansas State, I was not alone. Steve quickly became my closest friend and my best critic.

In late June 1981, I hitchhiked from Boulder to Missoula and stayed with Dick and Ripley Hugo to interview him for the book I had planned to do: *Landscapes of the Self: The Development of Richard Hugo's Poetry.* They were neighbors of Jim and Lois Welch, and Dick threw a tiny party for me, with some of the local literati. Around 9:00 P.M. I glanced over at Jim. He was awake but utterly still and remote, stoned in a way I had never seen before, and I thought of Dick's "Letter to Welch from Browning," the lines "but when drunk you shrug / away the world, . . . I'll simply nod and pour."

The year 1982 was a year when many of the eggs which I had laid began to hatch. That academic year we brought to campus Syd Lea, Stanley Plumly, and Robert Dana. With Lea, this visit began a great and important friend-

*Jonathan, with son, Zachary,
at Stephens College, 1975*

ship. Syd had read *The Rhetoric of the Contemporary Lyric* and devoted a long review/essay to it in the *New England Review,* praising my approach. It was the implicit morality of my approach which he liked, the notion of rhetorical accountability, my focus on the *ethos* of the persona of a poem, which in poems in the first-person singular I presumed to be a version of the author. Of course, my critical approach to poems reflected my own bias in favor of poetry like my own. I myself wrote highly personal poetry, and I had taken to heart Dick's words when he growled "if you don't risk corn, you're not in the ballpark."

Meanwhile, the various writing programs in the state of Kansas had formed an association modeled on the Associated Writing Programs. Each year, Kansas Associated Writing Programs held a creative writing festival, and that year I procured funds to have the festival at Kansas State. I invited for keynote speakers the great fiction writer Gordon Weaver (Steve Heller's mentor) and Mark Strand. Jorie had told me

that Mark Strand could be cruel, how once in the workshop he had slowly torn a student's poem into two halves and made an elegantly malicious remark about it. Driving Mark to campus from Manhattan Airport, I explained to him that the students here weren't all that sophisticated, that I hoped he would try not to hurt them but instead make them feel good. He nodded. "All right."

In the spring of 1982, I learned that my manuscript of poems *Leverage* had been cowinner, with Alice Fulton, of the AWP award series in poetry. Between the Devins Award (1972) and 1982, I had been submitting to university presses a manuscript of poems which had eventually become too long to be one book, so I had split it into two separate manuscripts, *Leverage* and a second manuscript, *Falling from Stardom,* which dealt with the darker aspects of my personal life. The *Stardom* of the title was a metaphor for male narcissism. Costanzo had expressed interest in publishing it with Carnegie-Mellon. When I was informed of the AWP award, I was relieved that the manuscript hadn't been taken earlier: my apparent bad luck had been good luck in disguise; I was being saved for something better.

In March 1983, I read from *Leverage* at the AWP Convention in St. Louis. I put greater care into preparing for that reading than ever before. I knew that I would be reading in front of perhaps hundreds of other poets and that every one of them would be bitterly wondering why he or she wasn't up there reading instead of Holden. Could such an audience be convinced? I decided to start with a sort of icebreaker, a poem that would induce laughter, my poem "Liberace." Alice Fulton went first, reading from *Dance Script with Electric Ballerina.* Although Alice is a genius, she seemed nervous and tentative. The audience gave her polite attention. After polite applause, it was my turn. I prefaced "Liberace" by proposing that only in America—a country that hated the feminine in men as much as we do—could a character like "Liberace" be invented. Then I began: "It took generations to mature / this figure. Every day it / had to be caught sneaking off / to its piano lesson and beaten up." The audience laughed. At the end of the poem, they burst into applause. They applauded after every single poem. After the reading, I was mobbed—as if I'd hit the winning shot at the buzzer.

That summer, I was invited to be on the staff of the Wesleyan Writer's Conference. Run by Anne Greene, it was, of the various conferences I've visited, the best, and some of the students have since then earned substantial reputations. Each year, there were two teaching fellows. My first summer there, the poet-fellow was Brooks Haxton, and the fiction-fellow was Susan Dodd. The next summer the poet-fellow was Andrew Hudgins, and the fiction-fellow was Sharon Stark.

In May 1983, I signed a contract with Associated Faculty Press for the Hugo book and delivered them the manuscript. I had queried a number of better publishers, but none of them had regarded Hugo's poetry as important enough to warrant attention. Linda Wagner Martin was a manuscript finder for Associated Faculty Press; I knew her work, and I knew that if she was associated with the press it must be good. We went through galleys and page proofs by December 1983. Then I waited. In 1986, I called Linda asking about the book. She said that several years ago she had severed connection with the press. In September, I called Richard Koffler, the new president of Associated. He asked if my department could support the publication of the book with a subvention. I wanted to laugh. On September 17, 1986, I wrote Koffler:

> If you do not send me, within fourteen days of the date above, a written, signed statement promising that my book, . . . will be published . . . on or before January 1, 1987, and giving a specific publication date, I will assume that you have agreed to let all rights to the book revert to me, and I will submit the book to another publisher. . . .
>
> Frankly, I almost hope not to hear from you, so that I can move ahead and give this book the quality of publication which it deserves.

In 1986, Associated finally published the book. It was a rushed and ugly book, on newsprint and containing dozens of typos. I received five author's copies. Hugo, of course, was dead. He had died on October 22, 1982, of acute leukemia. I sent one copy to Reg Saner, one to Ripley Hugo, one to Steve Heller. Nothing had come out well. I learned from Patricia Goedicke that Ripley Hugo now hated me, believing that

in the biographical introduction to *Landscapes* I had plagiarized from a book which Matthew Hanson was putting together of Dick's personal essays, *West Marginal Way.* Talking with my colleague Don Hedrick, who had done extensive work on John Berryman's poetry, I discovered that perhaps Ripley's behavior was typical of the widows of famous poets, but this was little consolation.

In the 1983–1984 academic year the poets I invited on our NEA grant were T. R. Hummer, Linda Gregerson, and Brendan Galvin. As judge of the John Williams Andrews Narrative Poetry Contest at *Poet Lore,* I had chosen Brendan's poem "The Last Man in the Quabbin" as the winner. Of the three, the poet I most liked was Brendan—a fierce, crotchety guy who is as good a nature writer as Thoreau. He gave an excellent reading, and we hit it off. We saw ourselves as fellow rebels, allies against the James Merrills, the Richard Howards, the whole fey New York poetry scene. Brendan, who is probably the best poet in Connecticut, had majored not in English but in biology. He had a life beyond academia and, like Dick Hugo, like Dave Smith in *The Fisherman's Whore,* an appreciation for local color.

In 1984, Carnegie-Mellon University Press published *Falling from Stardom.* Whereas *Leverage* contained mainly celebratory poems, many of them about building the dome and about my children, *Falling* contained a good number of darker poems, touching some of the darker aspects of my marriage (now entering its twentieth year) and on some of the less pleasant things I was finding out about myself.

As my parents aged, I found myself making increasingly frequent trips back to New Jersey to assist them. Jaynet was diagnosed with multiple myeloma, a form of cancer which mimics osteoporosis: the patient's bones begin to crack. Her illness raised the terrifying possibility of her death preceding Alan's, but Alan's health was failing too. He was suffering from severe emphysema. On warm afternoons, he would sit in a lawn chair bowed over a handkerchief for twenty-minute intervals as if in prayer while his nose and sinuses drained. Although Alan was stoical by nature, in June of 1985, as we sat at the kitchen table while he struggled with his inhalers, he burst out ruefully, "Don't get old, Son." The exclamation had in it a note of self-pity I'd never heard in him before.

By July, Jaynet and Alan were so weakened and dispirited that they required a live-in home-aid. I had tried to convince them to move to Manhattan, Kansas. There was and is an excellent facility here, Meadowlark Hills, and they could afford it; but they were insistent on staying to the bitter end in the house on Pleasantville Road. It was a kind of gamble. Jaynet's oncologist, Gary Gerstein, seemed to understand them better than I did. At one point he remarked to me, "Your parents really have a thing going," and he let them know that he knew and respected the special nature of their bond. They were still passionately in love. Between radiation treatments, he put Jaynet on the first of several courses of the steroid prednisone. It would alter her mood dramatically, and for ten days she would be cheerful, optimistic. His plan—though he didn't state it aloud—was to keep her alive until Alan died.

In late August, Jaynet called us in Kansas. She said, "I have some very, very, very bad news." I immediately flew back to join Stephen and Jaynet and to participate in the bureaucratic procedures of a death. Thirty-two days later, Stephen called me to say that Jaynet had been discovered fully clothed on the "playroom couch," dead. Though it was sad, it was also a relief. The worst-case scenario of her preceding Alan hadn't happened. In their last days, being alive had come to be nothing but a physical ordeal. And, indeed, Jaynet's death may have been of her own devising. We'll never know. There was no autopsy.

Meanwhile, my own professional life had been proceeding as usual: even before my parents' illness, work had been a sort of refuge for me—a refuge from a marriage which, under its surface bustle and apparent cheer, was fraudulent. Years later, after my divorce, I realized how Gretchen and I must have appeared to our friends and to the outside world—as if we had been walking around with a gaping, open wound from which everybody would politely avert their eyes. I wondered (and still wonder) if this isn't the case with most middle-class marriages.

But, though my marriage was a farce, my professional life was, if anything, more successful than ever. My life was proceeding almost exactly as I had thought it should, from studying my father's life: adulthood meant simply that one became very good at something that one liked to do. One went to work every day and did it, and came home to a nice supper. The house was a short walk to campus. I was (since 1984) a full professor and generally liked in my department. I had deliberately effected a sort of life plan: to be taken care of by a benign institution—just as Alan had been by the Bell Labs—an institution which would allow me time to be a writer. As I would joke to various friends, being at Kansas State was, for me, like being in a writer's colony. It was an ideal life: two classes per semester—Tuesdays and Thursdays—plus automatic prestige, plus all kinds of logistical and clerical support. It was almost like a scam, except that instead of coasting lazily into senility like other tenured drones, I would hold up my side of the bargain. I would produce.

In 1985, I won the Juniper Prize from the University of Massachusetts Press, and I published a book of essays, *Style and Authenticity in Postmodern Poetry.* Its title alluded deliberately to *Form and Value in Modern Poetry* by Harvey Gross; but the word "postmodern" was dangerously ambiguous. By "postmodern" I had intended not "postmodern*ist*" (like Ashbery) but only something chronological: "after modernist." I also received a twenty thousand dollar grant from the NEA in the category "Creative Non-fiction Prose."

In 1986, partly out of curiosity but more out of a desire to give some of my time and energy back to a profession which had given me so much, I ran for a place on the board of directors of the AWP. I was elected and got my first, close-up look at literary politics. It was like nothing I hadn't imagined, but still it shocked me. In 1986, AWP was in chaos, financially in the red and in need of leadership. Our first item of business was to find an executive director to replace Eric Staley, who had resigned. Of the candidates we interviewed, we chose Liam Rector. Rector would almost singlehandedly save AWP. The board of directors of AWP was, we had been warned, a "working" board, not an honorary board to rubber-stamp corporate decisions between rounds of golf. Some of the new board-elect took one look, saw this was going to be no fun, and resigned. Some on the board emerged as leaders: Ellen Voight, Reg Gibbons, and Ed Ochester were particularly effective. The work was nonstop, fifteen-hour days with meals wheeled into the boardroom, and the talk was almost exclusively about money. Those of us who remained grew close.

In my second board year, at an ocean "retreat," we received, from a husband-and-wife team called "The North Group," training in fundraising. By the third year, thanks to large infusions of money from the NEA, engineered by Liam, AWP was temporarily out of danger; but I will never be able to accept awards or monies again without realizing how much selfless labor goes on behind the scenes to make the ceremonies of culture "work." Giving a reading or a lecture at another university, I feel sorry for my hosts. I know too well how much it costs to make other people feel important.

In May 1988, I was made a university distinguished professor of English and poet-in-residence of Kansas State University. That same week, Stephen was invited to be a full-time staff member of the *New York Times,* reporting on popular music and drama. Was it fated? Important initiations always happened to us in pairs, simultaneously.

My poetry was gradually changing. I had always insisted that "change" in a writer's work could not be forced or anticipated. Development must be allowed to evolve naturally: organically. The times when, in my anxiety to publish, I had tried to force a poem always resulted in failure. To force a poem was like masturbation, a "mechanical operation of the spirit." You couldn't force a poem, but you had to be alert so that when a poem came to you, you could seize it. When a poem didn't come to you, it was best to turn to some other genre or write letters. Many of my better poems started out in letters, in essays.

I was dismayed to realize that, though I was nominally a poet, the reading I liked best wasn't poetry. It was novels and essays. What was it about a good novel or a nonfiction book like Lewis Thomas's *The Lives of a Cell* that made it more fun to read than poetry? It was subject matter. Novels and essays were a genre superior to poetry because, conventionally, they allowed a greater range of subject matter than the lyric poem; they allowed the writer—even encouraged the writer—to be discursive, to digress. In verse, the one form which most strongly encouraged attention to subject matter outside the author's personal feelings was the dramatic monologue. I formulated a hypothesis: any coming revolution in American poetry was going

With a portrait of his father, Alan Nordby Holden. Painted by Maurice Grosser.

to be in the domain of subject matter, not form, and the coming dominant verse form was going to be the dramatic monologue. All the possibilities for formal experiment had been exhausted. People were weary of reading about the poet's humid, horny, sweltering, little self. I put these ideas together in a book, *The Fate of American Poetry.*

As I was preparing the manuscript, I received a letter from the poet/critic Dana Gioia, a surprising event because I had just finished mentioning him in *The Fate* as "perhaps the acutest practical critic in America." Shortly after hearing from him, his essay "Can Poetry Matter" appeared in the *Atlantic.* He had scooped me. "Can Poetry Matter" created a hubbub among all the poets that I knew. Most of them were furious. I didn't care especially for Gioia's poetry—like most so-called "new-formalist" poetry it was overly decorous, and its subject matter was tamer than I liked. In *The Fate,* I had characterized "new formalist" poems as "elegant bottles without genies in them."

I remembered a story which Stephen Dunn had told me about running a poetry workshop with senior Woodrow Wilson fellows. Not only were they all closet poets, but their poems were quite well written. Yet the poems lacked some kind of *je ne sais quoi*. These scholars knew too well what they were doing. Dunn had concluded that "good writing" might be the enemy of poetry. I remembered Walker Percy's famous essay "Metaphor as Mistake" and Coleridge's lament in "Dejection and Ode" about the impossibility of discovering through "abstruse research" the "natural man": perhaps the best lyric poetry *was* somehow neurotic, the result of some kind of slippage. Frost had said it best: "No surprise for the writer, no surprise for the reader. No tears for the writer, no tears for the reader." But Dana was and is one of the most powerful and best educated minds that I have ever known: relentless, thorough, honest. The criticism in the book *Can Poetry Matter* that Dana spun out of the essay is the best practical criticism that I know of.

For the spring of 1991, I was offered, out of the blue, a visiting professorship called the Thrusten Morton Professorship at the University of Louisville: forty thousand dollars for one semester. I accepted it. I didn't ask Gretchen's permission. The money was too good to refuse, and we needed a break from each other. This would be like going off to college for the first time. I felt like an adolescent. Here I was, fifty years old, and I had never before set up a life for myself: Gretchen had done it for me. As the spring semester approached, I realized that what I was embarking on was really a trial separation. Shortly before I left, I received another letter from out of the blue. The envelope had only my name on it, but the handwriting made me dizzy. It was from an old lover, Anita Cortez Bond. I had heard that she was divorced. The letter began with the salutation "Dearest." Anita wanted to tie up a few loose ends, to say that she was okay now. I wrote back that we should talk, thinking that at some level I had always known that we would end up together, that it was inevitable, like the joining of Fermina and Florentino at the conclusion of Garcia Marquez's *Love in the Time of Cholera:* from day one, our compatibility and admiration for each other had been absolute.

The first weekend I arrived in Louisville, I called home. Nobody was there. I called other friends of ours and learned that Gretchen was in the Kansas City Marriott with one of her male coworkers. It was the straw that broke the camel's back. Gretchen had humiliated me too many times with extramarital affairs. I had her served with divorce papers. Anita visited me the same day that the Gulf War began and that Gretchen received the word of the divorce.

The divorce took place mainly by fax. Meanwhile, at the University of Louisville I was welcomed with relief. The poet who had preceded me had treated everybody so badly that I was given a wonderful advantage: there was nothing I could do wrong.

Back in Manhattan, I moved into an apartment, then into Anita's house, then, in August 1992, bought the house we now live in. In 1992, my sixth poetry collection, *American Gothic,* was published, and in 1995, my seventh collection, *The Sublime,* won the Vassar Miller Prize. The judge was Yusef Komunyakaa.

As I take stock of my life and of my work, right now, in June 1995, my general feeling is of comparative serenity. Although I am ambitious, I am less driven than I used to be, in less of a hurry. Thanks to psychotherapy and to Anita, much of my old anger—a furious impatience with the world—seems to have dissipated. Or maybe this equanimity, this welcome serenity, is a function of being middle-aged. I remember Alan's admonition (punctuated with a little throat clearing) "Many are called and few are chosen," and I feel incredibly lucky. The astronomical luck to have won five of the competitions in which I entered poetry manuscripts! If it weren't for the Devins Award, which I entered as a graduate student, on a whim, I might not have found the initial toehold from which to build a writing life. I could have been any one of the exhausted high school teachers I remember from my days doing Poets-in-the-Schools or when teaching at Carteret School, chain-smoking in the teacher's lounge, picking themselves up at the buzzer and starting stoically back into the hall toward a Room 204 or a Room 205 to try to infuse light and energy into thirty or forty glazed faces.

I was lucky to enter the job market at precisely the moment when the creative writing industry was in a state of maximum expansion, when every university had to have its poet. Now in the field of English literature and creative writing, after great expansion and the resulting inflation, we see the inevitable shakeout, along with a "de-centering" of the canon. As poetry and literature come under increasing siege from television and from the culture at large, I find myself feeling increasingly like an old fuddy-duddy. Reading itself is under siege. I distrust the flash and dazzle of poetry readings, believing more strongly than ever that poetry is an art constructed from the printed page.

William Dickey recently died of AIDS. Jim Folsom had several strokes. I remember him walking sideways in the halls of Hellems, his flushed face fixed in a perpetual glare. Then I learned he had died. Reg is the state poet of Colorado and has recently published a magnificent collection of essays, *The Four-Cornered Falcon,* with Johns Hopkins University Press. Ned Gatewood has married a pert, redheaded co-worker in facilities. Zachary is about to enter his senior year at Oberlin. Alanna, twenty-three, is currently living and working in Boulder. On July 18, 1995, I will be fifty-four, not "old" by any stretch of the imagination; yet every year I appreciate more than ever what Aristotle meant when, in his *Rhetoric,* he wrote that to appeal to the aged, one should appeal to their sense of caution, for they have seen how in the affairs of men "events seldom turn out well."

For me, so far they have.

BIBLIOGRAPHY

FOR ADULTS

Poetry:

Design for a House, University of Missouri Press, 1972.

Falling from Stardom, Carnegie-Mellon University Press, 1984.

Leverage, University Press of Virginia, 1984.

The Names of the Rapids, University of Massachusetts Press, 1985.

Against Paradise, University of Utah Press, 1989.

American Gothic, University of Georgia Press, 1992.

The Sublime, University of North Texas Press, 1996.

Nonfiction:

The Mark to Turn: A Reading of William Stafford's Poetry, University Press of Kansas, 1976.

The Rhetoric of the Contemporary Lyric, Indiana University Press, 1980.

Landscapes of the Self: The Development of Richard Hugo's Poetry, Associated Faculty Press, 1985.

Style and Authenticity in Postmodern Poetry, University of Missouri Press, 1986.

The Fate of American Poetry, University of Georgia Press, 1992.

Other:

Brilliant Kids (novel), University of Utah Press, 1992.

Contributor of poems and essays to numerous journals, including *American Poetry Review, Kenyon Review,* and *Poetry.*

Garrett Hongo

1951-

AMERICA SINGING:
AN ADDRESS TO THE NEWLY ARRIVED PEOPLES

Maybe you've seen the sign
On old Sepulveda. Tai Song,
Cantonese Cuisine, *on your way*
to or from the L.A. airport.

                                    Greg Pape

I've never been in Peking, or in the Summer
    Palace,
nor stood on the Great Stone Boat to watch
the rain begin on Kuen Ming Lake, the
    picnickers
running away in the grass.
But I love to hear it sung. . . .

                                    Li-Young Lee

I hear America singing, the varied carols I
    hear. . . .

                                    Walt Whitman

Garrett Hongo with his sons, Alexander, ten, and
Hudson, eight, Seattle, Washington, 1995

I'm fascinated and thrilled that there has been such a surge in new immigration from across the Pacific these past few years, that, as a country, we are again in the process of being renewed and reformed by the New Americans from Asia and elsewhere. These newly arrived peoples, I know, come not so much from Japan and Okinawa and Guangdong as did the ancestors of we third- and fourth-generation Asian Americans, but rather they are now coming, in increasing numbers, from Taiwan, Hong Kong, Korea, Southeast Asia, Tonga, Fiji, Samoa, the Caribbean, Central America, and the Philippines. Their presence has charged our society with energy and change.

When I visit California now, and walk about in the resurgent downtowns of San Jose and Santa Ana, I pass Vietnamese markets, Korean grocery stores, and restaurants for every kind of Pacific/Asian cuisine. When I was teaching at the University of Houston in 1988, I did most of my shopping in a huge super-supermarket run by Chinese for almost every Asian ethnicity—there was a Korean section, a section for Japanese foods (*nap-pa* cabbage, *daikon*, *kamaboko* fishcakes and *Kal-Pis* in the coolers), racks and racks of Chinese condiments like chili oil and oyster and plum sauces. I saw what I've always loved seeing—bins full of bean threads, bags of sesame seeds in various grades, cellophaned flats of dried seaweed, cans of black beans and bamboo shoots, fifty-pound bags of rice. The smells were gorgeous. The market was on its own little complex of shops—a big parking lot ringed with little storefronts for a travel agency, an optometrist, a records and tapes store, a bookstore, a coffee and *dim sum* shop, a casual restaurant, and a movie theater that showed *chop-sockie* Saturday matinees, mildly lurid *cheongsam* romances weekend nights, and serials all week long.

I was taken there by one of my master's students, Edmund Chang—a graduate of Tufts in Boston, who was born in Taiwan, who had grown up in Malta and Libya, who went to high school in New Jersey, and who had just become an American citizen the year before. He wanted to show me where to buy rice. We went with my two small sons, themselves half-Asian, who loved the sweet rice candies but wrinkled their noses at the carded, yellow circles of sliced, seal-wrapped octopus hanging on hooks near the check stand. And me—I loved the goddamn place. I loved the feeling of the throng of new peoples swirling around me. I loved the feeling that I was in a vortex of cultures, a new republic of exchange—the thrilled, New Americans all around me. I heard a new chorus—it was America singing.

When I left Houston in 1989, I got my car ready by getting it detailed. I didn't know if I was going to sell it or drive it to the West Coast where I was going to take a new job. I took it to a detail shop I'd noticed while driving by one day. The guy there was a young hot shot, a sassy white dude who could do everything—I knew it and he knew I knew it. I liked him. He had Benzes, Beamers, even a Maserati in his shop. There was a Volvo being vacuumed and shined up when I drove in. He gave me a guarantee and a good price. This was the place, I thought.

We made the deal and I handed the pup my keys. He leaned out of the little waiting room and yelled over to one of his employees inside the garage, busy shammying down a slick, black Riviera. The pup called him "Juan-Oh!" —a wiseass joke. Juan was a handsome, Native

American–looking guy with thick, crow-black hair who was to drive me home in the shop car. He and I climbed into a Jeep Cherokee, freshly shined and, inside, its plastic wiped down with Armor-All. We rode together in silence for a while, then, typically American, I'd stood about as much of it as I could, so I struck up a conversation.

"Where are you from?" I asked, typically blunt. His hair was jet-black, his skin rich and brown like stained Hawaiian *koa* wood. He held himself stiffly, and shifted gears with precision. He had the posture and build of a Navajo, I thought.

"El Salvador," he said to me, and turned his face to show me his grin.

"Oh," I said, surprised. In an instant, I felt redundant for being nosey. But I was curious too. "Are you here to save your life?" I said.

He told me *yes, mine and my mother's, my wife's, my children's.* "We all come," he said. There was silence again as we moved through traffic into the little university village near where I lived. I wanted to give him something.

"Do you know the phrase," I said, "El Pueblo Unído, Jamás Será Vencido?" I learned it from my Chilean friends who fled the murders after the coup of General Pinochet. It meant, "Our country, united, can never be defeated" and was a slogan used to rally the various splinter groups of the Latin American Left into unified coalitions. Hundreds of thousands chanted this as they marched in demonstrations through the streets of Santiago in support of the democracy of Salvador Allende, the doctor and Socialist who was the elected President of Chile and who was deposed and murdered by his own military and, it is frequently said, with some assistance from our CIA.

This El Salvadoran man next to me turned and grinned again, "Yes, sir. I know this saying. It is full of heart. We in El Salvador say it too, though we die for it."

What was chilling was his modesty, his resolve. Riding through Houston in that car, we were both humbled by the histories we carried and invoked.

Some folks—a lot of white Americans who fear people like us, who fear the oncoming change as weak, inner-reef swimmers fear the largest swells at sea beyond the reef—look to our renewed cities with anger and pessimism, consider them now as *terra incognita,* lands where monsters dwell and where they are no longer safe or welcome. Many of the people I talk with in so-called educated circles feel that the inner cities, the ghettoes, are a demilitarized zone to them, an unknown, an X or Mysterious Island where others belong, but not them, not the real Americans.

I remember a time—it was some years ago, in '82 or so—I invited another poet out to lunch. He is older than me by a generation or so, a teacher of mine in a way, one who was part of the '60s shift away from formal verse towards freer, more popularly accessible forms. I revered him a little and wanted to be his friend. He'd just moved to the suburbs east of Los Angeles, had a new job teaching at a private college there and, as one who had grown up very eastern in Philadelphia, was missing cities and their splendors. I called him up and offered to show him L.A.'s Chinatown, take him for *dim-sum* at the Jade Gardens, my current favorite, and then to an afternoon movie downtown or something. We made the date and met at some designated corner of the city that weekend.

Dim-sum started out fine. He marvelled at the variety, at the tastes, at the throng of Asians all around us at round tables, the dozen or so carts like street vendors making their way around the huge upstairs hall of the restaurant. He said, "Oh, this is wonderful. Oh, this is better than Philly. Oh, how has the world kept this a secret from me?" He, in exchange, told me about how he met Ezra Pound, the great and politically strange poet of High Modernism. He told me about the revolution against formal metrics during the '60s and the wave of interest in open forms, primitive and international poetries, and social justice. He believed in social justice. He might have joined the black and white Freedom Riders who rode together on the buses to integrate the South if he could've, but he was too young then, he said.

But there were things about him which were enormously troubling. At the same time as I enjoyed his stories of his apprenticeship in the afterglow of Modernism, the generous accounts of his time scuffling up the literary ladder and finding his rung on it, I was disturbed by his other anecdotes, his ample scorn for other poets of his generation, and his complaints. He talked incessantly about a rival, another poet he'd once been close to, but with whom he'd had a severe falling-out. He spent an entire course of

dim-sum bashing the other man's reputation, debunking a seriously arrived at politics as fraudulent, ridiculing his rival's lack of skill at "true" poetry, which was metric and lovely and free of politics. It was hard for me to listen to as, to me, ephebe in the art, both men were genuine heroes. He then recanted much of his own work at mid-career, done during the '60s when the two poets had been friends, calling his own poetry of that time—the poetry which I admired so much and had inspired me to seek him out—"sentimental, misguided and stupid— *another man's poems.*" I poured tea for him in a small porcelain cup decorated with dragons, and he leaned towards me and said, "I didn't know what I was doing. I was on dope all the time and chasing girls and nirvana. I thought life was a circus and I wasn't serious."

We paid the check—a small amount, five dollars each, another miracle—and rode a bus to a downtown theater, the old Orpheum, a once-lavish Fox palace gone the route of decay and semi-abandonment. Yet, miraculously, it was open and showing a Richard Pryor comedy for the four o'clock matinee late that afternoon. We went. My friend marvelled at the ornate appointments and plush chairs inside. He reminisced about his childhood in Philly. He laughed uproariously at the jokes, the sight gags, the crazy, convoluted plot that ended everything in a long chase scene. I relaxed and hoped the bitterness in him had been dispersed by our good time. We left the place euphoric, and, junior that I was, I was pleased I'd pleased him.

Outside, the city had turned dark while we were inside. The sidewalks, moderately trafficked when we entered, were now thronged with Friday-night cruisers, crowds of the poor and hustling. Buses and dirty cars jammed the streets. We heard rap music from a huge stereo boombox a passerby shouldered like a cargo sack as he sauntered before us. Like the calliope music of a carousel thrashes tidelike together with a Ferris wheel's countersongs and squeals from its riders, we heard disco pouring from the electronics store next door mingling with the car horns of traffic noise and hubbub from the passing crowd. A hawker in a red tuxedo and frilly dress shirt announced in Spanish that a ticket dance was fixing to start in the basement room below the movie theater. The New Americans surrounded us—Jamaicans in shiny polyester disco shirts, Cubanos and Puerto Ricans, El Salvadorans, blacks from Watts and Compton

Ministry: Homage to Kilauea

Thinking about volcanoes gives me hope—
           all the pure of it.
When my two boys were babies, to help them fall asleep in the
           afternoons,
I liked driving them out from the house we always rented in
           Mauna Loa Estates,
up the highway a mile or so through the park entrance,
then plunging down past all the micro-climates and botanical
           realities
until I got to the swing in the road just before the turnout to
           Kilauea observatory at Uwekahuna,
where I could pull over into a little gravel slot by the roadside
      and let all the air-conditioned tour buses
           and shining red rental cars
           and USGS Cherokees and geologists' Broncos
           swoosh by
while I took a long view
over the saddle towards the veldt-like lower slopes of Mauna Loa,
           my boys already asleep in the back seat.
    What I liked was the swoop of land,
the way it rolled out from under my beach-sandaled feet,
      and the swimming air,
           freighted with clouds
      that seemed the land's vision rising over it.
I could have been the land's own dream then,
and I liked thinking of myself that way,
as offspring come to pay it the tribute of my own thoughts,
           little brainy cyclones
that touched down in the lava channels
           or drained back into rivulets of wind.
"Cloud and Man differ not," I joked to myself,
"All is One under Heaven." And why not?

What if we were to recast ourselves as descendants
all gathered at the foot of our heresiarch mountains,
drawn by a love like primitive magnetisms and convection currents
    calling all things back to their incarnate sources?
Our lives might be ordered by a conscious abstinence,
a year of giving up to save for a trip home.
We would sacrifice for an earthbound commitment—
        homage to birthplace,
source rock come up from a star's living depth.

What would be the point other than to step into the sulfuric
    cleansing of volcanic clouds?
Our dithyrambs of dream-mountains not quite earth's equal
but more vague than that—like clouds around Mauna Loa,
drifting continents of vapor and dust
riding the gyreing wind-gusts over Halemaumau and Iki,
mantlings of evanescence on the tropical shoulders of an angel?

Aren't we the earth become known to itself,
we celebrants of a sublime not completely dreadful,
but companionable too, its presence like two sleeping children,
innocent dragons
    fogging the car's rear window with a visible breath?

---

and Inglewood, Chicanos from Whittier and East L.A. They were a processional of *penitentes*. The feeling was grand and powerful and strong. I felt the beat and wanted to dance.

My friend was terrified. A paranoid, he had panicked, running out to the street and hailing a bus down, making it stop, banging on the pneumatic door until the driver hissed it open. He stared blankly for a moment and then recoiled at all the Asian, black, and Hispanic faces he saw filling up the bus when he started to get on. It seemed to me, stupefied on the sidewalk behind him, that he fell backwards off the bus as he fled back to me, shouting. He pushed past me and ran for the street corner where he may have seen a taxi cruise by.

I let him go. There was more than a generation of difference between us. He had refuted all that I had loved about him. I recognized, finally, that he suffered from that Lethe-like, irrational wish, in poetry and in his concept of civilization, for an unblemished purity that can only be accomplished in death—that lavish extinguishment of desire and differences. There was in him a tremendous fear that may

*With friends from Anchor Books: Charles Flowers, associate editor,
and Martha Levin, publisher, November 1994*

have begun, innocently, as mild cultural disdain, a kind of antipathy-budding-into-intoler-
ance, which had eventually metathesized into
a powerful Kurtz-like horror for those of us
who come from struggle in the Heart of Darkness and want to help shape and belong to
the New America. The general term is racism.
And it grows strangely.

I remember one of my professors in graduate
school—a place I still refer to as "Apartheid
Tech"—sidling up to me at an afternoon reception and jostling me in a friendly way. I
turned and he was beaming a little, clearly
drunken from sampling the ample supply of
reception chardonnay (though we were a state
school, there was always money for things). "Hey,
Hahngo," he said, punching my shoulder, chum-
mily macho. The happy people in the room
around us were oblivious, abuzz with their own
excited chatter, our mentors in sensible shoes
and tweeds mixing with graduate students. I
overheard someone tittivating on the lyrics to
John Lennon's tunes, comparing them to
Spenser's *Amoretti*.

"Hey, Hahngo," said my professor, "I hear
you've got an interest in *Gook* Lit!" I felt the
skin on my face freeze. I was stunned. I couldn't
tell what he meant. "You know, that *minority*
stuff," he continued. He mistook my shock for
incomprehension. "I'm glad there's finally someone around here to cover it, fend off the Mongol
hordes." He gestured with his plastic wineglass
to the universe. He clapped me on the shoulder, turned away, and ambled over to the tray
of cheeses and grapes. The room with its
plateglass windows opening to a view of California eucalyptus and blooming jacarandas gyred
around me as if my place in it were the mirrors of a circus carousel. I was fixed to the
earth, speechless. And sickened.

I look upon the newly arrived peoples—
Hispanics, Carribs, Asians and Pacific Islanders,
refugees and refuseniks from Europe, our new
inhabitants of the inner cities, a new middle
class renovating and swelling the suburban sat-
ellites around our cities, our new workers in
the farm belts—with great hope and expectation. I know they are what my father was when

he arrived in Los Angeles from Hawai'i thirty years ago. I know they are what my great-grandfathers were when they arrived, tanned and thinned by seasickness and lousy food, crossing over the long gangplank of the Immigration Station at Honolulu Bay over a hundred years ago. My grandfathers were the immigrant poor who were rich in hope and expectation. They would give their bodies and their spirit to make a place for their children in this new land. They would give us their singing, a small legacy of pain and sacrifice, and they would give us some of their courage.

I rode from the Upper East Side of Manhattan once, leaving early for a plane back to Hawai'i or Houston or Missouri or wherever it was I was teaching or fleeing from teaching that year. My driver, a guy I simply hailed down as I stood on the street corner in front of my hotel that morning, turned out to be an elderly man from Greece. Other times the man was from Russia or Jamaica or Korea or Rumania. They each have a story. The Greek's was this: I glanced down at the identification shield hanging down from the visor over the passenger's seat in front, and I noticed his was a long, lavish name like Popoladopolous. "Mr. Popoladopolous," I began, "I am guessing you are a Greek. Can you guess where I am from?" It is one of my favorite games when I travel. The night clerk from Poland stationed at the front desk of my hotel guessed Singapore. The Egyptian cardiac surgeon who wanted to buy my freshly detailed car in Houston guessed China or Taiwan.

"You are right," my Greek driver said, "But you have the advantage over me—you know my name."

"I am Hohngo," I said, giving it the Japanese pronunciation, as I would back home in Hawai'i. On the Mainland, in "America," I give in and pronounce it "Hahngo," attuning myself to the dominant accent that calls my Senator Daniel Inouye, officially, "Inui."

"Oh," Popoladopolous said, "You are a complicated man. You are an American from California or Los Angeles, and you are Oriental. Your father maybe came from Japan?"

"Very good," I said. "You are almost perfectly right. I am from Hawai'i, and, yes, my *great-grandfather* came from Japan."

The traffic was intense. We ran into the infamous Manhattan gridlock as we crossed to-

wards the East River and one of the bridges. I asked him what he was doing in America. He told me he had been an attorney in Greece, a prominent man of his city, with a family—a wife and several daughters. Then the Colonels took over. "Do you know the Colonels?" he asked me.

I knew that there had been the terrible conflict between the different factions in Greece. The Costa-Gavras film *Z* is about that. The books *When a Tree Sings* and *Eleni* by my friends Stratis Haviaris and Nicholas Gage tell both sides of a tough story. I remembered the headlines about Greece when I was a teenager in Los Angeles, the exile of the king, the military dictatorship, the protest of the oppression by film star Melina Mercouri. I thought of the poet Yannis Ritsos and how he had lived long in exile. "Yes," I said, "I know the Colonels."

"I was an attorney in Greece, in Athens, a dirty but beautiful city. I was a leader and supported the wrong side. I came to America. I brought my family. My daughter, she is grown now, and she is next week taking the New York bar examination. She will be a lawyer as well. Here, let me show you. Come with me."

Popoladopolous jumped out of the taxi and motioned for me to do the same. The traffic was still locked around us. He went to the back of the car and lifted the battered trunk lid. There was a suitcase inside of it made of leather, badly scuffed. He opened it. There were clothes, books, a loose-leaf binder. He grabbed a small parcel. Inside were photographs and a certificate.

"See?" he said, pointing and holding up a snapshot, "Here is my daughter in red and my nieces and myself in the back." I saw buxom girls in party dresses and heavy makeup and Mr. Popoladopolous in a grey suit standing behind them. "This is her graduation party from Hofstra School of Law. We take her to the restaurant of my son-in-law." He shared his pride with me. Then he flipped through more photographs—his house in Queens, his old house in Athens, snaps of an island holiday on Eretria many years ago—and, finally, he held up the certificate I'd noticed, wrapped in yellowing plastic.

"To be an attorney," he said, "This is my diploma from Greece." For an instant, he held it up over our heads like a chalice and then handed it to me "So, you see," he said, "I am telling truth to you." I saw it was smallish, only

5"× 7" or so, but there were seals and signatures on it. I nodded yes, I believed him. "But why do you not practice here," I asked, though I knew the answer. It was ritual. "This is not possible," he said, brusquely. He could not return to law school, study for the bar, begin again as a clerk, then associate, and so on. "I must work for my family, bring them, feed them, send my daughters to school. Give them my future. I drive cab, make money. The house in Queens. We are Americans now. Greece is the past. I am lonely for it, but here I live."

The traffic loosened around us. We got back in his cab and sped away to La Guardia, feeling our common resolve.

Some years ago, on the way to Hawai'i on a leave from Missouri, I stopped over in Los Angeles to give some poetry readings. It was winter, January in southern California, and the great beauty of the place was in the snow-lined ridges of Angeles Crest and the San Gabriel Mountains, a stunning natural backdrop to the city that swarmed around us in its infinite patterns of distraction. You could be driving from the south up the Harbor Freeway, and the mountains would be constantly before you, blue behemoths splashed and lichened with snow. This time of year, the air was clear as summer in the Arctic, and visibility stretched from the pier at Long Beach to the Hale Telescope at the Cal Tech Observatory on the ridgeline above the city.

One morning, I gave a reading to a teenage audience at Alhambra High School, a place just east of Pasadena tucked in one of the canyon valleys against the San Gabriels. I drove up from the south where I was staying and parked my rented car on the street under an enormous palm tree next to a warehouse a few blocks from the school. I liked Alhambra. It was an older section of the metropolis, built up during the forties and fifties and the aircraft boom, the scale and vintage of the streets and buildings seeming to come straight out of a Raymond Chandler novel. I noticed small custom garages, a coin shop, bakeries, a few restaurants and diners, and one place with that classic extravagance of neon, stainless steel, asphalt and glass that meant a drive-in.

The day's event was sponsored by California State University, Los Angeles, an idea thought up by Carl Selkin—Director of the Poetry Center there and my host—as part of an outreach program by the university to the communities nearby, gone largely "ethnic." It was an experiment run as part of the celebration around Dr. Martin Luther King's birthday. At Cal State the day before, Selkin had explained that the poet on their faculty had not been interested in doing this, had found it impossible to reach an audience he deemed "largely illiterate." But the high school English teachers—many of them graduates of CSU's excellent education program—were thrilled with the idea. Two of them had studied with Zbigniew Herbert, the great Polish poet who had once taught at CSU in the '60s. They wanted me to come, so I agreed.

I was put in a large science classroom. I sat in front of a huge desk with a sink on one end and a kind of projector that looked like a clunky, off-scale microscope on the other. The teachers told me I would read to an assembly made up largely of Asians and whites—about a hundred students, most of them juniors and seniors. The Asians were a mixture of Chinese and Southeast Asians, they told me, some of them Vietnamese, some Cambodians, a lot of them from Hong Kong too. Some four or five English classes were put together to make up the audience, and the students trooped in and took their seats, the whites giggling and self-conscious, the Asians largely silent.

I read my poems about the inner city and my poems about Hawai'i, about my leaving there as a child, returning to it many years later as an adult, a poet, and seeking out the old places, the plantation lands, the sugar mills, the cane field and graveyard where I might have played as a child, the rough seashore which was like kin. I read a long poem about walking through the old Japanese cemetery in Kahuku on the plantation. I told them how it was placed on a promontory overlooking the sea, on a sandy point jutting into the ocean. I told them how we Japanese and Filipinos and Chinese put our cemeteries there because it was the land given to us by the growers, who needed the good land, the land that was arable, for growing the sugar cane and the pineapple. But what we didn't know, what the growers didn't know, was that the sea would come and take our dead from us then, in the periodic raids of rips and tidal waves from a swelling ocean. The Hawaiians knew this and took the bones of their dead to the high ground, to caves on the cliffs and rock mounds on the rainy plateau above

With members of his poetry workshop: (from left) J-son Woo-Chin, John Song, Sandra Vane,
Garrett Hongo, David Shih, and Brian Komei Dempster, Napa Valley Writer's Conference, August 1994

the shelves of land between the sea and wind-
ward mountains. But we immigrants, we newly
arrived laborers, placed generation after generation in the sand by the sea.

A *tsunami* came in 1946 and took over half
of our dead in one night. "Bones and tomb-
stones/up and down the beach," my poem said.
I told them of walking over the patchy carpeting of temple moss "yellowing in the saline
earth," the stinging sand clouds kicked up by
the tough, onshore wind. I recalled a story of
a murder committed out of outrage and shame—
it was an act of victimage committed *within*
the community—and paid homage to it as part
of my past. It was to the journey I paid homage, the quest and travail of it from an Asian
past to our American present. And it was to
its remembrance—as shame and pride—that the
poem was dedicated.

When I finished, I looked up. In the back
rows was a Chinese girl, or maybe she was Vietnamese, dressed in a plain white school shirt
and dark woolen skirt. Her hair was long and
hung in two thick braids against her ears and

jaw. Her eyes were shining. She wept, staring
at me as if I were a statue. I averted my own
eyes, glancing quickly across the row and throughout the assembly, and saw others weeping too,
wiping their faces. Some were embarrassed and
gazed down at the floor or at their shoes. A
few teachers nodded. I don't remember anyone smiling. Nothing like it had ever happened
to me before. There was a feeling in the room
and a momentary, heavy silence. I was surprised
and a little unsettled by it.

The assembly broke up, a teacher standing
and thanking everyone, gesturing towards me
and calling for more applause. The classes began filing out, and I remember beginning to
think about what to do for lunch. I dismissed
the thought of the drive-in immediately. An
Asian girl came up and asked me to sign her
Pee-Chee.[1] Then another had me sign a napkin.
A few more had xeroxes of my poems. I signed
them all. A boy with acne and hair cut close

---

[1]A notebook.

to his temples but thick with pomade at the top—it was a style then coming into fashion with urban rappers—asked if I'd be reading for "adults" anytime that week. He wanted his parents to hear me too. I phlumphered something about the Pacific-Asia Museum that Saturday.

I had lunch with the teachers. They took me to the cafeteria, and we sat at the long bench-tables I remember from my public school days. Over fish sticks or breaded veal and tapioca pudding, we talked poetry and the new Asian students. A youngish man dressed in brown tweeds then spoke. He had a light brown beard, neatly trimmed.

"I've never seen them respond like that," he said, "Never seen them act so openly, show emotion like that before. You really connected."

I was learning something, something new and strong. These children with so much passion, so much raw affection, were teaching me that I had an audience, that my experience and sensibility spoke for their experiences, that I could address a world of others like myself, of Asians newly arrived, of peoples wanting to make America their place too. Up until then, I'd pretty much felt embattled as an artist and took it as part of my identity. I saw myself as an individual presence up against cultural indifference or mild hostility, particularly because my subject—the history of Japanese in America—was something I thought few cared hearing about. Except for some wonderful exceptions—and most of these among my fellow poets—it had been so while in college, and even more so in graduate school. I'd felt that, even if I was allowed a place in academe or the literary world, it would be on sufferance, that no one was *intrinsically* interested in my obsession, my passions. I thought of America as an establishment aloof from me. But after that assembly under the Los Angeles mountains, signing the *Pee-Chees* and napkins and xeroxes those teenage students had of my poems, I sensed that I was beginning to belong to something, to join a throng of voices in need of their own singing.

When Walt Whitman, the great American poet of the nineteenth century, wrote his poems of robust American optimism, full of the democratic spirit and lust for challenges and union jobs, he shouted "I Hear America Singing!" and announced a theme that characterized more than a century of our history. Well, I look upon all of us here, now—we, the New Americans, among newly arrived peoples with their boat trails of memories from across the oceans, and, I think, I Hear America Singing too.

This essay originally appeared in *Parnassus: Poetry in Review,* volume 17, number 1, 1992, pp. 9-20.

BIBLIOGRAPHY

(With Alan Chong Lau and Lawson Fusao Inada) *The Buddha Bandits Down Highway 99,* Buddhahead (Mountain View, California), 1978.

Yellow Light (poetry; includes selections from *The Buddha Bandits Down Highway 99*), Wesleyan University Press, 1982.

The River of Heaven (poetry), Knopf, 1988.

(Editor) *The Open Boat: Poems from Asian America,* Doubleday, 1993.

(Editor) Wakako Yamauchi, *Songs My Mother Taught Me: Stories, Plays, and Memoir,* Feminist Press, 1994.

Volcano: A Memoir of Hawai`i, Knopf, 1995.

Under Western Eyes: Personal Essays from Asian America, Doubleday, 1995.

Also author of play *Nisei Bar & Grill,* 1976.

Mark Jarman

1952-

Nora

My maternal grandmother, Nora Pemberton, was a dedicated reader and writer. She loved Emily Dickinson, Dorothy Parker, and Samuel Pepys. She grew up with four brothers and a sister in Wiggins, Mississippi, where her father, Alonso Bodie, worked for the lumber industry. I have been told that her mother was a quarter Choctaw. The Native American features showed more in her sister's face than in Nora's, but the pictures I have seen of my great-grandmother, Allie Bodie, are striking. She had straight black hair and high cheekbones. Alonso Bodie's parents were from County Cork. Because he was not satisfied to be the engineer of a small lumber train, he would tell strangers he drove for the B & O Line.

Nora was not satisfied with her life, either. She divorced my mother's father, James Foster, when my mother was only four years old and later married Elmer Pemberton. After World War II when Granddaddy Pemberton, who liked to be called Pup Dog, got out of the navy, he started Dependable Maintenance, a caretaking and salvage company, in San Diego. His place of business, as Nora called it, was located on Newton Avenue. It included a bar known as the Total Loss Room where Pup Dog spent a lot of his free time. Nora sat at home writing stories and poems, chewing Pepsin gum, and smoking Chesterfields, or she took Yellow cabs around San Diego. She suffered from a mild form of epilepsy but also had nervous breakdowns periodically. Her epileptic seizures resulted in temporary memory loss. When she took her parakeet for walks around the neighborhood, attached to her wrist by a strand of yarn, it was usually a sign of a nervous breakdown. She had a fondness for horse racing. After she died at the age of fifty-nine, of a botched surgery for a blocked bowel, Pup Dog claimed that she had squandered a fortune gambling at Del Mar, the track north of San Diego.

Mark Jarman in Nashville, Tennessee

When I visited them as a child, Pup Dog would take me to the place of business, and I would be free to roam his warehouse, reading magazines or racy paperbacks from fire and flood losses while he worked or drank in the Total Loss Room. He had a collection of military rifles of all vintages, Japanese, German, and American. Once after work he set up a bucket of sand at one end of the warehouse and let me fire an M-1 rifle clip into it. I must have been eleven at the time. Usually I stayed home with Nora and played with a group of boys on her street who all called her by her first name. When she wrote, either she typed at her kitchen table or lounged on her recliner beside an enormous *Webster's* and revised typescript. She was thin as a slat. She would tell me, referring to the dictionary on its stand, that she lived in that book, and I could see her slipping easily between the pages. Toward the end of her life (I was twelve when she died) she acquired a dictaphone and would record her writing on belts of wide red tape. She wrote a story called "A Giant in the House" about an uncle living with his young niece and nephew, a poem about a lizard who was a dandy and made his money as a landlord, and she tried to publish a cookbook for husbands, *Serve While Hot,* "dedicated to men who like to play around in the kitchen." It was interspersed with jokes and poems, like the following that headed the chapter "Baked Goose."

> The goose appears to be
> As cheerful as a clown.
> But he is only bluffing
> For underneath he's down.

"My grandmother, Nora Pemberton," around 1955

I have the manuscripts of some of her stories and poems and I also have the dictaphone belts. After Nora died, Pup Dog moved the dictaphone machine that she had used to his place of business. Shortly before he died himself, Dependable Maintenance burned to the ground and, I believe, other manuscripts of Nora's which were stored there were also lost.

She published little during her life, but when she did she preferred to use the pen name Louise Verne. My parents regarded her as an oddity, and I never knew until much later, when I started to write, how much I owed her. In her presence, I must have learned that writing was something people did, people you knew, your own family members. I know I also learned the romance of embellishment, fabrication, and lying. She was proud, for example, of the fact that Pup Dog who had little schooling was even more widely read than she. Supposedly he had read Edward Gibbon's *The History of the Decline and Fall of the Roman Empire* before he was a teenager. Once I got into an argument with a boy in her neighborhood, one of my playmates when I visited San Diego, about the fall of

Rome. My friend had seen a movie in which it appeared that Rome fell in a day. I was certain that it had taken years, if not centuries. We asked Nora to settle our argument (I don't know why we didn't ask Pup Dog), and she took my side, informing my friend that, after all, *I* had read Gibbon's *Decline and Fall of the Roman Empire.* It was an impressive tactic. For a while I even believed her myself.

For many years I had the idea of writing a series of poems based on her dictaphone belts. My poem "Writing for Nora," included in my first book, *North Sea,* refers to them as "lost." Though I found them later, I could never locate the right kind of machine to play them. In 1987 when I began drafting my book-length, narrative poem *Iris,* which is based in part on Nora's life, I tried to give my character some of Nora's same interests as a reader, especially her passion for the diaries of Samuel Pepys. She loved his account of the Great Fire of London and at bedtime she would announce, "And so to bed." But reading the diaries myself, as I began to create Iris, I found it impossible to get excited about Pepys or imagine Iris, a college dropout from western Kentucky, reading him with Nora's enthusiasm. Instead I gave Iris an obsession with the poet Robinson Jeffers, no less outlandish, I admit, but an interest that coincided with my own.

Ray

I am the son and grandson of preachers. My father, Donald Ray Jarman, was ordained into the Christian Church (Disciples of Christ) in 1950, just after he graduated from Chapman College, which at that time was still located in Los Angeles, California. His father, Ray Jarman, was ordained into the same denomination, in 1912, in Kansas City, Missouri, when he was seventeen years old.

Ray Jarman's first pastorate was a little church in the mining town of Bevier, Missouri. He said that people came from miles around to hear the boy preacher and that when he left, the congregation had grown by 500 percent. Throughout his life, wherever he preached, he counted on the enthusiastic receptions of large crowds. As a young man he also traveled from church to church, as a kind of circuit rider. One night he had to share a hotel room and a bed with a man who returned late in the evening, wearing a gun.

Ray claimed that his mother's mother and Samuel Clemens's mother were sisters. Though the actual relationship is much more distant, it provoked Ray's lifelong interest in Mark Twain (my namesake). He made himself something of an expert on Twain's life and work, and in the days before Twain imitators, he would earn extra money lecturing on Twain, telling anecdotes based on the writer's life, reciting passages from his letters, and retelling his stories.

My grandfather had a phenomenal memory, one he had trained with a simple mnemonic technique that was taught to me by my father. He memorized by pacing back and forth, tracing and retracing his steps in a hall or in the backyard, sometimes extending his range and reversing direction, while adding passages as he established a physical rhythm. In this way he had memorized much of the New Testament. On Sunday when it was time to read the Scripture lesson, he impressed his congregation by saying the verses with the Bible closed. When

I was a child I thought he knew the entire Bible by heart. Along with Twain and the Bible, he liked to quote Kipling's poem "When Earth's Last Picture Is Painted," and Emily Brontë's "Last Lines" that begins "No coward soul is mine." One of his favorite passages, which I heard him recite numerous times even after he became a charismatic Christian evangelist, was Marie Corelli's description of the Crucifixion in her novel *Barabbas*.

After serving churches in the Midwest, Ray took his family to Los Angeles in the early 1940s where he was pastor of Huntington Park Christian Church. Ray had always had a fascination with what he called the transcendent or the metaphysical, which was often simply the supernatural or unconventional. In the pulpit he claimed that he heard the voice of his dead mother speaking to him. In the balmy, palmy climate of southern California, when towns like Huntington Park were still surrounded by orange groves and dairy farms, Ray discovered all kinds of unconventional spirituality. He built a church in South Gate and began a ministry that included a heady range of what today might be called new age theologies. He preached about the power of positive thinking, yoga, diet, clairvoyance, and dream analysis both from the pulpit and on his radio show, "The Shepherd of the Air." For a brief time he hired lecture halls around Los Angeles and gave talks about conquering the aging process with the help of a youthful looking elderly man who claimed to be so old he could not reveal his age. Finally, in the early 1960s, he took part in experiments with LSD.

Ray's experiences with the drug were religious and gave him something he had sought, a stronger, fuller sense of a spiritual life. His preaching was always passionate and able to overwhelm grown men with emotion. One man was persuaded to try the drug, had a bad trip, and sued Ray and the church. The consequences were disastrous. His church was in an uproar. His wife, my grandmother Grace, who had suffered since childhood from a heart ailment, grew ill and died. When Jesus Christ came to him in his office and asked why he had turned away from the gospel, Ray was born again. He lost his church—for them, his Damascus experience was the last straw—and spent the next fifteen years, almost until his death in 1980, witnessing to his redemption from modernist theology and the drug world.

Ray was an influential presence in my growing up, not so much because of his direct relationship to me, but because of his relationship with my father. During the years when he went further and further out, he and my father quarreled bitterly over the church and the nature of faith. After he was born again, his new embrace of the gospel, which my father had never let go, could make him insufferably righteous. Toward the end of his life, he was living in a home for senior citizens run by Amy Semple McPherson's Four Square Gospel Church, that quintessential creation of California balminess. There he came to loathe the pious superiority of his fellow inmates. Debilitated by strokes, aware of how he had alienated his son, he managed a partial reconciliation with my father. Yet when he died the same day as Groucho Marx and Mae West, my father took a grim satisfaction in knowing that the crowds greeting them in the next world would be larger than Ray's.

Ray's life and the conflict between him and my father have been the subjects of many of my poems. They form strands that begin in *North Sea* with the poems "History," "Altar Calls," and "Father, Son, and Ghost," and run through

my second book *The Rote Walker*, which takes its title from Ray's technique of memorizing while walking and tries to examine in poems like "1912" and "To Make Flesh" just what it meant to have both Ray's spiritual hunger and, as my father would say, his greed for recognition. In *The Black Riviera*, my fourth book, I tried to capture Ray's response to his wife's illness in the poem "The Death of God."

Scotland

In 1958 when I was six years old, my family moved to Kirkcaldy, Scotland, a linoleum factory town in Fife, on the Firth of Forth, across from Edinburgh. My father had been serving a church in Santa Maria, California, and that spring he had heard of a program called Fraternal Aid to British Churches. Our denomination was sending young ministers and their families for three-year stints to Great Britain to help keep alive its flagging brother churches. At the time, my father's church in Santa Maria was completing a large new sanctuary. Vandenburgh Air Force Base nearby was expanding and the word was that the whole area would enjoy a new

*"My grandfather, the Reverend Ray Jarman, and my father,
the Reverend Donald Jarman, at South Bay Christian Church," around 1962*

prosperity as a result, with many new members for Santa Maria's churches. My father had just turned thirty. He expressed his interest in going abroad to the church's head office in Indianapolis. On September 17, he, my mother, my four-year-old sister Katie, and I were aboard the *Empress of Britain,* a Canadian-Pacific ocean liner, embarked from Montreal to Greenock.

We lived for three years in a semi-detached bungalow, the church's parsonage or manse, at 19 Bennochy Road across from the town's cemetery and in the shadow of one of the Nairn's linoleum factories. Kirkcaldy, with about fifty thousand people, was known as the Lang Toon, for the way it was strung out along the Firth of Forth. It was said to have been built on the Devil. On mornings when the reek of linseed from the factories was especially strong, droll Kirkcaldians asked, "Can ye no smell 'im?"

The Church of Scotland was Presbyterian, of course, and the Christian Church (Disciples of Christ) was a small presence. My father served St. Clair Street Church of Christ, a very modest, very plain, gray sandstone building on one of Kirkcaldy's busiest streets. The congregation could not have numbered more than one hundred, but during the three years my father served the church, young people were more actively involved than ever before or since. The church elders would hear an innovative suggestion from my father and respond, "We dinnae do it that way." And yet he must have persuaded them to do a number of things "that way," at least for that time. Nearly twenty years later when I returned to Scotland for the first time, I attended a Palm Sunday service at St. Clair Street Church of Christ. The turnout was sparse and made up mostly of older people who had been the older people when I was a boy. I asked one member who had been a teenager when we lived in Scotland what had happened. He said simply, "Your father left."

Kirkcaldy was a dour place, but I only discovered that when I returned years later. It had a castle, Ravenscraig, a black, dangerous ruin on a sea cliff at the east end of town. On the town's west end, Michael Beveridge, a nineteenth-century linoleum magnate, had endowed a park. In the fall, just after school started, there was an evening festival in Beveridge Park. Lights and ornaments were strung through the chestnut trees, and the story of the Babes in the Woods was represented by illuminated figures that appeared beside the paths. Half-way between my house and Beveridge Park was Abbotshall Church where Pet Marjorie Fleming was buried. She was a friend of Sir Walter Scott and died before she was nine years old. A statue of her sat atop her grave. She wrote pious meditations, but also witty poems, one of which included the lines, "But she was more than usual calm, / She did not give a single dam." The inscription on her stone read, "The Youngest Immortal in the World of Letters." Down by the water was a long promenade where the wind blew constantly. It had been built to attract tourists. Once trees had been planted along it to create a bosky boulevard, but the wind uprooted them. Every April at the west end of the promenade the Links Market took place as it had since the twelfth century. The modern attractions included dodg'em cars, a haunted house, and tents for adults only. Best of all was the helter skelter, a dark wooden tower girdled with a spiral slide. You climbed up on the inside and stepped out at the top for the ride down on a rush mat. Not only could you see everything below, but if the day was fair you could look across the Firth of Forth to Edinburgh and the green saddle of Arthur's Seat with Edinburgh Castle and the Scott Monument set near it like black chess pieces.

Our house was heated by coal-burning fireplaces. The one in the living room heated the water. Instead of a refrigerator there was a granite slab in the kitchen pantry that kept things like milk and meat fresh for a couple of days. It seemed almost impossible to get laundry completely dry. In the morning before I went to school my mother would hang my damp knee socks (I wore short pants) on a small paraffin stove someone had given us and, if we weren't careful, the elastic around their tops would crisp like bacon. The night we arrived, the house was full of people from church who were there to greet us. My sister and I were put to bed by a woman who told us quite cheerfully before she put out the light that every house in Scotland had a ghost. The ghost in that house was the cold. One winter night it split the wooden toilet seat in the bathroom with a sound like a gunshot.

My father took up gardening in Kirkcaldy in order to have something to talk about with the church elders, who all gardened as a hobby. He grew roses and favored those with names like 49er, Texas Centennial, and Newport News. My mother kept house, shopping from the vendors who stopped by—the vegetable man with his horsecart and the fishman in a sea-green van—or walking into town with an enormous purse and a floral pocketbook, standard shopping equipment. At first she dazzled people, especially the wee wifeys in the church, with her bright California clothes, but then she eventually traded them for more subdued attire. Within a year my parents were both ready to return to the United States.

But living in Scotland gave them an opportunity to travel. We toured the Highlands, visited the Netherlands and Belgium, and during the summer of 1961 before we returned to the States, we traveled by car through France, Italy, Switzerland, Germany, Austria, and the principality of Liechtenstein. My parents loved Italy and my clearest memories are of our weeks there. In Milan we saw Leonardo's *Last Supper* and my father bought a copy painted on silk that he later framed and hung in his office at church. We saw the bones of ancient Christians in the catacombs outside of Rome, and Pope John XXIII blessed us in a huge crowd at St. Peter's.

My parents took a distinct dislike to their fellow American tourists, especially those who complained about the lack of American amenities. Yet when we visited Pisa, they decided we should spend the night in an American-style motel called The California Hotel. The name alone worked on their homesickness (we had been gone from the United States for three years). There were no rooms to accommodate the four of us, so we took two, with my father and me in one and my mother and sister in the other. That night we ate at a restaurant near the hotel. My parents drank Chianti and ate a baked dish made of green pasta. They seemed very happy and my sister and I were at an age when their happiness made us happy. We walked back to our rooms in a gay mood as a small black thundercloud, with brilliant horns of cartoon lightning, trolled toward us from the horizon. It was hot and muggy and we opened the louvered windows in our rooms. There were window screens in my mother and sister's room, but none in my father's and mine. Before dawn, my father and I were awakened by the downpour and the sound of thousands of mosquitoes that had taken refuge in our bedroom. A plump little boy, I was a mosquito feast. And for days after in our travels when people regarded my purple, poxlike mosquito

bites, my parents would say, "Pisa. Mosquitoes." They also reproached themselves for choosing a hotel because its name appealed to their nostalgia.

Later, in Vaduz, Liechtenstein, my father became ill from a meal of cannelloni. The woman doctor who examined him scoffed and said it was indigestion. His meal had not agreed with him, she said, probably because he was "a foreigner."

The experience of foreignness lingers from those years abroad. I learned to read in Scotland, sounding vowels out according to the instructions of my first teacher, Miss Reid, a large woman with wild white hair. She banished my American accent. Both my sister and I did not become bilingual exactly, but we spoke the Fife dialect at school and with our friends. My sister remembers the day she lost her Scottish when we returned to America. In answer to a question, she said, "Yeah, Mom" instead of "Aye, Mither." We adapted ourselves to holidays, too, but it was hard at first. Our first Halloween my sister and I dressed up and went from door to door, saying "Trick or treat!" We were greeted by puzzlement. One woman gave us an orange, another a sixpence. Then a gang of boys came to our house towing a strawman in a wagon and demanded, "A penny for the Guy!" They were collecting money to buy fireworks for Guy Fawkes Day on November 5. And to this day, when I think of past Christmases, the leaner, more somber figure of Father Christmas stands like a shadow beside Santa Claus.

Our second year in Scotland, around Easter time, I was walking to my piano lesson after school, behind a teacher whose son was in my class and who was walking with his mother. A group of older kids suddenly surrounded me and began shouting about something I did not understand. They wanted to know if I wrote to my aunties and uncles and grannies and granddads in America. If I did, I should tell them to take back their Skybolts. They pursued me for a block or two, taunting me about the mysterious Skybolt, then left off. I was in tears and mystified that the teacher and her son, who were only a few steps ahead of me, never turned around. Sobbing, I told my piano teacher, Miss Joy Clark, about what had happened and asked her what it all meant. Obviously she read the papers and knew about the pressure America was putting on Britain to buy their new nuclear missile, the Skybolt.

Joy Clark was a cheerful woman whose crooked back made her stand not much taller than I. She comforted me and said that it was not my fault, but she also advised me to ask my parents about it. She told me that America could be a very demanding friend.

North Sea takes its title from those years in Scotland and includes a number of poems about my childhood there. The North Sea itself, which in my mind is a chilly gray expanse with long wavering white caps like strings drawn across it, mirrors but does not reflect California's Pacific Ocean, the other body of water that appears in my poetry.

I have returned to Kirkcaldy a number of times. The chimneys of the linoleum factories and the factories themselves are gone, moved outside of town or closed completely, due to the lack of demand. The Christian Church (Disciples of Christ) no longer exists in the United Kingdom but has joined the United Reform Church. St. Clair Street Church of Christ along with an entire parade of shops on its side of the street was condemned in 1989 so that the street could be widened. Over the years when I visited I would stop by 19 Bennochy Road and see that roses of fairly advanced age, possibly my father's, were still flourishing where he had planted them. And yet the last time I was there, in 1992, his garden had been bricked over to make a patio. The house had become a bed and breakfast. I considered staying there one night, but thought better of it.

Redondo Beach

In 1961, when we returned to the United States, we moved to Redondo Beach, California. When my parents were growing up in Huntington Park, in South Central L.A., they considered Redondo Beach the sticks, an outlying, semi-primitive place. Redondo had a glamorous past as a tourist resort on the south end of Santa Monica Bay. There had been a pavilion, a boardwalk, and a roller coaster, but these were long gone before my parents' time. Once in an old drugstore near the Redondo Pier, I found a postcard advertising the city's charms. Redondo had been photographed from the air in black and white, and color tints had been added. It was an enclave, bounded on one side by the nearly purple Pacific and on three others by dense, green-black orange groves.

"My sister, Katie, and me, at 19 Bennochy Road, Kirkcaldy, Scotland," September 1958

This was the Redondo Beach my parents had known.

In 1961, Redondo was one of a string of slightly seedy beachtowns south of tony Santa Monica. Today, of course, the entire Santa Monica Bay is prime property and the population has been homogenized by upward mobility. My father took the pulpit at South Bay Christian Church. My sister Luanne, who had been conceived in Scotland, was born in South Bay General Hospital the same year. We lived at first in the parsonage on Vincent Street a few blocks from church. I could memorize an entire psalm or chapter from the Bible walking to Sunday school from our house. A few years later my parents bought their own house at the end of Knob Hill. It was too far from church to walk but close enough to the beach that I could carry my surfboard there, if I felt ambitious.

Returning to southern California, and especially greater Los Angeles, was important to both my parents. My mother's mother and stepfather lived in San Diego, her father and stepmother lived in the San Fernando Valley. My father probably would have preferred not to be so close to his father, but he had agreed with his sister, who lived in Ohio, that he would be the one to live near their mother, whose health was failing. As a result my sisters and I grew up surrounded by grandparents, pampered, spoiled, and fascinated.

Although I was born in Kentucky while my father was in seminary in Lexington, and my earliest memories are of the fields and euca-lyptus windbreaks near our house in Santa Maria, and my three years in Scotland are like an island of childhood, I think of myself as hav-ing grown up in Redondo Beach. And even though the contrast between the North Sea and the Pacific is profound, I still have the feeling that I should be living beside one or the other.

By 1961 the freeway system and the bed-room communities that sprang up around it filled in most of the open spaces between cen-tral Los Angeles and the beachtowns, like Redondo, Hermosa, and Manhattan Beach. I can remember driving through a dairy farm and an orange grove on the way to Ray and Grace's house, but those did not last much longer. Redondo was protected from the L.A. Basin's smog and heat by a range of coastal hills. When we moved to the house on Knob Hill in 1964, on the hill's crest just above us was a Nike missile base, part of our nation's defense against the Soviet Union's long-range nuclear bombers. Looking up from the end of our driveway we could see the finned white noses of the missiles on their launching pads. It could not have been much later that the base was dismantled and the missiles shipped away, made obsolete by intercontinental ballis-tic missiles. Hemmed in by a half-hearted hur-ricane fence, the abandoned site with its con-crete slabs like patios and its pale green stucco bungalow became a secret gathering place. It remained in the same condition for at least a decade. One night in 1971, home from col-lege, a group of high school friends and I took a jug of rosé to the missile base and watched the moon rise over Mount Baldy. On the ex-ceptional day when the smog had blown south to Riverside County, you could see from that hill all the way to downtown Los Angeles and the San Gabriel Mountains beyond. During the Watts riots it gave us a view of the smoke.

Many of the members of my father's church in Redondo were either in the defense indus-try or associated with it. They worked for com-panies like Northrop, McDonnell-Douglas, Hughes Aircraft, Garrett Air Research, and STL (Space Technology Laboratories), which became TRW.

They were a conservative bunch, and the 1960s polarized them as it did everyone. My father's attempts to integrate his church or at least to have the church participate in family exchanges with inner city churches drove people away. When he returned to seminary in Claremont to earn his doctorate, he was influenced by the younger students. After he preached the funeral of a boy in the church who had been blown to pieces in action in Vietnam, my fa-ther was soon making it clear from the pulpit that he thought the war was wrong. This too alienated a segment of his congregation. When he left South Bay Christian Church and the pulpit, if not the ministry, in 1971, he was battlescarred and his congregation was decimated.

I watched what was happening in that church and felt a keen partisanship on my father's behalf. Later, living in other parts of the country, I discovered that people actually believed that life in southern California was indulgent, worry free, sybaritic, and fake. This strikes me now as too stupid to rebut, but it angered me then and to this day when I write about living in that privileged place. Since it was beautiful and remains so, I feel moved to show the reality of life there, its urgency and validity.

At least a third of the children I grew up with were Hispanic, most of them Chicano. They were bilingual, the rest of us were not. The divisions did not become pronounced or in-flamed until we were in high school. My se-nior year I played center on the varsity foot-ball team and hiked the ball to a boy whose grandparents were from Sonora. Even then our team was mixed like the population of the school. Social pressure was applied increasingly by clubs, gangs, peers, and in the classroom. There were teachers at my high school who did not ap-prove of interracial couples and said as much. The irony is obvious. We were living in a state, a county, a town, and many of us were living on streets, like Juanita or Catalina, with Span-ish names. In my junior year, there were two brawls after post-game dances between Anglos on the football team and Hispanics who were members of car clubs. The bad blood festered. The next year a lunchtime incident in the stu-dent parking lot where cars had been vandal-ized led to a bizarre and terrifying spontane-ous separation of students on the campus. Groups of white and brown kids glared at each other until the bell rang to return to classes. On that occasion the eeriness of what had occurred,

St. Clair Street Church of Christ, Kirkcaldy, Scotland, 1958

though it did not lead to violence, eased tensions. But those of us who had been children together were not children or together anymore.

Life with its large resonances—racial strife, suffering in war—and its smaller ones—falling in love for the first time, discovering books—did go on in that place under ideal conditions, I must admit. If it wasn't spring, it was summer. The first day of high school I was waiting in line with a friend to be issued my student ID. My hair had been cut short for football, but my friend was still wearing his long. An officious vice principal (there were a slew of these creatures at our school) told him to get a haircut. It was a spectacular early September day, actually a typical day for where we lived, and my friend still had sand on his neck from his morning surfing. As soon as school was over that afternoon, he would be back in the water. Stunned by the vice principal's order, he said in a tone approaching outrage, "But it's still summer!"

I surfed but I was never very good. Yet I remember being in the water with some of the great surfers of that time, like Mike Doyle and Donald Takayama. It was the sport of truancy, if you were still in school. Huckleberry Finn would have surfed. The beachbreak in Redondo was excellent, until the city attempted to ex-

tend the sand to accommodate more tourists and dredged up the gently sloping bottom that allowed the Pacific ground swells to send in glassy breakers that peeled left and right most mornings almost until noon. Eventually the waves reclaimed what had been lost. I could never maneuver very well with the nearly ten-foot boards we rode back then, and preferred body surfing to board surfing. To be lifted, then launched down the face of a wave. To dive under a breaker as the tonnage of foam rushed overhead. To bask as the sun burned through the light morning fog and the water shifted and swelled and the next set of waves formed and came to shore. These were year-round pastimes for me and my friends. They are sensations that return to me in dreams.

Situated in a park above the Redondo Pier was the Redondo Public Library. I discovered truant reading there, the books not assigned at school. Though I did have excellent English teachers who pointed me toward poetry, I found a lot of it on my own, making it all the more precious. There were windows at the end of each aisle of shelves, so much of the place was filled with sunshine during the day. I can remember how the sun fell on the cover of James Dickey's *Buckdancer's Choice* when I first took it off the shelf. And I am sure I read Thom Gunn's "From the Wave," with its description of surfing, for the first time there and realized that I could write about that, too, maybe even better, though it was a long time before I tried.

My third book, *Far and Away,* is mostly about growing up in Redondo Beach. As the title suggests, it also concerns leaving the place behind.

Teachers

I have been lucky in my teachers, and that may be the reason I make my living as one.

In Scotland, at Dunnikier School, after a period of catching up under the instruction of the fearsome Miss Reid, I had the good fortune to be placed in a class taught by a young woman named Rachel Geddie. Miss Geddie liked Yanks, though like Miss Reid she insisted on the Scottish pronunciation of vowels. She was plump with short curly brown hair and wide set eyes. I could tell that she wasn't pretty (I measured all women's looks by my mother's who, according to my Scottish friends, was "the prettiest mother"), but Miss Geddie had such a spirit of fun and laughter that she seemed beautiful.

She was a musician and played the piano for the school assembly that took place every Friday morning. Singing was as important in our class as history, geography, and Bible study. She taught us Baring-Gould's "Now the Day Is Over." At the end of the day, when we placed our chairs atop our desks so the janitor could sweep, we sang it instead of saying a prayer. Once when the local Church of Scotland pastor was supervising Bible study in the next classroom, Miss Geddie led us in a rousing rendition of "What Shall We Do with the Drunken Sailor?" She taught us Scottish songs, settings of poems by Burns, and also showtunes from American musicals. She loved *Oklahoma!*

And she found me amusing. One morning she turned to me and said, "Mark, you must be very proud today." I didn't know what she meant. She told me about Alan Shepard's space flight. When another student mentioned that the Russians were still first in space, I challenged him. Miss Geddie was shocked to learn that I did not know or hadn't remembered about Yuri Gagarin. She told me that *The Scotsman* was a very good newspaper. I should read it. When I broke my ankle on the playground trying

to leap from a flight of steps, she phoned my mother, helped me to the hospital, waited with me, and told me about the famous leap of Wallace, the Scottish hero, who jumped from the East Lomond Hill to the West Lomond Hill, which was near Kirkcaldy. Wallace was foully murdered by King Edward I of England, but he was a man with strong ankles.

Miss Geddie spoke to me, as she spoke to all of her pupils, with a directness that made me feel grown up. Before my family left to return to America, she invited us to a party at her house. When I noticed a framed photograph of her wearing a tiara and an evening gown with bare shoulders, for some reason I asked her why she wasn't married. She didn't seem fazed by the question at all but answered, "Not everybody must be married."

One day while my parents were packing to leave she offered to get my sister and me out of the house by taking us on a walk into the country to Chapeltown, about two miles away. It was a grand adventure at first, on a day of good weather, and Miss Geddie sang and told us stories about growing up in Fife, which wasn't as dour as Kirkcaldy, but as we could see, very beautiful in the countryside. My sister and I faded after an hour. We were used to walking, but this seemed excessive. We never reached Chapeltown, and Miss Geddie insisted that we walk back ourselves. Finally she relented when we found a bus stop and let us ride the rest of the way. I have commemorated that day and Miss Geddie in a poem called "Miss Urquhart's Tiara" in *The Black Riviera.*

When I returned to America, at first we wrote to each other. Once she described a boy in her class who reminded her of me and asked me if I would write to him. I did but never heard back, and eventually I lost touch with her. While visiting Scotland in 1992 I stopped by Dunnikier School and spoke with a secretary who remembered Rachel Geddie. She told me Miss Geddie had played the piano for Kirkcaldy's Gilbert and Sullivan Society. But she had moved north over twenty years before to teach in a one-room school, and no one at Dunnikier had heard from her since.

I began writing as a freshman in high school and received encouragement, more than I ever deserved, from teachers and friends. I was invited to join the high school writing club and at one of its first meetings the senior English teacher, James Van Wagoner, spoke. He talked mainly about the necessity of learning to write, if one wished to be a writer, and of writing all the time. "Practice, practice, practice," he said. "Chain yourself to your typewriter." When I asked if talent didn't matter, he said it did not, unless you "practice, practice, practice." He made writing sound like virtuoso piano playing. Years later I discovered that Ezra Pound had the same advice for poets.

Mr. Van Wagoner was handsome, with a long face, wavy brown hair going gray, and a deep widow's peak, and often seemed to be laughing to himself about something. Those of us who admired him wanted in on the joke. He had had some talented students. I knew their work from the high school literary magazine. One of them, Lynne "Squeaky" Fromme, went on to national notoriety, but not as a writer. Her poems, which she had written for

"My parents, Bo Dee Foster and Donald Jarman, May 1950, two months before their marriage"

his class, impressed me. The poet Maurya Simon also studied with him. So did the novelist Rachel Hickerson. They were a couple of years ahead of me, part of a group that included would-be writers, reporters for the school paper, and our high school's version of political activists, all of whom seemed very glamorous to me. Mr. Van Wagoner had taught them all, and he was legendary for his knowledge of modern literature. He was also a poet and novelist, it was said, and he had sold screenplays.

He taught from the old Oscar Williams anthologies of modern and American poetry and let his classes wander through them as they wished. He loved the poetry of Thomas Hardy, Dylan Thomas, and Edna St. Vincent Millay and the fiction of Thomas Wolfe, and he talked about the writers' lives, emphasizing their dedication as artists. He was also a James Dickey fan. When I showed him my copy of *Naked Poetry,* which I had discovered at the Either/Or Bookstore in Hermosa Beach, he was interested. He let me write papers about Allen Ginsberg and Denise Levertov.

By the time I took his senior English class I was full of bad writing habits and myself. Yet he saw something in the poems I showed him. Perhaps it was only my avidness. Halfway through the year he told me that instead of attending class I could use the hour to write, but I had to show him my work. He became my first serious reader and critic, and that hour was the first time I had to face what it meant to "practice, practice, practice." I wrote in the teacher's lounge, which was always empty at that time, five days a week, for an hour. When I finished a poem I would show it to him. He would point to a line, or part of a line, a single image, and make a check beside it, and advise me to save it, throw away the rest of the poem, and build a new poem with that little part. He would write terse comments in the margins of poems, almost always having to do with clarity. I was not clear and I strove to be. He encouraged me to imitate difficult metrical forms by Auden. Once when I used the phrase "Ha, ha!" in a poem, unconsciously echoing God's laughter in "Channel Firing," he wrote beside it, "Too Hardy a laugh."

I don't know if I ever wrote a poem that he found successful while I was his student, but he let me know that he thought I had what it took to be a writer and told me when I graduated that if I stopped writing at any

Mark and Amy (center) at their wedding with Marjorie Simon and George Hitchcock, in "The House of Poetry," December 28, 1974

time for any reason in the next ten years, the muses should strike me deaf, dumb, and blind. It was a powerful admonition. Eight years later I dedicated my first book to him.

For an eighteen-year-old poet in 1970, the University of California at Santa Cruz was an exciting place to be. George Hitchcock had been invited to teach there at College V, the arts college, by the provost James B. Hall. I was enrolled at College V, having no idea what to expect except redwoods. Like a lot of other southern California students, I just wanted to get out of the L.A. Basin.

Hitchcock had been editing the little poetry magazine *kayak* for about six years when he came to Santa Cruz to teach. His press had been publishing books for half that time. My classmates from the Bay Area knew about him. One of them even had copies of some of Hitchcock's own beautiful, limited edition books of poems, *Poems & Prints* and *The Dolphin with the Revolver in Its Teeth.* At a welcoming party at the home of one of the faculty who lived

on campus, I found a copy of his latest book, *A Ship of Bells*, and read it curiously. I knew nothing about surrealism, at least as practiced by Hitchcock. I sat thinking what I could do if I could make poems with such images.

I discovered his magazine before I ever met Hitchcock himself. The bookstore had recent issues of *kayak* for sale. On my own I had already found the work of Philip Levine and W. S. Merwin, Charles Simic and James Tate, and *kayak* had new poems by them. There were also poems by Margaret Atwood and Nancy Willard, John Haines and Vern Rutsala, whom I had never heard of, but who were writing marvelous things. There were strange and hilarious letters to the editor, polemical reviews, and throughout, prints of people in Victorian dress involved in activities, like measuring a skull with calipers or simply standing in their underwear, that contrasted provocatively with the poems.

One night early in the school year a group of us who were taking a poetry writing class were invited to Hitchcock's house in Bonny Doon to read our work aloud and to meet other poets. Hitchcock had the bearing of an actor who could play Lear or Pozzo and seemed amused by the charcoal resonance of his own baritone voice. I think he was taller than anyone else that evening, with long gray hair that covered his ears, and a light in his blue eyes that was old-fashioned merriment. There were some very sharp, very witty young people present, and their remarks and poems delighted him. His house was full of books. On a coffee table where he had been working was a galley proof of Philip Levine's *Red Dust*, which kayak press would soon publish. We were allowed to roam around, even into his workroom in the back, and saw the mock-ups for the next issue of *kayak*. Outside the house was surrounded by redwoods, bay laurel, and madrone, and a stream ran past. Inside Hitchcock presided indulgently over our reading. I left with a borrowed copy of Mark Strand's *Darker*, another discovery. I began to think of George Hitchcock as the man who lived in the House of Poetry.

Over the next four years I took a couple of poetry writing classes with George and a course on George Bernard Shaw. But most important and most fortunate for me was watching him and eventually helping him to edit *kayak*. In one of George's poetry writing classes I met Robert McDowell, who had a sophisticated gift for writing in a bitterly funny, yet lyrical surrealist style that George encouraged in his students. I could never write that way and I admired McDowell's ability to do something I could not. We became friends, and the two of us began to spend as much time around George as we could and as he would permit.

He allowed us to go through the enormous number of manuscripts that were submitted weekly to *kayak*. It was understood that we knew his taste in poetry and that we were to look for things that might please him. I found increasingly that George and I did not agree about poetry. He shared Robert Bly's view of W. H. Auden and I held Auden's view of Bly. When I tried to find common ground with him, he told me it was more interesting to talk about where and why we disagreed. I developed my own preferences and honed my critical skills in argument with George. Subsequently he published my first essays and book reviews in *kayak*.

By the time we graduated from college, Robert McDowell and I were devoted to George and his companion Marjorie Simon. Their house on Ocean View Avenue was a mecca for writers and poetry lovers. My wife Amy and I were married there, in the House of Poetry, on December 28, 1974.

The Reaper

After college, Amy and I moved to Iowa City where I attended the Writers' Workshop. Robert McDowell entered the M.F.A. program at Columbia. I studied with Donald Justice and Charles Wright. Robert studied with Richard Eberhart and William Jay Smith. When we left graduate school we began to find ourselves increasingly at odds with the general drift of contemporary poetry. Robert had been doing a good deal of experimentation with traditional forms. I was writing a kind of autobiographical narrative verse. The small, imagistic lyric that focused on the poet's private feelings seemed exhausted, and it looked as if American poetry was headed in the direction of looser, often abstract, self-referential meditation, in the style of Ashbery. Robert and I knew we didn't fit in with any of this.

In 1980 circumstances brought us within close proximity for the first time since college. Robert was teaching at Indiana State University, Evansville (now the University of Southern Indiana), and I was at Murray State University, in Murray, Kentucky. The two places were about three hours apart by car. We felt isolated, though we were lucky to have jobs. We were angry because we didn't see anyone else writing or praising the kind of poems we were writing or wanted to write. Robert had recently attended a poetry symposium called "After the Flood" at the Folger Shakespeare Library in Washington, D.C., and listened to Harold Bloom, Donald Davie, John Hollander, Richard Howard, Marjorie Perloff, and Stanley Plumly give papers on the state of the art. He didn't like anything he heard and took copious notes. He shared his notes with me and I didn't like it either. We decided to collaborate on a rebuttal.

We had written collaborations in college, usually parodies, but for George Hitchcock's class on George Bernard Shaw, we had contrived a terrible play "in the Shavian manner" that read more like a bad script for *Columbo*. Still, both of us had a good sense of how the other thought, and we knew how to write a sentence together.

Then, Robert proposed that we do more than write a rebuttal, but that we start a magazine. He had pitched the idea of a literary magazine to his dean who liked it and said he would provide access to the school's printing and binding services and some financial backing. My tendency in the face of most radical departures that I haven't thought of myself is to say "No." Robert has always been ready to take a risk. He drew a parallel between *kayak* and what he envisioned: we would edit and publish a magazine devoted to our views of what poetry should be. Those views were not particularly clear, except that we were against the going trend. We would excite and anger people. We would castigate our enemies. We would publish our friends.

Robert has a depth of Irish persuasion and a Teutonic drive that for all my skepticism and dourness I find hard to resist. I agreed to start a magazine.

We called it *The Reaper* and imagined the grim figure as a symbol of change as much as death. Along with an essay on "After the Flood," we wrote a manifesto, "Where *The Reaper* Stands," for the first issue.

The Reaper is the great deleter, the one who determines when the story ends.

Most contemporary poets have forgotten him. Navel gazers and mannerists, their time is running out. Their poems, too long even when they are short, full of embarrassing lines that "context" is supposed to justify, confirm the suspicion that our poets just aren't listening to their language anymore. Editors and critics aren't listening much, either. Despite their best, red-faced efforts, their favorite gods—inaccuracy, bathos, sentimentality, posturing, evasion—wither at the sound of *The Reaper's* whetstone singing . . . *The Reaper* maintains that both the accurate image and the narrative line, two determining factors of the poem's shapeliness, have been keenly honed and kept sharp by the poets included here, whereas many of their counterparts, forgetting these necessities, have wandered into a formless swamp where only the skunk cabbage of solipsistic meditation breeds, with its cloying flowers.

Robert McDowell (right) and Mark Jarman on the Ohio River with Evansville, Indiana, in the background, May 1982

It is *The Reaper's* ultimate aim to drain the bog of American writing by providing a format for poems and stories that take chances and make squeamish the editors of most other literary magazines with more fashionable "tastes." . . .

The poems collected here in issue number one, unmannered, tell stories *which their imagery serves.* Their authors know when to stop, which acknowledges the role of *The Reaper.* They believe, in fact, in death, which gives us only so much time to tell our story, defining its necessity and making the choice of imagery urgent.

Do contemporary writers think they can wander the marshland forever? *The Reaper's* scythe is already whispering at their heels!

After she read our manifesto, whenever *The Reaper* was mentioned, Amy would say "Pffft! Pffft!" for his whispering scythe. Another friend warned us that after you drained a marsh, all you were left with was mud.

In issue one of *The Reaper*, we didn't really have the kind of poem we described in our statement. But it became clear to us that we were interested in narrative poetry. It took several issues before we started finding and publishing the sort of narrative poems we began to describe in our essays. By the time we finished doing the magazine in 1989, we had published major narrative poems by many younger poets who were working in the form, including Rita Dove, Garrett Hongo, Andrew Hudgins, Sydney Lea, Mary Swander, and Chase Twichell. Our essays, always written from the point of view of our persona, the Reaper, included an evaluation of the unfortunate influence of Wallace Stevens, an appraisal of Robert Frost as America's greatest narrative poet, "How to Write a Narrative Poem: *A Reaper* Checklist," and "*The Reaper's* Non-negotiable Demands." We also made up an exchange of letters between Homer and Dante on the art of epic and an interview with a highly successful po-biz couple, Sean Dough and Jean Doh. Many of the cranky letters to the editor we wrote ourselves. We managed to infuriate all of the people we had hoped to and more. We had a blast.

We tried not to take ourselves too seriously, but our conversations about the role of narrative in poetry, the necessity that a poem have some story to tell and that poems be about other characters besides the poet himself led us both to experiment with ways of telling a

"My parents, Bo Dee and Donald," in the mid-1970s

story in a poem. The result for Robert was his first collection of poetry, *Quiet Money*, published by Holt in 1987. Its title poem tells the moving and remarkable story of a bootlegger who flies the Atlantic solo before Lindbergh and later helps during the investigation into the Lindbergh baby's kidnapping. My own collection of narrative experiments, *The Black Riviera*, was published in 1990 and dedicated to Robert.

The Reaper died in 1989, but its healthy offspring, Story Line Press, lives on. In 1985 the Nicholas Roerich Museum in New York City proposed that we begin a poetry series that they would fund. From that beginning Story Line Press has gone on with Robert as editor and publisher to do more than one hundred titles in poetry, fiction, nonfiction, drama, and translation.

Children

Many of the poems in my first four books are about childhood, either my own or my parents' or my grandparents.' They are usually narratives and based on stories I have been told or I have told myself. When I write about my own children, I have the feeling that I am writing about strangers whose stories I can only guess at, countries with secret histories. My sense of childhood's power and ultimate secrecy, which has always been strong, has been increased by recent events in my mother's life.

My mother, Bo Dee, was born in Harlingen, Texas. Her name is a respelling of Bodie, her mother's maiden name. One of her earliest memories is of a Mexican woman in her mother's kitchen patting dough between her hands to make tortillas. Another, after her parents moved to California, is of taking the bus with her mother across country to Wiggins, Mississippi, to visit her grandparents, Alonso and Allie Bodie. Her clearest childhood memory is of her parents' divorce. Four years old she sits on the running board of her father's Hudson and asks him why he has to leave. She also recalls a day, after her parents were divorced, when her father came to pick her up at school. She is certain that he was not supposed to do that. He took her on a long outing and introduced her to the woman who would become her stepmother. Though her own mother never commented on the incident, my mother is sure that her father kidnapped her.

In 1983, after thirty-three years of marriage, my father left my mother. Recently we discovered that she had been suffering for many years from an excess of cranial fluid, a condition known clinically as normal pressure hydrocephalis. It is an insidious disease that gradually results in incontinence, short-term memory loss, and loss of balance. An operation in 1992 restored some of her faculties, but the n.p.h. and her grief have undermined her physically and psychologically. It is rare that she speaks of any event later than our three years in Scotland. She often revisits her four-year-old self on the running board of her father's car, as he prepares to leave his wife and his daughter.

After spending most of her life on the West Coast, my mother now lives in Nashville, Tennessee, where Amy and I moved with our two children in 1983 when I took a teaching position at Vanderbilt University. Since my mother prefers to talk about what for me is the distant past, when we are together I am put in touch again and again with events from my own childhood. When I was growing up in Redondo, my family's great aid to memory was that my father, who was an excellent amateur photographer, had an extensive slide and film collection of places we had lived and traveled. I know this kept my memory of Scotland and Europe sharp and clear. Now that I no longer

With daughters Zoë (front) and Claire in Redondo Beach, June 1993

have access to those pictures (my father lives in California), my mother's dwelling on the past often serves the same purpose. Her memory will suddenly project an image or a story that brings me or my sisters back as children, sharply, clearly, and, because of her deep depression, painfully.

I know that in raising our children we repeat what our parents did in raising us. Our first child, Claire Marie, was born May 15, 1980, in Mission Viejo, California, when I was teaching as a guest lecturer at the University of California, Irvine. At the end of that year, we moved to Kentucky, where I took a job at Murray State University. Though totally coincidental, still this move in some ways parallels in reverse my parents' move from Kentucky, where I was born, back to California. Our second, Zoë Anne, was born December 16, 1982, in Murray. Amy has often taken the girls with her to Colorado where her mother now lives, and Claire and Zoë have both gone to visit their grandmother there alone, just as when she was growing up, Amy would travel by herself to Colorado to spend summers with her grandparents in Greeley. In 1989, I directed Vanderbilt's junior year abroad program in England at the University of Leeds. Claire and Zoë spent a year in English schools and became friends with the four wonderful children who lived next door. They came home to America sounding like a pair of Yorkshire lasses. Before we went to England, I prepared the children by reading to them from a collection of letters that my father had sent to his sister between 1958 and 1961 while we lived in Scotland. I was creating a parallel between my childhood and my children's.

Claire and Zoë have the good fortune to have a mother who is a superb musician, a lyric coloratura with a heartbreaking voice, who has made music a central part of their lives. Claire plays the piano and Zoë is a violinist in the Nashville Youth Repertory Orchestra. They are both readers and are able to carry on poised, intelligent conversations with adults. At the same time, our daughters, as the poet James Wright would say, are their own secrets. At present, those secrets have to do with being teenagers. And we can only guess at them, as we overhear phone conversations or the emanations from their Walkmans. Because of their parents' nostalgia for California, they seem to think of themselves as Californians. Maybe they will be someday. Pulling up roots and crossing the continent, even crossing the ocean, is a family tradition. But for now they are growing up in Nashville, Tennessee. They are Southerners.

Amy and I have spoken frankly about my mother in the children's presence, perhaps too frankly. When we pick up their Grandmother Bo Dee for church on Sunday morning, they look at her with concern and pity. I have seen it in their faces. My mother is always delighted to see her granddaughters. She takes her seat in the car and begins almost at once to reminisce for them about Scotland or her own childhood memories of the South, in Harlingen or Wiggins. I think she will be an important part of Claire and Zoë's memory of childhood.

Faith

One evening in early November, 1973, during my senior year at University of California, Santa Cruz, I was on the phone to Robert McDowell when a person I had never met entered the house where I lived with a couple who were also students. She had come by to pick up the woman who was making costumes for a student production of *Jacques Brel Is Alive and Well and Living in Paris*. I remember that Robert asked what was wrong, because I had stopped talking.

The stranger was Amy Kane, one of the stars of the production. We had moved in the same circles in college for three years without meeting. I attended her first performance and made a point of introducing myself afterwards backstage. I attended the rest of the performances, too. Years later, when she was asked by an interviewer why she finally agreed to go out with me, she said, "I couldn't resist such devotion."

I don't believe we are destined to find our lifemate. I know too many people who never have. Maybe we only meet them if we're lucky, and perhaps for some, like my parents, it is not lucky in the end. But I believe when Amy Kane walked into that student house that night and I saw her and stopped talking, that I had an experience of the kind of luck that W. H. Auden called grace. Not to put too fine a theological point on it, I believe when I met Amy that something greater than myself but also deep within me said, "You have been given a gift."

Amy left college to come with me to graduate school. In Iowa City she worked as a waitress and in social services to support us. She also started taking lessons in classical voice. When I was appointed to my first teaching job at Indiana State University in Evansville, she entered the University of Evansville on a scholarship and earned a B.A. in music. In 1978 when I received a National Endowment for the Arts grant in poetry and quit my job at Evansville, we went to live in Italy where Amy studied singing at the Conservatorio di Morlacchi in Perugia. Today she sings opera, oratorio, and gives solo recitals throughout the United States and England.

In 1978 I had not been in a church for nearly seven years and had no interest at all in going to one. I nursed my father's bitter experience in Redondo like a grudge. Amy and I were living in Todi, in Umbria, and she had joined *il Coro di Todi* which sang regularly in the region's churches. One Sunday when Amy was singing with *il Coro* at San Fortunato, the Fransiscan church in the town, I attended. I had been reading Henry Adams's *Mont Saint*

Michel and Chartres and been moved by his depiction of how medieval Christians gathered in their churches, these great centers of power, to worship the Virgin. I realized on that Sunday that I was standing among many of the citizens of the town almost as Adams imagined them—there were no pews—and listening to them respond at places in the service, like the Gloria Patri and the doxology, that I recognized from my own upbringing. It began to occur to me at an inarticulate level that in my estrangement from the church and from God I was denying an essential part of myself.

In 1986, we had been in Nashville three years. I had tenure and Amy had begun teaching voice at Vanderbilt's music school. The girls had been attending the church where Amy sang in the choir, and she decided that it was time we all started going to church someplace together. Her decision was not religious, it had everything to do with our family. But for me it was a religious decision. It required admitting to myself that I still had a faith, complicated not only by what had happened to my father but, after my parents' divorce, by what my father had done to my mother. We decided to go together to a church in my denomination.

And things have become even more interesting and complicated in the intervening years. Amy is Jewish but was raised with very little sense of her religion. She and our daughter Zoë have joined the Reformed Temple in Nashville. Amy sings in the temple choir. We are all still members of Vine Street Christian Church, but usually only my daughter Claire, who has been baptized, my mother, and I attend. Amy also sings in the choir at Christ Church Episcopal. On Sunday morning, when Zoë goes to Hebrew school, we head in several ecumenical directions.

As an epigraph to *The Rote Walker* I quoted two lines from John Logan's poem "The Spring of the Thief": "When we speak of God, / Is it God we speak of?" I used to say flippantly that the answer to that profound question was "Yes and no." I no longer think the answer is flippant. It is just as profound as the question. When I met Amy Kane I began, without knowing it, a return to faith, not the faith of my fathers, exactly, but a faith *in* fathers and mothers, too, for that matter. It was a faith in custom and culture, the society that made me who I am, and the family that loved me. And it was a recognition that there was something greater behind these things.

In a little autograph book I owned as a child in Scotland and which I still have, my father wrote, from Micah 6:8: " . . . and what does the Lord require of you but to do justice, and to love kindness and to walk humbly with your God?" That passage has never failed to move me, even when I did not know who my God was. At this point in my life, with the help and love of my wife and children, I am finding out.

BIBLIOGRAPHY

Poetry:

North Sea, Cleveland State University Poetry Center, 1978.

The Rote Walker, Carnegie-Mellon University Press, 1981.

Far and Away, Carnegie-Mellon University Press, 1985.

The Black Riviera, Wesleyan University Press, 1990.

Iris, Story Line Press, 1992.

Questions for Ecclesiastes, David R. Godine, Inc., forthcoming.

M. T. Kelly

1946-

Until my father died just after my eighth birthday, and for a few years after that, we lived in an area of Toronto known as the Junction.

I was born on November 30, 1946, and trains were a factor in my childhood, even if I could not see, nor do I remember hearing them, from the one-bedroom apartment over a cigar store that I shared with my mother and father: 3103 Dundas Street West.

One of the memories I have of my father is his taking me to the Lampton roundhouse and putting me up in the cab of a steam locomotive. In a hallucinatory way I even remember being in one moving: fire, and the light of a very bright day, the men shifting about, a platform swaying. To this day trains reassure me in a profound way: I explain it now by describing trains as great benign beasts, monsters who will not hurt you: all this associated with a father.

There was anxiety too about going to the roundhouse, because we just walked in there and I feel, even then, that I worried about it. But as my mother has said, my father could "turn on the charm," everyone liked him, everyone liked Milt, and I do know that is one of the reasons we could walk in there and have me lifted into the cab. My dad in a suit, my dad who could talk to anyone. Many years later I was told how he even had Ernie the landlord "eating out of his hand."

That apartment was important. It was only two stories, and as you entered our unit there was a bathroom to your right, a long hall with a living room and a bedroom side by side facing the streetcars of Dundas; opposite them a large kitchen leading out to the back and an iron fire escape enclosing a U-shaped court and facing "the lane." I once tried to go back and look at the place but was met by a man nearly insane with anger and suspicion who would not let me in. I saw significance in the man's rudeness; he was an immigrant, and an echo from childhood came back: the "Maltese had driven

M. T. Kelly, 1995

us out." The man, however, was simply a paranoid jerk. Had I gotten into the place, the well-known but still constantly surprising recognition—not so much of things being smaller but, what is harder to acknowledge—of you being bigger would have applied. In the end it is what happened then and what I remember that has had such power.

I had no room of my own but a cot at the foot of my parents' bed, beside the wall, near the door. After my father died, the cot disappeared and I shared my mother's bed. I shared it before he died, as I remember being in bed with my mother and his coming home one night and putting a wrestling hold, a leg lock, on her. He must have been drinking, and the kind of joking he intended was the kind that went with a grin with a cigar stuck in it. I remember her whisper, "He'll kill us, he'll kill us," her nightgown, and a shriek.

Another time I was frightened was when my father sat on the side of my cot and I knew he had been drinking and he sang, I think it was, "Auld Lang Syne" and would not stop when my mother told him to, and the next day my father knelt and apologized to me in the kitchen: the kitchen with its yellowish walls where he used to have "doubles" and "singles"—bread folded over, or kept in slices and dipped in tea. The kitchen where he carried a fridge up the fire escape, and slapped me one time for having different coloured socks on; it was the place I left to go and buy steak for one of my mother's boyfriends after my father died. My mother was struggling with money and I was very aware of it, and when I came back with cheap round steak instead of T-bone,

and this was a chance for T-bone, there was laughter.

When my father apologized, I don't know if I was ashamed for him, or sorry, or aggrieved. It was complicated.

When he died, my father was a "customer's man" for a brokerage company. He had had many jobs. He knew some rich men and I met one of them. My mother had started a company called "Bridal China and Crystal" before he died and carried on with it after his death. She later got a job in a brokerage office herself, selling over the phone. There was never much money, and I was always aware of it.

In that apartment I waited for Santa Claus, seeing yellow light on snow on a deserted Dundas Street one Christmas eve, and it was looking down the long hall of that apartment, coming home with my mother happy after Christmas shopping, the freshness of the outside still on us, that I saw my father dialing for an ambulance that would take him away to die.

In writing this I am able to recall, perhaps for the first time, how sick he looked: am I half imagining, half seeing, how his always large forehead stood out? At last I deduce, over forty years later, that he was small from cancer; until this moment he had always seemed big. And what surprised and alarmed me because it disrupted things—his fumbling at the phone, looking at us with what I thought then was unnecessary crisis—I see now as shock and desperation. He knew he was going to die. Years later I saw a letter to him from his relatives in New York, which I think talked about his needing a miracle—it acknowledged his condition. But that moment: his eyes, looking at us. They were brown, dark, so big. I had forgotten his eyes. He and my mother used to talk and sing about eyes, hers were blue: "Beautiful beautiful brown eyes." My father's mouth, the thin Irish frog mouth: grim. So familiar now. How I remember things about my father, the optimism I had to make myself feel a sunny September as he drummed his freckled hand on the arm of the car seat—we had a new car, a '54 Ford. We were waiting outside a hospital. His hand.

So much comes back. Holding his pant leg tight when he asked me how I would feel if he went away on a trip.

Being in Grade Three and looking at the clock and thinking that now, this time of the morning, he was having his operation.

"With my parents, Sybil and Milton Kelly, outside my maternal grandmother's home," 1950

He got sick. I took the turkey carcass in to have him examine it with me after Christmas dinner: "Get it out, get it out, get it out, get it out!"

After all those years I conjure up so much, the details: his pyjamas and oxblood slippers. It is uncanny how the moment comes back.

That same phone table was where my mother sat when she told me my father had died. It was a brilliant January day; somehow I thought I was going to receive news that he was having a bath. Then crying and crying.

Writing this has allowed me to see that time and place; almost to re-inhabit my small body. It is a profoundly uncomfortable feeling, and I must reassure myself that I can leave some of the past behind. I must also not assume the connections I make will have the resonance for others they do for me; but writing is an act of faith in others' imagination, and I hope the brush strokes I make in this difficult art of autobiography will have some of the effect they can have in literature.

Baths. Because kettles had to be heated for bath water in that flat—and one of the few times I was left alone with my father he gave me a bath, then punished me—baths were significant. I recall the knobs of my mother's spine when I sat behind her in the bathtub and bathed with her. So many of my frantic feelings, so much of the agitation of that place, along with the grief and terror, come back. I remember walking down that same, to a child, long long corridor after the bath with my father. He was behind me and swinging his belt; lying across my parents' bed; the dim room. How that blue room would echo.

Well before I was nine, I know I was sick of the Junction apartment and neighbourhood, that it had changed, was over for me, and was glad when we moved, although to another one-bedroom apartment, this time a high rise in Parkdale. The grief of my father's death, so intense, would last and last, and aspects of it must last still. First, I formed an imaginary club of always victorious heroes, using his initials, the MTK's. And when I heard "Danny Boy" I would weep. But I grew and when I was about twelve or thirteen got my own bed and my own room. The numbers of the apartments where we lived are like names to me, and I can tell them over and over again: at 60 Tyndall Avenue in Parkdale we went from

Father and son, High Park,
Easter Sunday, 1952

apartment 302, one-bedroom, to 708, two-bedroom, to 901, two-bedroom. It was the same building my mother's boyfriend lived in. I did not live in a house until I was an adult.

Parkdale and the Junction were different neighbourhoods. Parkdale is located in the west end of Toronto and used to be connected to Lake Ontario through Sunnyside, an area south of Parkdale which served as an amusement centre. This all ended when the Gardiner Expressway's great trench cut the neighbourhood off from the lake. Parkdale was also one of the first areas of the city to experience massive high-rise development. The Junction was an old neighbourhood, one-story apartments over stores facing a busy street. No trees. Threadbare. Poor, really. From the Victorian to '40s architecture. Brick. There were houses on the streets off Dundas, some working class on the British model, some finer. Big houses on High Park Avenue, two blocks away.

It is difficult to say the Junction was Anglo-Saxon, but as I got a bit older it was certainly emphasized that "the Maltese" were moving in and changing things. But I was changing myself, very much outgrowing the place. How glad I was when we moved, when I was in Grade Five.

There seem to me now to be certain themes in both the Junction and Parkdale that give a feeling of the places. But these themes are also about my own psychic geography as well.

One of the themes was fighting. The Junction may have been more poor than tough, but my father had boxing gloves and he brought over a boy to box, or fight, with me in the living room. I half remember the chesterfield, the furniture: I remember the swarm and punching. It was with a smaller, or younger, boy, and I felt guilty about winning. There was also a fight where the courtyard joined the lane with someone "tougher," that my father watched from the top of the fire escape and did not interfere in. I wish he would have. I vaguely recall conversations about me doing okay and that it was understandable that I did not cry until I walked up the fire escape to get near him—but I didn't like the whole thing. The names of the boys I fought and played with are clear, I can recite them, like the ringing of a bell, but I will not list them here. After he died I found a book of my father's about self-defence that had in it the technique of gouging out an eye.

In Parkdale there were fights as well, it was very important. My best friend there was Jack Moore, from Cape Breton, who died violently. I met him when I beat his brother up. Jack came and beat me up. I went to fight him again, having read books of animals fighting to inspire myself, but made friends with him instead, and he didn't admit, or know, it was me he had beat up. We pretended we were "tied" in fighting. I didn't have to fight the guys he had "taken." The permutations of this system were unending, but I remember them. I wrote about Parkdale and its fighting, and glue sniffing, and ambience, in my play *The Green Dolphin.*

So much of where we have been and of what has happened to us we recreate as legends or myths whose meaning is received; part of a way in which we see and explain ourselves. I know the stories I tell, and have told of my old neighbourhood, are like that. Our narrative may not always take in other dimensions. For instance, Parkdale was certainly dis-

Mother and son, outside De La Salle Catholic School, 1957

tinctive in Toronto in the sixties for the emphasis it placed on rhythm and blues music. I once wrote:

> In spite of the devastation, the denizens of Parkdale have always had a special sense of themselves as a neighbourhood, which sense continues to this day. In the mid-sixties, Parkdale supported a subculture which many participants thought to be unique. While other teenagers looked to the Beatles, "the boys" (and girls) of Parkdale looked to black rhythm and blues and listened to Buffalo radio stations, such as WUFO. They dressed in clothes which, as one of their girlfriends commented, "made them look like apprentice pimps": stovepipe pants, silk and wool suits. They carried umbrellas. "The boys" had "Twist and Shout" by the Isley Brothers years before it was recorded by the Beatles. No one had a car, and the centre of this world was The Green Dolphin Restaurant.

This was true enough, but there is much more to it than that, and it was not as special as I thought. It was the people that were unique, not the sociology; if anything, what lights up a place is a certain timelessness in history, its ghosts, combined with nature, or what remains of it, and the present.

Naturally I made a legend of my father, and my mother encouraged me. She could never marry again, she would say, I was so sensitive. Without giving away too much, it is fair to say I became very special to her, a kind of husband—we had a "special" relationship, while she also had boyfriends.

Later I found out things about my parents that were surprising, not like the legend or the terrible grief of a child, but of interest.

At his death my father was fifty-eight, at least twenty years older than my mother. He could do "a hundred push-ups," swell out his chest so that milk bottles could be placed on it. He did this at parties, I was told. And every picture I have of myself in grade school shows a child, a year ahead in school because of his November birthday, small for his age, with his chest puffed out like a pouter pigeon. My father dressed "immaculately," and I do remember the smooth, nearly chamois-like quality of a beige sports shirt he had. Something of that shirt, a sliver of memory, still has in it weeping and love. He smoked White Owl cigars. He didn't want to take me, and only did once, to the women's softball he watched at Sunnyside in the evenings, because all I wanted to do was eat. I think now what else is new? All kids are like that when young.

Some research I have done (unlike the stories of relatives or my mother's "they came from the County Claire" in a rising voice, or "they came from the Isle of Mann") revealed that my father's paternal grandfather came from Ireland and settled in Markham Township, northeast of Toronto. My father's father was born there in the countryside—there were five children, two born in Ireland, three in Canada, to William Kelly, Labourer, RC, and his wife Bridget—but moved to Toronto quickly. I know very little about him. I think he worked for the transit company. My father's mother's maiden name was McInerney.

My father himself was born in the east end of Toronto in 1897, Milton Thomas Kelly, one of eight children, two of whom were stillborn. He had been married once before he met my mother and had lived in New York for a time. As a child I visited that city where I still had

Irish relatives and remember walking through a tough neighbourhood with my father. Again he wore a suit. There is a picture of this. I'm sure I was told to walk slowly and not to be anxious, not to worry. I'm sure I worried. I remember my father as big.

From this first marriage, which I didn't learn about until I was nearly twenty, I have a half brother named Ray. He was born in 1922 and I have never had any contact with him. The information was kept from me, I'm quite sure, so that the ideal I had of my father, and was encouraged to have, would not be spoiled.

Once my father had separated from his first wife (Ruby Smail, the spelling may be wrong), he came back to Toronto with the son, who was shifted about to live among my father's sisters. That must not have worked because eventually the boy went back to New York with his mother. My own mother saw this child once, my father asked her to find him in New York, and confronting Ray at a school yard she asked him if he wanted to see his father. Ray asked her "Why?" I am told Ray's mother moved after that and my father could never find the boy. A connection broken.

On his return my father lived in Toronto with different sisters, Margaret, or "Ummie," or Rhea, and he was living with the youngest,

In the kitchen, 1956

Doris or "Doe," and her husband and children when he met my mother.

My mother has always been extremely secretive about her age, but she was born in St. Catharines, Ontario, one of three children, all girls. Her father, Harold Preston Vores (1880–1945), had attended Cambridge and lost much of his inheritance, and in Canada, among other things, ran a candy store. He married my grandmother, Lucy Annie Jones (1879–1965), daughter of a stonemason, a skilled craftsman, in Toronto in the late 1800s. My grandfather was a member of the Masonic order. It is on his tombstone. There is a genealogy on my mother's father's side, going back to John Preston of Norwich, England, 1587–1628. The first name listed in the genealogy is Thomas Preston "of Norwich, published *Canabosis,* 1570." Another source has him listed as "Cambridge, England, 1537–98, published *A lamentable Tragedie, mixed full of pleasant mirth, containing the life of Cambises, King of Persia* (1569)." Canabosis and Cambises are so close, as are the dates, 1569 and 1570, I am sure it is the same person. My mother is much interested in such things, though I was deeply aware that her boyfriends, after my father's death, were not aristocrats.

I looked for father figures and didn't have too much luck. But at Lake Simcoe, north of Toronto, which I visited with my mother and her boyfriend Lorne Scobie, I remember being allowed to sit on the dock and fish with Steve Rocco, an ex-boxer and bookie. We talked. He had contended for the flyweight championship of the world. He fought Frenchie Belanger. He'd owned the Elmgrove Hotel in Parkdale. He didn't get nervous in the ring—which I found hard to understand. This only happened a few times, but I will never forget Mr. Rocco.

Scobie became the man in my mother's life; "Uncle Scobe," who bragged he was only a truck driver but a millionaire. He did not appreciate "perfessers—perfessers a' nothin'!" like me. The stage was set for many dramas with the ghost of my father, Uncle Scobe, and my mother's talk of my sensitivity. There were instructions on how to manipulate Scobie—such as calling him "Uncle Scobe"—and who I was informed had very clean underwear for a bachelor. A shorthand I use to characterize my mother's and my interactions with Scobie is jesters dancing around the court of an insane king, who would rouse himself occasionally to mutter, "I don't give a shit."

We, my mother especially, would become more hysterical and frenzied, yet for all her hysteria she was absolutely immovable and unchangeable in her methods and purpose. My mother had what I referred to as Nietzschean will. Implacable. She did not listen. She got her way.

After Scobie's death I came upon one of his business cards: Lorne (Buff) Scobie, with telephone numbers on one side and a joke so vulgar on the other that it can't be published here. Scobie died of cirrhosis of the liver, he was up to forty ounces of rye a day. He once bought one of my girlfriends "hot pants," and my mother, who had hot pants, an ankle bracelet. He referred to my mother as "little." Once I came upon a note of my father's that he wrote to my mother: "A PRESENT for the best little girl in all the world."

The drama of childhood is only part of the picture. Very early I went to an imaginative world. This was the world of, at first, knights and armour, and trains to balance it, but then, with great strength, animals and wilderness. Not that we had a cottage or that I went to camp, or ever experienced the wild—there may have been one visit to Georgian Bay to a cousin's cottage where my father made a battleship out of a two-by-four, and there was a story of how I burnt myself on coals at a Great Lakes beach—but my imagined experience was very real. I can remember discussing why I liked Ernest Thompson Seton's work over that of Sir Charles G. D. Roberts with Miss Alice Kane, the librarian at Lisgar Library in Parkdale. That kind of library is gone now, serious libraries with well-made hardbacks in open stacks. How I remember the way some of the books were made, how they looked and felt and were illustrated. The world of the imagination, and of the imagination combined with reading, was so powerful.

I also had a very good teacher early, in Grade Four. After my father's death I was sent to a Catholic school, De La Salle, staffed mostly by violent, strap-wielding Christian brothers. This was the Catholic order which figured in the extreme sexual abuse of children at Mount Cashel orphanage in Newfoundland. But Brother Richard, in Grade Four, was not like that; as I remember him, he was extremely aloof, and orderly, and exactly what I needed. I had a warmer teacher in Grade Five, Brother Terrance, perhaps the best year I ever had academically.

*"With my uncle Willie and my father,
at my First Communion"*

I remember reading a high school history text, *Ancient and Medieval History* right through in that grade, and I read it with enormous pleasure. It was also as early as Grade Four and Five that stories of the Jesuit martyrs sparked my life-long interest in native peoples. And I had been to the Martyrs' Shrine early in life: the broken wall in a farmer's field, piled stones, all that was left of the old mission, well before restoration.

There was also the lane behind the apartment building, empty, and I recall aspects of its silence on a summer afternoon, cinders catching the sun. If there were children's cries in that place, they are faint now, as of birds in the wind.

There was a musty garage, and garage roofs that gave access to trees in someone's backyard, climbed furtively. There was a broken fence, black mud and puddles, the light in the dead coal. I would go on bike-riding adventures on St. John's, where trees overarched, oily leaves from dark maples, great black trunks indifferent and comforting. The memories are mostly of summer there, but snow as well, no March light that would figure so prominently in my life in Toronto in later years. What there was of spring was the space between the trees in High Park before the grass had colour, spring

clothes, even the idea of which still gives me a headache, and talk of the Easter parade; empty, open, dusty spring, no lavender light, no sense of possibilities that would come later. Some of these memories may have led to what I have written about and felt, to what I finally saw in the new green on tundra hills, to the comfort I took: peace.

I had a few dogs, read dog stories, and one dog in particular, which did not last long and was returned to the pound, seems significant to my imaginative world. I named him Buck, after Jack London's *Call of the Wild*, which I read early. I used to fight him in an obsessive, repetitive way in the downstairs corridor of the apartment building. That tunnel, dark, all of it shiny as if even the walls were waxed, hardwood floor and linoleum, became a complete world. I was also influenced by Roderick Haig-Brown's *Panther*, but what was significant was an incredible, isolate, lonely interacting with the dog. There was feeling-sorry-for-myself sweetness, combined with a lonely yearning; as well as a deliberate craziness, going into another space or dimension. It wouldn't be accurate, however, to say that this was the beginning of fantasy, as expert as I would become at fantasy, because for all the isolation, the time out against the world, just me and the animal, I was looking for some kind of real connection.

The dog that we did manage to keep the longest was heartbreakingly stolen from me when I tied him up outside the Riverdale Zoo, to which I had gone alone. Animals.

The first poem I ever wrote and published was titled "Riverdale Zoo Is Closing," full of intense compassion for a psychotic polar bear.

My first literary experience—it's an inexact label but comes close, perhaps I should say self-conscious epiphany—occurred in the corner of the De La Salle library. This library stressed such books as the Hardy Boys mysteries, there wasn't much, but they had *The Old Man and the Sea* by Ernest Hemingway, perhaps thinking it was a safe book. I clearly remember holding the book and reading the opening. That moment. Here, I must have felt, was dignity. Later I argued with my mother about the part where the fisherman urinates over the side of the boat; but any shock value to me must have surely been that here was life—here was how to be in the world. A definition I have of literature that I came to like

The author, 1987

was that it was good advice touched with a breath of beatitude. I had thought it was something like that very very early: how to live.

Because of my particular background, a lot could be made of this: the search for "a way to be" in the world explains, in one way, my interest in native people (how did they do it, how did native people do it?), my interest in the searching aspects in the poetry of Yeats, in "exploration" writers such as David Thompson and Samuel Hearne. I have always responded to clarity; the prose of the eighteenth century I found much easier than great Victorian novels. My background could be used to explain my strong response to aspects of the Bible when I finally got to it, having read John Dominic Crossan's *The Historical Jesus:* the echo of the word abba, father: the sense of compassion that was completely absent from my religious training at De La Salle—as Catholics we never got near anything like that. I did not look at the Bible until more than half my life had passed. I had looked at Northrop Frye's *The Great Code* well before the Bible.

Is literature to be equated with religion? They're about the same things when they're at their best, but sweeping connections like this, relations to one person's particular circumstances, does not get it. The response is much more than that and cannot be explained here.

At De La Salle I again had good instincts and knew it was time to get out. At De La Salle there was a football team; at the public high school, Parkdale Collegiate, there was swimming, gymnastics, and especially track and field. At De La Salle there was a drum and bugle corps run by Brother Xavier, nearly psychotic in his explosive violence; at Parkdale there was a symphony orchestra. And Parkdale was co-educational. The usual injustices also occurred at De La Salle: I was denied a prize because another boy's mother was on the woman's auxiliary.

Parkdale was a better school than De La Salle, even though, because of prejudice against Catholics' schools, I was put back a year. There was a tendency for my marks to vary from the high nineties to the twenties at both schools. Later of course I settled down, again with the help of two very good teachers. I wrote a story that tries to create some of the feeling of what went on at Parkdale titled "All That Wild Wounding." It is the first story in my collection *Breath Dances between Them*.

Parkdale also gave me the chance to participate in track and field, and running gave me those two great aids: structure and order, something to do, not "just go and sit in the restaurant after school and eat chips and gravy and a coke." Running is something I like to do to this day. I was athlete of the year at Parkdale in 1967.

My imagining Canada may have lapsed at Parkdale, although in my earlier years there I did play "wolf lope," chasing down other kids on the Gardiner Expressway construction site as it was being built. The old, helpful pattern returned, and I knew it was time to leave the neighbourhood after seven years of high school. I did not want to live at home, "go to U of T then come home and hang out at the restaurant," but perhaps I didn't want to leave completely, so went to live in residence in Toronto, at Glendon College Campus of York University, "a small, liberal arts college," with an emphasis on Canada and current affairs. I was very conscious that a smaller school would be the best for me. And after my first year of university I got my first real job, with the help of a Parkdale history teacher: working up north for the Canex Aerial Exploration. Again, I have written about this. My work, of course, is imagined, but, of course, writers use their lives. And, again, it is complicated, but that first trip to the north is more than touched on in my book *The Ruined Season*.

I can remember vividly, before going away on that first trip, lying on the floor of Scobie's apartment in the dark listening to songs of the north, songs such as "Mush on You Malamutes" and "The Spell of the Yukon." Sentimental, gravelly voiced country and western music in the dusky apartment evoking a spruce skyline against twilight. I was happy.

It is difficult to say when I decided to become a writer. My mother had great ambitions for me but they were not literary. As a child I was told I could not be a train engineer but was going to become "president of the Canadian Pacific Railway." Later she would announce in a public way, her lipstick wet, "international law, or perhaps diplomacy." I bought into this,

in a strange way, in high school, reading such books as Howard Fast's *Power*, and thinking of myself as a tycoon, and saying such phrases as "splendid isolation" to myself. But as I have shown, literary influences were early and pervasive. Until the experience with Hemingway I tended to read historical novels, such as those of Thomas B. Costain. One of my favourite writers was Mika Waltari, author of *The Egyptian* and *For My Great Folly*, which featured tragic dying, the veins of legs cut to stain a robe the royal purple. I read and even wrote to Mary Renault, author of *The King Must Die* and *The Bull from the Sea*. I read Kenneth Roberts's *Northwest Passage*, lurking in the bushes of De La Salle, escaping. The reading helped. In Grade Nine a composition of mine was read aloud to the class, and I was shocked because all I had done was imitate either Charles G. D. Roberts or Jack London. In high school a great English teacher had us write every week, and I liked it.

A turning point was certainly in university when I wrote articles for *Pro Tem*, the Glendon paper, and *Excalibur*, the York paper. My first published piece was an interview with boxer George Chuvalo. I went on to B. B. King, Joni Mitchell, Phil Ochs. I worked hard on the pieces, still recalling what I wrote about Phil Ochs: "He was a baggy panted poet singing about the Universe ablaze, that's what mattered to me, not what cause his talent cried for." The political content of this remark is not what is important, listen to the sound. It was the sixties, but I was not a participating radical. The class I came from, and my home, had something to do with why. I was determinedly literary, however, which made me much more out of place than those with political involvement.

It was good to write those pieces about those people, to craft them, to have my name in print.

Again, the high school English teacher was in my mind when I wrote (and he was radical, son of an establishment family, extremely macho, totally competitive in all aspects of life, but encouraging to me), and he was in my mind when I thought of what I would do after university. It was fateful, as I had some of his talk in mind about writers writing, about how Hemingway had been a journalist. After those pieces, and some poems, I started to write a novel. I still have a copy of the novel, *My*

Vegetable Love. It remains unpublished, though my first published literary piece was an excerpt from that book and was published in *Northern Journey,* edited by Fraser Sutherland. I published this piece after I had left school. There were no creative writing classes in those days, but a sympathetic professor let me take a fourth-year thesis course and write my novel as the thesis.

And so I was a writer, and I have been all my life. I have had a number of jobs, but writing has always been at the centre.

There have been themes and, especially when I was younger, I went on what could be called literary pilgrimages; to the grave of William Blake, in London, England, to the Sligo of William Butler Yeats. Though Faulkner was not a big influence, I drove down to Mississippi. With my first car a friend and I drove to Ipswich, Massachusetts, and, unannounced and uninvited, visited John Updike who asked us, as we were leaving, if we'd like Salinger's address.

In England I went to Stratford on Avon and remember the quality of light over the fields at twilight. I bicycled to Oxford and looked into W. H. Auden's rooms. In Cuba I sought out Hemingway's house. On my second visit to Scotland I went to the Orkney Islands to see where the Hudson Bay ships had watered and to visit George Macay Brown. I loved Samuel Hearne's book *A Journey to the Northern Ocean, 1769–1772,* and retraced some of his route in the wilderness east of Great Slave Lake, publishing an article on it in *Saturday Night Magazine: The Land Before Time.* In Prince Edward County in southern Ontario, I drove past poet Al Purdy's place. Poet Gwen MacEwen, and Wayland Drew, author of *The Wabeno Feast,* influenced canoe routes. I don't make journeys like that anymore, but a couple of years ago, returning from a canoe gathering in Minnesota, I stopped at Hemingway's boyhood home in Oak Park, Illinois, and in the cold, dark, November evening thought of his boyhood. I remain interested in David Thompson, author of *Travels in Western North America 1784–1812,* and someday would like to follow some of his route.

In my twenties especially I was interested in Irish literature, or perhaps, more generally, Celtic culture. It may have been an attempt to connect with my father, because on my first visit to Dublin I remember saying aloud, and writing back home, "Everyone here looks like Uncle Willie." (William, Bill, Kelly was my father's older brother.) I cycled around Ireland, and one time led a literary tour of Ireland on a bicycle.

My first job was that of trainee writer for trade magazines.

That was followed by editorial work for *Who's Who in Canada* to get money for a trip to Europe, where I quickly tired of travelling and went to live in Edinburgh with my friend who was at university. On returning to Canada I got a job as city hall reporter for the *Moose Jaw Times Herald* in Moose Jaw, Saskatchewan.

These writing jobs could be seen as following naturally from my desire to be a writer, but that is not quite true. I almost had a job as a teacher, first, in Labrador, then in Watson Lake in the Yukon. I have often wondered what my life would have been like had I gotten those jobs. The one in Labrador fell through as it was a last minute thing and—the symbolism is heavy-handed—my mother had a D and C (dilation and curettage) and the gynecologist called me with all the details, and I had to visit her in hospital at the time, and missed the call. I just missed out on the Watson Lake job. What probably would have happened had I landed

Lynn King, "mother of our sons," 1991

"Our two sons Jay (elder) and Max," 1990

those jobs in the north is what happened to me in Moose Jaw. It is a pattern that I have seen in most of my life and is instructive.

My job up north with Canex after my first year of university was influential, so much so that on returning to my liberal arts university I even phoned the Halibury School of Mines to inquire about a career. More dreaming, but a deep interest. Anyway, the following summer I found a similar job with Inco, in the bush near Timmins. On arriving, I looked around at the rainy weather, the bare spring bush, and went right back to Toronto to a summer of being near a girl and driving a cab, a terrible summer. I left a perceived chaos that scared me to a chaos that was familiar.

This could be labeled a panic attack, but that doesn't quite get it. Similar behaviour had happened as a child: on the one overnight I attempted on a YMCA trip—I went back to the infirmary, claiming to be sick.

This quality of what I call bolting could be sometimes applied to my relationships with friends and peers. It might be explained in one way as an ambivalent, edgy relationship to having to perform. But then I was asked to entertain early in life, and, with warring feelings, did it. A shade of this has manifested itself in coming to terms with being a public figure as I have had success with my writing. It can be difficult. One thing is certain, solitude is essential.

I didn't bolt from my first job as a reporter in Saskatchewan, but a strike at the paper put me out of work. This is not to deny the early signs of dissolution at that job, manifested in drinking. And I certainly went quickly back to Toronto. I was hardly in the west for the fall (later examined in *I Do Remember the Fall*, my first novel). Returning to Toronto was one of the low points of my life, but the despair there must have seemed comfortingly familiar. With aspects of the terror which is at times at the heart of my being, who knows how long I would have lasted at any of the other jobs, such as the one in Labrador, had I gotten them? Yet through all of this writing, and literature, was a constant. Whatever was going on, I sent the manuscript of *My Vegetable Love* out—and I remember a book I was reading back then. At home, very depressed, I wrote a poem "Mother," later published in *Country You Can't Walk In.*

After returning from the prairies I applied to teacher's college, on the surface telling myself, "I can't write at night if I write all day," but also looking for stability.

Eventually I taught one year, from September 1976 to June 1977, in Levack, north of Sudbury.

Before I went to Levack, after my year at teacher's college, I lived with my girlfriend and wrote *I Do Remember the Fall*. In late August I realized Marilyn had kept me and that I owed her, and so took the first teaching job I applied for, which was the Levack one. Writing was the priority: I had to get the book done before I looked for jobs.

We moved to the north, and while there I sent my book out. It was accepted by a small press publisher, and I quit my job to return to Toronto for my thirties. I had given myself an artificial deadline of thirty to publish a novel, actually I think I was thirty-one, but I am sure I would have kept writing anyway. *I Do Remember the Fall* was a finalist in the *Books in Canada* Best First Novel of the year awards, then came out as a paperback, and this allowed me to get a column for the *Globe and Mail*—"Between the Sexes." An article would appear by me, then one by a woman.

I wrote in my thirties, publishing two more novels, and a book of poems, and the play. Through my column I met Lynn King, whom I interviewed, then became partners with. We have two sons. I wrote *A Dream like Mine*, which won the Governor General's award for fiction and was made into a movie, *Clearcut*, and has been translated into other languages. I was a busy father.

As I approached forty, I got a job teaching creative writing at York University one day a week, which I do know took away from my own writing—teaching is extremely tiring for me emotionally. The loss of that job worried me, but one day's teaching meant two days lost to my novel, one to teach and the other to recover. I was left with three days a week to write, and it took a bit too long for me to publish *Out of the Whirlwind* which, like *A Dream like Mine*, was the culmination of a lifetime's interest.

During the late eighties and nineties I was also a contributing interviewer to TV Ontario's literary show "Imprint." This gave me the chance to talk to many writers, and some of these conversations were published in the book *One on One: The Imprint Interviews*.

In my late thirties I corresponded with, then met, Alex Hall of Fort Smith, Northwest Territories (NWT), with whom I would canoe part of the route of Samuel Hearne, and also the Back and Thelon Rivers. He made it possible for me to visit the barren lands of northern Canada. Teacher's college had given me a prac-

tical interest in canoeing because of a course I did not want to take, Outdoor Education; again, never having experienced anything remotely like it as a child. I have loved canoeing a long time and canoed many rivers. It has been a passion.

In 1995, on a trip with Alex, our planes were separated and we were forced down on a lake called Powder Lake in the NWT. Had Alex's plane been with ours, things might have been different: we could have set up the tents, got a fire going, as I have heard others experienced in the bush say, and sat back and enjoyed life. There would have been order.

An aside. Earlier in this piece I mentioned my interest in how native people did it. After I had finished writing *A Dream like Mine*, I talked to a man named Gus Nahwegehbow, the father of a friend, who was one of the last native people to trap the French River in the traditional way; without motors or planes. When I spoke to him, he was a tiny man in his eighties. What he said to me impressed me so much that I have made an anecdote out of it, a kind of set piece, but nevertheless what he said to me was of profound importance. So how did he do it, carry such weight, winter out, deal with going upstream, portaging, carrying the canoe, someone as small as he was, what was the secret? (I embellish, in telling the story—

M. T. Kelly with his son Jay, North Shore, Lake Superior, 1992

oh guru, how does one relate to the country that way?) Mr. Nahwegehbow told me: "Well, the first thing you have to do is get organized."

With this most recent trip, the planes separated, the pilot we were with was without food, matches (I had some), proper clothes, even proper shoes. I saw a situation that, years earlier, I would have been enraged about but would have endured. This time, after writing in my journal "squalor + anxiety = the right choice," I bailed out of the trip. Standing at Powder Lake, stuck there, seeing the warnings about toxicity on the oil drums, I had semi-romantic thoughts such as "maybe there are some places people shouldn't go." The wind was blowing. But I dealt with that sort of thing, the landscape and place, in *Out of the Whirlwind*. What was really important about my decision was that the "man was father to himself" and I got myself out of there, not guilt free certainly, but having made a decision to "protect" a part of myself, a part that was not protected before.

I have not always protected myself; there was some intense drinking, especially in my late twenties, but I moderated early. I have entertained other people with shows of extremes, especially at parties, and hated myself for it. For someone with problems with boundaries, the two times I tried LSD in the late sixties was simple terror. Marijuana has no appeal; for a person like me it is a dangerous drug. I have also tried prescription drugs and I have been a street-corner pharmacist to myself. But nothing extremely severe, ever. Some damage may have been done. Once or twice I came close.

Themes, passions, a way of being, are much clearer in what someone writes than they can be in such histories as I have just laid forth. I can simply say I have been a writer most of my life, have worried about it, have done some work, maybe not enough, had a difficult childhood and an intense relationship with my mother—so often that seems to be the case with writers—have been a searcher, and suffered like everyone else, and have been touched by things which redeem. I have wondered about fathers and have loved being a father myself. And a writer.

BIBLIOGRAPHY

Fiction:

I Do Remember the Fall, Simon and Pierre, 1978, reprinted, New Press Canadian Classics/General Publishing, 1989.

The More Loving One (novel and three short stories), Black Moss, 1980.

The Ruined Season, Black Moss, 1982.

A Dream like Mine (also see below), Stoddart/General Publishing, 1987, Time Warner Books, 1992.

Breath Dances between Them (short stories), Stoddart, 1991.

Out of the Whirlwind, Stoddart, 1995.

Poetry:

Country You Can't Walk In, Penumbra, 1979, published as *Country You Can't Walk In and Other Poems*, Penumbra, 1984.

Other:

The Green Dolphin (play; produced at Theatre Passe Muraille, 1982), Playwrights Canada, 1982.

Wildfire: The Legend of Tom Longboat (screenplay), Canadian Broadcasting Corp. (CBC-TV), 1983.

Also author of play *McClusky and O'Sullivan*, 1983, and a filmscript for *Young Canadians and the Law*, CBC-TV. Contributor to anthologies, including *The Saturday Night Traveller*, Harper-Collins, 1990; *Best Canadian Essays*, edited by George Galt, Quarry, 1991; *Canadian Literary Landmarks*, edited by John Robert Colombo, Hounslow, 1984; *Un Dozen: Thirteen Canadian Poets*, edited by Judith Fitzgerald; *The Northern Ontario Anthology*, edited by Fred Mason; *Whale Sound* and *Whales: A Celebration*, both edited by Greg Gatenby; *One on One: The Imprint Interviews*, edited by Leanna Crouch, Sommerville, 1994; *That Sign of Perfection*, edited by John B. Blee, Black Moss, 1995. Author of column "Between the Sexes," *Globe and Mail*, 1979–81; reviewer, 1979–91.

Contributor to periodicals, including *Antigonish Review, Books in Canada, Canadian Forum, Globe and Mail, Northern Journey, Performing Arts in Canada, Poetry* (Chicago), *Queen's Quarterly, Saturday Night, Scotsman,* (Edinburgh), and *Toronto Life.*

Editor and author of introduction to *Arctic Argonauts* by Walter Kenyon, Penumbra, 1990. *A Dream like Mine* was translated into French, Japanese, Danish, and Polish, and also released as the movie *Clearcut,* Famous Players/Cinexus, 1991.

Maurice Kenny

1929-

ANGRY RAIN:

A Brief Autobiographical Memoir from Boyhood to College

Maurice Kenny, Brooklyn Heights, New York, 1986

For Lorne Simon . . .

> Whose life was cut so short
> that all the words he stored
> in his imagination
> few got to paper in time . . .

Foreword

Mountains surround me; white pine, hemlock, spruce, birch, the ever-beautiful tamarack; a coyote howls out of the night darkness; raccoons scurry up and down the hills near the house; a bear nibbles blueberries and blackberries; chipmunks cache their winter foods under the porch; a female cardinal alights on the telephone wire; a crow goes in the upper branches of an elm; a loon calls; a hawk wheels over the village below where the river gurgles and sings you to sleep across the balmy night. Pansy and forget-me-not, hawkweed and daylilies brighten the morning as the sun rises in the east behind the mountain range to slowly drift south.

The Adirondacks. The high peaks. Maple Hill.

I'm home. My blood family not too far away, my surrogate sons Dean and Jamie, and my surrogate daughter Lynn are a footstep from this machine. Friends: Brett, Peg, John and Eva, Ruth. Kathleen, Ophila/Renee, Gail and Bob, Joannie Debrun, Chris and Sue, John and Jeannie, Tim, Pete and Deborah, David and Mary, Nina, Bernice, Meg and Manny are all so close I could call down the hill to them in an emergency.

Adirondacks. Saranac Lake, the woods and lakes, the flowers and animals, the birds, the great and handsome mountains are here around me. Sweetgrass is braided and hangs from the wall; sage is in the drawer of the chest for burning if needed. When winter comes snow will pile up in blizzards to the windows and all the trees shall flower.

Long travels are finished; new lands explored; friends and acquaintances have come and gone in the light of day and the dark of evening. Mexico, the Caribbean, the Virgin Islands, British Columbia are over, the past, deep in memory and the thrills they gifted. New York City, Chicago, San Francisco are blots on the map . . . no longer necessary. Onchiota and Bloomingdale are more important to everyday living: J. J. Newberry's on Main Street, the Grand Union offers more surprises than Boston or San Juan . . . now. These days Mexico City and Vancouver, El Paso or Tucson, St. Thomas and Trinidad, Campache, the Yucatan, Barbados and Martinique, colorful, fruitful, crawling with poverty, no longer offer the incentive to roam. The wanderlust has cooled . . . awesome that travel has always been, will always be. The feet don't itch, the eye is dulled, the spirit is weak. The cool summer porch is more comforting; the winter supper in the kitchen . . . a chicken roasting in the oven, potatoes boiling on the burner, folks busy tearing lettuce for a salad and slicing tomatoes and mushrooms. The handshake is there,

the good morning rests on the lips, the church bells chime, the sirens blow, the canoe paddles down the lake, the river rushes over the dam, birds chirp, Lucy meows, mice scratch, the blare of reggae hurls out of the Water-hole, the library loans books, Mrs. Petty jams her jellies, Emily refinishes her huge kitchen, Pendragon plays another play, kids skate on the frozen lake as the artists chip huge blocks of ice and stack them into a castle of the winter fairyland festival.

Adirondacks, high peaks, Maple Hill, home.

*   *   *

William Faulkner, the Mississippi novelist, once wrote that we must be violated by life. The Lakota Holy Man Black Elk once said that we human beings must celebrate the greening of the day. I have celebrated that green spring and flowery summer, that russet autumn and snowy January. I have also been violated, and in turn violated life. The violation and the celebration have produced hundreds of poems and stories and made me acquainted with the night, the day, and more human beings than I can possibly remember, humans who have dallied with my mind and spirit, the creative process and the roast venison on my table; humans who have brought great pleasures to my many mornings, and burning pain to my darkest nights. Humans who have offered a way, a door, and those who stood a wall to passage. Some will be remembered always, others best forgotten as quickly as the rabbit hops into the bramble, the mole into its hole, the fox through the wild grapes. Many have been remembered here in this paper . . . those who deserve remembering from my childhood and young life.

No marigold grows without rain and sunshine, nor stalwart white pine, nor no child let alone a writer developing out of childhood joys and miseries grows without the rain of family and friends and the sunshine of the Creator and the world. I am no different from anyone else . . . farmer, mountain guide, tracker, student, teacher, poet, highwayman, window dresser, clerk, bank teller, priest, visionary, garbage collector, who have always been some of my favorite conversationalists, the old man on the park bench, the elderly spinster offering bread crusts to pigeons or squirrels. I have offered crusts: I sit on the park bench and talk now with students, with bank tellers, waiters from the local lunch counters and bars. I stroll through shadows and apparitions of those who came here to the mountains surrounding Saranac Lake to cure or die in a cough at the Trudeau TB sanitoriums. I live in a house with a boy-ghost who died in poorness and poverty of lungs and home. Swaddled in black cloth choking in a white shirt buttoned tightly at the collar . . . who comes at night and sometimes rocks in the rocking chair. What does he want to say, reveal, complain about? I must listen and write his story in a poem or fiction. I must listen the same way I have always listened to the voices which moved around me in dreams or nightmares, on the streets or in the classrooms where I have walked and talked, spoken to innocent minds . . . as though my mind was a receptacle, an archive of valued information. Listening we learn, and as we learn from dreams and the ghosts and the presences who visit us in the tombs in which we all live. Only a few are successful in breaking out of those tombs or walls which surround us, captivate our minds and spirits. Damn, I have been lucky, fortunate that there have been so many to give me the pick to break down the walls, break open the tomb, the grave which so many of us spend our lives in. Wanda put the pick in my hands, as did Werner Beyer, Douglas Angus, Quino, Mary and Fred, Josh, Joe and Jimmy, the horses I rode, the river I canoed or strolled, the mountains I hiked. Mexico opened doors as did St. Thomas, as did Indiana and Brooklyn. Paul and Ruth, Larry and the Brownings, Pete and Rokwaho . . . dear people who haunt the dream world, some of whom have been released into the echo of life such as Lorne and Donna, and some who remain on the right and left shoulder blade whispering, ever whispering . . . Rocco and Cigar, Aunt Flo and Etta, Uncle Jim who probably first teased me with the possible ownership of a horse. To all of whom I am so very grateful for the wondrous gifts brought to my hands and my imagination.

Surely I am indebted more to the beauties of Mother Earth than any other spirit. Surely my deepest of gratitude goes to my father who saw that I survived in the violent world and to my mother who brought me into the green celebration of life, and to my sisters who stung me into celebrating the ceremony and the violence. Surely I owe a deep and abiding debt

"My parents' wedding picture: Doris Parker Herrick Kenny and Andrew Anthony Kenny," Watertown, New York, 1918

to Quino who brought such hell into my young manhood but glory to the produce of my pen. I know the love which my niece Martha has always given and the joy and fun, so surely I owe her much, and I am thankful we are friends. I owe the winds, the rains, the roving clouds, the moon who has protected me all these years the way all grandmothers protect their children. I owe the stars, the waters, the turtle who has held me on his back, the beautiful poems of Wendy and Simon and Peter whose blue cloud with Dan's soft wolf robe have comforted and replenished; and the foods of George and Rochelle . . . their pear tree and their often funny words, and the generous words of Sarah and Frank, and Chad and Dan and Lori and Jen who have lent so much love and loyalty and given with their life-spirit, their life-blood, to excess.

Rain has fallen in torrents, but it has always been followed by sun. Blizzards have tormented but were also followed by a warm breeze.

Waters have always flowed in the river and quenched a terrible thirst, exhilarated, stimulated, activated.

The Adirondacks, the high peaks, Saranac Lake, home.

Very special thanks to Sharon Ofner of Writer's Voice of Silver Bay Association; Deborah Ott of Just Buffalo Arts Center; Jeannette Armstrong of the En'owkin Center in British Columbia; Paul Smith's college; Poets & Writers; and deepest gratitude to both the Lila Wallace and the Lannen Foundations.

One: Boyhood

Biting through the skin to the pulp of the flesh . . . my mother said I was born on the hottest day of any August she could remember. It was a dark night. She could not tell me the exact hour. Pain prohibited memory to function correctly, truthfully, or what was she hiding? My sisters, Agnes and Mary, were both autumn births, delivery is easier on cooler days, or nights. Perhaps it is for this reason that they received a bit more understanding from my mother than I was fortunate to know. I do not believe it was because they shared gender, and I did not. My mother, although she complained of the cold and hated winter, she always hated the heat of summer. I felt she blamed me for this heat . . . having been born on the hottest August night she could remember. It is possible through records to check that exact temperature that night, August 16, 1929, but, frankly, I don't care to. Some biographical background concerning my mother: she was born a farm girl in the township of Cape Vincent, New York, a few miles from the St. Lawrence River. The family Bible, still in the possession of her sister, my aunt Jennie Sanford, claims my mother to be descended from Robert Herrick, the English poet. Her father's people, the Herricks and Clarks, were in northern New York from the early 1800s. She was also a descendent of the Parkers: General Ely S. Parker is notated, if memory serves. Her mother, Leona, was both a Parker and an Oatman. She was born in Adams Center, New York, and an eighth blood Seneca. My mother attended the stereotypical one-room schoolhouse, and it was "red" she later would say. Exactly how far she went in school is debatable. From her knowledge of books, etc., I would guess

Maurice, age nine, with his sisters, Agnes (left) and Mary, Watertown, 1938

not further than what they used to call the Sixth Book. Not necessarily a strong religious woman, she had been baptized a Baptist, though I never can remember her reading or toting a copy of the "good book," yet she read most of her life: mainly women's magazines and, later, biographies of the rich and famous. She had no artistic abilities that I was ever aware of with the exception of crocheting. The house was choked by doilies. To almost the day she died she gave us presents of doilies for Christmas and birthdays. I have some still. She left the farm, as the other six sisters needed to do, and, as the others, became a scullery maid for the rich in Watertown, New York. From photos I gather she was a pretty girl, small and thin, but stylish or as stylish as her income would allow. She married young, bore her first child, my sister Agnes, young. Though no one has ever convinced me she did not love my biological father, I can't help but believe she thought always she had made a mistake in marrying so young and bearing children so young. I think my mother would have been much happier playing our childish games with us than making supper. She never seemed to take much pride in her cooking, nor was she a really fine cook. Her pastry was good, her roast, well, perhaps I should not comment.

My parents separated when I was nine years old. It was painful for all concerned. I went with her by choice . . . one of the many bad choices I have made in my life. She was not a good teacher . . . but more of this later. I think this marriage could have been saved had either of my parents considered a counselor. My father was stubborn and my mother wispy.

Andrew Anthony Kenny was born on a farm outside a small Canadian village in the province of Ontario. His father, Maurice, pronounced Morris, was not only Irish, but it was jokingly said he was born on the boat crossing the Atlantic. My grandmother was an Indian woman, Mohawk. I know little of her. She was a West. She died young, having birthed three children . . . the same as my mother . . . two older girls and one son, my father. I don't recall exactly how old my father was at his mother's death, but a young lad. His father married a second time, an Irish woman . . . so that there was as much Irish nationalism as there was "Indianism" in my father's rearing. His cousins have always taken pride in the fact that relatives still live and breathe in Ireland, and when younger they supported the idea I go and make my visit . . . which I have resisted all my life for varying reasons. My dad was reckless as a youth. He had constant conflicts with his Irish father, buried his head in his stepmother's bosom when his two older sisters were not binding his wounds. He was allowed to drive the horse and buggy . . . I cannot believe it was a surrey . . . to the church euchre game, but if he over-stayed his father's rule by a minute, his father, Maurice, was there at the church stable to take the horse and buggy home, forcing my father to walk the many miles late on a winter's cold night. My grandfather was a "mean" man. My aunt Julia, my dad's sister, said Maurice was *mean* in an Irish fashion. My father was never a mean man though he held the most outrageous temper that on occasion he would prove through his actions. He was, and often more than not, the lamb; had a soft smile, a twinkle in the eye, and a generous manner, unusually. My father enjoyed telling the story, especially when lecturing me on smoking cigarettes, of burning his father's haybarn down. He'd laugh and tell how he smoked one day, rolling his tobacco in some form of paper or possibly leaves, lit up, took a drag or two, and fell promptly asleep, having stayed out late the

night before at the church dance. That was one occasion when his father came to collect the horse and buggy. Naturally, in his doze, he dropped the lighted cigarette. The hay caught afire, and before long he was trying to stamp out the blazing furnace of the barn. Sometimes he would say that he stayed at the farm only long enough to receive the thrashing of his life. Other times he said he just hightailed it off the place as fast as his fourteen-year-old legs would carry him. The family down the road gave him sanctuary, and then he took off for the States, directly to Watertown where he first stayed with a cousin, Aunt Libby, and having the luck of landing a job, found a room on State Street in the home of one old lady, a Mrs. Collins . . . who mothered him like a blood son. He loved this lady greatly. She passed on before I had the opportunity of knowing her. He would never admit it, but I believe the act of smoking which caused the barn to burn to the rocky ground was accomplished through wish fulfillment: subconsciously he not only wanted to take some revenge on his father but was looking for an escape hatch. He hated farming . . . as did my mother. He was able to groom out the farmer in his character and style rather quickly. He took to city life . . . Watertown was then about 30,000 in numbers. He never spoke about it, but I can easily visualize him at pool halls and the bars which were then called "buckets of blood" due to the fact that vicious fights broke out nightly. A cousin was in the position to obtain a job for my dad. He became the waterboy on the gang of the Watertown waterworks department. He stayed at the waterworks for many years. When he left he had risen to the third-most-important position in that city department: foreman. My father was industrious, aggressive, competitive. He held many artistic bents but realized none except song. He loved to sing, particularly Friday nights when a beer or four encouraged the voice: "If I had the wings of a turtle / over these prison bars I would fly." It was impossible to convince him turtles did not have wings. He was either thinking of the turtle-dove, or he remembered something his biological mother had told him as a small child: that she was a member of the turtle clan. It stuck and those early stories came out, manifested through the turtle flying over the prison walls. He was a good storyteller, and was an excellent listener except when we children were in trouble and attempted to explain our way out to him. Then his ears were closed. He knew the reasons better than we did, and he acted upon them. He was not mean as stated above. He was usually considerate, generous, and warm. He rarely beat us. Again something handed down from his Mohawk mother. Indians do not beat their children. They teach bad from good via example. I had one terrifying beating from him. My sister, Mary, had one vicious beating from him when he was drunk. Agnes, his favorite, was never touched. He did slap my mother several times during arguments. She was a nagger. She had been given warnings. But he slapped her regardless. Thinking back now I have the tendency to think that she might have deserved the slaps. But using my head, reasoning, no, she did not. No woman deserves brutality. He was an extremely strong man: short, heavy, stocky, far stronger than the pitiful little creature my mother was . . . never weighing more than ninety pounds. No man is ever right in striking let alone beating a woman. He was wrong. I remember once he hit her, and I, a mere piddle of a runt, picked up a broom and tried to defend her womanhood and physical weakness. He held it against me all his life. Another example of his anger was one Christmas he was dressing the tree he had gone to the woods to chop. He enjoyed celebrating holidays, ceremonies of all kinds with the exceptions of birthdays, never accepting the fact that the celebrant should receive a gift for merely having been born. He observed this rite reluctantly. In those days, the 1930s, electric Christmas lights were not of the perfection they are now. They had, as it is often said, a mind of their own, when the bulbs of wire had the inclination to light up and spread the colored cheer around the living room. He had the wire strings strung out straight as a toothpick; the colored bulbs all screwed into the tiny sockets, male into female. Nothing happened. Not a single spark, not a single blue, red or green, or yellow, or white flashed against the wall where he sat puttering with the set. He worked for at least half an hour. Nothing. No color. No contact. My sisters and I sat near, delighted from the knowledge of the upcoming festivities, both the presents we'd receive and the goodies we would push into our young tummies: the homemade taffy my dad had made; the maple walnut fudge Aunt Francis, my mother's kid sister, had whipped up; the roast

duck my father had shot and my mother was cooking in the woodstove; the oranges we were given only on Christmas; the mincemeat pie; the cranberry sauce; the chocolate cake my grandmother Herrick had made and the ribbon candy Aunt Jennie brought one evening before. We knew where my mother had hidden the gifts Santa would have presumably brought the night before Christmas. We had watched her buy the wool stockings, the shirts and sweaters, clothes we would desperately need to cross the cold northern winters but in our hearts detested, and we hoped she had not forgotten a toy or two, at least books. Happiness glowed around the kitchen woodstove. My mother, Doris, puttered about slicing fruit for an applejack pudding; Aunt Francis was preening, applying makeup for her date that evening; my sisters and I were crumpled in expectation, delight, frozen in the coming act of celebration and joy. My father mumbled. Then he cursed. Took the name in vain. Called out something irreverent to my mother, like . . . I told you to buy these at Sears. He never tired of complaining my mother was a spendthrift, wasted rather than conserved. She bought packaged butter, rather than a pound from the grocer's tub which cost less than the packaged. Suddenly he rose from the straight chair, numerous sets of electric lights entwined around his body, arms and legs, whirling the loose wires over his head as if a lasso. He stomped off to the living room, and returned with the tree now tangled in the wire, went to the cellar door, and upon opening it, threw tree and wires and himself down the stairs. We all laughed, all but our mother. She knew better. She understood the consequence of our laughing in his face at his foolishness and his failure. In a few moments he crawled sheepishly up the stairs. We continued to laugh. With his hat, that he nearly always wore, and coat, he went to the kitchen door, and as he strode through turned and pronounced there would be no Christmas this year in the Kenny household, nor the next, nor the next. He kept his word . . . at least the following year. We ate hamburgers which Agnes cooked. My father and mother were not there. Later Agnes said they had gone to the bar Christmas Eve, were drunk, and had not come home.

I would suppose, due to this outrage and my father's temper, Christmas has never been important to me. First, the kitchen scene was to leave an indelible mark on my mind. This is a Christian holiday feted with pagan rite, much based upon myth and newly acquired pagan trappings . . . such as the tree itself, the lights. I have nothing against celebrating the birth of Jesus Christ. I honor Him, pay respect to His codes, words. My problem is that few Christians truly honor Him, pay true respect to His codes, words. Christmas can be and should be a spiritual day, the same as Gandhi's birthday, or Martin Luther King, Jr.'s, and, yes, Crazy Horse's, or the Iroquois Peacemaker's . . . if we knew his day of birth. That spiritual celebration need not stem from Christian reality. I am not a Christian, but a pagan. I was baptized a Roman Catholic but left those teachings at a very early age. I think it was in the third grade when I announced to the nun, my teacher, that I thought human beings descended from monkeys. She had no holdings with Darwinian thought. I think right then was the first time I was excommunicated from the church. Spirituality, spirit, religion, faith starts in the human heart, not as a catechism nor a black book (that can serve many needs by those seeking rational approval for wrong deeds).

Two: Life in the North

Childhood was not all celebration and lazy summer days, cool swims in the lake, picking sweet berries in fields or woods. My parents argued a great deal: there were arguments in my aunt Jennie's house, though those usually in the bedroom not in the kitchen in front of the children. My grandmother Herrick was not of honey nature. I think she did not like children, having had seven daughters and one son who died in infancy. We thought she was just being old-fashioned, but later I decided she was an embittered aging lady who had no real home of her own and visited her married daughters' homes in relays of three months. When she was at my father's house she constantly found fault with my sisters and me, and bided the afternoon when my father would return home for supper so she could report our mischievousness or what she thought our badness. He paid little attention to her complaints and she was chronic.

There was fun even on the farm though I had to rise early and milk cows, and often to

In New York City, 1960

my shame my aunt Ruth would hold me down while my uncle Frank, Jennie's husband, would squirt the hot milk from the cow's teat directly into my mouth. It hung dry, sticky and smelling. It seemed it never left my skin or my clothes. They laughed at my embarrassment. Some of my fun was really picking berries: the strawberries in the hot fields, the hickory nuts in the fall, the winter sleigh rides with hot bread and sweet jam or applejack which Aunt Jennie made for us with pleasure, placing cups of hot chocolate by the plate of pie still steaming from the oven. I had to help dig a water well once, and that hurt my sensibilities, but now these many years later I fully realize Uncle Frank was teaching a sense of work ethic and responsibility. It was for my own good. Haying was fun, though dusty, and even if I did have hay fever haying was fun . . . the cutting, gathering, storing off in the mounds. Aunt Jennie always made buckets of ginger beer which I could not drink because it was made with a fresh egg and a serious egg allergy would not allow me to participate with the frothy liquid in the pail. But I would serve it to the hayers and later thrashers. In the summer Uncle Frank would take us to the beach for watermelon picnics after chores were finished on Sunday. During the week he would take us into town, Three Mile Bay, a village of only a few hundred, and while he was doing business we could enter the huge store and buy candies. The store was marvelous. Filled with child treasures of

The author's father and stepmother, Ann McBride Kenny, Watertown, 1955

not only candies but pretty ribbons, shoestrings, yo-yos, paper and pencil and small workbooks, stationery, funny fishhooks, and naturally good things which adults enjoyed . . . bricks of cheddar cheese, smoked fish, fruit such as bananas and oranges which were difficult to find in the north country in those days, etc. Sometimes Uncle Frank would leave us for hours in his old Chevrolet. When he returned he always had a gift . . . perhaps a bag of pretzels, and he always had huge smiles, grins which spread from ear to ear. His face often flushed, his eyes utterly alive, and his breath smelling of a strange nutty odor. Beer, we found out. We arrived back at the farm . . . sometimes after the accustomed supper hour . . . Aunt Jennie would be in the master bedroom down the hall from the dining room and across the hall from the formal parlor.

Grandma Herrick would be arguing in the kitchen with Aunt Ruth. Periodically, Aunt Ruth would come out to shush our whispers. We could hear arguments going on behind two sets of doors. We were desperately trying to eavesdrop on these fights. Usually Aunt Jennie would not come out of the room until the words ceased hurtling. Uncle Frank would come out, having lost the flush to his countenance, he would then do the evening chores.

As a youngster, I spent most of my summers on that farm on Fox Creek Road. The farm was a few miles from Cape Vincent, along the St. Lawrence River. If we went visiting, it was in the winter, on weekends, or to funerals or marriages. It was more often to my father's people in Canada, to the homes of my aunts, Julia and Cecily, or to Uncle Eugene's farm, his half-brother. My father was born on Uncle Eugene's farm and it was at this farm where he burned down the barn.

In the early years, Grandpa Kenny was alive and a real teaser. He thoroughly enjoyed holding an Indian nickel out to my gaze. As I reached for it, he would snatch it away. This game seemed to go on forever and I was never allowed to claim the coin. The other game I played was with Uncle Jim. Not only was he a greater tease than my grandfather, he sparkled when he teased. He always told me I could take a horse home. I believed him. Constantly, my mother warned him he would need to deal with me the hour the car took off for the States. I could see no reason why we couldn't tie the horse to the car and let it trot behind us . . . yes, right onto the ferry or across the bridge. This bridge was built before the Second World War when Roosevelt was president.

All my relatives on both sides of the family really seemed to get a huge charge from taunting me. I've yet to figure out why. Was it because I was short and thin? Was it because I had bad allergies? Was it because I was a boy who lived with two sisters in a small city while they lived in rural areas? Was it because my cousins were all older and wiser than I and had formed an alliance with my two older sisters? Very easily, my sisters won games in the tomato patch, throwing rotten fruit as if they were snowballs. Consequently, they witnessed my punishment for being covered with streaming tomato juice, seeds in my hair, and skins hanging from my ears when I came back to the house kitchen. I have never liked a single one of my numerous cousins. Never! Not one. I was the enemy. This was true of both sides of the family. When I turned five, my father bought me my first tricycle. In a fit of jealousy, my cousin Morris, who was two years older than I, carried my tricycle onto the railroad tracks. The train was charging down the rails. Naturally, my tricycle was smashed. When my father came home from work, he spanked me. Never again did I have a tricycle. When I was in my mid-teens he did buy me a Sears Roebuck Elgin bike for my birthday. I think he made me clean out the garage before I received the gift. He didn't believe, as I said before, in being gifted for having been born.

I remember iris springs, chicory summers, maple-leafed falls, and snowdrift winters. Perhaps the best remembered are the chicory summers. The skies were as blue as my strange eyes; the eyes that always get questioned wherever I go. Even yesterday at lunch, an Okanagan woman asked if all my family had blue eyes. I told the story of how a strange man in Saranac Lake, where I live most of the time, one day stopped me on the street and asked if I was Maurice Kenny, the Mohawk poet. Naturally, my reply was "yes." "Where did you get those blue eyes?" he asked. "You know," I said, "that's exactly what my father asked my mother. And you know what she answered? She said, 'It's none of your business.'"

The world does not seem to want to accept the blood quantum I have in the veins. I'm always being questioned. My work is saturated with poems dealing with this theme. What is an Indian . . . blood, heart, spirit, colour?

I would spend iris mornings along the brown river shores with my father. Together, we would be fishing or netting the minnows. Later, he would sell to the fishermen who were touring from Utica or Syracuse. He made money. These mornings were special. It was time spent with a man I was attempting to understand and love, also whom I needed love from. It was a time in which he could speak and bring home values to me. As a young child, I could weigh and eventually accept these things. Although, as I grew into adolescence, this was unlikely. No teenager believes the parent; all parents are wrong. They do not understand boys' or girls' problems; they never had the same experiences. I spoke little in return to my father on those iris mornings by the river. I was shy and afraid. Some awe as well possessed and terrified me from confiding in him . . . much to my regret now, of course. It is always too late. He had much to teach. He did not have all the answers to many of my questions simply because there are no answers to all our questions. He taught me to love the river, the waters, the fish, the wild grass weaving in the current, even the rocks on the river bottom, and the flowers, iris, and pickerel. He taught me to enjoy the sun and sit calmly and qui-

etly, contemplating this free beauty. This lyric which nature and the Creator so bountifully has given and loaned to us all. One of the thoughts in my head that I kept from my father was an experience I suffered one summer at Aunt Jennie's farm. An older man, my parents' age, lived down the road on a farm. My mother had attended the red schoolhouse with him and knew him all her life. There were always cold whispers concerning this man. Somehow, my sisters and I received the impression that he was a dirty old man and that the girls should stay away from him. My aunts, Jennie and Ruth, always told us to come into the house whenever he approached us on the road, in the yard, or certainly in the field. My beagle hound was with me at the farm that summer. He had a tendency to run away at the first sniff of a rabbit. One day, he did just that. Aunt Jennie commanded I follow, find him, bring him home, and tie him up. I followed through my grandfather's abandoned apple orchard . . . mouldering in time. Uncle Frank cared little about husbandry duties to the fruit trees. The apples were small and wormy, even the small grape arbour at the side of the orchard was ignored. Only one apple tree behind the house shed was ever respected. This was a translucent tree that my grandfather took particular interest in. This tree was pruned and the apples were used in many delicious ways on the supper table. I followed Happy through the orchard and across a lot where Uncle Frank's pigsty stood. The odour was outrageous. As I neared, the pigs grunted, thinking I had slop or whey. Further on, I ambled into a kind of scrub brush jungle where there were cedars, crabapple trees, etc. . . . I found Happy. He was being held by the man who lived down the road. He had him on a rope. I don't recall our conversation other than him asking if I wanted to play a little game before I took the hound home. As a kid, I said yes. I liked games. All kids do. He said he had to tie me to the maple tree nearby and would show me how the game was played. In utter innocence, I smiled, laughed, and complied with his instructions. He tied me about the waist above the belt line with my hands to each side. I watched him drool, stand off, and approach me. He unbuttoned my pants, allowed them to fall, then pulled down my shorts and stooped in front of me. In all honesty, it did feel good. But shame covered me completely. I sinned. I knew somehow I had sinned or had given the right for this man to sin upon me. I was guilty as he was of the sin. Before he released me from the ropes, he said I must promise never to tell, not Uncle Frank, my father, or anyone. I promised and he released me from the binds.

That man followed my steps throughout adolescence. He would follow me down the street. He called me out of class during school hours. He would beg me to sit in his car when school was out. He offered to drive me home. It was impossible to get rid of him, but it was also impossible to tell my father who probably would have shot the man on sight. I never have told until now. And I'm still in fear that my father . . . dead these long years . . . is listening to my words and oiling up his deer rifle. Needless to say, this experience, frightening and shameful that it was, has haunted my life. It taught me to be wary and never trust a male adult. The iris springs and the chicory summers were spoiled. A wild thing had been bruised; a wildflower had been crushed. Many summers would be spoiled in the years to come, and winters, too.

I always loved horses. My uncle Jim's tease kept them in my sight. Among others, Uncle Frank had this one horse on his place. I didn't know it at the time, but this horse, due to long years of toil, was blind and put out to the pasture. I tried desperately to mount this black animal and ride off into the windy fields. I could never stand him still long enough to mount his bare back. Instead, I would try to ride the calves in the barnyard. That didn't work well either. One morning before going off to pick berries, I noticed the horse was standing below a wild plum tree. Nearby was a pile of rocks and one large boulder which he butted his hind end upon. I crept stealthily across the field. He did not scent me because the winds were blowing gently from the other way. I climbed the granite boulder. I had my hands onto his thick mane before he scented my flesh. I was up, on and away, but not for long! In mere seconds, he tossed me into a barbed-wire fence. To this day, I carry the scar on my left calf.

Childhood had its pleasure and pain . . . that I shall not deny. And now, looking back, I probably see it more golden than it truly was on those chicory days. There were many family problems that I was only half aware of, slightly interested in, or barely understood. They were family rows. I didn't quite understand death or birth. Marriage held an enigma. I did not understand why my mother didn't like to be near water when her belly was sometimes huge and round. My father bought an old summer cabin in Chaumont Bay on Lake Ontario. She fought because she did not want to go there even though my dad, my sisters, and I loved it. I figured it was because he was gone all week and was there only from Friday nights to Monday mornings. She was lonely in her weekly abandonment. She didn't really enjoy our company. It was years later when Agnes said he had her pregnant most of the time and she miscarried when she was near the lake waters. Perhaps she had a fear of him tossing her out of the fishing rowboat. He did this to me once, far out on the lake, when he attempted to teach me how to swim back to shore. She loved fishing, especially bullhead fishing, and didn't even squirm when she cleaned them before cooking. I have always hated bullheads (sometimes known as catfish) and refuse to eat them when served.

We loved the cottage/cabin. We loved the water, the rock shore, the picnic up the point, and the deep woods across the mud road. We wandered there picking hickory nuts off the ground, scampering and searching for guinea pigs or baby rabbits. Of course, we got into trouble when we brought them back to the kitchen and my mother screamed. We fought Labor Day's arrival and school with the nuns.

There is another story to be told about the nuns: the sisters of Saint Joseph. This is another story. For the first six years of my schooling I was forced to study with the sisters of Saint Joseph. It was hell at Holy Family School. It was not really a boarding school, but to me it had the earmarks of one. Mary was nonplused about it and got out fairly happy, even the convent high school. Agnes adored the school and the nuns. She wept broadly when she graduated from the convent high school. I shall never forget my sisters in their black uniforms with white round collars. Every morning they fought over their uniforms. The uniforms were costly and several were needed. Yet now, it seems like they never had a clean uniform to attend school. They did, but still complained bitterly. My father insisted that they graduate from that high school with an education equivalent to college. This was not true. Although, they did come out with some polish, some sense, some Latin and French. They did lose the northern New York accent. They could even sing pretty well, especially Agnes, who to this day maintains a lovely voice. Perhaps my sisters did not need to go through what I had to with the nuns. In today's school parlance, Agnes would be a brownnose. She had few problems with the nuns. Mary simply did her work and asked for nothing. Consequently, other than Latin, she had few problems. I could not wait to get out from under the nuns' black skirts and what they claimed as checkered aprons which were worn over the skirts. My oldest and strongest memories of the nuns are: pain, misery, and hate. Holy Family had been donated to the church by a very wealthy family whose name I don't believe I ever heard. It consisted of two coloured buildings: grey for grammar school and redbrick for junior high school. I never attended the red building which housed the principal or mother superior's office; although, I visited there often. It was not for a cup of tea or compliments. Behind the grey building was a marvellous formal French garden which we were allowed to stroll through during recess. BUT DO NOT TOUCH THE FLOWERS! If you picked one intentionally or by mistake, you were dead. To the right of the garden was a swimming pool. Most of the time, it was empty, which became another danger place. Beyond the pool was a high stone fence which enclosed a baseball lot. Here, they forced us to play baseball. It was in this lot that I learned to hate baseball . . . to this very day. I mumbled always that I was sick and dizzy and could not swing the bat, or run, or catch. I remember the lot was rimmed with a bed of yellow flowers. Being spring, they were probably dandelions. I do not hold that pain against those wildflowers. In third grade we were taught scriptwriting. I never really learned it with any precision or beauty. There was hell to pay if, when dunking the wood pen and point into the inkwell, you should spatter the ink on the braids of the girl sitting in front of you, or spatter and stain your shirt, or stain your fingers. You were taken downstairs to the cellar basement to stand on a wide, high wood platform before an enormous sink. The sink seemed nearly as huge as the swimming pool which was out by the garden. There you were washed and scrubbed clean until not a trace of ink was left. It was

also at this sink where the goodly sister toothpicked your head for lice. And should you have one . . . lo and behold, you were in serious trouble. How dare your mother allow you to come to school with lice in your hair. (Often, of course, our mothers were the culprits, the first hosts of the lice.) My mother particularly enjoyed going to J. J. Newberry's or Woolworth's trying on hats. She would bring the lice home to us. Once, when I gossiped on my poor mother, the nun told me I lied and washed my puckered mouth out with Fels Naptha soap. It was not especially tasty, and not really a sweet mouthwash. The students also had their mouths washed out with that vile soap more usually used for cleaning and curing poison-ivy infection. It was used if anything near a curse word be uttered, or if a word of Mohawk passed our lips. I taste that soap to this moment. When washing my face, I always do it with a washcloth so that my lips and mouth are not contaminated by any soap.

The most excruciating pain we felt from those sisters of Saint Joseph was when we were led to the boys' room, again, near the wood platform in the basement of the grey building. We filed into this dungeon-like room, with one lightbulb dangling from the ceiling, to find a long low trough against the wall. The good nun stood at the far end with a pointer stick in her hand. If a boy should spray the wall above the trough urinal, the thin pointer would come down onto his penis. Believe me it hurt.

With his mother and stepfather, Martin Welch, Bayonne, New Jersey, 1961

Why did they hate the penis so greatly? Again, this was something I did not dare take home to my parents, especially when no word of sex was ever mentioned in my father's house. I never once saw my father or mother naked. Only once did I witness my father urinate at the river shore while fishing one morning.

The sisters of Saint Joseph did a lot of damage to the boys. I have no idea what they might have accomplished with the girls. They were brutal and for the most part I found them to be insensitive to the needs of the children. You were even castigated if your parents did not have money and did not contribute to their fund with either outright cash or foodstuffs. I have no idea if my father complied. We were not poverty-stricken. It was the Depression, but my father always had a new Chevy. He bought the lakeshore cabin and we had warm clothes and good food. Even though much of our food was wild game, such as: fish, deer, rabbit, pheasant, etc. There was one nun whom I liked. Her name was Sister Dorothea. She was beautiful to behold. Her face was the colour of a very light honey and it shone under the light as if she were oiled. She was my fifth-grade teacher. She was also the music teacher and the conductor of the chorus. I might have loved her if it had not been for the horrible experiences I'd had with the other nuns at Holy Family School. She discovered my voice and had me sing. In fact, on one Christmas Eve in the church I sang alone. I sang "Silent Night." I was always terrified while in that church. The statues and icons put me off considerably. Were they real? At the left side of the church was the hanging cross of Christ's crucifixion. Did real blood flow from the hanging Christ who was pinned and nailed to the pillar? The nuns repeated many stories of the miracles of Christ and the saints. They told how Christ or perhaps God or the Virgin Mother would appear and reveal secrets to good people. Later, great monuments in honour of these good people were constructed and they became saints. I guess I wanted to be a saint and always looked for a sign, a message, or a visitation from either a saint, Mary, or Christ himself.

We were told to fast before attending Mass and taking Holy Communion which sometimes left us dizzy from hunger. Supper was always at five the night before and I did not always get a snack before going to bed. Sometimes I would get dizzy while sitting in the pew wait-ing for Communion hour. When a child is dizzy his mind wanders and often his eyes play tricks. I was dizzy. My eyes played tricks. I saw Christ move on the cross that was nailed to the pillar. Without a doubt, I was positive He moved. I called a nun and explained my most reverent spiritual experience. I was obviously bound to sainthood as Christ had given me a sign. He moved on the cross. Needless to say, I was ridiculed and shamed. The next morning I was spanked and had my mouth washed out. I was not a saint and never would be one. Christ would appear only to the innocent and I was surely not of that order. My soul was dirty from both lying and having a rich imagination.

So ended the nuns, Holy Family School, and Catholicism. I begged my father to allow me to attend public school where I could take various shop courses, such as: wood, metal, and print. He agreed knowing full well I was never going to be a saint or a priest. The nuns had convinced him of that.

Three: Peonies, Plums, and Passions

Butternuts and peonies; elms and bleeding hearts; maples and lilies of the valley; a trellis of roses canopy the veranda of the low charcoaled painted house, home of three ageing but nimble spinsters: Florence Graves, Etta Zeller, and Lena Butterfield. Three ladies who held a magic that attracted the neighbor children who lived next door by the railroad tracks in a squatty grass-colored house behind a fattening lilac bush which scented the neighborhood as its blossoms announced summer was on the way.

No secret, the side garden that sloped to the edge of the drive was exotic. Across the warm days of spring and summer, the yard was festooned with changing colors under rich shadows of the butternuts, elms, and maples, tapped for the sweet juices which would eventually end up on the dining room table of this musty old house crammed with antiques and cats. A daily visit was necessary to the yard to check the flowering and the changing of colors and species. The boy, of the next-door tribe, had the chore of watering one very special butternut tree given to him by Ms. Graves, better known as Aunt Flo. Adults laughed, and it was probably humorous to see this child of five or so with bucket in hand, strike out for the yard to water a tree of some twenty-five feet, a fully grown, adult tree. It was his duty: his obligation was one of pleasure. The tree was his very own, the only thing in life at that time for which he was responsible for caring. He was thrilled that Aunt Flo had such faith in his young abilities. Consequently he took an enormous interest in not only the butternut but the bleeding hearts, the iris, and the other flowers and shrubs that had been carefully nurtured by the elderly spinsters, his friends, and decidedly, they were his friends, and good friends of his sisters and their parents. The house was corralled by gardens and shaded by various fruit trees, such as wild plum at the far end of the vegetable garden, the crabapple between the summer kitchen and the more formal flower garden which every season was rowed with gladiolus, dahlias, zinnias, Veronica, and bee balm, etc. Often Etta, caretaker of the back garden, would fill his arms with flowers to take across the drive to his mother who was expecting company, grandma, or aunts from Canada, or aunts from New Jersey. After helping to pull weeds from around the carrots, the radishes, the various squash and other vegetables, Etta would allow him to pick raspberries and take some home for his own special dish, rewards for backbreaking labors in the rows of onions and melons. Etta was generous. She was also an educator. However, the real, true educator was Aunt Flo who showered marvels in the antiqued parlor in which she sat the two girls, Agnes and Mary, to the piano and taught them where finger and feet to the keys and pedals went. The boy! Well, he was a different student. His fingers never relaxed to the keys, frozen shut, they made noise not music. He was not to be abandoned. She observed how he enjoyed the Sunday comics, comic books, Tarzan books, whatever simple kind of reading materials came near those nonmusical fingers. Between the formal parlor and a bizarre dining room, in a kind of cubbyhole alcove, mountained on stout tables were newspapers. Yellowed, dusty, covered in cat hair, ageless, ageing, dated back to at least 1900, by then, perhaps 1934-35, collector's items. The boy looked to this ragged pile furtively. A journalist in the budding. A writer, she supposed, dreamed. When young, Aunt Flo had been a schoolmarm in the clichéd one-room red-painted schoolhouse. A schoolhouse to which she not only walked, trudged through winter blizzards, but chopped

wood for the potbellied stove and drew water from the creek so that her children would be warm but also would have water to drink. She always brought extra food in her lunch pail . . . just in case a student or two had arrived hungry and empty-handed. Even though it was a dairy-farming community there was poverty and hunger. Many of her charges lived on tenant farms, their fathers lazy, drinkers, or unable to eke out a living from the earth, for whatever reason. Aunt Flo thoroughly enjoyed telling the boy her mental anthology of stories about the schoolhouse and the boys and girls who attended. She had been an excellent teacher endowed with great compassion and outright love for the young. Each year she lived with a different farm family . . . part of her salary, or as we would say today, a perk. Now, I think of her stories in relation to some of the writings of both Willa Cather and Mari Sandoz. She was a storyteller and a good one. And she loved to read . . . the huge stack of newspapers in the alcove, and also upstairs stacked away in a forbidden bedroom, and books. The parlor was lined with glass-doored bookcases containing hundreds of books, many leather bound. Odd, but I don't recall titles on the shelves other than the classics: Shakespeare, etc. Often Aunt Flo would take a dusty but sweet-smelling leather bound volume out of the case and place it in my hands. That was a thrill and proved she trusted not only my hands but my mind which would one day contain the contents of that book. She taught me to love and care for the physical book and naturally the marvelous and magical words they contained. My fingers might be frozen on the keyboard, but they were not averse to turning pages. That parlor was a museum. No settee or couch. Straight chairs with soft cushions; the piano, of course, a handsome marble-top table in the center of the shadowed room . . . rarely did light filter into the space due to the rose trellis and low porch roof. I remember porcelain vases from Asia, Chinese silk hangings, brilliant in color under accumulating dust of many years. There were figurines: Japanese dolls which we children were never allowed to play with nor touch. Where they came from, how they were collected, I never learned that secret. There was an old-fashioned card table set up near the front window . . . the only light came from it, and at this particular table we played cards: "Old Maid" with Lena Butterfield, the oldest of the three spinsters. Lena came from a very prominent family of Watertown. On Washington Street, her family home stood for many years a gorgeous mansion, yellow and hugely impressive. Lena was retarded, a blood niece of Aunt Flo, and was fostered out in her care. There were times when Lena actually was spanked for committing some minor infraction of house law. She was then in her early seventies. But we, my sisters and I, regarded her as an equal as young as we were, except when playing "Old Maid." Confession is due. We always cheated the poor darling. She always lost. She was always crowned the old maid. She loved it. And would giggle for hours after that she was the old maid. Lena was the first of the three to die.

The parlor was magical, the foyer was dark and troublesome; the second floor forbidden unless you needed the bathroom and then you'd be taken by the hand and led quickly up and down with whomever escorted you staying in the room with head turned as nature took its course. The dining room, kitchen, and pantry were chaos and havoc. A ten-foot table stood dead center surrounded by chairs, of course. The table was littered and piled with all the condiments normally found in a refrigerator: mustard, catsup, mayonnaise, jams and jellies, pickles, apple butter, peanut butter, and dinnerware and silverware piled in the center under a large hanging tiffany lamp. Aunt Flo usually made us sandwiches of either catsup or mustard and we declared them absolutely delicious. In our father's house we would have never deigned to eat such food. No meat, no eat. It was joyful sitting at this huge buffet-like table with our catsup sandwich and a china cup of camomile tea . . . a drop of tea with two-thirds warm milk. It was truly sweetly delicious. We children preferred it to any other beverage. Later we learned, on reaching adulthood, that often those jams and mustards were moldy, and the bread was always green around the crust. My father asked how we could bear to eat such things. It didn't bother us at the time— the occasions were always of a party atmosphere. We were guests at that incredible table. Today, thinking back, I can't help but remember Dickens's audacious dining-room table set for a wedding in *Great Expectations.* A wedding which never took place, a wedding cake many years later hung with cobwebs, the cake rotting in disappointment, and in the movie a rat scampering in and out of the cake.

The kitchen contained only one huge round table which also collected newspapers and was ordained to be the eating spot for the cats allowed downstairs. These cats, and there seemed hundreds at the time, but obviously only a dozen or so, were cats neither pregnant nor in heat. Those cats were kept in the secrecy of the upstairs rooms . . . where there were not heaps and piles of ragged newspapers there were little tins and plates of cat food . . . mainly chopped boiled potatoes and perhaps a string or two of whatever meat or fish had been for dinner the night before. The pantry was a dark cave and contained the sink and dish closets and cabinets. I don't remember an icebox or refrigerator. Perhaps the reason for the molds. After Aunt Flo and Lena passed, Etta had the house exhumed. Nearly everything was tossed out including all the cats but one. It reeked of cat smells and stale food smells. Everything was cleaned, washed, polished, and sprayed with Lysol. As a college student I returned and couldn't quite accept the new beauty of the rooms, especially the parlor.

Etta Zeller was a very special woman. She worked as office manager for a paper company in Dexter, New York, until her retirement. She enjoyed greatly the company of young people . . . not children who always seemed to be underfoot, though she was never rude or unkind. She wished to share a more intelligent hour and pursued politics and the arts. Eventually she opened the second floor and turned it into an apartment and rented to young married couples until her own death in the late 1950s. She was an elegant woman. You might picture her as a character in an Edith Wharton novel or Henry James. Aristocratic, however landless and moneyless, but good blood. She was related to Aunt Flo on the opposite side of Flo's relationship to Lena. Etta was born in the Midwest. I believe Ohio.

Butternuts and peonies. They spell surprise, childhood enchantment, and we were levitated into a realm of not exactly fairyland . . . pulling garden weeds was very real and backbreaking . . . but there was a sensory, sensuous quality of life that beckoned and fascinated children's imagination needful of music and the thrill of books, stories. They were loyal women, unforgettable, kind in the offer of flowers and raspberries, understanding with the gift of the butternut, lovable in the music lessons, and their bosoms were a sanctuary for young tots already

Kenny in New York City, 1962

a fine aged wine. On sight an iris along my hometown lake today will reflect those delights of childhood in the charcoaled house. However to this moment I maintain a problem with eating catsup and drinking tea.

From the opposite side of the tracks I took my friends. The Audets, the Newmans, and the Youngs. We played on the railroad tracks when the trains were zooming down the rails, and placed our precious pennies on the rail to see what the great weight of the engine would do to the coin. It was the Depression and pennies came rarely into our hands. We also played in Etta Zeller's large stand of plum trees, a stand of sapling poplars in our own backyard, and a vacant lot across the tracks near my friends' houses which were nothing more than row houses, owned by a single but kind landlord who in those Depression days would knock on the separate doors and deliver over a basket of fruit and maybe some canned goods for Christmas. I can't but believe he often went without the rent. We played mostly in the vacant lot: marbles, mumblety-peg, baseball at which I was not too proficient and deserved the taunts and rancor of my fellow teammates, we camped overnight there with old pillows and ratty blankets too shameful to use on a guest bed, and we played cowboys and Indians. I, naturally, was always the Indian, even though Carl Young and his sisters were Indian as well. I was always chosen to be the Indian roped to a stake and set afire. Yes, a real fire with flames darting around my feet. Of course, my playmates always said they would not set the dry grasses around my feet to flame. But they lied. Many a day Mrs. Newman had to drop her work and come rushing out to the lot to save my life. She, indeed, scolded all of us . . . the others laughing, guffawing . . . and I was in tears . . . "They made me do it." Confession.

Carl had a much younger sister, I don't remember her name, and she was most ticklish. When she was tickled she wet her pants. Well, that proved great fun. In the poplar saplings behind my father's house also stood a huge railroad tie. We'd go there and drag the poor child with us and start tickling. She'd pee, wet her pants, crying embarrassed, and pull off her panties. That was the real fun because then we could see how she differed from us boys. Etta Zeller's plum trees were another grand place for scurrilous activity. Within the trees

confused by life and the times in which they were growing with the pains that all children know and suffer. Aunt Flo was a catalyst; Etta the strength of moral fiber and work ethic; Lena, oh Lena . . . do I dare say, the humor, the comic relief. She made my sisters and me think of ourselves as adults. They are inscribed on my brain, burned into my imagination, and chiseled into my personal sense of value. I don't think either ever went to church. I'm not sure that they belonged to a church, but they were the only true Christians I have ever known in my lifetime. From the bottom of my very being I thank them for having been our neighbors. If I plant a geranium today or pluck a wild raspberry, if I look up into a maple or dying elm, I know the focus was given to me by these three ladies in retirement. Soon after Etta's death the city bought the crumbling grey house with the rose trellis, the butternut and plum trees. It was torn down with sledge and hammer, bulldozed into memory alone. And the grass-colored house next door with the fat lilac bush which already belonged to the city, well, it too was torn down leaving only colored dreams.

The three ladies were non-Indian, most likely as WASP as you could be, but their morals and ethics were grooved, defined, and executed. They remain vivid pictures with the clarity of we were hidden by leaves and trunks and ripening fruit. Unless someone, a parent or Etta, were standing at the very edge of the stand we could not be observed. Even Aunt Flo could not have spotted us from the kitchen window or my mother from our back porch. It was there that we boys proved our manhood. It was there, every so often, down came our trousers and out came the penis ruler. We had to measure how large we were growing. I remember holding Jack's and placing the cold ruler against the foreskin. Two inches. Hadn't grown that week. However, a certain but weird sensation rose from my fingers into my loins and I flushed not realizing the reasons for blushing. He seemed to have no problem with measuring either mine or Carl's or any other young lad that hid in the plums with us. We were never caught. Our curiosity and manhood were safe. Years later, I learned from other male friends that they had accomplished similar acts of bravery out of dire necessity to see if one was truly a normal human being with all the proper male accoutrements. They were usually there . . . sometimes offering a great surprise to our bulging eyes.

Carl was Indian. It seems now that my father said his family came from Onondaga. Another family also had moved into the neighborhood and they hailed from Caugnawaga. So I may have Carl's home reserve mixed in my memory. Carl was dark. I was and remain light. His thick black hair was enviable as was his skin tone. He was a handsome young boy. He was my friend. In our clandestine rendezvous in the plum bushes, I never had the courage to measure his privates. We were close friends and that simply wouldn't do. Children are children and as children there were days when I would not share my playtime with anyone but Carl. We'd even sleep nights wrapped in those ratty blankets on my front porch. In his row house there wasn't room on the porch to sleep, barely sufficient space for a chair, but my porch was shaded into privacy by the great lilac bush. Very little sleeping was accomplished however. We talked, told stories, dreamed across the night which always ended in dampness, the fall of the dew. Our friendship ended in war. Two sides of the neighborhood boys decided to have a stone fight. Carl was on one side and I the other. Recognized enemies, we gathered stones and small rocks, marched to the railroad tracks in phalanx, aimed, and fired. Carl was the first to be struck . . . by my stone. I was the sec-

ond to be hit by Carl's stone . . . in the face. I bled. I cried and I ran home into the house where my mother was baking bread. She washed the wound, told me to stay indoors and find a book to read, and promptly told my father of the war the moment he entered the kitchen that evening after work. He didn't spank me but gave me a serious talk. You don't hurt your friends. Friends do not war. You must never pick up stones again because they fly home and strike back. What goes out comes around. He was right. He told me a story similar to our war which I simply cannot draw up out of the revery, a story of friendship. The tragedy was not so much our physical wounds, but that I never spoke to or saw Carl again. The next week his family moved away, his father needed to find work. I have looked for my friend all these many years to say how sorry I am to have thrown the rock and struck him. In fact, I have not seen any of those boys for these many years, and do not know if they still exist in this crazy world.

The Audets were French Canadian-Indian from somewhere in Quebec. Cree, I don't know. Mohawk from Oka or Caugnawaga. I don't know. I know only that they were a very large family, like the Youngs, and were very poor. The father, Mr. Audet, spoke little English, as did the mother, worked when there was work to be obtained on the Work Progress Administration. Remember it was the Depression. My father emphasized the fact that they were poor. He said when at their house I should never accept food as they didn't have enough to share. That if food was presented I should simply say I was not hungry, that my mother had just fed me, excuse myself from their company and go home. I held off from these invitations. Mrs. Audet was a good woman and couldn't bear to see any child hungry. One day she insisted I sit down at the lunch table. She served macaroni with lard. I had a hard time eating it. Figuratively, I held my nose, and gulped down, swallowing, a spoonful or two, sheepishly exclaimed I had to go to the bathroom, and ran across the tracks up the gully and into my mother's kitchen. She wasn't there. My sister Mary said she was downtown at J. J. Newberry's and Woolworth's trying on hats. (She had brought home lice to us on several occasions from those five-and-ten-cent stores much to the nuns' anger. Shame was heaped upon us.) My two older sisters were both tattlers, and Agnes told my father I had eaten food at the Audets when he had insisted we do not. I was whipped, and she was scolded strongly for having tattled. Actually the Audet children were not my friends . . . they were all much older, but as my sisters were friendly with their two younger daughters, I somehow figured into the Audet household.

After Carl Young moved from the area I became solid friends with Jack and his younger brother Bob. We had good times. Though Jack was never a hero to me he was important . . . after all his grandfather had been mayor of the town. I did have heroes as a small kid. Two heroes. Cigar and, well, let's call the other boy Rocco. They were both special, very special in my childish thinking. Rocco was a year or two older, but because he continued to fail his grades he ended up in the same classroom. His grandmother ran an Italian grocery store . . . what today is called a delicatessen. He was not hungry and his family was not poor but he dressed in rather raggy if not seedy clothes. Often he had holes in his pants and wore dirty shirts. He might have been a hippie long before that fraudulent style of dress became fashionable. I think the nuns despised him. I know he hated them. They were constantly spanking him for being truant, being sassy, gadding too long in the boys' rooms and spraying the wall with words. He never completed homework and usually refused to answer when called upon by the teacher. He was an all-out bad boy, or what today they would name and number a "youth at risk." He had been sent to the boys' reformatory once or twice though I have no idea what the crime was unless it was for truancy. He had a kind of nasty way of speaking from the left side of his mouth, and he smelled of garlic. I worshipped the ground he spat on, and walked in his physical tracks but dared not talk back to the nuns, or come to school in tattered clothes, pee on the bathroom wall, or play hookey. It would never do. My father would punish me after the nuns were finished with my backside. I certainly admired Rocco. When no one watched I aped his style, even said I loved garlic though I had no idea at that time what it was. There was a sensual quality to his walk, his sway, his undulation. I even attempted to copy that. I must confess, once I dared to rip my knickers behind a huge sign, a corduroy that I disliked intensely though was forced to wear . . . over

the knees covering brown woolen stockings. I felt I was the laughingstock of the classroom. Even Rocco laughed and that crushed me.

Years later I heard he had reformed and was most successful managing his grandmother's grocery store as proprietor. He did make a solid leap into adult society.

My second living hero was Cigar: a kid probably twelve years old, four years older than myself. I had no idea where Cigar lived. On Saturday mornings he always appeared at the skating rink at what was then called the ol' "Silk Mill" which formerly had been a box factory. He appeared but without skates. He'd stand at the edge of the ice, fists shoved into his pants pockets, and stare at us with certain hostility. He wouldn't stay the entire morning probably because he was cold, as he wore a very light fall jacket, and probably had had no breakfast, perhaps not even coffee. Cigar wasn't very tall, and it was said he had a mean and hungry look. My thought was that he was super . . . in today's parlance "cool." He didn't seem to give a damn about anything or anybody; he was his own man with or without ice skates. Spotting his leave taking, I'd sneak behind him and follow with wonder, curious where he was going, where he lived. Several times I caught him stopping by the entrance to the rink to unbutton his pants and pee his saffron waters onto the snow. Perhaps this is one reason that Denise Levertov's marvelous poem "To The Reader" remains a favorite, and a poem I use in creative writing classes. Why was Cigar called "cigar." There was one fact that I failed to mention: Cigar was black, an Afro-American lad, brown-skinned, and when I, or sometimes several boys, observed his saffron waters melt into the snows we naturally took particular notice of his privates. His penis was long and dark and shaped like a cigar . . . hence he acquired the nickname. I was proud that he could whip it out and pee publicly onto the crusted snow and feel no shame, no guilt. By then I was consumed by shame and burning with guilt. He taught me something about standing up against the world and sweet revenge.

Rocco and Cigar were celebrities.

*   *   *

My childhood . . . up to junior high school . . . had a sensuous quality enhanced by mother's baked bread in the oven, Aunt Jennie's blackberry pie steaming on the dinner table, Etta Zeller's fairyland garden of flowers, the Catholic nuns' rulers, the smelly fish and bloody game my father brought home from autumn woods and summer waters; the allergies to eggs, dust, goldenrod; my love of horseback riding and the good smell of horse flesh after a long canter. One of the most important sensations, and which I continue to remember, is the scent of wild June strawberries.

My mother's old family homestead years later had been sold to and demolished by two young hunters for a camp and the woods for deer and pheasant hunting. That demolition broke my heart. The house, always in need of paint, was a marvelous bastion of sensory impressions: tastes and touches, smells and hearing, and viewings. The old house contained many bedrooms and my favorite was my grandmother's boudoir, and it was a true boudoir. Rarely were we children allowed to spend a night in her great bed with the tick mattress, but it was a joyful event when Grandma said "yes." The room was at the front of the house, over the formal parlor which jutted out from the frame. It seemed to extend over the garden and to me became a part of the front lawn. Large, airy, the brightest room in the house, the windows faced the yard, the apple orchard to the left, and the drive rounded by a continuous circular yellow rosebush to the right. The fields of June ripened with wild strawberries bearing a contagious aroma. It made my senses more acute to apple blossoms, the roses Grandpa had planted years and years before, the mown grasses, the smell of freshly washed linen drying in sunny air. Given the rare opportunity of sleeping or napping in Grandma's room I became so affected between the fresh sheets by these scents, especially the strawberry, that I wrestled most of the night with my sensory glands overreacting.

This was before I learned the importance of the wild strawberry to Iroquois people. The first natural fruit of the eastern spring thousands of years ago came to be the symbol of rejuvenation and a property of healing.

Color, too, became an exquisite commodity; watermelon fattening in Aunt Jennie's garden near the peanut plants. She enjoyed experimenting with various exotic plants. Once she attempted a coffee tree to a crushing failure. Not a leaf sprang from the earth. Iris, blue chicory became favorite flowers, black elderberries dangling in the spokes of the after-noon sun; Uncle Bert's white mare pulling a sled load of wood through a thick emerald forest; the pink birthday cake I couldn't eat because of the egg allergy. I have disliked the color pink all my life.

The senses, without truly knowing, understanding, became utterly important to me as a child: flight of the bat under the porch roof of summer; electric storms; the feel of beach sand running through fingers; joy of a tick mattress; rich whipped cream on the tongue from Uncle Frank's cows; the craggy trunk of a hickory tree; a field of brilliant hawkweed; sweat on the hired men as they pitched hay or thrashed wheat; the acrid, nutty smell of human sweat; the shine of scales of a rainbow trout; all the beauty of a black willow; the rise of green hills; thin white rapids of Cold Creek; sails on the lake; my father's hunting boots and the shine on his rifles, oiled and ready for the kill, rabbit fur, the sheen of a beagle's fur.

When I was in high school I painted with oils. Not well, not interesting, but a poor imitation of Grandma Moses who was extremely popular at the time. My father and his friends seemed pleased, almost enamored, by my art, and encouraged me to go off to an art school. I knew better. Colorist I was, draftsman I was not. My horses looked like dogs and my dogs resembled stones in a field. There was a time in which I was quite taken with design and designed many floor plans. It was fun, but not to be taken seriously, and yet my father managed to sell for a small sum one of my plans to a friend. I think I was patronized.

No music, no art. I was stuck with being the budding journalist.

When I arrived at Shakespeare's plays and John Keat's odes and songs I was bowled over. My love of color, and use of the senses, had prepared me for these two great poets . . . encouraged by Aunt Flo Graves. They remain friends, heros in the same corner of my brain as do Rocco, Cigar, and the three elderly spinsters. Rocco gave me the strength to endure and survive the wrath and punishment of not only the St. Joseph nuns but the world in general; Cigar gave me a strong and lasting sense of pride even though my shyness may deny this characteristic. Aunt Flo, dear good Aunt Flo, brought beauty to my years.

* * *

Like all children I was bedded with illness . . . even though some were often manufactured. I was downed by measles, scarlet fever, the chicken pox that lay dormant for some fifty years and reared up into an ugly rash and piercing pain as shingles while teaching in British Columbia at the En'owkin Center. Colds often took their due, vertigo was a problem in the sixth grade and caused fainting spells. Once I fell down the staircase at Holy Family. Bloody noses occurred frequently, and, of course, my ever-present allergy to eggs and the others mentioned. And naturally, the toothache, the extraction and the fillings. But never has a wisdom tooth caused trouble, however my sisters suffered greatly with their wisdom teeth. Concerning fevers as a child I once wrote:

With Wanda McCaddon, Mexico City, 1962

Visitation

Fever and chill
chill and fever.

I knew what oranges were
though I had never sunk
a tooth into one.

Grandma Parker walked
into the room with an orange
  peeled
for sucking juices.

I lay back into my five years
and dreamed in death.

The morning sun healed
what fever and chill remained.

But my father growled:
"The kid's still sick.
Doesn't he know
she's been dead two years."

Odd, spectre-like it was, Grandma Parker had been dead two years. Oranges were most rare in northern New York in winter. In dreams all manner of acts can take place. If you believe, and the young have great faith, or certainly this young lad, cures may be received from the dead, the ghostly presence of the dead, especially one loved as deeply as a grandmother. Dreams are utterly important to Native American people, and particularly Iroquois, and especially to me. I think I have found the key . . .

with some help . . . to my dreams: the subconscious attempting to slowly inform the conscious mind of import . . . at times prismed, technicolored, miasmic, visionary illusions . . . the island in the stream, the creek flashing down the mountain shoulder, or in fantasy itself. I was always a dreamer, and at times remain a "daydreamer" distinguished from the real dream, the message of the real dream. Dreams are not to be toyed with, misinterpreted, ridiculed, mocked, or dismissed. Danger could be predicted, possible disaster.

Grandma Parker was conjured in my fever and chill, in the dream or in the vision. How deeply the illness was that night I cannot know nor remember, but it was serious. I believe it was a bout with scarlet fever which I continuously contracted by playing in the winter slush of the gully between the grass-green house and the railroad tracks. A fun place to slide and skate when the trickles of water had frozen. My mother could not keep me out of the gully. Grandmothers often exude love and strength, cures and comfort. Children are aware of these portentous qualities, and I summoned her to my dream to cure my illness . . . which she did.

Vision . . . the climb up hill or mountain to fast and dream, the study of spirit in wind or water, touching earth . . . has been written more successfully by others, such as Peter Blue Cloud and the classic rendering of the Lakota Holy Man, Black Elk. I can add little.

Most of my youth and adult life I was pretty much free of disease and illness. At age forty-four I did suffer a heart attack while living in Brooklyn, New York. This was very strange. I was working as a waiter in a neighborhood pub, and discovered the loss of feeling occasionally in my left hand, and some pain. I felt nauseous much of the time. So I consulted a local neighborhood doctor who insisted a brain tumor needed, demanded an immediate operation. I scoffed. A night or two later a friend conducted me to a hospital because of these recurring symptoms—Cumberland hospital in Brooklyn. There an East Indian doctor, young and cautious, responded that there were heart problems; his assistant, a white, Anglo doctor, said I was merely lazy and trying to avoid work. There was nothing wrong with me other than an ulcer pressing against the heart. Take antacid and return to work. The next night, at 3:00 A.M., rising out of a bed in sweat, nauseous and in dire pain, I called a friend and said I was going to the street, find a taxi, and enter Long Island College Hospital, a few blocks from my apartment. I remember being wheeled in, undressed and awakened (I have no idea when) by a cardiologist, Dr. _____, looking over me. No soft smile, no gentle hand holding mine, no eye comfort. Later, Dr. _____ inquired of my experience while blacked out. It was weird. Like Tantalus, I found myself in a shining green world, austere in sound, without smell. The green light bore down heavily into my vision. Something, without touching, continued to pull me upwards to a high pointed hill. I would fall back down. Again and again I would be tugged up the hill only to slip backwards. It seemed an eternity. Many weeks later, released from the hospital, my cardiologist asking me of the experience, and told as only a storyteller such as myself might tell, I related the green world. This time he smiled and responded: "I was pleading with you to live. You didn't want to stay in our world. I would not release you. I was determined not to lose you. You were totally exhausted which helped to cause your illness. It was my mission, and remains, to save a poet. I continued to plead until your eyelashes fluttered and you awakened." It had been a virus, he pronounced, causing a problem with your heart which affects men much older than you are now. A man of my then-middle age does not usually contract such a virus. It was the disease of an old man.

He saved my life. I did as he suggested. I wrote out my heart and pain.

Since then I have been comparatively healthy.

Four: Looking for Home

It rained the night I ran away. An angry rain.

The rain struck rooftops, sidewalks, autumn earth with such force I knew that I was not the only thing in existence which was troubled. Rain pelted against windowpanes, splattered down eaves, ran in whirls and circles through gutters, blustered down drains.

The world was drenched. My spirit was drenched.

My world and the world were coming apart, and this soggy world was neither of my own making nor of my desire.

*   *   *

The woman stood at her kitchen stove, the Onondaga woman; she was cooking fry bread for her husband, the children, and for me. Grease in the skillet spattered her apron, and hissed against exposed flesh of her arm. She called out a painful ouch. I watched her closely as she smiled down on her small children playing at her shoes. She was nice. She had been nice to me . . . the fostered boarder. They meant well . . . her husband, the little children, and naturally she meant to care very well for me. She'd given me a comfortable bed on the couch, fed me some good-tasting soup, made cookies, and now, that night, she was making fry bread for us all. We'd dip it in maple syrup. I remember she had made sausage and boiled potatoes smothered in the sausage drippings earlier for supper. It was good. She was good. She was young, not over thirty, pale complexioned; her dark hair was fluffy around her ears and cheeks. She was pretty, and her flower-patterned dress with white roses and bluettes accented her prettiness. The children, five and six, were pale-skinned like their mother, but black-haired with big brown eyes. She talked to me in soft words. She said how Halloween would be coming and she'd make candy for us, popcorn balls rolled in molasses, and we'd dress the children and go out trick-or-treating together. I was eleven, the second-oldest male in the house, and didn't think much of Hal-

*At the Tivoli II Club, St. Thomas,
Virgin Islands, 1966*

loween pranks anymore: cutting clotheslines, turning over garbage barrels, soaping windows. It wasn't that I had attained so much sophistication for those childish tricks, but I was standing near her at the stove thinking of how I could run out the kitchen door and run away from not just that family and house, the fry bread, but the abysmal world then surrounding my thin years and thinner body pained from loneness, hurt from having been cast away.

My parents separated when I was nine years old. Some years later they divorced. My father went to work in Rome, New York; my mother stayed in Watertown working at various jobs, renting apartments for her and me for the next two years following the separation. I enjoyed those years with her even though I rarely spent time with my mother. She worked nights and I schooled days . . . so that I needed to get my own supper and, after homework, tucked myself into bed. When I opened a can of tomato soup or fried hamburgers I thought I was really getting supper ready for the two of us. She rarely came home to eat. Bologna was good to a young boy's taste buds, but eating alone wasn't fun. So after the sandwich or soup or whatever can I'd open was ready to eat, I'd toss it out, and stayed contented on what the school cafeteria had served for lunch. We were then living in a dark apartment on Massey Street in Watertown that contained a strange smell. The sink coughed up an odd odor of, perhaps, old drain or garbage. But my mother's

bedroom smelled of her perfumes and rouge, her lipsticks and hair ointments. That was pleasant. I spent time in her room listening to her radio. I slept on a wicker couch in the living room, spare and frightening, with bare walls painted but the paint was so old and dusty that the several lamps could not brighten the room. One night she came home early from work. There was a man with her in an army uniform. She introduced us and said she had the night off and that they were going out on the town. Little did I know that years later he would be my stepfather. Martin was stationed at Pine Camp, now known as Fort Drum. He was in the tank corps, and his regiment was waiting orders to ship out to the European war. When at last his orders came, my mother announced broadly she was going to live with her three sisters in Bayonne, New Jersey. She couldn't take me with her. But would later send for me. In the meantime, I would go to Syracuse and stay with her girlfriend who was from there, and recently had been working in Watertown, being separated from her own husband. I'd have lots of fun in their house, and they would teach me Indian ways which my father had not as then done. She left. The Onondaga woman came by for me in her car, and helped me pack my few things. My mother had stored her things except the clothes she needed, cosmetics, things of that nature. I didn't have much, I remember, as most of my things, books, toys, and yes, clothes, had remained in my father's house. It seemed I lived with the Onondaga family an eternity, yet thinking back now, it was only a matter of days. When we left Watertown it was crisp October. Warm days. Cool nights. Leaves underfoot to be scuffled in piled-up play.

We arrived in Syracuse. I assumed I'd be registered for a school though it did not come up in any conversation, any talk between my new foster parents. I moped around all day while they worked. Then it rained. Rain is sad, depressing even to this moment. It means loneness, it means desperation. Truly it makes the April flowers, etc., but tell that to an aching boy who has first lost his father and then been abandoned by his mother. Orphaned. It won't work. I have never liked rain. It depresses still.

I stole out of the house never to return. My mother's best friend, Peg Greenwood, also lived in Syracuse, and her then-friend, Leo (?), I understood lived near the house where I had been dropped. I wandered the night looking for Leo's house; reading names at doors, ringing doorbells until at last I found him in an elegant apartment on James Street . . . at that time a posh neighborhood. He took me in. He'd been warned by Peg who had been warned by phone that I was on the loose and might show up at his door. I gather people were raking the streets for my rain-drenched figure.

When Leo opened the door I was sopping wet, shivering and cold. I had no jacket. A very tall man, he bent down and hugged my wet figure, pulled me into the room, stripped the wet clothes, poured me into a hot steaming tub, and soaked me until whatever fever and cold might be lurking behind the flesh was safely prevented from attacking. He swathed me in a shirt, his own, huge as a tent, and after feeding me hot soup, sent me off to bed. Peg Greenwood phoned my father my predicament. He phoned Leo and had him take me to Peg's house once there was assurance I had not come down with an illness from the drenching rain. I stayed with Peg several months . . . without attending school. Finally my father made the decision that if my mother did not want me . . . and she had been notified of my running away and then relocating at Peg's . . . that I should return north and stay with aunts.

I surely had assumed the semblance of David Copperfield.

*   *   *

As a child I was shy. My two older sisters certainly helped develop this particular characteristic I have suffered most of my adult life even though at times I appear loud and arrogant. The brawl, the bluster, the stomp was and continues to be self-defense. My mother was a rather quiet woman, my father usually soft-spoken except when angry, but his firmness, especially as he grew older, was frightening at times, and I often cowered before him. He was older, wiser, more assured, somewhat defiant not merely of certain conventions, but of humans. He was successful in his chosen work, not only successful but happy and proud. I was not proud, not happy, had no reason to feel successful as a child and had been deeply intimidated by my mother as to the maleness of men so that I acquired an offensive defense. Shyness. When quite small, after my sis-

ters had trudged off to bed involuntarily, my mother would take me into her bedroom, sit at the bottom of her bed, and we would stare out into the night. In winter we watched snow fall, tiny flakes as insignificant as myself. She would point off in the distance and beckon my sight to an automobile parked a block or two away. She said my father sat in that car. He wasn't alone. He was with another woman, a girlfriend. Many years later this woman became my stepmother. Mama would tell me how bad men were, thoughtless, inconsiderate, driven by sexual urges to commit the most heinous of sins and crimes. And my father was playing foul. I did not know if this was true, nor whether it was him in that car smooching with a woman other than my mother. I had only her word, her say-so, her fears. And her fears became mine. This indoctrination developed into a reason partly for my shyness, especially around women and particularly women of strength and authority, such as teachers. It also colored my imagination and intellect. I am much more comfortable with men than with women . . . after all we are "bad," capable of demolishing a woman's femininity. Perhaps she was correct in her assumption. Many feminists to this moment feel the same ideas rankle through their minds. Perhaps they are right. I can't really say. The only thing I can add is that I would probably have been a different man if my mother had not sat me on the edge of her bed on those snowy winter nights and programmed me into thinking men were "bad," or what people now might say "sleaze." Certainly what my father was doing was without a doubt wrong. If he no longer cared, let alone loved my mother, he should have been honest, forthright, and separated, or worked things out through some form of counseling. He did not. He was a womanizer. It didn't mean he did not love my mother. I have always believed he did. Or has it been simply necessary for me to continue, hold this belief for some handle on sanity. My mother, putting this guilt trip on me as a child, equaled the guilt trip the nuns at Holy Family indelibly burnt into my mind . . . Every morning after prayers, and before the structured class commenced, the nuns would tell us how Father Isaac Jogues was brutally slaughtered, beheaded by the Mohawk men, having been tortured by the Mohawk women, he was clubbed to death in the mid-1600s. Such a "kind good man," and how dreadfully savage the Mohawks had been to this saint, and didn't I feel ashamed of this history. I certainly didn't feel ashamed, guilty in the beginning of first grade. Certainly I became guilty as time wore on. Yes, it certainly was my fault that this good saint, Father Isaac Jogues, missionary to the Mohawks, had died so cruel and heathenish a death. Naturally the nuns failed to relate why he had been put to death by the Nation's chiefs. He was first French, not to be trusted, and the French had not only slaughtered Mohawks in ambush (1609), but later upon entering the Native villages brought all sorts of diseases which killed off large populations of Mohawks and other Iroquois people: everything from colds to smallpox. Once arriving in the village they systematically started to missionize, convert the Native people to Catholicism from a perfectly good and well worked-out religion. They attacked the minds of the women first; then the small children. They also relayed information to the French crown of the population of warriors, the quality of beaver and mink fur, trade routes by land and water . . . knowing the English crown

also had eyes upon the region for the same reasons, conquest and domination. Yes, the nuns failed to speak of these horrors upon Native peoples which the Jesuits committed.

The guilt stuck with me. Night after many nights throughout my life these horror stories and the guilt persisted in my dreams, or actually nightmares. Years later I wrote a series of persona poems and that collection of poems obliterated the guilt the nuns so steadfastly burnt into the mind.

My mother was doing the same. One mustn't forget the Jesuits were males. The Mohawk warriors were male as well. And my father was a male.

In those early years it was a house of women in which I was raised. My father was seldom home. He worked much of the time at his job with the city of Watertown, many overtime hours; weekends he hunted or fished, and weekend nights he was "out on the town." In the early days of my life my mother was often with him on those weekend night excursions, but a confrontation, obviously, sprang up between them

Julian Block, Richard Cornelles, Maurice Kenny, and Wanda McCaddon, 1984

and he started to leave her home, went out on his own, dressed in white shirt and tie in a tailored suit. She said he often came home near dawn with lipstick on his collar.

By the time my parents separated, my oldest sister, Agnes, had left my father's house. They heatedly argued over a boyfriend. He demanded she not see him as he was sure that the young man in question was not good enough for his daughter. The young man, a French-Indian, was loose, lazy, and would end up a bum. She disobeyed his command, and finally he asked her to leave. (A few years later she married him, and he proved to my father that he was utterly and completely wrong. John became a successful airplane mechanic and devoted husband and father straight through to his early death.) Mary, my other sister, was also seeing a young man of whom my father disapproved. What were his daughters and wife doing to him. Why did they go against his wishes, his better sense, his common sense, and his knowledge of these two young men. There were brutal arguments between Mary and my father. He lost a second time. She, also, a few years later married him, and Pat, as he was nicknamed, proved to be a good provider and good husband, at least to the outside world. My father was determined that I would listen to his better thought. I would not end up in a bad marriage. He did not seemingly keep me under complete control, chain me to my bedroom wall, nor beat me into submission. He attempted a different tactic with me by giving in to most of my demands, adolescent foolishness, and needs, and my peculiar, to him, character. I was sensitive and imaginative, and, unfortunately, both creative and shy.

Five: Broadway

My cousin, Dorothy, was far darker in complexion than myself. In the summer she was near black. Perhaps that is why she was so cruel when I reached Bayonne, New Jersey, at last, after my stay in rainy Syracuse and the few months as boarder with my aunts Frances in town and Jennie in the country on the farm.

All of which were troublesome days. My father at last came to the decision that as my mother had demanded me in the courtroom at their separation it was now not only her parental, motherly, moral, but legal obligation to assume responsibility of the small boy she had shrugged away into abandonment. My aunts were very kind even though whispers constantly assaulted my ears like sharp points piercing flesh. My grandmother Herrick, never terribly pleased with her second daughter, Doris, my mother, argued vehemently with Aunt Jennie and Uncle Frank as to the proper care and upbringing, raising this new burden on the household, an adolescent puberty-fraught boy. She was never crude but her sentimentality . . . gushing tears over my orphanhood . . . began to pall and pull. My grandmother was a sobber and a whiner . . . good woman that she was. As a young bride she had become accustomed to household help . . . demanding this and that of my grandfather. She had had seven daughters and one son, who did not live the year. She did have work, much work for a mother and a farmer's wife. But all women did in those early days of the century. Her lot was not much different with the exception that Grandfather Herrick still had some money left from the family fortune, such as it was, not much. Consequently it was paid out in fine furniture for the formal parlor and for household help . . . that exact word which was coined to call a maid. The money was spent. When Grandpa died he was in debt: farm mortgaged to the hilt, including his stock, cows and horses.

Aunt Ruth, one of two maiden aunts, my mother's younger sister, had stayed on the farm until her father died, and then continued living with her married sister, Jennie. Aunt Ruth was a few years older than Agnes, my oldest sister, and she was free and much fun. Hard worker, she spent her days in the fields, planting and harvesting . . . mainly hay. Evenings in the garden or berry patches after milking twenty-five head of cows. She put sprite into my days and games into my nights: jigsaw puzzles, etc. . . . Uncle Frank, the man of the house, was strong but sympathetic. He was my friend and bulwark against the ladies. His compassion was overflowing, and I was desperate for it. He came between all disagreements concerning my parental poverty, and often I would hear him reinforcing my mother's situation . . . in the sense that she had an absolute right to life, a life she chose to live . . . unfortunately she had a son.

The time sped by on the farm those months. One day Aunt Jennie announced it was necessary to pack a bag, and that I was leaving for

New Jersey. It would be fun . . . a train ride to New York City. I do not know how, but my father had coerced my mother to accept her responsibilities, and to her protest, she accepted my return to her bosom, in Bayonne. That proved somewhat unfortunate. I was entered in school . . . the eighth grade. They jumped me one grade even though I had missed many days. My cousin Dorothy was to take me the first morning . . . she was in the same class. Whispers behind cupped hands commenced almost immediately. The abandonment. The idea I was a quarter-blood Indian in a pretty much all Italian/Irish school. My cousin was smart and popular with the kids. I proved neither. Teachers came down on me like the horrid rains in Syracuse. I was determined to run away once more. Instead of taking up my hobo pack on the proverbial stick, I simply skipped school each morning. My mother gave me funds for the bus and lunch. And each morning I did board a bus, but not for school. Instead I walked out to what was then Hudson Boulevard, now Kennedy Boulevard, and went off to New York City, particularly Times Square. That's where the theater stage shows were, the legitimate theater and movie stars. Klieg lights, limelight, starlight-blinded vision. I soon found friends mutual to my thinking, and we were on the hunt. No, no, no. Not to star on stage and screen, but to hunt actors . . . movie stars especially, and savor their autographs. It wasn't long before my book was full with priceless signatures: Carol Landis, Victor Mature, Shirley Temple, Milton Beryl, Donald O'Connor, the gorgeous Maria Montez, Mary Martin who was starring in *One Touch of Venus,* Cornelia Otis Skinner, the Lunts, and hundreds more. Ginny Sims, the Hollywood/radio singing personality, was headlining a stage production at the handsome Capitol Theater on Broadway. I adored her . . . only Veronica Lake held more strings to my foolish boy-heart. I managed to save up some dimes and bought a camellia corsage and sent it up to Ms. Sims's dressing room at the theater. It wasn't long before a call came to the stage door asking the gifter to come upstairs. I went, shaking in my socks. Ms. Sims was between shows, it was lunchtime, and she was having a sandwich and coffee. She offered me food after thanking me for the lovely gift of camellia. We chatted a few moments. I was thrilled. She was stunning. She was gentle. She was intelligent, and wise. To paraphrase, she

"Sitting for a portrait by painter Julian Block,"
Ashville, Oregon, 1987

said something to the point that she had kindly granted me an interview as a favor to a young fan. Now I must grant her a favor. She conditioned that I must never be truant from school again. And proceeded to explain all the reasons that truancy was not only wrong, but foolish, wasteful, and could lead to serious troubles now as a lad and later as an adult. I wasn't thinking of adulthood. I was thinking of my pain in that school, and cold rain. I promised I would never skip school again. That I would venture into Times Square only on Saturday, with approval of my mother, and that I would concentrate on the studies I had missed, and make lost work up. Well, I lied to Ginny Sims. Because I did not forgo truancy, nor forget Times Square and autograph hunting, and I did not make up the lost work. Years later, the late Ms. Sims became a successful mayor of a California city.

When I arrived home that late afternoon . . . the precise time due from school . . . well, startling, there sat my mother at the kitchen

With Wanda McCaddon, Ashville, 1987

table having coffee and cookies with the truant officer. Again I made honest promises, and again failed to keep them. Shortly—the next morning—a letter arrived from the juvenile court stating that I must appear on such and such a morning with my parents. I had missed 280 days of the school year. My father went to court with me . . . he was, himself, then living and working in Bayonne, actually the Brooklyn Navy Yard on warships. He was not impressed with my conduct. He was not impressed with my mother's responsibility. I had become utterly undisciplined, obnoxious, a common criminal. I had not only skipped school, but had begun to both smoke and drink. I was twelve years old. He was very disappointed, hurt, angry, and somewhat feeling guilty for the advent of these early years of my adolescence. He did not have the words to say, but I knew then . . . I had at last become my childhood heroes . . . Rocco and "Cigar." I was very proud and pleased. I had defied not only schoolteachers, my cousin, but all authority and the world. I had peed onto the hard crust of snow wearing ragged knickers and smelling of garlic.

The judge was kind and lenient. He said that I would serve six months in a reformatory. My father intervened, blessedly, fatherly. I prayed, still a Catholic though weakening every day, to the Virgin Mother to save my skin. My father asked the judge should he take me from his wife's flimsy care, and cart me home to northern New York State where we were from . . . would the judge suspend the sentence. He agreed. Days later, packed up in his Chevy, we took off with Anne McBride, the woman who would a few years later become my stepmother. I was never again to live for any length of time in my mother's house . . . visits, yes, but nothing longer.

We went home north to Watertown with spring hawks, eagles, and robins. I was in time for school . . . it had not yet let out for summer vacation. Unfortunately, or perhaps fortunately, I was dropped down a grade. That was best. Naturally, I had failed all courses in Bayonne Junior High . . . even Latin which I enjoyed. The Watertown principal and his teachers had been duly warned of my proclivity to truancy. The first second I had not shown up, or was late, they were to phone my father. He would deal with me on that score. Needless to say, I failed to show the first morning. My addiction was stronger than my yearning to learn. I hid the day in my cousin Jewel Ortman's house. Jewel was my father's cousin, but she and her husband, Harry, were also his best friends. They two had come across the political border into the United States. To save a long story, Andrew Anthony Kenny never forgave, to his dying moment, Jewel Ortman her trespass against his will and wishes, having given me sanctuary that fateful morning. To her hundreds of pleadings he gave a deaf ear. They never spoke again, played euchre . . . in fact her name was not allowed in his house. The next time Jewel looked at his face he lay in his casket in death. The thought of skipping school or a class never entered my head again. I was clean. The drug was forfeited through cold turkey. I was no longer a slave to that addiction. But I continued to smoke . . . to this very moment, yet I gave up drinking until the last couple of years of high school, when with friends, to be smart . . . what we considered sophisticated, I took a gin fizz or two, sweet and sickening to this moment. When I seriously started to drink I went to vodka . . . straight on the rocks.

There were interesting stories connected to my truancy . . . other than discovering places to hang out all day and weird people I met at stage doors or hotel alleys. Once at the glamorous Sherry Netherlands I was lucky to be picked to celebrate Peggy Ryan's birthday. She then costarred with Donald O'Connor in a series of mediocre, cheap musicals. It was fun . . . especially to be photographed with such bright young Hollywood stars. Peggy has disappeared. Donald went on to great fame dancing in some of Hollywood's finest musicals. How meaningless that early experience seems today . . . when columned beside what I had lost from classroom. Probably the most exciting, original experience I had in those stagestruck weeks, and an experience or thrill I remember most vividly and tell to the young with relish and near pride, was that I had been horsewhipped by an exciting actor, one of the most important of his day, and now proven a true genius as not only actor, but director, Orson Welles. I never tire of watching *Citizen Kane.* And, leaning over to a friend, I delight in saying, "You know, he whipped me once." Of

course, to their amazed disbelief. But it was true. Orson Welles married the glamorous Rita Hayworth . . . star of *Rain, Cover Girl,* and many other films. She was the strawberry redhead of beauties. She was most beautiful, in fact I would guess more beautiful, off screen than on. They spent their honeymoon in the chic Sherry Netherlands . . . as did O'Connor and Ryan. We leeches, autograph hunters, were there at the swirling doors each morning and stayed all day waiting for them to exit or make an elegant entrance. We knew they had left the hotel and devised the idea they had left by a secret exit. Whatever, one bright, sunny morning I looked up and over to Central Park where at the street edge one might rent a hansom cab drawn by a horse for a pleasant spin through the park. I looked over, and as I did there were Welles and his lovely bride just mounting the first step of the cab. Silently I rushed the red light and crossed Fifth Avenue as the horse trotted up Central Park South. My short legs were motorized. I drew up to the cab, took a hold of the door forcing it to open, and trotted along fixing to take my autograph book from my pocket with pencil for their signature. I was perplexed. Instead of accepting my pencil, Orson Welles reared from the seat, grabbed the driver's whip, and proceeded to lash my flesh. For days the red welts refused to leave my back. But I had his signature. To prove to my cohorts that those slashes were given to my poor back by Orson Welles was another very difficult story. They turned away from what they thought a lie. But it was the truth. Unfortunately, now, those welts have long disappeared into the memory. Again Rocco and "Cigar" would have been proud of my effrontery and daring.

I did pretty well in junior high school . . . I even passed algebra with a decent grade. I began enjoying school and learning. There is a difference. I disliked gym because of the instructor, but the other teachers were fine. High school was enjoyed even more. I did very well, especially in Latin, English, history, and geography. Science and math no. Without forming a true philosophy, articulated intellectually, I must have realized that I was to become an imaginative writer and that science and math would not be needed. Science was passed but not with flying grades to be proud of and mainly because of my teacher, Miss Marie, who had also become my voice coach. I emptied her trash, raked the autumn leaves from her yards, helped plant spring flowers in the sidewalk gardens, and whatever light chores needed being done for free voice lessons. Hour after hour in her musty music room I stood at her piano and sang the scale, "Old Black Joe," and other gushy tunes. It was fun, and little did I realize she was teaching me a sense of discipline, voice range, enunciation, diction that is, and a love for the platform and podium. If I read poetry before an audience well today it is through Miss Marie's instruction. So science had been conquered. Geometry was something different. I failed it three times. Poor Miss Belle . . . with her short mannish haircut, her buck teeth, her scrawny frame . . . poor Miss Belle, she worked so hard on and with my non-mathematical brain to pass geometry. At the third try I failed again with a flat fifty points. Never was it passed. And I have proven to myself over and over again that it was not needed as an imaginative writer, a poet. Or so I have led myself to believe. Miss Belle may not have taught me geometry, even during the many after-school hours. But she taught me dedication, and that the student—not the school, not the college, not the Board of Regents—but that the student always comes first.

There was certain pleasure in high school. I had good friends, a very pretty girlfriend, we had lots of dances, basketball and football games . . . though rarely did I have the opportunity to attend these games . . . weekends in New York City allegedly visiting my mother . . . a used car my father bought for me, and horseback riding. I loved horses more than anything in life. They were friends, family, a whirl out of the misery of life, or what I thought to be misery of life, or what I thought to be misery.

Six: Horses

Symbol of freedom, wildness, mystery, symbol of beauty and grace, yet a beast of burden raised to pull the plow, the hay rake, milk wagon, the hansom cabs of Central Park, the village buggy, the stagecoach and the Pony Express, mail routes of the Old West; ridden by whiskered cowpokes, bucktoothed Billy the Kid, the U.S. Cavalry out to spread death across all Indian Nations west of the Mississippi River and between the Mexican and Canadian borders. Stolen by the Comanche of the Southern

Plains from the Spanish conquistadors, he became a noble beast to the Native American . . . image of art, symbol of warrior societies, on the buffalo hunt brought food, fur, and wealth to struggling Nations, beast of ceremony, and often in the mid- through late-1800s the means of survival for the Plains peoples of Oklahoma, the Dakotas, and elsewhere. The horse . . . so powerful a symbol, creature that the locomotive when first crossed the Far West the Native people named it the "iron horse" . . . out of wonder and respect.

As a boy I loved the horse, any horse, blind, crippled, bluegrassed, living, dead, in a photograph, painting, sculpture, under my loins, in memory, side by side as I curried its body or as it chewed hay or oats. But especially when I sat in the saddle trotting, cantering, galloping the high State Street hills outside Watertown. I was free of all bondage, of angry rains, of orphanhood, of Times Square weirdos, of hateful teachers and cold students who refused to make or offer friendship. The horse released me. Most teenage boys take to the rowboat, motorboat, or canoe to swiftly ride waves or down rapid rivers. I enjoyed boating but never considered boating a necessity. It was a way of whirling away a summer afternoon bored with fishing for trout which deliberately avoided your hook. Horseback riding was different. You were, first of all, one with the steed, your figure meshed with its body; you had six legs and the horse had two heads. And you were both free to race the rains, the grey mornings of boyhood, the sun-drenched afternoons of youth. The horse understood your emotions, your passions, the hurts and disappointments and the pleasures you knew on his broad back, fists clenched around his mane, knees buckling into his withers . . . your small, thin body no burden for his power, you were the weight of a wisp of wind. You, the young rider, knew his fatigue, his thirst, his need to wander through the ripe meadows. You knew his shod hoof, his frothy sweat, his smell, sometimes his bite as he turned his head, snorting, prancing, and nudged your leg with his flared nostrils and bit. Unlike your childhood dog, the horse rarely patronized with false love. Never did he sidle up, lick your hand, always begging for a bone or raw hamburg you might steal out of the refrigerator. If he followed after you in the paddock or field, if he allowed you to stay saddled or ride bareback, it was because the horse trusted and favored you, enjoyed your voice, smell, and the ride across the ridge or through a sweet clover meadow.

When very young I found the comfort of a stream which flowed past my house; the waters, trout within, the sand and rocks the waters leisurely flowed over, the black willows shading the ripples and standing guard along the shore, yes even the muskrat that lived in the waters and the hollows of the embankment; the muskrat who swiftly dashed across the brim of the creek like an arrow moving through heavy winds of the sky.

Seven: Silver Bay, New York, Lake George

Less than four hours ago I observed a mink race across the savannah along the lake shoreline; behind a small armada of three Sunfish sails navigated by teenage boys swiftly moved with the light breeze. Sparrows warbled in and out of a bush of juniper directly before the screened porch where I sat in a Kennedy-like rocking chair drinking coffee and peering into

a collection of short stories by Anthony Burgess, *The Devil's Mode.* From my porch I view not only the lake, a lake allegedly discovered in the mid-1600s by the famous Jesuit Isaac Jogues, but in historical reality the lake had been discovered long centuries ago by both Iroquois and Algonquians. Another blatant lie that history has proposed dealing with the early years of European contact with this very ancient world on the turtle's back. I see a number of trees such as a white pine, a huge weeping willow, and a long hedge of pink primroses.

Needless to say the foundation which supports my residency here, and the Writers Voice Association, has decidedly considered my needs and desires well, my comforts are worthy of deep appreciation.

I hear off at a slight distance down the shore the sweet voices of youngsters, boys and girls at play. The birds twitter, the radio gives the startling news of the day. The area and cabin, or what I prefer to call cottage, somehow give an English aura here. I must remember Sir William Johnson fought the French not far south at Lake George in the mid-1700s and

"Teaching a class at North Country Community College," Saranac Lake, New York, 1987

drove the French north into Canada making this area an important part of the English Colony. Hence the smell of Brits, the aura.

The cottage reminds me of the cottage my father long ago built on Chaumont Bay on Lake Ontario. The same feel: a kitchen, a living area, two bedrooms, and of course the usual bath; old furniture though perfectly serviceable. I've come a long way from that childhood cottage. A long way.

What would my dad now say? I journeyed to Mexico; I have flown to the Caribbean and South America. I have lived and taught in NYC, California, Oklahoma. I have even taught in British Columbia. What would he say? Unbelievable. A year before he died, sitting at the kitchen table, he wept, his face into his arms. I asked him why he was crying. His reply was that he feared for me: that I was effete, that I would not make it. That was in 1957. What would he say?

And watching the youngsters down the shore playing ball and hearing their fun and laughter, I can't help but wonder what my old heroes, Rocco and "Cigar," would say should they have any idea that here I am on this incredibly lovely lakeshore, ensconced in a charming cottage, watching a mink race across the burnt lawn. And more incredible, a wealthy important foundation was giving me money to sit here watching through the screened porch writing these words and lines. They would probably respond, "No way, Jose. You shy, cowardly, skinny, little cuss. Afraid to sass the nuns, afraid to piss in the snow on the world. You phony. Get out of there. You don't belong. Hit the road for the garlic fields."

On the road again, so to speak, I have just returned home to Saranac Lake from a long tour across the country with the beautiful poet Carolyn Forche, sponsored by another affluent foundation, and here I sit on the shores of Silver Bay pampered and swaddled like an important celebrity. And I think, attempt to recall the angry rains. I wasn't always pampered. No, not at all.

What am I doing here.

*   *   *

The author (fifth from left) at the Native American Women Writers Festival, Saranac Lake, 1988

Junior and senior high were friends and foes alike. Teachers I didn't cozy up to that much with rare exceptions. It was Pete Hyde who pretty much encouraged my trouble the very first session of wood shop. We were horsing around, as teenage boys call it, laughing or more like giggling over this piece of wood shaped like a penis that we were expected to carve into the fuselage of an airplane. That was the assignment given by Mr. Knapp, the teacher and school coach. Mr. Knapp was not at all thrilled with our actions and impertinence in his shop class. He threw us out, would not allow us to return, and flunked us to boot. It was fine by me. I hated carving anyway. I don't recall signing up for metal or print shop. It was the three shop classes through which I was able to convince my father to allow me to quit the Catholic school and enroll in the public. Pete and I made a mess of things. Carl Knapp became a quasi-friend. He was president of the class and a son of Mr. Knapp the teacher/coach. Carl was also editor of the student paper. He announced one day that I was the student reporter, and my duty would be to gather news (gossip he meant) for the paper as I was the budding writer and also something of a snoop. I was delighted. My closest male friends with the exception of Sherry Carr did not attend the public high school but rather were enrolled at the Catholic school, the Immaculate Heart Academy . . . where my two older sisters had graduated. Or in the case of Dick Paquin and Stuart Jones . . . neighbor lads . . . they attended high school in Copenhagen some seven miles away from our homes. My very best friend was Joseph White, son of French-Indian parents who originally hailed from the Province of Quebec. I could spend at least half this memoir telling tales of my relationship with Joe: the nights and days we spent together, the girls we double-dated (mainly Sally and Caroline Kelly who would neck in the back seat); how we learned to drive an automobile in Joe's dad's farm doodlebug on the flats of the back hay lots; the hours we pawed over our miseries dealing with parents, girlfriends, school, going off to college, work . . . Joe worked in a drugstore as a soda jerk (and he was no jerk) and I for my dad pumping gasoline; horses, as we both thrilled to ride and rode often the horses that were on the premises where Joe lived . . . the Longway farm where Doug Longway bought and sold or traded

mostly draught horses though occasionally a saddle horse showed its startled head in his horse van; growing pains, particularly sex, and it was Joe's smart mother who gave us all the instruction we would need, mainly "use a condom" before marriage, but as she knew we were both good Catholic boys (and Joe was a good son of the church) we would assuredly abstain until after a ring was safely and honorably placed upon a young woman's finger. That didn't stop us from necking with girls in the backseat of his or my dads' cars. We were virgins throughout our high school days, I think.

There was one problem I had which involved Joe. I was jealous. Not of him, not because he was better looking than I thought I was, not because he was probably more popular, not because he was better at math, or at dancing as I was mainly five-footed, not because he was tall and I was short, not because his parents stayed married and lived together until death did them part, not because his mother was a better cook than my stepmother nor that her nature was a bit sweeter than my stepmother who often fell to dark moods, but because of Jimmy Carr (no relation to Sherry). Jim came up from New Jersey to attend as boarder at IHA. He and Joe were classmates. From eight to four they were together sharing classes, teachers, girls, and other boys at the school, lunch, rides, secrets that I was not privy to, and that galled me. Joe was my friend most of the year. We were rarely separated especially over the summer. Many nights we shared the same bed in his father's house, and broke bread religiously together. There was no action that we did not share. To this moment I find it impossible to even consider that Joe shared his dreams with Jim as he did with me. Would he ever have confessed to Jimmy that he was positive he would die before reaching the age of thirty-six years, and that I was his sole heir. I was to receive his books and his class ring if he was not married. Nor did I ever tell anyone that I too would not live over the age of thirty-six, and that Joseph White was my sole and only heir . . . who would receive my books and horse if I had a horse at the time of death and was not married. We were quite sure that after college we would marry some brilliant talented young women of wealth. Neither of us died at thirty-six and only Joe married legally and raised children. To the best of my knowledge he is alive and yet has been a remarkably good husband, excellent father, and gentle grandfather. He did marry a pretty young woman whose father, though not extravagantly wealthy, had some money, certainly more than Joe's father. I was a better horseman, rider than Joe . . . I think because I cared, no loved their flesh and spirit more than Joe. I was also a much better singer than Joe who could not carry a tune. In our senior year the four of us: Joe, Jimmy, Sherry, and myself, would cruise down public square singing out our hearts to the pretty girls gliding along the street in their evening best . . . which were at that time flared printed skirts and pretty blouses or dresses tightly belted around thin waists. My voice rang the loudest in the silly ditties. I must admit that Jimmy also had a decidedly good voice. The nuns at IHA approved and he was given roles in the school's musicals.

I was jealous of Joe's friendship with Jimmy, and I was jealous of Jimmy's position and his voice and his wealthy background and family in New Jersey. I couldn't wait for the end of the school year so Jim would return to the bosom of his folks and I would have Joe all to myself with the exception of the young lady he was at that particular moment interested in: Sally Kelly, Mary Beth Hughes, Katherine Bolton who eventually married Sherry, or whoever. As we double-dated to the movies, summer dances, to swim at the lake, to picnic, to eat nightly at the diners, to sit porches, or neck in the cars of our fathers . . . there was no jealousy. Jim would be safely ensconced in New Jersey and was no threat until September of the new school year.

After high school I can probably count on my fingers the times I spent with Joe. Why? I haven't seen him for many years, over thirty, not since my own father died. Why? I have no desire to see him now, now as an old man probably bored with life, waiting for death as he sits in a porch rocking chair counting the floating seeds of dandelions or flakes of snow piling up around his feet. I have had no desire to see any friends of my youth: the Kelly girls, Sherry, Pete, Charles Major who played a minor part of my days in junior high, Virginia that sweet young girl I was foolishly in adoring love with at twelve or thirteen. I have met with a few but rarely and for only brief moments simply but quickly to say hello, good-bye.

My life has differed so very greatly from their lives . . . not just because I have pursued a literary career and they something perhaps more greatly common . . . if I may use that word, normal, pedestrian, bourgeoisie, Anglo. Joe was never concerned with his mixed blood as a young lad as I was; Jimmy I doubt went any further with his singing than cruising public square; Sherry went into the grocery business; all three girls, Sally, Caroline, Mary Beth, all married, some well, some not so well, I'd suppose because of the rules of life. I was different. I was on the outside, I was the outlaw, the uninhibited, something of the revolutionist. I wanted big things and to do big things. A gypsy woman foretold that I would hold books in my hands. Her prediction came true. I'm not sure what was predicted for Joe and the others, but I could conjecture a very average life of little pleasures under the Christmas tree, picnics on Lake Ontario, births and deaths and weddings, summer vacations in the Adirondacks or at Disney World or Pioneer Village, bridal and baby showers, boring cookouts, mowing the lawn, shoveling snow, working the same safe job all their lives, paying insurance, paying the mortgage, paying the installments on a new car they bought every three years, shopping in malls, eating at Burger King or the Red Lobster, burying their dead, attending Mass, giving to the United Way, voting Republican, going to war if there was war, perhaps keeping a journal, always watching for good, clear weather, attending church bazaars and never forgetting to bring the macaroni-and-cheese dish, praising local police for doing a great job protecting them, once in a moon attending a movie . . . before VCRs, repairing the grandson's bike, fixing the leaky sink; never being alone, never lonely, never having fear or at least showing fear, never taking a new challenge, never facing the threats of life or the dangers that lurk out there in the world, never being wrong but always right in the choices made.

Joe, what happened to the dreams. Your dreams. I have had to do it for both of us.

*   *   *

After high school . . . the end of the beginning or beginning of the end . . . depending on your perspective. I won't acknowledge which it was for me. After high school. It arrived one hot June morning. I had no Rocco to imitate, nor "Cigar" to observe and learn from. I was on my own with my own dreams and wishes, summer dreams and winter wishes. There was no Joe to share them with, or could he have accepted those dreams that began stealing into my nights as school days were coming to a close. Joe was becoming a physical man . . . he shaved, he had hair on his chest, he had a steady girlfriend and later fiancee, he attended college and then shortly dropped out, he got a job in a local factory, he married, had children, grandchildren, perhaps he still lives, but does he dream? Certainly did not dream the dreams I dreamt, nor certainly has not experienced the nightmares which have always chased me across the dark nights like the proverbial hound chasing the prey. I was the prey. Not that Joe didn't have dreams or nightmares, surely he did. But they must certainly have differed from mine as we have strolled down definitely different paths. I had time to tickle toes in a flowing stream; I had time to stop my hike and sniff the golden flower . . . the black-eyed susan; I had time to while away a day, a week, a month, a year on a foreign beach guzzling cold beers under tropical palm trees, had time to celebrate the day and to be violated over and over again. I had time to reconstruct my blood, my heritage, my family. Joe was not concerned. He needed to feed a family; he needed to buy a new car for work; he needed to pay insurance and save money for the vacation with the family. His dreams and nightmares were different. He stayed friends with Sherry and Katherine, with Sally and Caroline, with Jimmy and Mary Beth. He stayed in touch with the mundane, or what I think of as being the mundane, the corporeal, the Christian way of life and the pursuit of whatever joy life allows. Joe became composed and reverent, respectable and respected, believed strongly in the work ethic and family values, was a dutiful son and husband/father, became a pillar of the community and probably a bore. Though I was shy, I was extra shy, introverted but willful, secretly dared the violation and openly celebrated, I lusted to travel and I lusted to lust. In my heart I was uninhibited and longed, painfully longed to show the world, or friends at least, I was a revolutionary, that I could scar the world and time, the world I'd burn up as a bonfire as though the world and life, I mean, was merely a stack of cardboard boxes that one match could light and fire the heavens with the flames. I would do, I would

do . . . what none of my young friends would ever do including Rocco and "Cigar." Including Joe and Jimmy and the daredevil Pete who had me kicked out of wood shop and flunked. My heroes Rocco and "Cigar" had shown the way, how to rip my knickers and how to piss on the snow.

After school that June I hitchhiked to Alexandria Bay, a summer tourist village on the St. Lawrence River facing the famous Thousand Islands. Alex Bay, as the locals refer to it, was not far from the reservation at Akwesasne, though I dared not even consider going there. The thought alone was intimidating. Through friends I was given a garage to live in that summer. It had a bed with a mattress and the lady of the house, whose name I forget, gave me clean linen; her husband gave me a night job, after twelve midnight, as dishwasher. I ate very well at the restaurant and I was able to clean up the body there as well. No, that wasn't necessarily the attempt to fulfill the dream, not at all. The dream that summer was to become actively part of a summer stock acting company under the direction of Jack Harrington with his mother's money. The Harringtons came from wealth in Canton, New York . . . Jack himself had gone off to Broadway in New York and played the male children in *Life with Father* until he was too old for any of the sons' roles. Still a handsome young man he coerced his mother to open the playhouse in Alex Bay. She would be the firm hand behind the venture: money, know-how, the business smarts. His sister, Pat, would be one of his ingenues. The other actors he would contract out of New York City, and shortly college students would follow and take up the responsibilities of being apprentices. Though I was not a college student I did become an apprentice much, much to my father's chagrin. He tolerated my summer, my absurd rationale, my silly dream. I told him it was a way to writing. He thought I wanted to be a journalist and enter the School of Journalism at Syracuse University. He said I had no nose for news. I was utterly too shy for such an extroverted career. The truth was I had no desire to be a newspaper reporter. I wanted to write creatively, though at that summer's beginning I wasn't sure if it was to write fiction or relive fantasy/dreams into poems. Acting roles in dramas was creative. Some actors painted, sculpted, wrote novels or plays. This would be the road to writing and pub-

"Reading poems at La Raza," Sacramento, California, 1988

lishing. I would become a famous actor and of course overnight make lots of money and have then the time in which to create stories or poems, or plays if I wished. What a plus perfect arrangement. After all, fame came in the theater.

I stayed the summer with my father's wary and disappointed, his remorseful and better-advised approval. He came to see me once or twice and brought me bits of money, a few dollar bills so that I would not starve. He did approve of my dishwashing job, however. He did not approve of my living in a car stall of a garage which I had actually fixed up rather nicely . . . steaming hot at night that the garage became every night as the sun went down. When first arriving at the theater, Mrs. Harrington gave me rights to the playhouse. There was a cot in the theater and bathrooms and as I had a job at the restaurant . . . there was no problem about where or what to eat. She was generous, but her generosity was short-lived . . . through no fault of the kind, considerate, and overtaxed lady by not only her own children, Jack and saucy Pat, but by the company

as a whole and as individuals. She did not need more misery from me. The other apprentices . . . wealthy college students . . . lived in hotels. My second night in the theater sleeping in total darkness I heard footsteps nearing my cot. I could see nothing. It was a sepulcher, tomb, a Poe coffin. Terror began to grow in my stomach. The soft footsteps came closer to the cot. Fear welled in my guts turning and knotting over and over until my innards felt like a twisted rope. I burned to yell, scream. But my tongue and vocal cords were frozen. My tongue refused to move; my vocal cords would not respond to my urgent and fearful demands to scream. But who would hear? The entire company had left the playhouse: Mrs. Harrington had returned to Canton, the older players were either eating supper at a river cafe or chugalugging a beer in a local bar, or in bed. Jim and his sister, the two other apprentices, were who knows where. And where at that moment were Jack and Pat. I had no idea. I knew only the welling dread, terror that someone or thing was about to crush a sharp blade into my flesh, or blow off my head.

The footsteps ceased moving. The auditorium was totally and completely silent. Not a mouse scurried or a leftover fly buzzed. The black of the room engulfed my trembling body, young and vulnerable to whatever violation. Then I began to smell it, the scent of a human being: acrid and hot yet moist and sweet at the same time. I could smell armpits and crotch, I could also smell greasepaint. I could smell male sweat. At last I could move, finally my tongue could sputter and the vocal cords could scream. I edged away from the invisible figure standing over the cot. I edged further to the far side of the cot shaking and knowing death was only a second away. I screamed loudly over and over. And a hand reached out of the dark and covered my mouth.

"Don't scream. I am not here to hurt you. I promise I won't harm you. Don't scream and I will take my hand off your mouth. Promise."

A second hand moved in the black space above me and lowered. It touched my groin, fondled my genitals. I lay absolutely still but quivering, shaking, absolutely terrified by this horror, this nightmare.

"Don't scream. Be quiet. I won't hurt you. Relax."

I lay in death, rigid, frozen ice, a rock, stone.

The hand released from my mouth. The other hand continued to fondle my genitals.

"Please. Please." Pitiful, agony.

"Don't do that. Don't. Don't," I whispered.

"Please. . . ." And a face moved down out of the dark and rested its sweaty, flushed cheek on my groin.

And I was at Aunt Jennie's farm. She had sent me again out to look for Happy, my hound dog. I was racing through the woods after passing the pigsty. A man was in the woods. He stood there with the hound on a rope. "You want to play a game?"

I screamed. The face shot up, away from my prone body. The hand that had fondled my genitals moved off. Three, four, five, six seconds later a flash of light lit up the auditorium. A door slammed.

In the morning Mrs. Harrington said that I could no longer sleep in the theater. It was dangerous. I was a minor. She could not possibly be responsible in a tourist town with all sorts of weird men walking the streets. That is when the restaurant owner gave me his garage to sleep in.

This horrifying experience never happened again. Mrs. Harrington hushed things up. We never discovered who had entered the theater and abused me. I secretly, constantly was on the lookout. There were numerous male professional actors in the company. I stared them down. I listened intently every time they spoke lines while on stage either rehearsing or acting. I listened in restaurants, the green room, the dressing room, while boating on the river with various males. One asked me to go boating alone with him one day. It was him, I was sure. I said yes, and went into the rowboat. Nothing happened. Nothing, I was wrong. It was not the same pleading voice of that black night.

I never knew who this sex maniac was, the perpetrator of the heinous crime. But years later I think I have guessed. What would Rocco have done under the same circumstances? Or Joe?

*　　*　　*

At summer's end . . . having played a number of bit parts such as Oscar in *John Loves Mary* and been the understudy for the male lead, the sleazy hustler, in *Ladies in Retirement,* to this moment one of my favorite plays and films . . . I convinced my father to allow me to hit out for New York City . . . I had fallen in love with a preciously gorgeous ingenue.

I had fallen in love. Not so much with the spirit of the theater. I was short, not particularly handsome, though I was told my face was cute, skinny, carried a bad northern New York accent with much too much hay twined in my speech and choice of idioms, and I was very young. I wouldn't have a solitary chance to get a part in New York on Broadway . . . everyone in the company advised, and advised to go to college instead. Learn a trade. Go home and work for your father and pump gasoline. Forget the theater. You just don't have it, kid. Maybe in thirty years you can get character roles, but not now. You're what, eighteen . . . at best. Well, you look thirteen. And I did. But I had fallen in love.

Eight: Seeking or Escaping

The night I left the Alex Bay Theater it rained, dark and somber. My father came to fetch me. He was quite perturbed to learn that I had saved some dollars and would leave the next morning for New York City. I had no place to stay. I knew no one though my mother was still living in Bayonne, New Jersey. I could always show up at her door, if things were to go sour. He relented, "You can stay a year, and then I shall come for you." I stayed longer. He visited once.

The next morning I left town on a Greyhound bus. It rained all the way into New York City. Angry. Troubling rain, rain which frightened and depressed me. My spirits were soggy. My hope low. The rain beat ferociously against the bus windshield which I could observe from my seat. It slashed against the window at my seat. My fellow passenger attempted conversation. I was not interested in what the nice old lady had to say about her grandchildren even when she pulled out the plastic photo album. I was disconsolate.

Rain washed the bus clean, washed the road, washed the gullies along the road, lay a swamp in the fields. The rain was angry. I was running away again. The skies thundered.

I stayed that night in the Claridge Hotel in the Forties just off Broadway at Times Square . . . old stomping ground of the autograph-hunting days. The next morning I found a cheap room on Park Avenue South.

The rain had stopped. Pavements were fossil dry. It was late August. The hour was crowded with sun, and sultry. But it was not overbearingly hot for me. It was glorious. I was standing on Broadway in old New York, Manhattan, Times Square, surrounded by color and sounds, music of traffic and horns and feet shuffling. Who knew to whom that pair of loafers, those high heels belonged. Perhaps Robert Taylor or Greta Garbo. The city wheeled in magic. The signs of shows and movies burning high over the street, the Camel sign puffing out circles of smoke across the Square; the waterfalls over the Bond clothing store; the hot-dog shops where they sold cold papaya and pineapple drinks . . . cheap and delicious. Broadway and Seventh Avenue . . . the Palace Theater, the Capitol up the street, the Booth on the side street. I was indeed in heaven.

By sheer luck and adventure, I discovered the Actor's Exchange. For a few dollars a month you could have mail collected, use the telephone to check with agents, and simply sit around and talk shop, gossip over a Coke or coffee. The Exchange had a bulletin board of

casting calls for plays and films, it also had listings for needed roommates and apartments for rent. I paid my few dollars and instantly became an actor. The very first day I met Werner Klemperer who lazily sat around the office smoking and talking in a thick European accent about a certain play he'd seen the night before, how dreadful the weather was, and oh yes how he must, really must make the agency rounds. This was long before "Hogan's Heroes" made him into a star. Shortly I was informed that he was the son of the great, important German-born conductor Walter Klemperer. He had a way of upstaging everyone who entered and left the office. To the receptionist, I'm sure, he appeared a nerd. But I thought he was wonderful, an acting actor, spiffed and spanned, suave in dress and hair.

On inquiring about rooms, the young woman at the desk announced a David Forrest was looking to share a double bedroom, inexpensive . . . four dollars a week, no cooking, no bathroom in quarters but shared in the hall; short walk or bus ride from Broadway. I phoned but got no answer from the hall pay phone at Park Avenue South. The room sounded terrific, exactly what I needed. I could eat out of delis and the automat. There was a Horn and Hardets just up the street on Broadway from the Exchange. Naturally, disappointment met my dialing.

I had no sooner put the phone back into its cradle when the receptionist nudged me by nodding her head. There stood David Forrest in person. A short young man of twenty-one years; light blonde hair; a round moon-shaped shiny face; strong jaw; long arms with a dancer's stride. He was an actor presently out of work, at liberty as they say in the business, but was expecting a film job any minute as soon as his agent could work a deal, an army corps film. Quizzically David looked me up and down. Smiled but it was a hesitant movement of lips. He motioned to step outside into the corridor.

"Why did you run away?"

Before I could answer that I hadn't run away and that I was in New York with my father's approval, he said . . .

"How old are you? Fourteen, fifteen? Younger?"

It was difficult to convince him that I was eighteen on August 16th. I looked fourteen. No body hair showing, no body hair, I didn't shave as yet, no peach fuzz on the chin. Not a scar on what is said to be a rosy cheek which

At the University of Oklahoma, Norman, 1990

wasn't rosy but fairly dark in tone and summer tan. I offered my father's phone and address and told David he could call him collect to check me out. We shook hands and walked to Park Avenue South and Thirty-second Street where he showed the beautiful room with double beds, double dressers, one closet to share, and the bath and phone in the hall. He said the only two problems with the place were the bar underneath that played the jukebox most of the night, and the aging actress next door who thought she was on a set for a soft porno and smoked up a storm and when out of cigarettes and booze would knock on our door any hour, day or night. That was all fine with me. I liked the room, the price, the location, and I didn't mind sharing the bath. Also it was on impressive Park Avenue South, corner of Thirty-second Street. My dad would sure approve of that address and think I had made stardom already on my first day in NYC. I gave David eight dollars . . . my share of the rent for two weeks in advance. He took me out and showed me a Greek restaurant that sold a strange plate of

spaghetti; and also a deli where we could purchase salads and beans and baloney . . . standard food for starving out-of-work actors. The deli did sell a delicious macaroni and tomato goulash dish which I ate hundreds of nights after work sitting on the bed talking with David and his friends who stopped by often.

I'd died and gone to heaven.

"The first thing we must do . . . if you are going to be an actor . . . is to clean up your speech. Your diction is dreadful; you speak like an old farm hand from the Midwest. Sorry, northern New York. No one will cast you with that diction. Then we start reading plays, memorizing lines, etc. If you don't know the great plays of Shakespeare you are worthless. And read. Yes, you must read, read, and read more. Thomas Wolfe . . . *Look Homeward, Angel* and *The Web and the Rock* for example."

I was thrilled. This fairly handsome, fluffy blonde, wise, beautifully spoken young man would reshape me. And he did in many good, positive, helpful ways.

David was born and schooled in Southern California, Los Angeles as I recall. Part of his study was in the dramatic arts at the Actors Lab under the direction of Jessica Tandy and Hume Cronyn. When very young he was given parts in RKO Studio's "B" musical films. There he met many actors who became friends. He did not feel complete as an actor until he had made some small success, at least, on Broadway. His former mentor, Jessica Tandy, was starring on Broadway with the young Marlon Brando in Tennessee Williams's outrageous success *A Streetcar Named Desire*. David with a modicum of money left California and traveled to New York where we met only days after his own arrival. David had the luck to get a job as usher in the Midtown Theater on upper Broadway, a film house which screened art films, and mainly European. A week after we commenced rooming together he acquired a job as usher in the legitimate theaters on Broadway . . . which served both of us well. Not only did he make a slight bit more money (and tips) but we were able to see many Broadway shows on gift tickets. I saw Lee J. Cobb in Arthur Miller's *Death of a Salesman,* the Lunts, Irena Petina in a huge musical extravaganza, *Born Yesterday* with Judy Holliday, and Julie Harris in *Members of the Wedding,* and of course the magnificent production of *Streetcar* plus dozens of other memorable shows. When David exchanged usher jobs

I was in line for his position at the Midtown. I grabbed it instantly. I received fifteen dollars a week plus tips . . . if lucky. Some nights I would receive as much as forty-five cents. If really busy with a hit film I might make as much at $1.10. But it bought the hundreds of baloney sandwiches we ate and the little containers of macaroni goulash at the deli down the street from the rooming house. On any given night on returning home from the Midtown . . . which I usually walked to save the fifteen-cent subway fare . . . David would have brought friends home. *Lend an Ear* had just arrived in from Los Angeles and opened a tremendous hit on Broadway. David knew practically every actor, singer, dancer in the show. It starred Carol Channing and Gene Nelson. They may well have been sitting on my bed talking shop along with Bob Scherser. Some nights he would be conversing with Joan Lorring, the actress brought to great prominence in the film *The Corn Is Green*. She played the flighty young ingenue. Thrill after thrill. I sat tonguetied before these gods of the arts.

This youthful paradise did not last forever. Upstairs in the rooming house was a young lady, Jan Ffolks. She was a costume designer, also originally from California. David and Jan met in the corridor of our house. Shortly David was spending fewer nights in our room and more nights in Jan's. Several months later he announced that he and Jan were to be married and they would probably return to Los Angeles where he could get work in films. Broadway proved to be his nemesis. No agent could book him. He found small roles in movies such as *City across the River* and some signal corps films. (I, too, had a walk-on in *City* . . . I ran across a rooftop.) Bags packed, the married couple returned to sunny Cal. It was many years later while I was in college but visiting in New York City that I accidentally and literally bumped into David on West Forty-fifth Street, the heart of the theater district. We spoke briefly. He appeared utterly uninterested in my furthering my education. He wasn't working in either a play or film. He and Jan had divorced. I have never seen David Forrest since. And for all these years I have looked minutely at each and every cast list of films and plays. I have never seen his name listed.

David Forrest had a most important influence on my youth. He not only taught me how to speak, what to read, but also that I

was worthy of respect, and that I was not a complete idiot, and that one day I would know some success and happiness with my life and work. He knew fully well that I would never be an actor, but perhaps I had some of the stuffing to be a writer, a poet. His support, approval, aid of various sorts . . . elocution, therapy, etc. . . . were invaluable and perhaps helped save my mind and life, guided me through the maze and morass of dark confusion.

I remained in the city slightly better than a year. One day my father and stepmother, Ann McBride, arrived and drove me home to northern New York where I stayed slightly less than a year, and feeling the heat of wanderlust I took off not to return to home and my father's house until 1956.

The love of my life, the woman whom I followed to the city . . . a quick story. She was the vivacious Midge Longley, an actress with our summer stock company in Alex Bay. Midge was a graduate of St. Lawrence University. Met Jack Harrington through his younger sister Pat. Always the amateur ham, the cutup, the scene stealer, she had some fascination for the stage. Pat convinced her to audition for her brother Jack's company. He hired her. For the whole summer she was marvelous, successful in many of her roles, especially in *Ladies in Retirement* in which she played one of the wacky spinster sisters. I can visualize her now in costume and can't hold my laughter back. Josephine Hull I believe played the part in the Hollywood film which starred Ida Lupino. To me Midge was glamorous. I had no idea she was not a famous Broadway actress. I fell in love. I haunted her rehearsals. I never missed a performance. I was overjoyed to run for a glass of water or to fetch her forgotten script. I practically took up residence outside her dressing room and I mooned behind her wherever she walked. She lived in a brownstone on the Upper West Side in NYC. I traveled down and camped pretty much on her doorstep. It was only this very spring, May 20 to be exact, that I had the pleasure of her company at a formal dinner. We sat side by side . . . smirking little "I know's" at each other's glistening eyes. She was still wonderful, magnanimous. I fell in love all over again.

It must be added here that Midge did not return those same sentiments. She looked upon me as a confused kid brother, as did

"Telling stories at North Country Community College," Saranac Lake, 1990

David. She offered whatever succor she had to give . . . if only sharing slices of pizza on her brownstone's front stoop. A most remarkable woman who never did much in theater, but accomplished greatness at the *New York Times.*

Nine: Hitchhiking

So ended my theatrical career, and not with a flourish but with the Eliotian "whimper."

My eldest sister, Agnes LaMora, married her young sailor from home and after World War II was over, the smoke and fire extinguished, the blood mopped, and the guts sewn back into the innards of those brave young service people who had survived those horrible, relentless battles, Agnes and John moved their then one daughter, Terry, to St. Louis, Missouri, and shortly after to the old frontier town of St. Charles, Missouri. I knew they were there should I ever need them. And one day that is precisely what happened. I left my father's house. Returned for a brief spell to NYC. I went back ushering

at the Midtown theater; Mr. Bhiatt, my manager, hired me back. Mr. Bhiatt had been a burlesque clown, I believe, when young, though he professed he was a leading actor. He was a good man and treated me well . . . often buying me suppers at the drugstore across Broadway from the movie house. Many times he gave me subway fare so I didn't need to walk. One day he confided that he was to marry and would shortly thereafter leave his position as manager. He married the very young and pretty ticket seller at the Midtown. He was well into his fifties at the time, and she was still under thirty. They went off together. In a short time I went as well. Theater had proven it wasn't my forte. I couldn't act.

Many acquaintances, including David Forrest and Midge Longley, attempted to interest me in going to school, college. I chose not to listen. Other friends spoke of the magic, the mystery, the beauty, and the inexpensive life one could know in Mexico. I fired up. I used to fire easily. Fantasy overtook me. I put some dollars away, which wasn't easy on fifteen dollars a week earnings. I would Greyhound to Richmond, Virginia, and from there I would hitchhike to the border and somehow enter. I hadn't the foggiest idea of what I was doing. I did not even know of a visa, health cards, and the like. Mexico. I would go and live, write great poems, and become rich and famous. I had thirty-nine dollars when I left New York after my bus ticket.

In those years, it seems now, Richmond was a sleepy small city. But memory may well be clouded by years, or perhaps I've seen too many Civil War films. (Even Atlanta . . . boiling hot that Peach Tree Street proved, seems now small in the haze of memory.) I wandered down the main street, inquired as to where the highway was where I could commence my hike. On good information I was off and walking. Not many rides came quickly. I spent most of that hot summer afternoon with my thumb in breezeless air. Somehow I did discover myself in the state of North Carolina, and made a decision to go visit the birth house of Thomas Wolfe in Asheville. Wolfe had become, via David, something of an icon. His real and imagined suffering as a writer, teacher, lover while living and completing his novels in NYC appealed to my sense of the tragic. I spent only a day in Asheville . . . a charming southern city in the lower Smokies. I was off soon and thumbing. Luck would have it that along the road a friendly gentleman offered a ride. In conversing he recognized I was from the North, had not much money, and was on something of an escape route from reality. Mexico would never have dented the skins of his imagination. He kindly offered me supper and a bed in his home. His wife welcomed me grandly as though I was a young man of importance.

Much time passed. I traveled through huge blocks of hot weather with near-debilitating humidity of the South which did not appear hospitable. Suddenly I discovered myself standing outside the campus of the University of Alabama. It was a sultry but starry night. My thumb in the air, a limousine squealed to a halt. In the front seat two men, one young and dapper, the other middle-aged and moving to portly. They assumed I was a college student, or the older man did. We drove into Birmingham. The young college-Joe-type driver (who, incidentally, yes-sirred a great deal the older and wiser gentlemen) eyed me through the rearview mirror with some consternation and

certain hesitant doubt. I was pretty wild looking: dirty, soiled clothes, hair needing a good swipe with shears, and my skin was brown as berry. Also my northern accent gave me away. He drove straight to the State Capitol Building where the older man departed saying to his driver, "Take this boy to the Western Corral for some chow. Give him some money, too." We went to the restaurant. He parked but did not turn off the ignition. He slid over, leaned back, opened the door, and whispered, "Get out. You're a phony. You're no college student his excellency thought. Boy, do you know who that was?" I certainly did not, other than I knew he had to be a man of wealth and power. "You, boy, did not recognize that good man who offered you hospitality?" I was then living in the middle pages of a Thomas Wolfe novel although he wrote of North Carolina. At that time not much different from Alabama. "That was the lieutenant governor of the state of Alabama, boy. Now get out. And don't look back."

I had heard similar lines in western and southern movies. I knew what he was saying, threatening. I didn't look back. Nor did I have my supper at that elegant restaurant. Nor did the driver give me the money promised by the lieutenant governor. I hurried out of town as fast as my youthful legs and my thumb could get me.

*   *   *

A tractor trailer zoomed down the road. My thumb in the night darkness, I was sure the truck driver would not see me. I was wrong. He did. He pulled to a screeching halt a few yards down the black road. He opened the cab door and motioned for me to hop up and in. Instantly I fell asleep hardly giving him my name and destination, nor did I hear where the truck was heading, what depot. When I awoke I was on the outskirts of New Orleans. I still had nearly twenty-nine dollars in money. The cab driver was singing some western ditty about leaving Hilda back in the bar with another bloke and how he would return and take her back. He told me to reach down on the cab floor and I'd find a cup of coffee. He'd stopped only minutes ago but I was asleep. The coffee was great. I hadn't eaten for what seemed days, weeks, not since the generous North Carolinian family fed and bed me. The driver didn't have much conversation. But I blubbered wildly about my travels down into the South, what experiences I had thus far had, and where I was going. He frowned at the word Mexico as though I had said I was following Dante into Hades itself. In a few moments we were in downtown New Orleans, Canal Street where Tennessee Williams's streetcar plies the struggling surf of Louisiana humanity. It was not hot. It was torrid. Oppressive. The heat was blatantly belligerent. It was massive. And I stepped off the truck cab into Dante's hell. I found the train station not to buy a ticket but to home a waiting-room bench, gather my wits, and make huge choices. First I must call my father and warn him as to my whereabouts. Surely he was worried. Then something to eat . . . southern fried chicken, cornbread, a staple food in my father's house, or Louisiana traditional food . . . beans and cornbread or catfish. For the remainder of the day I leisurely strolled the old French Quarter in total fascination. I ate some food of sorts, some kind of soup and white bread, and found a shop which sold pralines. The sweetest candy I have ever stuck a tooth to. I became ill. The sugar overpowered by then a most sensitive stomach. I returned to the train station which is in the heart of downtown New Orleans. To this moment Amtrak sits in the very same spot though not identical to the station I bided my time in those long years past. I summoned courage to go phone my father. Why I took the route to a phone that I did I shall never understand the reasoning. Prolonging the confession, I'd suppose. Someone suggested a Western Union office was on such and such a street just off Canal. The station is at the end of Canal. Why oh why I decided to walk to the WU office through a back dim alleyway I cannot fathom. Foolishly I did. Nor did I get halfway down the alley when from out of the shadows stepped three or four men. They jumped me. Beat me severely but broke no bones. They emptied my pocket of my twenty-nine dollars and took the contents of my little gym bag which held not much more than a bar of soap, razor, a comb, brush and toothpaste, a change of underwear and a fresh shirt and two pairs of socks. I was left on the cement with a bloody nose and a tinge of luck.

The return to the train station was a walk in total humility, embarrassment, and pain. My nosebleed had leaked, dripped down my shirt. My face was a little puffy and my nose so sore I dared not touch it fearing it would unhinge and fall into my palm. At the station I cleaned myself as well as a men's room could possibly facilitate. I spent the night on the bench without anyone bothering me. Where were the city police protecting the sanity and safety of the station from what had become bums like me. I was a bum, vagabond, vagrant, homeless, cashless, exhausted, terrified, lonely, and frightened beyond thought. I was soon to be twenty years old and appeared to the world as a most vulnerable fourteen . . . who didn't yet shave and had no need of the razor those muggers stole.

In the morning I returned to Canal Street, found a pay phone, needing to borrow a dime to make the long-distance call from an officer of the New Orleans Police Force who stood by waiting to retrieve his coin as soon as the operator made the connection. I was grateful to his loan.

Where was David. Where was Midge. Where were Rocco and "Cigar"? Where were those friends who had convinced me I should hitchhike to Mexico. Where was my own head, intelligence, foresight, vision, common sense. I had none, and certainly had not used any common sense. I was indeed not just insane but stupid, moronic, blind.

I could imagine what my father would say. I doubt he would have traveled to New Orleans to save my life again. Incredible, impossible to ever consider he would be so wanton as I had been to scurry down the Atlantic Coast to the Gulf of Mexico to redeem my straggly, mutilated frame of rags and dried blood. The thoughts roaming through my mind as the operator continued to ring home and my father were anything but sensible or remotely resembling intelligence. How could I confess my mistake to him. Surely he would hang up the receiver in total disbelief. The operator rang and rang. No answer. She continued to ring. No answer. He was not home. What was I to do. He was always home. He never went anyplace. He was a businessman. Ann was always home.

"I'm very sorry, sir. But no one answers. Should I keep trying."

"Oh yes, yes, yes." No answer.

I hung up the receiver and strolled away from the phone. My starvation prowled Canal

Street. How was I to eat. I noticed a police precinct. Went in. Inquired at the front desk if the sergeant knew of any jobs I might get . . . washing dishes, floor mopping, carting whatever, running errands. He glared at me as though I were public enemy number one. "Get the hell out of my face, kid."

Canal Street was busy with pedestrians, shoppers. The street was peppered with book shops, record shops, curiosity shops, newsstands, fruit stands, and fortunately for me several five-and-ten-cent stores such as Woolworth's, Newberry's and the like. I wandered through the stores. In Woolworth's I could smell the cooked food coming from the restaurant counter. I wandered past the lunch eaters. I knew someone would take pity on a starving homeless lad. Naturally no one did. I went back into the broiling hot street, so hot the pavement wavered in fire. I stopped at a corner crossing. A huge wastebasket stood there inviting me to take out a newspaper . . . probably the *New Orleans Picayune.* I clutched it to my chest and returned to Woolworth's. Jaunting up and down the aisles I had noticed on a fairly low counter, spreading their beauty in wide and deep swaths, were enormous chocolate bars. Hershey's finest milk chocolate and chocolate almond, and bitter chocolate. The almond would serve nicely. I fingered the bars as though I couldn't make up my mind which to buy. I'd pick up first the bitter, then the milk, then finally the almond and then dropped each back in proper spot, and pretend to throw my attention elsewhere to other candies along the counter: bags of mint wafers . . . pink and white, jelly beans, toffees, etc. . . . . I swung around, put the stolen newspaper on top of the almond bars, snatched back the paper with two large candy bars beneath in the shadow, and slowly ambled off from the counter and without looking behind casually exited the store. God was with me. The high power was looking out for me. The supreme being was at my side. Providence watched over me as my guardian angel walked me out to the street where I ran as fast as my weak legs could travel back to the cooler train station. I gobbled the two candy bars . . . probably eight inches by three inches and a half inch thick in what seemed seconds. Gyrating with sugar, itching with sugar, I made up my mind as to what to do. I would go to Agnes and John in St. Charles, Missouri. They were kin, blood, siblings. They had to take me in

and give rest and food, perhaps direction and substance.

Ten: "That's All Ya Worth"

My sin of theft behind me; the bloody nose, the body ache and embarrassment of the beating/mugging, my loss back on Canal Street, I forfeited more torture from that city by climbing up out of the summer hellfires to the highway heading north to Jackson, Mississippi, and my sister's home and family in St. Louis.

With empty pockets, and an apple I had lifted off a fruit stand in the city, a smudged face, and dirty attire, I stood on the freeway with thumb in the air. I was tired not having slept that well in the train station. I stood in the broiling sun though I certainly cared more for sitting on the guy-wire fence, but what driver would stop for a lazy cur who would not stand. Various summer birds flew the airs, semitropical weeds bloomed the highway shoulders, and automobiles zoomed like spaceships up the road totally ignoring this suffering lad who more than anything in life needed to escape this land of Louisiana. Well, I really held no animosity to the land, the earth which indeed was beautiful and no cause of my anguish nor the beastly hospitality the humans of the area had dumped onto my body and mental health. Car after car surged up the road like lightning striking the sky, the roar of the motors the quick buzz of bees. 7:00 A.M., 8:00 A.M., 9:00 A.M. and then somewhere between 9:00 and 10:00 A.M. an old Chevy stopped two feet away. I had watched it slowly move up the highway chugging along. It was black or what color you can determine under a thick coat of dry mud. The driver had the doors locked though windows were open which didn't make much sense. For a solid two minutes he stared me down from head to toe, from toe to head. Then he unlocked and threw open the door. He said nothing, absolutely not one word crossed his lips. I climbed in. The innards of the car smelled of fried chicken. The man himself carried the scent of bananas. Strange I thought. He was nondescript, and though he was sitting at the wheel I could imagine he was short as he sat close, very close to the wheel, slightly hunched, and it seemed, looking down at his feet on the pedals, that his legs strained to reach the pedals. His head was topped with a ratty fedora, he wore bibbed coveralls, over a black-and-white checked shirt. His shoes were caked with mud and a tiny scent of manure wafted up from the floorboard. He was a farmer, sharecropper probably. Good. It meant he was safe.

I tried conversation but my attempt was met with a wall, or screen at least, of quiet insolence. The mood he was in or his attitude was that of I simply don't give a shit what your name is, where you're from, where you're going, why you're going, or anything else you might think I desire to know. I want to know nothing about you. So sit there in the passenger seat and shut up.

In moments I caught his attitude and remained quiet for a number of miles. Suddenly he turned off the highway onto a dirt road. Dust flared behind us. He accelerated, drove faster on this dirt road, much faster than on the highway. He was now in a hurry. We drove several miles and shortly came to a hamlet with a few houses and a gas station. He pulled up

to the gas station and asked the attendant to "fill her up." The attendant was an Afro-American, a teenage black kid. I looked about. The folks wandering around, sitting on small verandahs, porches actually on wood structured bungalows . . . most without curtains hanging in the windows . . . were also Afro-American. One elderly black gentleman walked over to the window to my seat in the car and stared me down. "Whatcha doin' there?" he asked. "Just out for the morning breeze?" As I made to answer, the old man turned and walked off.

The driver was soon back at the wheel. He had two bottles of soda pop. He offered me one. I think it was Orange Crush, or maybe wild grape or black cherry. Unimportant. Naturally, when he turned the key into the ignition, I had expected the driver to turn the car and wheel back to the main highway. He did not, but continued through the hamlet on down the dirt road. Well, he obviously knew a circular shortcut back to the highway. On the

The board of directors for the Coordinating Council of Literary Magazines, 1991: (front row, from left) Larry Peters, Jennifer Moyer, Lawson India, Wendy Rose, Janey Tannenbaum; (back row, from left) Bob Callahan, Lorna Dee Cervantes, Nicolas Kannelos, Eleanor Bender, Jerry Ward, Jr., Angela Jackson, Pamela Painter, Maurice Kenny

Kenny (center) with friends and former students at Writers' Week, Tupper Lake, New York, 1993

contrary, we drove further and further down deep into woods. Bayou country. Woods empty with the exception of hundreds of trees which I was not familiar with, and of course various grasses and wild blooms I did not know either. Here and there were spots of sun on the lay of the land, but mostly we traveled under and within shadow. It was eerie to say the least. Downright frightening. What ghosts were out there under those trees, zombies camouflaged by leaves. What wild beasts were ready to pounce. What old reprobate, furious with life and the world, was there with a twenty-two waiting for strangers to happen down his posted road, waiting to shoot someone's head off. I had read some Erskine Caldwell and I had seen the movie *Gone with the Wind.* This was the South of the 1950s. They didn't like strangers in these off-the-road parts. They might be moonshining out here at a still and did not recommend strangers driving through their territory.

My driver said nothing as we wound our way down into the bayous. It seemed hours that we drove down the dirt road, but perhaps it was my fear and the mystery that pushed the hands of my mental clock to revolve at such speed.

He stopped the car, pulled the hand brake, but didn't turn off the ignition. He reached over to the glove compartment, pulled back the door, and retrieved a pistol. I had been around rifles all my life. My dad had been a hunter. We ate his game: rabbit, pheasant, deer, etc. . . . He taught me not to be afraid of rifles but to know they can be dangerous. They kill at the slightest provocation. Don't play with guns. As I'm remembering my father's warning words, the man hunched back into his seat and pointed the pistol directly at me. And for the very first time spoke:

"Don't try anything funny. I'll shoot the shit out of ya if ya do."

I can only assume the gun was loaded, the trigger ready, and my driver, potential executioner, willing and able.

No response was offered through my lips. My vocal cords were not working. But my memory shot back to the theater in Alexandria Bay and the horrifying night in the dark house. I froze. Chill after chill passed across my shoulder and down my spine. My stomach began to bump. I knew I would retch the apple I had eaten only hours before and the soda pop this maniac had given me only minutes before. I was terrified.

He released the hand brake and rolled the car down the road. We went less than a mile when he pulled the old Chevy off the road onto a cutoff and we rolled further on the path into the woods, into absolute silence. Not a bird chirp; not a stroke or waft of breeze or running water, brook. Nothing but trees hanging over us.

The driver stopped the car and turned the ignition off. Pulled out the key and thrust it into his coveralls' pocket. Still aiming the gun at my head, he opened the door and backed out of the car. Once out he stuck his head into it again and ordered:

"Get out. Now. Hurry up."

He pulled out a hemp rope from behind his driver's seat, strode off a foot or two from the car, the gun still on me, and pointed for me to walk down the path. I walked several yards.

"Stop here."

He pushed me up against a tree. He turned my figure around and slammed me up against the trunk, and then proceeded to tie me to the trunk, the rope slightly above my waist. It is difficult to convey the horror and black fear which pounded through my entire essence, my body trembled as if I were naked in a winter blizzard, my mind did loop-the-loops. My legs weakened, would not stand straight. My arms went limp even though they were securely tied by the rope to my side at the tree.

When he had me . . . not me as I wasn't a "me" to this madman but a "thing," a "body," an "entity" to do at his will or whim . . . when he had me secure he stood back and just stared as if he wondered what part of my body, this young figure, should he first aim at and strike. Then he approached at a closer angle. He put the gun down. I could not see, but I could smell the banana scent on his clothes, the smell of the fried chicken became overpowering. I could even scent the wild cherry pop on his mouth and tongue.

Happy, Happy, my hound dog, was howling in the woods. Oh Happy, come home, now. Don't make me chase you. Don't make me run after you into the woods. Come home, Happy. And a man stood there in the clearing of the woods. Happy was tied to a rope he held in his hands. You want to play a game, son. Now don't tell anybody we did this. Don't tell your uncle Frank or your father. They don't like this game. Then you can take your dog home: Happy.

He pressed up against me.

Anything but happy.

As his figure pressed against mine, his smell became me. Banana, fried chicken. I could taste the wild cherry soda pop on my lips, his sweaty face so close to mine, his hair fallen and touching my cheek. It tickled my nose. I sneezed. He slapped me. I was sweating. He was sweating. He was taller than me. Small hands of raindrops, sweat from his forehead dripped onto my face.

"Shut up."

I said nothing. Not a word came out of my mouth. My tongue was tied. I may well have mumbled something. "Don't. Please don't." I may have groaned, whimpered.

I wanted to scream bloody murder, I wanted to scream until I was dead because I knew in a matter of moments I could be dead. My father would never find me here. Rocco and "Cigar" would never find me here. David and Midge would never be able to locate me. Joe would be lost himself seeking my dead corpse. Rocco, what the hell can I do. "Cigar," you don't want me to piss on the world. Teach me something else now. How to save my life and my body. I wanted to scream. I knew screaming would do no good. He wasn't about to untie and release me. He wasn't about to let me go free unharmed.

Happy.

I could feel the tip of the gun resting against my head, poking into my sweaty hair.

Until years later in British Columbia under the duress of shingles I have never in my entire life known and recognized such outrageous, unmitigated, unendurable, excruciating pain.

His weight sank against my backside, the gun at my head.

Shortly it was over though I knew he took hours.

He untied the rope from around my naked body. I stood there with my trousers on the ground and my underpants at my ankles.

Through reddened eyes, my tears, I could see him pulling up his pants. He had cleaned himself with a few leaves. He motioned to the tree leaves above my head and pointed to them as if I could use them to clean off. He walked nonchalantly back to the car, the gun now listlessly at his side. He placed the gun back into the glove compartment. Stored it away for another day, or another hour, another boy. He settled in his seat and turned on the ignition. He was going to leave me alive but alone in a strange world, a weird woods, the bayous of sweltering Louisiana. If I hadn't died from the gun and his utter brutality I would die of starvation and exposure.

Without looking at me struggling to pull my clothes back onto my soiled body, he called out:

"Get in."

By the time we reached Jackson, Mississippi, it was dark. No traffic until we hit the city. Along the way, without stopping to park, he pulled out a paper bag. It held fried chicken. Hunks of fried chicken between fat slices of plain white bread. I couldn't eat. I had been and remained nauseated for miles, certainly since the scene at the tree in the bayous. We drove slowly through the city, slowly enough for me to jump out of the car, but my wobbly legs, my weak stomach, my aching head would not allow it. At the northern edge of the city he pulled over onto the shoulder high over a gulch. He leaned over me. I was sure he was after the gun in the glove compartment. But he opened the door and proceeded to push me out. I fell on my side against the ground. I felt something metal hit my face, and heard him say:

"Here. That's all ya worth."

And the car sped down the highway.

In a moment I located the metal object he tossed. A coin. An American quarter. A U.S. two-bit piece. Twenty-five cents. And that's all I was worth. He was right. I was a worthless, useless, raggy bundle of brutalized nothing with less value than a bedraggled cat drowned in the Mississippi River in a grain bag.

My sins and the sins upon me multiplied.

Eleven: Brutes

That night, standing at the road edge in the dark, watching lights flicker and blink in the distance, I remembered my mother years ago saying men were brutes. Weak from both hunger and the bayou atrocity against my flesh, my boyhood, my youth, I could hear my mother. It was winter. Snow slowly fell to the roofs of the houses, the ground, the rooftop of the car parked in the lot beyond my house, the window from my parents' bedroom where I sat on the bed next to my mother. Her one arm around my shoulder, the index finger of her left hand pointing out and down the window at the parked car. Men are brutes. See, that's your father in the car down there. He is with a woman. And the snow continued to fall.

The memory, the pictures flashed across the memory of the angry rain in Syracuse when she orphaned me out to the Onondaga people, her friends.

And that night late in the dark of the theater, a hand coming out, reaching out of the blackness to cover my screams. And I remembered, redreamed, relived the other hand reaching down and covering my groin. And the voice, the pained, anguished voice saying:

"Please, please."

"Oh David, where were you? Daddy, why didn't you tell me? Mama, Mama, Mama. Mrs. White, there is much more to it than just using a condom, believe me."

And the plum tree stand behind Etta Zeller's garden where we boys, little tykes of four and five, Carl and Jack and the others, measured our penises under the plums. Was that, too, brutal, brutalizing each other. Or was it merely experimentation, curiosity.

My mother had convinced me men were brutes.

I stood in the dark. The night was balmy but moist. It was on a highway outside the city of Jackson, Mississippi. I was nineteen and had the look of a fourteen-year-old boy. This quarter-blood Mohawk . . . short, skinny, but "cute" as some folks were wont to say . . . especially girls in high school, particularly the girls I liked and necked with in the backseat of Joe's car or the front seat of my father's car high on the hill overlooking my hometown parked near the old cedar tree cemetery where I used to horseback ride, where I tied up the horse, gave him grass I picked, pulled, and a shot of water from a canteen I always carried for us on such days, such rides. And I would amble to an old stone under the cedar and dream. Even if it should rain, the horse and I would stay on the hill under the cedars. He

"With my friends Angela and Aaron Perkus at the opening of Kenny's Art Gallery,"
Saranac Lake, 1995

would chomp on the grass and I would dream, imagine what a good life I had in store and the great accomplishments I would make in life. How proud my dad would be, and Joe, and Rocco.

I stood in the dark a mutilated spirit, disgusting, smelling of filth and banana and fried chicken. I could still taste the soda pop. Wild cherry. I could hear Happy's whines as the man held him to the rope. And I could feel the driver slam my body against the tree trunk. I stood there on the highway a mutilated spirit, a ravished body, flesh smelling. Disgusting.

Many years later in New York City at the Living Theater on Fourteenth Street and Sixth Avenue I heard Julia Beck and Judith Malina scream out to a gathered audience in the theater how beautiful the human body is and how we should know no shame because of our nakedness. The beautiful body is beautiful.

At that moment in the dark on the Mississippi highway my body was ugly.

        *   *   *

Only a few years before the Beck and Malina wild proclamation of the body beautiful, sitting in my first modern poetry class, the instructor, Roy Marz, a poet in his very own right, proclaimed that to be a good writer one needed to feel intensely, but to write greatly one had to suffer.

I remember William Faulkner, the southern novelist, at winning his Nobel Prize said that we must be violated.

I give considerable thought to what all these people have said, and that Rocco had torn his knickers, and "Cigar" had pissed on the snow. And the memory of celebrating the greenness of the day, seize the day, the hour.

Standing on that road that night Etta Zeller's garden flashed before my vision. The image was plum trees at the end of her garden, and she handing me a bouquet to take home, bouquet of gladiolus, veronica, verbena. Aunt Flo stood near. She offered me a book, leather bound, old but in mint condition.

The night came down, embraced me, swallowed me. I was lost in its folds. I stood on the highway crying. Tears rolled down my cheeks. What would Etta and Aunt Flo say now.

*   *   *

"Hey kid, why you crying?"

I could manage to see only the whites of the eyes, and a white collar circling I would suppose a neck.

"Get down here . . . with me. They're coming and they is mad, man. They is blazin'."

A black man in a black suit with a white shirt lay against the rolling curve of the gulch. He held a plain cigar box in his fists. And he told me a strange story when I climbed down the gulch to sit at the bottom.

I could hear angry voices coming from the blinking lights, and doors slamming hard, and a faint whisper or what sounded a whisper coming from those distant lights: "We gotti kill the thief." Surely that wasn't me. "Shoot 'im."

His story was that he was a country preacher, an alleged reverend. He traveled the South, though mainly Mississippi, spouting the Christian sermon, reading the Bible and passing a cigar box for contributions in payment for his good works and his good words to the poor simple folks of the black communities. That night while sermonizing, as the cigar box passed through the congregation . . . which wasn't terribly large . . . a shot rang through the night. "Is that son of a bitch in that meetin' hall? String him up." He had somehow been committing crimes along his highway to Jackson. Obviously a body of humans, men, were on his scent. They had located him in the church just off this highway where only seconds before I had been hitchhiking my way to St. Louis. Now he was hiding in the gulch, his box pressed tightly to his chest, his torn Bible between his knees as he sat on the ground telling the tale. We could hear the anger, the voices going further south and further away. We stayed fairly quiet for an hour. Finally he pronounced it was over. The people had forgiven him and returned to their shacks. God, too, had forgiven him his rugged ways. And now he must be off.

Was this Huck and Jim?

And he proceeded to amble up the gulch, clutching both his cigar box tinkling with coins and his Bible. In moments he had completely disappeared in the dark.

Feeling somewhat safer with this preacher gone . . . hopefully to either heaven or hell . . . I returned to the road and, as a car was approaching the intersection where I had taken my stand, I stuck up my thumb. The car's lights lit me up with the dimmers. The car stopped. I looked in desperately hoping it would be a family or least a woman driver. It was an American serviceman, an army man. I think he was a staff sergeant.

"Hey kid, where you going. Get in. I'm going far's Memphis."

He opened the door and I climbed aboard. Surely an army man in the U.S. service of the government and the people would be a safe bet. Earlier I had resolved to board only a car driven by a man with his family. Smiles sprouted on my mouth and I commenced talking though I did not, would not reveal the bayou scene. We both chatted nicely along the way to Memphis. He was young, perhaps twenty-five or twenty-seven, had a pleasant but not particularly memorable face. He was slender, straight in his driver's seat. Appeared in command, confident. He wore a wedding ring on his left hand and a very wide smile on his mouth.

Managing to get me to confess to hunger he said he knew a roadside diner ahead and we could chow down there. Even when I professed I had no money . . . but the quarter hidden in my pocket . . . he exclaimed, "How much does a bowl of soup cost?" He'd splurge, be my Dutch uncle.

The diner appeared shortly. We stopped, parked, went in, ordered burgers and fries and cups of soup. Odd but it was corn chowder, an old Mohawk staple soup. We ate and talked and laughed at the waitress who was new on the job and having a hard time with a bunch of guys teasing her. We left, arranged ourselves in his car, and drove off.

He dropped me off just on the other side of Memphis and pointed the direction to St. Louis.

"Sorry I gotta leave you in the rain, kid, but I gotta get to the barracks. I'm a little on the late side."

It wasn't just raining, it was pouring a flood of water to the earth from the cloudy sky. In seconds I was drenched. Miserable. The rain would wash away the sins upon my flesh. I wanted to disrobe and allow the rain to cleanse me. I was on an open highway and, even though it was the middle of the night, the troopers would surely come by in their cars and arrest me. I stood in the rain. I stood in the rain. I just stood in the rain. The angry rain. And thought of Leo in Syracuse, how he hugged me when I finally found his house. And how he placed his oversized shirt around me after a hot bath. And the good soup he spooned into my mouth.

And it rained. It rained. Angry and cold, bitter.

My thumb was up. It never came down. I had to leave this horrible South.

A truck splashed up the road. Its lights flashing onto the wet pavement. It stopped. I looked. It was a man. A woman. And two small children. The woman was reading the Bible aloud to her family.

"Sorry, son, all we've got is the bed of the truck in the rain. But you are welcome to it. We're driving into St. Louis. You going that far, son?"

I rested in the bed of the truck all the way into St. Louis. I have no remembrance of how long it took. I remember only the rain gushing all the way up the highway. I sat huddled in a cold pool. But I was going to my sister's and I was traveling with a family. Safely.

I hopped out in downtown St. Louis. By then it was mid-morning. I inquired how to get to St. Charles from a woman walking in the streets on her lunch break. I walked from the center of the city to St. Charles. The police there helped locate my sister and her husband's house. I rang the bell. The police stayed in the car. She opened the door.

"Yes." She looked at the spectacle standing on her porch.

I was not only wet through and through, I was not only filthy with dirt, and abuse, but my hair was in my eyes, my shoes a wreck, somehow with magic of nature a scraggly beard had appeared from somewhere on my chin, and I was about to collapse.

"John," she called, nearly screaming. "John."
He was at the door swiftly.
"Get out of here."

They had not recognized me, nor could they see the brother under all the natural and inhuman abuse.

Immediately John had me in the tub, Agnes had hot food on the table, and the story that our father had recently left their house for home . . . that afternoon. That's where he was when I phoned from New Orleans.

Needless to say, they gave me good rest, good food, and a bed for nearly a year. I found a job carhopping in St. Louis at the Parkview Restaurant. Eventually my boss, Jack, transferred me with another guy to the store in Indianapolis, Indiana. It wasn't long before I was making friends and had some money in my jeans.

Twelve: By Hook . . . or by Crook

It rained a great deal that year in St. Louis, and it rained often in Indianapolis, but I stuck it out and remained at the Indiana store until fall. I took a sleeping room with the family of one cashier at Parkview. In the fall I registered at Butler University but continued living with the family until one night I brought home a fellow student. He was black, from Trinidad. He was a good student, a sharp writer, and a very fine young man who carried a fetching Trinidadian accent, colorful, flavorful, and yet suave. Birdi was a good person. We talked about writing poetry only. But in the morning the wife and husband stood at the front door as I was leaving for classes.

"We can't have that here," he pronounced.
"We have a baby girl," she added.
"You will need to find someplace else. . . ."
"Today," she added.

And I did. The Davidson home, a lawyer and the manager of a dress shop who had one daughter enrolled at Indiana University and married to a journalism major. I lived in that house until I left Indianapolis. They were beautiful people. They were like parents. For doing chores about the house they fed me often and asked very low rent. I did have a roommate in the two rooms . . . bedroom and study. Bill . . . he was then a pharmacy major though he had been a divinity student at a different college. He read the Bible constantly and over me at that. The next year they told Bill that there was no room. I had the quarters by myself. Bill had been okay in many ways. Bible he read but honeymoon bridge we played before going to bed to see who would lose and need to buy breakfast at the school cafeteria in the morning. Fortunately for me I usually won. I got a job at the Hagg drugstore downtown and sold sundries. Life was beginning to show sunshine.

College was something else. Why had I avoided it? I adored it. I adored my books, my study, my instructors, and my university. I studied hard, used gallons of the midnight oil. After the first year I received pretty good grades. Mostly A's. Soon I didn't miss David and Midge. I forgot about Joe. I didn't need Rocco and "Cigar" . . . they were out of my thought.

Youth was ebbing. I shaved fairly regularly now. I was getting too big for my clothes. I was broadening . . . mentally, intellectually, creatively. I signed up for writing courses with a Dr. Beyer who became a true mentor. I signed up for poetry and drama with Dr. Marz. I was sharp enough to sign up for an eight o'clock Saturday morning class with Alegra Stewart, surely one of the very best teachers in America of her day. I took every literature class the university offered. I reveled in literature. I read books all night. I was growing. I was getting too big for my clothes and I was shaving the fuzz on the chin. Dr. Marz said you had to suffer to write greatly. I thought I had to show suffering on my face. My countenance was rigid in the street. I was shy by nature, now I became stoic as I had read my Emily Bronte, but I was Mohawk, too. The history courses offered in the catalogue did not cover the complete history of America. Little or no reference to Native Americans nor the conflicts after contact with the European Anglo. It didn't have much to do with Afro-Americans either. I was greatly disappointed. I would need to study Native history on my own. Which I did. But I loved college, university life. I made friends but basically those were either fellow writing students or some frat boys who took me in because I was smart, fed me, and asked for tutorial help with their assignments, especially comp papers. I wouldn't be surprised if a few frat houses still had some of my papers in their files.

The end of a semester came. Dr. Beyer . . . I had taken every single course he taught over the years and he taught quite a few from one semester to another . . . finally said that he recognized a weed in his classroom some years before, but not then, that day he saw he was mistaken. That weed was really a flower, a rose blooming. He said he had taught me all he had to teach.

Under strained circumstances I returned to my father's house in Watertown, New York. That fall I entered St. Lawrence University, the ex-

tension in Watertown. I took classes from the fiction writer Douglas Angus. He was marvelous. He put me on the right road to poetry. I left determined to enter Columbia University that spring. However, I managed to find such good employment in New York City as manager of a Marboro Book Shop on West Fifty-seventh Street near Carnegie Hall that I forfeited Columbia, and later that fall of 1957 I entered New York University and had the great joy and pleasure of studying writing of poetry with one of the great lyric voices in American literature, Louise Bogan, a guiding light in my program, my history, my own poetry. Like Beyer and Angus; like Rocco and "Cigar"; like Etta and Aunt Flo; like David and Midge . . . a savior or in the least a beacon to my life.

On May 21, 1995, St. Lawrence University bestowed an honorary degree upon my name and career, Doctorate of Literature . . . with all the rights and privileges, as Dr. Patti McGill Peterson, president of the university, proclaimed as I was hooded in red and white. College was finished at that moment. But I was thrilled, perhaps more so than being knighted by the Queen of England or being the recipient of the Nobel Prize.

*　　*　　*

What happened to the man in the woods holding Happy on a rope? He is in my nightmares. Where did the young actor go who placed his hand over my mouth that terrifying night in the Alex Bay Theater? He is in my nightmares. How did that man in Louisiana fare after that shattering experience? He haunts my nightmares. They all walk in the angry rain and unfortunately they may still walk in that rain beside me.

What is truth? What is reality? What is verisimilitude? What is virtue? What is sin and who the sinner? . . . the child, the boy, the youth, or the man whose hand reaches out in the dark to touch, to change forever, to soil the flesh and the spirit and the mind of innocence, the wildflower blowing in the breeze, the chicory, blue and pure, at the edge of the road though near the gulch, the gutter.

Dates are rarely used in this brief account of my youth and childhood, but as much truth as possible to remember is here. The memory

Maurice Kenny, receiving an honorary doctorate of literature, St. Lawrence University, Canton, New York, 1995

is good, clear . . . helped by the nightmares. There are times when memory can and will play tricks on the fingers tapping the keyboard of a machine, but always the nightmare is there to keep the mind, the recollections straight. Needless to say but I never reached Mexico . . . until 1962 with Wanda, again in 1963 with Mary, and again in 1971 with Mary . . . our last trip together we made Mexico City. Magical. It was worth the attempts. Not the end yet, but finished for now.

Oh my father, you should have kept your son at thy side in thy house of labor. Oh my mother, thou should not have explained the flaw. Oh my schoolmates, Rocco and "Cigar," thou should not have tempted me to revolution. Oh Joe, my friend, my friend, I have abandoned thee. David, what can I say. Midge, lift the wine. Let us toast . . . it is coming to a close, and we made it . . . by hook or by crook.

© Copyright 1995 by Maurice Kenny

BIBLIOGRAPHY

Poetry:

Dead Letters Sent, And Other Poems, Troubador, 1958.

With Love to Lesbia: A Sheaf of Poems, Aardvark, 1959.

And Grieve, Lesbia, Aardvark, 1960.

North: Poems of Home, Blue Cloud, 1977.

Dancing Back Strong the Nation: Poems, illustrated by Daniel Thompson, Blue Cloud, 1979.

I Am the Sun: A Lakota Chant, White Pine, 1979.

Only as Far as Brooklyn, Good Gay Poets, 1979.

Kneading the Blood, illustrated by Peter Jemison, Strawberry, 1981.

Blackrobe: Isaac Jogues, b. March 11, 1607, d. October 18, 1646: Poems, North Country Community College Press, 1982.

Boston Tea Party, Soup, 1982.

The Smell of Slaughter, Blue Cloud, 1982.

The Mama Poems, White Pine, 1984.

Is Summer This Bear, Chauncey, 1985.

Between Two Rivers: Selected Poems, White Pine, 1987.

Humors and/or Not So Humorous, Swift Kick, 1987.

Greyhounding This America: Poems and Dialog, Heidelberg Graphics, 1988.

Selections: Poems, translated by A. Vaschenku, Korky Institute (Russia), 1988.

Tekonwatonti: Molly Brant (1735–1795): Poems of War, White Pine, 1992.

The Madness of Death, White Pine, forthcoming, 1995.

Other:

Rain and Other Fictions, Blue Cloud, 1985, expanded edition, White Pine, 1987.

The Short and the Long of It (chapbook), University of Arkansas Press, 1990.

Last Mornings in Brooklyn (chapbook), Renegade, 1991.

Tekonwatonti: Molly Brant (play of voices, first produced Strand Theatre, Schroon Lake, New York, 1992).

On Second Thought: A Compilation of Work (poems, fiction, essays, memoir), University of Oklahoma Press, 1995.

Backwards to Forwards (essays, historical, literary and personal), White Pine, forthcoming.

The author has also composed poetry for television programs, including *Today in New York,* NBC, 1984, and *Poems, Poets, and Song,* CBS, 1990. Contributor to anthologies, including *Native American Writing,* Greenfield Review, 1982, *Harper's Book of Twentieth Century Native American Poetry,* Harper, 1987, and *American Book Award Anthology,* Norton, 1991. Contributor to periodicals, including the *New York Times, Small Press Review, American Indian Quarterly, Saturday Review,* and *Beloit Poetry Journal.* Editor, *Wounds Beneath the Flesh: 15 Native American Poets,* Blue Cloud, 1983, new edition White Pine, 1987. Co-publisher of *Contact/II;* publisher of Strawberry Press; advisory editor of S.A.I.L., *Akwesasne Notes, Akwekon,* and *Time Capsule.*

James Laughlin

1914-

Byways

What follows are segments from a long poem-in-progress. The structure of Byways is contrapuntal. Two voices are speaking. The first, written in colloquial in the meter used by Kenneth Rexroth in his narrative Dragon and the Unicorn, *tells of things which the contemporary poet has done or seen. The second voice gives a correlative passage. This voice speaks in a tone which mimics the traditional translations, often for comic effect. This confrontation has two purposes. First is to show the persistence of classical literature into the present. The second is to show how an age-old theme is sometimes repeated today. Thus in the Dawn and Daphne pairing a modern girl is destroyed by men lusting for her bodily beauty, while a girl from mythology (the source is Ovid's account in the Metamorphoses the shy woodland nymph, Daphne, is pursued by the god Apollo, who has been inflamed with passion for her by an arrow from the bow of Eros, until she is exhausted and must save herself by being transformed into a laurel tree).*

James Laughlin—"The grouchy old man,"
Meadow House, Norfolk, Connecticut, 1993

I

Often now as an old man
    Who sleeps only four hours a night,
I wake before dawn, dress and go down
To my study to start typing:
Poems, letters, more pages
In the book of recollections.
Anything to get words flowing,
To get them out of my head
Where they're pressing so hard
For release it's like a kind
Of pain. My study window
Faces east, out over the meadow,

And I see this morning
That the sheep have scattered
On the hillside, their white shapes
Making the pattern of the stars
In Cans Major, the constellation
Around Sirius, the Dog Star,
Whom my father when we were small
Used to point out, calling it
For some reason I forget
Little Dog Peppermint.

173

About age ten. "At the ancestral home on Woodland Road, Squirrel Hill, Pittsburgh. I attended the Arnold Grade School."

What is this line I'm writing?
I never could scan in school.
It's certainly not an Alcaic
Nor a Sapphic. Perhaps it's
The short line Rexroth used
In *The Dragon & The Unicorn,*
Tossed to me from wherever
He is by the Cranky Old Bear
(but I loved him). It's really
Just a prose cadence, broken
As I breathe while putting
My thoughts into words;
Mostly they are stored-up
Memories—*dove sta memoria.*
Which one of the old Italians
Wrote that? Dante or Cavalcanti?
Five years ago I'd have had
The name at the tip of my tongue
But no longer. In India

They call a storeroom a godown,
But there's no inventory
For my godown. I can't keep
Track of what's in there.
All those people in books
From Krishna & the characters
In the *Greek Anthology*
Up to the latest nonsense
Of the Deconstructionists,
Floating around in my brain,
A sort of "continuous present"
As Gertrude called it;
The world in my head
Confusing me about the world
I have to live in.
Better the drunken gods of Greece
Than a life ordained by computers.

My work table faces east;
I watch for the coming
Of the dawnlight, raising
My eyes occasionally from
The typing to rest them.
There is always a little ritual,
A moment's supplication
To Apollo, God of the Lyre;
Asking he keep an eye on me
That I commit no great stupidity.
Phoebus Apollo, called also
Smintheus the mousekiller
For the protection he gives
The grain of the farmers.

My dawns don't come up like thunder
Though I have been to Mandalay
That year when I worked in Burma.
Those gentle, tender people
Puzzled by modern life;
The men, the warriors, were lazy,
It was the women who hustled,
Matriarchs running the businesses.
And the girls bound their chests
So their breasts wouldn't grow;
Who started that, and why?
My dawns come up circumspectly,
Quietly with no fuss.
Night was and in ten minutes
Day is, unless of course
It's raining hard, Then comes
My first breakfast. I can't cook

So it's only tea, Puffed wheat and
Pepperidge Farm biscuits.
Then a cigar. Dr. Luchs
Warned me the cigars
Would kill me years ago
But I'm still here.
Ne quid nimis wrote Terence
in the *Andria,* moderation
In all things. So I hold
It down to three a day:
One after breakfast, one
After lunch and one after
Dinner. A Bolivar is both
Stimulation and consolation.
They claim that what
Makes a Havana so mellow
Is the spit of the Cubans
Who lick as they roll them.
But the best leaf for wrappers
Is grown right here in the
Connecticut River Valley.

Yes, we have our wonders,
Our natural phenomena,
As witness the little man
In the Santa Claus suit
Right here in South Norfolk,
This when I first came
To live here back in 1930.
I forget his real name,
We just called him
The Santa Claus man.
In the heat of August
He'd put on his red outfit
And his white whiskers
And walk up to the green
From his shack in the woods
Where he lived on relief
To ask at the post office
For mail from the North Pole
But of course there never was any.
Everybody loved him,
Especially the children.
He'd get a bag of penny candies
(there *were* penny candies
in those days, they didn't cost
a nickel as they do now)
Handing them out to the kids
Who trooped after him singing
As if he were the Pied Piper

of Hamelin and like Mr. Finney's
Turnip that grew behind the barn
And it grew and it grew
And it never did no harm,
Mr. Santa Claus did no harm.
He was our local hero.
People came from other towns
To see and talk to him.
He was written up all over
The state . . . then suddenly
He stopped coming to see us.
They found him dead
With his head bashed in.
The state police went through
Their usual useless motions
But found no clue who'd done it.
We buried him in the woods
Near his shack, which had
To be burned down, it was
So filthy, he had never disposed
Of his garbage all those years.

Whom the gods would destroy
They first make mad
And whom they love
They rob of their reason,
Be it Oedipus who killed
His dad and slept with his mum
Or our beloved Santa Claus,
Now nearly forgotten.
Nobody believes me
When I tell his story;
But I have the news clips.
Does he sit up there now
On Olympus, another Ganymede,
Kidnapped like Ganymede
By the eagle of Zeus,
A cupbearer pouring out
The nectar for those
Drunken clots, the gods.
Who in the end will arise
From chaos to punish
And destroy them all?

And speaking of those
With whose destruction
The gods amused themselves
Notable was Dawn of Santo, Texas,
The most perfect face and body
That ever I beheld,

Each part perfection,
Modelled on the Venus of Milo
And perhaps, who knows for no one
Ever saw her, the Kyprian herself,
Aphrodite was born on Cyprus.
She violet-eyed, born of the seafoam.
Dawn's father began tampering with her
When she was ten; she was placed
In a home where there were
Brutish boys and little education.
Escaping at fifteen she reached Tulsa,
Got a job in a topless bar,
Met men, too many men
Who could see only the body,
Not the person inside it.
At last came one who was decent,
A man from New York
Who treated her kindly,
Showed her respect, a good man.
He took her to New York,
Set her up in an apartment,
Sent her to highschool,
Got books for her to read,
Bolstered her confidence,
Taught her how to dress.

But the cruel gods, bent on her
Destruction, caused him to die.
Back to the start, to despair,
Again the slave of her body.
When I met Dawn she was
Damaged goods. She cursed me
As I talked kindly to her,
Saying I was like the rest.
But I persisted. If it wasn't
Love it was an obsession.
In the end I know I gave her
Some happiness, some release
From her bondage, when we were
In Italy and Spain together.
One night in Milan when we
Were walking back to the hotel
From a restaurant she began
To cry in the street, at first
Softly and then violently.
She told me I had changed her.
That night she was indeed
A changed person, tender and
Passionate. We were happy
In Rome and Barcelona.
But I had not reckoned

On the spite of the gods.
They were jealous that I'd claimed
One they thought was their own.

In Burgos, cruel Burgos,
She suddenly became hostile
And silent, then catatonic.
I put her in the hospital
But their drugs didn't help her.
She escaped from the hospital
And threw herself under a tram.

I buried her in the cemetery
Of the Campo Sagrado, a long
Way from Santo, Texas. When I
Went through her suitcase
I found she had been writing
Little poems. Strange poems
That made no sense but they had,
In some of the phrases,
A kind of surrealist beauty.

And as it was in Greece so long ago

Phoebus Apollo, favoured son
Of Zeus, and Eros, god of love,
Whom later times called Cupid,
Were rivals in the power
Of their bows. Delian Apollo
Had struck down a great serpent,
The Python. He taunted Eros:
"What hast thou to do with the arms
Of men, thou wanton boy?" Eros,
Child of Venus, replied: "Thy dart
May pierce all things else, Apollo,
But mine shall pierce thee."
Forthwith he took from his quiver
Two arrows of opposite effect:
One blunt and tipped with lead
Puts to flight; the other sharp
And tipped with shining gold
Kindles the flames of love.
With the golden dart Eros pierced
The flesh of Apollo, pierced even
Into the bone and marrow. Straightway
Apollo burned with love. With the lead
Arrow Eros wounded the fair-formed
Daphne, a sweet nymph of the forest
Glades whose father was Peneus,
The river god. She hated the very name
Of love, rejoicing in the deep fastnesses

Of the woods and in the spoils of beasts
Which she had snared. A single fillet
Bound her locks all unarranged.
Her father rebuked her, pleading
For grandsons. O father dearest,
Grant me to enjoy perpetual virginity,
As you have done for Diana, the huntress.
But Daphne's beauty is irresistible.
Apollo loves her at sight and
Longs to wed her. He gazes at her eyes,
Gleaming like stars. He gazes
At her lips, which but to gaze on
Does not satisfy. He marvels at
Her fingers, hands and wrists,
And her arms bare to the shoulders,
And what is hid he deems still lovelier.
But Daphne flees him swifter than
The fleeting breeze. So does the lamb
Flee from the wolf, the deer
From the lion. "Nay, stay," Apollo
Cries, "Learn who thy lover is.
I am no unkempt guardian of
Flocks and herds. Mine is the Delphian
Land; Zeus is my father. By me
The Lyre responds in harmony to song.
The art of medicine is my discovery.
Alas, that love is curable
By no herbs." But the maiden
Pursues her frightened way, even in
Her desertion seeming fair.
The winds bare her limbs;
The opposing breezes set her
Garments aflutter as she runs;
But the chase draws to an end
For the youthful god would no longer
Waste his time in coaxing words.
So run the god and maid, he sped
By hope and she by fear.

Now is her strength all gone,
And she cries out to Peneus, her father:
"O father, help! If your waters hold
Divinity, change and destroy this beauty
By which I please o'er well."
Scarce had she made this prayer
When a down-dragging numbness
Seized her limbs and her soft sides
Were begirt with thin bark. Her hair
Was changed to leaves; her arms to
Branches. Her feet but now so swift,
Grew fast in sluggish roots, and her head

"With Gertrude Stein and her dogs Pepe (in my arms) and Basket (with Stein). I had worked for her at her summer place, Bilignin. My job was to write press releases for her American lecture tour," 1934.

Was now but a tree's top. Her gleaming
Beauty alone remained. But even so
In this new form Apollo loved her,
And placing his hand upon the trunk
He felt the heart still fluttering
Beneath the bark. He embraced the
Branches as if human limbs and pressed
His lips upon the wood. But even
The wood shrank from his kisses.
And the god cried out to her:
"Since thou cans't not be my bride,
Thou shalt at least be my tree. My
Hair, my lyre, my quiver shall always
Be entwined with thee. With thee shall
Roman generals wreathe their heads
When shouts of joy shall acclaim
Their triumph, and long processions
Climb the Capitol.

———————

Ezra

To Rapallo then I came,
  That was in 1934, a student
Bored with the academic conventions
Of Harvard, wanting to get to the source,
To learn about poetry from the best
Poet alive, and you accepted me into
Your Ezuversity where there was no
Tuition, the best beanery since
Bologna (1088). Literachoor, you said,
Is news that stays news,
And quoting from some old bloke
Named Rodolphus Agricola,
Ut doceat, ut moveat, ut delectet,
Make it teach, move the heart,
And please. You taught me
And you moved me and you gave me
Great delight. Your conversation
Was the best show in town,
Whatever you'd ever heard or read
As fresh as when it first got into
Your head. The books you loaned me
Were full of caustic marginalia:
Fat-faced Frankie (meaning Petrarch)
Had an assistant to put the adjectives
In the lines, it didn't much matter
Where they were placed; and
Aristotle was Harry Stottle,
A logic-chopper but so good at his
Job he anchored human thought
For 2000 years; and Aristophanes was
Herry-Stop-Her-Knees, good stuff about
Wasps and frogs.
          You believed
You were a revenant of Sextus
Propertius, your favorite Latin
Poet, saying that Propertius had
Rip-van-Winkled from 16 B.C., and you
Rewrote the best parts of your idol
In English, bringing the old boy's
Ideas up to date according to
Your own predilections. In your
Study, to keep from losing them,
You hung your glasses, your pens
And your scissors from strings
Over your desk. You had two
Typewriters because one was
Always being repaired from the
Beating you gave them; your

"*With Ezra Pound on the pass between Italy and Austria. I took leave from Harvard in 1944 to study with Pound in Rapallo. He made me his publisher and New Directions did about twenty-five of his books. Despite friction over his anti-Semitism, we were friends till his death in 1972. I finished Harvard in 1939.*"

Letters were often half full of
Capitals for emphasis.
          You read
My poems and crossed out half the
Words saying I didn't need them.
You advised me not to bother
Writing stories because Flaubert
And Stendhal and James and Joyce
Had done all that could be done
With fiction. They say you were
Cranky, maybe so, but only with
People who deserved it, stupid
Professors busy killing poetry
And international bankers making
Usury and *i mercanti di canoni*
Selling arms to start another war.

You elucidated the Eleusinian
Mysteries which were a key part of
Your composite religion, all about
Dromena and the *epoptea* and how
It was the *epoptea* that sent sperm
Up into a man's brain to make him
Smart. You loved cats and the cats
Loved you. Some days we would
Walk up the stony *salite* on the
Mountainside behind town, through the
Olive groves and the little peasant
Farms where the cats were perched
On the stone walls; they were
Waiting for you, they knew you
Would bring them a packet of scraps
From the lunch table. You would
Call to the cats: "Micci, micci,
Vieni qua, c'é da mangiare."
(Here's something for you to eat.)

One day when we were feeding the
Cats near the church of San
Pantaleone we discussed what you
Would do with your Nobel Prize
Money when you finally got it,
And you thought that a chef
Would be the best thing because
You were tired of eating at the
Albuggero Rapallo, but the Swedes
Never got around to giving it
To you, they were too dumb to
Understand the *Cantos.*

And when
Henghes the sculptor (id est
Heinz Winterfeld Klusmann)
Walked all the way down from
Hamburg to Rapallo to see you
Because he heard you had known
Gaudier, and arrived half-starved,
You fed him and let him sleep in
The big dog kennel on the terrace
(since there were no extra beds in
The penthouse apartment) and
You took him to the yard of
The man who made gravestones
And got him credit for a block of
Marble, from which he carved
His sitting-down centaur, and you
Sold it for him to Signora Agnelli,

The Fiat lady in Torino; and that
Was the beginning of Henghes' fame
And good fortune (and the drawing for
The Centaur became the colophon for
New Directions).

You said I was
Such a terrible poet, I'd better
Do something useful and become
A publisher, a profession which
You inferred required no talent
And only limited intelligence.
And after lunch you would
Stretch out on your bed with your
Cowboy hat shielding the light from
The window with the big Chinese
Dictionary on a pillow on your
Stomach, staring at the characters,
Searching for the glyphs of meaning
In the calligraphy. And years
Later the professor asked your
Daughter to define your ideogramic
Method of composition in the *Cantos,*
And she thought for a moment and
Replied that you looked deep into
The characters to find the truth of
Them, which was a properly Confucian
Answer. So you wrote your own
Versions of the *Great Learning*
And the *Odes,* which horrified
The sinologists, but the language
Is immortal. And you loved to
Quote from Confucius that:
"Anyone can run to excesses, it is
Easy to shoot past the mark it is
Hard to stand fast in the middle."

The Ancestors

And when we finally
Made it to Portaferry
Looking for ancestral graves,
Portaferry in County Down,
That is, an hour's drive south
Of Belfast, there was no trace
Left of the old hovel and
Potato patch, which they sold

In 1824 to take ship from Cobh
For Baltimore and the new life,
The two brothers, Alexander and
James, and the ailing old dad
Who was also James. No sign
Surviving as the parish church,
The fat little mayor told us,
Had burned with all the records
In '78. A pretty spot Portaferry
With a fine view out over
Strangford Lough, which the Danes
Called *Strangfjord* when they raided
There, God knows when; and Joyce
Had told me my name meant Danish
Pirate and that we had last met on
The battlefield of Clontarf,
Cluain Tarbh on Good Friday 1014.

Disappeared without trace as if
They had never existed. The farms
And fields bulldozed, along with
The stone walls and hedgerows,
To make way for condominia
For vacation homes for Germans.
Fat Germans hiking around in
Lederhosen and Tyrolean hats.
So with the money from selling the
Place the brothers bought crockery
And a horse and wagon in Baltimore.
Heading west they sold the stuff
To the farmers in Pennsylvania.
There was enough to start a store
In Pittsburgh. It prospered and then
There was a bank, then an iron foundry.
God-fearing people, Presbyterians,
Shrewd at deals, saving their money
To make more with it. Their luck was
The Civil War, selling rails
For the Northern armies as they moved
South. In the next generation
They sold pipe for the oil fields
In Texas, structural steel for
Skyscrapers, sheet for Detroit.

Five sons from James alone, five from
His son James, all working in the
Business, A Henry could draw and

Wanted to become an artist.
The old man would have none of such
Nonsense. No money in it. They built
Big houses on the hills of
Pittsburgh. Godfearing people who
Married their own kind, reproducing
Their own kind, until there was
Too much money. It spoiled most of them.
They moved east for the fancy living
In places like Long Island, They married
Rich girls from a better class,

Henry, my father, quit working
In the business at 40; he had been in
Charge of the company coal mines.
He devoted himself to golf, fishing
For trout and salmon, shooting birds
With an English shotgun; had his suits and
Shoes made in London, drove an
Hispano-Suiza; went to the races
At Auteuil and Chantilly, wearing a gray
Tailcoat and topper, as was the fashion;
Played *chemin de fer* in the casino
At Deauville, was often lucky at it.
Gave me a 30-foot power yacht
When I was 15, we sailed it up and down
The Florida inland waterway.
I called him "Skipper," he called me
"Mate." I loved him intensely. He gave me
The funds to start New Directions, though
He didn't understand the books I published.
His cousin, another Henry, got back to
Ireland by buying Castle Hyde. He rode
To hounds and kept fine horses,
One of which nearly killed him
By refusing a stone wall.
This Henry, the Boston one,
Once asked me, this was at lunch
At the Somerset Club when I was still
At Harvard, whether I was going to build
My life around skiing. "No sir,"
I told him, "I'm planning to be a writer."
"Not much money in that, I wish you luck."
Cousin Henry was right: no money in it
But a lot of satisfaction.

"Looking out into the garden from the alcove. The whole estate was on a wooded mountainside," 1937.

VI

My Aunt

Most mornings at Robin Hill
When I was living there on the
Third floor, that was before
My first marriage and when the
Office of New Directions was in
Her converted stable, she would
Summon me to her second floor
Sitting room after breakfast and
Sit me down by the fireplace for the
Daily monologue which usually
Went on for at least an hour,
Without interruption for I wasn't
Expected to say anything, just to
Listen and absorb her wisdom about
Life, of which there was a large
Supply. This sounds very boring
But it wasn't; it was endlessly
Fascinating. How had nature or

Some divine agent packed into
This little woman (she was my
Father's sister) such an intensity
Of feeling and such a capaciousness
Of spirit. She would have been in
Her sixties then and there she sat
In her Chinese silk peignoir
At the little table by the window
That looked out over the gardens
(She had attended a horticultural
School; in those days young ladies
Were not sent to college.) There,
She looked out at her beautiful gardens,
After she had finished her breakfast
Which consisted only of one uncooked
Egg which she downed in a gulp.
There I was, slumped in an easy
Chair (I was forbidden to smoke
In her presence) waiting for the
Lesson to begin, impatient to have
It over so I could get on with my
Writing but curious to know what
Would come from the lips of the
Oracle that day. And once she began
I was in thrall to her conviction.

These scholia took place long, long
Ago. My aunt has been dead for over
Thirty years. The great house and
Its gardens have passed out of the
Family. I am older than she was
When she was my teacher, Yet even
Now as I sit here typing, her figure
Is as clear as if she were still
Alive; she is standing in the doorway
Of my study, the not beautiful little
Woman with the insistent voice.
Her consuming love for me has
Penetrated time, it surrounds me
Like a sacred aura. She had great
Need of me, imperfect as I was.
She had no children of her own,
And I was named for the father
Whom she idolized. I was the
Receptacle. She was determined to put
As much of him into me as she could.

She had a store of stories to tell me
About her parents and the aunts and
Uncles, even about my great grandfather,

Who looks so fierce in the daguerreotypes
In the family album; about his house
Where wide lawns sloped down to the
Allegheny River as it came through
Pittsburgh to join the Monongahela
To make the Ohio at the Point where
Once Fort Duquesne had stood. Trips
In the buggy with her father to the
New mills on the South Side, where the
Eliza Furnaces were named for one of
Her aunts, the flames rising out of
Them against the sky at night.

Character studies of beloved servants,
Irish if they were "inside," black if
They were "outside." When the riverfront
Property was sold to make way for
Joseph Horne's department store, a new
House, rather ugly, was built on
Lincoln Avenue in Allegheny, which
Was becoming a fashionable neighborhood

For the quality. And much she had to
Tell about her father's place near
Zellwood in the central lake country
Of Florida. It had begun as pine and
Palmetto land for shooting quail; then
He developed it into orange groves
And an elaborate estate. "Sydonie"
He called it, named for his wife
Sydney Page. There were avenues
Bordered with live oaks and flowering
Shrubs. There were trees brought from
Many parts of the world; greenhouses
And slat houses. A dairy herd of
Jersey cows. There was a power plant
and an aviary of exotic birds. Two
Small lakes and a boathouse. Twenty
Cabins (without plumbing) where the
Black workers lived. (Remember that
All this was built before there was
An income tax.) The house was in
Spanish style, white walls and

"In the first New Directions office in Norfolk, Connecticut. It had been a cow shed on my aunt Leila's estate, but she got tired of the cows and turned it over to me," about 1943.

Red tile roofs copied from a villa
In Granada; terraces and courtyards,
Balconies & colonnades, bougainvilleas
Climbing the walls, separate apartments
For the families of each of the
Five children. There was, of course,
A track spur at the Zellwood station
For the parking of private cars.
(Today the place is a boarding school
For the children of missionaries.
Came the income tax and it couldn't
Be kept up.) The "Ariadne" was her
Father's two-masted schooner, crew
Of twelve, one of the prides of the
New York Yacht Club cruise. Each
Summer the cruise put in at
Nantucket harbor for a few days of
On-shore partying. That was where
My aunt met her consort, a Coffin
He was, descended from whaling ship
Captains, a gentleman through and
through, *sans peur et sans reproche*.
It was a long and happy marriage but
Without issue: the country gentleman
And the lady who loved gardens.

In her later years my aunt became
Interested in spiritualism. Through
A medium in Pleasantville she met
An angel in the beyond named Lester.
Lester was most sympathetic to the
Concerns of cultivated elderly
Ladies. It was a fervid correspondence.
My aunt would telephone her questions
To Pleasantville where they were
Communicated to Lester in séances.
His answers reached Robin Hill in
The medium's automatic writing. She
Consulted him about almost everything,
Except her investments which were in
The care of a banker in New York. The
Problems of all the young cousins
Whom she was educating, difficulties
With the servants, social problems,
Matters of conscience, her husband's
Health—it all went to Lester. It's
clear from Lester's letters (I have
Them still) that he really cared,
Particularly for what they called
"Going on to greater understanding."

Reading over some of the letters
I find that Lester's advice was very
Good; he was a sensible angel. He
was a great consolation to her. At
A certain point, when I was giving
Her a hard time, I became the subject
Of the exchange. She told him that
She was much worried about me. I was,
Making girls fall in love with me
With no intention of marrying
Them; what was to be done?
Lester's answer was very comforting
And rather accurate as I read it now
In the medium's jiggly script: "Don't
Worry, my dear, James will be all
Right; you have given him good
Values. It is normal for young men
To flirt, it's their nature. He will
Settle down soon and when the right
Girl comes along he will know it
And will make a good marriage. He
Will work hard and be a success in
His profession."

This remarkable
Woman "went on to greater under-
Standing" in her 86th year. The
End was hard for her but she bore
It stoically. There were many voices,
A clamor of Babel; a coming on of
Darkness, a struggle to hold the
Light; confusion and desperation;
Then bodily failures, waning of
Strength; days in silence, barely
Able to speak; the soul fighting
For life in her eyes; inanition.
Two of her men, young Leon and old
Theodore Sylvernale, the old man
Weeping, placing her gently on the
Wicker chaise-longue; her black
Maids who grew up on the family
Place in Florida, covering her
With blankets; she is carried, an
Egyptian mummy, out into the sun
In her garden to lie there for
An hour. She says nothing and
Seems to see nothing, moves not
Even her hand, is no longer a
Person.

Tom Merton

When I first went down
 To Kentucky to meet Merton
At Gethsemani, his monastery
Near Bardstown, the abbot
Had invited me for a visit
After I'd published *Thirty Poems,*
I was expecting gloom and obsession,
Grouchy old monks ponderous
In penitence, glaring through
Their sanctity . . . how wrong I was!
To be sure, the background
Was not prepossessing: a drab
Countryside, scrubby trees,
Dry fields, not verdant,
Shacks and billboards along the
Highway; the buildings
Of the compound behind
Its walls monstrously ugly,
Gray stone blocks set square
Without any architectural
Distinction, the spire
Of the church a tin spike
Poking up at the sky,
Over the gateway, in forbidding
Black letters PAX INTRANTIBUS,
It could have been a prison . . .
How wrong I had been about the inhabitants!
These brothers and monks
Were warriors of joy.
Happy and friendly, laughing
And joking, rejoicing in the
Hard life of work and prayer,
Seven services a day from Vigils
In the dark at 3:15 A.M. through
Lauds, Terce, Sext, None,
Vespers and Compline in the dusk,
These chantings of supplication
For the whole world, even infidels
Not just for the monks.
Such brightness, *lux in aeternitate,*

And Tom (his name now Brother Louis,
As a snake might shed his worldly skin)
The brightest among them, the merriest
Of them all, gaiety exuding
From him. One of the youngest
But already the intellectual
Pivot of the community with

His learning and his comprehension
Of what meditation was all about.
Tom never tried to convert me;
He said if I got grace
It would come from God
Not from his instruction.
He would answer my questions
About theology and the rituals
Very carefully, but no more.
One day we walked up
To the fire tower on the ridge.
Tom was the warden in fire season.
He was good at copping
The best jobs for himself.
He had declined to join
The cheese-making crew
Or work in the fields.
And he got out of sleeping
In the dormitory by learning
To snore very loudly,
They gave him an abandoned
Bishop's room all to himself.

We sat in the shelter atop
The fire tower and chewed the fat
About the literary scene, what
The writers were doing. No papers
Or magazines came to the monastery,
The abbot only told the community
In chapter what was suitable
For them to hear. We arranged
How the books of the likes
Of Henry Miller and Djuna Barnes
Would be mailed to the order's
Psychiatrist, who would carry them
To Tom. On the morrow,
By dispensation of the abbot,
Who knew that publishers could
Produce book royalties to the
Benefit of the abbey, Tom
Had leave for the day to be off
With me in my rented car.

When we went out the gate
Past Brother Gatekeeper
Tom was formally dressed
In an old bishop's suit
With celluloid backwards collar.
But when he had finished reading
The day's lesson in his breviary,

And we came to a wood, he said,
Stop here. He hopped out,
Carrying a paper bag. I thought
He was going to pee, but no,
He returned in blue jeans
And an old sweater. Near Salem,
He said, I've heard there's
A good bar. We found it and
Inside, although it was only 10,
A goodly company of jolly farmers.
They looked askance at me
In my city slicker clothes,
But Tom, talking farmer and
Even randy, was an old pal
In fifteen minutes. I didn't drink
Since I was driving, but Tom
Was belting down his first beers
Since he became a novice:
One, two, three . . . at four
I reminded him of our lunch date
In Lexington. Just one more, but
It was two more before I got him out.
Strangely, there was no sign
Of inebriation; he could have been
Drinking Coca-Colas. Our lunch hosts
In their little colonial
House-studio in Lexington
Were the Hammers, gentle
Victor, in his eighties,
In his youth a painter in
Vienna, doing elegant portraits
In the style of Cranach,
And later becoming in America
One of the great hand printers,
His *Hagia Sophia* of Merton's
Being perhaps his masterpiece;
And Carolyn, his wife, younger
Than he, a librarian at the
University who, under his tutelage
Had become also a renowned printer.

We ate in the garden, talking
About everything except modern art,
Which had to be avoided because
Of Victor's blood pressure.
There was a fine Pommard and after
Coffee Courvoisier, mostly consumed
By Tom but again no sign of his being
Tipsy. Our next stop, heading west,
Was Shakertown. No Shakers left

To do their ecstatic shaking,
But the old buildings and furniture
Well preserved. I started on the
Direct road home but Tom stopped me.
That ham, he said, I remember that
Wonderful ham laced with bourbon
I once had at the inn in Bardstown!
I turned the car and headed for
Bardstown. And it was indeed
A great Kentucky ham, a red-eye ham,
I think they call it, with a bottle of
St. Emilion to wash it down
And a few nips of cognac
To settle the stomach. And
Tom still sober as a judge.

When we got back to Gethsemani
There wasn't a light in the place.
Brother Gatekeeper was long gone
To his cot in the dormitory.
What to do? I remember, said Tom,
A place on the other side near
The cemetery where the wall
Isn't quite as high as it is here.
Tom was right, the wall was lower.
I got down on all fours
And had Tom stand on my back.
Can you reach the top? I asked.
Just with my fingertips, he said.
OK, hold on if you can,
I'll get up and push up your legs.
Tom was up, lying on the wall but
I couldn't reach his dangling hand.
I thought of my belt. I took it off
And tossed one end up to him.
Brace your legs around the wall
And I'll climb with my legs
The way Rexroth taught me on
Rock faces in the mountains.
Believe it or not, it worked.
We lay in the grass on the far side
Of the wall and laughed and laughed
And laughed. We have done the Devil's
Work today, Tom, I told him.
No, he said, we've been working for
The angels; they are friends of mine.
Keeping very quiet, Tom went off to
His bishop's room, I to my bed
In the wing for the retreatants.

III

The Wrong Bed—Moira

It was in London that I
Fell into the wrong bed.
I should have guessed she
Was paranoid but sometimes
You can't tell. She picked
Me up in the Gargoyle. It
Was the night Dylan tripped
And sprained his ankle so
Badly he couldn't walk. We
Got him to his place in a
Taxi, then went on to hers
In Chelsea. I think her
Name was Moira but I can't
Remember for sure now. She
Was a small girl, brown hair,
Lively eyes, nicely dressed,
An upper-class accent, quite
Chatty. She had some bottles
And we drank till we both
Passed out with our clothes

On. Next day, about noon,
She ordered a car with a
Driver and we drove down to
Bath. That's when the bad talk
About Americans started, but
I let it pass. She had friends
In Bath, a couple with an
Apartment in the Crescent.
We dumped on them; they said
We could have the sofa. We
Ate at a pub, then the drink
Began again. I think I was
The first to pass out. I woke
Up in the night. She was on
The sofa with the man. No sign
Of the wife, I went back
To sleep on the floor.

Next morning when the couple
Had gone off, they had a
Shop somewhere, she said,
"Well, you brought me down
Here, I guess I'd better
Let you have it." She sat
Down on the sofa and pulled
Up her skirt. By then I
Wasn't interested, but she
Jibed at me: "Come on, Yank,
Let's see what you're good
For." When that was over,
And it wasn't much, there
Was the only kind word I
Heard about Americans. She
Said, "You're better than
Most of the Johnnies around
Here." I should have left
Her in Bath to get herself
Home, but I felt sorry for
Her somehow. She was a mess
But sort of pitiful. I got
Her back to Chelsea. She
Didn't ask me in. The car
Hires ran me sixty pounds.

In the Italian alps, 1935

The Desert in Bloom

Why can't you remember the Nevada
   Desert awash with bright-colored
Flowers when we camped not far
From Tonapah that April long ago?
It was soon after we had met in
San Francisco and fallen in love.
You were George's sister, the
Beautiful poet's beautiful sister,
That's how I got to know you.
Surely you must remember how the
Desert, that was so harsh all the
Rest of the year, rocks and gray
Sand, had suddenly burst into
Bloom, a salute to Persephone in
Almost violent praise of spring,
A salute that would last only a
Few weeks till the snow moisture
In the ground would be exhausted.

Rexroth had loaned us a tent and
We gathered dry cactus to cook
Over an open fire. At night we
Heard the soft cooing of doves
From all around us in the dark
But at dawn they ceased their
Complaining. You said that they
Reminded you of the doves in
Provence when you were there
As a girl, the *roucoulement des
Colombes* that the troubadours
And their ladies once heard in
The castle gardens, recording
Their sound in their *cansos.*

The ground was hard under our
Sleeping bags, the desert gets
Chilly at night, so cold that
Sometimes we had to squeeze
Into one bag, skin to skin,
Enlaced together. At night in the
Desert the stars seem twice as
Bright as anywhere else; when
We lay on our backs we would
Look up into the vastness, trying
To locate the constellations
And remember the names that were
Given them by the Greeks in the
Myths how many thousands of years
Ago. Andromeda and the Dioscuri;
Cassiopeia, whom Perseus saved
From the sea-monster; Orion, the
Hunter, and Sirius his dog,
Brightest of all; the Pleiades,
Whose motions tell the seasons;
Bereniker, whose pretty lock of
Hair has lived in song; the lion,
The dragon, and the swan. Your
People were Jewish but your
Beauty was more of Attica, than
Of Phoenicia; great brown eyes,
Dark hair and olive skin. The
Girls of Lesbos would have adored
You but you were not of their
Kind. Your body is described
In the *Song of Songs;* not a
Fraction of an inch would I
Have changed in its proportions
If I were a sculptor. The desert
Was empty and I would ask you
To lie naked in the sun, now
And then changing your pose, a
Moving sculpture. You had the
Marks of Eros, a girl fit for
The Mysteries. Liquid as the
Fountain Arethusa. And you were
Funny and endearing and passionate.

Holding hands, we took walks on
The vast desert before the sun
Became too hot. I picked flowers
And made a multicolored garland
For your hair. The handmaiden
Of Aphrodite: *venerandam.* In the
Shade of the tent I read you the
Exquisite love sonnets of Louise
Labé, which aroused us to make
Love again, hot as it was, the
Sweet glistening on our bodies.
One day we drove into Tonapah,
Now the slumbering ruin of the
Old hell-&-damnation mining
Town, where once fortunes of
Gold were won and lost at the
Tables, and men killed for it.

"Skiing on the Ball Glacier, Mount Cook, New Zealand, South Island. With some boys from Dartmouth, I made a ski trip to New Zealand, in 1934, where we raced the locals. I was interested in skiing and mountaineering for many years. I made a business out of developing the ski lifts at Alta, above Salt Lake, which my children now own."

The streets were empty, but in
What is left of the Grand Hotel
California we found an old man
Dozing on top of the green
Gaming table; we woke him up
And shot craps with silver dollars
For chips. We stayed on the desert
For three days when we had used
Up the water we had brought in
Cans.

              *   *   *

Now after fifty years we're in
Touch again. You've had four
Husbands and I'm on my third
Marriage. You say that you
Can hardly remember our love-
Making on the flowering desert.
How can that be? For me it's
As fresh as if it only happened
Yesterday. I see you clear with
My garland in your hair. Now we
Are two old people nursing our
Aches. What harm can there be
In remembering? We cannot hurt
Each other now.

V

Melissa

Only "pretty," not "beautiful"?
She was almost angry about my
Half compliment. We were riding
In a cab to dinner in London.
It was about our third date and
I'd been looking down the neck
Of her dress; she never wore a
Bra, she was casual about such
Conventions. Melissa was from
Australia, from a town near Perth,
But her parents had transplanted
To England when she was about ten
So she'd finished her schooling
In Sussex. She'd made the move
Early enough so she'd entirely
Lost the awful Australian accent;
Everyone took her for a Brit. But
In her personality she kept the
Australian openness and ready
Friendliness with strangers. She
Could be a good friend after a few
Conversations. Yet there was
Sensitivity and a delicacy of
Feeling in all her relationships.
No coarseness such as Australians
Sometimes have. No rough talk.
I came to understand how she was
What she was when one Sunday she
Took me down to Sussex on the
Train to meet her "Mum." A small
House on the outskirts of a
Village. Her mother was living
On a pension, the father had died
Some years back, and she'd had a
Hard time making do for two girls.

But the garden was all trim,
Weeded and the borders edged.
The house was neat as a pin.
There was a pretty tea with
Watercress sandwiches and
Scones, a tiny vase of lobelias
On the tray. Her mother was
Relaxed and well-spoken, a sense
Of humor too. No touch of
Accent. Melissa's new accent
Was a bit Clerkenwell, the part

Of London past Holborn where
She lived, a district that
Borders on the slummy: little
Tawdry shops. She'd picked up
A bit of the way they talk
There because she thought it
Funny. A little slur of cockney,
But she could get her studio
There for a very cheap rent.
Five flights of steep
Stairs up to her place, but
She'd made a bower of it,
Pretty things picked up
At auctions. Pots of flowers
And climbing vines at the
Windows. Old prints, copies
Of pictures she loved cut
From art magazines. Sonia
Delaunay was one of her loves.
Some of her own abstractions,
Strait-edge drawings, lovely
Contrasts of subtle colors.
Believe this or not, she liked
To paint lying on her tummy
In the middle of the floor
With a sheet down to save
The carpet if a paint pot
Turned over. It was a hard go
With her work because she
Had no gallery though she
Sold a painting now and then
But for almost nothing. She
Made her living teaching at
The Royal College, and an
Odd job now and then at a
Shop. With her smile she
Could sell ice to the eskimos.

The first time we made love
Was in the bracken on a bluff
Overlooking the Channel in
Dorset near an ancient village
Named Little Piddle-on-Trent.
It was warm but clouds were
Riding across the sky. The
Bracken was soft. Our loving
Was soft and slow. It always
Was that way. We could be happy
Just looking and touching and
Stroking. Her skin was so white
And perfect. I teased her that

She had the proverbial skin
Of an English dairymaid. Gray
Eyes. Long reddish hair. To
Please me she'd sometimes put
Her hair up in a braid that
Hung down her back. It was a
Bother for her, but "all right,
James, if you'll take me to
Dinner at the White Tower, I'll
Put up my hair for you, you old
Fetishist." She would gobble
Up a good meal but one of her
Specialties was Heinz's baked
Beans served cold. She had
Tiny feet and one pair of
Shoes with heels. Only one
Long dress for going out.
Mostly she wore blue jeans.
She'd never let me buy her
Any clothes except once when
We were on a lovely long
Weekend in Paris to tour the
Galleries, she weakened when
We passed a boutique on the
Rue Saint Honoré. She found
A long swirling dress of fine
White linen which made her
Look like Joan of Arc in a
Wind storm, though when we
Went to dinner at the Grand
Véfours in the Palais Royal,
Where the other guests all
Stared at her, she looked like
A princess. Books she'd always
Let me give her. She was a big
Reader; she reads much more
Than I and always good
Things. With her love she
Gave me so much more than
I could ever give her. I used
To ask her to come to America,
But she wouldn't even consider
It. "New York would kill me in
A month," she said, "You're a
Dear man, James, and I'll not
Likely ever love anyone as much
As I do you, but I'm a London
Girl, a Clerkenwell girl, and
Here's where I belong, this is
The spot for me."

On the porch of the Alta Lodge in Utah, about 1946

Are We Too Old To Make Love?

Some fifty years ago, yes it was
That long, the summer when our
Families sent us to Munich to
Learn some German, and we met at
The opera in the Prinzregenten
Theatre, you were wearing a blue
Dress and blue shoes with little
White bows on the toes, we had a
Few dates and liked each other
In a childish way. (I was seventeen
And you were sixteen.) We decided
It would be fun to put our bicycles
On the local train and go up to
Mittenwald in the foothills of
The alps. We rode around the
Mountain roads for several days.
It was lovely, such views of the
High peaks, except when it
Rained, but we didn't have much

Money so we would take one room,
But with two beds with those
Funny feather puffs on them
Instead of blankets. It was all
So innocent, like little children
Playing house. We never kissed
Or even held hands the whole
Time we were in the mountains.
You would undress and dress
In the inn bathroom and I would
Dress while you were out of the
Room. When we had spent all our
Money we went back to Munich.

We went to the opera a few
More times, we liked *Magic
Flute* the best; we took to
Calling each other Papagena
And Papageno and we whistled
The flute tune. We took walks
In the wooded parts of the
Englischer Garten. I suppose
I could have tried to kiss
You but I never did. What was
Wrong with me anyway? Soon it
Was time to go back to the
States to get ready for college.

You were going to Vassar and I
To Harvard. They aren't far
Apart but for some reason I
Never tried to see you though
I thought of you now and then
And we sent a few postcards
Back and forth. That was fifty
Years ago. You married a man
In California and had children
And now grandchildren. With me
It's about the same except that
I've been married three times
And had more children. Fifty
Years ago. Then one day there's
A phone call from a lady in a
Neighboring town whom I know.
She says that "your old friend
Papagena from Munich is visiting
And would like to see you and
Meet your wife. Please come to
Lunch next Wednesday." The thought
Of seeing you again excited me.

What would you be like in old
Age? My friend had said on
The phone that your husband
Had died a few years ago.
What would you think of me
With my head getting bald
And my old man's fat stomach?
I imagined all sort of things
About you, how you would be
And what we might talk about.
Some of these thoughts were
Not rational. I imagined you
Were still beautiful and that
I asked you, quite seriously,
"Are we too old to make love?"

Yes, I really imagined that
Question being asked and
speculated on how you might
Reply to it. The meeting at
My friend's house was not
Embarrassing. It all went
Quite easily. You had white
Hair now, but you were slim
And moved gracefully. You
Still had your special smile,
A kind of enigmatic smile,
That I remembered. You and
My wife got along pleasantly.
We talked a bit about Munich
Days but not as if it were
Some big deal. Mostly we
Exchanged information about
Our children and grandchildren.

You asked about what books I
Was publishing. Up to that
Point it was all very
Easy, very comfortable. But
Then something happened that
Was astounding, something that
I still can't understand or
Interpret. We were alone in
The sitting room; the others
Had gone out into the garden.
You looked at me with your
Enigmatic smile and said, with
No more emphasis than if you
Were talking about the weather,
"You know, James, there's one

Thing I've always wanted to
Ask you if I ever saw you again;
Why when we were staying at
That little inn near Mittenwald
Did you tear the wings off all
Those moths and throw them on
My pillow?"

Is it possible I could have
done such a thing?

————————

The Yellow Pad

That's where it all gets piled
Up, on the blue lines of the
Big yellow pads, when I'm wakened
In the middle of the night by the
Pressure of images and words at
The back of my brain, ideas that
Are struggling to escape, to be
Liberated from the labyrinth of
Lost memories. The rush of them
Is strong enough to jolt me out
Of sound sleep.
            Last night the
Images were of Liddy and the
Words were the way she talked.
(This was forty years ago.)
She had a little resonant
Throatiness in her voice that
Set her apart from other girls
From Brooklyn. Poor Liddy, I
Treated her shamefully as only
A horny young man on the loose
Could do. She wasn't a beauty,
But she had a bright, pert
Look, a teasingness in her
Eyes that commanded attention.
Black hair and a dark com-
Plexion. Her body spoke to me
Like that of one of the girls
You read about in the Old
Testament. It was fecund. She
Moved in a way that made her
Hips glide. She was *attirante,*

As the French might say, she
Was seductive.
            Liddy was a
Clerk in the magazine office
Where I was then working.
My first job in the city.
It wasn't long before we
Were eyeing each other, then
Talking more than was neces-
Sary for work, then going
Out for lunch together and
Then after just a few weeks
Making love on the couch
That opened into a day bed
In my little one-room apart-
Ment on 73rd Street. She was
Far from being an innocent
Virgin. She suggested things
To do that I had never done
Before. She was proud of
Her skill and knowledge. It
Was all in a spirit of fun
And games. But there was
One strange thing: she never
Let me touch her breasts.
I could kiss them but was
Not allowed to play with
Them. Little spheres with
Nipples that went hard, but
She would slap my hand away.
But she was good inside,
Like honey. She was ready
For more than I could often
Give. But it came to me
Clearly after a month that
She wanted to be serious
About me that she hoped to
Get married. A good Jewish
Girl gets married even if
It's to a goy, as long as
He has a job and is making
Money. It became a conflict
Of wills, my lust against
Her determination. Oh, she
Attacked with great guile.
Nothing was ever openly
Said about marriage, but
She exerted all her sexual
Power. She began to invite
Me to spend a weekend now

And then at her apartment
On Cumberland Street in
Brooklyn. She was a good
Cook and she spoiled me.
Candles and wine on the
Table. Sometimes we would
Go to the opera or to the
Ballet. She read books
That were above her back-
Ground to please me. She
Had a good IQ and talked
Well about what she read.
In the mornings we would
Sleep late, then take our
Showers together, soaping
Each other under the spray
And rubbing our slippery
Bodies against each other.
Then she would do breakfast

*"Working on the Taggart Hut in Ashcroft,
Colorado. A group of us made a summer project
of reconditioning the old ruined prospector's hut
into a hut for ski trips," 1950.*

But without dressing. She
Would dart about her little
Kitchen without a stitch on,
Pausing now and then to kiss
Me intimately.

But all the while I was
Enjoying her, playing with
Her for my pleasure, I knew
Our relationship could
Never be altered. There
Was the barrier of class,
Of cultural background
Between us. I couldn't
Take her out with my class-
Mates from Harvard and she
Never took me to meet her
Parents. It was unthinkable
That I would have her meet
Mine. She understood only
Too well what worried me,
And she made a last effort
To convince me that what
We shared was enough to
Bind us together. Still
There was no discussion of
The problem. It was all
Intuitive, like a groping
Game of blindman's buff.

She had never been skiing
But she persuaded me to
Take her up to New Hamp-
Shire for a weekend. She
Bought a ski outfit at
Saks so she would look
Right. I put her in the
Ski class for beginners
And she didn't do badly.
The crisis came when we
Were in the pullman car
That night to go back to
New York. I asked her to
Take the lower berth but
After the train got going
And the other passengers
Had retired she opened
The curtains and pulled me
Into the lower berth with

Her. I couldn't resist the
Exotic temptation. At first
She was gentle but soon
She became violent. Her
Fingers were like talons
Gripping my body. She began
To bite me, then to engorge
Me. She wanted to mouth
Every part of me, to swallow
Me entire. She was possessed.
I was saved by the cries and
Groans of her frenzy. The
Black porter heard them and
Put his head into the opening
Of the curtains, "Everything
All right, suh?" he asked.
I told him it was all right
And he went away. Now Liddy
Went from passion to fright.
She began to shake as if
She were having an epileptic
Fit. I held her in my arms
For hours but the attack
Persisted on and off. When
We reached Grand Central
I found a cab and took her
Out to Brooklyn. Neither
Of us said much and when I
Tried to hold her hand she
Pulled it away. We both knew
That our relationship was
Over. It was the end of
The line for us.

When I got to the office
That morning Liddy was not
There and she didn't come
In all day. That night she
Came when nobody was there
And cleaned out her desk.
She never wrote or called
And I've never seen her
Again.

Poor little Liddy, I still
Think of her now and then.
I reproach myself for my

"Mountaineering atop one of the peaks in the Oetztal range of the Austrian alps. It was COLD up there," 1956.

Selfishness and for not
Having found a way to make
The parting less cruel for
Her. Now and then I'd hear
About her from the girls
She'd known in the office.
They told me that she had
Had to go to a shrink for
Many months to get back her
Peace of mind and her self-
Esteem. Through one of the
Girls I sent her a check
But she never cashed it.
Two years later I learned
That she'd married well, a
Professor of history at
Barnard. I hope Liddy is
Happy now and has forgiven
Me for making her a victim.
I used her shamelessly. It's
All down on my yellow pad.

The Rubble Railroad

It was October of 1945, only five
Months after the end of World War
Two. I was living in Paris, back
In my old digs on the rue du
Saint Père, trying to write a
Novel about life in Pittsburgh
In my youth, but the more I put
Down the worse it got. So I was
Glad when I had a letter from my
Old friend Herbert Blechsteiner
In Cologne saying that he had
Been able to wangle the use of
An Army car, with driver and
Gas ration, and would I like to
Join him for a week to inspect
What was left of Germany after
The bombing. Herbert, who was
Fluent in six languages, was
The greatest wangler I ever
Encountered. Anything he wanted
He would get, and at a bargain
Price. And he would do the
Same for his friends. This
Genius came from his years in
The Middle East. He had been
Born into a large family who
Were traders in antiquities.
There were branches of Blech-
Steiner Ltd. from Bombay to
Lisbon, all run by Herbert's
Uncles or cousins. London was
The province of Herbert's
Brother Ulrich, with a rather
Grand shop on Jermyn Street
Not far from the Cavendish
Hotel, where Rosa Lewis, one
Of the mistresses of Edward VII,
Still held sway. Herbert had
Served an apprenticeship at the
Shop in Damascus, where he
Picked up spoken Arabic, but
His heart was in languages and
Writing. He came back to Paris,
Where he lived with the uncle
There and did his time at the
Sorbonne in linguistics.

I took the Berlin Express but
Got off at Mannheim to board a
Steamer down the Rhine, this for
The sight of the Rhenish castles
Perched on the hilltops and
Vineyards cascading down to the
River. In Cologne I found a
Daimler-Benz sedan parked at
The Hotel Gruber. It had a
Little U.S. Army pennant on the
Front mudguard, so that would
Be Herbert. The driver, a sergeant,
Seeing my bag, leapt from the
Car to open the door and salute.
This saluting bit went on all
Through the trip. It embarrassed
Me because I'd managed with
Some effort to avoid the war.
"Can't you get him to stop the
Saluting?" I asked Herbert,
Who replied, "I told him you were
A bigshot in the OSS." I'd been
Wondering for some time why
Herbert stayed on with the Army
As only an interpreter. That
Evening at the Drei Hirschen
(Herbert would know the best
Place to eat in any city) over
A fine bottle of Gewurztraminer,
He explained that Germany was
Awash with displaced artworks.
Some were things that GI's had
Stolen. Others were things that
Starving owners who didn't have
Enough food cards for their
Families had to sell, often for
A song. Herbert's business was
To pick up such treasures and
Get them out to his relatives
In the Blechsteiner offices in
Army mail pouches which weren't
Censored. And how, I asked, did
He come by such an elegant auto?
Kindness of a Brigadier, he told me,
A charming fellow from New York
Who was a collector of etchings.
"I got him a prime Dürer, museum
Quality. He couldn't do enough
For me."

Next morning I accompanied Herbert
On his rounds. He needed some cash
And tackled a fat little dealer
Whose luxurious shop near the Dom
Betokened a sharpie set to catch
Tourists. Herbert was showing him
A superb Tibetan devil thanka he
Had picked up from one of the
Gurkhas in a British regiment that
Was stationed near Hanover. The
Dealer was no match for Herbert's
Salesmanship, which included verse
Quotations supposedly from the
Book of the Dead. Spotting me as
An American, Herr Plumps brought
Out a painting which he claimed
Was a Franz Marc, one of the
Blauer Reiter group, the man who
Did the famous bright red horses.
It was handsome, but Herbert
Pulled his ear to signal me that
It was a fake. And we left the shop.

Setting out for Frankfurt we
Stopped at the railroad station
To pick up the magnificent
Alexander who arrived from
Berlin to join up with us. I
Have selected the adjective
With care. Alexander Gruener,
Who had been Herbert's night
And day companion throughout
The war, was the embodiment
Of Hitler's prescription for
The ideal Teuton: nearly two
Meters tall, shoulders like
An ox but waist like a wasp;
Blue eyes, blond hair, and
A mien serious with determination;
His only shortcoming was that he
Was at heart a communist, which
Made him acceptable to Herbert as
A lover. The first few days we
Were together Alexander viewed
Me with suspicion, he couldn't
Quite place me in relation to
Herbert. Was I a rival? But he
Gradually got the picture that
We were just friends. He relaxed
And we got on well. His idea of
Amusements was to correct my

German and make the conventional
European's jokes about America.
He was soon calling me "der
Cowboy" and demonstrating his
Prowess in arm wrestling.

The bombing damage that we had
Seen in Cologne was slight; it
Had not been a primary target.
But Frankfurt was another story.
The center of the city had been
Flattened. Beautiful old quarters
Which I remembered from earlier
Visits were a desolation of
Destruction. The madness of war.
While we were in Germany I kept
A diary. When I got back to
Paris I put parts of it into verse:

> *In Frankfurt*
> Gray hungry men are loading
> debris from a blasted house
> into the little dump cars of
> the rubble railroad
> > this is
> the line that makes its run
> from death to hope
> > its tracks
> are layed on blocks in every
> German city & when one street
> is cleaned they move them to
> the next
> > it pays no dividends
> but runs all day and will for
> 7 years
> > their shovels probing
> hunger-slowly in the settled
> wrack turn up a twisted, rust-
> ing spoon. They all put down
> their tools and pass it around
> appraising worth or use
> > but
> it's too bad they toss it in
> the cart
> > I pick it out and put
> it in my pocket
> > I want that
> spoon
> > they stare I blush and
> offer cigarettes they take &
> thank and I walk off
> > I want
> their spoon I'll take it home
> back to the other world. I'll
> need it there to learn to eat.

The men, and there were women
Too in the work crews, were a
Miserable looking group. They
Were obviously undernourished,
Dressed in rags, some of the
Men in remnants of wehrmacht
Uniforms, all of them so tired
They had to rest, leaning on
their shovels every few minutes.

How Did They Look?
The face narrows
the skin tightens on the ckeekbones
the mouth & lips tighten
the cheeks suck in a bit
the eyes sink back into the skull
the eyes are dull seeming
the circles under the eyes deepen
& darken
the hair thins and grays
that's just the head
the body?
I couldn't bear to look.

Heading to Munich we couldn't
Go by the autobahn because it
Had only been rebuilt in sections.
Better to head south on small
Roads where we could enjoy the
Countryside, zigzagging from one
Rural road to another. It was
A welcome escape from the wreckage
Of the war. Pristine villages
Where the farming life was still
Going on. Hedgerows and poplar
Trees separating the meadows.
But there were few cows or sheep
In the meadows. They had been
Eaten. Where we stopped for
A lunch of kaiserschmarren in
An inn there was a small
Church beside the place, one
That had the slavic onion
Top on its spire. There a peasant
Wedding was taking place which
We watched for a half hour.
No cars about, there was so
Little gas. The bride and groom
Went off in a farm cart drawn
By a white horse so ancient he
Could hardly walk. We made a
Dip down to the Danube to see
The great gothic cathedral at
Ulm which had not been hurt.

In the New Directions office, New York City, 1973

In Munich we linked up with
An old friend of Herbert's,
The famous photographer Max
Faber. Max was touring around
Germany shooting the ruins for
The Air Force, which wanted a
Record of their handiwork for
The allied archives. He showed
Us his portfolio. Many of his
Shots were magnificent as art,
Giant sculptures in their way,
Especially where they dealt
With tall buildings that had
Only partially collapsed. The
Work depressed Max. In
His ebullient, gay way he was
A very jolly fellow, full of
German and macabre Jewish jokes
And stories. We spent a lot of
Time going around Munich with
Him. The sights of destroyed
Munich hurt me more than had

Frankfurt because I knew the
City well from the summer when
I had lived there, quartered with a
German family who were supposed
To teach me some German. I was
Only seventeen then, much more
Interested in the maedelis I
Picked up at the opera and in
The big English Garden Park.
Although the factories which
Were the targets for the air
Raids were outside the city
Proper, the aim of those who
Released the bombs was not
Good. Many of the cultural
Monuments were demolished.
Both of the pinakotheks had
Been hit, though fortunately
The paintings had been hidden
In saltmines and mountain
Caves. The buildings on both
Sides of the regal avenues,
The Maximilienstrasse and the
Ludwigstrasse, were smashed.
The Wittelsbach palaces were
Down, and in the business center
The Marienplatz and the rathaus
Town hall were in bad shape.

As we wandered about the city,
Where rubble railroads and
Their crews were working here
And there, we noticed another
Presence: large numbers of
American soldiers. They didn't
Seem to be doing anything except
Killing time. I talked to
A few of them to get a
Feel of how, as they waited
To be shipped home, they
Felt about their situation.
As conquerors of an old
Culture. And about the
Desolation their planes
Had wrought. Their chief
Expressions were of boredom
And of anger that repatriation
Was taking so long. I tried
Later to get it down in a poem.

Song of the GI's and the MG's

We are the lords of the cigarette
    & the green passport
      we do the best we can
we rule the world unwillingly
    & have good intentions
      we do the best we can
we are most of us sorry that you
    are always so hungry
      we do the best we can
we are unaccustomed to governing
    & make some mistakes
      we do the best we can
we often marry your girls after we
    have seduced them
      we do the best we can
we are hurt when you resist our plans
    for your re-education
      we do the best we can
we will help you try to clean up
    the bomb mess we made
      we do the best we can
we are the lords of the cigarette
    & the green passport
      we really do mean to do
      the best we can for you.

One evening Max invited us out to
His place in Schwabing, the artists'
Quarter out Ludwigstrasse beyond
The Siegestor. That is the quarter
Renowned for Oktober fests, a week
Of merriment and carousing as famed
As our Mardi Gras in New Orleans.
There wouldn't be one that year,
Of course, but I hear now that it's
Going strong as ever again. Max's
Residence could hardly be called
An apartment. One side wall of
The building had been bombed off,
But Max had made a false wall
With canvas nailed onto salvaged
Posts. Electric power had not yet
Been restored but there were half a
Dozen candles. Max had an Army friend
And there was Jack Daniels from the
PX. He had assembled some artists
And several pretty girls. It was
An eventful party as this poem
Tells it, not a happy one for the girl.

Max's Party

One of our new aristocrats
the knights of the air en-
thralls (he thinks) a half-
starved German tart with his
exploits while he gets drunk
then he passes out poor girl
she has to hit the street again
without a meal the MP's
cart him off in their jeep.

And one of the artists
Had a tale to tell.

Hard to Translate

My friend Klaus a German goes
to the MG travel office for a
permit to visit Switzerland old
          friends in Berne

have invited him they will feed
and fatten him for three weeks and
clear some of the misery mist
          out of his brain

The MG official feels like a little
joke and kids Klaus "why ever
do you want a trip? you Germans
          should stay here

at home and enjoy your hunger-
strafe" (that word is rather hard
to translate as it means hunger-
          punishment but it

also suggests the strafing that
God was supposed to give to the
English) Klaus winces but keeps
          hold of his tem-

per he patiently tells the man
(who is a Jew) about his impris-
onment under the Nazis in the
          end he gets his

permit all right the man is a
good egg and meant to give it
to him all the time he was just
          feeling like his

little joke but he should not
have said that Klaus tells me
such things go to the bone and
          they stick there.

My happiest day in Munich was
When I took the little local train
South to Gauting, a village which is
Halfway to the Starnbergersee,
To visit the Heys, the family
With whom I had spent the summer
Years before to learn some German.
When I had left them then, it
Must have been about 1931, they
Were in terror of the Nazis. They
Weren't Jews but the son, Fritzi,
Had been expelled from the Munich
University, where he was studying
Engineering. The father, whose
Profession was painting the art
Work for picture postcards (they
Were exquisite depictions of rural
Life) was in trouble because he
Had declined to paint the local
Gauleiter leading the parade of
Brown Shirts that toured the town
Every Saturday. When I left them
That summer I feared I might not
See them again. Not only Jews but
"Unsuzamanwirkends," those who
Didn't cooperate hard enough,
Were often being sent to the
Labor camps. But all was well
With the Heys when I walked out
To their charming little woods-
House from the Gauting station.
Nothing was changed except that
The fierce watchdog, Gunter, had
Expired. Herr Hey was painting
Away in his attic studio; he
Had received a commission from
The Prinzregenten Theatre to do
Cards of scenes from Mozart's
Operas. They read me letters
From Fritzi who had escaped
To India and was finishing
His engineering degree at the
University of Allahabad. And
There, my special blessing, was
Dear Frau Hey working in her
Beautiful flower garden. She
Was the one who was in charge
Of my German lessons. How I
Vexed her because I had
"Ungenügend anlegung"

For irregular verbs and things
That required memorization.
But she was gentle in her
Reproaches; she remembered
What it was like to be a
Student at seventeen. She
Imposed no penalties. I
Could take the train in to
Munich for the opera as often
As I wanted as long as I
Was back by midnight. My
Best friend was my bicycle.
After lunch I'd take off on
It riding for miles through
The manicured paths of the
Towering forests. Peasants
Picked up every stick and
Carted them home on their
Little handcarts. "Grüss
Gott," I would shout to the
Gatherers as I pedalled
Past them, and "Grüss Gott
Herr" they would reply from
The shadowy depths of the
Forest. If it was a warm day
I would ride down to the top
Of the Starnbergersee, a
A big lake that ran nearly to the
Foot of the Alps. There was
A schwimmbad there where I'd
Change into my trunks and
Rent a bathchair in which I
Could stretch out to sun
Myself as I looked up at the
Mountains, the Alps above
Garmisch and Mittenwald
With the top of the mighty
Zugspitz peering over them.
One day I fell asleep in
The sun. When the old man
Who ran the schwimmbad woke
Me up I saw that I was the
Last. "You should have
Wakened me," I told him.
"No," he said, "I looked you
Over and could tell that
You were having a good
Dream. That's what all of us
In this country need now, a few
Good dreams."

*In the New York City (Greenwich Village) office of
New Directions, 1975*

Herbert and Alexander wanted
Me to drive up to Berlin with
Them but I'd had enough of
Ruins and suffering people.
I took the train from Munich
To Paris and tried to buckle
Down to work on my novel.
But it was hard to concentrate.
Pittsburgh suddenly seemed like
A place that never existed
In real life. What I had seen
In Germany kept flooding my
Brain. It was a long time, even
After I'd returned to the States,
Before I was able to put my
Heart in the book. One day as
I was avoiding work, this little
Poem appeared on my notebook
Page. It had written itself.

O Frères Humains

The rubble railroad
carries freight
that's more than loads
of stone and dirt
it carries off
an age's hate
and puts it with
a people's heart

the cars are dumped
beyond the city
and then come back
to load once more
o brother men
at last learn pity
return them full
with love to share.

In Trivandrum

My next stop in India that year
(Which was 1953, as best I can
Recall) was Trivandrum, a little
But lovely city in the region now
Known as Kerala, which was in
Colonial times a princely state
Ruled by the Portuguese, then
The Dutch, and then the English,
Who called it Cochin. Vasco de
Gama landed his ships at
Cochin in 1502, reckoning it the
Finest port on the Arabian Sea
South of Bombay. Cochin has a
Heavy rainfall, making the land
Rich for rice, tapioca, pepper and
Vegetables. The landscape is set
With graceful coconut palms and
Many ponds and little ornamental
Waterways. The language mainly
Is Malayalam, but Trivandrum
Holds also a settlement of Jews
That boasts the oldest synagogue
In Asia. Christians of differing
Sects are scattered all over the
Sub-continent. Many myths tell
Of the coming of Christianity
To India. In Malabar they think

The Apostle Thomas ("doubting
Thomas") arrived in Cochin in
A.D. 52 to take up the work of
Conversion. But on the eastern
Coast people tell you Thomas
Built his church in Madras on
A hill known as The Mount.

I had come to Trivandrum to
Meet the novelist Raja Rao.
Along with R. K. Narayan of
Mysore, Raja Rao was, in those
Days and probably still is, the best
Indian writer working in English.
(How good the native writers,
May be, since they compose in
thirteen major languages, is
Hard to guess. Few of them can
Read the works of the others.)
But I had read Raja Rao's novel
The Serpent and the Rope and I
Had no doubt in my mind that
He was first class. I had heard
Rumors that he had finished
A new novel. I wanted to find
Him. The rumors were true.
After we had been together for
Two days, during which Raja
Had assessed my enthusiasm
For Indian life and culture, he
Placed the manuscript of his
New book, *Kanthapura*, in my
Hands, saying: "I think you'll
Like this. My friend Mr. Forster
Has been over it and says it's
A good book about India as
She is today, after Gandhi." I
Didn't need Forster's praise to
Convince me that this was a
Masterpiece. *Kanthapura* is
A book like no other I'd read,
A magical book that brings the
Spell of India to the western
Reader. New Directions brought
The book out at once, and after
Many reprintings it remains
As fresh and compelling as it
Was when I first encountered it.

"With the novelist John Hawkes, whom New Directions published, at a National Arts Club Award ceremony," about 1970

"Kanthapura" is a typical small
Village of southern India in
Which the changing life of all
Castes, impacted by Gandhi's
Revolution of independence
From the British, is the main
Force. Young Moorthy back
From the city with "new ideas,"
Works to break down the old
Barriers. Non-violence, as
Gandhi taught it, is his way
Of mobilizing the villagers to
Action. But his efforts are met
With violence from the police
And the rich landowners. The
Remarkable thing in the book
To me is its colloquial manner.
Rao's narrator is an old woman
Of the village who is imbued
With the legendary history of
Her region, the old traditions
Of Hinduism and the Vedic
Myths. She knows the past.
The stories of the villagers,
And her commentary on her
Neighbors is both pungent and
Wise. In her speech are echoes
Of the traditional folk-epics
Such as the *Ramayana*. But

How does Rao manage this
When writing in plain lucid
English? He has somehow
Made us hear native speech
In his narrator's extraordinary
Anglo-Indian language. He
Has a fine ear. He had known
The intonations and rhythms
Of the villagers as a child when
He was growing up in Mysore.
Then, because he came from
A prominent family, he had
Opportunities unusual for
An Indian, the University of
Madras and study in France at
Montpelier and the Sorbonne.

Traipsing about the countryside
With Raja as my guide was a
Great pleasure. The land is so
Verdant, and the busy life of
The inland waterways delighted
Me, the small open ferryboats,
Mostly motorized but now and
Then a boat with the red lateen
Sails of the ancient Arab dhows
That had first opened up the
Malabar coast. Raja had no
Car, but we borrowed bicycles
With which we followed the
Footpaths or the rough roads
Created by old bullock carts
Whose once-round wheels
Had been worn squarish by
Long use. We saw the villagers
Ploughing with their cattle,
Humped slaves who would work
Every day until they dropped,
Sleeping nights out in the rain.
Yet these cows seemed to live
A happier life than the sacred
Cows you find in Calcutta who
Live in the streets, sleep on the
Sidewalks and are fed by the
Faithful—once I was watching
As children gave candy bars
To a Calcutta cow—all this
Because the people believe
That cattle are descended, at
Least symbolically, from those

The Gopis watched over for
Lord Krishna at Brindaban.
We saw sheep and chickens
Around the hutments but no
Pigs. Little monkeys aplenty in
The coconut palms. The men
Distill a palm wine which they
Call "toddy." We were offered
Cups of it which tasted so awful
I could scarcely get mine down
Out of politeness. It looked like
Rotten eggs. But the intoxicating
Effect is said to be considerable.
Knowing Malayalam, Raja Rao
Was able to converse with the
People, who were not shy. They
Gathered around us to talk and
Raja interpreted for me. He said
They had never seen anyone
As tall as I (I'm six foot five).
They wanted to know where I
Came from and what I ate to
Get so big. Did I practice yoga?
Or some other occult mastery?
Some of them invited us into
Their thatched huts to show
Us with pride the rice-paste
Abstract paintings on their
Walls and thresholds. Raja
Taught me on that visit to
Eat curry and other Indian
Foods with my fingers, for no
Brahmin would ask for utensils.
It would be a breach of the rules
Of caste. But don't ask me to
Show you how it's done; I was
A poor pupil. The weather was
Hot in Cochin, of course, all
That moisture with the sun
Smoldering down through it.
Raja loaned me a dhoti, much
Better than my European pants
And shirt. But I managed more
Than once to get the skirt of
My dhoti caught in my bicycle
Chain, with resultant tumbles.
Our audience was amused. In
The evenings we had our curry
At Raja's home, which was for
Me a further trial of the fingers

In place of a fork. His was an
Extended family living in a
Small house in Trivandrum
And to this day I'm not sure
Who was who. Many women
In their saris smiled at me and
said nothing. Only the men
Joined us at table. The women
Ate apart, maybe in the kitchen
Which I was not shown. Then
Raja and I went out to wander
The streets of the old town with
Its Dutch-style buildings. Parts
Of it could have been Delft or
Nijmagen. No street lights, not
Much light from the house
Windows; it was eerie. Bare
Feet in the darkness making
No noise. It was enchanting
Too. We went to a show by
A troupe of Kathakali dancers
—Very exciting. Most of the
Dancing in South India, such
As the gliding style of Bharata
Natya, is tranquil, except for
An accompaniment of soft
Drumming; movement is
By the arms and hands, and
The "story" is told in classic
Mudras that have assigned
Meanings. Kathakali however
Is the opposite, violent motion
Most of the time. In a way it
Reminded me of the dramatic
Posturing in Japanese Kabuki.
For the westerner one of the
Attractions of Kathakali is
The costumes. Also the masks
Of the male dancers, sculpted
And grotesque. Vivid primary
Colors. Faces to scare children.
Demons and heroes. Men as
Tigers, as serpents. Terrifying.
Much magic, much death.

The plays are given outdoors
And always at night, often not
Finishing until the dawn. In
Darkness the great brass lamps
Flicker and add to the mystery.

The audience sits on the ground
(Though Raja Rao and I were
Honored with chairs). Men,
Women and children usually
Are separated. Two drummers,
Sounding their drums with
Their hands, often in very fast
Rhythms, provide the music.
The actors speak passages of
Verse that narrate the action
Of the play. The dialogue is
Sung by two singers who stand
At the back of the "stage." Now
The stories of the plays are told
In Malayalam rather than the
Classic Sanskrit, but they are
Still the ancient texts, epics like
The *Ramayana* (which reports
The heroic adventures of Rama
When he rescues his wife from
The demon-king Ravana of
Ceylon) or the *Mahabharata*
(Which recounts the endless
Struggle between two families,
The Pandavas and Kauravas,
Though the pre-eminent hero
Of the poem is the god Krishna)
Or the *Gita Govinda* (a cycle of
Poems about Krishna). These
Are traditional tales known
Almost universally in India
To all classes, just as Greek
Myths and Bible stories
Are known to us in the West.
In origin they go back perhaps
A dozen thousand years to
The oral tradition of village
Storytellers, the entertainers
Of that culture, just as our
Homeric epics are thought
To have been composed and
Revised and embellished by
Generations of warrior poets
Who recited them around the
Smoky campfires of ancient
Armies. At some point these
Original Hindu poems were
Transcribed into Sanskrit by
The pandits and gurus. Then
The final step was translation

Into the various vernaculars,
Hindi, Urdu, Tamil, Marathi,
Malayalam, and many others.

The evening of Kathakali was
Dramatic and thrilling though
Very long: it went on way past
Midnight. Raja Rao briefed me
On the unfolding motifs and
Actions as the play progressed.
Then the next day at dusk we
Experienced something even
More remarkable. Through Rao
I had met Professor Vivekananda
Who taught in the college at
Ernakulam on the coast north
Of Trivandrum. Vivekananda
Knew Sri Nalanda, a Vedantist
Guru from Bombay who was
Visiting friends in a
Village in the Cardamon
Hills. It was a rough trip
Getting there in a jitney
But we made it and the sage
Welcomed us cordially to one
Of the most intense occasions
Of my visit. I wouldn't have
Believed the background story
Vivekananda told me about Sri
Nalanda if we had been in any
Country but India, where the
Occurrence of wonders is so
Continual and many minds
Are saturated with the occult.
Gurus, holy men, sadhus, yogis.
Sannyasis all over the place,
Some with begging bowls, or
Smeared with ashes, or naked
In the streets. Being holy, being
A devotee of this god or that,
Depending on hand-outs from
The public, is a way of life. I
Was told by Vivekananda that
Nalanda came from a favored
Middle-class family. He had
Done well at school and had
Entered the railway service,
Where he had also done well,
Ending up as superintendent
At Bangalore. A faultless

Reputation, a married family
Man; no hint of any instability.
But his whole life was changed
When one night, while taking
A walk in the countryside, he
Met with a celestial messenger.
He knew by the godlike
Aura radiating around the
Old man's head that this
Stranger by the roadside was
Heaven-sent. The Ancient
Invited Nalanda to sit on the
Edge of a ditch and said that he
Had flown from Dharamsala
In the Himalayas to instruct
Nalanda, who indeed believed
It because like all Indians he
Believed in parakinesis. He
Knew that servants of the gods,
Like the apsareses, could move
Themselves over thousands of
Miles in the blink of an eye.

They talked together all night.
Then at dawn the messenger
Vanished, but not until he had
Laid on Nalanda the solemn
Injunction to make himself
A serious teacher of Vedanta.
Nalanda was careful to keep
What had happened a secret,
But immediately he began to
Study Vedanta with the wise
Men of the region, giving up
His worldly aspirations, and
He undertook long hours of
Meditation. In a few years he
Was renowned as an adept in
The doctrines of Vedanta and
Their significance, and also as
An eloquent elucidator of the
Ultimate meaning of reality,
Which, as it descends from the
Ancient Vedic texts such as the
Upanishads, concerns especially
The state of being beyond good
And evil, existence beyond and
Above mere knowledge. Then
Sri Nalanda was ready to begin
His teaching, and soon many
Devotees were attracted to him.

James Laughlin (left) with the famous bookseller Frances Steloff, owner of Gotham Book Mart and her partner, Andreas Brown, New York City. "[Steloff] lived to be one hundred," 1985.

On the night of my visit to him
With Professor Vivekananda
The setting for Sri Nalanda's
Lecture was not unlike that of
The Kathakali. It was outdoors
But a tarpaulin extended over
The bathchair in which the sage
Reclined as he talked. He was a
Small man whose somewhat
Birdlike features were belied
By a deep, almost hoarse voice,
More military than priestly.
His head was bald and glinted
As if astrally in the flaring light
Of the brass lanterns. He had
Piercing black eyes. He wore a
White dhoti and sandals. The
Professor and I were seated on

The modern New Directions office in Norfolk

Chairs near him but the others,
The devotees, sat on the ground
In a circle extending out into
The eerie dark. I felt that some
Kind of emanation was coming
From Nalanda into my own
Body, and I'd never had such
An experience before. It was
Not an unpleasant feeling. It
Was more like being a little
High on wine. I couldn't, of
Course, understand what he
Was saying, but Vivekananda
Whispered a word now and then.
I could see I was entirely out of
My depth. I'd had a course or
Two in philosophy at Harvard,
But the abstractions proposed
By Nalanda were from another
Thought-system, one for which
I was ill prepared. I caught bits
Of epistemology, whiffs of the

Philosophy of *Existenz,* but the
Frame was all alien. A different
Kind of mind, a sledgehammer
Of a mind, was at work. I gave
Up trying to understand and let
Myself drift as I watched, lost
In his gestures and intonations.
He lectured for about an hour,
Then rose to give his audience
The namatse blessing, with
Palms together, bowing in a
Circle to include everyone at
This gathering. Then came the
Gifts of food—bread, fruit, and
Vegetables laid out at his feet.
Nalanda asked Vivekananda
And me to stay on. The accent
Of his English was difficult, but
He was cordial, calling me "Mr.
Young America" with a warm
Smile. Vivekananda was well
versed in Vedanta; they talked

For a half-hour in Malayalam;
And when it was time for us to
Go, Nalanda asked me if I had
A question. But my mind went
Blank: what could I ask of the
Great sage? He smiled and said:
"So, let *me* ask *you* a question.
In America, tell me, what do
They teach you is between two
Thoughts?" I could think of no
Answer to that. I had no answer.
"No matter," said Nalanda. "In
Time you may be ready for such
A question. But fix it in your
Mind. Do not forget it before
You are ready." And all these
Years I've remembered, though
I know I can never answer the
Question. I scarcely understand
It. And is Sri Nalanda still alive?
Wherever he may be, what is
The space between his thoughts?

On my last evening with Raja
Rao we cycled out to the beach
To watch the sunset—a good
One, the sky blazing with many
Colors. At first the setting sun
Seemed a small, distant disk,
But as darkness fell it grew and
Grew into a huge ball of fiery
Red. "That is the great god
Agni," Raja Rao told me, "the
Eternal fire. He is many things.
He is the most important of
The Vedic divinities. First, he
Is the god of the altar fire and
Its sacrifices. Then he is the
Mediator between gods and
Men. And beyond that he is the
God of lightning and the sun."

As we pedaled back through
The dark countryside toward
Trivandrum, I began to smell
The loveliest natural perfume
I've encountered anywhere in
Any country. It's the evening
Scent of India. The people in
Their huts are cooking their

Last meal of the day, using
Cow patties to fuel their fires.
Every patty the cows let fall
Is picked up and saved by the
Children. The smoke rises in
The warm night air softly. It's
A pungent smell and a little
Sweet. It's the smell of India,
Primeval India of the first
Gods and the first real people.

[*The author expresses his thanks to Hayden Carruth for his editorial collaboration on "Trivandrum."*]

TWO VIEWS OF LONDON

I

My Shoelaces

My life has been a series of untied
Shoelaces, "Tie up your laces,
Dear, before we go to Granny's,"
My mother says, "Granny doesn't
Like untidy little boys," I didn't
Do it. Granny is an old wet hen.
She spends her days lying on the
Upstairs sitting room sofa, giving
Orders to the servants, who are a
Bunch of lazy Irish, except for
Thomas the butler who sneaks me
The Sunday funny papers, which are
Forbidden at home. I read them
With Thomas in the pantry and
He gives me ginger ale.

People always warn that I'll trip
Over my untied shoelaces and have
A bad fall. That only happened
Once. We were in New York visiting
Various relatives. I tripped and
Fell right in front of the Vanderbilt
Hotel. It was a bad one. I was cut
So deep I had to be taken to the
Hospital emergency room and have
Stitches. This made us late getting
To Aunt Patty's lunch party at the
Vanderbilt which put her in a pet.

What I did in the hotel dining room
Made her furious. It was the first
Time I had ever had an oyster. It
Tasted horrible and I spat it out
Right on the floor. Mother took
Me up to Aunt Patty's bedroom and
Gave me the hairbrush. And that
Was the end of the ten dollar
Goldpieces that used to come from
Aunt Patty every Christmas.

I won't bore you with any more
Shoelace stories, except for one.
We were in London on one of our
Summer trips "to acquire cultivation"
As they called it. Mother was off
In the country visiting a school
Friend, so my brother and I were
Alone with father. He said he was
Tired of the Burlington Hotel
Dining room, he would take us to
His club. That's what he called it,
"His club." It was a house in
Bulstrode Street, nothing that
Would tell you from the outside it
Was anything but some family's
House. A butler let us in and took
Us to the second floor in a small
Elevator. We were greeted in the
Sitting room by a handsome lady
Who looked somewhat like the Queen.
All dressed up. She and father
Seemed to be friends. They kissed.
We didn't sit down but the queen
Lady went out and came back with
The most beautiful girl I had
Every seen. "This is Winifred," the
Queen said, "she'll entertain you
Young men for half an hour." Then
She and father went off somewhere.
Winifred was a princess for sure,
She was wearing a rather scanty
Dress but it was made of gold.
This was many years ago but
I can still see how lovely she was.
And she was nice. "What will it be,
Gentlemen," she asked, "chess or
Checkers?" Neither of us had ever
Heard of chess, so we said checkers.
As she was going to get the checkers

Set she noticed my untied shoelace.
"Dear me," she said, "your man doesn't
Take very good care of you, does he?"
And, if you'll believe it (I still
Can't) this gorgeous princess knelt
Right down on the floor beside me
And did up not one, but redid both
Of my laces. Then we played checkers
And the butler brought us ginger
And bitters, as he called it. I
Should have been embarrassed,
But I wasn't. I'll never forget her
Or our visit to the house in
Bulstrode Street.

II

Someone Else

One of my best friends in my
Earlier days, though I don't
See him much anymore, is Hugh
Illingsworth. He's one of the
Suffolk Illingsworths, not the
Scottish lot. I met him first
At Winchester where he was head
Boy in his year. Everyone liked
Him. He put no weight at all
On his academic achievements,
In fact he made fun of them,
Claiming he got his good marks
By cribbing. At varsity, where
He was at Christ Church, it was the
Same story. Without seeming to
Grub he took a double first
One in lit, one in history. For
A few years after we came down
I didn't run into him but
Read with delight his witty
Book reviews in the *TLS* and
Various other establishment
Journals. By chance I ran across
A story of his that was bizarre.
It reminded me of the surrealist
Pioneer Raymond Roussel. It was
In a small magazine called *Ambit*.
It wasn't long till Illingsworth

Had begun to make his mark and
Was elected to the Garrick. It was
There I caught up with him one
Day and we sat down to lunch
Together. I learned that he
Had a clerkship in the city,
"To keep me in bitter" he
Said, and a little flat on the
Edge of Soho. These lunches
At the Garrick became fairly
Regular. I confess that I was
Enchanted with the man's talk,
And so were the friends whom
I asked to join us. "That chap,"
Said one of them "knows how
To keep the ball in the court.
He has you laughing about one
Subject, but next thing you
Know he's off on another tack
Which is just as comical."
I think it's impossible to
Define comedy. Either you
Have it or you don't. There's
No getting it up on demand.
I was becoming so fascinated
By Illingsworth's conversation,
The sheer glow of it, I began to
Listen to him carefully and
Gradually it grew on me that
There was a technique to it,
Or perhaps I should say
A stratagem of entrapment. In
A curious way it was the spider
And the fly. But please believe
Me, I'm not making this up.
The fly would begin to be
Another fly, or even some other
Bug. Illingsworth would get
His interlocutor interested,
Interested in the way he was
Being so much engaged in what
The charmer was making of him,
And then suddenly he would be
Addressed as if he were some
Other person. The whole tone
Would shift as well as the
Topic. He didn't do it to me,
He knew I knew him too well.
But with others, especially
Newcomers to the group, it

Would happen. Harry Crouch,
Who worked on the *Independent,*
Would suddenly become Jensen,
An under-curator at the Tate.
Everything Illingsworth said
To him was utterly right for
The Tate and quite wrong for
The newspaper office. Believe
Me I'm telling it as it was.

When Illingsworth first spoke
To Crouch in the role of Jensen,
Crouch was first startled, then
confused, then perplexed. What
Was going on? But he was too
Polite to challenge another
Club member. And he also hoped
To find out the meaning of the
Transfer, if that was what
It was, in psychiatric terms.
He was taken by the art of
The performance. How could
Illingsworth know so much
About a different milieu?
What a relentless voyeur.
It was almost supernatural.
The group of friends often
Talked about Illingsworth.
He obviously was a "case."
Was he a harmless one?
Was he some sort of con man?
Should the secretary of the
Club be alerted? But nothing
was done. Too much good
Entertainment was at stake.
Illingsworth ran through a
Wide range of professions
As other members were let
Into the game. We wished we
Could rig a wire under the
Table to record him, but that
Would have required assistance
From the staff.

At this point I had to drop
Out. I've had training in
Mechanical engineering and my
Company sent me out to Prague
As advisor on the latest methods
For manufacturing our washing

Machines. I liked it there. Prague
Is one of the most beautiful cities
In Europe, the food is good, and
The living is easy. I stayed on as
Long as I could. Letters from my
Sister Olive in Wembley kept me
Posted on her little doings. Then
An exciting one which announced
That Illingsworth was engaged to
A corker girl named Gwen Bland,
A good friend of Olive's, and there
Was money in the family. I sent a
Wire of congratulation, care of
The club but there was no reply.
I heard no more for several weeks.
Then Olive wired that it had
Been broken off. I was so curious
That I rang through to Olive for
Particulars. She was reluctant to
Talk about her friend, but I finally
Wormed an answer out of her.
Gwen had confessed that she
Really couldn't care for a man
Who always talked to her as if
He were talking to someone else.

© 1993, 1994, 1995 by James Laughlin

BIBLIOGRAPHY

Prose:

Angelica (novella), Grenfell Press, 1965.

Pound as Wuz (biocritical study), Graywolf Press, 1987.

Random Essays, Moyer Bell, 1989.

Random Stories, Moyer Bell, 1990.

Correspondence volumes:

William Carlos Williams and James Laughlin, Selected Letters, Norton, 1989.

Kenneth Rexroth and James Laughlin, Norton, 1991.

Delmore Schwartz and James Laughlin, Selected Letters, Norton, 1993.

Ezra Pound and James Laughlin, Selected Letters, Norton, 1994.

Henry Miller and James Laughlin, forthcoming.

Thomas Merton and James Laughlin, forthcoming.

Kay Boyle and James Laughlin, forthcoming.

Tennessee Williams and James Laughlin, forthcoming.

Poetry:

Some Natural Things, New Directions, 1945.

Selected Poems 1938–1985, City Lights, 1985.

Collected Poems 1938–1992 (contains all the early poems), Moyer Bell, 1992.

The Man in the Wall, New Directions, 1993.

The Music of Ideas, Brooding Heron Press, 1995.

Phantoms, Aperture, 1995.

The Country Road, Zoland Books, 1995.

Heart Island (epigrams), Turkey Press, 1995.

Editor of "New Directions in Prose and Poetry," fifty-five volumes, New Directions, 1936–91. Also editor of various numbers of Perspectives USA and "Perspectives" supplements to *Atlantic,* 1952–58.

Translator of numerous other books of poetry for publication abroad.

Carolyn See

1934-

Carolyn See, 1995

Now, in the month of June 1995, just three months after the publication of my autobiographical memoir, *Dreaming: Hard Luck and Good Times in America,* I'm beginning to wonder if readers—those who care to read it—won't have had enough of my personal life. My daughter Lisa See will publish, in a few weeks, *On Gold Mountain: The Hundred Year Odyssey of a Chinese American Family.* In the last pages of that serious social history, my first husband and I show up again—twenty-year-olds as comic relief, conducting a courtship notably lacking in organization and dignity. So maybe as a kindness to the reader, these pages should just be about how I work

as a writer—and why. In theory, I should let family facts alone.

But I can see that even here I have to go on talking about family. My father, George Laws, was a sometime journalist, would-be novelist. He really was what you'd call a *bon vivant:* he'd endured strong tragedy in his life but still, everything managed to strike him as funny. He slipped dimensions: one time after I'd grown up, I went with him and his fourth wife to a drive-in movie. One of the three offerings featured a pair of very embarrassed African-Americans dressed up in feathers playing real Africans in Africa. Their movie names were Maga and Futu. The next night, as Daddy fixed a salad and Lynda and I hung out in the kitchen drinking beer, Daddy got a wistful look. "I wonder what Maga and Futu are doing tonight?" He had a sense of life in layers, that you could slip *out.* He had literary dreams. He told me when I was eight to start reading the Captain Horatio Hornblower books so that I wouldn't get stuck, later, in the nautical details of *Moby Dick.* Dad left home when I was eleven and took the fun with him.

My mother got stuck with the bills and with me. She had an even disposition; evenly bad. When she laughed, it was at the expense of somebody else. She had a perfectionist, sadistic eye for detail. She would go off to work and I would clean the house and have dinner ready for her when she came home, trying, with this crazy role-tinkering, to restore balance to the household. She'd come in, take a look at the mopped kitchen floor, and tear into me about the baseboards: "What's the point of even *doing* it, if you're not going to do the *baseboards!*" I don't like it, but I never go into a house without checking out the baseboards, and a wrong word in a narrative, a sentence that sounds to me chunky or junky or out-of-tune, makes me nuts.

Every weekend, Daddy would come over to take me out. Often we went to afternoon literary parties—this would be in the late forties in L.A. The sun would be shining and the windows open, and witty Los Angeles journalists (Matt Weinstock, Gene Coughlin, Virginia Wright) would be knocking back scotch-and-sodas and laughing hard. They'd be talking about how, when they were writing their short stories, they'd weep from the pathos of it all. They'd tell stories from their City Side days. They worried about whether a magazine called *Fortnight* would continue. (It didn't, of course.) These afternoons were like paradise to me.

Then, as darkness fell, he'd take me home to Mother. She'd have been crying all day long. It didn't take a genius to see that fun was where the writing was; writing was where the fun hung out. Two other components go into this basic world view. My dad left three weeks after those atomic bombs got dropped. I had catastrophe dreams instead of abandonment dreams. Also, my mother was determined that our own relationship would be finite. "As soon as you hit eighteen, you're out of here," she remarked a dozen times a day. And, "You're just like your father." (Of course I was, but I was like her too.) For me to be able to leave

The author's mother, Kate Daly

home and support myself, she felt I had to take typing and grow up to be a secretary. Obstinately, I took academic courses at John Marshall High, in the ambiguous heart of L.A.

My mother couldn't wait, as it turned out. She married again, got pregnant, and kicked me out when I was sixteen. I lived with my dad and his third wife for a scant year, then went out on my own. I rented five-dollar-a-week furnished rooms, worked part-time at Van de Kamps as a waitress wearing big lace hats, and went to L.A. City College, a welcoming heaven on earth where the tuition was two dollars and fifty cents a semester. I should have been proud of myself. But the first story I ever wrote, in the back bedroom of my dad's house, was about a time at a youth dance hall in Hollywood, where I'd been working as a "bartender" dispensing soft drinks. A bunch of guys came up and asked me if I'd dance with a blind buddy of theirs. I didn't see getting out on the dance floor with a blind person, and I said no. Then I felt SO GUILTY, I had to write a story about it.

During my second year in City College, an old high school friend named Richard See came breezing back into L.A. This was during the Korean War, but he was serving in Newfoundland. We got married and I went to live with him in the deprived little town of Freshwater. It was the kind of experience I detested at the time, but it got better and better through the years. Whenever I feel lost or put-upon, I can think back to Newfoundland and just laugh.

When Richard was mustered out, we took the *Queen Mary* to Europe, where I had a couple of girlfriends waiting. I was twenty and pregnant. Life still seemed to me to manifest itself as either Heaven or Hell, but here was Paris and finally it was more complicated. Richard drank amazingly. I felt sick, but here were all these people coming and going and staying up late. I didn't get to party like the others; we were very poor and felt left out, but one afternoon in the hotel room when I was reading Robert Penn Warren's *All the King's Men*, a sentence leapt out at me. The paraphrase: Whatever you live is life—whether you're a family man with three kids and a dog or out there shooting the rapids of the Amazon, it's still *life* you're living, and all life has equal value.

I guess I thought then I could calm down a little, enjoy the guy we met who always had a suitcase full of bread-and-butter sandwiches and newspapers, in case he had to spend a

"My father and stepmom, George and Wynn Laws"

few days on the streets. We only went to two restaurants in Paris by and large, but they were good, and the people were nice to us. It was a good life.

We came back to L.A. and went to school: Richard in grad school, me at Cal State L.A. as a junior. They had a literary magazine at that little Quonset hut place called *Statement,* and I wrote a piece for them: "Nice Town, Paris." I think it was three or four pages long. I remember the exact minute I started to write it, sitting in a sunny, dinky little L.A. bungalow. The air was all sparkly and I thought, *This is it, this is it, I'm doing it, I'm doing it.* Of course even now my mother's voice chimes in: "Oh, sure, Mr. Big Man! Doing *what*? Like, did you ever consider going out and making a living? And what about those baseboards?" But for the first time in my life, without getting too dramatic about it, I'd done what my father sometimes did and I'd always yearned to do. I'd slipped *out,* gone from boring daily life into that better place. "We were all part of a continuous germ fugue," I wrote. I thought that was hot then, and I still think so now.

About a year later, Richard and I had moved with our baby, Lisa, down to a three-story tenement in downtown Los Angeles called the Sentous Apartments. We were back again, in Hell. In return for a rent-free two-room apartment, we got to manage the lives and the dwellings of thirty-five miserable families—the

neurasthenic wife of a convict who took to her bed and stowed her used sanitary napkins under it, the would-be suicides and almost murderers. Looking back, I think we were pretty brave. We had people over for dinner and cooked them burgundy beef. We listened to the very few albums we owned—Lee Konitz and Warne Marsh, Chet Baker and Gerry Mulligan.

Around that time, over at Cal State, I'd met La Monte Young—who would grow up taking a stab at being "the father of American avant-garde music," but who was a cute jazz musician then. He wore perfume and avoided socks. As a present he gave me some Pierre Boulez albums which I gave away, and also Ravel's Quartet in F Major. The liner notes said the Quartet had "no recognizable principle of construction," and also that "Ravel can make chords out of any notes that happen to be lying around." I loved those ideas, since I wasn't exactly in any cultural center. Looking back, I wonder that we could have been so extremely poor and still have had a pretty interesting set of cultural artifacts: a cardboard life-size cut-out of Gerard Phillipe, the whole set of the *Evergreen Review,* and original copies of most of the work of E. M. Forster and Virginia Woolf. (I have to admit, we stole a lot of the stuff.)

I read *A Writer's Diary* about a hundred times, finally getting over my dithering admiration of Woolf enough to see that she was a fretful worrywart. (No one had the idea of her actual clinical depression then.) I got the idea of *how* to write from Virginia Woolf: Five pages in the morning (but I cut it down to four), and *something else* in the afternoons. We didn't have her friends, but we could still have her dinners, and we did. I ignored what she said about children. And for what to write about, I listened to La Monte and read those album notes. Take whatever notes that happen to be lying around.

By the time I was in graduate school, about twenty-three, with Lisa about two, I knew I had to get out of the marriage. Richard was an empathetic person, but he was also a very mean drunk, and he drank astonishingly. At the same time, I was studying for the first qualifying exams in graduate school at UCLA, which would determine whether or not I could go on for a Ph.D. I began work on a first novel, *A Waiting Game.* Physically, I was as far away from where I wanted to be as it was possible to be. I sat in the stifling living room of the manager's apartment down at the Sentous. Across the street, in these lower reaches of downtown L.A., I could look across the street at a truckers' gas station, where someone was always steam-cleaning an engine. The two rooms where we lived were screamingly imperfect. There was a large living room with ivy-covered wallpaper. Richard had blow-torched plywood and gone over the wood with a wire brush. This was our wall paneling, but in places the ivy wallpaper showed through. There was a scratchy grey couch, homemade book shelves of the same blow-torched wood, and a forties modern desk from the Chinese side of the family, a bedroom dressing table with orange handles right there in the living room. Also, a huge painting of a nude with droopy breasts that the tenants thought was me. I deeply resented it. Richard *loved* it—and loved the bass clarinet he was teaching himself to play. The second room had an iron hotel bed in it, a linen bureau (more blow-torched wood), and another piece of blow-torched wood with metal legs that was our dining room table. Lisa's crib was in the closet. She had a piece of Sentous furniture for a dresser. We still have it down in the garage.

"Make chords out of any notes that happen to be lying around." I'm ashamed often of the bad mother I was, and sorry about the unloving wife I was, but I'm filled with admiration for the twenty-three-year-old who sat down at the Chinese dressing table at the corner of Twelfth and Sentous and started the pages of *A Waiting Game*. I wrote my thousand words a day, and there were days in the summer especially, when it would be about 120 degrees, and Richard would come home from studying, and Lisa would be pale and damp, and we'd sit down for dinner, and I'd be happy, *breaking even*, because I'd done my thousand words.

In that first novel, I preached a lot. I constructed hideous villains—because I was writing about the Sentous Apartments—I did background galore, but I couldn't figure out a plot, and I was terrified of breaking into dialogue. I couldn't make myself use those quotation marks and let my characters tell me what they wanted to say. My hero was the friend of a friend I'd known at LACC, a Greek Orthodox guy of great charm and melancholy—I just stuck him down in the Sentous because I was so lonely. My heroine was a beautiful waitress I'd known at Van de Kamps and already lost track of: she shows up again in *Dreaming*, thirty-five years later as

The author's first husband, Richard See, in the south of France, 1955

"Theresa." She'd been so much fun, and she was gone from me forever. So I put her in the novel.

I just wrote it. I didn't know what the hell I was doing. My studies at UCLA were all about Milton and Keats and Chaucer and Old English—and didn't pertain to what I was doing at all. I'd met a guy, Tom Sturak, and started a chaste romance. I sent Lisa during the day to the Salvation Army Nursery School, but Richard and I read her stories every single night and tried to pretend that this was some sort of living. I filled the pages of *A Waiting Game* with a lot of despair. I hate the thought that at the time my main influence was Nathanael West. I guess he was, considering what I had to work with.

Richard, Tom, and I all took our qualifyings in 1958. We got three master's degrees and one divorce. I'd entered my novel in the Samuel Goldwyn Creative Writing Contest at UCLA and came up with second prize—two hundred and fifty dollars. It would pay for my divorce. I believe that the prize also tipped the scales for me to pass the qualifyings to go on for the Ph.D., since I wasn't much of a scholar and the program wasn't exactly slanted to women. For a few weeks, life was a lot of fun: agents wanted to see me. I was such a dimwit that I told a junior agent at International Creative Management I wasn't interested in "being commercial"; that was the end of that. I gave the novel to a flaky lady agent who took it away for two years, Houghton Mifflin took it and lost it—but I was way too scared to call either her or them and lived in the delusion that for two years they were considering my manuscript.

Dumb! But sometimes it's good to be dumb, because if you knew the lay of the land you'd get so discouraged you'd die. At that time, John Updike published *The Poor House Fair,* and I was enraged at the sight of his picture on the back. I felt strongly that I was a better writer than he was, but I couldn't see the obvious: I'd gone to City College and lived in a slum, I lived on the West Coast, I was a woman, and—except for Virginia—women weren't a hot market item. I knew John Updike and Philip Roth with his *Goodbye, Columbus* lived somewhere in the East, and advanced their careers, and got published, but I was clueless about that whole thing.

By the time Lisa was three and I was twenty-four, I'd published two stories in *Statement,* a study of Kenneth Patchen's poetry in the *Arizona Quarterly,* and an account of Lenny Bruce's wedding in the *Carolina Quarterly.* I had a beautiful little girl, a marriage that was breaking up, and the chance to stick it out for my Ph.D. at UCLA. My goals at that time were to publish a novel before I was thirty, go to Europe, have a baby. I was batting more than 500 and less than 1000. At any time in any day I had less than five dollars in my pocket, no money in the bank, and a mother out there who hated my guts.

But I'd already learned to make chords out of any notes that happened to be lying around, write a thousand words a day, take characters that I was very fond of from other places and introduce them in the different world of my novel. I knew I was an addicted preacher and had trouble with dialogue and plot. I also knew that no matter what, when I sat down on the couch with a pen in my hand, there was an 80 percent chance that the world would begin to glow and shimmer, and I'd be away from the iron bed and the ten thousand cockroaches and the grim unhappiness that held poor Richard and me by the throat.

That's where I was when I left Richard in the summer of 1959 and ran off to Reno with Lisa and Tom Sturak to get a divorce and start a new life.

Then, for seven years, I didn't write fiction at all. I can't blame Tom for this, although I can blame him too. He was all for me writing—he'd turn down the music, tiptoe around the house, intercept my phone calls, then look over to where I was trying to write and say, "God! You do that so easily! How can you do that?" He'd walk over to adjust my light and look over my shoulder and say, "God! You never cross out anything at all!" He'd deliver long lectures on how any American who finished college would never have a literary career. He cited Hemingway and Faulkner and Fitzgerald to prove his point. He himself dearly wanted to write but felt in his bones he never would. He blamed the education he was getting.

But *I* didn't want to write either. Sometimes I thought it was because I was happy, or sometimes because we were fighting, but mostly because we were *doing* stuff. We were having a great time in graduate school, staying up late, dancing and drinking and giving parties and going to them. We drove to Mexico and did that again and again. Tom loved to drive, and we hit the road as far away as Oaxaca and Tampico and Vera Cruz. We lived for a year in Mazatlán. Tom spearfished. He ran. We yelled at each other. My hair got bleached white by the sun. We studied. I got the Ph.D. Tom was two years behind. We drove across the country and back. We hit Europe—seven countries in two weeks. I would have said I was living *life,* that there wasn't any reason to write. At that time, Alison Lurie, who'd begun to publish, asked me why I wasn't writing. I said that I was happy. She said quietly that *that* didn't seem to be a reason not to write. But in my heart, I knew that life with Tom and a life of writing weren't going to mix. It was just too rowdy with him. (It was fun though. I got to spend New Year's in the town of Villa Union, fifty miles south of Mazatlán on a chicken farm in the jungle.)

In 1965 my second daughter, Clara Sturak, was born. I was thirty-one. We were living by that time in a cabin in Topanga Canyon; Tom was working for the RAND Corporation. During the first week that Clara was home, I read *The Feminine Mystique;* I was one of the persons whose lives that book changed. Something else also kicked in. I remembered my father, who'd always "wanted" to write and carried that disappointment around with him. I was staying home with Clara, not teaching, through with school, housewife for the first time. I thought: now or never.

Tom Sturak with his portrait, in the 1970s

I started writing bad short stories and sending them out. I tried to write one thousand words a day, five days a week. I wrote when Tom was out, the way I'd done my doctoral dissertation. I didn't want him to see me work. They say now that "information is power," but withholding information can be power too. Once, Tom came home early, when I was struggling with pieces of a story, scraps all over the table, scissors and tape, trying to get these crazy scraps to go into a smooth narrative. He'd totally caught me, and so he could say, "Well, I suppose it's good therapy for you." I felt a wave of hatred, but also an awful blow to my soul. What if he was right? What if I was barking up the wrong tree entirely? What if I wasn't talented, just crazy? That's why at first I wrote in secret.

We weren't getting along. In the month after Clara was born, Tom had taken up with a girl at the office, though I wouldn't "find out" for about three more years. Tom came home from work, then, and looked out the window thinking dreamy thoughts. I had my thousand words to ponder over, but there wasn't quite the same magic to them, because they

had a fish-or-cut-bait feeling—a *do* it or get *over* it quality. If I couldn't write, I'd have nothing, nothing in my life to make me more than ordinary. It was a hard time for all of us— Tom, me, Lisa, Clara.

After two years of rejections from lousy little magazines, a friend told me the *L.A. Times* was going to be starting a glossy Sunday supplement. I had a thought. I remembered back to the year Tom and I had spent in Mazatlán, and the three *carnavals* we'd gone to. I wrote twenty pages on *Carnaval*—broken glass on the wide boulevards turning into polished sheets of glass as the whole city danced; a luckless American guy dying just beyond the surf line as inside the Bel Mar Hotel little girls sold *cascarones* so that everyone in the dining room could have a gigantic confetti fight. In a week I got back the familiar huge envelope and tuned up to cry. Inside was a letter saying they loved it, but that it ran too long. Could I cut it to twelve pages? It was almost as much of a life-changing moment as when I'd had my children. I drove home from the post office and called Tom. Something in my voice scared the socks off him. When I said I'd sold my first piece, he said, "Oh, thank God!" since he'd thought I'd found out about his girlfriend.

I had lunch with those editors and they sent me down to Watts, six weeks after the famous riots, to talk to women. I did it, and it got anthologized all over the place. *TV Guide* called me up and I began to do celebrity profiles. I was pathologically shy and pathologically bad-tempered. I was in way over my head, earning more money—though it wasn't much—than I'd ever had in my life. My husband was cheating on me blatantly, the kids were nervous wrecks. I was writing my thousand words a day for money. I caught poor old Tom coming home from a magic weekend with his girlfriend and the metaphor, *the shit hit the fan*, began to apply. It flew around pretty good for the next couple of years, but within the emotional chaos was the discipline of writing. By the time Harry Sions, a kind editor from Little, Brown, came out to L.A. on a scouting trip, took me to lunch at the Polo Lounge, and asked me to write a novel for him, I'd worked out a writing routine which I still use today.

That thousand words a day! (Or one "work unit," like two hours of revising.) Added to that, and just as important for a very shy person, one note to an editor, or a phone call that makes your hands sweat. Don't just write about "what you know," but write in a voice people will recognize as your own. Write to the reader as though to your best friend. I remembered the Sue Barton books, where all I wanted was to get into that chummy world. I remembered Elizabeth Enright and Kate Seredy, whose books had offered complete and enchanted worlds, and you could walk into them. Or E. M. Forster's first chapter of *The Longest Journey:* In front of a fire in a cozy student's room, a group of undergraduates argue the nature of reality. *The cow is there!* How great to be there with those students. You can't make your readers love your fictional world unless you love it too. (So much for Nathanael West.)

In the middle of all the flying gravel from the divorce, I'd realized all over again the value of having fun; if life was going to deal you these death blows, you'd *better* have fun. And it was good to travel: nothing was more fun

"Me, sulking and working in Mazatlán," 1962

"My second daughter, Clara Sturak, in her teens"

than to go on the road for a piece. I'd begun to write for *Today's Health,* where you went out and found a kid who'd die without drinking breast milk for the rest of his life, or kids who ate themselves to death. It was fun to get on a plane and fly away and into another person's life; to see their trials and sorrows, and the way they furnished their living rooms. It was fun to interview "celebrities." Sometimes they were Carol Burnett or Walter Brennan, but more often sweet girls with just a moment to enjoy fame. The *TV Guide* pieces were very useful to me and any other serious writer at that time. They paid the rent, and the West Coast Bureau Chief, Dwight Whitney, was a fanatic about structure no matter what the content—the end of every piece reaching around to kiss the beginning.

I wrote with felt pens on white, unlined paper, as I still do today. I sent the stuff out to the typist. (In Enneagram terms, I was and am a "Four." "Doing laundry—or typing—is beneath me." I think it's leftover rebellion from when my mother wanted me to type for a living in an insurance office.)

I knew that very few women did this stuff—wrote articles, or later, books, but I made that fact work for me. I'd hang around for a few days looking invisible and come home with material that I don't think assertive men could have gotten. And I learned immediately that you have to keep supportive people around you. My new boyfriends were easygoing and amused by this way of making a living. Only one asshole hated it, and after I saw he wouldn't stop by the post office to pick up his current issue of *Esquire* where I had a piece, I knew we were through.

After I started writing books, I knew that it would be necessary and probably even desirable to combine ways of making a living. A writer who only *writes* is a dull person. He's always thinking about what *he's* thinking: his only topic of conversation is his work. Or more accurately, himself. He sits in his office and he hasn't got a clue. He spends his time thinking lofty thoughts and telling other people to quiet down. He masturbates a lot because it's boring in that room of his. He often looks weedy and wan: he doesn't get out much. His natural shyness takes over. He becomes reclusive and aloof. He's tiresome about his wife and kids. In his mind, at least, he's chosen art over life. As a second-rate poet told a friend of mine, "I'm married to my art, but you can be my mistress." Silly girl that she was, she took him up on it, but left a few years later. He wouldn't play with the kids, he wouldn't help out with the chores, he didn't bring in any money, and his poetry wasn't so hot either. He wasn't any good in the sack, she said, because he only thought about himself.

Luckily, reality made writing different for me and most of my writing friends. It was *stupid* not to have a family. Virginia Woolf had been wrong as a three-dollar-bill about that. Kids got you up in the morning and got you out to the grocery store and kept you thinking about the house, and vacations, and schools, and money—the ordinary stuff that made you a human being instead of a twerp who went around saying, "I'm married to my art, but you can be my mistress." (That man had hair growing out of his ears too. He never bothered to go to a barber, because he was always thinking about his art.)

It was stupid not to have a family and treats and friends. And "writing" could be easily expanded to more-or-less mean "a life of art." That meant you could teach—and students went a long way toward keeping you sane and cheerful. You could do those magazine pieces, which were a hundred times easier to place than literary short stories, and—for a woman—were invaluable, since they got you out and about and into worlds you'd never otherwise see. You could do book reviews, the perfect exercise for when you wanted to write but had a short attention span. Also, those few hundred dollars a pop had a nice way of paying for restaurant dinners, and getting you to read the work of your peers, the people you should be keeping up with anyway. Once you had any success, you got to go out and speak at colleges and conferences—another way of getting out of the house and meeting the people who were going to read you, your "following," so to say.

Again, these paltry hundreds had a nice way of adding up. I know this sounds penny ante, but this is the year 1995 and for the last eight years I've been in the top 1 percent of single women earning money in this country. That says more about the pitiful condition of women in America than it does about my riches, but it's also true: despite the deliberate holding back of merit money at a small Catholic college where I worked, and the fact that as a book reviewer I'm never on staff and always do piecework; despite the fact that women routinely get paid less—in writing as in everything else—I have found that you can travel and play and send your kids through school and eat plenty of restaurant dinners when you take the wide view of writing in America. The novels? The novels were my "habit." I never expected to make money off them and didn't until very recently. They were my privilege and my calling, not to be too pretentious about it, and I spent money on *them,* rather than the other way around.

So! A thousand words a day, travel, felt pens and unlined pads, combining several tasks to make a "career," a supportive family and like-minded friends, and trying not to get too pushed out of shape about the unimportance and invisibility of women in America, because everything I did might change that, if only the littlest bit. I basically had that life-plan in place by 1969–70. I worked that program.

It was hard, though, when I first began writing for a living, which I did as soon as Tom left. I felt my mother's pervasive scorn

"My first daughter, Lisa See, in her twenties"

and lack of faith, and Tom's intolerably condescending: "Well, it will be good therapy for you," every time I sat down. To counteract these anguished feelings of inadequacy, I developed two other coping mechanisms. One might be thought of as "bad" in these puritanical nineties, but I don't think it was *that* bad. If I sat down in the morning after the kids went off to school and froze, I didn't think about it much. I got up and went to the refrigerator and cracked open a can of beer. It played hell with my girlish figure, but it made the ghosts of Tom and my mother curl up in a corner for a while. The other habit I had, and still use, was to turn on music, just below conscious audio level, and play the same piece until I finished what I was working on. The double album from The Band, "Last Waltz," got me through *Rhine Maidens* (Dr. John singing, "if I don't do it somebody else will!"); Lee Konitz and Warne Marsh and Gerry Mulligan for my first three books. Then, for *Golden Days* and *Making History*, Van Morrison—mostly "Hard Nose the Highway," "Astral Weeks," "Poetic Champions Compose," and "No Guru, No Method, No

Teacher." These and other Van albums and CDs got me through hard writing. They tapped into my chest and made tears fall out of my eyes. For my last book, *Dreaming: Hard Luck and Good Times in America*, the content was so emotional and potentially out-of-control that I went back to that beautiful, detached jazz: Lee Konitz again, and Warne Marsh, and Gerry Mulligan, Stan Getz, and Chet Baker singing. About a month ago the legendary journalist Grover Lewis lay dying, and I gingerly asked his distraught wife if there was anything Grover believed in; if he could in any way believe in a higher power. "I think Grover believes in Gerry Mulligan and Chet Baker," she said, and I think they're a good place to start, if you follow up with Warne and Van. That's where I am now and that's where I more-or-less was then, in 1968 or '69, when Harry Sions asked me to write a novel for him and Little, Brown, and offered me the princely sum of $200 as a retainer. I took it. And it left me feeling lighter than air.

I'm going to write now about my first three books and about choosing a subject, if you're a "serious," "literary" writer. I also want to say that I think American fiction written by men and written by women are two different things— *really* two different things, so they may come looking like print strung out on pages and bound between hard covers, but what's inside is *so* different that you get nowhere comparing them. It's also true, I believe, that up until very recently—like last week—men scorned to read novels by women, or they were afraid to. They didn't want to know the content. Beyond that, I believe men think femininity is catching— like herpes—and that if they read novels by women they'll start wearing panty hose, and that'll be the end of them. I know that until *Making History* and *Dreaming*, the only book of mine that men ever read was *Blue Money,* a nonfiction study of pornography as an American business.

But each time I chose a topic for a book, I was *absolutely convinced* that this was the book the American public was starving for. My book would transform them, exalt them, make them happy. (Nobody ever said writers were rational.) Every time I write a novel, to repeat, I'm *convinced* this will fill the ravening hole of longing so many of us are tormented by. It will alleviate loneliness, it will elevate the world. Conversely, I've never been able to get it together

to think about "career building," or holding to a theme, or investing wisely, or "this will make me rich." For my personal self I want:

and the heart-shape around it stands for elevating the consciousness of the world. "Delusions of Grandeur," my mother's voice is screaming, but I just have to say: Go ahead and scream, Ma. I want fun, love, fame, and money, in that order. And I want my work and my life as a whole to make the world a better place. Why not? There are plenty of people out there totally dedicated to screwing up the world, and nobody makes a fuss over that.

When I thought of my first real novel, to be written for Harry Sions at Little, Brown, I'd just gotten out of graduate school, as had most of my friends. Many of them, instead of going off to teach, ended up just across town, on the beach at the RAND Corporation. My own husband, anarchical Tom Sturak, worked at RAND. At home we had albums where folksingers strummed their guitars: "The RAND Corporation's the boon of the world, they think all day long for a fee. They sit and play games about going up in flames; for counters they use you and me, honey bee! For counters they use you and me." But there was Tom, going to work in the worst mood in the world, to sit and play games about going up in flames . . .

And at about the same time, one of my best and oldest friends had been called by the cops to pick up her husband down at the station. He'd been picked up for soliciting guys; he was gay. His wife was pregnant with their second child. There seemed nothing for her to do but take a lover, have a third child by him, and keep the two men in some kind of precarious balance. The story of *The Rest Is*

Done with Mirrors is the story of "growing out instead of up," as I say somewhere in the last pages, but it's really—I think—an exploration of what "adventure" or "adulthood" might mean in the West, in the middle sixties, in a society that was just beginning to gel into long-term postwar, military-industrial weirdness. For guys, education and culture meant the RAND Corporation. For women, the only "adventure" was to play one man off against the other until one of them cracked. I was absolutely *convinced* that the world was waiting for this glorious insight!

I'm still extremely fond of this novel. It seems to me I was right on the money about life in L.A. and life in urban America. But from the point of view of "reality," I was the wrong sex, on the wrong coast, and the wrong age. I was too young to know anything then. (One day about ten years later, I became too old.) Critics slammed my lack of knowledge about RAND and third-world spies, when in fact my husband came home every night and prattled on about our nation's dreadful secrets. They conceded I knew the squalid environs at UCLA veterans' housing pretty well, when in fact I'd never set foot in them. I couldn't believe the vitriolic reviews of this quite engaging little novel, although over the next couple of years—through teaching—I understood the dynamic. You always give your D's and F's to the people in the back row whose faces you can't see. You never trash someone you know. This set me on a path to simply *get to know* writers and editors and critics in America. Because when you know someone—know where they're coming from—you tend to read them with comparative understanding and recognition.

I want to flash forward for a minute, thirty years into the future, when I came up for a promotion at UCLA. The evaluation committee was very kind and generous about my teaching and about my work, but they opined that I had not succeeded in "breaking the barriers of the pre-Joycean novel." I know they said it, because I had to sign off on their written statement. I took a lot of kidding from my family. Couldn't the committee at least have said the *post*-Joycean novel? But that sentence led me to think about differences in how men and women (or maybe just how different kinds of writers) approach their lives and their writing. Not once in my life have I gotten up, stretched, yawned, poured myself a cup of coffee, and

thought—stand *back*, Jimmy Joyce! Today's the day I push those barriers down! I've read all of *Finnegans Wake*, because I had to. Just like I've read *Paradise Lost*, or William Gaddis's *The Recognitions*, or Thomas Pynchon's *V.* Those works, those writers, have nothing to do with me.

I guess I follow Forster and Isherwood, unmacho types. Forster cared about truth and love, or so he said, and Isherwood famously wanted to be a camera with its shutter open. I'd hope that my language would be like theirs at its best, so pure that you don't even see it, you see through it like vitreous fluid in the eye to the world you're creating, and that "world" is made clear to you through the events in your life.

After *The Rest Is Done with Mirrors* sank and died, I was devastated. My whole life *sucked,* there's no other way to put it. I was a woman divorced twice, with two children to take care of. I had to get a job teaching at Loyola Marymount University, and I was lucky to get it. The chairman, operating under affirmative action laws, asked me, "Don't you think it's *terrible* that I have to hire a woman?" Oh yes, I agreed, it was bad. (To be fair, I teased him about this for the next fifteen years, and he was a good sport about it.) The main thing was I was totally broke, terrified to start a novel, using magazine pieces to make ends meet, and going out with a lot of guys who looked like very weird fish at the bottom of the sea. If not for my wonderful daughters, I might have sailed off into a very different kind of life.

I became for the next two years an expert witness in pornography trials, a wonderful part-time gig that paid $200 a day, got me out of the house and into the courtroom, as well as the classroom. I met flocks of pornographers, attorneys, judges, other witnesses, and it was a great cure—or, at least, an anodyne—for a broken heart. It was all so silly! Lawyers swarming about, thundering, "*Well,* Dr. See! Perhaps you'd read this passage out loud to the court, if you think it's so harmless!" And it would be harmless, and everyone, *everyone* would get the giggles. The money flowed and flowed. I testified for both sides as we nattered on about the nature of language, how Anglo-Saxon words were part of "English," blah blah blah. A prosecuting attorney once approached me to tell me that he had learned his first word at the age of three. "I could say *car,*" he told me solemnly. "I could say *car.*" What kind of world *was* this? And how come men went so bats over pornography? It was all too evident what men "wanted," but what were they *like?*

Immersion in this world led me to write *Blue Money,* the title taken from the joyous Van Morrison song, where, after a day of putting together a blue movie, the singer suggests, "Then we'll go out and *spend* all this blue money!" I knew things about this industry that nobody else knew—the American outlaw quality of it all, the cops and robbers aspect of it, the cosmic goofiness of the porn kings. The last thing on their collective minds was sex. They were in pornography for the thrill of the chase, eluding the FBI, and having a good time. I was *convinced* the world needed to know about this! I interviewed half a dozen top pornographers in the country and their finest attorney (whom I followed all the way to the Supreme Court as he tried to get his clients off the hook). I met girls from movies, and dildo salesmen. They were all living a Bonnie and Clyde fantasy— adventurous outlaws in their own minds. The only one who ever hit on me was a prosecuting attorney who slid his hand up my leg in the Harvard Club. The pornographers treated me with gallantry, consideration, and charm.

Not too many people reviewed *Blue Money.* Libraries shunned it like the plague. The guy-magazines that might have been expected to like it were scandalized, since the book made light of all they held most dear—heterosexual sex without love. It was as if I'd made fun of motherhood and highway safety. No one liked *Blue Money* but me.

But I made enough money off that book to buy myself a silver Porsche (a 1969–911S) and felt my depression begin to lift a little. I was still living in the Land of Divorce, but I could begin to see its better side. Then, I got into a last, terrible, destructive "romance." He was a man whose sorry destiny it was to try to seduce one divorced woman after another away from her children. He tried it with two of my good friends and with me. (One of those friends was the heroine from *The Rest Is Done with Mirrors.*) Two of us spurned him; one did not, and her life changed fairly strongly. The central question of *Mothers, Daughters* was: If you're a woman with kids and you "fall in love" with one more guy, and the situation is wired so that you have to make a choice, which choice do you make?

Yes, yes, I know it's a cliché and a singularly womanish concern, but I'd lost my own mother—been unceremoniously tossed out on my ear when I was only sixteen—because of that cliché and now, here in the "present," in the early seventies when I was hitting forty, I was sorely tempted: to never have to work again! To live on a picture-perfect farm with two private lakes, in bucolic northern California! At the time it seemed a pretty good idea. All I'd have to do was give up the kids. Lisa was one year older than when I'd been cut loose. And what if I just let Clara go live with her father for a while? (Except that the gentleman in question was also painting a fairy-tale room for Clara up at that farm and had a son just her age, so everything would be sure to work out, wouldn't it? Wouldn't it?)

So, in the middle seventies, I wrote my mandatory divorce novel, *Mothers, Daughters.* It sold more than any of my other works had and was respectfully reviewed. It's my least favorite book because in my mind it has two big flaws. It's very weepy and whiny and tragic-seeming, and while that was "true" at the time, as true as I could make it, if I'd waited two more years I could have written it as comedy. Also the self-congratulatory martyrish last chapter makes me cringe. I didn't run off with a wrong-o! So what? Who cares? But many women loved this book, and wrote, and phoned, and told me so.

Which brings me to many "literary" novels written by women in the second half of the twentieth century. They are often centered in houses and are crammed with housekeeping details. There's often a white Protestant God hanging around. Characters are often gathering out in the back garden for afternoon tea. Husbands often show up as boors, and lovers have a short shelf-life. Heroines often make a fateful phone call to their best friend on the last page. The plots are full of domestic betrayal because those pesky husbands can't keep their flies zipped. Custody fights abound. Gail Godwin, Sue Miller, Anna Quindlen write these books. They're all marvelous writers, but for myself one novel of that lady stuff was enough. I guess it's because "woman's lot" is so depressing and so narrow. I admired Diane Johnson's novels about international terrorists, *set in a female context*—explosives hiding in jam jars, and so on. By now, and I hope I don't sound too egotistical, I'd begun to think of

The author between her daughters Clara (left) and Lisa, 1973

my literary life in at least semi-conscious terms. I wanted to write stories that both men and women might read. I wanted to write stories, that, at least half the time happened *out of the house.* I wanted to write about tragedy and terror and horror, but I wanted to be able to write in the comic mode, because it was beginning to seem to me that we created at least *some* of the tragedy we lived in. (But not all of it; that was the catch.)

In 1975 I'd begun living with John Espey, the writer and scholar, and we'd begun—again, consciously, and with an almost idiotic amount of effort—to put together a stable, civil domestic life. After some initial reservations, my children came to love John very much. Living so steadily and sweetly after forty-one years of heedless chaos brought up some questions for me. Lots of people complain about their unhappy childhoods, but mine had been a bit of a humdinger. *Why* had my mother picked up a barfly for a second husband, gotten pregnant right away, thrown me out at sixteen, driven the barfly to an early death and then pitched

out her second daughter when she was sixteen too? Why cause that kind of trouble? Why manufacture that kind of heartbreak? (The same question applied to the Wrong-o in *Mothers, Daughters.* If you hate kids, why go after women with kids? No good can come of it, so why do it?)

When I decided to write about my mother in *Rhine Maidens,* I didn't think of it as a "lady" book. There would be gardens in it, but snails would die awfully—melting down from salt. There would be a betraying husband, but he'd be a wimpy guy, and his wife would wreck his document shredder by jamming their daughter's diaphragm into it. That wife would have a mom, *my* mom, a creature of boundless, hateful energy, "a shark in a bathtub," the Devil Herself. How did she do it? *Why?* What was the dynamic with these scary people? It was my theory then that awful people simply haven't found their perfect place in life, and that if you could give them their perfect place in life, they might settle down and stop being awful. My mother had once remarked that all she really wanted to do was "drink and play cards." She lived alone now, in a perpetual state of simmering rage, and once, after returning from a European trip with a good friend of hers, she systematically trashed the great capitals of Europe: Paris was cold and boring, London tiresome and ugly, Rome disorganized and a great big drag. Finally I interrupted her: "Wasn't there *any*thing you liked about Europe, Ma?" She glared and then admitted: "The Rhine cruise was all right."

High praise. I took that "shark in a bathtub" and put her into a stable household—a fictional and very rich version of what John and I had cooked up. She hated it. She saw its flaws and saw some hidden "truth" in it— an unnerving habit my real-life mother had; she saw life as utterly monstrous and she was always "right." If you were an optimist, as I hoped to become, it could give you pause.

I took this fictional mock-up of my mom, let her tear through about three hundred pages, wreaking havoc on all the other characters in *Rhine Maidens,* then sent her on a Rhine cruise, where she could drink and play cards until the cows came home. Her last, reluctant words are: . . . "I think this could be fun." That's what you call fiction, but I'm glad I wrote it.

Peace is always harder to write about than war. Happiness becomes invisible.

"How ya doin'?"

"Fine."

Happiness and peace are conversation stoppers. So I guess now I must say that for the past twenty years nothing much has happened to me. I've gone from forty-one to sixty-one. My daughters have grown up and married well. I talk to them on the phone every day. John Espey and I live a very quiet life. If it weren't for the natural disasters that Topanga Canyon is so good about serving up, our lives would be peaceful to the point of coma. We have coffee in bed every morning. We talk and laugh. John is extremely learned but also one of the silliest people I know. He shares this trait with Lisa and Clara, so different in so many ways, but both absolutely able to transform the moment into a goofy charade. (Lisa's children have inherited this trait—the ability to come out with the unexpected sentence that shades the moment into *something else,* an echo of my father, pensive, wondering "what Maga and Futu are doing tonight.") My daughter Clara last week ranted about a fluff-blonde hyper-journalist who

writes how-to books for the Middle-Brow Masses, shouting rhetorically when she heard the journalist had made her book-tour escort cry: "For Christ's sake! Get *over* your damn self!" And then, because the sentence sounded so preposterous, Clara had to laugh.

Get over your damn self. That's what I've tried to do in my last three books, even though one of them is an autobiographical memoir. *Golden Days, Making History,* and *Dreaming: Hard Luck and Good Times in America* deal with the most horrific subject matter imaginable—or at least that I can imagine—but they've been written from a position of personal and familial peace. If I didn't have this peace, I don't think I could have attempted them. I think they are important and life-changing; I think "God" wrote them as much as I did, and I think if I died now, I might not be happy about it, but I wouldn't have a legitimate complaint. At least a third of my life has been very happy, and I've been lucky enough to have written these three books. Again, I don't think they came from "me" the way the first books did. I think that listening to Van Morrison— and praying shamelessly out in the Topanga patio with all the mountains and giant rocks and "Nature"—put me in another place.

I'm going to go out on a limb here and say that the first drafts of these three books came from a state of trance. I put my feet on the ground and pray to be connected to the center of the earth. I hold out my hands and pray to be connected to the wideness of the universe. I fluff out my hair to open the top of my head. I turn on Van Morrison just under audio level. The tears pour out of my eyes and I write. (The rest of the family just walks around me until my two hours or one thousand words are done. They don't mind it; they're used to it.) I sure don't put on this performance for a review or a magazine piece or an essay, but these books have meant the world to me; they're my gift to the world, my reason for being, and I know, no kidding, the world is better because of them. I've been lucky to be able to write them.

The "idea" for *Golden Days* came to me in the days just after Russia had invaded Afghanistan. Everybody and his brother had his turn to give a television interview, and finally some diplomatic attaché in New Delhi had his five minutes about how serious it was, and how this was the Beginning of the End and so on, and finally he flashed a huge, delighted smile. *"This means war,"* he said. My mother always said I was slow on the up-take, and maybe she was right, because it had taken me this long in my life to "get it," as they say: Men love war, they absolutely love it. It's their favorite thing, better than sex or hamburgers or Rocky Road ice cream. And every time they say they don't love it, they're over forty, they've already been gravely wounded in a war, or they're lying through their teeth.

I began to look at Dan Rather closely and see how much he loved that stuff. Back then, of course, he dressed up like an Afghan and thrashed around rocky embankments making a fool of himself. Hoping, I surmise, that all this would be leading to the Big Bang, or at least a chance to whack a few innocent women and children legally. And then I thought of "Another Mother for Peace" and how those bumper stickers played right into the ongoing macho dramas. And how even people like Jonathan Schell loved the part of the Apocalypse where the cows would gaze at the sun and their eyeballs would melt.

And I thought: To hell with all that. My lifelong fear of the bomb had had an up side: I'd read most of the major works on atomic energy (for the lay person, at least). I'd reviewed Thomas Powers's *Thinking about the Next War* and Mike Gray's *The Warning* and another terrific book about how Susan Hayward and Pedro Armendarez and John Wayne all went off to Utah to make a movie and had a swell time playing softball in the dust between takes, and ended up dying from cancer because they were downwind from the Nevada test sites. I thought: I can make up a narrative which will be absolutely scientifically correct, and which will be based on the lives of Samuel Pepys and John Evelyn during the Great Plague. While scores of wretches died around them, vomiting blood and ruining their best clothes, those men lived. Pepys because he had girls to fondle and dozens of oysters to consume, Evelyn because he was such a bean counter. He was too busy counting to keel over and die.

What if you constructed a world that was so beautiful and interesting and engrossing to live in that the bomb could come and go? People would essentially mutter *yeah, yeah,* and be appalled and injured and get radiation sickness, but their tropism toward life would be stronger than their tropism toward death, and they'd go on—*far differently*—but they'd go on?

I constructed a life as close to my own as possible, because essentially I was writing my own way out from under Dan Rather's sinister spell. I made up a working mother with two beautiful daughters and a great friend like John Espey and a wonderful girlfriend and some great neighbors. I wrote down the affluent *nouveau riche* life of west-side L.A. I put in independent producers (a great concept, I think, the *independent producer*), and female evangelists and made my southern California the most beautiful place on earth.

The novel itself is constructed like an atomic bomb: five consecutive linear chapters where a dreamy, easy plot is going on, with Edith Laughly, freelance entrepreneur, meeting and falling in love with Skip Chandler, a banker whose wife—terrified of war in the northern latitudes—has already taken off for Buenos Aires. On page 118 that story ends, interrupted by a "nuclear incident" somewhere in southern Mexico. The novel bursts into a little *blip* of narrative, like that *blip* halfway up a nuclear explosion. The blip is made up of essays, meditations: "Waiting Around," because what else do you do before the end of the world? And aren't we doing that now? "How Scared We Got," because for fifty years we've been living in fear—and showing incredible bravery, considering the mind set of war makers and fans of war. (Just this morning, June 29, 1995, I read John Sack, esteemed journalist, mooning around like a spurned lover in the *L.A. Times* over the long lost Vietnam War: " . . . everyone knows that a man who's not yet a KIA is more alive in a war zone than anywhere in the United States.") I addressed this mind-set in the third essay, "How Men Lived," which takes one man—very closely based on my ex-husband—and follows him through a day as he's "waiting around." As in *The Rest Is Done with Mirrors,* he's working for the RAND Corporation, part of the military industrial complex, but he's bored in his marriage, juggling a couple of girlfriends, going to a ball game with his buddy. If your days are numbered, you probably do what you've done all your life. This man is a runner, and from the narrator's point of view, he's spent his life running in the wrong direction, running toward death, destruction, mayhem, Hell.

Part III of *Golden Days* brings down that which we have been waiting for, the Blast, the

Doomsday, the peeling away of everything extraneous, the death of civilization as we know it. The fire comes and radiation sickness and plague. (My husband, when he was working for the RAND Corporation, once brought home a classified document that said the bomb would be incidental in the destruction of L.A.—the Plague, endemic in our scrubby foothills, would finish us off.)

But even Jonathan Schell, even Thomas Powers, couldn't figure out a scenario in which we would *all* be finished off. The main characters in *Golden Days* survive: "The ones I know who lived were the ones who had been making love, or napping, or fixing dinner, when the End came, or the ones at the beach—who still talked about the great Crystallization of the sand, the ones who dove beneath the waves and felt the whole Pacific turn lukewarm . . . as I say, the ones who decided to come *west* instead of east, were by and large the ones who made it."

But women are not supposed to know about such things. Science is supposed to be beyond them. They are only supposed to know about weeping and wringing their hands. In the last pages of *Golden Days,* Edith observes how "some people have questioned me. How come *you* get to tell stories? And why should we believe *you* can make fire, and why should we believe *your* version?!" Edith is cool. "In answer I say first, if a Caspar can destroy a world, why is it strange that an Edith should preserve it?" (That would be Caspar Weinberger, prissy-faced war-maker, a particular unfavorite of mine.)

It's my position that people can beat—not death, but the paralyzing *fear* of death—with magic, jokes, love, vitamins, and stories. They can't avoid Caspar and Dan, but they can check out their act and not be impressed. They can *prefer* life to death. *They can be more alive in the United States living life* than hanging around in a third-world country killing innocent bystanders, obsessing about whether or not they're going to be Killed in Action.

This is just a position, of course. A distinguished scholar who has written a book about nuclear fiction called *After Shocks* has dismissed my position as feminine "wishful thinking." I dismiss *his* position as *masculine* "wishful thinking." He'd like to see every cow with melted eyeballs, and women and children mashed out for good. But—just asking—what if some people, "hardy laughers, mystics, crazies" did live on

"through the destroying light, and on, into Light ages?" My! Wouldn't that irritate Caspar and Dan!

It took me seven years—with some distractions—to write *Golden Days.* It went from a 465-page first draft to 199 pages that—I hope—burn like a waffle iron. There was a while when I had the manuscript memorized, page one to the end. I knew it was important work. When it came out, the reviews were excellent, but many guys, including my own editor, asked me, "They all die, right? As soon as the book is over? Because everybody *knows* that . . ." and because of this mind-set, *Golden Days* is listed in many a science-fiction encyclopedia (with plenty of stars). But I think of it as social realism.

After you destroy the fictional world you've written about, you're up a creek without a paddle. Horribly, the universe gave me—slapped me with—my next novel. A few months after *Golden Days* was published, I got the phone call that every parent dreads most. July 19, 1986, my daughter Clara, still living at home and in her first year of college, had been in a dreadful car accident. She was "lucky." Her left foot had shattered, she'd lost several teeth, her face was horribly bruised. But she was still alive.

The accident occurred on Pacific Coast Highway at twilight. It was a phenomenon of the Pacific Rim. Her Australian passenger was counting money, and the money—blood drenched—scattered across the highway. An Asian couple had made a left turn in front of Clara. A drunk driver from Central America sideswiped her and fled. White Protestants got his license plate number, followed him, made sure he was arrested. Clara was incredibly brave in the emergency room. Her strength was beyond imagination. (But none of us had a real sense of the extent of her injuries.)

She "recovered," replaced her totaled car, and in a few months was driving again. Then, one morning about two or three, John and I heard a quiet knock on our bedroom door. I got up to open it, and Clara burst in, covered in shattered glass. Driving home in Topanga, she'd had a head-on collision with a galloping runaway horse. She wasted no time in weeping. "THIS IS A RANDOM UNIVERSE," she shouted, in tones that could be heard for miles. "THERE IS NO GOD!"

This second accident, though it left Clara physically unharmed, did harm to her heart and soul. There were two more very painful surgeries to be gotten through from the first accident, and we found ourselves—not struck by death itself, thank God, but in the Valley of the Shadow of Death, which I think is something else. Then Clara's first sweetheart died, of carbon monoxide poisoning. A group of kids from a very good high school nearby made a left turn on San Vicente, crashed into one of the trees that bisect that boulevard, and they all died.

Outside of the anguish our whole family was feeling for Clara, and the unspeakable, insupportable anguish *she* was feeling, on a purely solipsistic, novelistic level, I had to look at the idea that destruction, evil, madness, tragedy, had been going on a long time before Dan Rather and Caspar Weinberger. (Indeed, that accounted for a good part of their deep-voiced posturings; they had to know they were pissing in the wind. God had been creating havoc long before *they* ever got started.)

At about this time my son-in-law, Lisa's husband Dick Kendall, got involved in an enormous good deed, wresting a princely fortune away from Ferdinand Marcos in the Philippines and handing the millions of dollars he found over to Corazon Aquino. This errand took him all over the world, and he was heartened—I believe—by a vision he holds of a better world. There is a conflict inherent in this: Where does the duty of a good man lie? Odysseus certainly didn't make his reputation by staying home and mowing the lawn. But all over America, fathers seemed to be—not disappearing, exactly, but going out of focus. Unless you're the Two-Place-Swami, you can't be in two places at once.

In terms of nightmare, I realized that (unconsciously) I'd been fudging in *Golden Days*. What does it matter if the world goes blooie, as long as you have your family, your children with you? In *Making History* I wrote about what I believe to be the worst thing that can happen to anyone—the death of a beloved child. I tried to look further than just the splitting atom, at what was the real, random nature of the universe. And since, in my own later life, I'd been blessed to meet many honorable men, including John Espey and Richard Kendall, I wanted to take a look at the other of that spitting, atom-splitting male principle. I tried

John Espey

to see the male as order, or the yearning for it; women-and-children as carriers of ecstatic joy and boundless destruction.

I created another affluent, Los Angeles westside society, a combination of Santa Monica and the Pacific Palisades. I put my fictional family on another "safe" street, Georgina, perpendicular to the steep cliffs above the ocean. I let them live in Stephen Bochco's house. I made the most beautiful young girl in the world, good, exquisite, modest Whitney. I gave her the finest best friend a girl could have, spunky Tracie (actually very close to Clara in her temperament). I gave Whitney a tired working mom like me—except that Wynn had married very well, hooked up in a second marriage with Jerry Bridges, based on a kid with the same name minus an "r" whom I'd had a terrific crush on in the seventh grade. I put in Vida, a psychic, just as I'd put a slightly sociopathic young guru and a female evangelist in *Golden Days*. Because there had to be connections from this world to another one. All through the first draft, I kept asking myself: Who's telling this story? Who can know all this? Who's speaking in this tone of voice? It took a while to realize that it was Clara's young sweetheart, lightly and sweetly talking to me from another world.

The novel's narrative is based on two swipes of the random universe—two car accidents. The first one occurs very early, in Chapter 2, page 24. Whitney is hurt and the driver of the car killed. The worst has just begun, but the reader has every reason to think the worst is over. The middle is concerned with family stuff and traveling stuff. Jerry cherishes an unacknowledged affection for Whitney. Wynn finds a best friend. Jerry goes adventuring around the world. But—making different arcs and bridges—Whitney and Tracie have great adventures too, traveling as temporary secretaries over to Hawaii and down to Mexico, and just to downtown L.A. The world is so beautiful and new to them that everywhere is an adventure—even though Whitney has been smacked once by mortality and wears a cast on her arm.

The climax of *Making History* is a reconstruction of Clara's Pacific Rim accident—raised to maximum Sig Alert intensity. Although Whitney and Tracie drive a Volvo, the "safest" car in the world, Whitney and two little siblings are taken out by a divorcée skidding down Georgina off the cliffs of Santa Monica over onto the Pacific Coast Highway, pancaking on the Volvo. "Altogether fifteen people would die." They included that Asian couple from "real life," eight illegals driving south from Topanga, a French guy from a nearby circus, the suicidal divorcée. (The only person to narrate it is Robin, who's been dead since Chapter 2.) The agent of destruction? The Goddess Kali: "I am Nothing! I am Chaos! There is Nothing behind my eyes! And I myself am nothing! So much for all your hopes and dreams!" But she's the Goddess of Birth too. She stirs things up. She keeps things going.

One of the epigraphs of *Making History* comes from Bharati Mukherjee's *Jasmine:* "The scale of Brahma is vast, as vast as space in the universe. Why shouldn't our mission be infinitesimal? Aren't all lives, viewed that way, equally small?" I took the position that truly good men are rare in the world; they *are* heroes. Jerry has the capacity to be a world-changing hero of the modern age: He has every wonderful attribute *except* . . . a heart. It's there, but it's closed. In John Donne's words, it hasn't been battered open.

Lisa See, John Espey, and Carolyn See as "Monica Highland"

Just this week I spoke on the phone with a wonderful man whose son had just died—killed in a car crash. This man, ordinarily jovial, dear-hearted, light as a butterfly, was still the person he'd been, making word jokes, gossiping, even, but as he spoke of his son, he went with no transition into sobbing: "I remember the first time I saw him and the last time I saw him," he wept, and then went on, being himself. I felt as though, *through* the suffering, this man's heart had been cracked open. I began to consider that slightly wacky Catholic icon—the Sacred Heart—the *burning* heart, with thorns. The pensive expression on Christ's face as he invites the viewer to consider that heart. He's showing us his heart, a heart in fire and torment. No one cares to discuss it on a daily basis, but what if that really is the Human Condition?

Just as it takes a whole village to raise a child, what if it takes a flock of people to make a hero, not just a famous man, a brave man, but a *good* man? Vida, the clairvoyant in *Making History,* takes an eight-thousand-mile trip across the Pacific just to touch Jerry's life. Whitney, who's received so much love in her life that she's love personified, may have given her life for Jerry. He adores her but can't admit it in this world we live in—one reason he's a stranger to his emotions: if he looked at his emotions, he'd be scandalized and ashamed.

After Whitney's death, and the death of her little half-brother, Jerry's family is plunged into darkest grief. He finally gets what the universe has been trying to tell him all along. We live in a random universe. But within that fateful context, we still have the high duty to be human—as human as we can be.

Jerry tries, he goes through the motions, he accepts the ministrations of friends—including two great Japanese guys who've been partners in his dream of Utopia, his Heaven on Earth. But Whitney, together with the dead Robin, has been waiting, in air, for the right moment. When Jerry, driving on Pacific Coast Highway, finally breaks down and weeps like a kid, Robin hauls out some overworked Chumash Indian ghosts from Topanga Canyon who sweep into the window of his car: "This is a beautiful world just the way it is," they breathed. "Don't worry too much about it. You don't have to fix it up *too* much!"

Whitney speaks directly to Jerry: "I'm watching you every second of your life . . . You're such a good man. You know the right thing to do." Then she addresses Wynn, half-dead with despair. "There are good men everywhere, but you have to keep your eyes open. I bet one's coming home now. Hold out your arms to him, Ma! Don't be a lame shit *all* your life!" Out on the highway, "Jerry's ribs rattled. Whitney jumped right in." Robin, lighthearted as always, heads on out—because the scale of Brahma is vast—to see what will happen next.

Those guys at UCLA looking at my merit raise said I didn't push past the barriers of the *pre*-Joycean novel. I say again to myself and to them and to anyone who reads this that pushing pre-Joycean barriers wasn't what I had in mind. I was trying to explain how the world works, and what purpose suffering might serve, and why we *must* be joyous, as much as it lies in our power to be joyous.

By this time in my own life, two things had happened. My older daughter, Lisa, had begun work on her first book, *On Gold Mountain: The Hundred Year Odyssey of a Chinese American Family,* that beautifully researched and written history of the Chinese side of her family—because her father, Richard See, was one-fourth Chinese, and that fraction had influenced every aspect of his life and her life.

Then one morning in the early nineties, John Espey and I drove to the town of San Bernardino, about seventy miles east of L.A., to give a pair of speeches to four hundred high school teachers. I gave a—by now—fairly routine speech: We were all incredibly lucky; we were living, comparatively speaking, in Heaven on Earth. We all had a chance to teach kids the strong power of the written word. Wasn't that great?

Later, as John and I signed books down in a gloomy basement, I looked up and saw my mother, uninvited, coming downstairs. She had a look on her face that I knew too well. I believe she felt she should have been invited, because the town she lived in, Victorville, was just fifty miles away, over some mountains. (But John and I would be leaving within the hour, heading back for another speaking engagement at the beach.) But all this is "rational" fact, and what happened in that basement was irrational. She was there to make trouble, and she did. She told me, "You're bullshit, and everything you do or say is bullshit." (All this in front of good-natured school teachers waiting to get their books signed.) Then she began to talk to them directly: "When she was lippy, I used to beat her up pretty good. I guess they could put me in jail for that now."

I was devastated—not by what she said, because, in keeping with the tone of the day, this kind of remark was pretty routine for her. But the idea that she'd invaded my professional life to lay down her version of our early life was intolerable to me. She had always said I was "slow on the uptake," and I had been. My whole life I'd lived in a fiction that one day she'd say, "I'm so proud of you," instead of blaming me, my father, my half-sister, my stepfather, for all the sorrow and inconvenience in her own life. But she was the person in all the world who wished me the worst harm and had the lowest opinion of me. To deny this, as I had since the age of eleven, really did make me a moron, "slow on the uptake." I'd written about it obliquely in *Mothers, Daughters,* and directly in *Rhine Maidens,* but always felt that if I did something, the *right* thing, I might change that equation.

But . . . what if she was just a mean drunk who didn't like her kids? I began to think in terms of nonfiction. Lisa knew what shaped her father's side of the family: the implacable fact of being Chinese. What shaped both sides of my family? If you could bring yourself to look at it, it seemed to be a very steady diet of drink, suicide, terrible illness, early death, drugs, divorce. My family on both sides had been here since before the Revolution, and all they had to show for it was that my mother and father and two aunts were still alive.

My mother's mother died very young of TB. My mother had mentioned that her father died drunk in a snowdrift. My father's mother had blown her head off. (My father, at the age of fourteen, had discovered her.) His father had drunk himself to death. My uncle Bob on my dad's side graduated from high school, went to work in the sewers of Dallas, scratched himself on the first day of work, died two weeks later of typhoid. Dad's favorite sister died of TB in her early thirties. My mother went to meet her and fainted dead away. My parents were *poor kids* in every sense of the word—destitute, orphaned, very brave even to go on living. Then, when they got married and had a baby, what did they get? A kid with a birthmark. Bad luck!

You could react to this with chosen optimism, as my father did—although he lost it the last four years of his life—or with boundless, energizing bitterness, which my mother chose, and which keeps her alive to this day. You could drink to get through it, which they all did, and which I did. You could resort to hard drugs, which my sister did.

I began to write *Dreaming: Hard Luck and Good Times in America.* I began to consider that all this misfortune in the underclass might have some beneficial side effects for the ruling class in this country. I constructed two different worlds, the world of the golf course, where well-off church-goers whiled away their quiet afternoons, and the world of the abyss, where families like mine gasped in free fall. I discovered that paper money had been the currency of the ruling class in the thirteen colonies, but *rum* had been the currency of the middle and working classes; my ancestors had been paid in rum. And they drank it.

My sister reminded me that she'd had her first heroin-hit in Honolulu. Nixon was bringing our boys back from Vietnam, and their duffle bags were filled with the best Asian heroin. Funny how nobody noticed. Funny how the greatest nation in the world can put a man on the moon and make enough weapons to blow up the planet, but just can't seem to stop those pesky teenaged gang members from selling drugs on the street!

When *Dreaming* came out, four months ago to the day, critics were very kind, to put it mildly. But I came up against the same sticking point as when I'd written my first novel, *The Rest Is Done with Mirrors,* and they hadn't believed me about the RAND Corporation. They brushed off any thought that America might be divided into classes, that the gap between rich and poor has been widening dramatically for the past forty years, that black ghettos are littered with billboards advertising Colt 45, that marijuana is California's largest cash crop. No, lady writers got to write about families (and even particle physics, because no critic knew one damn thing about that). But Dan-Rather-stuff like the government and drugs? Michiko Kakutani dismissed that material as "turgid, silly and presumptuous," and queried, "Why should a reader want to hear these sordid confessions?" I answer tactfully: Because they're human, they're important, and they're the truth. (And I take some comfort from the fact that old Michiko suffers from the same gender prejudice. A startling amount of my very well-read friends think Michiko is a man. How else could she express such strong opinions?)

Government aside, people loved *Dreaming.* The University of California is publishing the trade paperback, for use as a text. Wynona Ryder has optioned it as a starring vehicle. I'm happy about it.

But it was very hard to write: A 700-page first draft pared down to a final 350 pages, a case of viral meningitis brought on by the strain of doing this hard work. Now—even as I'm still answering letters from readers who live in the abyss—I find that I feel empty and a little sad.

I'm sixty-one. I've been lucky and I count my blessings. My daughters, Lisa See Kendall and Clara Sturak, are the two funniest and sweetest women I know. My grandchildren are swell. My partner for twenty years, John Espey, taught me how to be civilized and decent. My best friend, Jackie Joseph, has been a friend since we were twelve. The people I've lost through quarrels or misunderstandings—the dads of Lisa and Clara, my two other oldest friends, Joan Weber and Judy Ross—are still friends at some level; I'm honored to have known them all. For thirty-one years I've lived in one of the most beautiful, most trying, places in the world—Topanga Canyon, where the land is ruled by fire and flood and surprise: we killed another rattlesnake last week, but we're blessed every day we spend here.

I'm lucky to have spent about five years in the eighties collaborating with Lisa and John on three books by "Monica Highland," two light-hearted historical novels and a nonfiction book. We had some fun and made some money. Magazine journalism opened up the world for me. Teaching—at Loyola Marymount University and UCLA—has been a treat. I love teaching, and my students have often seemed like a second family.

But I can't end this work-autobiography on a totally cheerful note. I want to say, as many writers have said before me, that writing is a devious and weird way to spend a life. When you're with people and need to write, you're frantic to get away by yourself. When you're by yourself and writing, you're desperately homesick for people. People in the world are disconcertingly willing *not* to buy your books. They'd much rather go out to dinner, or make love, or go to a ball game. In the end you're left with your fantasies of the writing life, and often they're the same fantasies you started out with. I still have a dream of sitting by a fire on a winter afternoon, plotting a novel, or opening a discreet stack of mail with a letter opener, sipping a glass of nice sherry. Pure Virginia Woolf! What I really do is sit in a tee shirt sweating my brains out on a hot Topanga day, listening to Van Morrison, writing-and-crying and hoping with part of my mind that the phone will ring to pull me out of this psychic vortex. When the mail comes, it's usually somebody wanting me to read an 800-page manuscript.

Sometimes my ideal life and my real life waltz around the room together—usually in New York, when I'm having lunch with my editor. But those times are rare. If I were more mature, I'd refurbish my fantasy life, but I don't think it's going to happen. I've written my books

to change the world for the better. That's overweening, self-absorbed, maybe crazy, but that's my position. I've spent my life writing, living the writing life. I think of other things I could have done, and choose this life all over again.

BIBLIOGRAPHY

Fiction:

The Rest Is Done with Mirrors, Little, Brown, 1970.

Mothers, Daughters, Coward, 1977.

Rhine Maidens, Coward, 1981.

Golden Days, McGraw-Hill, 1986.

Making History, Houghton, 1991.

Nonfiction:

Blue Money, McKay, 1973.

(With John Espey) *Two Schools of Thought*, John Daniel, 1991.

Dreaming: Hard Luck and Good Times in America (autobiographical memoir), Random House, 1995.

Under joint pseudonym Monica Highland, with John Espey and Lisa See Kendall:

Lotus Land (historical fiction), Coward, 1983.

110 Shanghai Road (historical fiction), McGraw-Hill, 1986.

Greetings from Southern California (nonfiction), Graphic Arts Press, 1988.

Contributor to *Atlantic, Esquire, McCall's, Ms., Sports Illustrated,* and *TV Guide*. Book reviewer for *Los Angeles Times, New York Newsday,* and *Washington Post*.

Lewis Putnam Turco

1934-

My father, Luigi Turco, was a Sicilian immigrant who came to America and was eventually converted to Protestantism by the missionaries of the Episcopal Church. These concerned Christians, however, did not really want Italians as fellow worshipers. As a result, he became the minister of the First Italian Baptist Church of Meriden, Connecticut. Early on, in my *First Poems* (1960), I wrote "An Immigrant Ballad," which, despite my mother's scandalized disapproval, Papa felt was rather accurate:

Lewis Putnam Turco, "At my Mathom Bookshop and Bindery in Dresden, Maine," 1986

An Immigrant Ballad

My father came from Sicily
    (O sing a roundelay with me)
With cheeses in his pocket and
A crust of black bread in his hand.
He jumped ashore without a coat,
    Without a friend or enemy,
Till Jesus nailed him by the throat.

My father came to Boston town
    (O tongue a catch and toss one down).
By day he plied a cobbler's awl,
By night he loitered on the mall.
He swigged his wine, he struck his note,
    He wound the town up good and brown,
Till Jesus caught him by the throat.

He'd heard of Hell, he knew of sin
    (O pluck that wicked mandolin),
But they were for the gentle folk,
The cattle broken to the yoke.
He didn't need a Cross to tote:
    His eyes were flame, his ears were tin,
Till Jesus nabbed him by the throat.

He met a Yankee girl one day
    (O cry a merry roundelay)
Who wouldn't do as she was bid,
But only what the good folk did.
She showed him how the church bells peal
    Upon the narrow straitaway,
And Jesus nipped him by the heel.

My father heard a sermon said
    (O bite the bottle till it's dead).
He quit his job and went to school
And memorized the Golden Rule.
He drained his crock and sold his keg,
    He swept the cobwebs from his head,
And Jesus hugged him by the leg.

The girl was pleased: she'd saved a soul
    (O light a stogie with a coal).
No longer need she be so wary:
Daddy went to seminary
To find how warm a Yankee grows
    When she achieves her fondest goal.
And Jesus bit him on the nose.

Lewis Turco with his parents,
Luigi and May, 1935

At last he had a frock to wear
    (O hum a hymn and lip a prayer).
He hoisted Bible, sailed to search
For sheep to shear and for a church.
He asked the girl to share his life,
    His choir-stall and shirt of hair,
For Jesus bade him take a wife.

My father holds a pulpit still
    (O I have had enough to swill).
His eye is tame, his hair is gray,
He can't recall a roundelay.
But he can preach, and he can quote
    A verse or scripture, as you will,
Since Jesus took him by the throat.

Pappagallo—as I liked to call my father, somewhat to his annoyance, for it means "parrot"—met May Laura Putnam—Mom May as she liked to call herself, because of the pun, I suppose—at a Methodist camp in Wakefield, Massachusetts, where she was working as a missionary. At the time she was an old maid in her thirties who had pulled herself out of rural poverty in Superior, Wisconsin, by sheer wit

and strength of will. Despite the desperate penury of her second-generation Danish mother, born Laura Christine Larsen; her shiftless father, William Herbert Putnam, descendant of an old New England family; her six brothers and two sisters; Mom May had made something of herself, becoming the only one of the Putnam siblings to graduate from college—Boston University School of Religious Education. I wrote about her in my first book as well:

Requiem for a Name

Believe it or believe it not,
    My mother was a Putnam once.
  On her ancestral tree she swears
The Lowells and the Deweys too
    Hang pendulous as lovely pears.
    My grampaw was a sort of dunce
Who rather let things go to pot—

Himself, his offspring, farm and wife.
    My grampaw was a sort of dunce.
  His homestead I remember well:
The floors were warped, the doors askew,
    And now and then the rafters fell.
    My mother was a Putnam once—
She led a less than social life,

So she went East from grampaw's West.
    My mother was a Putnam once
  Till she was married, woe O! woe.
No longer was she maiden free—
    She cursed her pa from pate to toe.
    My grampaw was a sort of dunce
To cheat the eaglet in its nest

By willing her a woman's form.
    My grampaw was a sort of dunce,
    But what a hefty name he wore!
He gave my middle name to me;
    It fits me like a saddlesore.
    My mother was a Putnam once,
I'd be one too, come sun or storm.

The Deweys and the Lowell hosts
    Are pendant from a hollow tree.
Now with this rime let them be felled,
    Let them be nothing more to me
Than windfalls blasted by the frosts.

    My mother was a Putnam once;
    My grampaw was a sort of dunce.

Mom May was wrong about the Lowells, but right about the Deweys.

So my parents married and I was born into their middle age. We lived a while in Buffalo near my father's sister, Vita Sardella, and her family. I was christened Lewis (my mother was having no other "Luigi" in the family) Putnam (hyphenated last names were not yet current in the U.S.) Turco, and then we moved to Meriden, where I was brought up unaware of how poor we were. Thinking back on my early life, I consider it remarkable that my parents, given their own histories, brought up their children as members of the middle class who had no doubt at all we were as privileged as anyone else. Though we had no money, the house was full of books of all sorts. My mother read to me from the cradle, and I soon learned to read for myself. Nor was writing an abstruse act: every week for as far back as I can remember I watched my father hunched over his typewriter hunting out and pecking at his sermons.

From an early age, also, I was aware that my mother's family had a long and fascinating, if not always distinguished, history. George Puttenham, back in the sixteenth century, had been the author of *The Arte of English Poesie*, a fact that was fraught with omens for me; Amelia Earhart had been married to George Palmer Putnam, the publisher (there were lots of writers and librarians and teachers among the Putnams; lots of farmers, too); and from my reading I knew of the involvement of the Putnam clan in the Salem Witch Hunt of colonial America. In high school I wrote a skit for the Fantaseers, our "science fiction reading club," about the trials of the Salem witches; much later, in my forties, I researched and wrote a 1200-page manuscript, still unpublished, titled *The Devil's Disease: A Narrative of the Age of Witchcraft in England and New England, 1580–1697*. I traced my grandfather Putnam's genealogy with some accuracy back to fourteenth-century Puttenham, Penne, and Aston Abbots in Buckinghamshire. Mother was a direct descendant of

Turco (fourth from left) with "the boys of the First Italian Baptist Church of Meriden, Connecticut," about 1944

Constable Carolina John Putnam of Salem Village, now Danvers, Massachusetts, who in 1692 was throwing the accused and hapless witches into jail.

But long before I discovered all this, when I was five years of age, my brother, Gene, was born in Meriden. His middle name is "Laurent"—probably the female version of "Laura"—and it was many years before I realized the derivation of "Gene": it is the American version of "Gino," which is short for "Luigi"—my father had named both his sons after himself! In my second collection of poems, a chapbook titled *The Sketches of Lewis Turco and Livevil: A Mask* (1962), I wrote about our childhood:

Gene

"Ragtail Gene, don't tag along here;
    scram on home or I'll bop your nose."
Brother, come the first of April,
    that was the word the second of May
    and all you heard when our lead pipe
      cannon
    swallowed a cherry bomb and belched
     a stone
    that boomed across the Fourth of July,
    nearly crocking you where you hid
    to spy on all the older kids.

If the world grew huger in your eyes,
    that was because they went wide
    to hear the clubhouse secrets told
    in the dark garage where gasoline
    smelled about good enough to swill.

For, the first you knew of going,
    you knew because we swore our raft
    was not a raft, but a ship to float
    a boy's body out of sight
    and a man's voice too deep for
      sounding.

That's the way that I am going;
    ragtail Gene, don't tag along here.

When I was in the eighth grade my father sent me off to Suffield Academy in Suffield, Connecticut. He told me that he was doing it to give me the best education he could, but he evidently told Gene that he sent me away to save my brother's life. I don't recollect that I was all that homicidal toward my sibling. The worst thing I remember doing was tying him to the porch of the parsonage on Windsor Avenue when I was supposed to be baby-sitting him. I wanted to play with my neighborhood buddies instead, and I knew he was safe because I could hear him screaming.

Turco (third from right) appearing in the Fantaseers' production of the Salem Witch Trials for Senior Skit Night at Meriden High School, 1951

My father's money and credit ran out after I had spent two years at Suffield, and I returned to Meriden to attend high school. By that time I'd been writing for several years. I had begun to publish in Suffield's student publication, the *Bell,* and when I returned home I won several writing prizes locally, including honorable mentions and a Key Award in the National Scholastic Writing Awards. In the local papers, the *Morning Record* and the *Journal,* I published poetry, articles, and even fiction, for I had become the *Record*'s morgue clerk, high school correspondent, and cub reporter. I also wrote for the Meriden High School publications and during my junior and senior years was first undergraduate editor and then co-editor of the *Annual,* the yearbook. Ray Staszewski and I collaborated on the Senior Class Poem:

Graduation

The morning years of life, for us, are through.
We leave a training-ground of mind . . . this
    school.
Our thoughts, diversified ahead, behind,
Find us more than a bit perplexed with life.
In retrospect, our memories are sweet . . .
Like morning sunbeams spread on dampened earth,
Or sparkle of a dew-dropped, dawning day.
Our free, young past we'll cherish close to us,
A bulky mass of mixed-up incidents
To be relived in later dreams of youth.
But ah, how swiftly change the tunes of life!
Our present soon becomes the passive past;
The future, perfect . . . yet, in all our hopes
There runs a thread of fear, for through the haze
Of college, working, fighting, on the road
That lies before us all, a question mark
Rears up its hoary head and asks, "But what
Of Age, of Death's cold, bony hand, whose slave
Is Time, with sickle cutting ever-widening swaths
Through youth, which cannot mend itself again?"
But still we look with firm, convincing thought
Into the foggy future that is ours . . .
Which holds some love, yet hate; some joy, but
    pain.
We therefore look to Fate and humbly say,
"Our lives are yours, harsh world. Please use them
    well!"

Neither Ray nor I could afford to attend college immediately, so we decided to join the Coast Guard for the Korean GI Bill. Through sheer laziness we wound up joining the Navy instead—not as safe, perhaps, but safer than the infantry. The point was moot, however, for before we got out of service school the war was over. Although my future wife and I had been members of the same crowd in high school, we didn't begin to date until she was a co-ed at UConn and I had gone to sea aboard an aircraft carrier, as I recorded in a poem from my chapbook *Curses and Laments* (1978), published under the anagram pen-name "Wesli Court":

Hornpipe Epithalamium

The sea blows high and the wind blows cold,
    The *Hornet* sails out to sting.
We bellbottom boys are bully and bold,
Young at the moment but growing old,
And it's no damn good that I bought Jean a ring,
    I bought pretty Jean a ring.

The Gunner's Apprentice is cute as a pin,
    The Yeoman can really swing.
Those almond-eyed girls all know how to sin
To make your eyes swivel and your head spin—
But I had to go buy Jeannie a ring,
    A yellowish diamond ring.

Davy Jones flirts with the mermaids below.
    Down there where Neptune is king
The seacows come swimming along in a row
With nothing more on than a green weed bow
While the drowned sailors gather around in a ring
    And dance till the fathoms ring,

For each wooed a maiden of iron and steel,
    Then took her out for a fling.
She had a pert hull and a lovely keel,
But one day she just wouldn't answer her wheel—
I wonder if Jeannie's still wearing her ring,
    That beautiful bargain ring.

The wind blows cold, the sea blows high;
    I stand here trying to sing,
But the salt spray rises to spit in my eye
Till I'm ready to kill and fit to die
While Jeannie sits home and stares at her ring,
    For I gave sweet Jean my ring.

"At my desk in the gunnery office of the USS Hornet*," about 1956*

It was while I was in the Navy, at the age of nineteen, that I published my first verses in 1953 in a national literary journal, the *American Poetry Magazine.* Shortly thereafter my work began appearing widely in the "littles." By the time I was discharged, married to Jean Cate Houdlette, and myself a student at UConn, I was heavily involved in the literary scene. My friends included my fellow undergraduate James Scully and a graduate student, Alexander Taylor, both poets—Sandy Taylor had been the editor of *Patterns,* one of the magazines that had published my early poems.

Two of my instructors were Norman Friedman and John Malcolm Brinnin, the man who had brought Dylan Thomas to America. I emulated him by getting myself put in charge of the Student Union's Fine Arts Festival committee, which brought visiting writers to campus to read their work: e. e. cummings, Richard Eberhart, Donald Hall, Philip Booth, James Wright, James T. Farrell, and many others. As editor of *Fine*

Arts Magazine I published original work by some of our visitors, and as president of The Connecticut Writer, the undergraduate literary organization, sponsored events by student writers, including a Beat reading at which everyone wore white bucks. Jean worked for the university (on the information desk at the administration building—people enjoyed calling her "Miss Information," and when she told them she was married they said, "All right, then, Mrs. Information!" and laughed and laughed); we lived, therefore, in the Northwood Apartments faculty housing. Still, the winters could be bitter:

Letter from Campus

It somehow seems the campus owns no end,
No boundaries save those of season's change.
The students make no bones at fall, but wend
Their leaf-run courses out of shouting's range

And in again, four sheets to compass lawns
Extending, dun on green, toward the rout
Of hill on which this world is built. The tawns
And hint of fawn in autumns hereabout

Extend no hint of leniencies of snow
This winter. There will be the ague to pay:
The weather holds three mortgages on woe
Till March steps in to steal the march on May.

June's like a pregnancy not long conceived:
More wonderful in dreaming than in fact,
Perhaps. Yet, none of pain may be perceived
Except in execution of the act

Of proving life. I must believe the warmth
Is worth the winter, worth this boundless hill.
The third month has transpired. So will the ninth.
Leaves fall no longer and the wind is still—

The blizzard's will is stronger than my own.
This letter wrinkles on and must be done,
For chill has breached the window, scorned the stone
Around my room. December has begun.

Graduating in mid-year of 1958–59, I applied to attend the Iowa Writers' Workshop in the fall and was accepted. I spent the spring semester at UConn as a graduate assistant and part-time instructor of English teaching an introduction to the short story/composition course to sophomores, then several weeks during the summer as the youngest resident of Yaddo, the artists' colony at Saratoga Springs, experimenting with writing unrhymed quantitative syllabic poems. Yaddo is located next to the Saratoga Raceway; this poem is from my third collection, *Awaken, Bells Falling: Poems 1959–1967* (1968), and it depicts an actual event:

Raceway

I.

    My raceway of sheets last night became
a cool trotter, unwinding with grace. Today,
    autumn peeps imponderably out of
        the soggy drought July had posted
            on the foothills. It is August

        here in Saratoga; the races
open tomorrow. Yesterday a filly
    worked out her own odds, snapping two of her
        ankles while we watched. She was done in
            by a green syringe. She lounged on

        the turf, staring from one farthest eye,
both her forehooves angled like ballerina
    slippers. With her, summer has staggered: it,
        too, soon will drop and the jockey sun
            grow gray above the world's brown hide.

II.

    When a thoroughbred loses its
        pins, there's no more running. Snort if you
will, but reason, too, exhausts itself when
cause falters. Men have run down when barred from
    the
        race. Summer is a fragile courser

        here in the North; our racers are
    all imports from the southland. Summer
will not slow for falling leaves, nor haul our
sleighs: it will linger, pawing its reluctance
    to leave, but its strength is of only

        short will, meant for one swift effort.
    Watch the summer run its oval, it's
a winner now—nothing can stop it! The
stands urge their encouragement upon open
    air; shouts fall and rise like the fall wind

        that moves out of the foothills now, sure,
    pervasive, wild.
            Blooded summer shies.

At Iowa some of my fellow students were George Keithley, Robert Mezey, Vern Rutsala, Morton Marcus, and Kim Merker; Curtis Harnack was there with his wife, my fiction professor Hortense Calisher, and Verlin Cassill labored away in the quonset hut where the poetry work-

shop was held. My professors were Paul Engle, director of the workshop, and Donald Justice, who has remained a lifelong friend—in fact, I am writing these words on the fifth of May 1995, having returned to Oswego this morning from Oneonta, New York, where last evening I witnessed Don receive a well-deserved Doctor of Humane Letters degree from Hartwick College. I reminded him that at Iowa I had asked him whether he thought a comprehensive handbook of verse forms traditional to English and American poetry might be useful, as no one, incredibly, had ever compiled one before, not even George Puttenham. Don had said he thought so, and with that encouragement I'd begun working on the book that would be published eight years later as *The Book of Forms: A Handbook of Poetics* (1968) and later still as *The New Book of Forms* (1986).

Influence is reciprocal sometimes, however, even between student and teacher. When he

With his wife, Jean, at the University of Connecticut, about 1956

saw my new workshop poems back in 1959 Don said, "But, Lew, you're cheating. Your poems don't rhyme." Dylan Thomas and Marianne Moore had been writing rhymed syllabics, but no one other than haikuists had been writing just plain syllabics. A few years later I couldn't help noticing (because I was asked to review it) that Don's second book, *Night Light*, consisted of unrhymed syllabic poems.

I didn't stay at Iowa as long as I might have wished, though, for I needed to find a position and begin earning some money:

Old News

"Six weeks gone," the doctor said,
that odd good luck look walking his lips along

the trail blazed by the tip of
his tongue. "Six weeks gone, son. She'll be fine. Lousy

in bed, though," shaking his head.
"You'll be used to the idea come daylight,"

and off he went, his eyes propped
wide with a good call's work—blasé, not quite bored

by the old wonder with which
I was left: the old bride whose acquiescence,

I now find, can swallow down
this house with its carpet silences; stillness

of pillows; the couch couching.
Outdoors, the dark lies in the hollows of trees.

Night descends like a muffled
lamp. These eyes seize on ancient things: the roadway

sleeping between its curbs, the
lurking swell of a still flat belly, and the

lidded moon risen, unwinking, on the world.

I left without taking my degree, but my publication record was strong enough to land me a job at what was then Fenn College in Cleveland, later to be Cleveland State University. My *First Poems* was published, and in Meriden our daughter, Melora Ann, was born the summer of 1960:

A Carol for Melora's First Xmas

When I came out of the bunting's hive
I stung the world with my bumble eyes
    With a hey! ho! rockabye boy,
And it was a kick to be alive—
I dug this chuckle and mammary jive
    Come dumpling, precious, dear little goy.

When I hopped out of the cradle's croon
I counted the cash in my purse of skin
    With a hey! ho! rockabye boy,
And I spent my time like a new doubloon
On liquid propellants to the moon
    Come thumper, jiminey, jumping for joy.

When I blew off to my windy school
I kissed Miss Tuttle and told her lies
    With a hey! ho! rockabye boy,
For I played the scholar like a fool,
And she broke mine, and I broke her rule
    Come cunning, clever, fresh little goy.

But when father preached, he tried to tell
Me the last damn word in the works of sin
    With a hey! ho! rockabye boy!
I caught on quick, and the breezy bell
Went swinging above us halfway to hell,
    Come organ, keyboard, an end to joy.

When I buzzed out of that web of pain
Death was a spider, we were flies
    With a hey! ho! rockabye boy,
And Christ dripped blood on the windowpane
From a sky of tears and a world of rain
    Come sad, solemn, sorrowful goy.

Now my Melora has bumble eyes
That prickle and prod my purse of skin.
Shall I say there's fear in the belfry's din,
And the flesh of the world is a bag of lies?
Shall I teach her to love, but teach her to sin,
To look for Hell in her grandfather's skies?—

    With a hey! ho! goodbye, old boy!
    Come sweat, sweet, as you stretch for joy.

During the summer of 1961 I went as a Poetry Fellow to the Bread Loaf Writers' Conference in Middlebury, Vermont, where I made the acquaintance of John Ciardi, director of the conference, who remained a friend and mentor until his death. Others there stayed

"Some of the Bread Loaf Fellows," 1961: (from left) A. R. Ammons, Robert Huff, Lewis Turco, and Richard Frost

friends as well: Richard Frost, whom I introduced to Robert Frost one evening in Treman Hall and whom I saw at Hartwick College yesterday; Richard Emil Braun, with whom I had been publishing in the little magazines for years (people at Bread Loaf thought I ought to be much older than I was, as Dick Frost reminded me; I told him that I'd caught up with and passed myself); A. R. Ammons, and Miller Williams, who, many years later, as director of the University of Arkansas Press, would publish two of my books: *Visions and Revisions of American Poetry*, which in 1986 won the Poetry Society of America's Melville Cane Award for criticism, and in 1989 *The Shifting Web: New and Selected Poems*. I've just finished revising an essay for a forthcoming Arkansas book edited by David Baker, *Meter in English*, and some years back I contributed an article to another, *John Ciardi, Measure of the Man*, edited by Vince Clemente.

When I got back to Cleveland in the fall of 1961 I founded the Cleveland Poetry Center aided and abetted by Loring Williams, Hart Crane's uncle by marriage and publisher of

American Weave Press. Before either of us knew I would be coming to Cleveland, Loring had been one of the members of the board of editors of The Book Club for Poetry, which had made my *First Poems* one of its selections. He presided over the center's Poetry Forums, which soon became a major focus for literary activity in the city. I put the UConn experience to good use by bringing William Golding for a reading that founding year, followed, first by John Crowe Ransom, who read the first poem he had written in forty years at a session of the Ohio Poetry Society convention, and then by a Jazz Poetry Benefit reading. Subsequent visitors included Richard Wilbur, Robert Huff, W. D. Snodgrass, Donald Justice, Hollis Summers, Mac Hammond, Howard Nemerov, Richard Frost, Don Petersen (also an Iowan and Oneontan), Alberta Turner (who eventually succeeded me as director), and many others.

In 1962 Loring published *The Sketches* from his own press and I returned to Iowa briefly to finish my master's degree. In 1964 I left Fenn to go to Hillsdale College in Michigan where, in the fall, the nation completed a year of mourning for its fallen president:

Ode on St. Cecilia's Day 1964

For J. F. K., One Year Later

I. Of the Past

Some music, then, for this day. Let it be
Suitable to the mood of fallen snow,
The veil of a virgin saint. Quietly
Let it come now, out of the silence; now
While the birds inexplicably forsake
The elm, the oak, the seed in the lilac. . . .
Instead, drumrolls muffled in an old year,
An echo of trumpets in the streets. Clear
But muted, there is a ragged tattoo
Of hooves, image of a sable horse, wild-
Eyed, resisting the rein, skittish among
The twin rows of witness citizens who,
Their voices frozen, give up to the cold
Air of the marble city an old song.

II. Of the Present

But it's another year, Cecilia's day
Again, another part of the land. So,
Let the phantoms of those dead days lie
Under these new burdens of snow. Allow
That chorus of stricken men to dim like
Shadows into blackening film, the dark
Merging with the riderless horse. Feature
By feature, let the scene fade into near
Distance, into perspective, then shadow.
This is music for St. Cecilia. Yield
To her the lyric due her. Let us sing
For her patronage—her martyrdom grew
Out of a summer heart: she is our shield
Against the winter. She is always young.

III. Of the Moment

Here beyond the window the campus lies.
The students pass in mufflers and coats, eyes
Almost hidden against the wind. The sound
Of radio music settles around
The furniture, into the carpeting.
Choral voices: a requiem. Distant
And urgent, the November church bells ring.
Outdoors a dog rags something. An instant
Pause in his play—he has caught a squirrel
Which tosses and tosses in the gray air.
The mongrel, in the midst of his quarrel
With life, is assaulted by three girls. There,
At the base of a tree, the limp ruff falls
From insensate jaws, starts to inch up walls
Of oak bark toward some invisible
Sanctuary. The dog begins to howl.
The girls watch the squirrel into the limbs.
Cecilia's radio has no more.

I stayed at Hillsdale just long enough to produce the Conference of Midwestern Poets during the summer of 1965. The morning after the conference was over, a portion of the town was destroyed by a tornado while I slept. In June "While the Spider Slept," a ballet choreographed by Brian Macdonald to music by Maurice Karkoff, titled from and based upon my poem "November 22, 1963," was debuted by the Royal Swedish Ballet in Stockholm. Subsequently the Royal Winnipeg Ballet performed it in Canada and throughout the United States. My family moved to Oswego, New York, where I began to teach in the State University College.

During the summer of 1968 I returned to Bread Loaf as a member of the teaching staff, and in the fall my family moved temporarily to Potsdam, a sister college in the SUNY system, where I was visiting professor for a year. No sooner had we settled in than my father died in Meriden. Mom May said he had been sitting watching the news on television when suddenly he pitched forward and was gone, a circumstance that gave rise to a recurring dream which was not exorcised until I wrote this sestina:

The Obsession

Last night I dreamed my father died again,
A decade and a year after he dreamed
Of death himself, pitched forward into night.
His world of waking flickered out and died—
An image on a screen. He is the father
Now of fitful dreams that last and last.

I dreamed again my father died at last.
He stood before me in his flesh again.
I greeted him. I said, "How are you, father?"
But he looked frailer than last time I'd dreamed
We were together, older than when he'd died—
I saw upon his face the look of night.

I dreamed my father died again last night.
He stood before a mirror. He looked his last
Into the glass and kissed it. He saw he'd died.
I put my arms about him once again
To help support him as he fell. I dreamed
I held the final heartburst of my father.

I died again last night: I dreamed my father
Kissed himself in glass, kissed me goodnight
In doing so. But what was it I dreamed
In fact? An injury that seems to last
Without abatement, opening again
And yet again in dream? Who was it died

Again last night? I dreamed my father died,
But it was not he—it was not my father,
Only an image flickering again
Upon the screen of dream out of the night.
How long can this cold image of him last?
Whose is it, his or mine? Who dreams he dreamed?

My father died. Again last night I dreamed
I felt his struggling heart still as he died
Beneath my failing hands. And when at last
He weighed me down, then I laid down my father,
Covered him with silence and with night.
I could not bear it should he come again—

I died again last night, my father dreamed.

In 1968 also *Awaken, Bells Falling* and *The Book of Forms* were published. When I returned to Oswego I took up the directorship of the Program in Writing Arts which I had put together before I left for Potsdam. It became eventually one of the largest undergraduate writing programs in the nation, and I directed it until this year, 1995, when I stepped down on January 1. The college subsequently appointed me poet-in-residence, perhaps to comfort me, though I needed no consolation—I'm not J. Edgar Hoover, and more than a quarter-century of doing something is long enough. My colleague and fellow (but much younger) Iowan, Leigh Allison Wilson, is the new director.

At Oswego in those early days I met and began working with the printmaker Thom. Seawell. We did several poemprints together and then, in 1970, we collaborated on a book of prose poems and prints, *The Inhabitant,* about a man who, in mid-life, discovers he no longer understands who he is and begins to wander about his house in search of himself:

The Hallway

The Inhabitant stands in his hallway. A long
way from the door, still the gentleman has
a distance to go before he can leave, or enter, or simply resume.

Here there is small illumination. The only window
is of squares of stained glass, in the door
behind him which is closed.

Things wait in the narrow aisle. Objects be-
guile him—each has its significance, in and
beyond itself; each is an obstacle in a way
to be touched and passed:

Touched and repassed, and with each touching
to become more than the original substance.
The Inhabitant stands in his hallway, curiosi-
ties looming ahead and behind.

It is as though, almost, this furniture had become organs, extensions of his body. If he
listens, the gentleman may find his pulse boom-
ing in the hallseat, under the lid, gently,
among artifacts and mathoms.

Let him proceed; let his footfall say *clum,* silence, *clum.* Let the stained light lie amber
on a black umbrella in its stand, fall scarlet
on the carpet, make a blue haze of a gray
hatbrim rising in shadow to the level of his
eye to rest on an iron antler in the hall.

The Inhabitant is home. Let him go down the
hallway, choosing to pass the stair and ban-
ister this time, pass these things of his, lev-
elly, moving from light to light, shadow to
shadow.

In the same year my monograph bibliography, *The Literature of New York,* appeared—books at opposite ends of the spectrum, no doubt—and SUNY published a study guide for a correspondence course, *Creative Writing in Poetry.*

In 1971 *Pocoangelini: A Fantography and Other Poems* appeared; it was followed in 1973 by an expansion of the study guide as a college text, *Poetry: An Introduction through Writing;* a second study guide, *Freshman Composition and Literature;* and a chapbook, *The Weed Garden;* but the most important thing was the birth of my son, Christopher Cameron.

Minotaur

In my dream there is light
in the underground passage
turning between stone block walls.
The floor is a shallow stream.

How have I come to be
here in this place with my son,
not yet a yearling? Danger
waits nearby—one can feel it.

He must be preserved. At
the end of the passage there
is safety—another thing
I know, but cannot tell how.

The water moves slowly,
but it can bear him in this
frail shell in which I place him.
And he has been set afloat.

As he drifts through stone, through
light, he rises, leans upon
the rim to fathom water.
It is true: Pain is depthless.

My feet move to follow,
to seat my child again, but
the fluid drags at my flesh.
I call; he does not look back.

As he diminishes
in the curve of his passage,
I sense the beast I have feared
in the distance between us.

This is the place where a stone,
given its occasional career, could disturb
    little with an arc and fall,
  for the pond would swallow all voice
and shrug circling ripples into its banks until
    moss had absorbed this small wet gift,
      showing a fancy darker.

This is the place where one may
abet his heart's romance, deceiving his eyes by
    unconsciously confusing
  slow change with no change. But even
here, dream makes way for declensions of
    wind and sun.
    The alders will grow, moss will dry.
      Wings will pulsate, then plummet.

This is the place where peace rests
like ferns beyond lilies. The trick is to wear it
    as a mantle, but to know
  cloaks for cloaks, shelters for shelters.
Beneath this revery of surfaces, fish wait
    for the dragonfly's mistake. The
      trick is to lose, but to own.

This poem is from a chapbook, *A Maze of Monsters,* with illustrations by Louise Dickinson, published in 1986, but the series from which the chapbook was culled is an unpublished (in its entirety) alphabestiary, *A Book of Beasts,* which had fostered an earlier chapbook in 1978, *A Cage of Creatures.*

"Wesli Court" published his first chapbook in 1977, *Courses in Lambents: Poems,* from Mathom Publishing Company of Oswego, whose founder, Charlie Davis, had at one time been a jazz musician and composer of the all-time jazz classic "Copenhagen." On a second sojourn at Yaddo that year I lived and worked in the Tower room, and I reacquainted myself with the millpond about which I had written on the first occasion:

Millpond

Yaddo, Saratoga Springs, New York

This is the place where peace grows
like a green frond set among waters aerial
  with dragonflies. Where, at noon,
  the trees section the broad falling
leaf of light, and space color upon the millpond,
    yet do not move because motion
      might be lost upon silence.

Curses and Laments, another chapbook, followed in 1978, as did a children's storybook, *Murgatroyd and Mabel,* illustrated by "Robert Michaels" (Robert Sullins), and a third chapbook, *The Airs of Wales,* modern versions of Medieval Welsh poems in the bardic forms, all by "Wesli Court." In Maine, on the farm where my family and I spent nearly every summer, my father-in-law, John Cate Houdlette, who had been my seventh-grade shop teacher in Meriden, died just before Christmas. The summer before, the family had spent one lovely day at the beach before learning the diagnosis:

Cancer

We did not know, then, what the wen
    was on his heel. The gulls wheeled
in the summer sun, the combers
      broke and broke; the sand siled.
  On the beach the grandchild ran
  and stopped, dug wells, ran again

while the old man slept in a round
    shadow cast against the light.
The old wife dreamed beside his dream,
      wound in a shawl, as shade
    fretted the edge of waking.
  But all the while, as the tide

pulsed, moving by moments toward
    the drying seaweed of high
water, through the web of his veins
    the crab sidled, stalking.
The day was perfect, then. Now
    a sea-change has taken it;

rather, it has become two days,
    that fair one and another
in which sandworms rise from the child's wells,
    segmented, mandibled.
The beach umbrella sends its shade
    casting over the rising surf

to meet the east wind. The seabed
    is calm and murderous with
life. The boats toss like dreams, their nets
    seining the undertow.
Now the ocean is almost
    upon us—our eyes are stars

       with spines; our minds are eight-armed; they
grope and coil in the darkness of the sun.

Loring Williams, publisher of The Sketches of Lewis Turco and Livevil: A Mask, *with the author's daughter, Melora Ann Turco, Cleveland, 1962*

The following summer while Curtis Disbrow, a Houdlette son-in-law like me, Jean's cousin Joe Packard, and I were converting the ell and shed of the ancient Dresden farmhouse into heatable living quarters for Bertha Houdlette, my newly widowed mother-in-law, and Jean's oldest sister Nathalie Ahern, I began a seasonal enterprise, The Mathom Bookshop, in Dad Houdlette's tractor garage. (Joe's brother is named "Putnam Packard," for the Packards and a branch of my mother's family had intermarried generations before.) My bookstore is still operating, and this summer I will move it into a newly renovated section of the barn, as the garage has become too small and the sills have disintegrated. Because many people ask, I will record here that "Mathom" is a Tolkien word meaning "useless treasure."

My chapbook *Seasons of the Blood,* poems on the Tarot, appeared in 1980, and I began collaborating with a second Oswego printmaker, George O'Connell, with whom I have been working ever since. My old Yaddo poem, "Millpond," was coupled with his intaglio "Dark Light" in *The New York Landscape: Poems by Twenty State University of New York Poets, with Visual Responses by Twenty SUNY Artists,* an exhibition that opened at the Plaza Gallery in Albany in 1981 and subsequently toured the State, with reprises in 1982–83 at the Pratt Manhattan Center Gallery

in New York City and at SUNY Plaza in the fall of 1994. This collaboration led to a permanent exhibit, the Jeffrey Sisson Memorial, in the lobby of the Aurelia Fox Memorial Hospital in Oneonta, which I had the pleasure to see for the first time when I went down to the investment of Justice this week. Also in 1981 *American Still Lifes,* a book of poems with drawings and design by O'Connell, was published by Charlie Davis.

In 1982 I was Bingham Poet-in-Residence at the University of Louisville, and in 1983 an awardist in the NEA/PEN Syndicated Fiction Project. *The Compleat Melancholick,* supported through a grant from the National Endowment for the Arts, was published in 1985 and exhibited at international book fairs in Europe. The next year I returned to Cleveland for the first time since 1964 to participate in the Poetry Center's silver anniversary. The same year, 1986, saw the publication of *A Maze of Monsters, The New Book of Forms* (which was introduced to the world by its publisher in a reception at the MLA convention in New York City with a dinner afterward at the Algonquin—ah! if only poets could live like that a bit more often), and *Visions and Revisions of American Poetry.*

However, in Connecticut my mother died—she was the same age as the century, and in Oswego I was a pallbearer several times.

The Shadowman

This is the year when everybody died—
This is the year when friends and neighbors died,
Took that short trip or ended the long slide.

Jim shot himself on Cemetery Road,
Left an ironic note beside the road.
No one heard his desperate heart explode.

Our frightened former next-door neighbor went—
Rita, the fearful widow from next-door went
To join her husband John in the firmament.

Paul's heart quit because his cough would not.
His life went up in smoke, for he could not
Stop smoking soon enough—so he would trot

Along our streets slower than folks could walk,
Jog the streets slower than we could walk
And slower than the shadowman can stalk.

Cooper's blood sluggishly turned to whey
In his pale veins—slowly turned to whey
Beneath the translucent skin now turned to clay.

Kermit and Dorothy lost this chilly spring
To the sickle and the crab—lost the spring
To the dim weather and the scorpion's sting.

And Mag, our neighbor on the other side,
Next door toward the lake on our north side,
Father of my son's best friend, has died

Because he loved his beer more than his life,
Loved his suds more than his very life,
Let alone his daughter, his son, his wife.

The shadowman comes tapping down the street,
His feet come stuttering along the street.
Nobodaddy's patrolling, walking his beat.

Hear him, townsmen, between the curbs of night,
Among our yards, towing the craft of night
Whether the hour is dusky or dark or light.

Listen to him breathing in the walls
Of all our houses, breathing in the walls,
In our kitchens and in the empty halls.

Stop when you listen and whisper to the dust,
"These are the names of neighbors scrawled in dust,
Whistled to shadow, scattered in a gust."

One of our high school crowd, Alice Van Leuvan, had married the Dutch composer Walter Hekster. When the Twents Conservatorium in Enschede, Holland, wanted to commission a chamber opera on an English script, Walter asked me for one. The result was *The Fog,* published in 1987 in Amsterdam. In 1989 both *Dialogue: A Socratic Dialogue on the Art of Writing Dialogue in Fiction* and *The Shifting Web: New and Selected Poems* appeared.

For many years, all of my married life, I had been writing family poems about the Houdlettes and the Getchells of Dresden, Maine, most of whom I loved as though they were blood relatives rather than in-laws, but I had never been able to develop a format into which I might fit them in an organic manner. At last I evolved a sequence titled *Voices in an Old House,* in which people who had lived on the farm for over two centuries, since 1754, spoke with one another across the generations. From this I culled two chapbooks of poems, the first of which was *A Family Album* in 1990. This was the prologue:

Albums

The ancient albums lie
behind the parlor door spinning fine
tintype fables between plush covers: straight stares
line out over handlebars and whalebone

stays. They were familiars,
once; now the summer eyes of the old
farm run through evenings of conjecture, try names
against heydays, trace the features of these

generations peering
over collars and boas. A jowl
sags here, beneath this rafter. An eye is gray,
like the sky over the hill. A fire

flickers at the grate, flares
and settles. Someone lights a pipe. Now
the pictures come to life and walk the halls: this
bone is the old lady's, that tooth the man's.

Whose child is this that sits
in the dusty shadows—whose dust, whose
shade? Who made the bed of webs above the ell?
Who sleeps, who wakes, whose footfall on the floor

disturbs the carpet beetle in its lair?

The following year, 1991, I was writer-in-residence at Ashland University in Ohio, which published a series of talks I gave there during my tenure, *The Public Poet: Five Lectures on the Art and Craft of Poetry.* A British edition of *Dialogue* was published in London as well, and a poem from the manuscript *Voices,* "Priscilla Bourne," was chosen to appear in *The Family,* a national juried visual art and poetry exhibition mounted by the Peconic Gallery of Riverhead, Long Island, New York. For four years in a row different judges took poems from the manuscript for the annual Peconic exhibitions. In 1992 a second chapbook culling from *Voices,* titled *Murmurs in the Walls,* was published, and "Francis Pullen" was chosen to appear in the Peconic exhibition titled *Heroes.* In 1993 "William Mason" was selected for the *Imagination* exhibition, and in 1994 "Jason Pullen" hung in the fourth Peconic show, *Passion,* which subsequently traveled to the Rathbone Gallery of Page Junior College in Albany, where I read from the chapbooks at the gallery's reception.

In the spring of 1992 the Alumni Association of my alma mater, the University of Connecticut, presented me with a Distinguished Alumnus Award, and later in the year *Il Dialogo,* the Italian edition of *Dialogue,* was published in Milan in a translation by Sylvia Biasi. Although I'd not been overseas since the USS *Hornet* had made its world cruise during 1953–1955, I'd always meant to go to England, but at the last moment something always seemed to go wrong: the roof blew off the house, the driveway sank out of sight in spring mud, the ancient sewer system collapsed. In 1992, however, Jean and I actually managed to go. We spent a week in London, and then during the second week drove around the rest of Britain, up to Wales and Scotland, in a whirlwind trip with two friends from Oswego, Tom and Mary Loe.

The following year I was granted a sabbatical, and I went back for a month, Jean joining me for the second fortnight. I spent the first two weeks in London, and then we went to visit friends in the Lake District and in Devon, where at the University of Plymouth at Exmouth I participated in the opening day class of a course in Modernism conducted by the English poets John Daniel and Tony Lopez.

In London I renewed my acquaintance with Gavin Ewart, who had read at Oswego in 1986, and got in touch with Ian Hamilton, for whom I had been writing entries on American poets for his *Oxford Companion to Twentieth Century Poetry.* He was associated with the literary periodical *Agenda,* and I made a point of attending its silver anniversary celebration at the Turret Bookshop, where I heard various people read and chatted with some of them, including William Cookson and Sam Milne. It was there also that I made the acquaintance of a young American poet who had been living in England for eight years and had published two collections of poetry with Oxford University Press, Michael Donaghy. A few days later Michael took me to another reading at the Terrible Beauty Coffee House where I met some young expatriate Americans and Canadians and talked at some length with one of the readers, Charles Boyle. Then it was my turn to introduce Donaghy to David Ricks of the King's College, London, with whom I had been corresponding. At last Jean joined me, and when we got back to Oswego it was winter. I went back to work in my attic study with its huge window that looks out over our neighborhood:

The View from a Winter Garret

Skies are gray and winter is settling down
Past my attic window as I write.
I see my neighbors' roofs adrift through town

Blown by the wind winding them in white.
The current of my mind begins to spill
Into a fault of time. I watch a flight

Of gulls come rising out of chimneys, fill
A fold of sky that falls in siftings there
Into Ontario below the hill.

I hear the wind build palaces of air
And ice along the shore of Whitman's lake.
Only silence will make a dwelling where

Music must turn to crystal to survive,
And seagulls scull like snowfall come alive.

Since 1982 I had been living inside Emily Dickinson's head, reading her work and writing about her in my garret on West Eighth Street in Oswego. At last, in 1993, *Emily Dickinson,*

Turco (far left) on the porch of Treman Hall, Bread Loaf Writers' Conference, 1968

Woman of Letters, was published; it included "A Sampler of Hours: Poems and Centos from Lines in Emily Dickinson's Letters":

Brown Study

His son's dinosaurs surround me.
Overhead in his attic study
    antique maps slant away
    between me and the stars.

The kneewall set into the eaves
is sated with books. Down the garret,
    charts and prints cascade from
    the eastern wall—its slit

window—to the western
door with a panel of glass stained
    green and faint lavender,
    the *fleur-de-lis* aqua

in a field of frost. The gable
end displays portraits of him, the boy
    whose ancient animals
    walk this landscape of books,

that pause of space which we call 'Father!'

Also published that year was a chapbook, *Legends of the Mist.* Though I liked the poems in it well enough, it was so badly produced that I got rid of every copy I could find. In October I was installed in the Hall of Fame of my home town in Connecticut, an event that was belittled by a fellow workshop poet. I wrote him a letter that read in part,

I saw your remarks in the Iowa Workshop *Newsletter* and feel constrained to write. Meriden, Connecticut, a city of about 50,000 souls, is the place where I grew up. When one's home town chooses to confer upon one of its sons or daughters its highest honor it is, indeed, an *honor,* because those people know you; they watched you walk the streets and play in their back yards; they noticed you in your best and worst moments over a period of years. The standard by which they judge you is stringent and personal.

The man who nominated me was my high school choral director, Tony Parisi, now nearly blind. The person who seconded the nomination was the ancient editor of the *Morn-*

ing Record, for whom I had worked as a cub reporter, morgue clerk, and high school correspondent forty years earlier. The people who attended were citizens for whom as a child I had delivered newspapers, my classmates and schoolmates and playmates, the parishioners of my father's church including my Sunday school teacher, the organist with whom I had sung in the choir, the man with whom as a student I had collaborated to write the Meriden High School Class of 1952's graduation song [Walter Carey].

The day I was installed in the Meriden Hall of Fame alongside the diva Rosa Ponselle and my classmate Tomie DePaola, winner of the Caldecott Award, was without a doubt the most gratifying day of my life. When another classmate [Jim Masterson] asked me whether I had truly enjoyed the day, I told him my only regret was that it could never come again.

My acceptance speech was a poem that I had written years earlier in Meriden about the family, the town, Hubbard Park, and Castle Craig, a stone tower on East Peak that looked down upon the place where Jean and I had grown up.

A Family Celebration

That fourth of July a sly laugh
       dogged our fancy. Uncle John,
the old wag, taled off again. The children
  clamored in bushy shadow, and green
     grass grew all around all around

     under the vintage windows, rosé
      with the last of the sun. Like
time shrunken and drawn taut across the evening,
  the lawn tapped out its cricket sounds and
     Melora rapped her doldrums on

     the tabletop. Muzzy Aunt Nat
      turned over turning forty-
one, gave the women the once-over, thumbed
  down the thought. Who'll describe it? The park
     that day was ducks like sparks about

     the pair of snowflame swans burning
      out of blue sconces. The kids
had crackers and quacks—as many as they
  could swallow or toss; the trees had leaves
     thick as Moorish rugs. Their silhouettes

At the New England Poetry Conference, Harvard University, 1985: Charles Osgood, Herbert Coursen, and Lewis Turco

blotted sunlight, drank it off thick
    banks and gravel walks. And flowers!
Bows of them, beds massed beneath Old Glory
    poling it over the bandshell, green
        benches applauding its rustic

        orchestration: flagstone, sandstone,
        half-timber. All told, it was
a period piece, a dash of Edward—
    a pause. But not ours, and surely not
        the children's. Perhaps we elders

        could remember when it was like
        this all day long, nearly, day
in, well-nigh, and out. And what were we to
    say when the night came mooning? When light
        lay draped lightly about the hill,

        and on the hill the old stone tower,
        in it the four flights of iron
stair that we climbed counting that afternoon
    to see the world unroll there beneath
        the parapet? Not even the world,

        merely our town: a tall tale told tongue-
        in-cheek—to a child holding
buttercups and clover—by a sly old
        mountebank, it well may be.

During the winter of 1995 Tony Parisi died. Both Jean and I had sung in many of his choruses and a production of Gilbert and Sullivan's *H.M.S. Pinafore* while we were high school students and shortly afterward. We still sing in productions of the Oswego Opera Theater; just this spring we were in the chorus of William Schuman's *Mighty Casey*, a tortuous piece of music. Afterward we went to Meriden during spring break and made a point of visiting Tony's widow Tata, the Warren Gardners, the Jim Mastersons, Dorothy Van Leuvan, the mother-in-law of Walter Hekster, and others of our friends.

Recently I have been working on several projects, notably a manuscript volume of memoirs titled *A Book of Leaves,* of which this essay will become an integral part, and *The Oxford Handbook of Literary Forms,* a test draft of which, on a Faculty Development Grant from SUNY Oswego, has been given a field test this spring in various classes and schools. George O'Connell is working on a portfolio of prints incorporating my ancient "Bordello" series, and if all goes well we will exhibit them at the Rathbone Gallery in Albany during the spring of 1996.

Reading through this brief account of my professional life, I can see one might get the impression that all has been clear sailing for me during the last forty-five years or so. Such is far from the case. For instance, no one publisher has published more than two of my books, which means that I have had to sell each manuscript separately, without benefit of an agent. Early on there were long dry periods—eight years passed between the publication of my *First Poems* and my next full collection, *Awaken, Bells Falling*. I don't want to leave the reader with the notion that the writer's life is anything but frustration and rejection . . . but then, what life isn't? It's much more like this:

Canzone

"Whatever you set your mind to, your personal total obsession, this is what kills you. Poetry kills you if you're a poet, and so on. People choose their death whether they know it or not."

                     —*Don DeLillo*, Libra

Canto Uno. Obsessive Ottavi
It's said we choose the thing that will destroy us:
The plumber picks the scalding pipe that bursts.
We seize upon the obsession to employ us
All our days—the butcher among his wursts
Will gasp his last on the sausage he embraces,
The cobbler strangle in his own shoelaces.
The tease will die in a way that will annoy us,
The sweetie-pie in a manner sure to cloy us.

The fiddler will pass away in some vile inn
Between gigs on the road. The hypnotist
Will suffer stroke and spend a little while in
Staring into nothingness; the dentist
Will feel the drill slicing through his sinus,
The banker's columns add at last to minus.
The model shall come to end her days in style, in
Styli the engraver; the clerk shall file in.

Who makes these rules? One wishes it were so,
But only poets smother in their words
That spill like cottage cheese out of their vents
In swollen streams throughout their lives. Although
The words are for the world, the world says, "Hence!
Take back this whey, take back these pallid curds."
And so we eat our words all our lives long,
Stifling finally in a mound of song.

Canto Due. Terminal Capitolo

Why is it when we've worked our will and won,
Some goomba comes along and trips us up?
Just when we're on our toes he knocks us down.
The ewe's in place, and now here comes the tup—
The ram is blind! He misses by a mile!
Basta! It does no good to mope and gripe—

We ought to groan and berate with a snile;
We ought simply to turn the other cheek,
But when we do we're met with another snarl
And batted from today into next . . . month.
That's to the good! for there we'll find the sun
Filling the halcyon sky with light and warmth.

Basta! again—smoke rises between our toes!
Just when the eyes have it, so does the nose.

Canto Tre. Aria Gone Awry

Everything is gall and bile at last,
A dagger in the liver or the spleen,
A splash of acid from the acrid past,
A dash of bitters in life's chipped tureen.
No matter what we do it comes out wrong,
Our voices crack in the middle of the . . . aria.
The world is a martini mixed, not stirred,
Its twist of lemon sere as August's rind.
Search as one may to find the proper word,
A synonym will have to do: "behind"
Becomes *arrears* and smells a little strong,
And that's the short of it, the short and . . .
    interminable.

So, what to do? Drink up the curdled broth;
Quaff the quotidian cocktail at the sink;
Choke down the peel that tastes like pickled moth;
You'll never swallow finer food or drink—
For future food becomes what you have passed,
And everything is gall and bile . . . in the final
    analysis.

Commiato. Elegiac Barzeletta

No one can tell which way the wind is blowing
Unless it's snowing; then the eyes can wrinkle
And an inkling—just a hint—of the future
Lash its way beneath your eyelid. Your cornea
Will be abraded. You will be all but blinded.
You'll long for California, or perhaps you'll
Wish that you'd been born dead. You take my
    meaning?

The weather of the world's demeaning, *non e
Vero?* The temperature is zero even
On a summer evening: Here comes the sunset;
The azure of the heavens slowly deepens
To violet. The sun on the horizon
Cloaks itself in velvet mists. It is lovely . . . ,

Until the hailstones fall upon our foreheads
As we look up. The wind comes whistling meanly
Among the fuschias, knocking down the bluebirds'
Happy house. Outstanding among the headstones
We find our fortune: "He who lies here sleeping
Cares not for hail or gallstones, earth or ether,
Nor for songs of the plaining poet's making,
But for dreams that rise from a gravel pillow."

BIBLIOGRAPHY

Poetry:

First Poems, Golden Quill Press, 1960.

The Sketches of Lewis Turco and Livevil: A Mask (chapbook), American Weave Press, 1962.

Awaken, Bells Falling: Poems 1959–1967, University of Missouri Press, 1968.

The Inhabitant: Poems, with Prints by Thom. Seawell, Despá Press, 1970.

Pocoangelini: A Fantography & Other Poems, Despá Press, 1971.

The Weed Garden (chapbook), Peaceweed Press, 1973.

A Cage of Creatures (chapbook), Banjo Press, 1978.

Seasons of the Blood (chapbook), Mammoth Press, 1980.

American Still Lifes, Mathom Publishing Company, 1981.

The Compleat Melancholick: Being a Sequence of Found, Composite, and Composed Poems, Based Largely upon Robert Burton's "Anatomy of Melancholy," Bieler Press, 1985.

A Maze of Monsters (chapbook), Livingston University Press, 1986.

The Shifting Web: New and Selected Poems, University of Arkansas, 1989.

A Family Album (chapbook), Silverfish Review Press, 1990.

Murmurs in the Walls (chapbook), Cooper House, 1992.

Emily Dickinson, Woman of Letters: Poems and Centos from Lines in Emily Dickinson's Letters, State University of New York Press, 1993.

Legends of the Mists (chapbook), New Spirit, 1993.

Nonfiction:

The Book of Forms: A Handbook of Poetics, Dutton, 1968, expanded edition published as *The New Book of Forms: A Handbook of Poetics,* University Press of New England, 1986.

Creative Writing in Poetry (study guide), State University of New York, 1970.

The Literature of New York: A Selective Bibliography of Colonial and Native New York State Authors, New York State English Council, 1970.

Poetry: An Introduction through Writing (textbook), Reston Publishing, 1973.

Freshman Composition and Literature (study guide), State University of New York, 1974.

Visions and Revisions of American Poetry (criticism), University of Arkansas Press, 1986.

The Public Poet: Five Lectures on the Art and Craft of Poetry, Ashland Poetry Press, 1991.

Under pseudonym Wesli Court:

Courses in Lambents: Poems (chapbook), Mathom Publishing Company, 1977.

Curses and Laments (chapbook), Song Magazine, 1978.

Murgatroyd and Mabel (for children), illustrated by Robert Michaels, Mathom Publishing Company, 1978.

The Airs of Wales (chapbook), Poetry Newsletter of Temple University, 1981.

Contributor:

Riverside Poetry 3, Twayne, 1958.

Japan: Theme and Variations, Tuttle, 1959.

New Campus Writing 3, Grove, 1959.

Poetry for Pleasure, Doubleday, 1960.

Anthology of Contemporary American Poetry (record album), Folkways, 1961.

Midland: Twenty-five Years of Fiction and Poetry from the University of Iowa Writers' Workshop, Random House, 1961.

Doors into Poetry, Prentice-Hall, 1962.

Of Poetry and Power, Basic Books, 1964.

Best Poems of 1965: Borestone Mountain Poetry Awards, Pacific Books, 1966.

The Kennedy Reader, Bobbs-Merrill, 1967.

The New Yorker Book of Poems, Viking, 1969.

Best Poems of 1971: Borestone Mountain Poetry Awards, Pacific Books, 1972.

Contemporary Poetry in America, Random House, 1973.

America Is Not All Traffic Lights, Little, Brown, 1976.

American Poets in 1976, Bobbs-Merrill, 1976.

Realms of Light, photographs by Ernst Haas, Walker, 1978.

Poets Teaching: The Creative Process, Longman, 1980.

Beowulf to Beatles and Beyond, Macmillan, 1981.

Tygers of Wrath, University of Georgia, 1981.

A Green Place, Delacorte, 1982.

Poeti Italo-Americani/Italo-American Poets, Antonio Carello Editore, 1985.

Available Press/PEN Short Story Collection, Ballantine, 1986.

Patterns of Poetry, Louisiana State University, 1986.

Seems Like Old Times, Iowa Writers' Workshop, 1986.

Strong Measures, Harper, 1986.

Contemporary New England Poetry: A Sampler, Sam Houston State University, 1987.

Ecstatic Occasions, Expedient Forms, Macmillan, 1987.

John Ciardi: Measure of the Man, University of Arkansas, 1987.

Conrad Aiken: Priest of Consciousness, AMS Press, 1990.

The Hampden-Sydney Poetry Anthology 1975–1990, Hampden-Sydney Poetry Review, 1990.

American Fiction 2, Birch Lane, 1991.

Miller Williams and the Poetry of the Particular, University of Missouri, 1991.

Best American Poetry 1992, Scribner, 1992.

Dictionary of Literary Biography, Volume 120: American Poets Since World War II, Third Series, edited by R. S. Gwynn, Gale, 1992.

Scarecrow Poetry, Ashland University Poetry Press, 1994.

Two Worlds Walking, New Rivers Press, 1994.

Yo Words, One Reel, 1994.

Other:

The Dark Man (play), first produced at the Jorgensen Little Theater, University of Connecticut, Storrs, 1959, later produced as *Dreams of Stone and Sun*.

While the Spider Slept (ballet scenario), choreography by Brian Macdonald, music by Maurice Karkoff, decor by Rolfe Nordin, first produced by the Royal Swedish Ballet, Stockholm, 1965.

The Elections Last Fall (play), first produced at Tyler Hall Experimental Theater, Oswego, New York, 1969.

The Fog: A Chamber Opera in One Act (libretto), music by Walter Heckster, first published in Amsterdam, the Netherlands, 1987.

Dialogue: A Socratic Dialogue on the Art of Writing Dialogue in Fiction, Writers Digest Books, 1989, Robinson Publishing, 1991, Italian translation by Sylvia Biasi published as *Il Dialogo*, Casa Editrice Nord, 1992.

Also contributor to *Collier's Encyclopedia, Contemporary Literary Criticism, Dictionary of Literary Biography Yearbook, First Printings of American Authors, Masterplots II: Poetry*, and *The Oxford Companion to Twentieth Century Poetry*. Contributor of poems, stories, essays, and reviews to many literary journals and periodicals, including *Atlantic, Hudson Review, Kenyon Review, Nation, New Republic, New Yorker, Poetry*, and *Sewanee Review*. Turco's work is also available as a sound recording, "Lewis Turco Reading His Poems with Comment," Archive of Recorded Poetry and Literature, Library of Congress, 1979.

Gerald Vizenor

1934-

VISIONS, SCARES, AND STORIES

The unnamable:

My visions, scares, and stories are traces of the unnamable; that eternal nature and countenance of narratives. Native stories and memories mean more to me than aesthetic romance, or the antidote to ruinous silence. The native author bears the unnamable, the ironies of contested creations, the mortal wounds of dominance, simulation of names, the sanctions of mean discoveries, and the common treasons of transitive histories.

The unnamable is that sense of *presence* created and heard in a narrative; that instance when the internal turns of words, visions, and memories of an author bear the same traces and coincidence of the eternal. That moment when the unnamable is *heard* in common stories and in the ironies of remembrance. The unnamable presence in stories is not the mere antithesis of absence or silence; the unnamable is eternal and has no absence or truancies to measure, because the absence of the eternal would be a simulated representation, otherwise a museum.

Stories *are* remembrance, histories, as *historia*, and *storie*, oral presentations, the transmutation of the native trickster, and more: stories are narratives, as some narratives are aesthetic, the art of the written, the simulations of romance, and the burdens of heroic tragedies. In my stories and narratives the unnamable is the chance *not* the cause to overcome silence with memories, remembrance, and a sense of presence. Every new story is my start and chance to be heard in the ruins of cultural representations.

I directed a social service center more than twenty years ago on Franklin Avenue in Minneapolis, Minnesota. Daily, many native people who had moved from treaty reservations and those who lived on the "urban reservation" came

Gerald Vizenor, Oakland, California, 1995

to the storefront center in search of work, housing, medical care, and the unnamable in stories. That sense of native presence was heard in many casual stories at the center. Stories that were ironic and comic, others might have considered careworn and tragic at the time.

One man, for instance, who was born in an automobile on a reservation, told a story about a social worker who asked him where he would live until he received his first paycheck. The man said he would live in his car. Naturally, the social worker was troubled by his circumstances. "People don't sleep in their cars, that's not a residence," she said to the native. "Something wrong with that?" he wondered. She was not certain, but insisted that a car was not a proper residence. "Why not, I was born in the back seat of a dead station wagon on the reservation, and that's what it says on my birth certificate."

The memories of that time are continuous scenes, not ethnographic transcriptions or translations of the moment; the traces of a native presence in one story must be created in other stories, as the stopover of one story is the natural start of another, and another, in the eternal shadows of the unnamable.

I was weary, distracted by personal troubles at home, and the last to leave the center that humid summer evening at the end of the week. A native couple entered the center, just as I was about to lock the door, and sat down in my office. He tried to smile, but his face was mean. He leaned over my desk to shake hands. His hand was rough, hard, and hesitant. She was drunk and silent on the couch at the other end of the room. He told me they had been in a hot boxcar, riding the rails across the prairie, for two days. They had no money, of course, and no place to stay for the night. They were neither expatriates nor victims; they were in motion, a natural manner and burden of native sovereignty.

I told them the center was closed, but arrangements could be made for them to stay overnight at a transient hotel in the city. I offered a small amount of cash, which the center made available for such emergencies, and referred them directly to the Salvation Army.

He was very angry, turned his head to one side, and accused me of doing what I had once criticized other agencies of doing, the generous "perpetual referral" from one agency to another. I shouted right back about my own fatigue, but he was right about the evasive referral. "You got me at a bad time, this is the end of a long week." I handed him the cash and a note with the name and reservation at the hotel. "You've got a place to stay, and I don't want to hear any more stories."

He was suspicious, but smiled, an ironic turn in his gestures, and watched me at a distance. Then he turned to the woman on the couch. He was at the center for the money, to be sure, but he was there for the stories, to be heard in motion, the chance to create a sense of presence with a few words. She sat in silence, showing no signs that she was even aware of the conversation, much less capable of hearing a story. She wore a man's shirt, oversized, unevenly buttoned, and stained with vomit. Her hair was twisted, gray, and wild. The stench of her body, breath, urine, and stale beer was unbearable. I covered my nose with one hand to resist the reek of humid air and was distracted once more by memories of the many nights of drunks in my own family.

"You're no Indian," he roared.

"I wish that were true right now." The aim of his curse never connected because such execrations were common maneuvers in the course of services at the center. My manner, nonetheless, was turned around by his comment. I was ready to leave, my mind was already on the road, the late drive north to the lakes. If for no other reason his words and her stench bothered me enough to leave, but at that moment my concentration turned to his mean presence and the ironies of native identity.

I was there with them, mean or not, to bear the chance of that moment and hear the unnamable. I can see him now, as he leans back in the chair, certain that my manner was no longer elusive and the perpetual referral had ended. I moved closer and mocked his loud voice. "So, what makes you an Indian?"

He was always ready, it seemed to me then, for a performance of native identities that were intended to invoke converse nostalgia and shame in the listener, and so he told several tragic stories of pain, poverty, and long suffering, an admirable appearance in a world that does not listen to much more than the extremes of success and victimage. He cocked his head to the side and blamed his troubles on racial hatred and the white man. He was right, of course, but his stories claimed too much of the past and were a tedious cover without a hint of ambition or courage. "Indians never get anywhere, and every time we try the white man holds us down."

"So, your trouble is being an Indian?"

"No, we never get a chance because we're Indian," he said.

"Why be one then?"

"I can't be anything else."

"Standing Bear would never say that."

"Never mind, he was a movie actor."

"Not Keeshkemun either."

"Who's that?"

"Charles Eastman, he'd never say that either."

"He's a doctor and married a white woman."

"Wait a minute, if being an Indian is the only cause of your troubles, then why not be someone else, why go on living the life of the victim?" I watched him closely across the desk. He frowned, his neck muscles were tight, and his cheeks moved when he breathed, thin and bluish. I was not pleased with my tone, but the contradictions of victimage and identity were an invitation to dare his overstated pity.

"I could never stop being an Indian," he said firmly. His voice wavered at the end, and, for some unheard reason, the woman on the couch raised her head and turned toward the door of the office. He was very nervous. We both paused to follow her moves, as if someone was about to enter.

"What if you never were an Indian," I said and waved my hands. "Suppose I could chase the Indian right out of you, that would be the end of your troubles, no one would hold you back anymore, you would no longer have any excuse to be a victim."

"I *am* Indian," he insisted.

"With blue eyes?"

"What about you," he shouted at me.

"So, you're not a victim then?"

"Listen," the woman whispered. She pointed to the door, and as she rose from the couch she was no longer the same drunk who had entered the office a few minutes earlier. She announced that we should stand because the native flag was about to enter the room. The flag she envisioned was a native staff of eagle feathers.

"No, no," the man pleaded, "don't do this to me."

"Now, we must sing an honoring song," she said in a clear voice.

"No, no, not now," he shouted.

Facing the door, she sang an honoring song. Her voice was strong, and the room was transformed by the sound of her vision. I remember the peace and presence of that moment, but at the time my heart raced, and my body trembled at the sound of a native honoring song.

She stood in silence for a few minutes and then turned toward me. "It feels good just to talk again," she said and then gathered her hands to her face. She was drunk when she sat down on the couch, but then, at once, she recreated the moment with an honoring song, the coincidence of a native presence. She smiled, turned toward the outside; he followed her in silence out of the office. No one said another word as we parted at the door. I am forever moved by the memories of that moment, a chance to hear another story, and another one here, an unnamable native presence.

The namable:

The Anishinaabe have been active for many centuries in the northern woodlands and waterways. Anishinaabe, the name, means a native person or human in the oral language of the families who lived in that area; however, in the eighteenth century the name was recorded by missionaries, colonial factors, and government agents as variations of the Ojibwa and Chippewa Indians. Anishinaabeg is the animate plural ending. Most writers use the singular form as the name of that native past and present, and in some instances, for natives in general.

Names, and the stories of nicknames, are ancestral distinctions; national and historical connections, to be sure, but names are more than mere representations of identities. Names are traces of a native presence. English invented names, transposed native names for more than a century. Indian is a nominal simulation of racialism and colonialism, an invented name, unheard in native oral languages. The name is unbidden, and the native heirs must bear an unnatural burden to be so christened in their own land. I wrote more than two decades ago in an editorial essay that we must return to the use of original native names.

The Anishinaabe are an unnamable native presence. The same elemental traces are not heard in invented names, the tiresome names of dominance. The discoverers, in other words, must bear the burdens of separation and simulation, not the natives.

Anishinaabe families were once the necessary political and economic center in the woodland and the essential sources of personal identities. Now, of course, native identities are determined by peers, institutions, constitutional democracies, and the diverse policies of communities and nations.

The Anishinaabe are my ancestors. I am a crossblood descendant of these families and, by chance, and vision, bear the narratives of

The author in Minneapolis, Minnesota, 1962

native reason and the associations of both co-lonial and national dominance. My ancestors were active in the fur trade, as were most natives at the time; that enterprise, the consecration of missionaries over native healers, territorial wars, national treaties, and other separations of names, land, and time have forever recast the traditions of native families. My native inheritance was an oral presentation, recorded on birch bark scrolls but unwritten until the fur trade, and my experiences were neither romantic revisions nor tragedies. Others, however, have noticed my crossblood survivance otherwise. One more native heir in the great stories of natural reason and motion, an incomparable sovereignty.

The Anishinaabe were once honored in oral remembrance, and by other nations, as the scions of the crane, loon, bear, martin, and catfish clans, the five original totems or families. I trace my native descent to the crane totem, the orators and inspired leaders of many woodland families.

Keeshkemun, the grandson of the first traditional leader of the crane families, resisted colonial domination, and, at the same time, he wore a George Washington Peace Medal. The crane leaders in "former times, when different tribes met in councils, acted as interpreters of the wishes of their tribe," wrote William Warren, the nineteenth-century crossblood historian, in *The History of the Ojibway Nation*. "They claim, with some apparent justice, the chief-tainship over the other clans" of the Anishinaabe. Warren used the name Ojibway, which later became Chippewa, the legal designations of the time, but he comments on the native name. The crane "loves to soar among the clouds, and its cry can be heard when flying above, beyond the orbit of human vision. From this 'far sounding cry' the family who claim it as their totem derive their generic name" of the echo makers. Many of my distant relatives were echo makers.

Englishman, said Keeshkemun, "You ask me who I am. If you wish to know, you must seek me in the clouds." Michel Cadotte, a crossblood member of the crane families, was the interpreter at the time. The British tried to enlist natives to fight against Americans in the War of 1812. Cadotte reported this encounter to the historian William Warren.

"I am a bird who rises from the earth, and flies far up, into the skies, out of human sight; but though not visible to the eye, my voice is heard from afar, and resounds over the earth."

Englishman, continued Keeshkemun, "You wish to know who I am. You have never sought me, or you should have found and known me. Others have sought and found me. The old French sought and found me. He placed his heart within my breast. He told me that every morning I should look to the east and I would behold his fire, like the sun reflecting its rays towards me, to warm me and my children. He told me that if troubles assailed me, to arise in the skies and cry to him, and he would hear my voice. He told me that his fire would last forever, to warm me and my children."

Englishman, "You have put out the fire of my French father. I became cold and needy, and you sought me not. Others have sought me. Yes, the Long Knife has found me. He has placed his heart on my breast. It has entered there, and there it will remain." Long Knife, or *gichimookomaan* in the language of the Anishinaabe, is the name of the military officers who carried swords, the Americans.

"You say true," replied the British officer. "I have put out the fire of the French men; and in like manner am I now putting out the fire of the Long Knife. With that medal on your breast, you are my enemy. You must give it up to me, that I may throw it away, and in its stead I shall give you the heart of your great British father, and you must stand and fight by his side."

Englishman, said Keeshkemun, "I shall not give up this medal of my own will. If you wish to take it from me, you are stronger than I am. But I tell you, it is but a mere bauble. It is only an emblem of the heart which beats in my bosom. . . . You are stronger than I am. You can do as you say. But remember that the voice of the crane echoes afar off, and when he summons his children together, they number like the pebbles on the Great Lake shores."

The Americans "are stealing away your country," the British told Keeshkemun. William Warren noted that the orator's "influence may be chiefly attributed to the fact that the Ojibways of Lake Superior and Mississippi remained neutral during the progress of the last war." The federal government claimed vast areas of native land, "negotiated" treaties, and removed thousands of natives to woodland reservations in the next two generations. The White Earth Reservation, located in northwestern Minnesota, was established in 1867.

Alice Mary Beaulieu, my paternal grandmother, was born on January 3, 1886. The following year she was removed with her parents to the new reservation. She married Henry Vizenor on the reservation in 1905, and by that time the communal native land had been allotted to individuals by the federal government. My grandmother, not trained to read the metes and bounds of survey maps, never located one of her allotments. That land she leased several times to a timber company, sight unseen, but as it turned out, the land was a marsh and had no timber value.

The Great Depression was even greater on the reservation; there were no markets to crash, but the depression never ceased. My grandmother, who had been demeaned in many ways by her husband, moved from the reservation with her seven children in search of employment. They lived in Detroit Lakes for a time and then landed in downtown Minneapolis.

My grandmother inherited the remembrance of the crane totem, a natural native presence; she told stories of the heart with generous humor and carried on the wild comedies of tricksters, but the beat of the crane would be silent for at least a generation in the city. She was concerned with other measures of survivance.

Clement William Vizenor, my father, was a crane descendant. He was born on the White Earth Reservation. Twenty-six years later he was murdered on a narrow street in Minneapolis.

My father died in a place no crane would choose to dance, at a time no tribal totem would endure. One generation later the sound of the crane returned in native names, remembrance, and in my narratives.

The silence:

Laurel Hole In The Day moved her mouth in silence. I was a native community advocate when she came into the social service center for the first time that morning at the Waite Neighborhood House. She could not speak. She could have been my grandmother thirty years earlier in the city. That unnamable presentiment, natural caution, and a wise sense of an escape distance in an institution are not uncommon sources of native silence.

Laurel held an extreme silence, not even humor could break it that morning. She moved her mouth and tried to speak several times; the gestures were earnest, honorable, but the silence decisive. My grandmother was more certain with humor than silence, but then, the depression was so monotonous that silence would have been another burden of the time. Minneapolis in the thirties was not the same as in the sixties. For that matter, the reservation was never the same either. The stories of courage in one generation are not the same in another.

"Would you like coffee?" She nodded in a positive manner and we both knew that neighborhood houses were not the best places to break down and then wait for the spirits to return.

"Would you like to *talk* about something?" I said and then laughed. Laurel nodded with her head forward on ,her chest. She looked down and held the coffee cup in both hands. Outside the sun rushed the trees.

"Too serious to speak about?" Laurel nodded once more in a positive manner with her head down. I leaned over, my face close to the level of the desk, and tried to catch her eyes. I said, "You must be pregnant." At last she smiled, but turned her head away. Later, when she revealed the nature of her silence, she told me that she was *not* pregnant.

Laurel Hole In The Day is a protective name; she is a real person, and since that morning in the neighborhood house she has become an outstanding leader in social service programs on reservations. Laurel was married with nine children. She was in the city to be with her youngest child who was having surgery to correct a cleft palate. Public health officials on the reservation had made the arrangements.

Laurel had once lived in the city, when she was seventeen. She moved from the reservation at the end of the war to work as a laborer in a federal defense plant. Then, when her future husband was discharged from the military, they moved back to the reservation because he had seen too much war and wanted to live alone with his family in the woods.

"Do you have work?" Laurel nodded in a negative manner for the first time. She and her family had no money, and yet, like my grandmother, wanted to move to the city. Laurel had nine children and a husband; my grandmother had seven children and no husband when she moved to Minneapolis.

"When will you return to the reservation?" Laurel showed me five fingers. "Five days and you want work and a place to live?" She nodded with enthusiasm and then lowered her head once more. "Impossible, an impossible dream," I said and walked back and forth in the office. I opened the window and looked outside at the trees.

"Is your husband a bear or a bird?" Laurel looked at me, she moved her mouth, the silent words of doubt or suspicion, and then smiled. She covered her mouth with her hands. She knew that only a native advocate would wonder about birds and bears in the context of social services.

I placed two pieces of blank paper on the desk in front of her and told her to list what she wanted on the first paper, her impossible dream, and then on the second piece of paper what she thought would be the problems. "Write about the bear and the dream first," I said and left the room. She wrote in a clear and articulate style, a practice she had no doubt learned in a federal or mission boarding school.

"We want to live with our children in the city together," she wrote of the dream. "We need a place to live and my husband wants to work so to pay the rent on time. This is all. Did your dad work for the tribal council once?"

Then she considered the problems of such a move. "My youngest daughter is in the hospital ward getting better now. She is very sick and she will be able to talk when she grows up because of the operation. Peter is there with her, we do not have money and no work

so we could not pay the rent right away. Peter has a bad back from the woods. I hope you can help us, we got to go back next week on Monday. The public health nurse takes care of us now, and the children at home." She ended the note with the word *miigwech,* which means thank you.

They would both have to work to support their family and, as they were unskilled with no work record, the hourly wage would be very low to start. A company that manufactured and assembled plastic caps for glue bottles agreed to hire them, and on different shifts so that one parent would always be home with the children. I located an apartment in the urban reservation, not far from their work, a few blocks from Franklin Avenue. Several people helped me paint the apartment, and we fixed the locks and windows. Laurel and Peter were very happy when they moved into their new home in the city. Their children came down from the reservation and in two months the couple found better work, with insurance and other benefits. They were employed by a larger company.

The small apartment was not secure, and the couple were rightly worried about their children. Soon they wanted to live in a better apartment. They moved out of the urban reservation to a much better neighborhood. The new apartment, in fact, had more space and the rent was lower. The couple saved money and bought a used car. Their lives had changed for the better, most everyone would assume, but in six months' time they were lonely, and together they returned after work to the urban reservation. The couple found other natives from the reservation in bars, and they drank together, and told stories that created a sense of presence.

Peter was absent from work several days a week. Shortly after he was fired he left with the car and did not return. Laurel moved back to the reservation with her children, back to their cabin. There she found her husband alone in the woods. Silence teased the unnamable, and nothing, as it turned out, was insurmountable.

The great river:

The Mississippi River starts at the end of a lake in the stone faces of the birch in motion, the waves of summer clouds, the turns and shimmer of the reeds, and shiners that tease the slow march of cranes; native trickster stories are the origins of this great river.

The Anishinaabe named the river the *gichiziibi,* the big river, and that river was mine in our seasons. Wicked to the ears in winter, cruel on shore in the spring, warm and treacherous in summer, a hidden peace, and clouded with the manners and moods of leaves in the autumn. The river intersected the politics of discovery and nationalism. Natives were driven to the separation, to the other side of the river, their families disunited by nationalism and the cruel measures of civilization.

The *gichiziibi* was my ocean as a child, the heart and motion of my interior landscapes; the rise and run of the seasons, and the treasures that washed ashore on my personal borders, were the traces of stories and native remembrance. I carved endless roads and names in the fine wet sand, and nothing has lasted but the stories.

Rivers, tricksters, mongrels, and the weather were the outright real to me as a child in the city. Trickster stories were transmutations of the obvious, something of a religious experience at the time because the best stories, those that were not translated as moral lessons, told that the trickster was the very wind of lust with an erect penis bigger than his own leg, that his brother was a stone, and his breath was in the stones, that trickster faces matured in roses, and his elusive presence could be heard in the continuous migration of birds. That was too much to consider then; nonetheless, our stories were a chance at the unnamable. Mongrels were some of my closest friends, my brothers at the river, at hand with dreams and at the starts of imagination; my mongrels healed loneliness, separation, and abandonment. The weather watched over me, and taught me to hear natural motion, the motion that would later become my common sense of native sovereignty.

Winter teased me to the last breath on that thin ice. The crows never rested on the road, a consummate sense of the last moment. I shouted at thunder and traced with one eye the lightning cracks healed in the oaks. My

Gerald Vizenor with his wife, Laura Hall, at an autograph party at Savran Books, Minneapolis, 1981

uncles pushed back the autumn a week at a time with their stories and waited for me to catch my own seasons. I tried to overturn the winter, once, twice, and more each year, and beat the trees to bear fruit earlier in the spring. The birds hurried to the same trees, but left little more than green apples every year. I must have lived on bitter berries, tiny carrots, warm tomatoes, and the hearts of cabbages stolen from the nearby truck farms. Nothing was ever certain but the run with my mongrels down to the motion and sensations of the river.

"Childhood is given to us as ardent confusion, and the rest of life is not time enough to make sense of it or explain to ourselves what happened," wrote Michel Tournier in his memoir *The Wind Spirit.*

Likewise, the ardent selection of names, chances, and persuasions is an unreliable representation of that confusion, not to mention the courtesies of the roads not taken. My grandmother, uncles, and other relatives who told stories encouraged me in a roundabout way to become a writer. Their stories were tricky bonds of the past, the real, and the imagined; the

uncertainties of humor, and traces of that unnamable presence. Native humor never ends, and humor never lasts long enough either.

My father was murdered, one of many unsolved crimes that year in the city, and the newspaper accounts of his death were racist, causing my relatives needless heartache. My rage over these distracting reports would motivate me later to become a more humane writer. Many of my stories as a journalist were about the experiences and burdens of native people. My life, in a sense, is heard in others, in the unnamable presence of others in stories. Curiously, my first personal association with a newspaper, other than my duties as a delivery boy, was not a daily in the city but an iconoclastic newspaper on the reservation. At the turn of the last century my relatives published *The Progress,* and later *The Tomahawk,* the first newspapers on the White Earth Reservation.

Theodore Hudon Beaulieu, editor of *The Progress,* announced in the first issue, March 25, 1886, that the "novelty of a newspaper published upon this reservation may cause many to be wary in their support, and this from

At Pueblo Bonito, Chaco Canyon, New Mexico, 1985

a fear that it may be revolutionary in character. . . . We shall aim to advocate and withhold reserve, what in our view, and in the view of the leading minds upon this reservation, is the best for the interests of its residents." Theodore was my grandmother's uncle. His courage and dedication is an inspiration to me as a writer.

T. J. Sheehan, the Indian agent, confiscated the newspaper and ordered the removal of the editor and publisher from the White Earth Reservation. The second issue of the newspaper was published about six months later on October 8, 1887, after a federal district court ruled in favor of *The Progress.*

"The United States district court," wrote the editor in the second issue, "decided that we were entitled to the jurisdiction we sought. The case came before him, on jury trial. The court asserted and defended the right of any member of a tribe to print and publish a newspaper upon his reservation just as he might engage in any other lawful occupation, and without surveillance and restrictions."

The Anishinaabe are honored with more published writers than any other native nation or community; this too, encouraged me as a writer. Some of my most memorable teachers were native writers. George Copway, for instance, who was born in 1818 near the Trent River in Canada, published *The Life, History, and Travels of Kah-ge-ga-gah-bowh* in 1847. Three years later *The Traditional History and Characteristic Sketches of the Ojibway Nation* was published in London. Copway was one of the first native writers to reach an international audience.

Anishinaabe writers have published histories, autobiographies, essays, and fiction in the past two centuries, but one of the most honorable native historians was William Warren, who was born at La Pointe, Madeline Island, Lake Superior, in 1825. In January 1851, two years before his untimely death, he became a state legislator in Minnesota. His notable *History of the Ojibway Nation* was published posthumously in 1885 by the Minnesota Historical Society. Warren's dedication and sense of native presence in history has been very important to me as a writer. Had he lived another thirty or forty years to witness the removal of natives to federal reservations he might have turned to autobiography, or written an ironic or political novel.

The measure:

Clement William Vizenor, my father, must have teased evil too much in the city. He had heard trickster stories on the reservation about the evil gambler, the horrible one who made sounds of scorn and ridicule, but stories were the chance of humor, a liberation not a curse. The trickster, in one version, was warned by *nookomis,* his grandmother, about the wicked one who stole the wind and ate humans. The trickster wanted to hear the hideous measures of evil, and so he entered the *wiigiwaam* of the evil gambler. My father, in the figurative sense, entered that measure of evil in the city.

The Anishinaabe trickster, *naanabozho,* watched the evil one, a curious white character with preposterous manners. "All of those hands you see hanging around the *wiigiwaam* are the hands of your relatives who came to gamble," said the evil gambler. "They thought as you are thinking, they played and lost their lives in the game." The trickster was young and not worried about anything.

"I demand that those who gamble with me and lose give me their lives," hissed the evil one. "I keep the scalps, the ears, and the hands of the losers, and the rest of the body I give to my friends the *wiindigoo,* the flesh eaters." The native *wiindigoo* is a gruesome character in trickster stories, a specter that eats children. "The spirits I consign to the world of darkness."

My father was murdered on a narrow street in the city. I was not yet three and would learn much later, as a college student, about the homicide in newspaper stories. My grandmother buried her bereaved memories of the murder with her favorite son. He was buried in an unmarked grave in the city. She lost two of her five sons that same summer. My mother, who was nineteen years old at the time, never mentioned the death of my father, not to me, not to anyone.

I turned the withered back issues of the *Minneapolis Journal,* the same newspaper that had hired me to be a home delivery boy twelve years after the report on the murder of my father, and found the stories on the front page with a photograph of my father. I might have heard the horrible scorn of many evil gamblers between the lines that morning in the library.

"Giant Hunted in Murder and Robbery Case," was the headline on the front page of the *Minneapolis Journal*, June 30, 1936. "Police sought a giant Negro today to compare his fingerprints with those of the rifled purse of Clement Vizenor, 26 years old, found slain yesterday with his head nearly cut off by an eight-inch throat slash," the newspaper reported.

"Vizenor, an interior decorator living at 320 Tenth Street South, had been beaten and killed in an alley. . . . He was the second member of his family to die under mysterious circumstances within a month. His brother, Truman Vizenor, 649 Seventeenth Avenue Northeast, was found in the Mississippi River, June 1, after he had fallen from a railroad bridge and struck his head.

"Yesterday's slashing victim, who was part Indian, had been employed by John Hartung, a decorator. One pocket had been ripped out of the slain man's trousers. His purse lay empty beside him. Marks in the alley showed his body had been dragged several feet from the alley alongside a building."

My father and his brothers worked for the same contractor as house painters and paper hangers. The reputation of their excellent work would favor my own contracts as a painter in the summers as a college student. The police investigation and report contained not much more information than was published in the newspapers. I learned to love my father later, of course, at a heartsick distance. He was twenty-six years old at the time of his death. I was the very same age when I first read about his death in the newspapers, and in the same month that he was murdered. That coincidence is a measure of his presence. He was my father then in his stories. I am his father now in my stories. Twice, since then, my father has spoken clearly to me in dreams. His presence is unnamable.

The *Minneapolis Journal* reported that the arrest of a "Negro in Chicago promised to give Minneapolis police a valuable clue to the murder of Clement Vizenor, 26-year-old half-breed Indian, who was stabbed to death in an alley near Washington Avenue and Fourth Street early June 27. Vizenor's slaying was unsolved."

The murder of my father was never solved by the police, and no motives were ever established. Racial violence was mentioned in most of the newspaper stories, but there was no evidence in the records or investigations that race was a critical factor in the crime. There was no evidence of resistance, no struggle. He had not been robbed, in spite of the newspaper stories, and the police never established a motive for the murder. My father was a gambler, a cardplayer, and he could have been a victim of organized crime, as there were more than thirty homicides, and several were unsolved, that year in Minneapolis.

The picture of my father published with the newspaper stories was severed from a snapshot that shows him holding me in his arms. This is the last and only photograph, taken a few weeks before his death, that shows us together. Clement wore a dark fedora and a suit coat. His smile is natural, and his wide right hand is on my shoulder. I must have been teased to smile for the camera. We are outside, my hands are covered, coat is buttoned. Spring, no snow, but nature is not obvious in the picture. The tenement in the background is our home; we lived with my grandmother. Closer, a heap of used bricks, some stacked under the windows. My memory of that moment is unnamable. My grandmother held the camera, the last pose of her son, my father.

The *Minneapolis Journal* reported later that the police had "arrested a half-breed Indian in a beer parlor near Seventh Avenue South and Tenth Street and are holding him without charge for questioning in connection with the slaying, early Sunday, of Clement Vizenor. . . . The man who, according to police, was drunk, was picked up after making statements that indicated he might know who Vizenor's assailant was. He is alleged to have claimed knowledge of who Vizenor's friends were, and of many of the murdered man's recent activities. . . . The murder was blamed by police upon any one of a growing number of drunken toughs roaming the Gateway district almost nightly, armed with knives and razors. The killing of Vizenor climaxes a series of violent assaults upon Gateway pedestrians in recent weeks by robbers who either slugged or slashed their victims."

In another newspaper story the police "sought the husband of a former New York showgirl for questioning in connection with the knife murder of Clement Vizenor. . . . The man sought is believed to be the same who left with Vizenor from a cafe at 400 Tenth Street South about five hours before the murder. Alice Finkenhagen, waitress at the Tenth Street Cafe, gave police a good description of the man who called Vizenor to come outside. Detectives partially identified the showgirl's husband as that man. Also, they learned this man had resented Vizenor's attentions to his showgirl wife.

"Vizenor was called from the cafe at about 12:30 a.m. Sunday. Later he appeared at his home, then left again. His body was found at 5:30 a.m., his throat slashed, in an alley near Washington and Fifth avenues south. Police also were holding three half-breed Indians for questioning in the case. Vizenor was a half-breed."

The murder story continued that a "former New York showgirl and her husband were released by Minneapolis police Thursday after questioning failed to implicate them as suspects in the knife murder. . . . Police learned that Vizenor's attentions to the showgirl had been resented by her husband. But that difference was amicably settled long ago, detectives found out." None of this, of course, even had much to do with real suspects or police investigations. These stories doubtless were based on obscure sources of reportage that would show how active the police had been in solving crimes. Showgirls, giant Negroes, and halfbreeds as dubious suspects, and the later tease of a jealous husband, cuckolded by a native from the reservation, are simulations of a homicide that received minimal attention and investigation by the police.

The *Minneapolis Journal* reported that "Captain Paradeau said he was convinced Clement had been murdered but that robbery was not the motive. The slain youth was reported to have been mild tempered and not in the habit of picking fights. Police learned he had no debts, and, as far as they could ascertain, no enemies." In other words, the police had closed the case, another unsolved homicide.

Minneapolis police officials allowed me to review the complete records of their investigation. I was, that summer, the same age as my father when he was murdered. There was some resistance by the police, of course, some concern that my intentions were not personal but political. The police must be defensive about homicides that were never solved. A thin folder was recovered from the archives. Inside, the chief of detectives was surprised to discover that his name was on the report. He remembered that he was the first officer called to investigate the crime. The coincidence seemed to please him for a moment, as he explained that he was a new police officer then. His mood turned

when he defended his trivial report. "We never spent much time on winos and derelicts in those days. . . . Who knows, one Indian vagrant kills another."

"Clement Vizenor is my father."

"Look kid, that was a long time ago," he said and then looked at his watch. "Take it on the chin, you know what I mean?" I certainly did know what he meant. Homicide investigations are political, and notice of my father, a descendant of the crane and native newcomer from the reservation, was minimal in the city. That detective could have been the same man who told my mother to move out of town, and, as she told me later, "forget forever what happened." She tried to forget, and in so doing, left me with my grandmother in the tenement.

*

The *Minneapolis Journal* ended and the *Minneapolis Star and Tribune* hired me as a delivery boy with a route on the north side of the city. I delivered the morning, evening, and Sunday newspapers to more than a hundred houses in the neighborhood.

The *Minneapolis Tribune*, a daily morning newspaper, hired me, some twenty years later, as a general assignment staff writer. That chance was not so unusual as many journalists have eclectic experiences; mine could have been more uncertain than other new reporters. I am a descendant of the crane, a high school dropout, a seasoned house painter, and had been a university graduate student in Asian area studies. I was the only journalist, at that time, who had once delivered with distinction the same newspaper that would bear his name and date line as staff writer.

I had served honorably in the military as an entertainment director in Japan. My first job as a college graduate was as a social worker in the state reformatory, and then, for several years, I was an advocate in native communities on the urban reservation in Minneapolis. I was dedicated, organized, and angry enough to demand substantive changes in education, medical care, criminal justice, and federal services to natives in the city.

Surely, few other staff writers were hired because they had accused the executive editor, advertisers, and owners of the newspaper of racism and elitism. I did just that, and never mentioned once the "halfbreed" and "giant Negro" reports on the murder of my father. There was no need to at the time because the morning newspaper was never without cultural, racial, and gender distractions in advertisements and stories. I had been invited to address a conference of publishers and editors held at the university; the session was on racism and cultural stereotypes in newspapers and magazines. My presentation to the editors was passionate, unstudied, and accusative. I roared a few times, as a missionary might have done, but with secular intensities, that their editorials were cultural curses and moral crimes; that the editors maintained the treasons of cultural dominance in their newspapers. Moreover, native communities were denied a distinctive presence in news and feature stories; natives were the *other* in most reports, separated and mastered, in most instances, by anthropological discoveries and "scientific" evidence. I demanded that the "editors be tried for crimes against humanity." The editors sat in silence at the end of my lecture. Later, outside the auditorium, the executive editor of the *Minneapolis Tribune* introduced himself and handed me his business card. "I want to talk with you, call me," he said and turned away. His invitation was not significant to me at the time. He sent a reporter to find me, to summon me to meet at the newspaper. I had been working on the capital punishment case of Thomas White Hawk in South Dakota.

Bower Hawthorne was direct about his invitation; he wanted me to become an editorial writer for the *Minneapolis Tribune.* I was an advocate, to be sure, but editorials were not in my measure of experiences. I could write, but not editorials; so, instead of the exposition pose, we agreed that I should start as a general assignment staff writer and then, later, consider writing for the editorial page.

The stories:

Frank Premack, the curious city editor at the *Minneapolis Tribune,* assigned me a desk and typewriter in an enormous newsroom on Monday, June 3, 1968. He was a wild man with a keen sense of news, and he tormented me to write better stories about natives. I would pay, more than once, the price of my lecture to the editors at the university. He soon told me

that the second coming of Jesus Christ was worth no more than a page and a half, "so, let that be your guide in writing news stories."

Robert Kennedy died of gunshot wounds in Los Angeles on June 6, 1968. Sirhan Sirhan was indicted the next day for murder. Premack ordered me to write a feature news story that the nation was *not,* in essence, violent. My first assignment, three days into my career as journalist, was an extreme view at the time. James Earl Ray had been arrested about the same time for the murder of Martin Luther King, Jr.

My first story was published on the front page of the feature section on Sunday, June 9, 1968. The story was based on research and an interview with Luther Gerlach, who was then a professor of anthropology at the University of Minnesota. He argued that violence grew not only from a sense of powerlessness but out of a need to achieve political power. He declared that acts of assassination were not evidence that the nation was inherently violent. The potential for violence, he pointed out, may be built into the traditional structures of the society. "The problem is how to deal with the reality that violence produces power," said Gerlach. "We cannot simply classify the movement, the quest for power, as a collection of civil disorders and law enforcement problems." He asserted that "we are involved in a revolution," and that we cannot be "bought off" with federal grants or welfare payments "simply to expunge guilt feelings as a substitute for action."

Premack told me to cover the funeral of Dane Michael White in Sisseton, South Dakota. I was on assignment in northern Minnesota at the time, and drove most of the night. I arrived at dawn, attended the funeral, two family receptions, and then telephoned my story to the city desk that afternoon. I stayed there for more than a week to continue my investigation of the cruel and unusual circumstances that caused this young man to take his own life.

The American Indian Movement, too often the faux prosecutors ready to prey on coincidence and headlines, accused the county sheriff of racism and other crimes. The accusations, as usual, were insurgent, fetishist, and wieldy. I had already learned that the good sheriff and his wife were very troubled that a juvenile was detained as a criminal in their jail. The sheriff was bound by a court order, and yet the couple reached out, as best they could, to be parental and protective.

American literature conference, University of Erlangen, Germany, 1992:
(from left) Luci Tapahonso, Andrew Holleran, Gerald Vizenor, and John Williams

Dane White was lonesome, separated from his grandmother, and brave, as his crime was no more than truancy. He must have heard the voice of the evil gambler, but he had not yet learned how to play to native chance; instead he lost the paternal game of harsh lessons and court time. Dane was not put behind bars to win, he was there to be sure he lost. I wish he had heard native trickster stories that last night, but he was alone. He might have waited to outbrave the evil gambler at the bearable end of his own stories.

"Kin, Friends Attend Rites for Young Indian" was the headline on the front page the following morning, November 21, 1968. Sisseton was the dateline and my story was concise. "Catholic funeral services for Dane White were held here Wednesday in English and in the Dakota language at Saint Catherine's Indian Mission Church. Following the service, attended by seventy-five people, all but six of whom were Dakota Indians, Dane was buried here in Saint Peter's Catholic Cemetery.

"Born in Sisseton thirteen years ago, he took his own life Sunday in the Wilkin County Jail, Breckenridge, Minnesota, where he had been held since October 7, awaiting a juvenile court hearing.

"The Reverend William Keohane conducted the service. Two hymns were sung in the Dakota language. 'Dane is here, in the background of the banquet table. Lord, remember Dane in your Kingdom,' Father Keohane said in prayer, pointing to the large picture of the Last Supper behind the altar of the small Indian church.

"Six of Dane's school friends carried his gray metal coffin from the church. Fifteen cars formed the procession to the cemetery on the edge of town. Following the service at the grave, the six young Indian pallbearers removed their honoring ribbons and placed them on the coffin. A cold Dakota wind blew across the slope of Saint Peter's cemetery. The six pallbearers were the last to leave the grave."

I completed several more articles that week about the suicide, the families, the court delays, and expressions of concern that were too late. Later, I wrote a critical narrative on what had not been said in my stories published in the *Minneapolis Tribune.* Dane White had entered my heart; he is an unnamable presence.

Dane White was separated by two cultures and stranded between families in both life and death. His natural parents were divorced and both had remarried. Divorced parents and separate families attended separate functions following the requiem mass and burial.

Dane's father, Cyrus White, lived in Browns Valley, Minnesota, at the time. Burdell Arnell, the boy's mother, moved to Chicago, Illinois, leaving the children with their father. Marian Starr, the maternal grandmother, lived in Long Hollow, seven miles west of Sisseton, and it was there, in the old house near an abandoned church on the worn rim of the town, that Dane seemed to be the most comfortable. There in the generous nurturance of his native grandmother the police officers found the truant child and returned him to his father and stepmother across the border to Minnesota.

Cyrus, who was born near Enemy Swim Lake, north of Waubay, South Dakota, worked as an auto mechanic in Montana before he married his second wife, a divorcée with five children, and settled in Browns Valley. Eleven children, ten from two previous marriages and a new infant, shared the space in a neat, clean, rented frame house. The father entertained relatives and visitors in the kitchen at a large marbled Formica table. The windows were dressed with print curtains, pinched in perfect pleats over the white windowsills.

Marian Starr sat in a large wooden chair, the cushion was torn at the seams, near the space heater. "Dane liked it out here." She smiled at the first memories of her grandson, but then there was a distance in her face. "He was happy, laughing, joking around with the other boys." Stiff small trousers, worn by her other grandchildren, moved in slow motion on the clothesline over the stove. Cracked and worn linoleum covered the floor, but it was too short to reach the end of the room. Two of the three wooden chairs in the room, turned toward the stove, were backless. Behind the stove there was a cardboard box filled with pieces of plaster, pieces of a puzzle that had dropped from the ceiling lath during the night.

Grandmother Starr seldom traveled, but she was ever in motion. The world and her grand-children came to her with their dreams, adventures, and humor, to the native memories and nurturance of the old house. She carried a sense of native humor and could have been my grandmother; there, in that worn house the world seemed to make sense, and with no pretensions. Dane was there, outback in the shadows; blue clouds carried his native bones unnamed in the distance.

Dane White was locked in the Wilkin County Jail in Breckenridge on October 7, 1968. The day before Herb Mundt, the Roberts county sheriff in South Dakota, found Dane with his native grandmother in Long Hollow. He held the child overnight as a truant fugitive. That sheriff seemed to rule the border as he abused native rights. Arliss Schmitz, the good sheriff of Traverse County in Minnesota, transported Dane from Sisseton to Breckenridge because he had been charged with truancy and running away from the home of his father to the home of his grandmother. For that he was held in jail for forty-one days without a juvenile court hearing.

I interviewed both sheriffs and the father and examined school and juvenile court records in an effort to discover who was responsible for the heartless decision to isolate a child in jail. A foster home placement may not have been satisfactory, but his choice to live with his maternal grandmother had been denied because she lived in a "substandard" house that was located across the state border. Dane was cornered by the very policies that were initiated to protect children from abuse.

Sheriff Mundt was asked "to pick him up and give him a good scare," said the father, Cyrus White. He leaned over the kitchen table on his bare elbows. "Dane was never in school," he explained. "The kids teased him, calling him dumb and stupid. Sheriff Schmitz said he wanted to take Dane to Breckenridge and decide from there what to do with him." Cyrus could have ordered his son released at any time, but he waited for the court to act.

Mundt announced that "Cyrus came in here and said he wanted me to pick him up" from his grandmother's house in Long Hollow. He racked his boots one over the other on his desk. Mundt seemed to be a man who was never uncertain about his authority. The train of his eyes was memorable, a gaze that was seldom overlooked in his border county. The sheriff heard the reasons, that native warriors were overcome, their traditions and motion a burden; some natives, on the other hand, endured the ruin of market economies, but not providence on the prairie.

Dane was in jail a month when the court appointed an attorney to represent the interests of the child. The attorney was familiar with court procedures; nonetheless, five hearings were scheduled and then postponed for one reason or another.

"I wanted a foster placement immediately to get the boy out of jail," said the attorney. "I had been told that placing Dane with his grandmother, Marian Starr, had already been decided." There is no record that the attorney appointed by the court ever visited his client or grandmother; rather, the attorney postponed the next scheduled hearing to prepare for the case. Sadly, the father, the attorney, and the court took too much time to ever be pardoned for their insouciance. My native grandmother never tolerated such abasement of children.

Dane White, meanwhile, was alone, a truant child treated as a criminal, with the horror of the evil gambler at night and no humor of trickster survivance. He wrote the word "love" on the back of his belt, and "born to lose" on his tennis shoes. He was thirteen when he buckled his wide belt around his neck and hanged himself from a shower rod in the jail. I weep for him now. He was brave, and so young to lose his stories.

The Minnesota attorney general read my stories and ordered an investigation of the suicide. "Dane saw no one on any regular basis," the report indicated, "other than the Wilkin county sheriff and his wife, who delivered meals to the boy's cell." Dane shared the cell block with two other boys for four days, but the rest of the time he was alone, in isolation. "Dane was visited by members of his family twice, once for less than an hour by his father and once by his stepmother for about half an hour." The report concluded that "without a more exhaustive study of how juveniles are treated . . . it is impossible to say conclusively that this excessively long jailing was because Dane was an Indian."

With his granddaughter, Emma Dale Vizenor, Oakland, California, 1993

Minnesota Senator Walter Mondale, then the acting chairman of the Subcommittee on Indian Education, after the death of Robert Kennedy, attributed the suicide of Dane White and other young natives to an "identity crisis" resulting from education experiences "depicting the Indian as pagan savages. . . . Indians find themselves alienated from their own culture."

Senator Mondale invited me to travel with him on a tour of federal boarding schools in Arizona and New Mexico. He compared federal schools to the very first school administered by natives, the Rough Rock Navajo Demonstration School. At Tuba City the children marched past the window in neat columns; their hair was tossed by the wind, but nothing else seemed spontaneous. The principal said, "These children aren't as unhappy as people say they are . . . they're only lonely for about a month."

Two weeks later, during a session of the Subcommittee on Indian Education, Mondale told the commissioner of Indian Affairs what he saw and felt at Tuba City and Rough Rock. "It was the difference between a semi-military setting and a setting which was the kind that one would want to educate his own children in. . . ." The Tuba City dormitories were "cold, really humaneless structures for these children." At Rough Rock, a native community school, parents "live with the children so that they had a friend, a supporter, counselor and adult, just like every child needs at that age." More than that, and "in an indefinable way, I saw a spirit and pride and excitement of people who realized for the first time they had something to say about their own lives."

The prisoners:

Alice Beaulieu Vizenor was abandoned by her husband after sixteen years of marriage and seven children. Henry Vizenor, my native grandfather, married Margaret Porter and moved to Chicago. Alice endured many heartaches on the reservation, and even more later. When she heard the wicked backbiters, and the rumors of the evil gambler, she leased her government land allotments to a timber company and moved with the children to Detroit Lakes, a small town south of the White Earth Reservation. Later, the family moved to a tenement in downtown Minneapolis.

Detroit Lakes was not much better for the survivance of the children than the reservation or the city. Maybe it was worse. Jeek and Bunny, two of her sons, my uncles, were nicked by racial abasement and sentenced to the same reformatory that hired me as a social worker about thirty years later. I first learned about this coincidence in the course of my duties at the institution. Understandably, the family never mentioned that my uncles had served time in the reformatory.

The Detroit Lakes District Court records indicate that Joseph Henry Vizenor, born July 24, 1906, "then and there being at said time and place, did willfully, wrongful, unlawfully, and feloniously carnally know and abuse one Ona Peck." Jeek, my uncle, was sentenced to "hard labor" for one year because he had sex with the woman he loved. Ona was white, seventeen years old, and she loved Jeek, who was reservation born, attended school to the sixth grade, and wanted to be a baker.

Truman Paul Vizenor was convicted of grand larceny about the same time. He had stolen candy and cigarettes worth about sixty dollars from a store near Detroit Lakes. Bunny was twenty years old, three years younger than Jeek. They were sentenced about the same time, for one year, and worked as trustees at the farm outside the walls of the institution. Alice wrote to the warden, "Please do something to get Truman out for he knows his mistake and I know he has learned a good lesson and will be not so full of mischief as before. Some boyfriend would happen along to coax him to go with him and he'd come back not the same Bunny at all and my heart would just sink." She continued to the warden, "So it's the use of intoxicants that turns the mind into false doings like one in a dream. Just like an insane man does things which land him in the insane asylum. Their body follows their crazy mind what another crazy mind suggests." Truman and my father died in the same month in Minneapolis.

My grandmother brought Timmy, the family mongrel, along on one visit to the reformatory. Naturally, the mongrel was left behind with the boys on the farm. Timmy was actually hidden in the barn that first night to avoid the guards, but the warden was soon informed about the dog.

"Dear Madam," the warden wrote to my grandmother, "our day turnkey informs me that upon your recent visit to this institution that you lost a dog belonging to your son. The dog has been found and is here. . . . You may have him by calling here."

Alice wrote back to the warden that her boys loved their dog and that she would soon return to the reformatory. Naturally, my grandmother managed to leave the dog behind each time she visited her sons. Timmy, meanwhile, had become the mascot of the inmates at the institution. When my uncles were released at the end of the year the dog stayed behind at the farm, the first canine trustee at the reformatory. Several years later the warden wrote to my grandmother, to inform her, with regret, that Timmy had died a natural death and had been buried at the institution.

I was behind those same bars thirty years later at the Minnesota State Reformatory at Saint Cloud. In 1961, a few months after my graduation from the University of Minnesota, the state hired me as a social worker and corrections agent at the institution. The reformatory was not my first choice, but there were only two positions open in social services at the time. I was fortunate to have a job, and later to discover the coincidence that my uncles had been there as inmates. I studied their records in the archives and discovered letters, generous entreaties about her sons, written by my grandmother to the warden. There were also letters in the file from my father to his brothers, and notations on visitors. Once more the coincidence of an unnamable presence.

The warden learned that two of my relatives were convicted felons and had served time in the institution. He decided that my family history was a moral and legal issue and, in no uncertain terms, asked me to resign my position to avoid the embarrassment of an investigation. There was no chance that a persecutional warden would use my uncles to nick me with the same racialism thirty years later. My promise of a lawsuit, and a news release on the matter, seemed to resolve his concerns.

I was the first in our families of the crane to earn a college degree, and there, in the warden's protected sanctuary, my new sense of racial and cultural tolerance was no more secure than when my uncles were sentenced to the reformatory. The manners of the warden were captious, and his spurious sanctuary yet another prison. Thirty years ago my grandmother touched the warden with the stories of a mongrel, the best she could do at the time with native cultures and other measures of civilization.

The associate warden, who was responsible for custody, endorsed me without hesitation. His manner was persuasive, as he had been at the reformatory for more than thirty years and told stories about my uncles that gave me a good name. "I remember your uncles, they worked at the farm, good boys, hard workers, they always had a laugh on being here." He had been hired as a guard in the same year that my uncles were sentenced and remembered the mascot Timmy. "That dog's buried here, outside the wall," he said. "The name's gone but the wooden marker's still there." My grandmother might have had a good laugh over that coincidence. Our family is traced to the reformatory, you could say, as inmates, visitors, and, most recently, as a social worker.

The fosterage:

That old man with the clean forehead, with a frown deep and white, never was a soldier. Otherwise he might have died once more in the war, a hero to women and children, but he was disabled, an unseen warrior deformed by poliomyelitis, and he was wasted by alcohol at the bar. He used that one shriveled arm and hand to beat his biological son. That man was my first foster father.

I lived with my native grandmother for about two years after the death of my father, and then, my mother *claimed* me, only to place me in several informal foster homes. The tenement with my native grandmother, aunts, and uncles, was crowded and warm, a tricky bond of humor, nicknames, and the tease of stories. Most of the foster homes were crowded too, some with children my age, but the humor was strained and there was namable violence.

One foster father, the lame warrior, would crash daily into the back door; once inside, he accused his biological son of various urchin crimes and beat him with that wizened arm. He beat his son more and more as other men went to war. My foster father became more sullen, abusive, violent, because he could not serve his country in the Second World War. The enemy became his children. I was the unready witness, not the intended victim of corporal punishment. My fosterage was for the

The author (left) with A. Robert Lee, editor of Shadow Distance: A Gerald Vizenor Reader,
University of California, Berkeley, 1994

money, not the nature of parental love, salvation, or moral restoration.

About twenty years later my foster brother, the one who was beaten as the enemy, was convicted of a felony and sentenced to the reformatory. I became his social worker at the time; a chance encounter, or coincidence of my fosterage, because new cases were assigned to several social workers at random. The warden would have been thrice worried had he learned that one more relative was on my caseload; two uncles, and then a foster brother. I had not seen him since the war, but we were both aware that we had met somewhere. The namable violence of my last foster home became yet another coincidence at the reformatory.

There were no common associations in his personal record but he was convinced that we had met. We reviewed schools, military service, reservations but found no familiar intersections or connections in our lives. At last, we reached back into childhood and our miseries, his father, and my fosterage. Slowly, in our remem-

brance that day in the reformatory, we decided that he was a victim of a family war. My fosterage was for the money, a curious neutrality.

The fortunes:

Chester Anderson, a professor of literature, invited me to contribute an autobiographical essay to *Growing Up in Minnesota*, a collection that he edited for the University of Minnesota Press. I said no at first, but he persuaded me to write in any style that pleased me. I could not, at that time, twenty years ago, imagine myself as the narrative voice of my own stories. "I Know What You Mean, Erdupps MacChurbbs" was the title of my essay in the collection. MacChurbbs is the name of a trickster in my childhood memories and stories. I wrote, with limited omniscience, thirteen short narratives about selected events in my life. I described, for instance, my mother's unusual response to my inquiries about how she met my father, a newcomer from the reservation. I thought she might say at least something about natives. Instead, she said, "The first time I saw your father he looked like George Raft, not the gangster but the dancer. He was handsome and he had nerve." Nerve, or survivance, in my stories was notable and memorable, native or not, during the Great Depression.

I continued my style of selected memoirs, the author as one of the characters, in *Interior Landscapes: Autobiographical Myths and Metaphors.* For that book, however, my attention to time and other details demanded extensive research to place my family in a historical or institutional context. My father's murder, the reformatory, military service, a typhoon, for instance, had to be critical, literary, and accurate histories. I created the mode of *autocriticism* to comment on earlier essays, the author's critique of his own autobiographical stories. I wrote that the best autobiographies are imaginative histories, a remembrance past the barriers, and wild pastimes over the common pronouns in "Crows Written on the Poplars: Autocritical Autobiographies," published in *I Tell You Now*, edited by Brian Swann and Arnold Krupat.

"My memories and interior landscapes are untamed. The back stoop of that tavern where I fed the squirrels, while my grandfather drank in the dark, breaks into the exotic travels of Lafcadio Hearn," I wrote in *Interior Landscapes.* "Tribal women in sueded shoes and blonded hair mince in my memories over the thresholds into the translated novels of Kawabata Yasunari, and Dazai Osamu."

My grandmother was in her sixties when she married a blind man twenty years younger because he told her she "*looked*" beautiful." Now, out there in my remembrance, perched in the paper birch, with bears, crows about, and a moist wind, their adventures in the suburbs to sell brooms and brushes overturn the wisdom of common families and histories. The blind man and his native stunner were there to entertain lonesome women in pastel row houses, the new suburban healers, and no one bought a broom from the blind man.

The haiku envoy:

The United States Steamship *Sturgis,* with more than three thousand soldiers on board, was bound for the port at Inchon, South Korea.

Peace negotiations were down and there were no indications that the war would end before we docked. We were the soldiers of counterpoise, the most recent warriors of democracies. The *Sturgis,* however, was anchored in Tokyo Bay, because a hospital ship was held in the last berth at Inchon.

We were, as usual, told to wait for instructions. Thousands of soldiers were mustered at dawn and dusk; about three hundred names were called each day from the top of the alphabet for flights to Korea. The slow muster to combat was unbearable and became more worrisome the closer my name came to the war list; then, near the end of the T's in the alphabet, there were no more musters. We waited and silence turned rumors into paradise. One week later, by chance once more, the soldiers with names at the end of the alphabet boarded a train for Hokkaido, the northern island of Japan.

The names at the lower end of the alphabet, about two hundred soldiers, were assigned to the Seventieth Tank Battalion, First Cavalry Division, a celebrated unit that had been decimated a few months earlier in Korea. My honorable discharge, after close to three years of service, was dated August 31, 1955. I bought a used car, a new suit, three shirts, and a winter coat with my military savings and drove east to visit friends. I was an army veteran with two volumes of pictures to show my stories as a tank driver, theater director, survivor of a typhoon, and at home with the bears in the Imperial National Forest on Hokkaido. My friends convinced me to attend the first day of classes with them. I was curious, twenty, and, by chance, a university student at the end of the day.

Look Homeward Angel, and other novels by Thomas Wolfe, encouraged me to become a writer. His narratives, unions of impressionism and the real, moved me as traces of the unnamable. I first read *A Stone, A Leaf, A Door,* at a military library, a "stone, a leaf, an unfound door; of a stone, a leaf, a door." Coincidentally, his former faculty office was occupied at the time by Eda Lou Walton, my first teacher of writing at New York University.

Thomas Wolfe should be read on a train, as his enthusiasm for trains was unbounded; his prose was a landscape on a parlor car, an interior rush and double vision on the train windows. "Few buildings are vast enough to hold the sound of time, and now it seemed to him that there was a superb fitness in the fact that the one which held it better than all others should be a railroad station. For here, as nowhere else on earth, men were brought together for a moment at the beginning or end of their innumerable journeys," he wrote in *A Stone, A Leaf, A Door.*

I have published more than twenty books in the forty years since then, including narrative histories, an autobiography, and five novels. My first books were collections of haiku poems, and my most memorable haiku teacher was Edward Copeland at the University of Minnesota. He started a literature course that summer with haiku in translation. That sense of impermanence is in the weather, he said, the seasons, and in haiku; at the same time, we must be aware of culture and tradition.

Copeland translated, in class, a haiku poem by Basho: *furuike ya,* the ancient pond; *kawazu tobikomu,* frog leaps, or jumps; *mizu no oto,* sound of water, or splash. He invited us to consider the direct show of the season, the subtleties of tradition, motion, and impermanence. Copeland paused over the lines, a natural sense of literary motion, as a poem would score, and then he continued with the seasons.

The Plains Book Bus, loaded with books published by small presses, scheduled poetry readings in rural towns. The bus was funded by various foundations and was a great success in several states. I was honored to read, or say, some of my haiku poems in Ellsworth, Wisconsin.

Main Street was the start that afternoon as we looked for an audience. A television crew was there to record the event; later, my show in a restaurant became part of the film *A Nest of Singing Birds.* I approached a man who was delivering the local newspaper and asked him if he thought it would be all right for me to read poems out loud in the town.

"I wouldn't do that," he said in a gentle tone of voice, truly concerned about what might happen to me, and my poems. He seemed concerned and watched me, not at a critical distance, but in a sense to warn me, to protect me.

"Why not?"

"Well, not poems."

"How about at the Coast to Coast store?"

"No, not there," he insisted.

"Why not?"

"They might think you were queer."

"But my poems are short."

"I like your poems," he said.

"But you haven't heard them."

"I like you."

"Join me for pie and coffee, and we can try my poems out in the restaurant down the street." The television crew was at our sides. The delivery man was warm and curious as we walked, and then very cautious as we entered the small restaurant in the center of town.

The owners, an older couple, gave the crew permission to film me at the counter in their restaurant. They were friendly but did not want to be part of the film. I ordered strawberry pie and asked the owner's daughter to listen to my short haiku poem and then respond with "whatever comes to your mind." Sound levels were tested, lights were focused, the camera was ready. I said one of my best haiku poems over the counter.

fat green flies
square dance across the grapefruit
honor your partner

I said the haiku twice and the owner's daughter listened to each word, and with each word a hesitant smile moved across her face. She turned to her parents for some assurance, raised her shoulders, and then she said, "Well, that's not what we do with flies around here, mister." That scene was part of a public television production.

Donald Keene observed in *Japanese Literature* that a "really good poem, and this is especially true of haiku, must be completed by the reader. It is for this reason that many of their poems seem curiously passive to us, for the writer does not specify the truth taught him by an experience, nor even in what way it affected him. . . ." What haiku poems have sought, he continued, "is to create with a few words, usually with a few sharp images, the outline of a work whose details must be supplied by the reader, as in a Japanese painting a few strokes of the brush must suggest the world."

I drove back to the city later that night. The moon was bright, and the shadows named me in natural motion at the side of the rural roads. I was alone and thought about the haiku poems that had first moved me in Japan. The haiku that ascribe the seasons with shadow words, the sources of creation and a sense of pres-

Gerald Vizenor, in Georgetown, Guyana, 1993

ence. Later, these same traces seemed so natural to me in the translations of native stories and songs. "The sky loves to hear me sing" is a heartened invitation to the dreams songs of the Anishinaabe. I remembered, on the road that night, other translations at the turn of the last century by Frances Densmore.

> *as my eyes*
> *look across the prairie*
> *I feel the summer*
> *in the spring*

Matsuo Basho was born near Ueno in Iga Province. He wrote his first poems when he was eighteen years old, but his best haiku and haibun, or travel poems, were composed during the last ten years of his life. He wrote about the common experiences of the world in a serious manner. Basho created his haibun at the same time that my native ancestors encountered the colonists and their diseases.

Basho visited Matsushima and wrote his haibun diaries about the moon over the pine islands, the treasures of the nation. I was there three hundred years later, touched by the same moon, and the master haiku poet. "Much praise has already been lavished upon the wonders of the islands of Matsushima," wrote Basho in *The Narrow Road to the Deep North*, translated by Nobuyuki Yuasa. "Yet if further praise is possible, I would like to say that here is the most beautiful spot in the whole country of Japan."

My haiku poems are read in the four seasons. There are three attributes of my style, and my haiku trace a sense of nature and presence in my novels and other narratives. The haiku in my first three books, *Raising the Moon Vines*, *Seventeen Chirps*, and *Empty Swings*, were common comparative experiences of nature, created in the past tense. Later, in *Matsushima: Pine Islands*, my haiku images were more metaphorical, concise, and with a sense of presence.

> *wooden bucket*
> *frozen under the rain spout*
> *springs a leak*

> *march moon*
> *shimmers down the sidewalk*
> *snail crossing*

> *hail stones*
> *sound once or twice a summer*
> *old school bell*

> *bold nasturtiums*
> *dress the barbed wire fences*
> *down to the wild sea*

The third attribute in the style of my haiku widens the sentiment and manner of the poem with an envoy, a prose concentration and discourse on the images and sensations. This practice combines my experience in haiku with natural reason in native literature. Native dream songs and haiku are heard as a natural presence. For instance, the haiku poems that follow have an envoy, or a comment on the touch and motion of haiku, and the natural reach of native survivance. The envoy is a narrative trace of the shadows in the haiku, that unnamable presence.

> *calm in the storm*
> *master basho soaks his feet*
> *water striders*

The striders listen to the wind, the creation of sound that is heard and seen in the motion of water; the wind teases the tension and natural balance on the surface of the world. The same wind that moves the spiders teases the poet who tries to soak his feet like a water strider.

> *those stubborn flies*
> *square dance across the grapefruit*
> *honor your partner*

Fat green flies dance on the back of spoons, turn twice, and reach for the pink grapefruit. The flies allemande left and right in a great breakfast dance, but the owners of the spoons in the restaurant would terminate the insects to save the grapefruit, and without a serious thought otherwise. We are the lonesome dancers over the remains of so many natural partners in the world.

BIBLIOGRAPHY

Poetry:

Born in the Wind, privately printed, 1960.

The Old Park Sleepers, Obercraft, 1961.

Two Wings the Butterfly (haiku), privately printed, 1962.

South of the Painted Stone, Obercraft, 1963.

Raising the Moon Vines (haiku), Callimachus, 1964.

Seventeen Chirps (haiku), Nodin, 1967.

Empty Swings (haiku), Nodin, 1967.

(Contributor) Kenneth Rosen, editor, *Voices of the Rainbow,* Viking, 1975.

Matsushima: Pine Islands (haiku), Nodin, 1984.

Novels:

Darkness in Saint Louis Bearheart, Truck Press, 1973.

Griever: An American Monkey King in China, Fiction Collective, 1987.

The Heirs of Columbus, Wesleyan University Press, 1992.

Dead Voices: Natural Agonies in the New World, University of Oklahoma Press, 1992.

Contributor:

Chester Anderson, editor, *Growing Up in Minnesota* (autobiographical stories), University of Minnesota Press, 1976.

Jan Katz, editor, *This Song Remembers* (autobiographical stories), Houghton, 1980.

Earth Power Coming, edited by Simon Ortiz, Navajo Community College Press, 1983.

The New Native American Novel, University of New Mexico Press, 1986.

The American Indian and Problems of History, edited by Calvin Martin, Oxford University Press, 1987.

From Different Shores: Perspectives on Race and Ethnicity in America, edited by Ronald Takaki, Oxford University Press, 1987.

I Tell You Now: Autobiographical Essays by Native Americans, edited by Arnold Krupat, University of Nebraska Press, 1987.

Harper's Anthology of 20th Century Native American Poetry, edited by Duane Niatum, Harper, 1988.

The Illuminated History of the Future, edited by Curtis White, Illinois Sate University and Fiction Collective Two, 1989.

A Gathering of Flowers, edited by Joyce Carol Thomas, Harper, 1990.

American Indian Literature, edited by Alan Velie, University of Oklahoma Press, 1991.

The Interrupted Life, Museum of Contemporary Art, 1991.

The Lightning Within, edited by Alan Velie, University of Oklahoma Press, 1991.

Native American Testimony, edited by Peter Nabokov, Viking Penguin, 1991.

Talking Leaves: Contemporary American Short Stories, edited by Craig Lesley, Laurel Paperback/Dell, 1991.

The Before Columbus Foundation Fiction Anthology, W. W. Norton, 1992.

Partial Recall: Photographs of Native American North Americans, edited by Lucy Lippar, New Press, 1992.

Without Discovery, edited by Ray Gonzales, Broken Moon Press, 1992.

Inheriting the Land, edited by Mark Vinz and Thom Tammaro, University of Minnesota Press, 1993.

Sacred Trusts: Essays on Stewardship and Responsibility, edited by Michael Katakis, Mercury House, 1993.

Harper American Literature, edited by Donald McQuade, HarperCollins, 1994.

An Other Tongue, edited by Alfred Arteaga, Duke University Press, 1994.

(And editor) *Native American Literature* (anthology), HarperCollins College Publishers, 1995.

Other:

(Editor) *Escorts to White Earth, 1868–1968: 100 Year Reservation,* Four Winds, 1968.

Thomas James White Hawk, Four Winds, 1968.

The Everlasting Sky, Crowell, 1972.

Anishinabe Adisokan: Stories of the Ojibwa, Nodin, 1974.

Anishinabe Nagomon: Songs of the Ojibwa, Nodin, 1974.

Tribal Scenes and Ceremonies (editorial articles), Nodin, 1976.

Wordarrows: Indians and Whites in the New Fur Trade (stories), University of Minnesota Press, 1978.

Summer in the Spring, Ojibwa Songs and Stories, Nodin, 1981, new edition, University of Oklahoma Press, 1993.

Earthdivers: Tribal Narratives on Mixed Descent (stories), University of Minnesota Press, 1984.

The People Named the Chippewa: Narrative Histories, University of Minnesota Press, 1984.

Crossbloods: Bone Courts, Bingo, and Other Reports (essays), University of Minnesota Press, 1990.

Interior Landscapes: Autobiographical Myths and Metaphors, University of Minnesota Press, 1990.

Landfill Meditations (short stories), Wesleyan University Press, 1991.

Manifest Manners: Postindian Warriors of Survivance (essays), Wesleyan University Press, 1994.

Shadow Distance: A Gerald Vizenor Reader (selected fiction and essays), edited by A. Robert Lee, Wesleyan University Press, 1994.

Work is represented in numerous anthologies. Contributor of poems, short stories, and essays to magazines, including *American Indian Quarterly, Caliban, Chelsea Hotel, Chicago Review, Exposure, Fiction International, Genre, Halcyon, Indian Youth of America, Japan Times Weekly, Native American Literature, Native Peoples, Neeuropa, Northeast Indian Quarterly, Notes from Native California, Oshkaabewis Native Journal, Tamaqua, Wicazo Sa Review,* and *World Literature Today.*

Tobias Wolff

1945-

EDITOR'S NOTE: The following passages are excerpted from Tobias Wolff's memoir *In Pharaoh's Army: Memories of the Lost War*. Some of the references raise questions that are answered in the book as a whole, which we recommend to those interested in Mr. Wolff's life, along with an earlier volume, *This Boy's Life*. By presenting these sections, the author means to give an impression of a young writer's formation through his experiences of war, family life, and personal struggle, and his growing commitment to the art of fiction, which he represents here as a clarifying, restorative vocation.

Tobias Wolff, 1989

Command Presence

When I was eighteen I worked on a ship, a Coast and Geodetic Survey ship out of Norfolk. As I sat on my bunk one night, reading a book, I became aware that one of my shipmates was staring at me. My face burned, the words started swimming on the page, the tranquillity in which I had been imagining the scenes of the novel was broken. For a time I blindly regarded the book and listened to the voices of the other men, the long shuddering surge of the engine. Finally I had no choice but to look back at him.

He was one of the ship's mechanics. He had rabbity eyes and red hair cropped so close his scalp showed through. His skin was white. Not fair. White, the pallor of a life spent belowdecks. He hardly ever spoke. I had felt the weight of his scrutiny before, but never like this. I saw that he hated me.

Why did he hate me? He may have felt—I might have made him feel—that I was a tourist here, that my life would not be defined, as his had been, by years of hard labor at sea relieved now and then by a few days of stone drunkenness in the bars of Norfolk and Newport News. I'd been down to the engine room on errands and maybe he'd seen me there and seen the fastidiousness that overcame me in this dim, clanking, fetid basement where half-naked men with greasy faces loomed from the shadows, shouting and brandishing wrenches. He might have noted my distaste and taken it as an affront. Maybe my looks rubbed him wrong, or my manner of speech, or my habitual clowning and wising off, as if we were all out here on a lark. I was cheerful to a fault, no denying that; glib, breezy, heedless of the fact that for most of the men this cramped inglorious raft was the end of the line. It could have been that. Or it could have been the book I was reading, the escape the book represented at that moment and in time to come. Then again there might have been no particular reason for what he felt about me. Hatred sustains itself very well without benefit of cause.

279

Not knowing what to think of him, I thought nothing at all. I lived in a dream anyway, in which I featured then as a young Melville, my bleary alcoholic shipmates as bold, vivid characters with interesting histories they would one day lay bare to me. Most of what I looked at I didn't really see, and this mechanic was part of what I didn't see.

I worked on cleanup details in the morning, scraped and painted in the afternoon. One day I was scraping down the hull of a white runabout that was kept on davits for the captain's pleasure and as a partial, insincere fulfillment of our lifeboat requirement. It was sultry. The sun beat down through a white haze that dazzled the eyes. I ducked under the boat and pretended to take an interest in the condition of the keel. It was cool there in the shadows. I leaned back, my head resting against one of the propeller blades, and closed my eyes.

I slept for a while. When I woke I felt heavy and dull, but I couldn't go back to sleep. In this muzzy state I heard someone stop beside me, then walk to the stern. I opened my eyes and saw a pair of bell-bottom pant legs ascending the ladder. Boards creaked overhead. My nap was done.

I sat up and shook my head, waited for clarity, was still sitting there when a great roar went up behind me. I looked back and saw the propeller I'd just had my head on spinning in a silver blur. I scuttled out from under the boat, got to my feet, and looked up at the mechanic, who was watching me from the gunwale of the runabout. Neither of us said a word. I knew I should go after him, even if it meant taking a beating. But he was ready to kill me. This was a new consideration, and one that gave me pause, excessive pause. I stood there and let him face me down until he decided to turn away.

I didn't know what to do. He'd given me no evidence for a complaint to the captain. If I accused him, the mechanic would say it was an accident, and then the captain would ask me what the hell I was doing down there anyway, lying against a propeller. It was pretty stupid. That's what my shipmates told me, the two of them I trusted enough to talk things over with. But they believed me, they said, and promised to keep an eye on him. This sounded good, at first. Then I understood that it meant nothing. He would choose the time and place, not them. I was on my own.

The ship put in a few days later to take on supplies for a trip to the Azores. The weekend before our departure, I went to Virginia Beach with another man and ended up on the first dark hours of Monday morning propped against the seawall, trying to make myself get up and walk the half mile to the motel where my shipmate was waiting for me. In an hour or so he'd have to begin the drive back to Norfolk or risk having the ship weigh anchor without him. I sat there in the chilly blow, trembling with cold and sunburn, and hugged my knees and waited for the sun to rise. Everything was cloaked in uncongenial grayness, not only the sky but also the water and the beach, where gulls walked to and fro with their heads pulled down between their wings. A band of red light appeared on the horizon.

This was not the unfolding of any plan. I'd never intended to miss my ship, not once, not for a moment. It was the first cruise to foreign waters since I'd been on board, and I wanted to go. In the Azores, according to a book I'd read, they still harpooned whales from open boats. I had already made up my mind to get in on one of these hunts, no matter what. All my shipmates had the bug, even the old tars who should've known better. When they said "Azores" their voices cradled the word. They were still subject to magic, still able at the sound of a name—*Recife, Dakar, Marseilles*—to see themselves not as galley slaves but as adventurers to whom the world was longing to offer itself up.

I didn't want to miss my ship. Forget about far-off places, the open sea; the ship was my job, and I had no prospects for another. I didn't even have a high school diploma. The prep school I'd finagled my way into had tolerated my lousy grades and fatuous contempt for its rules until, in my senior year, having pissed away my second and third and fourth chances, I was stripped of my scholarship and launched upon the tide of affairs, to sink or swim. I appeared to be sinking.

Where to turn? My mother lived in one small room in Washington, D.C., where she worked as a secretary by day, by night as a restaurant hostess. She had just begun to accord me, with touching eagerness, the signs of respect due a man who pulled his own weight in the world. Unteachable optimist that she was, she drew hope from every glint of gravity in my nature, every possibility of dealing with me as an equal. I didn't want to think about the look on her face when I turned up at her door with some tomfool story about the ship sailing without me. Where else, then? My brother Geoffrey and I were good friends. He might have been open to a visit except that he was in England, doing graduate work at Cambridge on a Fulbright fellowship. His good luck; my bad luck. My father was also unable to play host at just this moment, being in jail in California, this time for passing bad checks under the name Sam Colt.

I had to join my ship. But I stayed where I was. People with dogs began to appear on the beach. Old folks collecting driftwood. When there was no longer any chance of meeting my shipmate I got up stiffly and walked into town, where I ate a jumbo breakfast and pondered the army recruiting office across the street.

This wasn't a new idea, the army. I'd always known I would wear the uniform. It was essential to my idea of legitimacy. The men I'd respected when I was growing up had all served, and most of the writers I looked up to—Norman Mailer, Irwin Shaw, James Jones, Erich Maria Remarque, and of course Hemingway, to whom I turned for guidance in all things. Military service was not an incidental part of their histories; they were unimaginable apart from it. I wanted to be a writer myself, had described myself as one to anybody who would listen since I was sixteen. It was laughable for a boy my age to call himself a writer on the evidence of two stories in a school lit mag, but improbable as this self-conception was, it nevertheless changed my way of looking at the world. The life around me began at last to take on form, to signify. No longer a powerless confusion of desires, I was now a protagonist, the hero of a novel to which I endlessly added from the stories I dreamed and saw everywhere. The problem was, I began to see stories even where I shouldn't, where what was required of me was simple fellow feeling. I turned into a predator, and one of the things I became predatory about was experience. I fetishized it, collected it, kept strict inventory. It seemed to me the radical source of authority in the writers whose company I wanted to join, in spite of their own coy deference to the ugly stepsisters' honesty, knowledge, human sympathy, historical consciousness, and, ugliest of all, hard work. They were just being polite. Expe-

rience was the clapper in the bell, the money in the bank, and of all experiences the most bankable was military service.

I had another reason for considering this move. I wanted to be respectable, to take my place one day among respectable men. Partly this was out of appetite for the things respectable men enjoyed, things even the dimmest of my prep school classmates could look forward to as a matter of course. But that wasn't all of it, or even most of it. My father's career, such as it was—his unflinching devolution from ace airplane designer to welsher, grifter, convict—appalled me. I had no sense of humor about it. Nor, for all my bohemian posturing, did it occur to me to see him as some kind of hero or saint of defiance against bourgeois proprieties. He had ruined his good name, which happened to be my name as well. When people asked me about my father I sometimes told them he was dead. In saying this I did not feel altogether a liar. To be dishonored and at the end of your possibilities—was that life? He appalled me and frightened me, because I saw in myself the same tendencies that had brought him to grief.

The last time I'd lived with my father was the summer of my fifteenth year, before I went back east to school. We were taking a walk one night and stopped to admire a sports car in a used car lot. As if it were his sovereign right, my father reached inside and popped the hood open and began to explain the workings of the engine, which was similar to that of the Abarth-Allemagne he was then driving (unpaid for, never to be paid for). As he spoke he took a knife from his pocket and cut the gas line on either side of the filter, which he shook out and wrapped in a handkerchief, talking all the while. It was exactly the kind of thing I would have done, but I hated seeing him do it, as I hated seeing him lie about his past and bilk storekeepers and take advantage of his friends. He had crooked ways, the same kind I had, but after that summer I tried to change. I didn't want to be like him. I wanted to be a man of honor.

Honor. The very word had a martial ring. My father had never served, though he sometimes claimed he had, and this incompleteness in his history somehow made his fate intelligible and offered a means to escape it myself. This was the way, the indisputable certificate of citizenship and probity.

But I didn't join up that morning. Instead I went to Washington to bid my mother farewell, and let her persuade me to have another try at school, with results so dismal that in the end she personally escorted me to the recruiter.

I never made it to the Azores, and even now the word raises a faint sensation of longing and regret. But I was right not to go back to my ship that morning. So many things can happen at sea. You can go overboard at night. Something heavy can fall on you, or something sharp. You can have your hat size reduced by a propeller. A ship is a dangerous place at any time; but when one of your shipmates wishes you harm, then harm is certain to befall you. In that way a ship is like a trapeze act, or a family, or a company of soldiers.

I went through basic training at Fort Jackson, South Carolina, during a heat wave, "the worst on record," we kept telling one another, on no authority but our opinion that it was pretty damned hot. And it was. The asphalt streets liquefied, sucking at our boots, burning our eyes and throats with acrid fumes. Sweat gleamed on every face. When they packed us into Quonset huts for lectures on "homoseshality" and "drug addition," the smell got serious enough to put a man down, and many went down. Passing out came to be so common among us that we awarded points for the drama of the fall. The big winner was a boy from Puerto Rico who keeled over while marching, in full field equipment, along a ledge on a steep hillside. We heard him clanking all the way down.

The drill sergeants affected not to be aware of the rate at which we dropped. They let us understand that taking notice of the temperature was unsoldierly. When a recruit in another company died of heatstroke, our company commander called a formation and told us to be sure and take our salt pills every day. After he'd given his speech and gone back to the orderly room, our drill sergeant said, "Shitbirds, why did that troop croak?"

We had the answer ready. "Because he was a pussy, Sergeant." We were mostly volunteers. A lot of men regretted the impulse that had brought them to Fort Jackson, and all of us whined unceasingly, but I never heard of anyone writing to his congressman about the treatment we got, which was pretty much what a boy brought up on war movies would expect, and maybe a little better. The drill sergeants rode us hard, but they didn't show up drunk at midnight and lead us into swamps to drown. The training seemed more or less purposeful, most of the time. The food was decent. And there were pleasures to be had. One of my pleasures was to learn that I was hardy and capable. I'd played team sports in school, and played them doggedly, but never very well. Military training agreed with me. My body was right for it—trim and stringy. Guys who would have pulverized me on the football field were still on their third push-up when I'd finished my tenth. The same bruisers had trouble on our runs and suffered operatically on the horizontal bar, where we had to do pull-ups before every meal. Their beefy bodies, all bulked up for bumping and bashing, swayed like carcasses under their white-knuckled hands. Their necks turned red, their arms quivered, they grunted piteously as they tried to raise their chins to the bar. They managed to pull themselves up once or twice and then just hung there, sweating and swearing. Now and then they kicked feebly. Their pants slipped down, exposing pimply white butts. Those of us who'd already done our pull-ups gathered around to watch them, under the pretense of boosting their morale ("Come on, Moose! You can do it! One more, Moose! One more for the platoon!") but really to enjoy their misery, and perhaps to reflect, as I did, on the sometimes perfect justice turned out by fortune's wheel.

Instead of growing weaker through the long days I felt myself taking on strength. Part of this strength came from contempt for weakness. Before now I'd always felt sorry for people who had trouble making the grade. But here a soft heart was an insupportable luxury, and I learned that lesson in smart time.

We had a boy named Sands in our squad, one of several recruits from rural Georgia. He had a keen, determined look about him that he used to good advantage for a couple of weeks, but it wasn't enough to get him by. He was always lagging behind somewhere. Last to get up. Last to formation. Last to finish eating. Our drill sergeant wasn't from Brooklyn, and he came down hard on this cracker who didn't take his army seriously.

Sands seemed not to care. He was genial and sunny even in the face of hostility, which I took to be a sign of grit. I liked him and tried to help. When he fell out on runs I hung back with him a few times to carry his rifle and urge him on. But I began to realize that he wasn't really trying to keep up. When a man is on his last legs you can hear it in the tearing hoarseness of every breath. It's there in his rolling eyes, in his spastically jerking hands, in the way he keeps himself going by falling forward and making his feet hurry to stay under him. But Sands grinned at me and wagged his head comically: *Jeez Louise, where's the fire?* He wasn't in pain. He was coasting. It came as a surprise to me that Sands would let someone else pull his weight before he was all used up.

There were others like him. I learned to spot them, and to stay clear of them, and finally to mark my progress by their humiliations. It was a satisfaction that took some getting used to, because I was soft and because it contradicted my values, or what I'd thought my values to be. Every man my brother: that was the idea, if you could call it an idea. It was more a kind of attitude that I'd picked up, without struggle or decision, from the movies I saw, the books I read. I'd paid nothing for it and didn't know what it cost.

It cost too much. If every man was my brother we'd have to hold our lovefest some other time. I let go of that notion, and the harshness that took its place gave me a certain power. I was recognized as having "command presence"—arrogance, an erect posture, a loud, barky voice. They gave me an armband with sergeant's stripes and put me in charge of the other recruits in my platoon. It was like being a trusty.

I began to think I could do anything. At the end of boot camp I volunteered for the airborne. They trained me as a radio operator, then sent me on to jump school at Fort Benning, Georgia. When I arrived, my company was marched onto the parade ground in a cold rain and drilled and dropped for push-ups over the course of the evening until we were covered with mud and hardly able to stand, at which time they sent us back inside and ordered us to be ready for inspection in thirty minutes. We thought we were, but they didn't agree. They dumped our footlockers onto the floor, knocked our wall lockers down, tore up our bunks, and ordered us outside again for another motivational seminar. This went on all night. Toward morning, wet, filthy, weaving on my feet as two drill sergeants took turns yelling in my face, I looked across the platoon bay at the morose rank of men waiting their

"Mr. Wizard"—guessing ages and weights, Seattle World's Fair, 1962

ration of abuse, and saw in one mud-caked face a sudden lunatic flash of teeth. The guy was grinning. At me. In complicity, as if he knew me, had always known me, and knew exactly how to throw the switch that turned the most miserable luck, the worst degradations and prospects, into my choicest amusements. Like this endless night, this insane, ghastly scene. Wonderful! A scream! I grinned back at him. We were friends before we ever knew each other's names.

His name was Hugh Pierce. He was from Philadelphia. It turned out that we'd gone to rival prep schools. To come across anyone from that life here was strange enough, but I didn't give the coincidence much thought. We hardly ever talked about our histories. What had happened to us up to then seemed beside the point. Histories were what we'd joined the army to have.

For three weeks the drill sergeants harried us like wolves, alert to any sign of weakness. Men started dropping out. Hugh loved it. The more fantastic the oppressions, the greater his delight. He couldn't stop himself from grinning his wiggy grin, bouncing on the balls of his feet as he waited for the next absurdity. Whenever the drill sergeants caught him smiling they swarmed all over him, shouted dire threats directly into his ears, made him do push-ups while they sat on his back. Nothing got to him. His pleasure in the ridiculous amounted almost to a pathology. And they couldn't wear him down, he was too strong for that—immensely strong, and restless in his strength. Unlike me, Hugh made a habit of helping men who dropped back on our runs, mostly out of generosity, but also because to him exertion was joy. He liked making it harder for himself, pushing the limits however he could. At night, when the last drill instructor had exacted the last push-up and pronounced the last insult, we fell into our bunks and made wisecracks until sleep got us. But for me the joke was wearing a little thin. By now I was mainly trying to keep up.

In the last week we jumped. We jumped every day. For hours each morning we waited on the tarmac, running in place, doing push-ups and equipment checks while the drill sergeants went through all the possibilities of getting lunched. They dwelt in loving detail on the consequence to our tender persons of even the slightest accident or mistake. Did anyone want to reconsider? Just step to the side. Always, some did. Then we boarded the planes, facing one another across the aisle until the green light came on and the jumpmaster gave the order to stand and hook up our static lines. To psych ourselves for the plunge we sang "My Girl" in falsetto and danced the Stroll, swinging our shoulders and hips, flapping our wrists feyly as we made our way down the cargo bay to the open door of the plane. The planes were C-130 turboprops. The prop blast was tremendous, and you jumped right into it. It caught you and shot you back feetfirst spinning like a bullet. You could see the earth and sky whirling around your boots like painted sections on a top. Then the chute snapped open and stopped you cold, driving your nuts into your belly if you didn't have the harness set right, snatching you hard even if you did. The pain was welcome, considering the alternative. It was life itself grabbing hold of you. You couldn't help but laugh—some of us howled. The harness creaked as you swung back and forth under the luminous white dome of the silk. Other chutes bloomed in the distance. The air was full of men, most quiet, some yelling and working their risers to keep from banging into each other. The world was laid out at your feet: checkered fields, shining streams and ponds, cute little houses. For a time you belonged to the air, weightless and free; then the earth took you back. You could feel it happen. One moment you were floating, the next you were falling—not a pleasant change. The ground, abstractly picturesque from on high, got hard-looking and particular. There were trees, boulders, power lines. It seemed personal, even vengeful, the way these things rushed up at you. If you were lucky you landed in the drop zone and made a good rolling fall, then quick-released your parachute before it could drag you and break your neck. As you gathered in the silk you looked up and watched the next stick of troopers make the leap, and the sight was so mysterious and beautiful it was impossible not to feel love for this life. It seemed, at such a moment, the only possible life, and these men the only possible friends.

In our last week of jump school Hugh and I signed up for the Special Forces and were sent on to Fort Bragg.

The Special Forces came out of the OSS teams of World War II. They'd worked in German-occupied territory, leading partisan brigades, blowing bridges and roads, killing enemy officers. The membership was international. When I came to Fort Bragg some of the old hands were still around: Czechs, Poles, Ukrainians, Brits, Hungarians. We also had a number of Germans who had signed on after the war, more attached to the uniformed life than to any homeland.

This accented remnant gave a legionary feeling to the unit, but most of the troops were young and American. They were also tough and smart, and savvy in a way that I began to understand I was not. I could keep up with them physically, but I didn't get the hang of things as easily as they did—as if they'd been born knowing how to lay a mortar, blow a bridge, bushwhack through blind undergrowth without ever losing their sense of where they were. Though I could do a fair impersonation of a man who knew his stuff, the act wouldn't hold up forever. One problem was that I didn't quite believe in it myself.

There was no single thing I had trouble with, no skill I couldn't eventually learn. I simply ceased to inhabit my pose. I was at a distance, watching this outrageous fraud play the invisible bushman, the adept with knives, the black-faced assassin willing at the drop of a hat to squeeze the life out of some total stranger with piano wire. And in that widening distance between the performance and the observation of the performance, there grew, subtly at first, then intrusively, disbelief and corrosive irony. It was a crisis, but I hardly recognized its seriousness until one achingly pure spring day at the sawdust pit where we practiced hand-to-hand combat.

We were on a smoke break. I lay on my back, staring up at the sky. Our two instructors were sitting behind me on the wall of sandbags that surrounded the pit. One of them had just received orders for Vietnam and was saying he wouldn't go back, not this time. He'd already done two six-month tours, and that, he said, was enough. The other sergeant murmured commiseration and said he could protest the orders but it probably wouldn't do any good. He didn't seem at all surprised by this show of reluctance, or even falsely sympathetic. He sounded troubled. I'm not going, the sergeant with the orders kept saying. I'm not going.

Both of them were dull the rest of the session. They just went through the motions.

This set me thinking. Here you had a man who knew all the tricks and knew them well enough to teach them to others. He'd been there twice and been competent enough to get home. Yet he was afraid. He was afraid and didn't bother to hide it from another man who'd been there, certain it wouldn't be held against him. What sort of knowledge did they share, to have reached this understanding?

And if this sergeant, who was the real thing, had reason to be afraid, what about me? What would happen when my accounts came due and I had to be in truth the wily, nerveless killer I pretended to be? It was not my habit to meditate on this question. It came to me unbidden, breaking through the bluff imitation of adequacy I tried so hard to believe in.

I never unloaded my worries on Hugh. I didn't hide them, but when we were out on a tear they ceased to trouble me. We patrolled Fayetteville on our nights off and spent the weekends cruising farther afield in Hugh's Pontiac, to Myrtle Beach and Chapel Hill and down to Fort Gordon, Georgia, where his brother was stationed. Yak, yak, yak, all the way. Girls. The peculiarities of our brothers-in-arms. Books—

at least I talked about books. And of course the future. We had big plans. After we got out of the army we were going to get all our friends together and throw the party of the century. We were going to buy motorcycles and bazooka through Europe. We were going to live. It's been almost thirty years now and the words are mostly gone, but I remember the ecstatic rush of them, and the laughter. I could make Hugh laugh pretty much at will. It was a sight: crimson circles appeared on his high cheeks, his eyes brightened with tears, he wheezed for breath. He could do the same thing to me. We were agreed that the world was a comical place, and that we'd been put here for the sacred purpose of being entertained by it.

And we sang; how we sang. Hugh had uncanny rhythm. He could do scat. He could imitate a bass, a muted trumpet. He had a good voice but preferred to sing harmony and backup while I took the lead. We did old Mills Brothers songs, the Ink Spots, Sinatra. A couple of the girls we went out with were always after us for "The Best Is Yet to Come." That was our big gun. I laid down the melody while Hugh did crazy riffs around it, shoulders jumping, eyes agleam, head weaving like a cobra's. We might have been pretty good. Then again, maybe we weren't.

This was 1965. The air force had started bombing North Vietnam in February. The marines were in Danang, and the army had forty-four combat battalions on the way. Plenty of guys we knew were packing up for the trip. Hugh and I were going too, no question about that, but we never talked about the war. I can guess now that the reckless hilarity of our time together owed something to our forebodings, but I didn't suspect that at the time. Neither of us acknowledged being afraid, not to each other. What good would that do? We had chosen this life. My reasons were personal rather than patriotic, but I had consented to be made use of, and in spite of my fears it never occurred to me, nor I'm sure to Hugh, that we would be used stupidly or carelessly or for unworthy ends. Our trust was simple, immaculate, heartbreaking.

That fall Hugh got sent for medic's training to Fort Sam Houston in Texas. I was at loose ends and bored. My company commander had been working on me to apply for Officer Candidate School, and I finally agreed. I took some tests and went before a panel of generals and colonels who took note of my command presence and pronounced me officer material. They told me I'd be on my way in a month or so.

While I was awaiting my orders I got a letter from one of the girls Hugh had gone out with. Her name was Yancy. She said she was pregnant and that Hugh was the father. She knew he'd left Fort Bragg but didn't know where to find him, and asked me to send her his address and let him know the situation. I got this letter on a Saturday afternoon. The building was empty. I sat on my bunk and tried to think what to do. Yancy was the friend of a girl named Trace I'd gone out with. The two of them roomed together, tending bar and living it up on terms as hedonistic as ours, or so it seemed to me. I hadn't seen either of them since Hugh left, and I didn't know what to make of this. Was I honestly supposed to believe that Hugh was the only man Yancy had been close to during the time in question? I supposed it was just possible. But what would Hugh think if I gave her his address, or if I sent him the message she wanted me to send? Would he think I was meddling, taking her side? Judging him? I understood that the strongest friendship can be spoiled by a word, a tone, even an imagined tone.

Why had she written me, anyway? It didn't matter where he was, if she'd addressed the letter to Hugh it would have been forwarded. Maybe she didn't know his last name. Did he not want her to know?

I put the letter away. I would consider it, then come to a decision. But I never could decide. The standard by which Hugh and I tried to live was loyalty, and I'd always thought it was a good one. In the face of the Other we closed ranks. That worked fine when the Other was a bullying sergeant or a bunch of mouthy drunks, but it didn't shed much light here, where she was a girl in trouble. I could sense the insufficiency of the code but had no stomach for breaking it, at the risk of betraying Hugh. In the end I did nothing. I let other matters claim my attention.

My orders came. Instead of sending me to the infantry school at Fort Benning, they assigned me to artillery Officer Candidate School at Fort Sill, Oklahoma. I felt both guilty and relieved. Since the Special Forces had no howitzers they could not reasonably send me back

At Fort Bragg, North Carolina, 1965

there. My logic was impeccable, but six months later, with twenty years of life under my belt and new gold bars on my shoulders, I opened my orders and saw that I was going right back where I started, to Fort Bragg and the Special Forces.

My position was absurd. While laboring to become an artilleryman I had acquired a body of skills now utterly useless to me—trigonometry! calculus!—and lost or grown clumsy in those I needed. It was going to be hard for the troops at Fort Bragg to take me seriously as an officer when some of them had known me not long before as an enlisted man, and as something of a fuck-up. I couldn't even take myself seriously. In my OCS class I'd finished forty-ninth out of forty-nine, the class goat—like Custer, as no one lost a chance to tell me.

It wasn't as disgraceful as it looked. There'd been one hundred twenty of us to start with. But it was still pretty bad. I barely passed the gunnery course, and then only by pulling all-nighters in the latrine. I was chronically late and unkempt. My jocose manner amused only a few of my classmates and none of my training officers, who in their reports labeled me "extraneous" and "magic"—not a compliment in those circles—and never failed to include me in the weekly Jark, an hours-long punishment run in full field equipment, which was so effective in producing misery that people used to line the streets to watch us stumble past, as they would have gathered to watch a hanging. Some bystanders were actually moved to pity by the sight of us, and slipped us candy bars and words of encouragement. The true Christians among them threw water on our heads.

In the end I finished OCS only because, mainly to amuse myself, I had written a number of satirical songs and sketches for our battery to perform on graduation night. These revues, in the style of Hasty Pudding or the Princeton Triangle, were a tradition at Fort Sill and a big headache to our training officers, whose talents did not lie in this direction. Along with hundreds of other visitors, the post commandant and his staff would be in attendance. There'd be hell to pay if the show was a flop. When the time came for the final cuts to be made in our class it was discovered that I was the only one who could put the whole thing together.

They kept me on to produce a farce. That was how I became an officer in the United States Army.

One by one Hugh and my other buddies disappeared into the war. I kept waiting for my own orders. At last I did get orders, but instead of Vietnam they sent me to the Defense Language Institute in Washington, D.C., to study Vietnamese for a year. Most of the students were young Foreign Service officers. So I wouldn't stick out too much, I was detached from the army and put on civilian status. I could live where I wanted to live. I reported to no one, and no one checked up on me. My only duty was to learn Vietnamese. On top of my regular salary I got per diem for food, housing, and civilian clothes. Before leaving Fort Bragg I was issued a pamphlet showing in detail the kind of mufti an officer should wear on different occasions, from clambakes to weddings. Each "Correct" picture was paired with an "Incorrect" picture—goateed beatniks in shades and sandals, hipsters in zoot suits, doughy proles

in bermudas and black socks. The correct guys always wore dark blue suits except when they were doing their morning run.

It wasn't a hardship post. My mother still lived in Washington and so did my brother, Geoffrey, and his wife, Priscilla. I had some good friends in town as well, guys I'd known from school days and kept in touch with during my leaves home. Laudie Greenway, in town for a last fling before joining the army himself. George Crile, studying at Georgetown and working as a stringer for Drew Pearson. Bill Treanor, about to open the first home in Washington for runaway kids. We threw in together and rented a house not far from Dupont Circle. Our landlady was Jeane Dixon, the newspaper sibyl who'd become famous by predicting the deaths of President Kennedy and Dag Hammarskjöld. She collected the rent in person, but not from me. As soon as her car pulled up I went running out the back door before she had a chance to see me and start prophesying. In all the time I lived there I never once let her lay eyes on me.

I bought a Volkswagen and took girls to Wolf Trap and the Cellar Door. I smoked dope. I began a novel, which, somewhat to my surprise, I managed to work on in a fairly disciplined way. I fell in love.

Her name was Vera. She was related by marriage to a Russian prince, and had grown up among expatriate Russians and come to think of herself as one of them. She had their wounded gaiety, their air of romantic, genteel displacement, their manners and terms of address. Her grandfather she called Opa; her brother Gregory, Grisha. She hated to cook, but when she had no choice she made great borscht. She favored high boots and bright skirts and scarves such as a Russian princess might wear while at leisure among her beloved serfs, picking mushrooms or hunting bears or dancing to the balalaika. She drank like a man and ate like a wolf. I fell in love with her the first night I saw her and pursued her for weeks afterward. I loved her name, her odd swinging stride, her dark wit and mad laugh, her clothes, her pale skin and antique, heart-shaped face. She had a steady boyfriend but I kept after her anyway until finally she surprised us both by falling in love with me. Her best friend, the girl who'd introduced us, took me aside and told me I was in way over my head. I didn't know what she was talking about, but I began to learn.

She could be very funny, my Vera, but her humor was desperate and biting. She was obsessed by a single terrible truth, that everything and everyone you love will someday be taken from you. For Vera all other truths were frivolous; this was the one that mattered. Her father had been her closest friend. He had told her his secrets. They had conducted ESP experiments together—successfully, according to Vera. She had lost him suddenly, without any warning, when she was in her first year of boarding school, and the pain that came upon her then had never left her. She saw everything through it.

And as if it weren't enough by itself, this unhealing wound was endlessly abraded by anger, anger at the world for being a place where such a thing could happen. She wouldn't have said so herself, but her father's death left her feeling deserted. And because she was convinced that everyone else would desert her in the end, she was always looking for the first signs. Just about everything was a sign. A quizzical look, failure to agree, reference to experience not shared with her, private sorrow, old loyalties. Anything could qualify. And her rage at such betrayals was uncontainable.

We were driving across the Chesapeake Bay Bridge late one night. It was hot in the car, and I asked Vera to crack the window. She looked at me curiously. I asked her again. *What?* she said. *Crack the window?* Please, I said. She screamed *Here!* and struck the windshield with the heel of her hand. She did it again, and again, as hard as she could. *Here! Here!* I grabbed her wrist so she wouldn't hurt herself and asked what I'd done wrong. *You know,* she said. She stared ahead, hugging herself. Finally she declared she'd never in her life heard the expression "crack the window," and said further that I *knew* she'd never heard it. Why, she asked, did I like to mock her? Exactly what pleasure did it give me?

I thought it best not to answer, but my silence goaded her to fury, and the injured sound of her own voice served as proof that I had wronged her, that I was vicious, disloyal, unworthy, hateful. Vera was still going strong when we got to my place. She hadn't moved in with me yet; that opera had yet to open. My friends and I lived in a black neighborhood where people didn't observe the white protocol of seeming not to hear what was going on around them. I tried to hush Vera but she was in full cry, and before long our neighbors joined in, yelling at us from up and down the street. They were inspirational to Vera but not to me. I told her she had to go home, and when she refused I simply got out of my car and went inside.

It was well after midnight. My friends were in their rooms, gallantly pretending to be asleep. I opened a beer and carried it to the living room.

The first crash wasn't that loud. It sounded like someone had kicked over a garbage can. The second was louder. I went to the window and parted the blinds. Vera was backing down the street in her mother's old Mercedes. This was a blocky gray diesel made, no doubt, from melted-down panzers. Vera went about fifty feet, stopped, ground the gears, started up the street again and rammed my car head-on, caving in the hood. Her undercarriage got caught on my bumper as she pulled away. She couldn't move but kept trying anyhow, racing the engine, rending metal. Then she popped the clutch and the engine died.

"I'm going to kill you," I told her when I reached the street.

I must have looked like I meant it, because she locked her door and sat there without saying a word. I walked back and forth around my car, a yellow Volkswagen bug, the first car I'd ever owned. It was cherry when I bought it. An unusual word to use about a VW, but that's what the ad said: "Cherry, needs tires, runs good." Gospel, every word. It was a good car but a soft car, no match for the armor-plated Überauto now parked on its hood. Before landing there Vera had nailed the bug twice on the driver's side, caving in the door and breaking the window.

I kept circling it. As I walked I began to tote up the damage, translating it into words that offered some hope of amendment. *Crumpled fender. Dents on door panel.* A phrase came to mind that I tried to dismiss and forget, because the instant I thought of it I knew it would undo me. *Cracked window.* I sat down on the curb. Vera got out of her car. She walked over, sat beside me, leaned against my shoulder.

"You cracked the window," I said. "I'll think twice before I ask you to do that again." And we sat there laughing at my ruined car.

This sort of thing became routine, all in a day's work. At first I was able to see Vera's fits as aristocratic peculiarity, and even managed to believe that I could somehow deliver her from them and help her become as squared away as I was. After all, she looked as solid as a rock compared to her brother Grisha.

I never actually met Grisha. Just before I started going out with Vera he had quarreled with their mother over something so trivial she couldn't remember it afterward, except that she had said something about not liking the look on his face, whereupon Grisha declared that he wouldn't inflict his face on her or anyone else ever again, and locked himself in his room upstairs. He refused to come out except when there was no one to see him. Vera's mother left Grisha's meals on a tray outside his door and carried the dirty dishes away when he was done. The same with his laundry. That was the situation when I first visited the house. Vera's mother was a fond and patient woman who had long ago surrendered her authority in the family. She accepted this business with Grisha as she accepted everything her children did. Anyway, it couldn't go on much longer. Summer was almost over. Grisha had another year of school left, and he would have to leave the room once classes began.

That's what she thought, but Grisha thought otherwise. Just before Labor Day he left a note with his dirty dishes announcing that he planned to stay right where he was and get his diploma by correspondence.

He trusted his mother to arrange the details. She called a family council to discuss the question, and asked me to sit in. I was glad to do it. It was a sign of favor and I did my best to be worthy of it.

When she asked for my view I gave sound military advice, which was to lay siege to Grisha. Starve the brat out, I told her. She had to show him he wasn't the center of the universe.

When I finished I looked at Vera's mother and saw that I'd been wrong: Grisha *was* the center of the universe. She seemed embarrassed and a little amazed that I didn't know this. She thanked me and turned to Vera, then the talk turned serious. They reasoned together and after sober consideration reached their decision. Grisha could do anything he wanted to do.

Vera's mother signed him up for correspondence school and continued to minister to him. But one night Grisha opened his door just as she was picking up his dinner tray. For a breathless moment they were face-to-face. Then Grisha slammed the door and immediately took measures to ensure that no such accident ever happened again. He wrapped his head completely in gauze, leaving little holes for his mouth, eyes, ears, and nostrils. Once he was all covered up he became less reclusive. I could sometimes catch glimpses of him at the end of a hallway, or retreating up the stairs as I came in the front door. And once, after dropping Vera off in the early morning, I came across Grisha out for a walk. He flared up suddenly in my headlights, his bandage a white ball on his narrow shoulders. It wasn't at all funny. It was as if I were seeing not Grisha but some terrible future, the future of my fears.

I made up my mind to live with Vera's moods, as I wanted to think of them, even while they grew more outrageous. I tried to see them as evidence of a rich, passionate nature. What other girl had ever cared enough about me to destroy my car? She'd even threatened to shoot herself once, pulling a pistol out of a desk drawer as I was about to leave her house in the middle of a quarrel. It was pure theater, I understood that, but a small doubt remained, and a small doubt was too much for me, so I gave in and stayed. I nearly always gave in. This became part of the trouble between us. Once she got her way she despised me for letting her have it, and immediately started pushing again. She had to find that line I wouldn't cross, where my cussedness was equal to hers. On this ground we fought like sworn enemies. We held nothing back, and once we were exhausted, after we'd given and taken every hurt, we came together with a tenderness that lasted for days, until the next round began. It was a hard way to be in love, and not the way I'd hoped for, but it was our way.

To be out of the barracks and the uniform. To be young and in love, surrounded by friends, free in a great city. To have my own time, to read, to loaf, to see plays, to hit jazz bars with Geoffrey and stay up until dawn talking about books and writing—all this was to forget for hours, even days at a time, that I had a bill coming due. But I found reasons to remember.

This was late '66, early '67. The news kept getting worse. More troops going over, more getting killed, some of them boys I'd known. I was afraid of the war, but I had never questioned its necessity. Among the soldiers I'd served with that question didn't even get raised. We took the official explanations on faith and did not ask for details. Faith carried no weight in Washington. My brother and most of my friends believed that the war was an atrocious mistake and ridiculed the government's attempts to justify it. I argued with them, furiously at times, but I didn't have command of the subject and my ignorance got me in trouble, never more than when I locked horns with I. F. Stone one night at Geoffrey's house. With exquisite gentleness, Stone peeled my bluster like an onion until there was nothing left but silence.

I began to attend Professor Carroll Quigley's Vietnam lectures at Georgetown. I went to a teach-in, but left after the first couple of speakers. They were operating out of their own faith system; faith in the sanctity of Ho Chi Minh and his cause, faith in the perfidy of those who were unconvinced. Mostly I read: Bernard Fall, Jules Roy, Lucien Bodard, Graham Greene.

The Quiet American affected me disagreeably. I liked to think that good intentions had value. In this book good intentions accomplished nothing but harm. Cynicism and accommodation appeared, by comparison, almost virtuous. I didn't like that idea. It seemed decadent, like the opium-addicted narrator and the weary atmosphere of the novel. What really bothered me was Greene's portrayal of Pyle, the earnest, blundering American. I did not fail to hear certain tones of my own voice in his, and this was irritating, even insulting. Yet I read the book again, and again.

In time I lost whatever certitudes I'd had, but I didn't replace them with new ones. The war was something I had to get through. Where was the profit in developing convictions that would make it even harder? I dabbled in unauthorized ideas, and at the point where they began to demand a response from me I drew back, closed my mind as if it were a floodgate, as if I could control the influx of doubt. But I was already up to my neck in it.

My mother lived within walking distance. We had dinner together at least once a week. She liked making a fuss over me, and I liked letting her do it. One night I was sitting in her living room while she cooked up some spaghetti. Her husband, Frank, was out somewhere. She moved around the kitchen, humming along to the radio—101 Strings, Mantovani. Easy listening. The apartment was warm and smelled

good. She had filled it with mementos of her travels: Spanish dolls and Brazilian puppets, posters, goat-hair rugs, a camel saddle from Morocco, where she'd spent two weeks driving through the Atlas Mountains with a friend. I sat on the sofa with my legs crossed, drinking a beer and reading the newspaper. While I was in this state of contentment I saw Hugh Pierce's name among those of the dead.

It was no mistake. His name, rank, and unit were all there. I kept reading the words, and each time they floated farther away from my comprehension. I understood only one thing: This shouldn't have happened. It was wrong. I knew it at that moment as well as I know it now.

I called out to my mother. She came to the kitchen doorway and stood there looking at me. She was on guard, she knew something was up. I told her Hugh had been killed. I said it reproachfully, and my mother frowned and pushed her lips together like a girl who'd been scolded. Then she crossed the room and sat beside me and touched my wrist doubtfully. "Oh, Toby," she said.

I knew there was something I should do, but I didn't know what. I began to walk back and forth while my mother watched me. She told me to go on home if I wanted to be alone, we could have our dinner another time. But I discovered that I was hungry. Famished. I sat down and cleaned my plate and let my mother fill it again. I didn't talk and neither did she. Afterward I sat there and tried to form an intention. I couldn't think at all. I felt weightless. My hands were on the table as if I were about to push myself up decisively, but I stayed where I was. My mother looked on, stricken and afraid. For her sake I knew I had to get out of there. I said maybe I'd better go home after all.

I didn't remember Yancy's letter until late that night. I got out of bed and opened the top drawer of the dresser, where I kept my correspondence and receipts. I riffled through the pile. She had loopy, girlish handwriting, and she'd used a pencil. I could recognize the envelope at a glance and often did, with a pang, when I was looking for something else. I knew it was there, but I didn't come up with it the first time through, nor the second.

I slid the drawer out and put it on the floor and knelt beside it. One by one I lifted every letter, turned it over, set it aside. When the drawer was empty I still hadn't found it. I was close to panic. I sat back and imposed calm on myself. The letter had to be somewhere in the room.

Taking care not to hurry, I searched the other drawers. I looked under the dresser, then pulled it away from the wall and looked behind it. I emptied my duffel bag, went through the pockets of my civvies and even my uniforms. I ran my hands over the shelves in the closet. When I heard myself panting I sat on the edge of my bed and forced myself to think back to when I'd last seen the letter. I couldn't. I got up again, took stock. Quietly, so I wouldn't wake the house, I began to tear my room to pieces. I left no inch of it unexamined. Nothing. Yancy's letter was gone. Had I thrown it away? Could I have done that—just thrown it away?

I couldn't even remember her last name.

A few days later I thought of calling her friend, the girl I'd taken out, but the number had been disconnected and her name wasn't listed in the directory. I called the bar where they'd both worked. No one knew any girls named Trace or Yancy.

I don't know exactly what I would have done if I'd found Yancy. Given her the news, of course. Tried to find out if she'd had the baby. I wanted to ask her about the baby—lots of questions there. And I would have said I was sorry for sitting on her letter, because I was sorry, I am still sorry, God knows I am sorry.

Vera and I fought more riotously every week. She took offense at something during a party and hewed out great clumps of her hair with pinking shears. One night she climbed the tree outside my bedroom window with a rope around her neck and threatened to hang herself. The outlandishness of our quarrels isolated us, and made reconciliation harder. We had to keep upping the ante, promising more of ourselves, to put the last one behind. Just before I finished language school we got engaged.

And then my year of grace ended. At the end of it, scared, short-winded, forgetful of all martial skills and disciplines, I was promoted to first lieutenant and posted back to Fort Bragg to await orders. Just after I got there I was assigned to a training exercise being played out in the mountains of Pisgah National Forest. I didn't know any of the men whose temporary

commander I became; I was filling in for their regular team leader, who had other business to attend to. Our job was to parachute in and link up with another team and make a show of our expertise.

It was over a year since I'd been in the field. In that time I had done almost no exercise, nor had I worn a uniform, carried a rifle and pack, or given an order. I hadn't read a compass or used a map except on drives into the countryside. On the day before the drop I locked myself up with plenty of coffee and every field manual I could get my hands on, like a student boning up for a chemistry final.

We gathered on the airstrip well before dawn. I tagged along with the first sergeant while he made the equipment check, looking on as if I knew what he was doing. It was still dark when we boarded the plane. I sat with the others until we entered the forest, then I hooked up my parachute and stood in the open doorway, trying to follow our position on the map. There was light breaking on the tops of the hills but the land below was still in darkness and the map kept flapping in my hand. Our pilot was supposed to flash a green warning light when he saw the smoke marking the drop zone, but I knew better than to rely on him. We were moving fast. If out of distraction or malice he was even a little slow giving us the signal we could end up in impossible terrain, miles from the drop zone and the men we were supposed to meet.

We were flying up a long valley. The slopes were awash in light, the plain was turning gray. We passed a cluster of houses. I tried to find the village on the map; it was unmarked, or I was looking in the wrong place. In fact I had no idea where we were. As the valley began to narrow, the plane descended and slowed. This was the usual prelude to the jump, but the green light still hadn't come on. I braced myself in the doorway and looked out. Smoke was rising off the valley floor a mile or so ahead of us. Our smoke was supposed to be yellow, and this was black, but it was the only smoke out there. I turned to the first sergeant. His eyes were closed. I looked back out the door and confirmed what I'd seen. Smoke. But still no green light.

A decision was required. It was my duty to make it. I gave the order to hook up, and as the first man came to the door I smacked him on the rump like a quarterback breaking the huddle and shouted "Go!" Then the next man, and the next, until everyone was out but me, and then I jumped.

Sudden silence. Mountains all around. The eerie, lovely sight of the other canopies, the men swinging below. My men. I'd gotten them out in good order, and with no help from the pilot. If I could manage this, I could manage the next thing. That was the secret not to think ahead too much, not to rehearse every single step in advance. Just do what was needed as the need arose.

Then the man closest to the ground gave a shout and I looked down and saw him hauling like crazy on his risers, trying to change the path of his fall. The others started doing the same thing, and a moment later, when I got a good look at what lay below us, so did I.

We were not, as I had supposed, drifting down upon a field marked with signal grenades, but over the expanse of a vast garbage dump where random fires smoldered, sending greasy coils of smoke high into the air. I caught my first whiff a couple of hundred feet up and the smell got worse the closer I came. I pulled hard to the left, making for a patch of ground not yet covered with junk. I was lucky; being last out, I was fairly close to the edge. Almost everyone else landed in the soup. I watched them go down as I drifted to port, and listened to them bellow and swear, and heard the crunching sounds they made as they slammed into the dump.

We were several miles from the drop zone. To get there took us most of the day. No one spoke to me. It was as if I did not exist. We maintained this arrangement until our part in the exercise was over.

Two weeks later I was in Vietnam.

White Man

A week or so after Sergeant Benet and I made our Thanksgiving raid on Dong Tam, the division was ordered into the field. The plan called for our howitzers and men to be carried by helicopter to a position in the countryside. I was sent ahead with the security force responsible for preparing the ground and making sure it was safe to land. My job was to call in American gunships and medevacs if any were needed. I could even get F-14 Phantom jets if we ran into serious trouble, or trouble that I might consider serious, which would be any kind of trouble at all.

The designated position turned out to be a mudfield. We were ordered to secure another site some four or five kilometers away. Our march took us through a couple of deserted villages along a canal. This was a free-fire zone. The people who'd lived around here had been moved to a detention camp, and their home ground declared open to random shelling and bombing. Harassment and interdiction, it was called, H and I. The earth was churned up by artillery and pocked with huge, water-filled craters from B-52 strikes. Pieces of shrapnel, iridescent with heat scars, glittered underfoot. The dikes had been breached. The paddies were full of brackish water covered by green, undulant slime, broken here and there by clumps of saw grass. The silence was unnatural, expectant. It magnified the sound of our voices, the clank of mess kits and weapons, the rushing static of the radio. Our progress was not stealthy.

The villas were empty, the hooches in shreds, but you could see that people had been in the area. We kept coming across their garbage and cooking fires. Cooking fires—just like a Western. In the second village we found a white puppy. Someone had left him a heap of vegetable slops with some meat and bones mixed in. It looked rotten, but he seemed to be doing okay, the little chub. One of the soldiers tied a rope around his neck and brought him along.

Because the paddies were flooded and most of the dikes broken or collapsed, we had only a few possible routes of march, unless we moved off the trail; but mucking through the paddies was a drag, and our boys wouldn't dream of it. Though I knew better I didn't blame them. Instead we kept to what little remained of dry land, which meant a good chance of booby traps and maybe a sniper. There were several troops ahead of me in the column and I figured they'd either discover or get blown up by anything left on the trail, but the idea of a sniper had me on edge. I was the tallest man out here by at least a head, and I had to stay right next to the radio operator, who had this big squawking box on his back and a long antenna whipping back and forth over his helmet. And of course I was white. A perfect target. And that was how I saw myself, as a target, a long white face quartered by crosshairs.

I was dead sure somebody had me in his sights. I kept scanning the tree lines for his position, feeling him track me. I adopted an erratic walk, slowing down and speeding up, ducking my head, weaving from side to side. We were in pretty loose order anyway so nobody seemed to notice except the radio operator, who watched me curiously at first and then went back to his own thoughts. I prepared a face for the sniper to judge, not a brave or confident face but not a fearful one either. What I tried to do was look well-meaning and slightly apologetic, like a very nice person who has been swept up by forces beyond his control and set down in a place where he knows he doesn't belong and that he intends to vacate the first chance he gets.

But at the same time I knew the sniper wouldn't notice any of that, would notice nothing but my size and my whiteness. I didn't fit here. I was out of proportion not only to the men around me but to everything else—the huts, the villages, even the fields. All was shaped and scaled to the people whose place this was. Time had made it so. I was oafish here, just as the Vietnamese seemed oddly dainty on the wide Frenchified boulevards of Saigon.

And man, was I white! I could feel my whiteness shooting out like sparks. This wasn't just paranoia, it was what the Vietnamese saw when they looked at me, as I had cause to know. One instance: I was coming out of a bar in My Tho some months back, about to head home for the night, when I found myself surrounded by a crowd of Vietnamese soldiers from another battalion. They pressed up close, yelling and pushing me back and forth. Some of them had bamboo sticks. They were mad about something but I couldn't figure out what, they were shouting too fast and all at once. *Tai sao?* I kept asking—Why? Why? I saw that the question infuriated them, as if I were denying some outrage that everyone there had personally seen me commit. I understood that this was a ridiculous misunderstanding, that they had me confused with another man, another American.

"I'm the wrong man," I said. "The wrong man!"

They became apoplectic. I couldn't get anywhere with them, and I soon wearied of trying. As I pushed my way toward the jeep one of them slashed me across the face with his stick and then the rest of them started swinging too, shoving for position, everyone trying to get his licks in. I fought back but couldn't

hold them off. Because of my height I took most of the punishment on my shoulders and neck, but they managed to hit me a few more times in the face, not heavy blows but sharp and burning, as from a whip. Blood started running into my eyes. They were swinging and screaming, totally berserk, and then they stopped. There was no sound but the feral rasp and pant of our breathing. Everyone was looking at the bar, where an American lieutenant named Polk stood in the doorway. He was the one they were after, that was clear from his expression and from theirs.

With an unhurried movement Polk unsnapped his holster and took out his .45 and cocked it. He slowly aimed the pistol just above their heads, and in the same dream time they stepped back into the street and walked silently away.

Polk lowered the pistol. He asked if I was all right.

"I guess," I said. "What was that all about, anyway?"

He didn't tell me.

I was halfway home before it occurred to me that I could have saved myself a lot of trouble by pulling my own pistol. I'd forgotten I had it on.

Sergeant Benet cleaned my wounds—a few shallow cuts on my forehead. Sergeant Benet was probably the biggest man in this part of the province and certainly the only black man. He had a touch as gentle as a woman's, and feeling him take me so tenderly in hand, dabbing and clucking, wincing at my pain as if it were his own, I started to feel sorry for myself. "I don't get it," I said. "Polk doesn't look anything like me. He's almost as big as you are. He doesn't have a moustache. He's got these piggy little eyes and this big moon face. We don't look *anything* alike!"

"Why, you poor nigger," Sergeant Benet said. "You poor, poor nigger."

Which is all by way of saying that even as I composed my face for the sniper, making it shine forth my youth and good nature and hope for years to come, I had no illusion that he would see anything but its color.

We found the second position to be satisfactory and set up camp for the night. Though the troops weren't supposed to build fires, they did, as always. They dropped their weapons any old place and took off their boots and readied their pans for the fish they'd collected earlier that day by tossing hand grenades into the local ponds. While they cooked they called back and forth to each other and sang along with sad nasal ballads on their radios. The perimeter guards wouldn't stay in position; they kept drifting in to visit friends and check on the progress of the food.

Nights in the field were always bad for me. I had a case of the runs. My skin felt crawly. My right eye twitched, and I kept flinching uncontrollably. I plotted our coordinates and called them in to the firebase and the air support people, along with the coordinates of the surrounding tree lines and all possible avenues of attack. If we got hit I intended to call down destruction on everything around me—the whole world, if necessary. The puppy ran past, squealing like a pig, as two soldiers chased after him. He tumbled over himself and one of the troops jumped for him and caught him by a hind leg. He lifted him that way and gave him a nasty shake, the way you'd snap a towel, then walked off swinging the puppy's nose just above the ground. After I finished my calls I followed them over to one of the fires. They had tied the puppy to a tree. He was all curled in on himself, watching them with one wild eye. His sides were heaving.

I greeted the two soldiers and hunkered down at their fire. They were sitting face-to-face with their legs dovetailed, massaging each other's feet. The arrangement looked timeless and profoundly corporeal, like two horses standing back to front, whisking flies from one another's eyes. Seeing them this way, whipped and sore, mired in their bodies, emptied me of anger. I shared my cigarettes. We agreed that Marlboros were number one.

I motioned toward the dog. "What are you going to call him?"

They looked at me without understanding.

"The dog," I said. "What name are you going to give him?"

The younger of the two gave a snort. The other, a sergeant with gray hair, stared at the puppy and said, "Canh Cho. His name is Canh Cho."

Dog Stew.

The one who had snorted lay back and shrieked like a girl being tickled, banging his knees together. Some other soldiers wandered over to see what was happening.

I addressed myself to the sergeant. He had a thin, scholarly face and a grave manner. When he spoke to me he lowered his head and looked up from under his eyebrows. I said, "Are you really going to eat him?"

"Oh yes." He smacked his lips and made greedy spooning gestures. Then he turned to the newcomers and repeated our conversation. They laughed. Gold teeth flashed in the firelight.

"When are you going to eat him?"

"Oh, tonight."

"Tonight? He's pretty small, isn't he? Don't you want to wait until he's bigger?"

"No," the sergeant said. "Now is the best time. The meat is best now." He made the spooning motions again. He said, "Let's eat!" and stood and untied the puppy, then picked him up by the tail and carried him to the fire. Looking at his friends and dancing a clownish jig, he dangled the yelping little wretch over the flames.

"Don't do that," I said, and everything changed, or became clear. I saw it in the sergeant's face, felt it in the hardening silence of the others. Up to now we'd been a couple of soldiers messing around in a soldierly way. But I had drawn a line, or at least called attention to the line already between us. I had spoken in absolute confidence of my mastery here. Now he had no choice but to show me—I could feel it coming—his own view of the situation.

The sergeant pulled the pup away from the fire and studied me. Then he hung it over the fire again. It gagged in the smoke and raked the air with its paws.

"Stop it!" I said, and got up.

He moved the puppy back long enough to let it catch its breath, then swung it like a censer back and forth through the flames. All this time his eyes were on me. I knew I should keep my mouth shut, but when the pup started choking I couldn't help myself. I ordered him to stop. Again he pulled the pup back, again he held it to the fire, again I told him to stop. And again. He wasn't playing with the dog, he was playing with me, with my whiteness, my Americanness, my delicate sentiments—everything that gave me my sense of superior elevation. And I knew it. But knowing did not free me from these conditions, it only made me feel how hopelessly subject I was to them.

Please, what was I doing here? If I'd been forced to say what I was doing out here in this alien swamp, forced to watch an ignorant man oppress a dog, could I, with a straight face, have said, "I am an adviser"?

I couldn't win. My only choice was to quit. I turned and walked away, until I heard a howl of such despair that I had to stop. It seemed I didn't have a choice after all. Nor did the sergeant, grimly waiting for me with the singed and gasping pup. He was locked in the game too, as much as I was. He had to take it to the end.

I could think of only one way out. I said, as if this had been the question all along, "All right. How much?"

The sergeant was no dope; he saw his opening. He looked at the puppy. "A thousand piastres," he said.

"A thousand piastres? Too much. Five hundred."

"A thousand."

I made an aggrieved face but got out my wallet and paid him. It didn't kill me—five dollars and change. He took the money and gave me the smoking dog. The other soldiers had been stern and watchful, holding him to his task, but now they were joking around again. They were satisfied. Profit was victory.

"Good-bye, Canh Cho," one of them called.

I took the puppy back to my tent. His fur was scorched and greasy with soot, his eyes bloodshot, his nose blistered. He smelled like rancid bacon. I cleaned him up as well as I could and tried to calm him. He trembled convulsively. Every time I touched him he yipped in fright and shrank away. I spoke to him in low, gentle tones and when he continued to cringe I began to dislike him. I disliked him for being so unlucky. I disliked him for involving me in his bad luck, and making a fool of me. I disliked him for not seeing any difference between me and the man who'd hurt him.

But I held him and petted him and finally he fell asleep in my lap, his nose tucked between my knees. While he slept I went on stroking him, and my hands grew slow and gentle with the memory of all the other dogs they'd known, Sheppy and Tyke, Ringer, Banana, Champion, and without warning tenderness overcame me. It spread through me like a blush, like the sudden heat of unexpected praise—an exotic sensation, almost embarrassing in its intensity. I hardly recognized it. I hadn't felt anything like it in months.

The radio operator brought me a plate of rice and fish. He looked at the pup and made the same eating gesture the sergeant had made. He rubbed his stomach and laughed, and walked away laughing.

From that day on it became the custom of our troops to greet me with spooning motions and signs of ravenous appetite, especially when I took Canh Cho out for a walk. He seemed to understand their meaning. He was a sad little pooch. I tried to teach him a few tricks, bring out some personality, make a proper mascot of him so he'd have a place in the battalion after I was gone. Nothing doing. He wouldn't even chase a ball unless I smeared hamburger on it. All he wanted to do was lie under the big wicker chair with his head sticking out and snap at flies. This engaged his interest, and he was certainly good at it, but it seemed a raw, unfriendly sort of pleasure.

Shortly after Christmas Vera wrote to tell me she'd been seeing someone else, "seriously." She thought it best to suspend our engagement until things were clearer. I read the letter many times over, not sure how to respond. Though I managed to strike a note of offended trust and virtue in my letter back to Vera, I didn't really feel it, and knew I had no right to it. The truth was, I'd been unfaithful to her ever since I got to My Tho. I made resolutions, and renewed them now and then, but they never survived any temptation worth the name. Nor had I given Vera much to hang on to. My letters home were by turns casual and melodramatic, and had little to say of love. If, as she'd asked me to do, I had written truthfully about my inner life, I would have written about boredom, dread, occasional outright fear, and the sexual hunger that fear left boiling in its wake.

Still, Vera's letter gave me a knock. It caused me to compare myself to the other fellow, Leland. We had never met, but I'd heard Vera speak of him as an old friend. Though only a year my senior, Leland was a college graduate with a good job. She had once said that he was brilliant. The word went down hard even then, as if I'd sensed how it would come back to judge me later.

Using Leland's blazing sun to take my bearings, I looked around and found myself exactly nowhere. No marketable education, no money, no prospects. My writing, my "work" as I'd begun to call it, was supposed to take care of all that. Mindful of the feckless dropout Scott Fitzgerald leaving the army with a finished draft of *This Side of Paradise* in his duffel bag, about to feed lifelong dust to his classmates, I had promised myself that I would use my nights to finish the novel I'd begun in Washington; but it soon came to seem romantic and untrue, and I conceived an implacable hatred for it.

Probably it was romantic. Most first novels are. As to whether it was untrue, that's another question. I believed in it when I first started writing it, believed in its story and the view of things that held it together. The truth of a novel proceeds from just that kind of conviction, carried to extremes. I had it, then I didn't. The ground shifted under my feet; the old view vanished and of the one still taking shape I could make neither poetry nor sense. I put the novel out of sight. Eventually, ceremonially, I burned it.

I was unable to write anything else. Instead I tried to read the books Geoffrey took such pains to choose and send me, but over the past several months my passion for them had gone flat as well. It became a duty to read each sentence, and the books themselves felt awkward and foreign in my hands. Before long I'd catch myself staring off. This was my signal to join Sergeant Benet for Bonanza or The Gong Show, or brave the road for a run into town. The best thing I had to say for myself was that I was still alive. Not impressively, though. Not brilliantly.

Strange, how the memory of that one word— she didn't use it in the letter—could give me so stark a picture of my condition. Even more than the letter itself, even more than losing Vera, whose loss, to tell the truth, did not seem impossible to bear, that word cast me down. I called Canh Cho over, thinking it would be agreeable to have him lay his head on my knee and look up at me while I stroked him and pondered my state. But he didn't move.

"Come here, damn you."

He pulled his head back under the chair.

I stood and lifted the chair to show him he couldn't hide from me, anywhere. He looked up and understood, then lowered his head in the woe of his knowledge. I put the chair back down. I was sorry, but what a sad dog. I had to conclude that he probably would have been happier with the Vietcong, unless, of course, they ate him.

Civilian

I was discharged in Oakland the day after I stepped off the plane. The personnel officer asked me if I would consider signing up for another tour. I could go back as a captain, he said. Captain? I said. Captain of what?

He didn't try to argue with me, just made me watch him take his sweet time fiddling with the file folders on his desk before handing over my walking papers and separation pay. I went back to the bachelor officers quarters and paced my room, completely at a loss. For the first time in four years I was absolutely free to follow my own plan. The trouble was, I didn't have one. When the housekeeping detail asked me to leave I packed up and caught a taxi to San Francisco.

For over a week I stayed at a hotel in the Tenderloin, hitting the bars, sleeping late, and wandering the city, sharply aware that I was no longer a soldier and feeling that change not the way I'd imagined, as freedom and pleasure, but as aimlessness and solitude. It wasn't that I missed the army. I didn't. But I'd been a soldier since I was eighteen, not a good soldier but a soldier, and linked by that fact to other soldiers, even those long dead. When, browsing through a bookstore, I came across a collection of letters sent home by Southern troops during the Civil War, I heard their voices as those of men I'd known. Now I was nothing in particular and joined to no one.

In the afternoons I put myself through forced marches down to the wharf, through Golden Gate Park, out to the Cliff House. I walked around the Haight, seedier than a year before, afflicted like the faces on the street with a trashed, sullen quality. Sniffling guys in big overcoats hunched in doorways, hissing at passersby, though not at me: a clue that I was radiating some signal weirdness of my own. No hug patrols in evidence. I went there once and didn't go back.

As I walked I kept surprising myself in the windows I passed, a gaunt hollow-eyed figure in button-down shirt and khakis and one of my boxy Hong Kong sport coats. Without cap or helmet my head seemed naked and oversized. I looked newly hatched, bewildered, without history.

There might have been some affectation in this self-imposed quarantine. I didn't have to stay in a seedy room in San Francisco, broodingly alone; I could have gone on to Washington. My mother and brother gave every sign of wanting to welcome me home, and so did my friends, and Vera. She had parted ways with Leland soon after they took up together, and her most recent letters had spoken of her wish to try again with me. All I had to do was get on a plane and within hours I would be surrounded by the very people I'd been afraid of not seeing again. But I stayed put.

I thought of my friends and family as a circle, and this was exactly the picture that stopped me cold and kept me where I was. It didn't seem possible to stand in the center of that circle. I did not feel equal to it. I felt morally embarrassed. Why this was so I couldn't have said, but a sense of deficiency, even blight, had taken hold of me. In Vietnam I'd barely noticed it, but here, among people who did not take corruption and brutality for granted, I came to understand that I did, and that this set me apart. San Francisco was an open, amiable town, but I had trouble holding up my end of a conversation. I said horrifying things without knowing it until I saw the reaction. My laugh sounded bitter and derisive even to me. When people asked me the simplest questions about myself I became cool and remote. Lonesome as I was, I made damn sure I stayed that way.

One day I took a bus over to Berkeley. I had the idea of applying for school there in the fall and it occurred to me I might get a break on admission and fees because of my father being a California resident. It wasn't easy to collect hard intelligence about the old man, but since the state had kept him under lock and key for over two years, and on parole ever since, figured his home of record was one thing we could all agree on.

I never made it to the admissions office. There was some sort of gathering in Sproul Plaza, and I stopped to listen to one speaker and then another. Though it was sunny I got cold in the stiff bay breeze and sat down by a hedge. The second speaker started reading a list of demands addressed to President Johnson. People were walking around, eating, throwing Frisbees for dogs with handkerchiefs around their

Tobias Wolff, 1981

necks. On a blanket next to me a bearded guy and a languorous Chinese girl were passing a joint back and forth. The girl was very beautiful.

Microphone feedback kept blaring out the speaker's words, but I got the outline. Withdrawal of our troops from Vietnam. Recognition of Cuba. Immediate commutation of student loans. Until all these demands were met, the speaker said he considered himself in a state of unconditional war with the United States government.

I laughed out loud.

The bearded guy on the blanket gave me a look. He said something to the Chinese girl, who turned and peered at me over the top of her sunglasses, then settled back on her elbows. I asked him what he thought was so interesting and he said something curt and dismissive and I didn't like it, didn't like this notion of his that he could scrutinize me and make a judgment and then brush me off as if I didn't exist. I said a few words calculated to let him know that he would be done with me when I was done with him, and then he stood

Relaxing with friends: (from left) Richard Ford, Raymond Carver, the author, and his brother, Geoffrey, 1981

up and I stood up. His beautiful girlfriend pulled on his hand. He ignored her. His mouth was moving in his beard. I hardly knew what he was saying, but I understood his tone perfectly and it was intolerable to me. I answered him. I could hear the rage in my voice and it pleased me and enraged me still more. I gave no thought to my words, just said whatever came to me. I hated him. If at that moment I could have turned his heart off, I would have. Then I saw that he had gone quiet. He stood there looking at me. I heard the crazy things I was saying and realized, even as I continued to yell at him, that he was much younger than I'd thought, a boy with ruddy cheeks his beard was too sparse to hide. When I managed to stop myself I saw that the people around us were watching me as if I were pitiful. I turned away and walked toward Sather Gate, my face burning.

I got to Manhattan Beach just after sundown and surprised my father once again. He was in his bathrobe, about to pop some frozen

horror into the oven. I told him to keep it on ice and let me stand him to dinner at the restaurant where we'd eaten the year before. He said he wasn't feeling exactly jake, thought he might be coming down with something, but after we had a few drinks he let himself be persuaded of the tonic potential of a night on the town.

So we gave it another try, and this time we got it right. Again we stuffed ourselves with meat and drink, and again my father grew immense with pleasure and extended his benevolence to everyone in range. The old rich rumble entered his voice; the stories began, stories of his youth and the companions of his youth, rioters whose deeds succeeded in his telling to the scale of legend. He found occasion to invoke the sacred names (Deerfield; New Haven; Bones; the Racquet Club), but this time I managed to get past the lyrics and hear his music, a formal yet droll music in which even his genuine pretensions sounded parodic. I asked no questions about Hadassah. I let him roll. In fact I egged him on. I didn't have to believe him; it was enough to look across the table and see him there, swinging to his own beat.

I had come back to Manhattan Beach, I surely understood even then, because there could no longer be any question of judgment between my father and me. He'd lost his claim to the high ground, and so had I. We could take each other now without any obligation to approve or disapprove or model our virtues. It was freedom, and we both grabbed at it. It was the best night we'd ever had.

I paid the next morning. So did he, and then some. Late into the day he was still in bed, flushed and hot, and I finally realized that he really had been coming down with something. I called his doctor, who stopped by the apartment on his way home that evening, diagnosed the flu, and prescribed something to bring the fever down. He wouldn't let me pay, not after my father sneaked it in that I was just back from Vietnam. I followed the doctor to the door, insisting, wagging my wallet, but he wouldn't hear of it. When he left I went back to the old man's bedroom and found him laughing, and then I started laughing too. Couple of crooks.

That night and the next day he was too sick to do much of anything but sleep. In his sleep he moaned and talked to himself. I came into his room now and then and stood over him in the dim slatted light cast by the streetlamp. Big as he was, he looked as if he'd been toppled, felled. He slept like a child, knees drawn up almost to his chest. Sometimes he whimpered. Sometimes he put his thumb in his mouth. When I saw him like that he seemed much older than his sixty years, closer to the end and more alone than I wanted to think about.

Then he started coming out of it. He liked being babied, so he wore his invalid droop and mopery as long as I let him. When I helped him in and out of bed he groaned and mewed and walked as if his joints had rusted shut. He had me buy him an ice bag, which he wore like a tam-o'-shanter, his eyes tremulous with self-pity. All day long he called out his wishes in a small desolate voice—cheese and crackers, please, some Gouda on stone-ground Wheat Thins would be swell, with a little Tabasco and red onion, if I wouldn't mind. Palm hearts with cream cheese, *por favor,* and this time could

I skip the paprika and just sprinkle a little onion salt on them? Thanks a mil! Ginger ale, old son, over ice, and would it be too much trouble to *crush* the ice?

He was relentless and without shame. Once he pushed me too far and I said, "Jesus, Duke, suffer in silence awhile, okay?" This was the first time in my life I'd called him by that name, and the sound of myself saying it made me cringe. But he didn't object. It probably reassured him that I was ready to vacate any outstanding claims on him as his child and accept a position as his crony. I never called him Duke again. I wanted to feel as if I still had a father out there, however singular the terms.

He started feeling better after the second day, and I was almost sorry. I liked taking care of him. I'd blitzed the apartment with cleansers, stocked his cabinets with cans of stew and hash and clam chowder and the treats he favored—Swedish flatbread, palm hearts, macadamia nuts. I had a new muffler put on the Cadillac. While he was laid up sick the smallest acts felt purposeful and worthwhile, and freed me from the sodden sensation of uselessness. Out running errands, I found myself taking pleasure in the salt smell and hard coastal light, the way the light fired the red-tiled roofs and cast clean-edged shadows as black as tar. In the afternoons I brought a chair and a book out to the sidewalk and faced the declining sun, chest bared to the warmth, half listening for the old man's voice through the open window at my back. I was reading *Portnoy's Complaint.* Geoffrey had sent it to me some time before and I'd never been able to get past the first few pages, but now it came to life for me. I read it in a state of near collapse, tears spilling down my cheeks. It was the first thing I'd finished in months.

My father took note of my absorption. He wanted to know what was so fascinating. I let him have it when I was through, and that evening he told me he'd never read anything so disgusting—not that he'd finished it. Come on, I said. He had to admit it was funny. Funny! How could such a thing be funny? He was baffled by the suggestion.

"Okay," I said. "What do you think is funny, then?"

"What b-book, you mean?"

"Book. Movie. Whatever."

He looked at me suspiciously. He was stretched out on the couch, eating a plate of scrambled eggs. "*Wind in the Willows*," he said. Now there was a book that showed you didn't have to be dirty to be humorous. He happened to have a copy on hand and would be willing to prove his point.

More than willing; I knew he was dying to read it aloud. He'd done this before, to Geoffrey and me, one night in La Jolla seven years earlier. It was a dim memory, pleasant and rare in that it held the three of us together. Of the book itself I recalled nothing except an atmosphere of treacly Englishness. But I couldn't say no.

He started to read, smiling rhapsodically, the ice bag on his head. I was bored stiff until Toad of Toad Hall made his entrance and began his ruinous love affair with the automobile. "What dust clouds shall spring up behind me as I speed on my reckless way!" he cried. "What carts shall I fling carelessly into the ditch in the wake of my magnificent onset!" Toad had my attention. I found him funny, yes, but also familiar in a way that put me on alert.

Toad is arrested for stealing a car, and in the absence of any remorse is sentenced to twenty years in a dungeon. He escapes dressed as a washerwoman and manages to commandeer the very car he was imprisoned for stealing, after the owner offers a lift to what he thinks is a weary old crone. Toad pins the Samaritan with an elbow and seizes the wheel. "Washerwoman indeed!" he shouts. "Ho, ho! I am the Toad, the motorcar snatcher, the prison-breaker, the Toad who always escapes! Sit still, and you shall know what driving really is, for you are in the hands of the famous, the skillful, the entirely fearless Toad!"

By now I knew where the déjà vu came from. My father was Toad. He wasn't playing Toad, he was Toad, and not only Toad the audacious, Toad the shameless and incorrigible, but, as the story gave occasion, good-hearted Toad, hospitable Toad, Toad for whom his friends would risk their very lives. I'd never seen my father so forgetful of himself, so undefended, so confiding.

He read the whole book. It took hours. I got up now and then to grab a beer and refill his glass of ginger ale, stretch, fix a plate of crackers and cheese, but quietly, so he wouldn't break stride. The night deepened around us. Cars stopped going by. We were entirely at home, alone in an island of lamplight. I didn't want anything to change.

But Toad couldn't keep up the pace. The hounds of respectability were on his neck, and finally they brought him down. He had no choice but to make a good act of contrition and promise to keep the peace, live within his means, be good.

My father closed the book. He put it down and looked over at me, shaking his head at this transparent subterfuge. He wasn't fooled. He knew exactly what Toad's promise was worth.

I'd meant only to touch down in Manhattan Beach, but day followed day and I was still there. In the afternoons I sat by the water and read. At night I went to a bar down the road, then came home and sat up with the old man, listening to music and shooting the breeze. We talked about everything except Vietnam and prison. Only once did he mention his life there, when I asked about a livid scar on his wrist. He told me he'd been cut in a fight over which television program to watch, and that stupid as it sounded he'd had no choice, and didn't regret it. I never heard him mention another inmate, never heard him say "the joint" or even "Chino." He gave the impression it hadn't touched him.

I was drinking too much. One night he asked me if I didn't want to give the old noggin a breather, and I stalked out and came back even drunker than usual. I wanted it understood that he could expect nothing of me, as I expected nothing of him. He didn't bring it up again. He seemed to accept the arrangement, and I found it congenial enough that I could even imagine going on in this way, the two of us in our own circle, living on our own terms. I had nearly six thousand dollars in the bank, a year's worth of unspent salary and hazardous duty pay. If I enrolled in the local community college I could milk another three hundred a month from the GI Bill. They didn't check to see if you actually went to class—all you had to do was sign up. I could get a place of my own nearby. Start writing. By the time my savings and subsidies ran out, I'd have a novel done. Just a thought, but it kept coming. I mentioned it to the old man. He seemed to like the idea.

It was a bad idea, conceived in laziness and certain to end miserably for both of us. Instead of masquerading as a student I needed to be a student, because I was uneducated and lacked the discipline to educate myself. Same with the novel. The novel wouldn't get written, the money would all get spent, and then what? I had intimations of the folly of this plan, though I persisted in thinking about it.

I'd been in town about a week when I met a woman on the beach. She was reading and I was reading, so it seemed natural to compare notes. Her name was Jan. She did speech therapy in the local schools. She had four or five years on me, maybe more. Her nose was very long and thin and she wore her blond hair mannishly close. She was calm, easy to talk to, but when I asked her out she frowned and looked away. She picked up a handful of sand, let it run through her fingers. "All right," she said.

Grand Illusion was showing at the local art theater. We got there early and strolled to the end of the street and back until they opened the doors. Jan wore a white dress that rustled as she walked and made her skin look dark as chocolate. She had the coolness and serenity of someone who has just finished a long swim. As we were going inside I noticed that her zipper had slipped a few inches. Hold on, I said, and slowly pulled it up again, standing close behind her, my nose almost in her hair.

I had seen *Grand Illusion* before, many times. My friend Laudie and I had memorized Pierre Fresnay's death scene with Erich von Stroheim and used to play it out to impress our dates. But that night I couldn't even follow the plot, I was so conscious of this woman beside me, her scent, the touch of her shoulder against mine, the play of light on her bare arms. At last I figured do or die and took her hand. She didn't pull away. A little while later she laced her fingers through mine.

When the lights came on I was awkward and so was she. We agreed to stop somewhere for a drink. She didn't have anyplace in mind so I took her to the bar where I'd been going, an alleged discotheque frequented by former servicemen and some still in uniform. The moment I saw Jan inside the place, in her white dress and cool, manifest sanity, I saw it for what it was—a hole. But she claimed she liked it and insisted on staying.

We'd just gotten our drinks when a hand fell on my shoulder.

"Hey, Cap'n, you trying to keep this lovely lady all to yourself? No fuckin way, man."

Dicky. Dicky and his sidekick, Sleepy.

Chairs scraped. Lighters and cigarettes and glasses descended on the table, a pitcher of beer. They were with us. Jan kept trying not to stare at Dicky, and kept failing. Dicky was clean-shaven but he had a big curly mustache tattooed above his lip. I couldn't tell whether his intention was serious or jocular, if he actually thought he resembled a person with a mustache or was just riffing on the idea. He claimed to have been with a marine recon team near the DMZ, even to have operated in North Vietnam. I didn't know what Sleepy's story was.

They were there every night, hopping tables. The last time I'd seen them they were trying to break into Sleepy's car after he'd locked the keys inside. Dicky rigged up a wire of some kind and when that didn't work right away he went into a rage and smashed out the driver's window, but not before he'd kicked some dents into the door panel and broken off the radio antenna. Sleepy stood there with the rest of us who'd come out of the bar to watch, and didn't say a word.

Dicky caught Jan looking at him. He looked back at her. "So," he said, "how'd you get to know this cabron? Hey, just kidding, the cap'n here's numero fuckin uno."

I told him we'd been to see a film together.

"*Film?* You saw a *film?* What happen, your specs get dirty? Hey, Sleepy, you hear that? The cap'n says he saw a film, I say, What happen, your specs get dirty?"

"I laughed," Sleepy said, "didn't you hear me laugh?"

"No, I didn't hear you laugh. Speak up, asshole! So what film did you see, Cap'n?" For some reason sweat was pouring out of his hair and down his face.

I gave Dicky the short description of *Grand Illusion*.

He was interested. "That was some bad shit, man, Whirl War One. All that bob wire and overcoats and shit, livin like a buncha moles, come out, take a look around, eeeeeeeerrr, boom, your fuckin head gets blown off. No way, man. No fuckin way. I couldn't get behind that shit at all. I mean, millions of assholes going south, right? Millions! It's like you take the whole city of L.A., tell 'em, Hey, muchachos, here's the deal, you just run into that bob wire over there and let those other fuckers put holes in you. Big Bertha, man. And poison gas, what about that mustard shit, you think you could handle that?"

Jan had her eyes on me. "Were you a captain?"

I'd told her I'd just come back from Vietnam, but nothing else. I shook my head no.

"But I tell you straight," Dicky said, "no bullshit. If they'd of had me and my team back in Whirl War One we coulda turned that shit around real fast. When Heinrich starts waking up in the morning with Fritzy's dick in his hand, maybe they decide to do their yodeling and shit at home, leave these other people the fuck alone, you hear what I'm saying?"

Sleepy's chin was on his chest. He said, "I hear you, man."

"What were you, then?" Jan said to me.

"First lieutenant."

"Same thing," Dicky said. "Lieutenant, cap'n, all the same—hang you out to dry every fuckin one of 'em."

"That's not true."

"The fuck it isn't. Fuckin officers, man."

"I didn't hang anybody out to dry. Except maybe another officer," I said. "A captain, as a matter of fact."

Dicky ran a napkin over his wet face and looked at it, then at me. Jan was also looking at me.

As soon as I started the story I knew I shouldn't tell it. It was the story about Captain Kale wanting to bring the Chinook into the middle of the hooches, and me letting him do it. I couldn't find the right tone. My first instinct was to make it somber and regretful, to show how much more compassionate I was than the person who had done this thing, how far I had evolved in wisdom since then, but it came off sounding phony. I shifted to a clinical, dead-pan exposition. This proved even less convincing than the first pose, which at least acknowledged that the narrator had a stake in his narrative. The neutral tone was a lie, also a bore.

How do you tell such a terrible story? Maybe such a story shouldn't be told at all. Yet finally it will be told. But as soon as you open your mouth you have problems, problems of recollection, problems of tone, ethical problems. How can you judge the man you were now that you've escaped his circumstances, his fears and desires, now that you hardly remember who he was? And how can you honestly avoid judging him? But isn't there, in the very act of confession, an obscene self-congratulation for

the virtue required to see your mistake and own up to it? And isn't it just like an American boy, to want you to admire his sorrow at tearing other people's houses apart? And in the end who gives a damn, who's listening? What do you owe the listener, and which listener do you owe?

As it happened, Dicky took the last problem out of my hands by laughing darkly when I confessed that I'd omitted to offer Captain Kale my ski goggles. He grinned at me, I grinned at him. Jan looked back and forth between us. We had in that moment become a duet, Dicky and I, and she was in the dark. She had no feel for what was coming, but he did, very acutely, and his way of encouraging me was to show hilarity at every promissory detail of the disaster he saw taking shape. He was with me, even a little ahead of me, and naturally pitched my tune to his particular receptivities, which were harsh and perverse and altogether familiar, so that even as he anticipated me I anticipated him and kept him laughing and edgy with expectation.

And so I urged the pilot on again, and the Chinook's vast shadow fell again over the upturned faces of people transformed, by this telling, into comic gibbering stick-men just waiting to be blown away like the toothpick houses they lived in. As I brought the helicopter down on them I looked over at Jan and saw her watching me with an expression so thoroughly disappointed as to be devoid of reproach. I didn't like it. I felt the worst kind of anger, the anger that proceeds from shame. So instead of easing up I laid it on even thicker, playing the whole thing for laughs, as cruel as I could make them, because after all Dicky had been there, and what more than that could I ever hope to have in common with her?

When I got to the end Dicky banged his forehead on the table to indicate maximum mirth. Sleepy leaned back with a startled expression and gave me the once-over. "Hey," he said, "great shirt, I used to have one just like it."

I called Vera the next morning from a pancake house, my pockets sagging with quarters. It was the first time I'd heard her voice in over a year, and the sound of it made everything in between seem vaporous, unreal. We began to talk as if resuming a conversation from the night before, teasing, implying, setting each other off. We talked like lovers. I found myself shaking, I was so maddened not to be able to see her.

When I hung up, the panic of loneliness I'd come awake to that morning was even worse. It made no sense to me that Vera was there and I was here. The others too—my mother, my friends, Geoffrey and Priscilla. They had a baby now, my nephew Nicholas, born while I was in Vietnam. I still hadn't laid eyes on him.

I made up my mind to fly home the next day.

That last night, the old man and I went out to dinner. For a change of pace we drove down to Redondo Beach, to a stylish French restaurant where, it turned out, they required a coat and tie. Neither of us had a tie so they supplied us with a pair of identical clip-ons, mile-wide Carnaby Street foulards with gigantic red polka dots. We looked like clowns. My father had never in his life insulted his person with such a costume and it took him a while to submit to it, but he came around. We had a good time, quietly, neither of us drinking much. Over coffee I told him I was leaving. He rolled with it, said he'd figured it was about time I checked in with my mother. Then he asked when I'd be coming back.

"I'm not sure," I said.

"If you're thinking of going to school here, you'll want to give yourself plenty of time to look around, find some digs."

"Dad, I have to say, I've been giving that a lot of thought."

He waited. Then he said, "So you won't be going to school here."

"No. I'm sorry."

He waved away the apology. "All for the b-best, chum. My view exactly. You should aim higher." He looked at me in the kindest way. He had beautiful eyes, the old man, and they had remained beautiful while his face had gone to ruin all around them. He reached over and squeezed my arm. "You'll be back."

"Definitely. That's a promise."

"They all come back for Doctor Wolff's famous rest cure."

"I was thinking maybe next summer. As soon as I get myself really going on something."

"Of course," he said. "Filial duty. Have to look in on your old pop, make sure he's keeping his nose clean." He tried to smile but couldn't, his very flesh failed him, and that was the closest I came to changing my mind. I meant it when I said I'd be back but it sounded like a bald-

faced lie, as if the truth was already known to both of us that I would not be back and that he would live alone and die alone, as he did, two years later, and that this was what was meant by my leaving. Still, after the first doubt I felt no doubt at all. Even that brief hesitation began to seem like mawkish shamming.

He was staring at my wrist. "Let's have a look at that watch."

I handed it over, a twenty-dollar Seiko that ran well and looked like it cost every penny. My father took off his Heuer chronograph and pushed it across the table. It was a thing of beauty. I didn't hold back for a second. I picked it up, hefted it, and strapped it on.

"Made for you," he said. "Now let's get these g-goddamned ties off."

Geoffrey noticed the chronograph a few nights after I got home. We were on his living room floor, drinking and playing cards. He admired the watch and asked how much it set me back. If I'd had my wits about me I would have lied to him, but I didn't. I said the old man had given it to me. "The old man gave it to you?" His face clouded over and I thought, Ah, nuts. I didn't know for sure what Geoffrey was thinking, but I was thinking about all those checks he'd sent out to Manhattan Beach. "I doubt if he paid for it," I said. Geoffrey didn't answer for a while. Then he said, "Probably not," and picked up his cards.

Vera's family owned a big spread in Maryland. After a round of homecoming visits, I left Washington and moved down there with her to help with the haying and see if we couldn't compose ourselves and find a way to live together. We did not. In the past she'd counted on me to control my moods so that she could give free rein to her own and still have a ticket back. Now I was as touchy and ungoverned as Vera, and often worse. She began to let her bassett hound eat at the table with her, in a chair, at his own place setting, because, she said, she had to have some decent company.

We were such bad medicine together that her mother, the most forbearing of souls, went back to Washington to get away from us. That left us alone in the house, an old plantation manor. Vera's family didn't have the money to keep it up, and the air of the place was moldy and regretful, redolent of better days. Portraits of Vera's planter ancestors hung from every wall. I had the feeling they were watching me with detestation and scorn, as if I were a usurping cad, a dancing master with oily hair and scented fingers.

While the sun was high we worked outside. In the afternoons I went upstairs to the servants' wing, now empty, where I'd set up an office. I had begun another novel. I knew it wasn't very good, but I also knew that it was the best I could do just then and that I had to keep doing it if I ever wanted to get any better. These words would never be read by anyone, I understood, but even in sinking out of sight they made the ground more solid under my hope to write well.

Not that I didn't like what I was writing as I filled up the pages. Only at the end of the day, reading over what I'd done, working through it with a green pencil, did I see how far I was from where I wanted to be. In the very act of writing I felt pleased with what I did. There was the pleasure of having words come to me, and the pleasure of ordering them, re-ordering them, weighing one against another. Pleasure also in the imagination of the story, the feeling that it could mean something. Mostly I was glad to find out that I could write at all. In writing you work toward a result you won't see for years, and can't be sure you'll ever see. It takes stamina and self-mastery and faith. It demands those things of you, then gives them back with a little extra, a surprise to keep you coming. It toughens you and clears your head. I could feel it happening. I was saving my life with every word I wrote, and I knew it.

In the servants' quarters I was a man of reason. In the rest of the house, something else. For two months Vera and I tied knots in each other's nerves, trying to make love happen again, knowing it wouldn't. The sadness of what we were doing finally became intolerable, and I left for Washington. When I called to say my last good-bye she asked me to wait, then picked up the phone again and told me she had a pistol in her hand and would shoot herself if I didn't promise to come back that same night.

"Vera, really, you already pulled this."

"When?"

"Before we got engaged."

"That was you? I thought it was Leland." She started to laugh. Then she stopped. "That doesn't mean I won't do it. Toby? I'm serious."

"Bang," I said, and hung up.

A week later I traveled to England with friends. When they returned home I stayed on, first in London, then in Oxford, reading, hitting the pubs, walking the countryside. It was restful: the greenness, the fetishized civility, the quaint, exquisite class consciousness I could observe without despair because as a Yank I had no place in it. My money stretched double and nobody talked about Vietnam. Every afternoon I went back to my room and wrote. I saw little to complain of in this life except that it couldn't go on. I knew I had to make a move, somehow buy into the world outside my window.

Some people I'd met encouraged me to take the Oxford entrance exams in early December. That left four and a half months to prepare myself in Latin, French, English history and literature. I knew I couldn't do it alone, so I hired university tutors in each of the test areas. After they'd made it clear how irregular this project was, how unlikely, they warmed to it. They took it on in the spirit of a great game, strategizing like underdog coaches, devising shortcuts, second-guessing the examiners, working me into the ground. After the first few weeks my Latin tutor, Miss Knight, demanded that I take a room in her house so she could crack the whip even harder. Miss Knight wore men's clothing and ran an animal hospital out of her kitchen. When she worked in the garden birds flew down and perched on her shoulder. She very much preferred Greek to English, and Latin to Greek, and said things like, "I can't wait to set you loose on Virgil!" She cooked my meals so I wouldn't lose time and drilled me on vocabulary and grammar as I ate. She kept in touch with my other tutors and proofread my essays for them, scratching furiously at the pompous locutions with which I tried to conceal my ignorance and uncertainty. All those months she fed her life straight into mine, and because of her I passed the examination and was matriculated into the university to read for an honors degree in English Language and Literature.

Oxford: for four years it was my school and my home. I made lifelong friends there, traveled, fell in love, did well in my studies. Yet I seldom speak of it, because to say "When I was at Oxford . . . ," sounds suspect even to me, like the opening of one of my father's bullshit stories. Even at the time I was never quite convinced of the reality of my presence

Wolff with his sons, Michael and Patrick, 1984

there. Day after day, walking those narrow lanes and lush courtyards, looking up to see a slip of cloud drifting behind a spire, I had to stop in disbelief. I couldn't get used to it, but that was all right. After every catch of irreality I felt an acute consciousness of good luck; it forced me to recognize where I was, and give thanks. This practice had a calming effect that served me well. I'd carried a little bit of Vietnam home with me in the form of something like malaria that wasn't malaria, ulcers, colitis, insomnia, and persistent terrors when I did sleep. Coming up shaky after a bad night, I could do wonders for myself simply by looking out the window.

It was the best the world had to give, and yet the very richness of the offering made me restless in the end. Comfort turned against itself. More and more I had the sense of avoiding some necessary difficulty, of growing in cleverness and facility without growing otherwise. Of being once again adrift.

I was in the Bodleian Library one night, doing a translation from the West Saxon Gospels for my Old English class. The assigned passage was from the Sermon on the Mount. It came hard, every line sending me back to the grammar or the glossary, until the last six verses, which gave themselves up all at once, blooming in my head in the same words I'd heard as a boy, shouted from evangelical pulpits and the stages of revival meetings. They told the story of the wise man who built his house upon a rock and the foolish man who built his house upon the sand. "And the rain descended, and the floods came, and the winds blew, and beat upon that house; and it fell; and great was the fall of it."

I'd forgotten I'd ever known these words. When they spoke themselves to me that night I was surprised, and overcome by a feeling of strangeness to myself and everything around me. I looked up from the table. From where I sat I could see the lights of my college, Hertford, where Jonathan Swift and Evelyn Waugh had once been students. I was in a country far from my own, and even farther from the kind of life I'd once seemed destined for. If you'd asked me how I got here I couldn't have told you. The winds that had blown me here could have blown me anywhere, even from the face of the earth. It was unaccountable. But I was here, in this moment, which all the other moments of my life had conspired to bring me to. And with this moment came these words, served on me like a writ. I copied out my translation in plain English, and thought that, yes, I would do well to build my house upon a rock, whatever that meant.

BIBLIOGRAPHY

Fiction:

Ugly Rumours (novel), Allen & Unwin, 1975.

In the Garden of the North American Martyrs: A Collection of Short Stories, Ecco, 1981.

Matters of Life & Death: New American Stories, Wampeter, 1983.

The Barracks Thief, Ecco, 1984, published as *The Barracks Thief and Other Stories,* Bantam, 1984.

Back in the World, Houghton, 1985.

Collected Stories, Picador, 1988.

The Liar, Engdahl Typography, 1989.

Biography:

This Boy's Life: A Memoir, Atlantic Monthly, 1989.

In Pharaoh's Army: Memories of the Lost War, Knopf, 1994.

Other:

Picador Book of Contemporary American Stories, Picador, 1993.

(Editor) *The Best American Short Stories,* Houghton, 1994.

Interview with Kay Bonetti, American Audio Prose Library, Columbia, Missouri, recorded 1985.

C. D. Wright

1949-

My Story is not important, but odd like horses lying down.

For seven years my brother, Warren, was the only child.

On the night our mother gave birth to me, they had friends over for steak dinner. Mother kept removing herself to the kitchen with contractions. It was an incredible source of pride to proceed with the dinner party at the start of labor. I was a breach; it could not have been merciful. Women tried to stay slim to the end in those days. Medications were in favor, and only the poor gave suck.

While she did not actually win the White River Carnival Beauty Revue, Mother came in second or third to whomever accepted the tiara and the gladioluses, along with one of the McClure twins, which McClure she could no longer be sure.

My mother's body was strong, and she was a pleasing weight, but I never knew her as the bony, darkheaded lady with the squinting, towheaded boy at her knee and the squinting, towheaded baby in her arms. I never knew my mother's breasts before their fall. Or her waist before it thickened and began to fold. I never knew her nearly black waves of heavy, shoulder-length hair. As I came to know her, she was not a bathing beauty, but a groomed and busy professional woman. She was nevertheless beautiful.

Here we are under the Cotter bridge. Warren is barefooted on the rocks, Mother in a bareshouldered sundress holding me aloft, and Papo, her daddy, young then himself, confidently slouched. The car bridge was built by the Works Progress Administration. Parallel to the car bridge is the railroad bridge—the one from which our great-grandfather fell embracing a girder and from which a first cousin tumbled while taking in some air on the caboose.

By the time I entered first grade, Mother had given up flying, which she had learned to do in the first place on a whim and contrary

C. D. Wright and her husband, Forrest Gander

to my father's "instructions." Not to be outdone, once Mother soloed and showed him her license, my father learned to fly. She was the better pilot; he the better navigator. Her passenger had to be on constant alert for the wind sock before she gracefully set the two-seater Cessna down in one grassy runway or another. Our father's passenger held a ticket to ride the big potholes in the sky.

When the work is progressing at its best, one labors absorbed.

She was a court reporter, rather The Court's (my father's) reporter, and she loved her work.

She sat straightbacked and purposeful at the stenotype machine, compiling transcript on transcript, then typing them up word for word, in perfect copies. Her typing was astonishingly fast and accurate. She worked among a swarm of men, and I am sure she enjoyed this, under my father's presiding eyes as he peered down from his black drapery on the bench. From my perspective, her daily absence from the house enhanced her mystique. Few of my friends' mothers worked outside of their homes in the fifties.

Needless to say, he enjoyed his work, the Judge. A juryless court, he loved the autonomy, and the word of law.

Even after her vitality began to drain and her drinking eclipsed her clarity, my mother remained, and still is, utterly unchanged in her letters.

Certain writerly traits must have flowed my way from her: to begin with, a notion of being professional, rather, undomesticated. I caught her distractedness in everything except what I took to be my bona fide work. Perhaps, seeing her at her post, I glimpsed a picture of my future self, stationed at a desk for hours at a stretch. I copied her readiness to take out the dictionary to check the spelling, her compulsion to start a new page if a single errant word marred the one on which we were working. And without a doubt her penchant for gossip—all that he said, she said stuff—without which, no story.

The particulars of hill society have shaped my work more than any certain somebody.

Mountain Home, Arkansas, Grey Street: white clapboard exterior with brown trim, a beige roof. One story. No basement no attic, no garage no shed. Unshaded. It stood on the corner just in front of the government village, a little hamlet of identical GI Bill housing.

One picture of me on Grey Street. Ruffled panties. Studying a mangled toy in my hands.

My pedal car was a Buick.

I have an actual photograph of my mother on top of an actual bull. I was never so physically intrepid.

The master bedroom had a grey carpet and grey drapery. Everything about it spoke adult. I sometimes tiptoed in to snoop.

My high chair was painted over white. I recall kicking at the rungs with my white shoes. Having what Mamo, Mother's mother, called a hissy fit.

Three relatives held my attention: Lottie, Sonnyman, and Audie. They were naturally if a little perversely mesmerizing because Lottie had a hump on her back, Sonnyman was missing, and Audie killed in action. I was never in fact to meet Sonnyman or Audie, and Lottie I met but a single time.

Lottie fell off a post. Sonnyman stepped out for the proverbial loaf of light bread and kept going. After a period of years, his social security number was traced to a couple of towns in Texas. Audie was shot down over North Africa, end of the war.

In the living room on Grey Street we had twin lamps with shades that looked like strapless evening dresses.

Little Rock, 1949. Shortly after my birth the family left Mountain Home for a year. Something about a state commission, a gubernatorial appointment. And Mother in business school learning to be a court stenographer? The house in the one photograph was buff brick. I am in the picture, in a coat but barelegged, hair combed up from both sides to a crest of curls on top, combed as bald men do. Straddling the ample hip of a youngish, dark-brown woman with hot-combed bangs. When Mother pulled into the driveway early in the evening, she said she could hear our combined laughter before she turned off the motor. When she entered the house, we would be on the floor, laughing. I adhere to this nonmemory. This nonmemory of her, Orevia, the one who got down on a hard floor on all heavy fours and brought the laughter up and out of me.

Returned to Mountain Home, College Street, 1950. A freckled, pigtailed girl named Jodie lived in the sandstone shotgun house on the other side of us. She moved to the country, and I spent one night with her there. Used an outhouse for the first time.

The house on College Street was a step up. Never mind that the college of College Street had already been converted into a funeral parlor. Phony dormers made the new house appear to have a second floor. A flying squirrel found itself prisoner in the attic when Daddy was out of town. Mother hustled us to the Danhusers, convinced it was a bad man. Roy Danhuser was not overly brave himself. I don't recall him going back to bring the intruder to heel, only imploring us to stay over. I could be confused. Maybe Roy did what man had to do, dashed up the attic ladder with a loaded gun. By this writing I never expect to see another flying squirrel.

I dragged the cardboard dirty-clothes box out of the closet to fish out some favored, wrinkled, soiled item and left the box on top of the floor furnace to catch on fire. Even then, I wasn't spanked.

 è&

In the **Oxford English Dictionary,** *the page succeeding the one headed* **loadstone** *is the heading* **loaf-eater,** *"one who eats the bread of the master." I would accept* **poet** *to be written here in apposition.*

On a ferry from Tiburón to Angel Island, my recently divorced brother admitted having taken my tricycle from the yard on College Street and disposing of it in some bushes some thirty years earlier. Though the parents had looked high and low and the theft had been reported to the police, it was never found.

è&

In the Oriental ideal, neither practice nor art has been set apart from either living or thinking.

A man who paced the sidewalk in front of our house was said to be a dog poisoner. He would bare his own scummy teeth and growl back at our mongrel, Rosemary. One litter later, Rosemary was poisoned.

Sally and Dinky King lived to the left of us with their mother. Oh the envy I felt for Sally and Dinky's fluffy, handsewn Easter dresses compared to my trim, store-bought suit. Year after year I proposed look-alike dresses to my mother, a pair of margarine-colored, dotted-swiss numbers with stiff, flounced slips. It didn't happen.

A man named Snake Maynard played the guitar at our house one warm evening. He

Parents, Ernie E. and Alyce E. Wright

dressed Western. The lightning bugs rose and fell in the heavy air.

Mother's friend Doris had two boys. I thought her Sydney was the living end. So he was at four or five. He came back from Vietnam in a wheelchair. Drove into a tree a few years after that, snuffing the rest of his lights out. Mother drove Sydney and his younger brother, Clark, and me in the Christmas parade in a white convertible loaned by the dealer for the occasion. We were Santa's elves. When she hit the power brakes she threw one Fletcher over the backseat straight into the dash. Lucky for him his daddy made dentures.

A television was installed on College Street. We all sat facing it.

ଏ

In my book poetry is a necessity of life, what they used to call a taxable matter.

The house on South Cherry Street in Harrison was sided with pink shingles. Otherwise it would have looked like a farmhouse which sprung up in the middle of a town or one which simply withstood the town springing up on all sides of it.

Directly opposite our house was a divorced woman who had male visitors, everyone noted. On the other side of us lived a shut-in. A saintly woman named Winnie looked after her. Every afternoon I roller-skated the broken sidewalk past the shut-in's. On the same short sidewalk I learned to ride a bicycle. It had a silver frame.

Warren's dog Blazer was a good-sized, good-natured mongrel. He became rabid and had to be put down, prior to which Blazer was in every picture Warren was in. One simply did not see one without the other.

I could hear Warren confiding in Blazer as I lay in the living room propped up on pillows with the curtains drawn, hot and crusty with the pinkeye.

The house on North Cherry Street sat on a double, heavily treed lot. There were three varieties of oak: pin oak, Arkansas oak, white oak. Dogwood, blue spruce, cedar, magnolia, and volunteer hackberry and mimosa. Before the Wrights pulled into the drive, a yard-of-the-month sign was frequently planted in the front yard. There were borders of phlox, spirea,

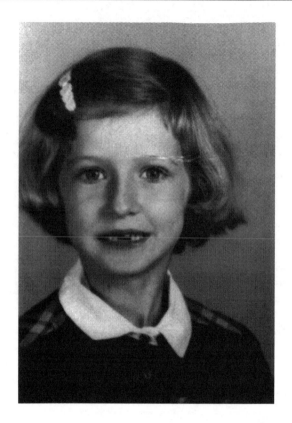

C. D. Wright in second grade,
Central Elementary School, Harrison, Arkansas

japonica, tulips, forsythia; fans of climbing roses and a lilac bush which the Judge kept trying to eliminate and under which Mother would eventually bury her beloved dog Puddles (in his Santa Claus suit). The lilac finally fell to the wild rose that took it over from the inside. A tree swing hung from a high oak limb.

ଏ

I don't know if I think art is capable of realizing ambitions such as revelation. Art articulates. In so doing, it can change you (hopefully on the side of enlargement).

On a typical lonely afternoon behind the white house on North Cherry, I was there. Early fall, bronze but still hot. My dress dragged in the worn spot of earth under the tree swing. The swing had been hung by the previous owners, rumored to have been accomplished with arrows—so that I could pump perilously high and ever so slowly descend; slowly slowly come to a full stop. Then I could begin to busy myself as architect of stick towns for the fat, black ants. The towns were complete with canals, cafes, three-storied houses, and burial grounds crowned with a june bug bier.

I quit pumping and started to drift down toward my ant kingdom. Leaves of oak passed downward, then surprisingly upward, opening and closing in their passage, becoming winged. They lighted on the rusted chains of my swing. By the thousands, tens of thousands, the monarchs materialized in certain migration. The entire eastern population fluttering through our backyard on Cherry Street en route to Mexico. The yard noiselessly exploded with their black-veined pinions. I filled the lap of my dress and stroked the settled ones while countless others extravasated in the splotches of sun about me. I sat still. Silent. "I did not move my arms so much. It was an exotic moment without rush, without engines . . . ," wrote Neruda. Maybe such an occurrence cannot be called numinous. Or can it?

≥•

It is not a blasphemy, at least no blasphemy intended, when I say I look to poetry for supernatural help.

The best-liked feature of the house was the glassed-in back porch. Six months of the year all waking indoor hours were spent on the porch. We ate there at an imitation marble table, seated in hateful, wrought-iron chairs. We filled the glider to watch TV. The turntable was there, and I held my one boy/girl party there which I very nearly enjoyed until someone drew the blind in the bathroom while I was on the stool exposing me to the entire sixth-grade class twisting on the porch. At night Mother and I labored over 1500-piece puzzles on a card table. Daddy pored over the *Congressional Record*. There I waited on Warren hand and foot when the parents were out.

On the high cabinet above our mother's vanity table the gun was kept. Loaded. I would climb up on the table and stand on my toes to take it down to show a friend whenever the parents were out and the gun's presence asserted itself in my mind. We would spin and stroke the barrel, return it to the holster; then

I stretched to shove it back under the heating pad on the shelf.

When the time seemed to have arrived to ensure its operation, the Judge would take down the gun, take it to the backyard, and fire it skyward or into a dead television tube in the incinerator. Daddy's cousin Lester maintained a costly arsenal in his basement. Upstairs, Lester's wife, Cecil, raised tropical flowers in aquaria. For every weapon Lester brought home, his wife brought a bloom. When Lester met Cecil she was a rope lady in the circus.

While my brother was loning it through high school, playing taps and doing the quarterback sneak, I was reading my way through grade school. Precocious in that and in no other respect. I was nose-to-page, reading both at and beyond my understanding; understanding before I knew what it was I had been reading: Dickens, Alcott, Austen, the Brontës, Twain, Hawthorne, Lawrence. And a fair supply of pulp, primarily Nancy Drew.

Art was not part of our curriculum. Nor did it run in the family. Mother played "On the Road to Mandalay" with lyrics by Rudyard Kipling. She played "The Naughty Lady of Shady Lane" and "Star Dust." Warren played at funerals. I gave up the piano with the third teacher. Not one Wright sang. Nor painted. Nor danced. Until my brother and I came into the family, the privilege of growing up in a spell did not exist.

Not that we knew we were in a spell much less that we could wilfully prolong this condition a lifetime.

≥•

Writing is a discretionary activity; it follows that reading is also.

Judge and I were the readers. Warren read a good deal, too, but not constantly as Judge and I did. How reading is learned is still rocketry to me. I know the words sucked me in as much as the illustrations. My Mother Goose book was a pop-up book, and after I had torn off all the extras, I devoured the rhymes.

I was keen on putting every letter down right in the Big Chief tablet with my left hand clenching the fat, soft-leaded pencils. There was a pleasing tension associated with learning to print. In second grade I failed a spelling test.

I had not misspelled any words, but the letters were so minute the teacher could not read them. I blazed with shame. Shredded the test in my catchall bag, never to mention or forget the failure.

Once I could read, I could never not be reading. My father hypothesized that we turned to books because we were nearsighted. We could not recognize a friend waving from across the street. We could not even see the waving. But a book, we could hold close, instantly become intimate with. It is true, I had a reputation for being unfriendly before leaving grammar school. The blackboard was blank; on the playground the ball just a blur. I failed my first eye test, but this failure had mistakenly been attributed to the fact that I had conjunctivitis at the time the exam was administered. I was not examined again until I discovered my father's army glasses when I was eleven, put them on, and saw that the glow from across the street emanated from the widow's television screen. I saw that the oaks were defined to their tips. By then, I was a confirmed introvert. Books were my company.

Strategies by which I could extend my reading periods into darkness were my stock and trade. I fastened old, adult belts together to make a chain that ran from my bed to the closet string. Then I could put my head at the tail of the bed and read by the closet's far-off light. When I heard one of the parents headed my way, I could yank on the belts to throw the room back in the dark without the risk of being overheard running from bed to closet and back to bed. Eventually the ruse was discovered, and I was forced to fashion a nocturnal reading nest inside the closet. Travelling, when it became too dark to read in the dark, I would stretch out on the ledge behind the backseat and wait for the headlights of cars behind us to highbeam the page. It was an avidity verging on the neurotic.

❧

I do not know if I am trying to do something new, but I know that I am trying to learn something new. The doors fling themselves open. Follow the light of your own skull.

In a doll store in Eureka Springs, Arkansas, a clerk introduced me to a powdery woman in a fine fur collar. She was said to be a children's book author. Mother must have told them I read a lot. She smiled at me, the "authoress." That was a spark.

My father took me to the Legion Hut to hear Kenneth Simmons speak. He hailed from Texarkana and had written a prisoner-of-war novel titled *Kriegie.* He signed our hardbound copy. That was a spark.

Poetry was the news from Pluto. *Forty Best Loved Verses,* a selection by Major Bowles, was in our bookcase. I memorized one of its maudlin verses, "I Have a Friend," about a buddy who croaks before the speaker ever makes it to the friend's door for a long-intended visit. My freshman year in high school, Seymour Krim's Beat anthology was pressed on me by a sophisticated senior. That was a spark.

By the time I was out of junior high, I had become inordinately difficult. I floorboarded the Desoto at every opportunity. Heavy petting took up my spare time—fending my boyfriend off at the last possible second—and battling the parents whenever we were obliged to come together for more than a few minutes. To the relief of all, I was sent to All Saints Episcopal Preparatory School for Girls in Vicksburg, Mississippi, for the summer. There, I took up cussing like my father before me, hitching obscenity onto his profanity. I learned to smoke and fell in with a dark, bardic girl from Baton Rouge who referred to herself as a neuter, like a mule, and a gorgeous, suicidal albino from Jackson.

At All Saints, the history teacher interrupted himself to write "Buffalo Bill's Defunct" on the board, signing it *ee.* I was pulled up by the hair roots. Years later a sybaritic poet told me he had achieved nirvana eating a market tomato under a tree facing the flying buttresses of Notre Dame, but my nearest brush came in Amzi Barber's American history class, scrunching my eyes to read the chalkboard during one of the futile bouts when I was trying to get along without glasses.

I reached college having read my childhood away and only four women authors: Louisa May Alcott, Jane Austen, Emily and Charlotte Brontë. I would graduate from college without more than doubling the female figure: Flannery O'Connor, Katherine Anne Porter, Eudora Welty, Carson McCullers. I read American, English, Irish, French, and Russian authors. Men only.

Much as I was afflicted with longings to write, I cannot pinpoint and can barely accept how long I bore the affliction without realizing I could act, instead of being so burdened, so preemptively silenced. Before making up my mind I would write, I was anxiously checking all the egresses, seeing if there weren't somewhere a knoll of sweet-stemmed grass I could chew without getting yelled at, and perhaps looking to share the loaf of the master. When I began to write, it was in fits and starts, contorted with uncertainty. I entered the arena of written words not as a robust challenger, but besotted with fear.

❧

For a long time the critical question has been, can poetry survive?

My South was not The South per se. Arkansas did, after considerable resistance, secede. But the mountain people were not slaveholders and rejected secession time and time again. Until the sedition laws were set in blood, many

C. D. Wright (left) with her first cousin Pamela Jo Collins, in Cotter, Arkansas

would not enlist. Then the hillfolk fought the gentry's war. Owners of twenty slaves were exempt from conscription. A sizable number of hill soldiers fought with the Union. And allegiances were divided officially in the latter part of the war as two civil governments were set up, roughly following the Arkansas River.

Grandma Wright told me her grandfather was beaten within an inch of his life by Confederates for allowing a runaway to sleep on his hearth. I prayed this was a true story—that some white man had taken a risk on behalf of some black man somewhere in the traces of our bloodline. Supposedly, abolition accounted for the origins of Republicanism in the family. I doubt it, though my grandmother continued to vote Republican, making an exception only when my father appeared on the ballot. No one could persuade her that her party had become the party least representing her interests (as if either party cared).

My father told me his great-uncle John killed two young black men when they veered in his direction on the tracks heading into town. Great-Uncle John was a known dandy, not much of a farmhand. On this particular morning he was walking into town along the railroad tracks to avoid having a wagon throw mud on his suit. He was dressed to do business. He carried a derringer for protection or, more likely, as part of his ensemble. Two young men approached from the opposite direction and the opposite side of the tracks. They veered; he fired. That was his defense. If formally charged, he was quickly acquitted; it was his word against that of two dead black men. I wrote a poem making the two young men twin children, a boy and a girl, carrying sacks through "a field drifting with bluets." I never brought myself to read the poem aloud. Based too much on fact, it hectored me.

❧

I would be solidaristic with poets, but that does not mean vertical relationships do not abound in this and every other human enterprise, utopic, heretical, or otherwise.

For no specific reason, I was an eager integrationist before I had met anyone of another race, color, or creed. I was also propink. But not to confuse the two: walking down

*Son, Brecht Wright Gander, and catfish head,
near Horatio, Arkansas*

the streets of Little Rock at night with my parents, window-shopping in the fifties, we passed a black man, and I rushed forward to say hello. My mother called me back. She said I was not to talk to strangers on the street, especially at night, in the city, most especially to a black man. The last *especially* did a flip in me. I had rushed forward to say hello, especially, no, solely because the man was black. I wasn't in the habit of speaking to strangers. I wasn't even in the habit of speaking to familiars first. But I was burning to make contact with The Other. I continued to make of myself a honky fool in subsequent years. Because I was determined to know every black person I met, I could not understand why every black person who had the chance did not want to know me.

From the start, I was attracted to anyone from any realm other than the one in which I was narrowly defined by birth. No doubt, an element of boredom entered in. Wherever you turned you saw another set of grey eyes, another head of fair hair, another straight nose, straight mouth, another sharp chin. "Grim-vis-

aged," the Works Progress Administration Guide to Arkansas describes hill people.

After I was given an ivory-colored clock radio for Christmas and tuned in Chicago, I was probably a goner for my hometown. Once I discovered "Randy's Record Review" in Baton Rouge, once I heard the "Gospel Hour," I was ready to catch the first thing smoking.

Furthermore, I was a hothead. Injustice inflamed me. I had a nose for it, and it smelled the worst to me on matters of race. My outlets were admittedly weird. Through my one art-school-bound friend, I met the town's antivivisectionist. I had never before known anyone with a cause.

Dee Dee Smith lived off Highway 7 with her shell-shocked husband. She wrote tracts on vivisection, and she multiplied them with her mimeograph. On the subject of vivisection she was expert. But she was bonkers on most other matters: the unseemly sketches of models in the *Arkansas Gazette,* school taxes, race. When my friend Stephen brought us together I don't think he knew that she was racist; he brought us together because she was a crusader. Within minutes we charmed one another, within seconds more we were in an irreparable fight about miscegenation. We did not meet again, but I occasionally sighted her tooling around the square. Without benefit of a stencil, she had painted across the doors on both sides of her car: IN 1957 DOCTORS BEAT DOGS TO DEATH AND CALLED IT SCIENCE ISN'T THAT ENOUGH TO MAKE YOU VOMIT.

❧

Does the writer have a mission? Yes, to write. And to recognize the total absence of this particular activity's neutrality.

If I did not have such a wealth of crimes of my own doing to expiate, I would not write. If I had not stomped my foot and screamed at my mother, "I hate you! I hate your guts!" If I had not stomped my foot at my shy, buck-toothed neighbor, "I hate you! Everyone hates you." If I had not told on my brother for stealing my tooth fairy money. If I had not used my girlfriend to get close to her brother. If I had not teased my boyfriend only to refuse him. If I had not eloped with him to Salem, Arkansas, only to have him rush me home before dark, before the justice of the peace opened his door. If I had not accepted the diamond ring he gave me, put it in a Band-Aid box, and returned it to his base in Da Nang. If my first trip to New York City had not been for an abortion. If I had not loved a married poet only to have love end in the bottomless tragedy of his suicide, I would not write. Not that when I do write, I feel compelled to confess. I feel compelled to selectively confess when I sense that the literal truth is relevant. As a writer, I am not interested in my self as a burning matrix of material. I am interested in my self, as sociology, someone whose early stimuli were necessarily fixed but whose responses vary. I feel much more at liberty to examine my self than the self of a bail bondsman or of the woman who sold Dutch Masters cigars out of the back of her stationwagon in my hometown, either of whom would offer far more opportunities for dramatic involvement. And in which case I would write fiction. As a social organism who needs to write in order to begin to understand, I will serve.

It is a function of poetry to locate those zones inside us that would be free and declare them so.

Nevertheless, when I began to write, I insisted upon making up everything, every incident, every one. I wanted to story. Stories were at my disposal, the difficulty was in the words, the order of the words; then learning which to use, which words not to use. I worked within this rude field. I did not have an inkling as to how many other challenges there were between the place of torment and the place of pure light and fire of poetry.

By Jude Jean McCramack Goddamnit to hell dog's foot: the unappeasable Mrs. Vittitow.

I was seventeen when I met her. She's the one who made me want to be a writer more than any other living one. There were of course The Great Dead. They made me want to write but failed to persuade that I could be one among writers. And the Judge, himself a great

reader and wordswright. But a lawyer, a judge, and at bottom negative to the imagination. And school, which neither aided nor contained the calling of writing. If I were among writers customarily asked, if anyone were interested in what kind of mud I am made or whose thunder I stole, I would point to her.

That's her. Solid silver straight hair, in a thick-banged dutch cut. Probably a towhead to start with. Bad posture. Double-jointed. Eyes set a little close. Like a Siamese cat's. The very same blue as a Siamese cat's. Nothing in her icebox but Hershey's Kisses, and that is no exaggeration. After work she picks up a White House burger. Eats something green once in a blue moon. She would much rather smoke than eat. Barely into her fifties and toothless. On the phone she talks to you without her dentures, which is as close as you will come to seeing her with them out. Always in a loose-fitted chemise and pants. Black or bone to be the more invisible. Also because she is classical as well as poor. Mrs. Vittitow—I would not say of her there is anything she would die for now, but I can say there is something she risked her life for once, and most would conclude that she lost.

The events of Vittitow's own personal freedom ride—which include a bitter boycott of white businesses, her husband's radio-broadcasted repudiation of her activities, a poor people's march to Little Rock, rioting whites, the torching of her car at police headquarters, a government escort out of state—provide the dramatic fulcrum of a life in which Mrs. Vittitow has always been an embroiled participant. Again and again she has refused the role of tragic player which the consequences of her involvement might suggest. An image of her walking the rest of the distance across the Mississippi River (the Arkansas-Tennessee line halves the bridge) shorn of husband, seven children, house, and pocketbook toward the Memphis skyline peers from an old residence hotel pane in my eye. At every juncture, her life has been riveting—not only when an *Arkansas Gazette* stringer, a band of Feds, and a heavily armed, white citizenry were obsessed with her whereabouts.

If her grandfather had not lost their Kentucky farm gambling on dogfights, she would have been landed gentry. This she dates with characteristic irony—two months before Roosevelt declared a moratorium on farm mortgage foreclosures. The house she remembers as Hopperlike, gaunt. But it was a genuine spread complete with outbuildings, animals, woods, tennis courts, and she has lived in dignified poverty ever since. Of her mother there are no memories since she died of cancer when Margaret Kaelin was three. She was to be raised by aged and remote adults: a severe German grandmother; an errant Swiss grandfather; the servant named Wordan who was born on the farm, son of a slave; her Irish father, an all-but-silent alcoholic; and her mother's sister, whom her father eventually married. She recalls giving her lunch money away in kindergarten—anything to nab the attention of other children. Her eyes would go to theirs as if a string were connecting them.

Books were her defense against a wall of adults.

It is among Vittitow's curious literary claims that Oscar Wilde perverted her. She read Alcott and *A Girl of the Limberlost.* The *Golden Bough* opened doors though she read it, she claims, without comprehension. Her house held the Harvard classics; she read out of them. The set was missing the third volume of English poets, but she read Swinburne in the Sacred Heart Library. Browning she reacted against because he was her father's favorite. The Brontës, Austen, Galsworthy, Cellini's autobiography ("I love it when he is forgiven for all murders 'past and to come'"). Cyril Cusack came to her school to lecture on Hopkins. *Macbeth* played one year as did an all-girl production of *Julius Caesar.* She was smitten with Mark Antony. She memorized Cardinal Wolsey's speech. And recalls being shepherded into the auditorium to watch General MacArthur on a little, snowy television mounted on stage.

She was raised on heavy guilt and Catholicism. Pregnant seven months in her freshman year at Nazareth College, she could no longer conceal her condition and dropped out. Sex education was taught her by a botany teacher who pulled the shades down to tell them about chromosomes. Christ, the botanist insisted, had only twenty-four, and he was the spitting image of his mother. Thus parthenogenesis had its exponent in Kentucky. It is a truism to say Mrs. Vittitow is a radical, an upstart, and an autodidact, but it is more honest to say she was educated to an important degree by the Ursuline nuns who pressed a sense of justice on her through the law of antithesis, and a love of literature through the parochial canon. It should also be manifest, hers is an insatiable mind.

A friend in my dormitory, Cecelia Grubmeyer, had grown-up next door to Mrs. Vittitow and was fully aware of her genius. She was playing poker and drinking bourbon. It was midday. Her kids were swarming. Sam, one of the triplets, was rocking on his foot a few inches from the blasting television. Vittitow was chasing broadsides against the Church—along with all instances of pretense, hypocrisy, and bigotry that had recently fallen on her ears—with Jack Daniels Black and a losing hand. The slow burn. She monitored her children with the eyes in back of her head. There were staggering but utterly contextualized references to Joyce, Hopkins, Waugh, Greene, Merton, O'Connor—she knew all the Catholic writers. That was for openers. She could quote anything from the lyrics of "Abdul Abulbul Amir" to lengthy passages of *Ulysses;* from "The Prisoner's Letter to the Governor" to the last words of a sentry at Pompeii. There was always a context; she never simply held forth. She conversed; she engaged.

When I was a college senior, Mrs. Vittitow lived with a den of us, her acolytes, in Memphis (after we lured her away from a run-down residence hotel downtown). We were reading Camus and Nietzsche and Dostoyevsky and Tolstoy. Vittitow was devouring John Barth, Thomas Pynchon, and Hunter S. Thompson. It was when she was reading Pynchon that we began to call her V. Fifteen years our senior, we were reluctant to drop the courtesy title even though Mr. Vittitow had divorced her. He had gained custody of the children on slippery, even insidious grounds. I made my first pale effort to write about her in a few lines about a person of every possibility who lacked every opportunity and so "settled into a box with a man / who fixed clocks fixed clocks / fixed clocks."

V is now ensconced in a housing cooperative in Hell's Kitchen. She is among the key people responsible for the community garden across the street from her apartment building. Finally she lives in the one town in the country customized for her. In fact a walk down Forty-eighth Street and through the garden with V is like being on Cleopatra's barge.

When I met Mrs. Vittitow in 1967 I was convinced that Arkansas was the center of the universe, that the house V occupied was the center of Arkansas, that the poker table was the center of the house, and that V was the Buddha. I have since seen her lose control over everything from her children to her bladder. I have never had a second's doubt but what the revelation was genuine. When I talked to her on the phone, telling her I wanted to write a personal history of her, she seemed amenable to recounting the business boycott she instigated in Forrest City, Arkansas, and has saved the newspapers for the purpose. For her, her whole history has significance only in terms of that moment, when her life was at risk. I am reminded of Yeats, a poet she knows thoroughly, of the advent of the real that must come with the circus animals' desertion, "Character isolated by a deed / to engross the present and dominate memory."

BIBLIOGRAPHY

Poetry:

Alla Breve Loving, Mill Mountain Press (Seattle, Washington), 1976.

Room Rented by a Single Woman, Lost Roads (Fayetteville, Arkansas), 1977.

Terrorism, Lost Roads, 1979.

Translations of the Gospel Back into Tongues, State University of New York Press, 1982, 1994.

Further Adventures with You, Carnegie-Mellon University Press, 1986.

String Light, University of Georgia Press, 1991.

Just Whistle, Kelsey Street Press (Berkeley), 1993.

Tremble, limited edition, Ziggaraut Press (Providence, Rhode Island), 1994, Ecco Press (New York), forthcoming.

Nonfiction:

The Lost Roads Project: A Walk-In Book of Arkansas, University of Arkansas Press, 1994.

The Reader's Map of Arkansas, University of Arkansas Press, 1994.

Cumulative Index

CUMULATIVE INDEX

The names of essayists who appear in the series are in boldface type. Subject references are followed by volume and page number(s). When a subject reference appears in more than one essay, names of the essayists are also provided.

INDEX

INDEX

INDEX

INDEX

INDEX

INDEX